THE PRESIDENT'S SERIES
IN ARKANSAS AND REGIONAL STUDIES

volume two

TULIP EVERMORE

TULIP EVERMORE

Emma Butler and William Paisley
Their Lives in Letters, 1857–1887

Edited by Elizabeth Paisley Huckaby and Ethel C. Simpson
With an Introduction by Ethel C. Simpson

The University of Arkansas Press
Fayetteville, 1985

Library of Congress Cataloging in Publication Data

Paisley, Emma Butler, d. 1887.
Tulip evermore.

1. Paisley, Emma Butler, d. 1887. 2. Paisley, William.
3. Arkansas—Biography. 4. Arkansas—Social life and customs.
I. Paisley, William. II. Huckaby, Elizabeth.
III. Simpson, Ethel C., 1937–   . IV. Title.
CT275.P314A4 1985   976.7'051'0924   84–27873
ISBN 0–938626–34–5
ISBN 0–938626–35–3 (pbk.)

This project is funded in part by a
grant from the Arkansas
Endowment for the Humanities.

To my family,
because the Butlers and their kin have renewed my consciousness of all the
ways that family relationships have influenced and enriched my life.
Ethel C. Simpson

To those great-grandparents, grandparents, great-aunts, and great-uncles
whom I never knew but who wrote these letters; and to their descendants
whom I have met only recently through *their* letters, so helpful in the
completion of this book, and to my more immediate family:
my parents, brothers, sister, aunts, uncles, cousins,
and in-laws who have continued the tradition of
letter-writing to the enrichment of all of our lives.
Elizabeth Paisley Huckaby

CONTENTS

INTRODUCTION

by
Ethel C. Simpson

"Dear Sister: Papa tells me that you think hard of my not writing to you. I will not say it is strange if you do; for I confess that a letter was due you from me long ago." These phrases, written 12 March 1857 from New York, are the beginning of a remarkable chronicle of family correspondence that was to span four generations over thirty years and to extend from coast to coast of the American continent.

That first letter in the correspondence was written by Lewis Butler, then eighteen, who had gone on a trip with his father and was seeing the sights of New York before proceeding to Chapel Hill to attend college. He wrote to his sister Emma, then about twelve and a half, living on the family farm in Tulip, Arkansas. Emma kept this letter, and ultimately kept about six hundred others to and from her brothers and sisters, her parents, her husband, and her children, as well as from other relatives and friends. After she died in January 1887, the letters, contained in a small trunk, passed first to one and then to another descendant. More than ninety years later, they became the property of Emma's granddaughter, Elizabeth Paisley Huckaby. It was she who set in motion the machinery which has produced this book.

Emma Butler Paisley was particularly well situated to be the custodian of a family chronicle. She was a daughter of Alexander Butler, a prosperous Tulip merchant and farmer. He was one of the leading men of the community, generous with his hospitality, devoted to family, church, and the conduct of business. Born in Boydton, Virginia, in 1807, Alexander Butler settled in Henderson County, North Carolina, where he worked as a plantation overseer. In 1832 he married Mary Wyche Reavis, and in 1848 or 1849 they emigrated, like many of their fellow citizens of North Carolina, to begin a new life in the west. They settled in Tulip, Dallas County, with their eight children, including Emma, then four years old. By the end of 1857, the year of the first letter in the Butler-Paisley documents, there were twelve living Butler children, the eldest, Sarah, having died of burns as a young child. Emma was one of the middle children. The baby, James Oliver Butler, born in September of that year, was twenty-two years younger than the oldest surviving child, Martha, known as Sister Mattie. When Emma was still a young girl, her big brothers and her oldest sister went off into the world, to marry, to attend college, to fight in the Civil War, to teach school. When they wrote home, she was old enough to receive some of the letters. But in contrast to the letters they might have written to their parents or to each other, those that were written to Emma are preserved, still folded neatly away in their envelopes. A few are worm-eaten and faded, but the assembly of more than six hundred letters provides a richly detailed picture of a single family living during one of the most dynamic periods in the history of the country.

Tulip, the home of the Butler family for more than forty years, was a remarkable village in mid-nineteenth-century Arkansas. It was a rural community rather than a town. The first settlers had arrived just a year or two before the Butlers, and from then till the outbreak of the Civil War, Tulip thrived. It always had a reputation for good schools. In the 1840s, the first of a succession of academies opened in Tulip. In 1860 the Arkansas Military Institute and the Tulip Female Collegiate Seminary were successful enterprises, and could look back to locally famous occasions when the likes of Albert Pike and W. D. Lieper delivered speeches in the grove on their grounds. Then as now in the rural community, the schools were the center of social and cultural life, the scene of recitals, demonstrations of elocution, picnics and political events.

The Butlers' children attended the local schools, and some of them, like Lewis, went to college in North Carolina or Tennessee. In the next generation, after the war, Sister Mattie's children attended universities in the Ivy League and even abroad in Europe. But sooner or later, they all came back to Tulip, "the dear old home," as one of the girls called it. When they married, as they all did, they brought spouses and children home for visits at special times, such as holidays and summer vacation. Sometimes the daughters came home to have their babies, or to be nursed in various illnesses, or to help nurse those still living at home when they were sick. The Butlers reared two orphaned cousins, the Phillips girls, as members of the family, and a constant stream of overnight, weekend, or other short-term company passed through the house. They often entertained the Methodist itinerant preachers who served the churches in the area. The house, after all, was large, and Alexander Butler was prosperous. The Butlers convey in their letters that they were never more content than when the house was aswarm with kinfolk and that they felt lonesome when everyone was gone.

The Butler-Paisley correspondence is a document of the life of the extended family so much discussed in social commentary on the nineteenth century. Alex Butler is the patriarch, but there are references to members of the preceding generation, his aunts and his wife's mother, for example, though none of their letters are in the present collection. Next come his twelve children: Martha, who married George Hughes, a banker and businessman; Henry, his father's partner in the mercantile business, who married Mollie Coulter; Mary, who lived with her parents till she was past forty, married a widowed clergyman, and ultimately returned with him to continue living at the old home place until her death; Lewis, a lawyer, who married Jennie Bowman; George, a minister, who married Julia Moores and emigrated to California; Charles, who farmed, drove a wagon, and did other work, and married Kate Colburn, a music teacher; Emma, who married William Paisley, who had worked in the family store from his boyhood and left Tulip to start his own business in the next county; John, a storekeeper and farmer, who married Malinda Clardy; Annie, who married Olin Moores, a merchant, would-be politician, and "drummer"; Ira, a merchant, who moved to Texas, where his bride, Fannie John Smith, died before the year was out; Alice, second wife of Olin Moores, following the death of her sister Annie; and James, farmer and merchant, who married Mariah Moores, sister of Julia and Olin.

In the next generation, the children of Mattie and George Hughes were contemporaries of Alex and Mary Butler's youngest children. They went to school and college together and spent wonderful summer vacations at the old home place. They also served as additional "uncles"— as if any more were needed—to the younger members of their generation, like the children of Emma and William Paisley. When the youngest Butler son, Jimmie, had a son, he received the name of Jimmie's uncle and contemporary, Walter Hughes, son of Sister Mattie. Thus the circle was complete.

The family of Emma Butler's husband William Paisley was less numerous, but a similar extended structure is evident. Billy's Aunt Minerva, widow of his father's brother, wrote the news of the family who remained in North Carolina, and Billy occasionally visited them when he was in the East. Minerva's sons also wrote to their Cousin Will, who was just enough older to be something of a hero. Billy's mother and stepfather represented the earlier generation closer to home in Arkansas. And Billy's sister Mary Ann, married to Charlie Scott of Pine Bluff, figures occasionally in the family story, along with Billy's half-brothers and sisters from his mother's second marriage.

Although all these Butlers, Paisleys, Mooreses, and others have their place in the chronicle of the letters, the focus is naturally sharper on Emma and Billy Paisley and their children since Emma kept the letters.

William McLean Paisley's father, the Reverend John Paisley, graduated from the University of North Carolina and from the theological seminary at Princeton, New Jersey. John Paisley married Eliza Bradshaw, a Tennessee woman who was the daughter of a Presbyterian minister. Two of their three children, William and Mary Ann, survived to adulthood. John Paisley died in 1845, when Billy was three years old. Two years later, Mrs. Paisley married Captain Lorenzo Dow Lipscomb, a tailor, and the family went west to Tulip. When Billy was fourteen, he went to work in the Butler store, and worked there till he left to join the Tulip Rifles, afterward Company I, Third Arkansas Infantry, along with many other Tulip youths. When he returned from the war, he and Emma married, and Mr. Butler took him into the family business. But after a short time, they moved to Clark County, Arkansas, where Billy entered a partnership with Joseph Doby, yet another North Carolina Presbyterian transplant, at a crossroads known as Dobyville, about forty miles west of Tulip.

Emma and Billy had nine children. They were John Alexander, William Butler, Emma, Henry Lewis, Mary Eliza, Martha Wyche, Lula Grier, Annie Orr, and James Ira. All lived to adulthood except for Annie, who died before she was a year old.

Billy's mother and stepfather, the Lipscombs, were much beloved by the Butler family and inspired the older Butlers with their piety. After Billy moved to Tulip, they followed him there, and after Mrs. Lipscomb's death, the captain moved to Texas.

The families are extended in another sense, one that may be surprising. Both the Butlers and the Paisleys had connections over the face of the continent and kept in contact with many relatives. One of Emma's brothers, George Emery Butler, moved to Southern California to join the first Methodist conference there in 1871, and after that various members of the family, including their in-laws, the Mooreses, moved to or from California. The North Carolina correspondence of the Paisleys, as well as the letters in the early 1860s from Sallie Kittle, Emma's "Southern Belle" cousin, illustrate the ties that extended across considerable distances despite the shortcomings of the postal service.

The postal service was not the only way that letters were transmitted in rural America in the nineteenth century. Letters as well as oral messages were sent along with travelers who planned to stop in the desired vicinity. During the Civil War, sending letters by any means was a very uncertain matter, and the boys in the army complained incessantly about the dearth of news from home, even while acknowledging the possibility that their kinfolk might have written letters that went astray. They sent letters by other soldiers who were going across the Mississippi, hoping that they might eventually reach Tulip. Even after the war, many letters continued to be sent by this informal post. For example, when someone in the Dobyville community stopped at Billy Paisley's store on his way to Malvern or to Tulip, Billy would often dash off a hurried note to his wife visiting "at home." Traveling ministers and "drummers"—traveling salesmen—often carried spoken or written messages or simply general news from one part of the family to another.

Letter writing was a highly conventional activity in the nineteenth century. There were formulas for the expression of many kinds of sentiment, from condolence to the announcement of a wedding or the birth of a baby, who was nearly always referred to in such an announcement as "the little stranger." Formulas for the opening portion of a letter included apologies for tardiness in writing, a brief discussion of whose turn—sender's or recipient's—it really was to write, and sometimes an apology for writing with a pencil, something that no conscientious correspondent was supposed to do.

The body of the letter typically covered both sides of each page of a folded sheet. The Butlers and their correspondents considered it important to "fill the sheet" even if it meant apologizing for the lack of news. Occasionally cross-writing, the bane of editors and transcribers, was used, usually by an emotional young woman like Cousin Sally Kittle, describing an affair of the heart to Emma. After she had filled out the sheet, she turned it sideways, or occasionally on the diagonal, and laid on another layer of writing in that direction. Sometimes the second layer was done in pencil, which did not make the letter any easier to read. Generally, cross-written letters contained several admonitions not to let anyone else read them.

In the closing remarks of an ordinary family letter, the writer usually requested that the recipient "write soon and often," and sent love to the members of the household, with kisses for the little girls and babies. Older people and the pious of all ages also sent blessings or promised prayers. More times than not, the writer signed his full name, even when writing to a spouse or a close relative. When women used a middle initial, as they usually did, it was that of their second Christian name rather than of their maiden name as is now the custom. Emma, for example, is "Emma E. Paisley."

For all the conventions, however, the personalities of the letter-writing members of the Butler and Paisley families come across very clearly. Aunt Minerva Paisley could not be mistaken for Ma Butler. Captain Lipscomb could barely write at all, but his letters convey a striking character and frequently a poetic turn of phrase. George Butler, who was a Methodist preacher in California, had a different style from his more worldly brother Lewis, the minor politician from Cairo, Illinois. The Harvard-educated Walter Hughes wrote Emma a charming and literate letter complimenting her sons' behavior, and Hughes's superior advantages are evident when his letter is compared to those of his uncle Ira, just three years his senior.

The Butler-Paisley letters have much to teach us about the history of Arkansas in the nineteenth century, for they show the effects of national developments on a family and a community. During the three decades covered by the letters, steam power and railroads revolutionized transportation, the nation fought the Civil War, slavery was abolished, and various economic crises changed the American way of doing business. For Tulip, these and other events virtually destroyed any chance the town might have had to fulfill its promising beginnings as a regional center of culture, religion, and education. The war dismantled and diffused many of Tulip's families. Those like the Butlers that were spared any loss of life were nevertheless dispersed over the next twenty years by the lack of opportunity in rural Arkansas and the prospect, or hope, of doing better elsewhere. Some of Emma's family moved on to Texas or to California, and others settled in Little Rock or Malvern, which had transportation and other facilities that promised a brighter economic future.

Some of the lessons of that period of Arkansas's history have been learned and relearned through the past hundred years. Economic and social changes have continued to depopulate rural Arkansas, so that today parts of Dallas and Clark counties seem nothing but pine forests. The most interesting part of Tulip in the 1980s is probably the cemetery, and Dobyville has disappeared altogether. Arkansans have made other treks to California and Texas in search of a better life and greater opportunity, despite the call of home and kin that continues to summon them back to the Ozarks or the Delta.

The attachment to home and kin pervades the Butler-Paisley letters. The Butlers all felt it for the "dear old home" at Tulip. Emma and Billy Paisley managed better than the others to move out on their own, but even they saw Tulip as a place for refreshing the spirit by renewing the old family ties. These attachments were inevitably changed with time as the members of Emma's generation died or left, but while they lasted, they were the central fact of family life.

News of the family is the heart of the correspondence, the most interesting topic to the writer and to the recipient. For the twentieth-century reader, however, reading the letters as a social and historical document, the letters provide information about the function of the church in people's lives, about the many kinds of work they did, both at home and away, and about the kinds of recreation and leisure activities they enjoyed.

On the Arkansas frontier in the nineteenth century, the church provided a kind of focus that it no longer has for most members. The Sunday services, weekday prayer meetings, and revivals gave people some place to go. The preachers—at least in the Presbyterian and Methodist denominations—frequently displayed a better-than-average education, with training in oratory as well as theology. The community greatly enjoyed the return of a favorite preacher, and the Butlers and Paisleys apparently were comfortable attending sermons of either denomination. Churchgoers did not object to hearing the same skillfully delivered sermon more than once, any more than a concertgoer might object to hearing a repeat performance of a violin sonata. The music of both denominations was very simple on the frontier, and the old favorite hymns were remembered with much nostalgia by the boys in the army, singing them as they did around their campfires far from Tulip.

Religion also occupied a considerable place in the home life of the Paisleys and the Butlers. Many of the households had group prayer at night for all the family, guests, and servants. Emma's obituary stated that since her marriage she had read the Bible through fifteen times. One of her brothers was a Methodist preacher, and three of her sons were Presbyterian ministers. Her sister Mary married a Methodist circuit-rider, the Reverend George Matthews, who had frequently been a guest in the homes of various Butler households on his circuit. The church was a vocation and a profession, as well as a set of beliefs and rituals.

William Paisley's North Carolina family had always been Presbyterians. A number of years after Emma married him, she decided to leave the Methodists and join her husband's church. She announced this decision to her parents in a letter that probably caused her as much pain as it did them. Even though the Butlers were on cordial terms with their non-Methodist neighbors and revered Billy's parents, Captain and Mrs. Lipscomb, they reacted emotionally to Emma's announcement. Ma Butler actually wrote that she felt as if someone had died. But in 1873 Emma joined her husband's church anyway. Her brother George similarly followed his own convictions in the Southern California Methodist conference and became a leader in the more evangelical wing of the church, despite the disapproval of the bishop and some of the laity.

The structures of the Methodist and the Presbyterian churches in Arkansas provided other opportunities to combine spiritual development and recreation. At the Annual Conference of the Methodist church, preachers received their assignments for the coming year. The bishop presided, and both the clergy and laity attended as many of the sessions as they could. In those years the Conference convened in various towns throughout the jurisdiction. Tulip had the Arkansas Conference in 1853 and the Ouachita Conference in 1862. At other times, members of the Butler family, especially Ma Butler, traveled to Little Rock, Arkadelphia, Washington (Hempstead County), Pine Bluff, or Hot Springs to participate in the event. Ma Butler even attended the General (that is, national) Conference in Nashville in 1882. The Presbyterians had similar administrative structures and meetings in the Arkansas Presbytery and regional synods.

Since the towns where religious meetings were held had few public accommodations, the visitors stayed with their relatives and friends. The Butlers had several well-to-do relatives in Nashville who lavished their hospitality on Ma and the other members of the family. In some cases, several families virtually took over a rooming house for the duration of the meeting. When Emma acted as hostess to people attending the synod, she kept so busy with the duties of hospitality that she scarcely had time to attend the sessions. Attendance at a conference or a synod became a reunion with old friends and kinfolk, a religious revival, and a recreational excursion as well, somewhat resembling a medieval pilgrimage.

The Methodist camp meeting also combined social and recreational experience with religious renewal. The Butlers, with scores of their friends and neighbors, loaded children, servants, and provisions into wagons and journeyed to a grove or a spring where many "tents" (simple board cabins) surrounded a "tabernacle" (central pavilion) that contained a pulpit and primitive benches, brightened by torches or tallow candles. As many as five services a day were held, with preaching, singing, and prayers. At these meetings, the three generations of Butlers joined friends and relatives for a week or more, listening to the outstanding preachers who conducted the services and catching up on the news of all the scattered communities from which they had come together.

The social aspect of church life was clearly very important, but the Butlers also embraced the spiritual and moral teachings of their faith with sincerity and fervor. Especially in bad times, as when someone had died or when economic news was bleak, they wrote letters suffused with the rhetoric of Victorian American piety. In good times they remembered to be thankful to the Almighty. In the presence of natural wonders, like the Pacific Ocean, they remembered the power of the Creator. Their religion provided comfort, inspiration, and emotional satisfaction at many points in their lives and an ethical and moral framework for their daily conduct. Ideals of duty, fidelity, honesty, and unselfishness arose from their religious training.

The letters also reveal much about the everyday work of rural and village people. The writers of these letters worked as farmers, storekeepers, homemakers, a lawyer or two, schoolteachers, and a Methodist minister. When they wrote home, they expressed concerns about their work very similar to those found in the same occupations a century later.

Another occupation, found only in the earliest letters, is that of soldiering. Four of Alexander Butler's sons served in the Third Arkansas Infantry, CSA, from 1861 to 1865, as did William Paisley. Few letters written by Billy, and none written by Emma, remain from these years. But her brothers wrote to the loved ones at home and to each other, and Henry Butler wrote with considerable faithfulness and some irritation to Billy, who did not reply regularly. During these years, the faith and piety of the young minister George were put to the test, and Lewis, whose career as a schoolteacher had just begun when the war broke out, resolved to be a more faithful Christian. Charlie was captured by the Yankees and imprisoned in Fort Delaware. Johnnie, born in 1846, managed to serve for a few months at the end of the war and wrote enthusiastic letters home from Texas. The soldiers' letters employed the rhetoric of patriotism and the kind of Christian piety that often accompanies it. They described the hardships they experienced and bragged about their units and about the superiority of certain Confederate forces over the enemy. George conducted prayer meetings. After Billy was wounded, he went on leave to visit some of the Paisleys and indulged in the soldierly pastime of girl-watching. Henry was continually anxious about his sweetheart, almost totally unnamed in the letters, until he received a letter that solved the mystery of her uncommunicativeness: she had heard that he was dead, and also that he had married a relative of Robert E. Lee. But he finally resolved the confusion, and soon after, he and Mollie Coulter were married.

Many of the Civil War–period letters were addressed to Billy Paisley from Henry Butler, who had been his lifelong friend and became his brother-in-law. Throughout the letters, Henry chides Billy for his poor performance as a correspondent, but his real affection for him always moves him to forgiveness. The Civil War letters also include an interesting vignette of Billy's character. According to a family legend, Billy borrowed money in Richmond to buy a mule, which he rode home to Tulip when the war ended. The correspondence contains two notes from James T. Johnson, who loaned the money, thanking Billy for his prompt repayment of the debt.

After the war, Tulip, like the rest of the South, underwent many changes. The schools that were once her pride faded away. From time to time, letters disclose that a teacher has come to have a school, usually boarding with one of Tulip's families. Kate Colburn, who married Charles Butler, taught music at Tulip and boarded with the Butlers. Some families who had left during the war never returned, and some just dwindled away.

With the loss of slave labor, farming also changed. Alexander Butler had fifteen slaves, according to the 1860 census, and his property was valued at $41,000. The 1865 tax report for

Dallas County valued his estate at $2710, including 562 acres of land. The Butler sons farmed some of the land, and tenants farmed on shares. The system of crop-liens, begun soon after the Civil War, made it possible for farmers to pledge their crops for food and other necessities. Landowners as well as tenant farmers were frequently obliged to do so, and the Butlers were caught in this system both as farmers and as merchants. It is not surprising then that Henry Butler's New Year letters to Billy almost always include a lament about hard times and financial embarrassment. Weather, the volatile cotton market, and variations in interest rates could mean the difference between a good year and disaster.

Aside from the economic considerations of farming, it was very hard work, seemingly without possibility of getting caught up. When the mules were in good physical condition, they might escape through a weak place in the fence, and hours would be lost in catching them. Or the plow might break in a way that was impossible to repair, with the nearest replacement miles away. If rain came at the wrong time, a field might have to be replanted. If no rain came, all the work might be lost. In harvest time, all family activity was in thrall to the dictates of the weather. Since the horses and mules worked hauling the crops, the ladies of the family could not "get a conveyance" to take them visiting, to say nothing of a male escort to see them safely to their destination.

From time to time Billy turned his hand to the plow, but not till his older sons could manage some of the farm work did he devote much space in his letters to farming. Then he was careful, especially when he lived at Gurdon, to give them instructions on how to proceed and on how to deal with the hired men who worked his farm land at Dobyville.

Storekeeping was what Billy Paisley liked best. For a young man returning from the war, storekeeping was often a good alternative to farming, whether as a merchant with his own establishment or as a hired clerk. With the passing of the plantation store from the scene, communities needed mercantile establishments, and every little town in the South had several. The Butlers had been merchants even before the war, and afterward most of the sons tried storekeeping sooner or later. A familiar pattern developed: Alex Butler took them into his store in Tulip, where they learned the business, and then he set them up in another place, such as Malvern, Center Point, or, in the case of Billy, Alex's son-in-law, in Dobyville. This arrangement was sometimes less than ideal, for the patriarch attempted to influence the operation of the business after his sons or sons-in-law believed themselves able to run things independently. As he got older, Alex became more difficult to deal with, and Henry sadly broke off their partnership and went it alone.

The fact that Billy Paisley and some of the Butlers were merchants provides an important dimension to their correspondence, because their business required them to travel far more than the typical Arkansas farmer. As a result, some of Billy's letters contain many details of the everyday life of a merchant. His activities provide the reader with a view of the outside world, as the large extended families of Butlers and Paisleys provide the view of home and hearth. Over the years, he traveled to several major trade centers: New York, Cincinnati, St. Louis, and New Orleans. He made his first trip in the early spring of 1867, just a few months after he and Emma were married. The young couple were living with the Butlers in Tulip, and Emma remained there while he made the arduous journey.

On their twice-yearly buying trips, merchants like Billy, Alex, and Henry had several kinds of business to attend to. They had to stock their stores for the coming season with everything from crockery and farm implements to drugs and ladies' bonnets. Then they had to execute various commercial transactions, paying off loans from the previous year and arranging for the shipment of cotton from Arkansas to ports on the various rivers where it was purchased and shipped to the manufacturing cities of England or the Atlantic coast. Finally, they had "bills" or "commands" to buy for their friends and relatives. The Butler girls asked Billy to buy their hats, and he purchased such things as furniture, sewing machines, and even a carriage and horses in Saint Louis for shipment back to his customers.

Billy also took in the sights of the cities he visited, sometimes including a parade, a speech, or a great fair. Usually he attended church in an important sanctuary and reported on the sermons and music he heard. When the women went along, Billy and Henry enjoyed escorting them to places like Shaw's Gardens in St. Louis or to the fashionable streets of fine houses. These sights they recorded for the family back in Arkansas.

After the merchant had returned from a buying trip, he was probably fatigued by the rigors of the trip and possibly half ill from eating strange food. Billy's travels sometimes seemed a martyrdom to him, torn as he was by the pangs of homesickness and the desire to be with his wife and children. When he got back to Arkansas, he still had to contend with the complicated tasks of getting the goods from the port or the railhead to the store, unpacking everything, and getting it on the shelves. This work often went on late into the night, for during regular hours he had to conduct his usual business. Sometimes he worked so late that he would simply eat and sleep at the store, particularly when Emma and the children were visiting at Tulip.

The accounts of Billy Paisley indicate that he succeeded at his business. The letters hint at a few rough times, including a lawsuit, though no details are provided. Since Billy's letters were addressed to Emma, he did not dwell on the negative aspects of his business dealings, and from his letters it appears that he enjoyed good credit with his suppliers. Henry's letters to him, as well as references made in some of the other correspondence, indicate that the family thought very highly of his business sense. Henry wanted a partnership with him, but Billy always evaded the issue. Perhaps he did not wish to be too near the strong guiding presence of Alexander Butler.

Lewis Butler, though he started adult life as a schoolteacher, became a lawyer after the Civil War and lived in Cairo, Illinois, where he held a minor office in the city government. His office provided contacts from whom he obtained private work as well, and he lived a comfortable life in various St. Louis suburbs until he contracted tuberculosis. Lewis's earliest letters, as well as those of Lacy Paisley and John Carothers later in the chronicle, tell something of the life of schoolteachers in the rural South. Many aspects of their lives did not change substantially until after the Second World War. Teachers were generally single, though in some cases a married woman taught in the same school as her husband. They were as a rule not well paid, and they had no job security or guaranteed annual salary. The teachers frequently boarded or rented rooms in the community and, at least in the case of the Paisleys, enjoyed the fellowship of the other teachers in their free time as well as during the work day. In the years after the Civil War, teaching was a very uncertain profession in Arkansas, for the state provided little support and most schools operated by subscription. Teachers were as vulnerable as farmers and businessmen, who were their patrons, to the vagaries of the weather and the national economy.

None of Alex Butler's sons became doctors, but one of his grandsons was completing his medical training as the chronicle of letters ended. Medical science in the nineteenth century was still rather primitive, and in rural areas, the doctor had a difficult life. A distressing amount of time and effort was spent in nursing the sick. The Butlers fortunately could afford good care, for they were not a robust lot. Alex and his wife had fairly good health and considerable stamina well past middle age, and except for Sarah, all their children lived into adulthood. However, they and their children and grandchildren had a great many spells of sickness, and in the case of serious illness sometimes had a doctor in attendance night and day, aided by the women of the family. But the healing resources available were extremely limited. The letters generally do not name the illnesses in any fashion useful to twentieth-century readers, but from the symptoms, malaria, tuberculosis, typhoid, and pneumonia can be inferred to be rather common. Today drugs and sanitation have almost eliminated them as serious threats, but in the terrible lingering illnesses to which Lewis, Annie, and Alice succumbed, the treatment appears to have been limited to keeping the patients comfortable until they died. The childhood diseases struck more seriously than now, and whooping cough especially was dreaded, though a light case was considered a good thing, inasmuch as the child was then immune to it. Pregnancy was in the category of sickness, and Emma referred to giving birth as "being sick."

It should be noted that the occupations and professions mentioned were open only to men, with some exceptions made for female schoolteachers. In the Butler and Paisley families, no married woman worked outside her home. After Lewis's death, Jennie, his widow, decided to send for her schoolbooks and brush up on her teaching skills. But following her second marriage, there is no mention of her teaching. Indeed, in these families, even the unmarried women remained at home.

And as a matter of fact, in large households like Alexander Butler's and William Paisley's, there was more than enough for one or two women to do. Housekeeping sounds like hard work in Tulip in the nineteenth century. There were virtually none of the labor-saving devices we know today for doing laundry, for preserving or preparing food, or for keeping things clean. In Alex Butler's household, the family divided the labor as much as possible, and even after Emma left he had three daughters at home to help Ma with the chores. In addition, the Butlers generally kept some hired help, usually a cook-laundress. The Butlers were apparently convinced that white women were unable to cook in very hot weather, or to "do all their work" at any time. And indeed, since Emma was pregnant or nursing an infant for a good part of nearly every year from her marriage till her death, it is a relief to know that she usually had a "girl" to help. Sometimes the hired girl was herself a mother, and she and her offspring both might be on the payroll, the child being charged with getting kindling, tending a baby, or other light labor. Mary, Annie, and Emma all expressed the traditional doubts of homemakers about whether hired help were really worth the extra trouble and expense.

As one might expect, the men performed few of the inside chores of maintaining the home, although Billy did cook a bit. In 1868, Charlie and Johnnie Butler tried for a while to farm and keep house, but they soon decided that at least one of them would have to get married. Considering that men spent long hours in the fields and that Billy often worked a twelve-hour day in the store, it is not surprising that they expected someone else to take care of the domestic arrangements.

In addition to preparing the family meals and maintaining the kitchen and the rest of the house, the women usually tended the vegetable garden and gathered the small fruits that might be grown or harvested from the wild. The men of the household, or a hired hand, generally did the heavy work of plowing, and children often had gardening chores like pulling weeds or gathering berries. Families procured seed from commercial houses in the city, and there was a certain amount of consultation in the letters as to which house provided the best varieties. Sometimes the seeds of a particularly fine specimen would be saved for the following season, as in the case of watermelons.

Ma Butler showed a strong interest in cabbage, and others in the family reported with great pleasure on the first mess of peas in the spring or the earliest strawberries. A late frost, a drought, excessive rains, or an infestation of garden pests was a real disaster to these people, for their diets depended on the success of their gardens; there were few means of preserving vegetables for later use. When Mary Butler married the Reverend George Matthews, his enthusiasm and skill as a gardener made him a favorite among the family still living at Tulip, the more so since most of Ma Butler's sons had left to make their own homes elsewhere.

The women also raised poultry. Ma Butler's turkeys form a motif throughout the correspondence. She also raised chickens, but the turkeys were her chief enthusiasm. Emma Paisley also raised poultry, and the California branch of the family, living near abundant supplies of water, had geese and ducks as well as the barnyard fowl. The children helped with the poultry chores, feeding the chickens or gathering the eggs. On festive occasions, roast turkey or guinea was the featured dish. The customary standby for unexpected company was chicken. Whenever possible a woman sold her surplus poultry or eggs at the store.

In addition to the henhouse, the rural homestead contained a smokehouse and a dairy. Hog-butchering time was a major event throughout the neighborhood, and generally men had to do the heaviest work connected with slaughtering the animal. The members of the family generally assembled to share the work as well as the results, and the host family sent portions of the fresh meat around the neighborhood. Sausages, hams, and other portions that could be preserved were stored in the smokehouse. The letters contain some discussion of various techniques for preserving meat. The women usually tended the cows, and one letter describes a dramatic encounter between a cow and Ma Butler. They also made butter for home consumption and sold the surplus. There is no reference in the Butlers' letters to either cheese or clabber, two staples of the rural diet.

Fruits were as great a pleasure in nineteenth-century America as they are today. Everyone welcomed strawberries as a springtime treat. Women and boys picked wild berries for pies and preserves, and orchards yielded apples, peaches, plums, and pears. In addition to making preserves, the Butler women dried apples for winter use. Many summertime letters report on a routine favorite, watermelons, telling how many have been picked, how many are in the fields, and the top weight. It bears remembering that Dobyville is not far from Hope, today's watermelon capital of Arkansas.

The homemaker was responsible not only for feeding the family, but also for making many of

11

their clothes and virtually all the linens and other cloth goods used in the house. When Billy Paisley and Henry Butler went on their buying trips, they sent back reports on the quality and cost of various types of cloth goods. Captain Lipscomb, Billy's step-father, was a tailor and made men's clothing to order. But most clothing for women and children, and a considerable amount of men's work clothes and linen, were made at home. The Butler sisters bought and exchanged dress patterns, and their letters show that they were very sensitive to changes in style and wanted the new fashions. When the women referred to "buying a dress," they meant buying the cloth. Then they had to "get it made up." Ma Butler fondly made pants for her little grandsons, for whom the departure from dresses was a real milestone in their lives. When a new baby was born, his aunts usually sent a bib or dress, though occasionally they sent only a pattern. Around 1870, they all began acquiring sewing machines, which lightened this aspect of their labors considerably. In addition to clothing, they also made quilts and rag carpets and made and remade mattresses, pillows, and feather beds.

Despite this formidable description of the everyday lives of the Butlers and the Paisleys, they found time for play as well. They had books and newspapers to read, though there is little evidence of what they read except for devotional tracts and, of course, the Bible. They had music. Billy frequently purchased sheet music for the Butler girls on his trips to the city, and sometimes the letter writer mentions that "Sister is playing the piano." The family gathered around the instrument to sing hymns as well as secular music. For a time in the 1870s, croquet was as popular with them as it was in the country as a whole, and sometimes they built fires on the lawn so that they could play after dark. They had fireworks on the appropriate southern occasions, which included the Christmas holidays as well as Independence Day. Once, a large group of young Tulip folk assembled for a buggy ride nearly all the way to Princeton, eight miles south. Another time, following an unexpectedly heavy snowstorm, Alex rigged up a sleigh, and the adults and children alike took turns riding across the property.

Like many large families, the Butlers' recreation almost always involved other members of the family. But they also had many visitors, including neighbors, friends from other communities, traveling clergy, and widows or orphans in need of a place to visit en route to live with a relative. They had parties to celebrate weddings, birthdays, and holidays, with much food being prepared and consumed, though no hard drink. Their religious scruples forbade having or attending dancing parties. In fine weather people of any age might go fishing or take a picnic to the riverbank. In the late 1870s, the word *sociable* came into use to denote a party with refreshments, later called a tea.

The social aspects of church life, and the communal effort involved in chores such as corn-husking or quiltmaking, also provided recreation, as did some of the public activities at the schools in the community. For some of the Butlers, there was also the exciting possibility of travel. Since they had the opportunity of taking twice-yearly business trips, Alex Butler, Billy Paisley, and Henry Butler knew their way around the big cities. They had business contacts, knew where the good hotels were, and could negotiate trains, streetcars, horse-drawn cabs, and hall porters. From time to time, they enjoyed escorting some of the women of the family on these trips. Emma went with Billy to Saint Louis, leaving her mother-in-law to take care of the children in Dobyville. Billy and Henry took the younger girls, Alice and Annie, and also Sister

Mary, to visit their brother Lewis, leaving them for some weeks while they went about their business. Another relative later escorted the girls back to Arkansas.

One of the most interesting facets of the correspondence is to observe the improvements in transportation between Billy's first trip, made in the spring of 1867, and 1886, when things had become so much better that he actually made three trips. In 1867 he rode a horse to Rockport, where he got a stagecoach to Little Rock, which is roughly seventy miles from Tulip. From there he boarded a steamboat to Memphis, and "the cars" from Memphis to Cincinnati. At any point along this tortuous route, disaster threatened the traveler. The wheel might fly off the stage-coach, never to be found. Or a delay in the departure of the steamboat might cause one to miss the train. Once Billy was asleep in a railroad car that was uncoupled and left behind when the rest of the train pulled out of the station.

When George Hughes and Olin Moores worked for railway companies, they had passes and could ride very cheaply. Sister Mattie Hughes traveled extensively in the late 1870s and the 1880s between Little Rock and Malvern, and she sometimes arranged to meet Ma Butler at Malvern, where they both visited some of the Butlers who lived there. The Hugheses were the most affluent members of the family and had sons in eastern colleges. They took several long train trips to visit their sons and to attend the American centennial observances in Washington and in Philadelphia. George Hughes traveled widely in search of better health, once leaving Mattie behind in Arkansas while he went to Honolulu.

Even Ma Butler traveled fairly extensively for a woman of her generation. She attended the Methodist General Conference in Nashville and made an extended trip to California to visit her son George and the family of Jennie Butler, the widow of Lewis, who had died soon after he arrived there.

In some respects, traveling between Tulip and Dobyville, a trip of some forty miles, appears to have been more difficult than between Tulip and Cincinnati. Heavy rains in the winter and early spring made the roads impassable, and the creeks frequently rose without warning. One letter reported the death by drowning of a circuit preacher who was washed away trying to cross a river. In the early years of their marriage, Billy sometimes warned Emma that she should walk across bridges instead of remaining in the wagon or buggy. Then in the summertime, the dust and heat made a trip very unpleasant. At any time of the year, there were no commercial accommodations for travelers except along the most frequently used roads, and some of those were rather dubious. The men, traveling alone or in a group of two or three, often camped out-of-doors in good weather. Once Billy borrowed a coffeepot from a woman to use at their camp-fire and greatly offended her by scouring it carefully before he used it. Billy's anxious letters and notes to his wife often contained several alternate routes of travel, arrival times, and contingency plans. Without access to any form of reliable communication, and often without knowing when he set out whether the streams would be in or out of their banks, he was understandably uneasy, and all the more so when it was Emma who was about to set out on the trip.

Toward the end of the chronicle, however, the railroad had advanced to Malvern and to Gurdon, making it possible for the families to visit more frequently and more conveniently. The women could even travel alone for some distances, as when Alice returned from Texas on the train. Emma summoned the courage to take the train from Gurdon to Malvern with several of her young children, an adventure to be remembered. But the Arkansas roads, from the beginning of the story to the end, consistently discouraged any but the most determined travelers. That only began to change with the invention of the automobile.

The reader who looks to the Butler-Paisley correspondence for a complete picture of nineteenth-century life will be disappointed. Naturally, in a collection so large, there are a great many details, and many of them are interesting for all sorts of reasons. When the family traveled, they reported what they saw. The first letter in the collection contains a description of Barnum's Wax Museum and of Fifth Avenue. There is an account of the wide-open style of New Orleans's Sabbath—shooting galleries, band concerts, and every sort of business operation, just a few blocks away from a splendid program that included little girls reciting religious poetry before a large audience. There are all the letters in which Billy describes his adventures on steamboats and trains and in hotels and rooming houses. And Ma Butler's letters from California recount her impressions of the Pacific Ocean, orange groves, and the streets of Los Angeles.

However, these details tend to remain just that—small pieces of a larger picture. They do not necessarily add up to anything more than themselves. The same observation can be made about the picture that the letters provide of everyday life at home. There is a great deal of information in the letters, but in order to obtain a more complete picture of the family, they must be supplemented with census records, tax rolls, and other documents. For like all letter writers, the Butlers and their correspondents selected the details they wished to present. As a general rule, they did not criticize one another in their letters. Wives are virtuous and good; babies are generally sweet and pretty and very little trouble to their mothers; husbands, especially immediately after marriage, are reported to have a perfect understanding with their wives and to be models of kindness, generosity, and good temper.

In addition to this emphasis on the positive, another factor prevents a twentieth-century reader from obtaining a complete historical reconstruction from these letters. He is an outsider to the life of the family, and the letters are written by and for the insiders. They have no need, for example, for extended physical descriptions of each other. Lewis asks whether one of the Paisley babies has "that white eyelash of yours," but whether it is Emma's or Billy's is not clear. There are very few other physical details, except for weight, which varies considerably with their health. Their descriptions of their physical environment are equally vague. From the letters it is impossible to state how many rooms Alex Butler's house had, or where the store was located with respect to the house. Billy writes of watching Emma's window from the Dobyville store, but whether their house was painted or not, where the garden was, or how far they lived from the road does not come across in the letters. They refer to their neighbors by incomplete names, and the latter-day reader may be completely mystified as to the identity of these people.

Thus there are many unknowns, many unanswered questions about the lives of the Butlers and the Paisleys. Nevertheless, the letters capture glimpses of this remarkable family. They wrote about the things that mattered to them—the activities of the churches and schools that they attended; their work in the fields, in the stores, and at home in their kitchens and gardens; the good times of parties with their neighbors and friends; and the sad times watching with those neighbors and friends in sickness and in death. If the story of Tulip lacks the neatness and completeness of an epistolary novel, it is after all a work of chance rather than of art. Chance determined which letters would be preserved when Emma began to keep her cache of letters. Chance rather than art determined what her correspondents wrote, for certainly none of them expected that historians would care about what they did or thought. But although they were not writing for the future, Emma and Billy and the other Butlers and Paisleys did leave to the future the record of a life, in fragments that can be fitted together into bigger pieces to add to the historian's storehouse of equipment with which to explore and understand the past.

Fayetteville, Arkansas
June 1984

EDITORS' NOTE

The text of the correspondence has been edited for greater clarity, with punctuation, spelling, and paragraphing standardized in most cases. Frequently original nonstandard usage has been preserved to illuminate a writer's personality more fully. Standard letter format has replaced the practice of "filling the sheet" usually followed in the nineteenth century. Undated or incorrectly dated letters have been supplied with dates from internal evidence whenever possible, and these are indicated by brackets. The entire Butler-Paisley Family Correspondence, from which this selection has been made, is in the manuscripts repository of Special Collections, University of Arkansas Libraries, Fayetteville.

The editors acknowledge the help of many persons as they worked on this book. Miller Williams and Willard Gatewood of The University of Arkansas Press brought us together for this enterprise, a collaboration that has become a friendship. The Arkansas Endowment for the Humanities provided a grant that helped to make this publication possible. The University of Arkansas Libraries provided support. Special thanks to Mary Wagoner and Cindy Geels of the library staff, for their help in collating the text and typing the introduction and appendices, and to Elisabeth Grant-Gibson, who typed the final version of the manuscript.

Jonathan K. T. Smith, author of *The Romance of Tulip Ridge*, the ultimate authority on Tulip, Arkansas, generously shared his knowledge with us. Sarah Brown's report, "Historic Resources of Dallas County," prepared for Arkansas Historic Preservation, provided useful information about the Butler homestead. Illustrations are from Special Collections, University of Arkansas Libraries, Fayetteville, with assistance from the graphics unit of the Center for Instructional Media.

Special thanks are due to many members of the Butler and Paisley families, who contributed family records, photographs, and information. Jerry and Martha Hammett gave Mrs. Huckaby the letters, which had been saved by Emma Paisley's daughters after her death. Emma Hayley Hawkins donated Emma Paisley's photograph album, which contained pictures of many of the family. Anne Butler Paisley Boyd provided information about names and dates, and boundless enthusiasm for the entire project. An extensive network of cousins also shared information and photographs: Shirley Morrison Allen, Mary Louise Bixby, Elizabeth Bramlett Braswell, Richard Colburn and Gertrude Butler, Richard C. Butler, Jr., Ruth Knickerbocker Chedsey, Ruth Boddie Farmer, Mary Knickerbocker Glenn, Elizabeth Butler Knapp, and C. Barrett Knickerbocker.

Mrs. Huckaby acknowledges the support and assistance of her immediate family: her sister Clara Paisley Doyle, her brother and sister-in-law Clifton Lewis and Joy Smith Paisley, and her sister-in-law Eleanor Rhodes Paisley.

The staff of The University of Arkansas Press have been helpful and encouraging to us at every stage of this undertaking, and we gratefully acknowledge their support.

BEGINNINGS: 1857–1860

Lewis Butler to Emma Butler in Tulip

New York March 12th, 1857

Dear Sister

Papa tells me that you think hard of my not writing to you. I will not say it is strange if you do; for I confess that a letter was due you from me long ago. I do not take my pen this morning mearely because I am pressed to it by your complaints of neglect; although this quickens me to tell you that I am sorry for not having performed this duty, and that by not writing to you I have only *concealed* my love for you. Nevertheless, my affection for my sister Eliza is as great as it would have been had I answered both of her letters on their reception.

Perhaps I can approach nearer to interest in my letters, now that I am in the city of *wonder* and of *wonders*. I have written home twice since we have been here, and have nearly exhausted my ideas concerning New York, for howsoever few ideas and descriptions my letters contained, yet they ment much more than they expressed, and any subject howsoever fruitful will grow insipid by bad management of it, when it is not half exhausted. For instance, if I sit down and write home that New York is a wonderful city, that I have been up 5th avenue, down to the 5 points and seen the place they call old Bruery and the lik, without ever describing what I saw in these noted places, I say if I write these about the city, skiming the subject over without giving you a single idea concerning what I had seen, the subject will grow trite and will cloy although by no means exhausted. I have written two letters home since I have been here, and in a general way told what I have seen. Now you may hear some of the particulars. You must excuse the above *parched* page.

Last Sunday we attended preaching four miles down in the city, and walked about six coming back in order to get a view of New York. Fifth Avenue is a broad street along which a great many rich people reside in the most magnificent dwellings, surrounded by evergreen shrubery arranged with all the care and niceity of art. The buildings are mostly of stone or granite 5, 6 or 7 stories high. We continued our walk all along 5th avenue, with on each side a wall of such grand buildings as I have described, and after gazing at the wealth and splendor of the upper tendum, decended imediately to what is called the 5 points from the circumstance that 5 streets point directly there. This is the center of all the poverty, misery, vice, and their attendant train, that New York affords. A gentleman remarked the other day on my telling him I had been to the 5 points that 5 years ago a man that had been there was considered as having accomplished a fete, but now it was so changed that almost everyone went there. It is somewhat dangerous; and very dangerous at night. Mr. Pulliam said he thought about takeing a Police with us but concluded that we would be in no danger. To one ignorant of the habits and vices of large cities, it is very dangerous to go far without haveing someone with you.

Yesterday evening I went in Barnum's museum, and saw more curiosities than I ever saw before in all my life. Images of great men, looking almost as natural as life, and if you were not aware before hand that they were only representations you would be almost certain to be deceived. Daniel Webster, H Clay, Lord Byron, Kossuth and others, at full hight, not painted on canvass, but represented by an exact likeness made of a substance hardly distinguishable from the human skin, stuffed, with eyes as bright as the original, hair peculiar to each one, in a word so exactly like the real, that the most practised eye could not detect any defect. You may know it resembled the living man when dressed as it was in his usual style. Another interesting scene was our Savior when brought to be questioned by Pilate, with the crown of thorns on his head attended by the train mentioned in the Book, all dressed and fashioned after the maner I have described, you may know it was an interesting sight. I saw what is called the "happy family" composed of various kinds of animals naturally hostile to one another, but tamed and rendered as friendly and peaceable as a human family.

I came very near starting for Henderson [North Carolina] this morning with Mr. Lewis Smith of Granville, but Papa concluded I had better remain one day longer. So I expect to leave for H tomorrow morning. We left there exactly a week today. I do not recon Papa will get off before the middle of next week. He thinks of returning through NC, and if so will stop in Virginia a day or two.

It makes me feel like going home when I see him going back, when I hear descriptions of the prosperity of our state and see so many people from out there, but I think it is better that I should undergo the pain of being separated from those dearest to me for the sake of improving my mind. If I were to consult feelings alone, the speed of the electric wire would not be too great to bear me home; but reason and judgement tell me that I should forego the pleasures of home and association for a season to obtain that which when obtained will make me a better, greater, and more useful man every way. I expect to go to Chapel Hill. Papa seems to prefer it, and says that Mama does, and for many reasons I do too.

I will write shortly after I arrive at Henderson. Give my love to all. Write to me and I will hereafter number you among my correspondents.

Your affectionate brother Lewis P. Butler.

Lewis Butler to Emma Butler in Tulip

Lisbon [Arkansas]. 27 March. 1859

Dear Emma,

I am happy to see, that instead of waiting a long time, you have returned to me so promptly your reply to my letter, and I sincerely hope that you will treat this and all my future letters with the same respect. Well what shall I write? I am getting tired of repeating in every letter "that my school is getting on very well", though I am sure I should dislike very much to have to change my tone and say that it was getting on very badly—so let me be content with a good thing.

But my school has not been going smoothly on without any interruption. One of my schollars— a little girl of about twelve years, died week before last of Pneumonia, and the mumps getting out in the neighborhood has for a while thined the number of my pupils, though I believe it is pretty well over now.

You are curious to know how many of my schollars I have whipped yet, as if you doubted that I would whip at all. Well I tell you—I haven't kept any account, but I believe I have gone as high as four a day. Though by the by you need not inform Miss Josephine of this fact, as it might give her a rather harsh idea of my really good nature. I hardly know whether to say that you sent me Miss Jos.'s love yourself because you knew it would be pleasing to me, or that she really sent it herself. I hope the latter, but you must take the pains to assure me of this fact, which you see is a matter of great concern to me, in your next letter. Give her my love, and my blessing attend her at the trying day of your Examination.

You ought to be writing your composition—ought you not? Make haste and write it off and send it to me. I would like to see it before you have to read it. Have you learned to play that tune yet— "Be kind to the loved ones at home?" I recon your concert will be a real treat.

I have nothing new to write—except that Maj. Coulter starts for New Orleans tomorrow. He will be gone about three weeks, I recon. Today is Sunday, or rather Sunday night—and you will say that I ought not to be writing letters, but really Sunday down here is the dullest day of all others to me, and I have to keep my spirits up somehow. Now at Tulip, Sunday is always the most welcome day. There we always have preaching convenient to go to, and at night down at home, to sit and talk with you all or to sing a song or two, what is more pleasant!

Miss Anna Watson intends coming down with Miss Mollie to spend the vacation. I will not be here much of the time, but I would enjoy their company very much.

I received a letter from Sister Mat a day or two since. She was well, and I was glad to know that she was in good spirits, and likely to enjoy her stay up at Benton fishing with Mr. John Hughes and his lively, young wife. Now I recon is the most pleasant part of the year up at Benton. 'Twill be so fine to fish on the Saline.

But in the Summer—at your examination, she must certain to be at Tulip and spend all the Summer with us, for I have seen so little of you all since I returned, that sometimes it appears that I have not been home at all.

I have nothing more to write and I recon you will excuse me for stopping right here, for I have not in fact written you anything that you will take pleasure in reading. I must answer Sister Mattie's letter tonight.

So with giving my love to you all, Miss Jos. included. I am your brother Lewis

George Butler to Emma Butler in Tulip

Randolph-Macon College
March 3, 1860

My dear sister Emma,

I dreamed the other night papa went on after goods and left brother Henry to take care of the Store &c, but I reckon my dream can not be relied on as true: for I think if brother H. had been at home all this time, I should have had a letter before now. I have been expecting one a long time. I received a letter from brother Lewis only a few days back.

I have visited our relatives around here but little since I have been at college, and reckon they think rather hard of it, but it is almost impossible to visit much here, and especially in the winter season. I will try to visit them more frequently now that the spring has begun. I love them all very much, and if I should consult my pleasure and inclination would spend most of my time with them, but you know that it would not do even for one going to school at home, to visit a great deal if he expected to keep up in his studies, and for one boarding out it would be much worse.

Aunt Eliza is very kind to me. Sends me apples, cakes &c. I have on now a warm pair of socks which she knit for me. I go over there oftener than to any other place because it is nearer than any of the others, and also there I can see the face of my dear mother, yours, Mary's and others, that I love to look at.

We are now carrying on a protracted meeting, but there seems as yet to be but little feeling on the part of the ungodly. Members of the church are not generally warm, and I have heard here no such sermons as those we had at camp-meeting from brothers McKensie, Hunter &c. I look back upon that meeting as the most pleasant and truly happy time I have ever spent. May the Lord bless the young that are growing up around Tulip and give to them the spirit and religion of their parents.

O! Emma, how valuable do I find religion far away from home at college. When my soul without it might be oppressed with gloom and melancholy, with it I am made to rejoice and feel happy trusting in Jesus. What sweeter name than that to a soul conscious of his pardning love. Hold fast to your religion, and be not content to live a cold professor, as I believe you will not, by the grace of God. How I would like to be at Tulip, Home, tonight for it is Friday night and I reckon the church is lit up. Don't think, though, that I am discontented or low spirited; on the contrary, my heart is "lit up" with joy and consolation by our religion, which says "All things shall work together for good to them that love God." So confiding fully in this prommise we will go forward and "turn not to the right hand nor to the left" for we are sure

> "He shall direct our wandering feet,
> He shall prepare our way."

Much love to all. Your affectionate brother George

George Butler to Emma Butler in Tulip

Randolph-Macon College
December 28th, 1860

My *dear* sister Emma,

It is Friday night. The Frank Society has just closed its weekly meeting, and I hasten to my room to answer your kind, sweet letter, which was handed me a few moments ago by a fellow Frank while the Hall was in session. You may be sure I sought the first opportunity to retire to my room, and reading the letter which I saw, from the stamp, came from some loved one at Tulip. Quickly did my eyes run over the pages which your own dear hand had written! and quickly did I return to the Hall to prevent being fined for staying out over my time. But now, as I have said, I am free: and would, loved sister, that I could write you a letter which would give you as much joy and satisfaction as yours did me: But if I fail in doing this, I trust to your good nature to excuse me; for in the first place it is not very easy to do; in the second place, it will not be because I have not the *will*.

Christmas is nearly out. We had but one day given us here; but I took another in addition to that. Uncle Joseph sent for me pretty late on the first morning of Christmas, and advised me to spend the next day with my relations in the country. I did so, with the consent of the president, Dr. Smith. I had quite a lively time with cousins Ann & Ginnie Walker and several other young ladies. We had several very laughable plays. Uncle Joseph participated in them, and all, old and young, laughed until our heads fairly ached. Well, if there is "a time for laughter," we all thought that it was then.

We have had a protracted meeting going on at college for two weeks. Six or eight have professed pardon, and there are yet several seekers. How I would liked to have been with you all at camp meeting: It is with pleasure that I look back to that one which I attended just before leaving. I live in hope of seeing yet again happy times at the same camp ground. May the Lord bless *evermore* the Christians around Tulip!

Dr. Walker requested me to ask brother Henry what property it was that Dr. R. wishes to sell. Does it include more than his office and what it contains?

It is time I had finished your letter. If I had a good pen I would rewrite it; for I fear you can hardly read it. Much love to all. Write soon to your devoted brother

George

29th Dec.

P.S. I did intend to inclose a letter to Sister Ann, but can not now conveniently. I will write again soon, when I hope to have a smoother pen than this, to answer sister Annie's letter.

Affectionately
Your brother George

WARTIME: 1861–1865

Lewis Butler to Emma Butler in Tulip

Camp Alleghany, Va.
August 12th. 1861

My Dear Sister Emma:

Brother Henry received your letter yesterday written to us both and we were equally rejoiced to hear from home and to receive a letter from our dear sister Emma. Brother Henry went down to Camp Bartow this evening and did not return until near night, and as he is now writing and I have a better opportunity than I will have again soon, as we contemplate removing tomorrow, I have determined to write to you.

Last night was Sunday night, a night always commemorated by you all by singing the sacred melodies which have been hymned in our house since childhood. Billy Paisley, Dunkan Durham, Mr. Jones, and myself gathered around one of our camp fires and made the camp ring with some of the same good old songs which we have learned to love for their very age, and which I doubt not you were singing in that same hour. I remembered you all then, and imagination showed me the lighted parlor, and my ear caught the sound of my mother's voice as she sang the treble to some of those time honored songs, and my heart ran out in sighs that I might be permitted once again to be with you all at home, dear home.

Emma, you can hardly estimate how our love for home and its inmates has increased since we have entered upon this life of hardships and uncertainties. You have often heard tell of the corrupting tendencies of camp life, but another good result I have experienced since we left you all is that I have read my Bible more and with greater pleasure and profit than ever before, my thoughts have been more constantly turned towards *the hereafter*, and so far from suffering any temptation to do wrong, I have felt that my conduct was more especially under the inspection of God than ever, and that now I had need to look constantly and entirely to our heavenly Father in this hour of especial need, if I expected from him protection and defence against the numberless dangers by which we are assailed. I am conscious that my conduct since I left you all has been more scrupulous than before, and in my case at least, the dangers attending camp life have but served to arm me more securely against them. But the corruption in camp has not been exaggerated as I can see all around. So far as morality goes, I think ours is far the best company in the regiment.

I have written what I have written, my dear Emma, from the impulses of my heart, and because I thought this would be of greater interest to you than aught else I could write. It is now growing late at night, it has been raining hard upon our tents for hours and many a sick soldier is now suffering and moaning as the rain borne on the wind beats upon the thin covering above him and sends the damp to his weakened and languishing frame. Brother Henry is now writing on the other end of the table with the candle and inkstand between us. We have both been remarkably blessed thus far above our fellow soldiers, and I know you will continue to pray God to preserve your brothers and lead them with honor from the field of their country's glory safely back to those they love so well.

Tomorrow we leave here to go in the neighborhood of our enemies, and in a short time we expect to meet and conquer them. How pleasant it would be to be with you all this Summer enjoying the luxuries of the season, but we willingly yield up this when a more important work calls us away, and if we can be instrumental in speedily establishing our government in peace and prosperity we shall be content.

We see no fruit at all in this country—it is almost uninhabited—the only delicacy, we look upon it as such—we have is maple sugar, which the inhabitants of the mountains make in large quantities. I have written a long letter this evening to George Hughes giving all of any interest— it is now late and I must cease writing. May heaven bless you my dear Emma and all the dear ones at home is the prayer of both your brothers. Write again and often.

Yours affectionately, Lewis P. Butler

P.S. God bless you my dear Sister Emma. Henry

George Butler to Emma Butler in Tulip

Randolph-Macon College
December 4th, 1861

Dear Emma,

I would like to have time this evening to write you a long letter as I have put it off so long, but the Sun is almost down and I have to walk two miles, you know, before I get my supper. Besides, it is quite cold; Snow on the ground, and it seems hardly to melt at all. There was hardly enough here to cover the ground, and sticking to the trees almost from top to bottom on the north side.

Oh, how hard it must be on our noble Soldiers who are encamped on the bleak and cheerless tops of the Allegheny Mountains. 'Tis almost enough to make a body shudder to think of it. God preserve our dear brothers. I received a letter from brother Lewis a day or two since, but it was a long time getting here, long enough to have reached Ark. They were expecting to leave the Mountains soon for a more comfortable climate to winter in. I do hope they may not be required to spend the winter where they are.

I received Pa's letter about the same time I received yours. I have since received one from Ma and one from Sister Hunter. Aunt Eliza had just written to Ma and Pa before Ma's reached me, and perhaps this will account for my not writing sooner. You can better imagine than I can tell you, how I felt when I received your letter & Pa's. You know what feelings and emotions it kindles in the heart to receive letters from those we dearly love. But this pleasure is greatly increased when one is far away from home and, so to speak, alone.

We have now in college thirty three students, a small number for a college, but the reason is plain. We drill every evening, near an hour. It is the very best kind of exercise, and a double quick for a few minutes is not disagreeable these cool evenings. We have no regular military instructor yet; but our Prof. in Chemistry drills us. It is getting so dark I can hardly see. So you must excuse this short worthless letter. Aunt Eliza and all our relations are well. My love to all, servants included. Write me soon.

Really it is dear postage, paying ten cents for such scribbling as this. My health continues to be very good. I enjoy my morning and evening walks finely these cool frosty mornings. If perchance the northern blasts should be most too cool, I can draw on my large thick overcoat and warm yarn gloves and thus be protected securely from the cold. How thankful I ought to be to God for all his blessings temporal & spiritual, and to my kind beloved parents. Well, I do feel grateful.

How beautiful the stars shine out from their homes in the skies these pretty nights. O that my heart were as pure and free from sin as they. I sometimes think the Virginia skies are bluer and clearer than ours in Ark. But the gems of night are already showing their faces, and the crescent moon is sinking in the West. Goodbye. Sweet Emma, write soon. George

Phenie Finly to Emma Butler in Tulip

Jan 26, 1862

Dear Emma—

This will make the second time I have written to you within the last three months. I have also written to Puss Brown twice. I am very anxious to hear from Old Tulip, and I wonder very much what can be the matter with you all, you must surely receive my letters; if you knew, Emma, how anxious I was to hear from you all, you would surely write to me.

I wish to hear from the school, how does Mr. Barcus and Borden get along—do they *scold very much*. Tell me all about yourself and schoolmates, especially Puss—all the news. See what a long letter you can write me, Emma, oh! it will give me so much pleasure to read it.

It has been a great while since I have seen any of you. I have almost forgotten how some look, but not you, Emma. I never can forget your sweet little face. Have you quit going to school yet? Tell me all about yourself. Have all the young men gone to war; all from here are gone—there is only one or two left. They are both unfit for service. One has one hand, the other one eye. Oh, this war is terrible, 80 young men left here last May 12 of them have died. I am afraid more will die with disease than Lincoln's balls will kill. Emma, I do declare it is a wicked wish, but I do hope that Lincoln, Sewed [Seward]—and all of his cabinet may sink into the lowest depths of torment even they are planing against us, no torment is too good for them. If I could only see him burnt by piece meales, I think it would do me a great deal of good. Now don't think me two wicked. I cannot help it, but I speak the truth.

I will tell you something of myself. I have been going to school at home to a teacher pa employed to teach us children, all except brother Jimmie. I have been going to her all the time since I left Tulip, until this last Christmas she left us. I cannot tell where I will go next. Pa says I must go one year longer at any rate. I have been taking music lessons all the while. Pa employed a teacher last week to come every day and teach me but I do not think I shall like him—he reminds me of Mr. Barcus not that he scolds, oh no, I dare not do that, but he talks like him. I am very unhealthy, and he had the audacity to tell me 'twas all put on just to get pa to pet me. I guess he got sick of it before it was done with. I am not well now, I am so nervous I can hardly write, I do not expect you can read this now. I will close. *Emma do please please* write to me soon, and a *long* letter as long as you can write. Give my love to our friends, tell Puss Brown to write to me. I remain your friend
Phenie Finly
P S Please do no[t] show this to any one. There are so many mistakes and it is written badly—be sure and write

Phenie

Henry Butler to Emma Butler in Tulip

Winchester, Va.
Feby 10th, 1862

My sweet sister Emma,

On looking over some old letters on yesterday I came across one from you, and although I have answered it, yet it was such a nice, sweet letter it deserves *two* of mine. It is now late at night, all is quiet save an occasional cough from the tents around me. I am sitting by *a bright fire* in the *same chimney* I had to my tent before we left this place for Romney. So we are again *at rest*, occupying the same ground we were encamped upon more than one month ago.

But alas, we all are not here, for the severe marches, and hardships experienced since we left this place on the 1st day of the year has sent some of our soldiers to their homes, and *many* to their *long homes*. I am glad to learn, however, that the sick in the various Hospitals are doing well, and a great many are returning to duty. We went into camp at this place last Thursday evening, and although the ground was covered with snow, we have raked out the snow, and got some nice dry straw for our beds, and we fare finely. Of course the boys are in good spirits, at once more quieting down in camp, and are allowed to visit town to buy a *cigar* or a *pipe* or chewing tobacco, or something of the kind. We are now quite busy making out Muster and Pay-rolls so that the Quarter Master can pay the soldiers some money. Another thing is occupying the attentions of many, that is *furloughs*, a certain number from each company (according to the size) being permitted to go home for a month or so. I have no idea of getting a furlough this winter, so *I* need not trouble myself about it.

Brother L. is quite well, and is very well contented. He is much better satisfied than he used to be, owing no doubt to the fact that he has something to do now more agreeable. Billy P., Dick S., Jim R. and the boys generally are well. Billy P. was boasting this evening about eating such a fine dinner out in the country, and seeing some pretty girls too.

Give my love to Cousin Mat, though I reckon she has returned home. I received a day or two since two *very nice comforters* knit and sent by *a young* lady, one for brother L. and the other (the *prettiest* of *course*) for myself. O they are so *very* nice. Mine has several colors, purple, green, crimson, light and dark red. They *are* quite *comfortable*. Can you guess who sent them to us? I don't know how to thank the *fair donor* sufficiently for *such kindness*.

Kiss the little children for me, Little Jimmy who Ma use to love so much. I would like so much to see him. Walter and Henry West are interesting little fellows too. So buss them for "Nunc," and tell them to be good boys till I come to see them. O how delightful 'twould be to walk out to see brother G. and sis Mattie again!

Give my love to "cousin" and ask her to write, and so do you very soon. Tell Annie I have not *forgotten her* by a *great deal*.

Your loving "Brun-ry"

P.S. I cannot close this without at least writing Alice's name. She in sister Mary's last letter said "Put in a few words for me", O how much is expressed in those words. God bless the dear child. Kiss her *twice* for her brother Henry.

W. S. Marshall to William Paisley in the 3rd Ark. Inf.

Richmond, Va.
Nov. 22, 1862

Dear Paisley—

I received your kind letter on the 16th inst, which was not only satisfaction to me, but to the entire company, to hear that you were so fortunate as to be able to travel as soon as what you were.

In answer to your letter, you owe no apology for anything. As regards my clothing, that is all right. Something of myself and the company. I am well and here at the Chimborazo Hospital waiting for the Regt. I was left behind on rear guard at Orange C. H. [Courthouse]. I thought then that I would take the train for Gordonsville and meet the regiment there. There I learned that it would not pass in 10 miles of the place. I saw Capt. Stone, and he said the regiment would be at Hanover Junction the next day, and for me to go on there. As there was no train going out that evening, I reported to the hospital to get lod[g]ing for the night. In the morning I got aboard of the train with the sick going to Richmond and when it got to the place of my destination, the guard would not let me off the cars, brought me on and placed me here.

I have been from the Co. 4 days. At that time they were all well, and tolerably well clothed. I expect they have gone to Fredricksburg. Doc Lewis of Co C is also here, and got here the way I did. Dick Smith is well and expects to go to the Co. soon.

Paisley, as I know nothing of the general movement of our grand army, of course so can say nothing. Jackson is supposed to be near Staunton, Longstreet & Lee in the direction of Fredricksburg. Yesterday was a day set apart by the enemy for the shelling of the town. Peter Craig is appointed Hospital Steward. Rand as 2nd Lt. Adjt. Butler is on Brigd. Gen. Cook's staff. Louis is appointed Adjt of the regiment. Some little change in the Co. James Joyner orderly. Watson 2nd Sergt., Tysie B., 3rd, Lofton Little 4th, Tommie 5th, Sam Pryor 1st Corp. Latham 2nd, Paisley 3rd, Sims 4th.

As I have given you all the news I think of at present I shall close. Give my love to J. M. Somerville and any of the boys you may see. Write soon. Respectfully yours friend W. S. Marshall

Paisley I want you or someone to bring my trunk from Ark to Jackson, Miss., and send it to Father's.

H. Marshall
Thomaston, Miss.

Henry Butler to Emma Butler in Tulip

Hd Qrs Cooke's Brigade
Near Fredericksburg, Va.
Nov. 24th, 1862

My dear sweet Sister,

I have written to Ma and George H., but will try and finish one to you if possible. I am in a position now requiring more attention, writing &c than heretofore. Consequently I am interrupted every hour during the day. In looking over some old letters the other day I came across one from you and you addressed me so affectionately that I determined I would write you next. You know there are so many of you at home to write to, that it is impossible to write a letter to all, when we have so few opportunities of sending letters across the Mississippi. I have received one or two letters by mail from Arkansas, but as it is uncertain about their crossing the river, we have been slow to write and send by mail. Major Stone leaves tomorrow morning for Arkansas. He is a friend of mine, and if he calls to see you all you must be *very* kind to him. I regret having to part with him. He has shown me many favors.

Well, sister Emma, have you become accustomed to the war, to seeing soldiers with muskets and artillery. Or do you ever see any cannon passing by Tulip? I don't know how I would feel to get out of sight of troops marching to and fro, to leave the camp all tents and go again to living in houses. But you must not think that I wish to live always in the army. No, I love to be at home. I sincerely wish this cruel war was over, but so long as the enemy menaces our beloved country, I want to be a soldier, doing all I can to beat back the insolent foe that comes to despoil our once happy land. I have never wished yet to be out of the service.

I am in good health, have not been sick in a long time, for which I *do feel* thankful. Charlie is well. You would be astonished to see how dextrous he uses the musket in going through the manual of arms. He is ahead of some of the oldest soldiers in drilling and many other things. I have not heard from Brothers L & Geo since I wrote to Ma. This is owing to our marching about so much recently. I look for Lewis every day. This evening brought me a letter from Bro. Caldwell. Why some of you all did not write me about Eaton I cannot see. Mr. Caldwell wrote me *a good* letter. I wish I could receive more of them. Do you all have sugar in your coffee, or do you have any coffee in Arkansas? We have just purchased one hundred pounds of sugar at seventy-five cents. We bought so much because it was *cheap*. We live well but it costs something. Do you ever [hear from] my sweetheart? You must write to her and tell her "Brunry sends his love."

I do not know where we will winter. I would like to write to you all every week and receive letters as often. Tell sister Mary she must excuse me for not writing to her this time. I believe I owe sister Annie a letter too. Well tell her that I will write her some of these times.

Goodbye, dear sister Emma. Pray for us that are absent but often think of you all at home. May the good Lord bless and preserve us to meet again. Give my love to *all*.

Your loving brother Henry

Orders for Corp. Wm. Paisley, Dec. 30, 1862–Feb. 20, 1863

Regimental HeadQrs
December 30th 1862

Spcl Order No. 1

In pursuance to Genl. Order No. 135 from the General Commanding this Army, the following named officers and men are ordered to report, without delay, to the Conscript officer nearest their homes or present abode for duty, *until sufficiently recovered to return to their commands.*

Corpl. William Paisley Co I. 3rd Ark. Regiment

By Command of Col.
Van H. Manning
Comdr 3rd Ark. Rgt.

L. P. Butler
  Lt. & Adj't.

[On reverse]
Enrolling Officer Clark Co.
Corp. Wm. Paisily [*sic*] reported to me
this day, and is ordered to report to
Maj. G. D. Alexander for duty.
                  W. D. Neely Capt
                  And E. O. Clark Co.

Arkadelphia, Arks.
Feby 20th 1863

[Written vertically
across the above]
Apl. 13, 1863
Paid two months pay
to 31 October 1862
$26 Maj J Ambler
S Duckwall Capt

Post, Arkadelphia March 9th 1863

This may certify that Corp Wm Paisily has been employed as Clerk in my office at this Post, and that now having recovered sufficiently of his wounds as to be able to return to his company in the Army of the Potomac, he is hereby directed to report for duty back to his regt. All Officers along his route are respectfully requested to give him transportation, and facilitate him in reaching his destination.

        Geo. D. Alexander
        Maj. Ord & Arty &
        Comy Post, Arkadelphia, Arks.

George Butler to Emma Butler at Tulip

Camp near Fredericksburg, Va.
January 1863

Dear Emma,

I believe I have not written you a letter nor received one from you since I have been in the army. But I can not think that this is due to a want of affection in either of us. However, I cannot let the present opportunity of sending you a letter pass unimproved without doing violence to my feelings. I am now sitting in my cabin, with a cheerful fire blazing in the fire place and a board in my lap to write on. The day is pretty cold but not too cold for the season.

Cook's Brigade, to which brother Henry belongs, has left us, for what place we have not yet heard. I am sory that we could not all remain together, but we have great cause to be thankful that is has been as well as it has been with *us four* since the war commenced. All of us are yet alive and very comfortably situated. To God our Father and Preserver be all praise for his goodness. Brother Lewis, as you know, now holds the position which brother Henry had before he left our regiment. He makes a good Adjutant, and Col. Manning seems to be much pleased with him.

Our Col. is a nice man, makes an excellent officer, but I am sorry to say is not a Christian, and like most of our officers, curses and swears when he gets vexed at the conduct of the men. He admits afterward that it is wrong and seems to regret it. It is a great pitty that men in office and exerting so much influence should set so bad an example before their inferiors.

I am glad to say that I have never known one of my brothers to be guilty of thus profaning the holy name of God. Doubtless this is due in great measure to the manner in which we have been brought up by our dear parents, and to them, under the grace of our Heavenly Father, we owe a *large* debt of gratitude for exemption from this as well as many like sinful practices. To our God we owe eternal thanks for giving us such parents. We shall never know their full value until the light of the eternal world shines upon our mental vision; when "this corruptible shall have put on incorruption and this mortal immortality." Then shall we see more clearly than we ever have yet the value, the *untold value*, of the immortal soul & see how we ought to have valued its rescue from sin and eternal death.

Sister Emma, you must be sure to write me, and send your letter by some of those who will be returning to the regiment not long after you get this.

Brother Charles & I have a cabin now to ourselves, and will have a good opportunity for religious exercises if we remain here during the winter.

Much love to all. Good by

Your brother
George E. Butler

33

Henry Butler to William Paisley

Hd Quarters Cookes Brigade
Coosawhatchie, S.C.
Apr 22nd 1863

Dear Billy

I was glad to receive your interesting letter from Mcleansville, N.C. I regret that the circumstances were such as to prevent your coming by and spending a few days with me. Your cousin would also have been much pleased to have seen you, and no doubt you could have passed a few days with us quite pleasantly. Your cousin is quite well, also the young man Clark who was rooming with you at the Jordan Springs near Winchester.

The 27th is fuller and in a better condition every way than it has been for twelve months, numbering about *five hundred* men for duty. The Brass Band has improved very much and is now one of the *best* in the service. And, by the by, the 27th N.C. is one of the best Regiments I have seen, can *surpass any* in the manual. It is a real treat to witness their dress parades. I am acquainted with most of the officers of the 27th and find them *all* gentlemen. Genl. Cooke thinks there is no such Regt as the 27th and the 3rd Ark.

At the same time the letters you sent me came to hand, I received several more by Capt. Smith, and another from Sister Mary mailed at Atlanta Ga., dated Apr. 1st. I wish I could make some arrangement whereby letters could be sent across the Mississippi regularly. Do you know whether the mail communication is opened as yet? I wrote to Foster on yesterday. Tell Lewis to write to him. His address is 9th Tenn Regt (Co "C") Maneys Brigade, Chatanooga or Tullahoma.

What is old man John Pattillo and Wm doing? Is John Eaton subject to the conscript law? If I could have seen you, you would have been troubled with *a thousand* questions about the people around Tulip.

We are in a fine country surrounded by magnolias, orange, and palmettos and living well—fish and oysters in abundance, though it is getting too late for the latter. We are surrounded too by snakes, musketos, gnats and Aligators. One of the soldiers killed one of the latter yesterday morning measuring *seven feet*.

I go down to Savannah occasionally, being only a few hours ride on the cars. I don't think we will remain here long, since the cause which brought us here has in a great measure been removed. The Yanks will hardly make another "reconnaisance" in Charleston harbor this spring. There is some talk of our being sent back to Wilmington, N.C. I wrote to Brother Lewis several days since. I am anxious to hear from you all, for Charlie was sick when I last heard. Have the Arkansas prisoners arrived yet? *Paul Coulter* and John Drake were among the captives. I reckon "Paul" is a hard looking customer as a soldier. *You need not tell him so*, however, for I really think *some* of his family are *good looking*.

Billy, I would like to see you promoted. What do you think of your chances? I could probably get you in with Major Hayes, our Brigade Commissary, but that would amount to but little, only 25 cents per day in addition to pay as private.

Col Manning has asked me to be his Brigade Commissary *provided* he is promoted; in that case, I would like to have you with me if you cannot do better.

Give my love to my brothers and *our* friends. Write to me at Pocolaligo, So. Car.
Yours, Henry

Henry Butler to William Paisley in Charlotte, N.C.

Head Quarters Cookes Brigade
Kingston, N.C.
May 21st, 1863

Dear Billy—

I herewith send you two letters from your sister, which were handed me by your uncle James Paisley who is now with the Brigade. He came in yesterday and was much disappointed in not seeing his son, who had been sent off to Johnson County with a detail of men to look up deserters from *Daniels' Brigade.* We sent out a party of one hundred men to arrest deserters from that Brigade—*two hundred* of the scoundrels having deserted within the past month or two. Your uncle dined with me today, and he expected to leave tomorrow for home as it was uncertain when Sergeant Paisley would return—but as good luck would have it, a squad of deserters were sent down and your cousin in charge of the party. So your uncle will probably remain with his son a day or two longer.

Your uncle is quite a clever gentleman, and thinks a great deal of you. I think I can see a likeness between him and yourself. I was glad to see your cousin return this evening. He brought in eighteen deserters. One deserter was shot yesterday belonging to Daniels' Brigade. It was the first execution I ever witnessed. The whole brigade was present to witness the scene.

I am at a loss to know where to direct this, but suppose it will reach you sooner or later.

Genl Lee sent an order to Genl Hill to "send him Cookes Brigade," but he (Genl H.) took the authority to send Daniels' in our stead. Genl Lee then telegraphed. "I have ordered Cookes Brigade—why has it not been sent?" What further occured I know not, but there is still a probability of our being sent to Va. The enemy are leaving Newbern and Washington, and Genl. Hill thinks of advancing to draw them out if possible. But I think nothing of importance can be gained in this country. The enemy have such advantages in position &c.

I have received no letters from home during the past month, and but one letter from my brothers—in which you added a P.S., which by the by was *longer* than *the letter itself.*

I wish we could go to Va. I think Genl Lee will make an advance on Hooker before long, and I would like so much to be in the campaign. Of course Genl Cooke is *very* anxious to go to Va. I wrote to brother Lewis a day or two ago. Give my love to my brothers.

Affectionately your friend H. A. Butler

Your uncle sent you the within printed letter—it is a good epistle, read it.

Lewis Butler to Emma Butler in Tulip

Regt Head Qrs.
Northern Virginia
June 3rd, 1863

My Dear Emma:

I wrote a long letter to mama some days ago by Dr. Chambers who I thought would start in a day or two; but he has been delayed until the present time, and it is necessary that I write a few lines, or what is already written will be old when you get it. I have read over again your letter of 14th April to day that, with several other letters mailed on this side the Mississippi river by bro. George Hughes, are the last we have received from home. You cannot exaggerate the pleasure your letter gave me. It was one of the most interesting I have received.

We are still encamped near the Rapidan River, in the same locality where we were when I wrote last, though we have changed camp. We leave here tomorrow morning at daylight, in what direction none of us know, though all of us expect a move of importance, may be an advance into the enemy's country. Our army here is very strong and in a very efficient condition. I will let you hear from us again as soon as we stop and opportunity offers. We are all well now. George is doing his duty as chaplain, preaches quite often. Charlie is the same old seven & six. I have not heard from brother Henry right recently. He was well when I heard. When you write Miss Phenie Finley give her my compliments, and tell her she ought not to allow any young man *at home* to win her affections so long as the war lasts. The poor fellows in the army are at a great disadvantage, I am afraid. We are all in great suspense in regard to Vicksburg, but we are hopeful that she will be able to stand.

It is now late—we have Reveille tomorrow before day. Good by. Write to me often as you can, and with love to all, I am your affectionate brother

Lewis P. Butler

Direct as heretofore: Robertsons Brigade
Hood's Division
Longstreets Camps
A.N. Va.

Henry Butler to William Paisley in Charlotte, N.C.

Hd Qrs Cookes Brigade
Gordonsville
Sept 26th 1863

Dear Billy

I saw your cousin a day or two since, from whom I learned that you were now at Charlotte. You run about so much, I know not where to write. Two Regts of our Brigade arrived here day before yesterday. The other two, 27th and 46th, will reach here this evening. We were ordered up in much haste, this place being threatened by a raid from Yanky Cavalry. We have immense stores here—in fact the Army of Nor. Va. receives all its supplies by this place, and it would discommode Genl Lee very much should the enemy get possession. We are eight miles from Genl Lee's HdQrt, the bulk of the army being just in front and on the right and left. We are now a part of the Army of N.Va. We will remain at this place for the present.

I am quite anxious to hear from the 3rd Ark. Of course they were in the hottest of the battles of Chickamauga. I earnestly hope brother L and Col. M. have escaped again. I have heard nothing further from George or Charlie. The privates are being exchanged slowly, while I hear of no officers being exchanged at all.

I have not heard a word from home since July 22nd. Your folks were all well then. It seems the Yanks have at last taken Little Rock. At least their papers say so. I am glad to hear that your pay has been increased. Your cousin William says you think of procuring a situation in one of the departments as clerk. You could realize more money in that way.

We are only twenty miles from Charlottesville. Miss Offul is staying there. I need not say that I am going up soon.

Remember me to your uncle when you see him. Write to me.

Your friend truly—H. A. Butler

Henry Butler to William Paisley in Charlotte, N.C.

Hd Qtr Cooke's Brigade
Near Brandy Station, Va.
Oct 31st 1863

My dear Billy

I was glad to hear from you again, also for the letter from your sister. That is much later than any letter I have received. I am much moritified to learn of "Jay Hawkers" being in Dallas Co., Ark. Who would have supposed that that old gray headed sinner (though he professed to be a saint) Hinchley would ever lead a band of dislegalists right at our homes.

I suppose you have heard the particulars of our campaign the battle of Bristoe Station &c. Our Brigade which acted gallantly losing seven hundred. The 27th rgt lost most.

The General was again badly wounded, though he is getting along quite well. He will be kept out of the field several months, much to my regret. I shall miss him. O you can't imagine how much. It is quite a fall to come down from General C. to such a man as Col Hall.

I received letters from brothers Lewis and George a few days since. The former wrote from Selma and was just about starting to his rgt. Lewis has tendered his resignation in anticipation of going over to the trans-Miss Dept. Brother George wrote from Henderson, from where he expected to visit our relations in Mecklenburg for a few days. He wrote me an interesting account of his sojourn in Yankydom. I have heard nothing from brother Charlie. Poor fellow, if he has not escaped he will not see service soon, as all exchange of prisoners has been stopped.

I saw your cousin and showed him your sister's letter, for which he seemed very thankful. Your cousin is a good boy. Old fellow, you are lucky in getting into such a situation as you have and making some money. Write soon

Your friend truly H. A. Butler

George Butler to Emma Butler in Tulip

Camp near Knoxville, Tenn.
Dec 2nd 1863

My ever dear Sister Emma,

I have another opportunity of sending a letter across the Miss., and gladly embrace it to let you all hear from us again. We have received letters from home of as late date as Oct. 3rd. We have written to you since, but do not know that you ever received our letters. We write every opportunity, notwithstanding we have heard that you have no mails at Tulip now. The last letter we received from home was from brother George H. He gave us a full account of the state of affairs in Ark., and a very sad and lamentable one it is. We were glad to hear the truth although it was an unpleasant one. From a Captain Jones who has just returned to the regt from Ark, we hear that the Yanks have been at Princeton and Tulip, but did not stay there long. We are very anxious to hear from you all, to know how they treated you. Capt. Jones left the 1st of Novem, and we somewhat expected letters by him. Brother Lewis wrote to you by him and requested you to send letters to him to bring to us; but I suppose you had no mail to send them to him by.

I have not heard a word from brother Hunter in a long time. I do not know whether they still live at Tulip or not. I have written to Sister Hunter since I returned from Yankeedom, but do not know that the letter ever reached you. Sim Williams received a letter from his sister of date 7th of Oct. I suppose bro. Hunter has left the neighborhood of Tulip, as none of the latest letters say anything of him or family. Our Quartermaster Capt. Bust will leave us for Drew Co., Ark., this evening, and I will send this letter by him.

Brother Lewis is not with the regiment. He is in Nunen, Ga. on furlough. He left us about three weeks ago. If his resignation is accepted, he will come over to Ark. I am afraid he will not better himself much by the change. But he is anxious to go, and can hardly be satisfied here now.

The weather is so very cold I can hardly write at all. All our ink froze up night before last. I have heard nothing from brother Henry in some time. Brother Charles I suppose is still in Ft. Delaware. I am afraid he will suffer this winter. I believe the Federal government has determined not to have any more exchange of prisoners.

We have conflicting rumors here about an engagement between Gen Bragg and Thomas at Chattanooga. Gen Longstreet, with about twenty thousand men, has Knoxville almost surrounded. The Federal force within the town is said to number between fifteen and twenty thousands. We have had some fighting since we have been here, but have accomplished little as yet. The place is strongly fortified. A good many of the enemy are Teneseeans. About one half of the citizens around here are Union. Brownlow and Burnside have made their escape from the place. It is said the latter resigned before he left, leaving the command to Gen Foster.

Ally and Sim are well. Billy Paisley is in N.C. He has a very pleasant position and makes a trip about once a month on business to parts of the Confederacy. He has some position in connection with the Medical department. Jim Watson is about well of his wound, but has not been exchanged yet.

Sister Emma, you have no idea how much wickedness is carried on in the army. A great many of our soldiers curse and swear, lie and steal as if they had no consciences. Since we have been in Tenn. it has been no uncommon sight to see hogs lying about in the woods and along the roadside, where the soldiers have shot them dead and gone off and left them there to waste. Some of the citizens say that the soldiers have robbed them of their last hog and left them not a mouthful to eat. Our soldiers are worse here than they were in Pennsylvania. They try to excuse themselves by saying that the people are nearly all Union and ought to suffer. I do not mean to say that all or even a majority of our soldiers are thus wicked, but it prevails to an alarming extent.

On the other hand, there are some noble characters in our army; men who amid all the toils, privations, hardships and temptations of camp life have maintained their Christian characters. Jim Robertson is trying to get a furlough to go to Va. and get married, at least this is his plea for wanting a furlough. If he gets his furlough he says you may look for him in Tulip by March. Poor Jim! he has backslidden entirely, but is not yet lost to shame. I gave him a talk the other night about his unfaithfulness to his God, and he seemed to feel it a good deal and said he would be all right again after a while. I suppose he meant when the war was over. I told him that might be after he was *dead and lost forever*. He said that was so. He has been doing better since.

The Chaplains of Longstreet's Corps had a meeting last week. It was a very interesting and I hope a profitable time to me. There were twelve present. The reports which the chaplains made of the work of God in their regiments was especially gratifying in some cases. There was a glorious work in our army last summer and fall, but we are moving about now so much and the weather is so cold, that but little can be done in the way of preaching. We have some wounded at our hospitals, and can labor with them to advantage. We have lost one man killed from our regt. since we have been here, and another is now very sick, at the point of death.

I would like to write more and a better letter but you must excuse me with this, as the weather is cold and I am very poorly fixed for writing. My love to brother and sister Hunter if they are in the neighborhood. Give my love to all the servants also. With much love for you all, I remain

Your affectionate brother George E. Butler

George Butler to Emma Butler in Tulip

Morristown, Tenn.
Jan 21st 1864

My dear sister Emma,

Tomorrow a member of the 3rd Ark Cavalry will leave for Ouachita Co. Ark., and I gladly avail myself of the opportunity of writing you a hasty letter. But I do not promise that it well be a *short* one, nor do I promise it will be a *long* one. I am just going to write to you freely and carelessly as things suggest themselves to my mind. When I get tired I shall quit, and it may be before.

Well, to commence at the present time. We are now in winter quarters in East Tenn. on the rail road between Knoxville and Bristol, about forty miles from the former and ninety from the latter place.

I say "we" but I do not mean myself and brothers, for I am now the only one of the four that is still with the third Arkansas regiment. Brother Charles is yet a prisoner in Ft. Delaware, unless he has been lately released. I see that (500) five hundred prisoners have been brought up to City Point for exchange. Brother Charles may be among them. I received a letter from brother Henry a few days ago. It was written to brother Lewis, but as he was not present, I opened and read it. Brother Henry was well and with his Brigade at Orange Court House in N. Va. He said he was going to write a letter home and send it over by one of the Congressmen from Ark. As to brother Lewis, I suppose he will be in Ark. before you receive this. He has not written me a word since he left the regiment near three months ago, or his letters have miscarried. An order has been received here notifying the Co. that brother Lewis was relieved from duty here.

There has been of late much talk of our Brigade's being sent across the Miss, but I believe expectation is rather on the decrease. Nearly all the men are very anxious to be sent across, with the expectation of being furloughed for several months. I would like very much to be at home a while and to be where I could hear from you all and for these reasons would prefer, if I had my choice, to go across the river.

But there are many advantages that a soldier has here, that he would not have over there. The army over here is under much better discipline than the soldiers in the Trans Miss. Department. Here we can get much more reliable news than you can get, and are not troubled with so many wild rumors. Here too there is hardly where we stop to camp that we cannot get plenty of good dry wheat straw to make a bed with. This is a great advantage when we are moving about in wet weather. The farms in this country are numerous, and every farm has a large pile of wheatstraw.

The society in East Tenn is for the most part very poor, and it is quite significant that this part of the state is largely Union in sentiment. It is nothing uncommon for girls and women to chew and smoke tobacco, and some even curse and swear. I should not like to have to find me a *partner for life* in East Tenn. when the war is over. But of course there are some even here in East Tenn. who are ornaments to the female sex. A few there are who are not wanting in that unaffected modesty which forms one of the brightest jewels that adorn the female character.

I shall leave to brother Lewis to inform you all of the general news on this side the river. If you ever do get an opportunity of sending a letter across the Miss., you must be sure to write me a full account of how things are going on in the neighborhood of Tulip. How did the Yanks treat you all?

Sam Smith is still at his uncle's in N.C. getting well slowly. I saw a letter from [him] several days since. He said it would be some time yet before he would be able to come to the regt. Sim

Williams and Ally McNeill & Z. Lantorn are well. Sim makes a good soldier and a good non commissioned officer.

I had a pleasant meeting with Mr. Foster just before our Corps left Chatanuga [Chattanooga]. He is the same noble-hearted young man of former days. Pompey Matlock I saw some time since. He is in 3rd Ark. Cavalry. Lieut. Lenham (lawyer from Princeton) was with him. They were both looking well.

I am very anxious to see the close of this dreadful war. But peace is not so dear, nor is life so sweet, as to be purchased at the sacrifice of liberty. Several men who deserted the regiment some time since and tried to get home to Ark have been caught and returned to the regt. I would not be surprised if some of them should be shot. This *looks* like a very severe punishment, and I will be glad if a milder one will answer.

Well, my chum tells me that I must wind up my letter and get to bed. So I close for tonight. Good Night

G. E. B.

Morning. If I had time I might finish this page, but the man will start in a few minutes. Probably you would like to hear how I get on as chaplain. Well I confess, rather unsatisfactorily to myself. I am pleasantly situated, and get on very well with the officers and men, but is seems to me that I am doing but little good. Last summer, the most favorable time for preaching, I was confined in Ft. McHenry. Now it is winter, and too cold to have public preaching in the open air. The best that can be done is to visit the men in their winter cabins and talk with them and have small prayer meetings.

Shortly after I got back from Yankeedom, we had a good prospect for a revival. Some thirty mourners presented themselves as seekers of religion, but our meeting was soon broken up by the movement of the army. I long to see the happy time when in quietness and peace I can pursue my calling on some quiet circuit. Pray for me, sister Emma. My love to all. (Servants included) Remember me kindly to Sister Hunter, if you ever see her, and to all enquiring friends.

As ever I remain your affectionate brother

George E. Butler

George Butler to Emma Butler in Tulip

Camp near Bull's Gap E. Tenn
March 17th 1864

My dear sister Emma,

I have not an opportunity just now of sending a letter across the Miss. but as I feel like writing to someone I have concluded to write part of this letter to you and finish it when I hear of an opportunity to send it to you. My last letter home was written to sister Mary by Capt Thrasher. If he ever returns to us again, I hope you will all send letters by him.

We have commenced a "protracted meeting" in our Brigade. Our Brigade has four regiments in it, three from Texas. We all camp near together so that men from the four regiments can meet for preaching at the same place. We have only two chaplains in the brigade, myself and a Baptist minister from Drew Co. Ark., by the name of Vick. We get on together in entire harmony so far.

41

We have had thirteen to present themselves as seekers of religion, five from our Regt. For the last two days the weather has been very cold, snowing a little, very unfavorable for meetings in the open air. Still we are keeping them up, as the men seem anxious and interested on the subject of religion. There are now about fifty professors of religion present for duty. I will write more about the meeting after a while.

I feel greatly encouraged in my duties as chaplain. About a month ago, I commenced having daily prayers in the Regt. and I think, under the blessing of God, I am doing more good than I had been doing before. The men attend preaching better, and there appears to be a better state of feeling among the members of the church. Early every Sabbath morning I hold public prayers in the regt. immediately after the Band has played several sacred pieces of music. I find that the way to enjoy religion is to go to work and labor for the salvation of souls, being diligent in the use of all the means of grace. Fasting is too much neglected as a means of grace. I know from experience that I cannot neglect it without suffering loss. I try to observe every Friday as a day of fasting and prayer. On last Friday morning I took my Bible and went out to a private spot in the woods for the purpose of meditation and prayer. After sitting a while in silent meditation I took up my Bible and wrote the following on a blank leaf. "Camp E. Tenn. Mch 11th 1864. I have now been a professor of religion for more than ten years. I feel that I have yet a heart partly sinful. Unbelief, pride, vanity, love of the world and desire for human applause still find a lodgement in my heart and at times make their presence felt. O Lord, I mourn over and lament these things. I would repent of indwelling sin. I desire the mind of Christ. I call Thee O God to witness that I hate these heart-sins. O God, cast them all out of my heart!" "Mar 11, Friday, near noon"

"*Glory be to God!* My soul is very happy. God has greatly blessed my soul this hour. I never before felt so *peaceful, calm* and *happy.* I feel now that God approves me *through Christ* without the *shadow* of displeasure. I set apart this day as a day of fasting and prayer, especially to seek a *pure heart* and to be filled with the *love of God.* God has not disappointed my expectation. He has fulfilled his promise 'Whatsoever ye shall ask in prayer, believing, ye shall receive.' Blessed by the Lord Jesus Christ, *My Saviour,* My Redeemer! My Love my All! May I never grieve Thee more. It is all the *grace,* the unmerited favor of God, to me a sinner saved by Grace."

The above were my feelings at the moment as I then wrote them, as I have said, on a blank leaf in the Bible that Ma gave me. The last part was written several hours after the first. Sister Emma, remember me at a throne of grace. I scarcely ever go to God in prayer that I do not think of Pa and Ma and brothers and sisters who are far away and subjected to so many anoyances from the enemies of our country.

Mch.24th. I received sister Mattie's letter to bro. Lewis a few days ago. It was very short but intensely interesting as all letters from home are now. I will send it to brother H. by tomorrow's mail. At night after I lay down to sleep I remained awake for some time thinking of the condition you were all in at home. May God bless and protect you all.

Before this time I reckon brother Lewis has been with you. Prisoners are now being exchanged, and I expect brother Charles to come in in a week or two. I heard from him a short time ago. Aunt Eliza has written to me since brother Henry paid them a visit. They were all well.

A snow about twelve inches deep has interfered with our meeting. There was one conversion, and two or three others not fully satisfied. There are about fifteen others who are seeking religion, and I hope by the grace of God to see them converted before long, even if the weather does not permit us to resume the meeting. I have their names and intend to converse with them, and to pray with them and for them. Lieut. Gibson expects to start to Ark. next month, so I will not write more at present.

Evening of the 24th Mch. A man from our regt. (Segt. Williams Co K) will start for Miss. to-morrow and he may go across the river to Ark., so I have concluded to send this by him and write another to send when Lt. Gibson goes next month. Ally MacNeill, Sim Williams, Zac Lantorn are with the company, all well. Lts. Brown & Prior and Capt. Smith are all absent recovering from their wounds, also Jim Watson. There is some talk of our going back to the army of N. Va. If we do, I will be able to see brother Henry occasionally. I wrote to sister Mary by Capt. Thrasher, and will continue to write to some of you every opportunity, expecting you to do the same. I have written many more letters home than I have received, but I reckon many of them never reach you.

I will bring my letter to a close. Remember me kindly to all enquiring friends. Hoping that you all, dear Emma, will not let the visits of the Yanks cause you to live any the less devoted Christians, or to destroy your peace of mind, and hoping also that this year may witness the close of the war and the joyful reunion of long absent ones, I remain forever

Your affectionate brother
George E. Butler

George Butler to Emma Butler in Tulip

near Richmond
June 9, 1864

[begins with p. 2]

We have been fighting in Va. more or less every day for one entire month, and still the fighting continues. Cannon are now booming in the distance. Bro. Henry is still safe. He had one horse killed under him. You just ought to be thankful to God that none of your brothers have been killed in so many battles. I have heard (indirectly) from brother Charlie. He is certainly in Ft. Delaware, and is well. He wrote a letter by flag of truce to Mr. Kettle dated April, I believe near the last of the month. So you see, the four of us are still living and in health. Richard Smith is with him, but he did not mention him because Mr. Kettle is not acquainted with him.

And now, Emma, I will make a few general remarks. Our soldiers have fought well since the commencement of these fights. Gen. Lee, by the blessing of God, has not been driven from any position he has taken. If he has repeatedly left a line that he had established, it was only when the enemy refused to come out and fight him. Our loss has been very small in comparison with that of the enemy. They have lost four or five times as many men as we have. Thousands of them were left unburied on the field of battle. The inhumanity of Gen. Grant to his own men, well, wounded, and killed is beyond question. Our men are in good spirits and never more confident of success.

But I must close. My sheet is full. Goodby

Your affectionate
brother G.

Henry Butler to William Paisley in Charlotte, N.C.

Hd Qrs Cooke's Brigd
Near Chaffins Farm
June 24, 1864

My dear friend Billy—

I received your letter written from Rocky Point soon after the opening of the campaign, and I answered though by a brief note a few days thereafter, I think from Spotsylvania Court House. Thought or hope you would write again. Out of the past fifty days our Brigd has been [in battle] forty at least, and of the forty we have been under fire I think thirty. So you see we have had but little rest. I will not attempt to portray to you the part we have taken in this stupendous campaign, though the papers have not noticed us. I reckon you remember my horse, a nice dark bay. I will not be able to replace him soon. I am now riding one marked "C.S." About the 14th inst we lost ninety men down below White Oak Camp driving the enemy's cavalry.

I saw your cousin *Wm.* on a litter borne out badly—but I hope not mortally—wounded. I afterwards learned he was wounded through the left lung. But I am glad to be told, the surgeons are hopeful of his recovery. I had become attached to your cousin partly on your account. Our Brigade was at Petersburg, just this side of the Appomattox several days, but three days ago we [came] to Chaffin's Bluff in the very hills we formed on about two years ago in front of Malvern Hills. You remember the place, do you not? We are now in the same line above New Market, and the same distance below Chaffin's Bluff. You will see from the papers that the enemy are at Deep Bottom. You ask what I think of Mr. H—'s offer of two hundred per month? You must consult your own judgement.

And you have seen my cousin Sally K[ittle] have you? I think she is a sweet girl, judging from her letters which I receive occasionally. I did not see her while on leave in Feby. She had left a short time previous for Duplies County where she has a small school. I have not seen her since she was a little girl (with "bib") about seven years of age.

I am the more anxious to see her when you declare her to be something like Miss M[ollie] C[oulter] of Texas. Did I write you that she had certainly left for the state? If not, I do so now. The old "Major" [Coulter] sold out and left Union County last August, and is now or was a few months since settled in Anderson County. You will be surprised when I say that I have not received a letter from her since I saw you last summer.

I have seen brother Geo. several times during the campaign, but as our Corps are generally on opposite wings of the army, I see him but seldom. He was well when I saw him. On yesterday I received a letter from Pa, the first letter from home in several months. It was dated Feby 5th and that time things looked "quite blue" out there, so you know Pa was despondent. All the family and neighbors were well. Pa mentioned your mother and family. George Hughes has to go [into] the service at last, and I know he hates it. I use to tell him he ought to go.

There was a meeting at Little Rock to take steps to get the State back into the loving embraces of "Old Abe." Dallas County was represented by Harrison Stanfield and old Young's son and motherinlaw. So you see what *class* is deserting us.

Billy, I don't often offer excuses, but really, after looking over this scrawl, I must ask you to pardon me for sending such. I have written it with the soldiers all around me, to say nothing of the crack of the skirmishers' rifle. Do write to me. When I think of you my heart warms up. Genl. Cooke, by the by, has recommended my promotion to the majority under the recent Act of Congress. Goodby, Billy. Write to me soon.

Your friend
H. A. Butler

George Butler to Emma Butler in Tulip

Near Drury's Bluff
Aug. 16th, 1864

My *own sweet sister Emma,*

Your letter with sister Mary's reached me evening before last, bringing joy and gladness to my spirit. Two officers of our Regt. will leave for Arkansas in a few days, to bring back all absent without proper leave of absence. I gladly avail myself of the opportunity by writing to "the loved ones at home." I have written to sister Mattie and send this in the same envelope.

For a week past I have been pretty sick, barely able to get about, fever and headache with uncommon weakness. The fever and pain are gone, and I am regaining my strength. My mouth quite sore yet but think that will soon pass off. I regretted being taken sick at that time, because I was assisting in a very interesting meeting in our Brigade. But could not help it. It was of the Lord who doeth all things well. The meetings were broken up last Sunday by an advance of the enemy on this part of our lines. There has been some fighting every day since.

The men appear to be much interested in religious worship. I never saw men pay better attention at preaching, and that too when there is no "great preacher" present. Several were converted and probably fifty or sixty more are seeking religion. God grant they may soon find the "pearl of great price." 'Tis an interesting sight, one that makes me feel solemn, yes like weeping, to witness a large congregation of these hardy, sunburnt, *noble hearted warriors* listening attentively, seriously to the preaching of the Gospel. In less than twenty-four hours that congregation may be called upon to face death upon the bloody field of battle. Will they accept of Christ now and get ready to meet death anywhere at any time? Or will some refuse Jesus? O 'tis sad to think that any of those brave fellows, who have spent three long years of self sacrifice for their country's good, and who for this have faced death on many a field of battle, O 'tis sad, to think that they should reject Christ and go down to eternal woe! But I dare not preach as some talk, that their sufferings in their country's behalf, will atone for their sins, and that their souls will be saved in Heaven because they are killed in battle. I know of but one atonement, one sacrifice for sin; and that our blessed Saviour made. *There* I have found peace; and there every *sinner may* obtain *pardon* and *purity* and *Heaven.*

Our largest congregations are at night, when the men have nothing to do, and nothing to draw on their attentions. It reminds me then of Camp Meeting. Our lights are made by pine knots &c burnt on stands erected for that purpose. I sometimes wonder if the days of camp meeting will not come again, by and by when this war is over. I believe they have done great good. I look back to

Porters camp ground with great pleasure. I remember the sweet soul feast sermons that the holy McKenzie preached to us on that occasion. He has passed away to his reward. Blessed is his memory. May a double portion of his spirit fall upon me. He had the "Tongue of Fire" the *power of the Holy Spirit* in his preaching. My warmest Christian love to brother and sister Hunter if you see them & to brother Winfield, and remember me to all enquiring friends.

> Your loving brother
> George

P.S. I have written twice to Sister Hunter since I received her last letter. I will write to her the next opportunity.

Henry Butler to William Paisley in Charlotte, N.C.

> Hd Qrs Cooke's Brigade
> Petersburg, Va.
> Aug 23, 1864

Dear Billy,

Last April you wrote me a long letter in which you pitched into me extensively for not writing you as you supposed. Now old fellow, it is permissible to pitch in, but well not to do so—suffice it to say I have not received a letter from you either in that time—though I have written two if not three letters to you. Since your cousin's death I have been unable even to hear from you. I wrote you not long after your cousin's death, and expressed my sincere sorrow at the sore affliction to his parents. I liked him exceedingly.

We have been in several battles since I wrote you, and I owe many thanks to the Giver of all good for preserving my life through all. I have certainly escaped remarkably. Our Brigade was in the fight on day before yesterday below the city. Genl. Heth, with three Brigades, attacked the enemy in front while Genl. Mahone [?] with six Brigades made a detour around the enemy's left flank and rear. Genl. H drove them from one line of works in front, but Genl. Mahone failing in the assault in rear, we did not pursue. The enemy was too strong both in position and numbers, having had two days to fortify and bring up reinforcements. This is the only repulse their army has met during the campaign. We—our Brig.—lost only seventy men. Among them, however, were three captains who were all good officers.

I received a letter from Foster a day or two since. He was quite well, still a private in the 9th Tenn. Regt. Maney Brigade, Cheatham's Div., Atlanta Ga. I gave his address in order that you may write to him. He would be delighted to get a letter from you. I know he would. I received also letters from home last week dated June 20th. All our family was well and your Ma's were all well. Rev. Jesse McAlister, Mr. Littlejohn and Sam'l W. Smith are all dead. Brother Johnny had joined the army, a member of Capt. Will Jones Somerville's Company. Lewis is in Austin, Texas, in the Commissary Department. This I learned through Bart Johnson's brother, who received a letter from Bart in Ark. Charlie is still in Fort Delaware but is getting along well, as he says in a letter rcd the 4th of May at home.

Billy, I am quite much hurried or I would write a long letter but I don't know that you receive my letters, consequently it is not very encouraging to write. Do write to me and give me one of your excellent epistles.

> Very truly your old friend
> Henry

Foster rcd a letter from Miss B. sent by sister Mary. Jo Littlejohn and Ella Drake are married. I (poor me) have not had a letter from MEC since I wrote you.

Henry Butler to Emma Butler in Tulip

> Hd Qrs Cooke's Brigade
> Near Petersburg Va
> Oct 10, 1864

My dearly loved sister Emma,

On last week I received two letters which occasioned much joy to my anxious heart. One of the letters was from you and of *May 24th*, and the other from our dear parents written to their "soldier boys," dated July 23rd. Why these letters should come together I can't imagine—You see they were written *two months* apart. I wrote to Pa and Ma not long since, so will try and write you—if I will be undisturbed long enough.

I have written home every opportunity to send letters by hand and several times by mail. In one of my letters, (in April, I think) I sent my photograph to Ma for the receipt of which has never been acknowledged. I suppose it was lost.

I am now in good health. Have not lost a day from any cause since the opening of this *mighty campaign*—consequently have been in every battle and skirmish in which the Brigade has been engaged. O how thankful I ought to be for being so mercifully spared, while so many of my comrades in arms have fallen victims to this cruel war. I believe I owe it in a great degree to *the prayers* of the "loved ones at home." This campaign has already exceeded *any thing* we have ever had or *thought of* before. Scarcely a single day since the 3rd of May have we felt entirely secure from being called upon to meet the enemy. It is enough to wear out the patience and *even patriotism* of the soldier who has to trudge along with musket and knapsack through five long months of such hardships. But we have the greatest soldiery in the world.

Our Brigade is now about four miles south of Petersburg, confronting the enemy in his attempt to push his left to the south-side Rail Road. I sent the letters from you and Pa to brother George who is on the north side of the James, near Richmond. It has been several weeks since I received a letter from him. I have received one letter from Charlie since he has been at Fort Delaware. Cousin Sallie Kittle writes me an occasional letter, and she writes a very good letter. I have not seen her since you have—as she was either at school or teaching on the two occasions I visited Henderson. Mr. Kittle is quite desponding, thinks the Yankees will finally whip us out and compel the south to re-unite with them. He is thought by some to be *a traitor* or only lacks the opportunity to prove so. He always was a strange sort of a man.

I have not heard from brother Lewis since he left Tulip. Brother George says one of the 3rd Ark received a letter from his brother, who informed him that brother Lewis was in Galveston, Texas, in the Commissary Department.

Well sis Emma, what do you think of my not having heard from M. E. C. in *sixteen months*? I sometimes get out of all patience waiting for a letter from *her*, but then I know there is some good reason for the long, *very* long silence. Can't you write to her? I wrote her one letter, and sent it to Foster, who knew of a soldier going to Texas. I also have written by mail since I found out the Post Office.

Your account of the soldiers marching past sister's, and the battle of Jenkins Ferry was quite interesting. Genl Cooke was acquainted with General Randall who died of wounds rec'd in that battle. I think the Yankees treat our people much better out in Arkansas than they do here. I could give you some accounts of the suffering of the good people of Virginia, that would astonish you. I have some warm friends in Virginia, and would regret to sever my connection with the army, particularly with Genl Cooke, but I do *so long* to see you all at home I would accept a position in the western Army if I was tendered one. I could then have an opportunity to *visit Tulip*, which seems impossible so long as I remain here.

I reckon you all think I *could* have come home before now. What do you suppose it would cost me to visit home? Certainly not less than *one thousand* dollars and that is more money than I could have raised. I could do so now by selling my horse. At the battle of Sharpsburg I lost my horse, for which the government has never paid me any thing. I lost another horse killed in the battle near Cold Harbor on the 3rd of last June, for which I only received eight hundred dollars, about one third the worth or what I would have to pay for one to replace him. I have another horse now, which through the kindness of a friend I obtained at quite a moderate price, about twelve hundred dollars.

I have just been interrupted by two ladies who have walked about one mile to see Genl Cooke to get some wagons to haul their goods and chattels from their home which is between the opposing lines. A day or two since, we had a skirmish in the yard of their home when a negro woman was killed, and themselves almost frightened to death. The Yankees carried off *all* their servants. I have just made an arrangement to haul their property to a place of safety. They are nice looking young ladies and doubtless never had to work before, but now all the servants are gone and all their brothers are in our army, while their parents are helpless, even to themselves.

Give my love to all our friends—brother Caldwell, how I would like to see the *good brother*. Kiss all the loved ones at home for me and sisters. Tell all to write. Sister Mary has been very kind and punctual in writing heretofore.

Goodby, sweet sister. May the Giver of all good grant us to meet again.

With much love I am always

your affectionate brother
Henry

Henry Butler to William Paisley in Charlotte, N.C.

Hd Qrs Cooke's Brigade
Near Petersburg, Va
Oct. 30th 1864 [?]

Dear Billy

I have just received a letter from your Uncle James in answer to one I wrote a few days ago, making enquiries as to your whereabouts &c. The last letter I rec'd from you was in May or June, although I have written three different letters since your last was received. I supposed from your not answering that you was either sick or had gone to Ark; and now that your uncle informs me that you was at his house about the first of August, and left there, well I cannot but express my surprise at your neglecting to write to one who has ever felt and I think expressed real friendship for you. I trust your silence has not been from doubt on your part of the interest I feel in your welfare. I do assure you the friendship I ever felt for you has not abated in the least, and that friendship has ever been great. Of this I cannot but think you are satisfied. But, let's hie away to something else.

We have just witnessed the most complete failure the Yankees ever made. On last Thursday morning about two o'clock our scout reported the enemy active and moving troops to our front and right. (It is proper to state that our Brigade was then next to the right Brigade of infantry of the army and about five miles from Petersburg.) At early dawn the crack of the skirmishers' rifles rung forth on our right and soon we were on the move by the right flank. The enemy, as soon as he supposed he had flanked the infantry, made an advance on our lines, but were repulsed quite easily, when the enemy continued to move troops to our right while we continued the same movement, constantly confronting him.

The enemy felt our lines repeatedly, but accomplished nothing till they reached the cavalry across the Rowanty Run when the line was broken, and the enemy quickly advanced to the Boydton plank road. Here the enemy accumulated part of three corps in a few hours, but two Brigades of Rebels attacked and broke through their lines, but were so completely enveloped by the enemy as to be compelled to retire with the loss of the artillery which was captured from the enemy with some prisoners. Night put an end to the conflict. During the night several Brigades were massed (among them Cooke's) to attack the enemy at daylight. But the enemy "skedaddled" during the night in much confusion, leaving their dead and many wounded on the field.

There is no doubt that we would have made a complete "smash up" of the Yankees. Such was the disposition of our forces and those of the enemy that I am certain we could have captured most of the army. Our losses in the army were insignificant, not one sixth of those of the enemy's. Our Brigade now occupies the extreme right of the line and about six miles from Petersburg. The enemy has taken up their old lines.

You doubtless have seen accounts of the engagements in which we have participated. Our Brigade has lost over sixteen hundred in killed and wounded during the campaign. We now number eleven hundred guns. Cooke's Brigade is regarded throughout the Army as one of the best, while some say *it is* the finest in this Army.

The latest news from Ark I have is contained in letters of August 1st. All the people around Tulip were well, and the feeling of despondency which had been brooding over our people so long was fast disappearing. Crops good and less damage had been inflicted by the enemy than could have been expected.

I have received two letters from Charlie, one about two weeks since. He is still in Fort Delaware. He and Dick Smith were well.

Brother George is now on leave of absence to attend the Virginia Conference, which convenes at Lynchburg about the 13th Nov. I suppose you have heard of the changes around Tulip. Let me know the latest news you have from there. Joe Littlejohn and Ella Drake are married & Mr. Littlejohn is dead, also Sam W. Smith and Rev. Jesse McAlister.

Write me soon

Your friend
H. A. Butler

Henry Butler to William Paisley in Charlotte, N.C.

Hd Qrs Cookes Brig'd
Petersburg, Va.
Nov 15th, 1864

Dear Billy,

Your highly prized letter of the 4th inst. gave me much satisfaction dispelling every doubt—*if any existed*—of your kindly feelings toward me, and brought back to Memory "*the past*" with its many hallowed associations.

"Ah! *those* days were very bright—Billy
And *now* they seem to me—
Like some fair enchanted isle
As seen in a desert sea."

But is not well to think too much upon the past. It is *the present* with which we have to deal—*that* and the future demands *all* our zeal—all our strength. That we as a nation shall be equal to the occasion I doubt not.

I am glad to know that you are so pleasantly situated and enjoying the confidence of your employer. I can imagine your appearance as you strut through your commodious ware-rooms with your thumbs in the armpits of your vest, hat cocked, and cigar—for I suppose you (in your responsible position) have discarded the pipe—carefully inserted in the corner of your mouth, looking the very picture of a New Orleans Commission Merchant. I almost envy your position and really think you ought to congratulate yourself on your good fortune. You did not mention your *income*.

You ask "if my health has been impaired by hardships of the past six months campaign"? I think not. On one or two occasions I thought I was going to have an attack of fever—but it passed off, and I can say what few officers in this army can—I have been in every battle and skirmish in which this Brigade *ever was* engaged, and during the past six months have not lost a day's duty on any account.

We have orders to erect huts for winter quarters, but have not commenced as yet. I think it rather soon. However we are making ourselves comfortable so far as having chimneys already.

We are on the extreme right of the lines, and seven miles from Petersburg, our right resting on Hatchers Creek just below Burgess Mills, which are on the plank road. We are quite fortunate in being in the woods where big fires can be had, besides being rid of many other annoyances such as mortar shells and Minnie balls, which are to be had in the trenches in front and east of the city. I hope we will not get back in those abominable trenches again this winter. General Cooke has been absent four days—consequently I have had considerable business during the day and have been quite lonely at night, being *entirely* alone, excepting an occasional visitor. Lieut. Patton went with the Genl., and Majors Broxton & Hayes being in the bomb proof department, are "well to the rear." I expect the Genl. back tomorrow.

We are living very hard just now—*pickle pork* and bread with an occasional issue of coffee and sugar and rice constitutes our fare. The bread is quite good "baker's bread" which is baked every two days. I think we will have sorghum issued to us soon. I am very fond of the latter—like it better than molasses. It would be quite a treat to get down into the Old North State this winter to get hold of some potatoes and pea-nuts for which the country down toward Wilmington is noted.

I have not received any letters from Ark. or Texas (in fact I have *never* rec'd any from the latter) of later date than July 24th. The last letter from Lewis I send you, which after reading you can destroy. All were well around Tulip July 24th. Johnny had joined Will Jones Somerville Cavalry Company, making five of us in service. Pa was doing pretty well, had on hand a sufficiency of bacon.

Well, I hardly know what to say or think about my not receiving any communication from my sweet heart, and yet I cannot believe she has wilfully neglected me. What do you think when I tell you that the last letter I have from her is dated March 3rd, 1863? Such is the fact. Foster met with *Lieut. Paul Coulter* who is in the Army of Tenn., who told him his father's family were all well when he last heard from them, which was sometime during last spring. I have written a letter or two and sent them to Foster to have them forwarded. I also requested Foster to write to her himself merely on the score of being old friends &c. Of course I feel much anxiety to hear from *her*, but I shall never despair till the fact is beyond any dispute that she has intentionally neglected me.

[no closing]

George Butler to Emma Butler in Tulip

Trenches 5 miles from Richmond, Va.
Decem 1864

Dear Sister Emma,

Your letter of 15th August has been received. Also one from pa & one from sister Mary, written in Sept and sent across the Miss. by Dr. Smith. Bro. Henry sent the last two to me, and I have just received and read them. I need not stop to tell you that we were glad, *very glad* to hear from you all. Letters from our dear home always give us great satisfaction and joy, although some things we hear from there may make us feel sad. 'Tis sad, for instance, to hear that the friend once so dear to us, and who contributed so much to the happiness and desirableness [of] our boyhood have left their homes and moved to a distant place. 'Tis sad to hear those friends are, one by one, leaving earth and never more to return to us again. 'Tis sad to hear that those beautiful homesteads are desolated and defaced and some even laid in ashes. To think that the home, *the pleas-ant happy home* of our youthful days is *so changed* in a few years! That we shall never again behold that home in its former beauty and loveliness! 'Tis sadder still to think that its loved inmates, the dearest and nearest friends on earth, are so liable to disturbance and fear at the hands of a vandal foe.

These and other reflections would make one feel *gloomy*, if his desire and hopes were fixed on earthly objects: if he looks for no higher, no purer enjoyments than those which this world can give. But thank God! that as professors of the religion of our Lord and Saviour Jesus Christ, our hopes and aims are not bounded by the fleeting, evanescent and unsatisfying objects of time and sense. "We seek a city that hath foundations whose builder and maker is God." Thither *our blessed Saviour* has gone before us *to fit up a home for us.* And O what must be the beauty and grandeur of that home which *God* prepares, of set purpose to make his children forever happy! Some of the homes prepared and decorated by the hands of feeble and shortsighted men, in this sinful fallen world, are beautiful to behold. What then must be the appearance and nature of that place, that celestial city, the heavenly Jerusalem, which the *Almighty*, the *allwise God* is fitting up for the *eternal dwelling place* of his redeemed, his beloved children? The beauty of that home shall never fade. Its attraction shall *never* grow less. Its pure and happy inmates shall never be pained by a parting farewell! Sin, with its inseparable companion misery, shall never find an entrance there. The feet of the unclean, the impure shall never walk on those hallowed, shining shores. O sister Emma, let us always love and adore *that blessed Jesus* who has purchased for us such a sweet happy Home in the Skies! Let us always be ready to go up and meet Him there. And let us pray that God may give us our friends to go with us. And pray for me, your unworthy brother who am trying (but alas! how feebly) to preach to others the *unspeakable riches of Christ.*

We had about sixty to profess religion in our Brigade last fall. We have built us a chapel to worship in this winter, but it is too small to hold all the congregation. The brethren have gone to work today to enlarge it. If we are permitted to remain here this winter, we expect to have a good time, the Lord willing. Our regiments are so small now that we all meet together and hold Brigade meetings. This does very well in our Brigade as some of the regiments have no chaplains.

I got a leave of absence, some time since, and spent about thirty days with our relations in Mecklenberg and Granville. Cousin Sallie Kittle rode with me over to Gar river to see aunt Hallie and our cousins. We found them all well, except one of Patsy's sister Fannie's children was sick. Fannie was very glad to see us, and sends her love to her sister Patsy and all. Her oldest daughter is married and has a child. Cousin Eliza was going to school, and all the boys that were old enough. Aunt Hallie made me think often of my own dear mother. Cousin George was off on his circuit. I spent four days over there.

On our way there we stopped and spent two nights and a day with Cousin Betsy Marable. Her brother Alexander was with her. He was in the war of 1812. Cousin Betsy's health was quite feeble. I reckon she will not live very much longer. We also stopped at cousin Sam Reavis' about an hour. He has three daughters grown. Aunt Fannie is declining right fast. She is going to break up housekeeping and go to live with Ben Wyche's wife. He has gone into the army.

Aunt Betsy was just about the same as she was three years ago. Her sons William and George are nearly grown. Lewis is in the army. Emma and Bessy, the two youngest, are growing rapidly, especially Emma. Cousin Hallie is becoming more fleshy and more like her mother. She is very good company, quite intelligent, and performs splendidly on the piano. She is now teaching a class in music. Cousin Parry and Uncle George are the same as they were years ago. The latter is called into the service of the State.

Our relatives in Virginia are all about well. Uncle Joseph's health is bad, but he is called into service again. I spent some time very pleasantly at Mr. Walker's. Cousin Tom Walker and Miss Sallie Homer were married while I was there. Cousin Roberta lost her second child, Mattie, a week or two before Tom married. She was quite young, about four or five years old, but shortly before she died she opened her eyes and said, "Ma, I see Heaven." Cousin Roberta bears her death like a Christian.

Aunt Eliza is very kind to me and to us all. I have on new socks, pants, coat, and vest which she made with her own kind hands. She furnished the cloth to make the pants. Uncle Theo is living several miles from Mr. Walker. He told me to give his love to you all. I believe he is getting on somewhat better than he did at Tulip, but it appears to be next to impossible for him to bridle his tongue. Uncle Joseph and Edmond make plenty to eat, and sell a good deal and buy very little, for they make nearly everything they need at home. They each made three or four hundred gallons of sorgum (molasses) and good crops of potatoes and enough corn and meat to do them, and some to sell. Uncle Edmond is "bonded" and has to furnish the government with a quantity of meat.

Emma, I have written the last page or more, not because I thought it would interest you but thought pa and ma might desire to hear of their relatives. I reckon if George Hughes had to read this he would think me nearly as bad as Cousin Peter Wyche.

Why are you all so silent about brother Lewis? I have about concluded that he has left the Confederacy. Sim Williams is about the only one of the Tulip boys now with the company. Yes, there is Jim Robertson. I forgot him. Jim Watson has gotten a pleasant position as chief clerk in an office in the quartermaster department in N.C. Capt. Smith expects to be retired and come home in about a month. I will send a letter by him when he goes if I can. He expects to start from N.C.

Well, my sheet is nearly full. I may write more if the man does not leave tomorrow. Is bro. Hunter still living near Tulip? My love to him and sister H. Also to Maj. Borden, bro Barcus and families. If you ever see bro. Caldwell, my love to him. Remember me to Aunt Mollie and Uncle Albert and to all enquiring friends. Please send the enclosed letter to its destination.

As ever your affectionate brother
George

Henry Butler to William Paisley in Charlotte, N.C.

Hd Qrs Cooke's Brigade
Burgess Mill
January 6th, 1865

Dear Billy

Why in the world don't you write? I have not received an answer to either of my two last letters. The last letter from you was written just after your uncle had written you about my anxiety concerning your welfare &c. In that letter you promised to *do better* in the future, and seemed to be quite *penitent* for past negligences in the way of writing. As above intimated I have written my two letters since—in one of which—the last I believe—I sent you a long letter from brother Lewis written from Tulip. The latest letters from Tulip are of Oct. 25th though *I* have not *seen* them. They were sent to brother George—who mailed them to me, but our mail carrier lost the entire mail. 'Tis hard, isn't it? I receive so few letters, and some of them to be lost after getting almost in my hands. Of course the mailbag was picked up by some unprincipled scoundrel, and that is the last of it.

But Billy, I have received *one* letter from a certain little Nymph, away over in the "Lone Star state" that is worth *all* other epistles in Christendom. She is "all right," though she tells me she came *very near* being *married* & now what do you think of that? It had been *fourteen months* since she rec'd my last letter, during which time she heard from soldiers crossing the river that I *was married—certainly* married to a Miss Lee, niece of Genl. R. E. Lee. Then she heard that I was *dead*, killed in one of the battles in Maryland or Pennsylvania. At last she received the letter I gave to our friend Foster to have conveyed to Texas. This letter was received last August (20th) on her birthday, which she answered on the same day. She confided every thing to me. How she was addressed by this gentleman & that gentleman and finally a certain surgeon from South Carolina, a man of intelligence. It is a long story and I cannot tell you all. Suffice it to say that she has revealed to her parents since the reception of my letter the long-hidden "secret" and they "raise no objections" to her choice. Now Billy, I am fearful this letter will not reach you, or I would write much more.

Brother George and Charlie were well when last heard from. The latter still at Fort Delaware. Do write me a long letter.

With sentiments of the highest regard

I am ever
Your Friend
H. A. Butler

I think of making an effort to see my "sweetheart" this winter—If I fail, will get a leave and visit my relations in N.C. and Mecklinberg, Va. Remember me to your uncle.

Henry

Henry Butler to William Paisley in Charlotte, N.C.

Hd Qrs Cooke's Brigade
Feby 15th, 1865

Dear Billy

I rcd yours of the 1st on the day of the fight (the 5th inst) just as we marched out to meet—or attack—the enemy, and did not finish reading it until the fight was over for that day. We lost something over one hundred men, having driven the Yanks about half a mile through the woods, but coming upon another line entrenched, we *ceased to advance*, in consequence of a Brigade to our left having "played out" and our right being exposed a flank fire from another line of battle. This thing of charging breastworks either by Confederates or federals may now be numbered "among the things that were." Our Brigade at Reams Station charged the enemy works with abattis &c in front, and that too after the other troops had failed. I believe they would do it again, but the troops *do not fight* as they *use* to. We can whip the enemy two to our one in an open field any day—an easier job I don't wish, but there is something *repulsive* about advancing through abattis or "chancerade" while the Yanks are popping away, making a perfect hail storm of buck and ball.

While there is this sort of feeling among *our* troops, the Yanks are far worse and have *never* taken works from the army defended by a line of battle. A skirmish line can, behind works, whip two lines of battle of the enemy. The enemy gained *nothing* in the recent move. They have moved their lines to try the left, but that could have been done two months ago. They essayed to get to the plank road but were driven back in the greatest confusion. —So much for *that*.

I have but little to write you to day. Sent up an application for leave of absence, and will be most delighted to meet you in Somerville Co., and I will write you again in regard to the time &c. I must say I do not anticipate a great deal of enjoyment visiting my relations in Somerville. Some of them are not very *loyal*, and besides, they are not by any means the *elite* of the country. The most pleasant anticipation is in visiting my relations in Mecklenburg.

Very truly
Your friend
Henry

Henry Butler to William Paisley in Charlotte, N.C.

Feby. 16th [1865]

Dear Billy

Since writing, my application for leave of absence for thirty days has returned, "approved for 18 days" much to my surprise and annoyance, for I hardly feel like leaving camp upon so short a time. It was approved for thirty days by Genls. Cooke, Heth & Hill. But the "General in chief" cut it down. Well, we all say that what *he* does is *right*. I must flatter myself with the belief that Genl. Lee (seeing the campaign about to open) is persuaded that my *valuable*—I might say invaluable services, cannot be disposed of in this critical juncture of affairs.

But feeling aside, I do think it is a little hard that while officers of the 3rd Ark Regt. are allowed thirty days, I who have had but one leave of absence in *four* years and have been present during the entire past campaign should be refused. This cutting down of my leave will deprive me of the privilege of visiting Granville, for I would not have time to visit both places. I am very sorry I cannot see you. Can't you meet me at my Aunt's near Boydton? If you will come up by Granville R. R. to Keysville I think—yes, I am certain there is a line of stages from the latter place to Boydton.

Write to me and direct your letter to Boydton, care of Mr. Edmond Dane [?]. I will not leave camp till the 21st, and will go direct to Keysville.

I shall expect you.

> Yours truly
> H. A. Butler

If you will visit me at Mecklenburg, I will endeavor to make your stay as pleasant as possible.

Henry Butler to Captain William Paisley in Charlotte, N.C.

> Hd Qrs Cookes Brigade
> Hatchers Run, Va.
> March 10th 1865

Dear Billy—"Captain"

I congratulate you on attaining to the *very respectable* rank of "Captain." Why didn't you let me know of it before? I am glad to know of the honor conferred, and doubt not that you with the sixty-five men of your command will do good fighting whenever the opportunity offers. "Captain Paisley"—that sounds well and allow me to say is well merited. Your letter was *read last night* which I found on my arrival, but as it is likely you did not receive my last letter I will tell you *where I have been.*

I left camp on the 19th ult. with an *eighteen day* leave in pocket, which was

Billy you will have to excuse me for not finishing the above sentence, for I was interrupted and have forgotten all about what I intended to write. I was called for by Genl. C to answer a flag of truce from the enemy in our front. You know I suppose the "modus operandi" in regard to a flag of truce. The object of the Flag was to receive within our lines the body of a North Carolina soldier who was killed on the 5th of last month. I met the Yanky officer, by the name of Capt. Wister of Gen Humphries staff. He was quite civilized, disposed to talk. During the interview he asked me to *drink* with him which I refused to do, much to his embarrassment. He *appeared* to be quite a gentleman but was a "Yankee."

I will—after the above digression finish telling you about my absence.

I wrote you just before leaving and asked you to meet me in Mecklenberg Co. I was very much in hopes you would do so. I know you would have enjoyed yourself very much. I have four *pretty cousins* down there who are fine girls, full of life and fun. They are second and third cousins, but I insisted on kissing them. At first some of them refused to kiss me, but on my leaving, I received a sweet kiss from them all. To tell you I had a splendid time would not be conveying to your mind a proper degree of my enjoyment. I could not visit Granville, my time being too short. I rode through the country on horseback and encountered much mud and high waters on my return trip.

Since you wrote, the Yankeys have advanced quite near your town—near enough, I suppose, to give you something to do in the way of manning the fortifications with your "sixty-five invincibles." Everything in regard to the movements of the contending armies around Charlotte is kept quite dark, consequently we know *nothing*. You must write me and give me the particulars. What you thought of Wheelers cavalry? If the remnants of the Army of Tenn. is near you, try and hunt up Foster's Co. "C," 9th Tenn. Manly's Brigade. Also Paul Coulter, who is a Lieut. in the 2nd Ark Regt, Capt Laney's Company. The Regt has been consolidated with (I believe) the 9th, and I don't know how that may have affected his status.

Nothing more from *Texas* or Arkansas nor from Charlie, except that brother George received a letter from him in Feby. I hope he will be with us soon. Prisoners are arriving daily, but it seems but few have been taken from Ft. Delaware.

The spirit of our army has very much improved, desertions less frequent than a short time since. Yanky deserters still continue to come over.

Well "Old Bragg" has met with a *success* at last, and by the way, very close to the house at which we were assigned our Hd Qrs when you came to see me in the spring of 1863.

Billy (you must not expect me to call you Captain), I am under many obligations to you for the proposed gift. I am certainly *very* much obliged (even if I never receive the present) for your kind intention. The package will come up safely if directed to me by express to Petersburg. Quite a number of our Brigade visit and pass through Charlotte on furlough. Write to me as early as possible. Excuse this scrawl which is written very hurriedly and under the most unfavorable circumstances, the tent being crowded with company.

Good bye. Sincerely yours

H. A. Butler

AT HOME: 1865–1871

John R. Butler to Emma Butler in Tulip

Marshall, Texas
May 16th 1865

Dear Sister Emma,

I left home the third day of May and arrived here on the fourteenth, which was eleven days' travel. On the way I stopt at Parson Moors one of our Methodist preachers; he sends his respects to Pa. I saw Mr. Gant who says he traveled with Pa to New York before the war. He says he would like very much to see him. I went over to Maj. Alexander's quarters this morning and saw Mr. William Hunter. He got his leg broken not long since, but it is now most well. I had a look at the works, which are very curious the way they make hardware and any thing else they try almost.

I do not think I would like the Infantry service as well as the cavalry, which is one thing I am pleased with here. I have a better time to read my Bible now than I have had. I've a very good mess: Mr. Night's Son, cousin John Butler, Till Harrison—no relation of our Van Harrison I believe. John Nix wants to go on to our old com, which is some fifty or more miles west of this. We went to the commander of the post, and he gave us an order, him saying that our command would return in a few weeks at most. It would be a long walk for nothing. I expect to remain here until this struggle is over, which is thought will not be a long way off.

I heard that our dear brother Charley had gotten home, which I hope may be so, but we hear so many things that are not so, we cannot tell when to believe a thing. Our Capt'n's name is Wright, who seems to be a talented man. The men of our Brigade are going away most every night, four left last night, eight night before, there is nothing to make them leave in the world. They (the leaders) say the soldiers will be paid a part of their wages in silver. Confederate money is now selling I heard for ten thousand dollars for one in specie, which is nothing very few will like. Cotton is down, selling for seventy-five cents in the currency. I recon Bro Henry and George will be at home soon if living I hope.

Col Reid has been arrested for a speech he made a few days ago telling the boys that our confederacy was gone, and called for all that wanted to go to Mexico to fight. He is now ordered to Shrieveport to attend court martial. He will leave in the morning and Jim with him who got here to-day. He says the thing is too near over to join now and so he will start for home. Cousin Johnnie is as strong a rebel as his ma, would be willing to fight ten years longer if it was necessary. Most all the boys are willing to surrender as it is. A great many thinks we are ready to be delivered to our enemy now.

Sister Emma, I feel that I have lived far beneath my privaledge, but my determination is settled to serve the One who made us and has provided for us so much more than we have deserved. How shall we ever pay the debt we own him, only by serving him. Pray for me that I may have more of his grace bestowed upon me. I long to see the day we may go to hear the Word of God in our old Chapel where we with our dear Parents, Brothers, and Sisters have spent many a pleasant hour in worship to God. The more I contemplate on his works the more I feel like adoring him. One ought to try to live more religious in days to come.

I must say goodby, dear Sister, hoping to see you all soon. As ever your loving and affectionate brother

John Reavis Butler

Much love and respect to all at home.

I saw Goodloe Patillo. Daniel Borden is staying with him sick. Joseph Cooper is over at his uncle's. Jim is waiting on him, he has been, I heard, very sick though I think he is improving. Lawrence is here in town.

Sallie Kittle to Emma Butler in Tulip

Henderson, No Ca
Sept [Probably 1865]

Dear Cousin:

I must really thank you for the long interesting letter I received a few days since. Why did you complain of a want of something to interest me? Why not write as I do, the first thought that enters your mind, and if you cannot find something sensible tell something unsensible. If you are as lenient as I am, all will be well; then do not hesitate to write, saying you know nothing that will interest me.

I am all alone tonight in my room and feeling so lonely. I conclude to write you a short letter. I do not think it will ever reach you. Brother Louis has gone out to call on some of the girls. He asked me at the tea table to go with him. It is so disagreeable walking I declined going. We have had no rain for nearly eight weeks. Fevers have prevailed extensively during the summer. I have lost a dear friend, Sue Hammer, who died in July. Cousin Charlie remembers her. I saw her only once after he left. Sue was a pious girl and I trust has made a happy exchange. How grateful we should be that our home circle yet form an unbroken number, while so many have lost a brother or father. We are indeed ungrateful creatures and so sure to be discontent with present blessings. Our necessary wants are few, but our imaginary necessities are unlimited.

I have had much company during the last few weeks. A friend from Virginia has been with us some time. He is now in the country. Cousin Peter Wyche's son Tom seems anxious that I should accompany him home the first of November, says he will take me straight on to Ark. Ma thinks I had better wait until the communication is regularly established. I believe she would expect a letter from me twice every week. I rarely stay out at Uncle's more than two days before Ma will send for me. I leave Aunt Martha scolding because I will not stay some time with her.

Cousin, you cannot be more anxious to see me than I am to see you, and when I do visit Ark you may conclude to come home with me, for I intend to keep you twelve months. I cannot tell when I shall see you. I hope to spend next summer with you but have no idea when I can go out there. Cousin Mattie Reavis and I wish to make a "flying visit" together but we may be disappointed. She has an Uncle near Princeton, I believe.

Pa is wedded to Henderson. I frequently tell him I wish we would by some magic means transfer him away. Pa expects to leave soon for N. York, and wants to take me with him. I expect a friend to meet me there. She has written to me recently, and will expect me to spend the Winter, but I have no particular desire to stay so long in yankeedom. I have some sincere friends North and thought perhaps they had changed, but I have proof to the contrary. I detest some Yankee principles but endeavor not to entertain personal hatred. It is a trial to hate the act and yet have a kind regard for the person. After the Army passed, a Yankee Capt. had the impudence to write to a lady expressing many kind wishes, and desiring to know whether her Father had suffered much from the Army. She of course did not reply. Such presumption did not deserve a passing notice.

I have just received a ticket to a Tournament and Ball, which will come off next week. I do not think I shall be in H. then. Balls and Tournaments are raging now. They have sixty knights practicing every day Sabbath and night.

We have had a quantity of grapes and peaches. I enjoyed the grapes so much. A gentleman sent me nice apples last summer but he has neglected me entirely this season. I think he is a little angry. Alas! that I should offend anyone and unintentionally. You are entirely mistaken, Cousin, I have not a beau at this time. It is true there are two here which Madame Ramsey says are sweethearts, and I heard the other day that I was married, but regret to hear so, don't you think? We are good friends and that is all. One of them they have teased me about since I was fourteen. I will admit he wanted to address me then, but while I respected him highly I would of course not receive his or any other gentleman's attention while I was a school girl—since the surrender we have come to a decision of the question. I could not marry a man of his religious principles.

And you have a new sister & I know you are proud. Please remember me to her as an affectionate cousin. But cousin, if you do let anyone read the letter woe be to you. I would write on, but scarcely think this will ever reach you. Please write to me soon, and a long letter too. I am at a loss whether to direct this to Little Rock or Pine Bluff. If you will answer this soon, I will be more punctual. The post office here is opened now—it seems like old times to receive letters.

Pa has been very busy for the past two weeks collecting his cotton so I believe he has secured the larger portion. Ma says tell Aunt she is waiting patiently for a letter. All send love.

Be sure to write soon.

My love to all.

> As ever most affectionately
> Your Cousin
> Sallie

William Paisley to Emma and Annie Butler

December 20th 1865

Misses Emma & Annie

I saw a man from Princeton yesterday who told me that the party at Princeton was not to be a dancing party—but that it would be managed in such a manner as to receive the approval of the most scrupulous lady or gentleman. He said it was possible they might have a dance, as there would be several young ladies there who sometimes indulge in that kind of amusement, but that it was not probable, and even if they did, it would take place in a room separate and remote from the main parlor so that none need see it, except those who participate.

> Very Respectfully yours &c
> Wm Paisley

[On back of this note]

The nicest ladies in and around Princeton will attend the party, and I think that fact alone is sufficient evidence of its character. Resply &c W. P.

P.S.

I am so well satisfied the party will be "all right" I insist on you going, and with your permission I will be pleased to accompany you. W. P.

Sallie Kittle to Emma Butler in Tulip

[Henderson, N.C.]
Saturday Evening
[Winter ? 1866]

My Dear Cousin—

This has been a dark cold wintery day and I have been compelled to stay indoors all day. I miss my usual promenade so much. I like to get a company of girls and walk out about one mile—we certainly have rare fun. Sometimes we will not let any of my brothers accompany us. Not long ago, a crowd of us while walking came to an old house. I was surprised to find a small hut in an old field. We concluded to go in. Pretty soon an old woman came in. One of the girls asked her if she could tell fortunes. She replied yes, and then came round to me and took my hand. I laughed and then asked her if she discovered anything mysterious in regard to my future destiny. She commenced telling what had happened and what would come to pass in future. I could not begin to tell you all she said—some true and more false of course. There were eight of us—she told each one—and one gentleman's besides. We had a merry time with the old lady.

I was out to see Mrs. Marable not long since. She always speaks in high terms of Uncle and Aunt—sends her best love to them, also to Cousin George and Charlie. She would be perfectly delighted to receive a letter from Uncle. Aunt Martha has named her youngest son Charles Emory—she has four sons—quite a little company of spoiled children. Uncle George is a perfect child spoiler. Cousin Sallie will soon be grown in size—she is a sweet cousin. Uncle says he is glad the negroes are free and Ma is a perfect abolishionist—says she can see the hand of Providence in the issue of this war.

Pa and Ma enjoy good health. Our minister will come today, I guess, as the meeting will commence out at Rock Spring Sabbath. Brother Riegrid is a capital man—both in the pulpit and around the social circle we all like him very much. I have visited the family once since they came to Ridgeway. They have had protracted meetings all around us this Summer. I heard the other day that one of my soldier correspondents had embraced religion. I was agreeably surprised, for I thought him a hard case.

I do hope it will rain tonight—then it will be so much more pleasant traveling. I have a friend in Washington City I wish to call on as we pass. I wish you could see some of her drawings. They are beautiful. Brother Louis and David Speed clerk for Cousin Parry Wyche. I have some Cousins who are either merchants or clerks in Henderson.

Please write soon and do not let anyone see this letter. Direct to Henderson, and if I am not there it will be forwarded immediately.

> With much love and a kiss
> I remain as ever
> Your loving cousin
> Sallie

Sallie Kittle to Emma Butler in Tulip

Henderson
April 30th [1866]

Dear Cousin,

Your letter came some several weeks since, a pleasant surprise I assure you. When returning from a walk, I found two letters awaiting me—yours, also one from Cousin Nellie Fraser in Ala. We are strangers—but I really love her—guess I shall call by to see them when on my way to Ark. I scarcely think I will disappoint you, Cousin, for I do not like to incur the displeasure of a good friend—even if I do at the same time, act contrary to the wishes of *one* who argues that *he* should be consulted in a matter so important.

Pa is in New York—will be about three weeks—I fear it will be stormy weather during his stay there—Henderson is as dull as can be now—new goods are coming in every day—great quantities. I think the present style of bonnets and hats is so homely—Cousin William Wyche is in town—I expect Ellen down soon—to purchase bonnets &c for them—I will return home with her and stay one week, I guess. I am sure you were delighted to visit Cousin L [?] I know he has a sweet wife, her [tin]type told that—I hope to see her one of these days.

All our fruit I think is destroyed. Ma's garden is flourishing but we will not have vegetables very early this year—we have had a quantity of rain—it is so cool for this season—fire is quite pleasant. Our minister & lady have been round to see us today. Mrs. R. is one of the sweetest little ladies I ever saw—I fell so in love with her that I felt obliged to give her something—so I sent out a jar of pickles to the cars when they left for home. They have a melodeon in our church—I do not think it a great addition by any means.

I guess there will be a picnic out in the country about four miles from here the 1st of May—a large crowd will be there—Two gentlemen were around this afternoon to give me the order of programming. I engaged to ride out with one of them—will have music & dancing. Of course, I never participate in that amusement. Yet we rarely see one who does not dance—indeed it is carried to great excess, I think, and at present renders a person anything but graceful or fascinating—I have not visited Uncle's in some time—little Jimmie was quite ill last week—it is the loveliest place in the world I think.

Cousin Peter Wyche sent in his sweetheart's [tin]type a short while since—I would like to see it—hope he will be more fortunate in his second selection—or rather that he will find a more congenial companion—he has a good heart with all his pecularities—It seems that the cholera & small pox will rage throughout the land this Summer—they are scourges indeed—

I expect two friends to visit me soon—old school mates—it will be quite a treat to see them. There are a few young ladies in H. but a number of young men, and they are very sociable—great ladies' men generally—always have amusement of some kind on hand.

Cousin Annie must excuse me for not answering her question—in regard to Valentine—I did not send or receive one—did not think of it in time. I feel really languid tonight—in consequence of late hours observed last night—and I imagine this is a terribly dull letter—besides I do not feel encouraged to write more—thinking it will never reach you.

With much love and many kisses I bid you good night.

Sincerely—
S—

James T. Johnson to William Paisley in Tulip

Richmond
May 29th 1866

Dear Paisley—

I have just recvd your letter, enclosed in one from Mrs. Johnson. She says it was accompanied by a check for $65 for which please accept my thanks. I left your note in Mo. and will send it to you upon my return. My family are still there at my wife's Father's. I am here trying to establish a nursery and seed business, similar to that in which I was engaged before the war. My address here is "P.O. Box 438" and I shall be pleased to hear from you.

I am writing this in a hurry, just on the eve of leaving town for a few days. Upon my return I will write to you more at length. Do not fail to let me hear from you, what you are doing and what your prospects are.

Yours truly
Jas. T. Johnson

"Louie" Elliott to Emma Butler in Tulip

Forest Home
June 3rd, 1866

My dear friend,

I received your letter but a few days ago, not knowing of your return from "Union" [County]. I was not looking for a letter at the time, thinking you would not write until you got home again, but as it was I was very glad to get a letter from you. I did not see Mr. Barcus, consequently did not get your letter as soon as I should have done. We are almost lost down here, surrounded by so much water, I do not believe I ever saw as much water upon the earth before. How and when did you get home, who was with you? Why did you not come by to see us?

I got a letter from Mary Thacker a week ago, the first I have received in a year. She was still at her old home, and anxious to visit me, and wants, when I move home to live with us, to teach the children. She has two little sisters, whom she must educate, and of course she has no means, only what she receives by teaching. I guess she will come. We will move home in the fall, and then when you are passing through [to] Henry's, I know you will call, now won't you? I will be right glad when I get over there, for then I will sometimes see you and many others, who are old friends. Where is your Sister living? Mary wrote me, she had heard that Miss Annie H. and Maj. P. Smith would be off very soon. Is there anything to it? "Aint" none of you never going to marry? It seems not. Who is your beau? I know you won't tell me.

I am going over in the neighborhood of Aunt Ebb's house before long, and I shall certainly visit her before my return, I would like so much to meet you there. Our next quarterly meeting is at Sardis. Find out when it is and come down. I have forgotten when. It is some time this month, probably I will be in attendance, if the water ever subsides. I saw Ruth and Mary yesterday, at a dining given by the citizens of Holly Springs at the "Female Academy" to the male school, which closed, the day before. They had an elegant dinner, a variety of most every thing, every one seemed to enjoy it. But I was sad notwithstanding the gaiety around me, tho' I thought it was in consequence of Mr. Elliott's absence, so far away on the other side of the "big water." I know you will say I was brave, when I tell you I came home across the water, it sometimes running into the buggy, but I was determined to come "sink or swim." I have not been to church in a long time, and Oh I do love to go, but am so situated that I can never attend. I understand that Mr. Barcus will bring Mary down his next round. I will be so glad to see her.

Dear Emma, write me again soon. I love to hear from you all. Tell Annie not to let Mr. Watson fall in love with her, as he generally falls in love with his pupils, from what I can hear. Write me who you saw in "Union," what you done while there. Did you stop in Camden? Well I've run out of something to say, so I will close by saying think of me and love me always. May heaven bless you is my wish. Love to all.

Your friend
"Louie"

Emma Butler to William Paisley in Tulip

At Home
June 19th, 1866

Mr. Paisley,

After considering the question proposed on last night I have concluded to answer it by note. I have been troubled for some time to know *what* to do. You know that this is a subject which should be well weighed by both parties concerned. In other matters I have always liked to leave for my ma or some more experienced person than myself to decide; but *this* decision is to be made by myself. I have prayed that I may be guided by my Heavenly Father in all things; and if there *ever* was a time when I needed *His* direction it is the present. I have long thought it to be my duty to marry a Christian and before your conversion, this was my principal objection to becoming your partner through life. A man without religion would be a poor companion for me. If you can get the consent of my parents, then, I will be yours. But till ma is entirely willing *we* can never be one.

Your friend,
Emma Butler

[Written on the back of this letter]

Precious letter may our children preserve it, and with the help of their Heavenly Father, be governed by the same principal that influenced their most excellent mother before they were born: honor their parents & look to God for guidance in all things.

Aug. 11, 1876   Wm Paisley

Jas. T. Johnson to William Paisley in Tulip

Richmond
June 25, 1866

Dear Paisley,

I wrote to Mrs. Johnson to look among my papers for your note but she could not find it, and consequently the matter was delayed until I could visit Mo. myself. I have just returned, and now enclose the note—again thanking you for your prompt remittance. We often spoke of your long journey, undertaken under such unfavorable auspices, and would like, when you have the time, to hear how you got through. I have no doubt it was full of adventure.

In looking over my old papers, I find the paroled list of all officers & men at the Purveying Depot. If it would be of any interest to you, I will have you a copy made. Do you know what has become of Serg. Little? If you ever meet with him please give him my address & tell him I should be very glad to hear from him. I have a high respect for his integrity of character and am under a personal obligation to him for an important service which he rendered me about the close of the war.

Mrs. Johnson and Roger desired me to send their kindest remembrances & best wishes and I am, as always

Very truly your friend
Jas. T. Johnson
"Box 438
Richmond
Va"

Wm Paisley Esq.
Ark.

William Paisley to Emma Butler in Tulip

July 19th 1866

Dearest Emma:

If the fates or *Miss Carrie* do not prevent, I hope to see you this evening after supper. My *well disciplined pleasure* came very near breaking over all restraints yesterday evening, and I commenced preparation to visit you, but on reflection I concluded that the pleasure of seeing you alone would more than repay me for waiting *twenty-four hours longer*. Together with a great many other items of interest, I shall expect a full account of your Princeton visit, the number of conquests you made &c.

W. P.

William Paisley to Emma Butler in Tulip

Aug. 22nd 1866

Dear Emma:

Your old friend Mrs. Rozell and her husband passed through Tulip this evening on their way to Dr. Colburn's, where they will spend the night. Mrs. Rozell has come down for her health, and will spend several weeks in the neighborhood—will board either at Dr. Colburn's or Mrs. Hughes'.

Many thanks for the basket of nice peaches you sent me the other day, the reception of which would have been acknowledged immediately, had I known they were intended for me & that you were the fair donor. But the peaches had nearly all been eaten by "loafers" when I found the basket, & I didn't know who they came from or for whom they were intended, until Johnny returned from school. Notwithstanding all that, they were none the less appreciated by me, for the fact of their being a token of your kindly remembrance *more than repaid me for the loss* of the fruit.

> Ever and affectionately
> Your William

P.S. I send you some old [Arkansas Christian] Advocates that came yesterday to Mrs. Taylor's address.

> Truly
> W. P.

Mattie Phillips to Emma Butler in Tulip

Montroy, Arkansas
August 25th, 1866

Dear Cousin Emma,

I have just been reading some of your old letters written during the war, and am ready to give you a scolding. Your letters then were so much more affectionate than the last two or three. However I don't suppose that your love for me has diminished, only, you know when daylight comes the flame of the candle, though the same, waxes dim. "The greater glory dims the less." How have you all been getting on since I left? You may be certain that it is with some impatience that I wait your promised letter by Dr. Colburn. I suppose ere this your brother George and Mr. Tannyhill (is that the way he spells his name) have gone.

Now that we have such delightfully cool weather I supose you have sent for Mamie. I say "delightfully"—these last few mornings have been really *unpleasantly* cool—that is without a fire. Isn't it fine for the sick folks? When I came home nearly *every*body on Washitor was either sick or had been so. Even Miller Gibson, who never was sick before in her life, has had an attack of fever. I found mother had been quite sick and was very feeble. She is better now. Ellen has been sick too. There has been a great deal of sickness in Arkadelphia and several deaths. Among others, tell Mary Pryor that Mrs. Heard is dead. She had just returned from New York, where she had been for her health. The night after we got to Mrs. Littlejohn's, Sallie was taken sick and was quite sick all the next day, so Mr. Foster did not bring me home till the day after.

You will be surprised to learn that some time ago when Capt. Cooper was down here, he told his aunt that there was a marriage in prospect at Tulip between Miss Emma Butler and Mr. Paisley, but that it would not come off in four or five months. In consequence I have been quizzed most unmercifully. I find that the report is very general indeed down here. I have something else to tell you on that subject when I see you. Dear Bremma, can't you come down soon? I want to have a visit from Emma Butler once more. Cousin Annie, too, knows how glad I would be to see her, & all of you. Joe Somerville passed here a few minutes ago going hunting with Mr. Haywood, so I supose he is not married.

> My best love to all.
> Affectionately,
> Mattie

September 20th

My dearest cousin,

I wrote the above nearly a month ago, but did not have an opportunity of sending it then, and have not time to write an entire letter now, so will send it anyhow. I only received yours of the 26th ultimo the other day, was very much interested, of course, though if it had been of a later date I would have been glad. However, I look for another day after tomorrow. I suppose ere this the important day has been fixed on, and various arrangements pertaining thereto. I would like so much to see you and have a long talk, I am so sorry you were disappointed about your trip down here, I still hope you will come, though.

I was down at aunt Eveline's yesterday—went after mother. Her health has not improved much. Saw Maj. Coulter down there. I am *so* anxious to see or hear from you, want to know all your plans &c. Heard that you expected to invite about a dozen of dear friends and relations, if so, let me know all about it. I would like very much to come up a few days before the eventful night. Was very glad to hear that Aunt Mary had become reconciled.

I have written very hurriedly which must be my excuse for every thing.

> Truly yours
> Mattie

Sept. 23rd

Dear Bremma,

don't laugh at this third date. I have just received yours of the 21st instant. Was *very much* interested, but my dear child, do tell me about what you are all going to wear.

Write to me by every opportunity. If you would write and send your letters up to Tulip, *he*—as you call him—could find plenty of chances.

What does Mannie [Annie Butler] do with herself, just heard she had got home, nothing more. You say nothing of cousin Mattie's health. Hope it has improved. Give my best love to all.

> Most affectionately
> Mattie

Sallie Kittle to Emma Butler in Tulip

Near Baltimore
August 28th 1866

My own sweet Cousin:

Indeed I was glad to receive tidings from my dear Cousin once more—for do you know that I had concluded—you would not write again soon, if ever. At last, however, a surprise greeted me this morn—in the form of a letter from "the loved ones at home" containing your missive.

As you discover, I am some distance from H—on a visiting tour—to meet old friends &c—left home with Pa and Sister Emma several weeks since—from Washington came on here. I need not tell you how much I have enjoyed myself—not an accident or incident to mar my pleasure—have met many strangers and formed many acquaintances of course.

The ladies I find are quite gay—I do not select my companions from among the gayest of the gay, you may be sure. They ride horseback a great deal—make excursions all around. I cannot tell you the number of elegant rides we have taken.

The young gentlemen are so gallant that we girls find no trouble in procuring horses. We have quite a visit in contemplation for next Tuesday. A large party of us will ride about eight miles to spend the day. The residence is in a romantic situation and the scenery around beautiful, they tell me. I anticipate a nice time. A gentleman was in a few moments since, and wis[h]ed to engage my company. He is a nice kind of man—rather boring—and I do wish he would condescend to excuse me. There is another gentleman with whom I would rather ride, but unfortunately he does not yet know when we are going. I am pretty sure he would have put in his card first. The ladies have full costumes of black, and you have no idea how striking to see fifteen or twenty with as many gentlemen, sweeping past on their splendid steeds.

Sept. 1

I have not felt well for two days, am now writing on a cot, hence you must excuse all—have been out a great deal at night, and now I cannot leave my room. I would be so delighted if I could only see you this bright evening—so much to tell you—I could not attempt to write the half I wish to say to you. I have written few letters since I left home. We expect to leave here soon, and after spending a couple of weeks among the mountains of Northern Va., Pa will meet us in Baltimore, and take us on to New York. I have met several ladies from Brooklin. They will leave with us, I guess. We hope to reach home by the fifteenth of Oct., in time for our Fair. Oh! do come out.

Many times do I think that I would be happy—yes inexpressibly glad, could I visit you—but I will never say again that I shall do so. Sis joins me in love to you all.

I certainly will remember you in my prayers—and will you do the same. May Heavens richest blessings ever attend my own dearest Cousin.

> As ever—
> Your
> Sallie

[On separate sheet]
Let no one see this, no one—

My dear Cousin, I cannot bid you a final adieu until I tell you—that I was not surprised at the secret which you committed to my keeping—long ago I mistrusted—why or how I shall not tell you now. You spoke as though I did not like Mr. P—and I am sure you had no reason for such a conclusion—I have met him once on a short occasion—and I will tell you frankly that I came to [the] conclusion that he was a perfect gentleman in every sense of the term. Do you wish me to say more? No indeed, you cannot. I thank you for the confidence—and shall not betray—or divulge—I would be so delighted if you could visit us—I certainly wish you a life of perfect happiness. Mr. P—is a Presbyterian is he not? Tell me all—please.

The gentleman I spoke of—as not knowing that we were going to visit—is a Mr. Thomas Carter—from Baltimore—a merchant there—he and I have been engaged some time, and he expected it would be consumated by the first of October—but his health has been declining for the past two months and nothing seems to afford any relief. He wishes to accompany Sis and I to the mountains in a few days—I do not think a mountain climate congenial to a consumptive— that disease has not shown itself perfectly. No one has hinted to me that Mr. Carter is declining— but I am sure—Cousin, that we can never marry. The barrier is insurmountable—a thought I cannot realize when I see him so noble, pure, refined and bright, vowing a love which I have every reason to believe springs from a pure heart. Be sure, my cousin, my trothplight will never be broken save by the iron hand of death—which I already imagine I see not a great way from the one to whom blushingly I gave my heart and hand—I feel now that I can never love another so entirely as I have Mr. C—. I must tell you that he is everything I would have frail human nature to be—remember this is a "profound" secret—please show or let no one read this sheet—lock this in your own heart and keep it for me, will you not? Mr. C. has rode to a friend's on business. He was exempt during the war on account of health—I could tell you many little secrets of myself if you were only by my side—it is not interesting to me to write them.

Sept. 3rd

A dark dismal day Cousin, and I am indoors, of course. Mr. C. left us very reluctantly Tuesday— he hopes to meet us again in Flint Hill—but he looks wretchedly now—so feeble—and yet he strives to appear cheerful—I hope all happens for the best—Hallie Swain, the lady I am visiting is sick—and I tell her it is half pretense. She is love sick. I have visited several battle fields, recalled many recollections of the past. I recently read a history of the war by a Carolinian, a complete little work. Please let no one on earth see this, keep it to yourself. I would tell you a great deal if you were with me.

A kiss I send you—with much love and a great many kind wishes.

> Write me soon—
> As ever—
> Devotedly—
> S—

[Cross-written in pencil on the last three pages of this letter]

Dear Cousin Please write to me soon but do not say anything about this secret yet. I will tell you more one of these days. I do not wish it known in our place, and I do not wish you to mention a word about it in your next letter. You cannot imagine how bad I feel when I allow myself to think of Mr. C.'s health. At first I had no idea that he was delicate—so large and fine looking—is said to resemble cousin Henry very much. Cousin, what do you think? I had an old widowed beau not long since—fifty years of age—do wish you would have seen him—he said he would not expect me to love him, but he had every thing in the way of this world's goods to offer, and he is immensely wealthy—lives in a brick mansion—I need not tell you that I had no hand to surrender *him*, for another had a prior claim—I have been out riding, taking a survey—a Mr. Moore was my escort—a nice man. Must return some calls out in the courts this afternoon—Come over and take a ride with me, do—a friend has called.

I do wish I could have attended your revival. I feel the need of religious friends so much— do write me often for your letters always contain so much sweet consolation. I feel sometimes as though there is not a Christian in existence, and that sin has unlimited sway. Strange that nearly all my pious friends are dead, and why I am spared, I cannot imagine, for it seems that no good have I ever done but I am certain that I love to inhale the most heavenly atmosphere which always sustains a circle of Christian friends. Friends are calling in and I bid you a lingering good bye. Let no one read this, please.

Devotedly,
S—

Sallie Kittle to Emma Butler in Tulip

Henderson [N.C.]
Oct 4th [1866?]

My dear Cousin;

I have received your sweet missive; laughed heartily to think I had committed so many blunders and was caught, but if you only knew the circumstances under which I wrote you last, I am sure you would laugh & not wonder that I should write at such random. I have heard from Va. since we left—just received quite a little volume of good news from a friend—let me quote a message she writes for a gentleman—"he says" Tell Miss Sallie that her beauty, genial and pleasing manners—sweet expressive eyes and soft smile are not forgotten, but have made an impression that time shall not efface. The pleasant recollection of that last visit will constitute an oasis in the desert of time—yes, the greenest spot in memories waste"—Now Cousin, I scarcely know what to think of such a tribute of flattery—but enough of this, let it pass. Willie comes in with another letter. Another friend writes that she has not forgotten me. Well Cousin, I shall have writing sufficient to keep away loneliness this Winter Season. My dear Cousin, how much I would enjoy a long chat with you. This quiet bright day Ma sits alone downstairs singing one of Grand Pa's favorite hymns. Bessie is at school, Sis sits by me on the bed looking through her Photograph Album. The fair draws near—I guess we will have company.

I would be delighted to witness your marriage, but it cannot be as we wish—consequently you must accept my sincere congratulations. I trust your marriage vow will bring you both none but bright days of unalloyed happiness—No vain regrets of disappointed hopes and misplaced affections. You remember the little poem ending "God pity them both and pity us all—who vainly the dreams of youth recall For of all sad words of tongue or pen These are the saddest "it might have been.'"

Oct. 8th

Cousin duties and company have interrupted me as you will see—I hope to hear from you very soon. I heard from Mr. C. last week. His health has not improved. He seems very much depressed, does not think of recovery—he is now in Va. with relatives. I find consolation only in the belief that there is wisdom and good design in every mysterious dispensation of God. To him we should look for aid in every trial—on our best friend rely and, my dear Cousin, when nearly overwhelmed with despondency, I hear a voice of inspiration pleading—Come unto me all ye who are heavy laden and I will give you rest—a volume of sublimity I see in those little Words "I will give you rest."

We expect our dear beloved minister this week—think him near to a saint. Our elder is a fine man also, but I do not think him so devoted as Uncle Ricard—he has five children, and they stay with us a great deal. I mean the Elder—their mother died three years since.

All join me in love to each and all. I saw Miss Martha Robertson the other day. She sends love to all, and complains that her brother does not write.

Believe me as ever most affectionately

Your cousin
S.

Mattie Phillips to Emma Butler Paisley in Tulip

Rose Dale, Arkansas
October 23rd 1866

Mrs. Paisley,

Dearest Bremma,

We arrived home safely Saturday evening and found mother a good deal better—was almost sorry I had not stayed longer at Tulip. What did you do on Sunday; church I suppose was out of the question. I slept nearly the whole day. In the evening Col. & Mrs. Whitaker and Kate Cooper came down and brought a separate horse for me to come and see the last of them, so I have been here ever since.

How are you getting on? Finely, of course, you would say now. But remember you are to tell cousin Annie and me six months from now whether you are any happier. I expect you will be like every body else though; if you are not you will not acknowledge it.

You will be surprised to hear that Ella Wilcox is dead. She died very suddenly, was taken sick last Friday and died Sunday morning. Dr Mitchel is also dead. I merely write this short note for the sake of writing to Mrs. Paisley. Tell cousin Annie when I have any thing to [say] I will write to her, now you are old married folks. No, Bremma, you know I will answer every letter you write to me.

My best love to all.

Affectionately,
Mattie

William Paisley to Emma Butler Paisley

Tulip
Oct 25 1866

For My *Wife*:

> The treasures of the deep are not so precious
> As are the concealed comforts of a man
> Locked up in woman's love. I scent the air
> Of blessings when I come but near the house.
> What a delicious breath marriage sends forth
> The violet bed's not sweeter.

My dear Emma

The above lines by another are so expressive of my own feelings and sentiments produced by the relation we now sustain to each other that I can but copy them for your eye.

> Yours with much affection
> W. P.

J. A. "Louie" Elliott to Emma Butler Paisley in Tulip

Forest Home
Dec. 2 [1866]

Darling Friend;

The first letter you have written me since your marriage, has just been handed me by Bro. "Harvey." I was indeed glad to hear from you again, and hope you will not delay writing again so long, but *dearest Emma* (you are frequently called by this name now, I guess) I readily forgive you for not writing sooner. I am pleased to hear you are so happy, may you ever continue so; a dear kind husband is better than anything on earth, and really you deserve such a one, as you are such a dear good creature yourself. This is not flattery but a real truth. Now we are all married, that is your most intimate friends, and mine too, all except Mary Thacker, yourself, Sallie Vaughn, Phenie, and myself, we have taken to ourselves kind good husbands. I hope to meet with you every one before I die.

Yes, it was a mere accident that I met with Bro. Henry and Mollie, I was delighted to see them. Mollie looked as natural as ever, and that dear little babe, how sweet it was, I hope some day to meet with you, when I get home. We would have moved ere this, had not the creeks been up so very high that we could not cross. You have heard that Mary Mc & Mr. Juniel [?] were married and living in Holly Springs, happy pair, so they say. I have never met her since the marriage.

Oh, Emma, I would be delighted to visit you all, more particular now since you are married; to see how you look. I guess your ma was glad to have her children all together once more. I know I should have been, tell Annie she will be stepping off, before any one knows it.

Emma, you treated me real mean, I know you have been loving Mr. Paisley all this time. Why didn't you tell me? I was slightly acquainted with him, I always thought he was handsome, now don't you think so! yes I know you do. Well, to tell you the truth I have a most excellent husband, so good I never want for any thing, and strange to say, I never asked him for any thing in my life, and we have been married almost three years. All that know me say I have every thing that heart could wish! Come to see me some time and you can see for yourself.

Sis has gone home. Ma went with her to stay a week or two. She would be glad to have Annie visit her while at Pine Bluff. I feel quite lonely since they went away. Sis has a sweet little boy named Willie. Fannie, my little girl is a sweet child, bad—very bad—sometimes, is afflicted though with something like a goitre on her throat. I have had the advice of every physician that I know nearby; none know what it is, neither agree. I have been using a treatment for almost a year, I can't see that it has any effect. Emma, you say Sallie R gave you her photograph and her husband's. Now you send them to me to look at. I will send them back. I would love to see them, does she seem to be happy? Where is there home? Write to me very soon.

My husband always asks to be remembered to my friends, kindest regards to Mr. Paisley. Love to all inquiring friends, a kiss for the *children*.

> Yours lovingly
> "Louie"

You will see that I have torn a leaf from my old composition book to answer your letter immediately, as I went to write, I found I had none, so before I would delay I take this leaf. I will have some paper in a few days. All well.

> Farewell
> J. A. Elliott

William Paisley to Emma Butler Paisley in Tulip

[as he begins his first buying trip after their marriage]

Rock Port, Ark.
[Feb 25, 1867]

My dear one:

While Mr. Johnson, Charlie & "uncle Nick" are talking about things generally I am thinking about my dear Emma, and as it is impossible for me to interest myself in the conversation, I will write her *just one line*. You will not expect a note from me so soon, but I have been thinking about you so much & loving you so hard today, my dear one, that I feel to night like I would give anything if I could only slip back to Tulip and see you one more time before I leave, but unpleasant as it may be, I will have to reconcile my self to the thought of being separated from you for four or five weeks. How could I live without my darling! The very thought of separation pains me. Your Pa will perhaps call this *foolishness*. If he does, tell him I *glory* in such folly & hope I may always be guilty of it.

Mr. J. and I had a very pleasant trip together. He was unusually agreeable. We reached Mr. Miller's this evening about half an hour before sundown, & found Charlie just coming from school. Charlie is well & looking some better than when at home. I will leave early in the morning on the stage. Mr. Johnson will go with me to Benton. Charlie went with me over in town this evening, when I went to secure a seat in the stage, & we found the "city" alive with young men preparing for a "grand ball" that is to come off in the Coach House to night. The country girls were pouring in on all roads approaching town, dressed in white, as cold as it was & looking as gay as geese, & are now dancing like their lives depended on their making a "big fuss."

I will get to Little Rock to morrow evening & will lose no time there unnecessarily. I will write to you every opportunity, & be assured my sweet one that you are ever uppermost in my heart & thoughts. Pray often for my safety & protection. Our Heavenly Father will always hear our prayers, and we know that he doeth all things well, and if it is His will, there is nothing that can prevent our meeting again & spending a long and happy life together.

Love to all and much love & many kisses for your dear sweet self

Ever yours affectionately,
W. Paisley

P.S. Please tell your Pa that the horses did so well, I concluded to buy the 20 bushels.

William Paisley to Emma Butler Paisley in Tulip

Steamer "Guidon" in sight of
Helena on Mississippi
Feby 27, 1867

My own dear Emma:

You no doubt expected a note from me at Little Rock & indeed I expected to write from there, but when I got off the stage at the "Anthony House" Saturday night, I was so tired from being cramped up & jolted on a crowded stage that I was unfit for anything. Besides, I met with Dr. Kelly, Col Cameron, Capt. Deadman & others, whose company would have kept me from writing, even if I had been in "trim." We arrived at Little Rock just before dusk. Dr. Kelly was the first man I met, and as it was then after "Banking hours," I got him to go round with me & show me the different Brokers' offices. We only found one open (Tucker's) & you will please tell your pa & Henry that I disposed of the silver at 122 & bought New York Exchange at par. I invested all of Henry's paper. We were so late getting to the "Rock," I was fearful I would not be able to attend to my business, as the next day was Sunday, but I got everything arranged satisfactory & what was better, found the "Guidon" there ready to start out the next morning. So I lost no time. *The business part will interest your pa and Henry.*

And now my dear one I will talk with you & tell you something of my trip &c. The stage agent at Rock Port informed me that the stage would start before or by day break the "next morning" & cautioned me to be ready by times. Mr. Johnson having concluded to go on with me as far as Benton, we got up very early the next morning, & (as might have been expected) were at the Hotel long before the stage was ready.

At the Hotel I met an acquaintance, Cap Simpson, a St. Louis merchant. He told me the stage would be crowded & that he was one of the passengers, but I was not prepared to see the crowd that I found when we all commenced getting in. Let me see, I will give you a list of the passengers inside & commence with the Ladies. There was Mrs. Gus Garland, her little boy & waiting girl, & Miss Cook of Arkadelphia, making four, then there was Mr. Johnson, Mr. Royston, Capt. Simpson & myself all packed into a little stage with but very little more room in it than your ma's carriage, besides the driver & two other passengers on top. I was cramped up on the middle seat without any back to it. But notwithstanding we were all suffering from cramp & jolts, we found a good deal to laugh at, & altogether had quite a jolly time. I was introduced to the men and had no difficulty in forming a travelling acquaintance with the ladies, both of whom I found very pleasant.

I went aboard the "Guidon" between nine and ten o'clock, & after looking around and finding that I had no acquaintances on the boat, together with the thought that I would then be "wafted more swiftly" away from my dear Emma made me feel quite lonely & sad, a feeling that I am not entirely rid of yet, tho it is not as oppressive as at first. Oh my dear one, how delighted I would be to have you with me. The boat I am on is a very good one & I could have such a nice time with you & you would enjoy this kind of traveling, the scenery &c so much. Our crew and passengers has been somewhat improved since we left Little Rock, but at first it was made up almost altogether of those cold-natured, inquisitive Yankees. If you were with me I would not have to depend on them for enjoyment or rather I would have some company for I have none that is congenial—as [it] is "David Copperfield" has been my companion since I got on the boat.

We are due at Memphis tomorrow morning, & I will leave the same evening at ½ after three for

Louisville. I will take the cars from Memphis which will prevent my going by Cairo & seeing Lewis. I regret this very much as I fully expected to see Lewis on this trip, but it would take me several days longer to go by River & I am now so late I haven't the time to spare.

I haven't recovered my health entirely yet, but feel that I am improving. For the first two days after leaving L. Rock I feared that I might have another spell of sickness, but I feel so much better today that I am not at all uneasy now. The weather has been quite cold since I got on the River & I fear it will be very severe up north. Do not, my sweet one, give yourself any uneasiness about my being sick. I promised you that I would be candid & would not deceive you & I expect to be as good as my word.

I met Mr. Garratt—formerly a merchant of Pine Bluff—at Napoleon last night. He is just returning from Kentucky with a new wife—was married just nine days before we were. He told me that he intended going to Tulip in the course of a week or ten days & would go to see your pa's family. I shall wait very impatiently for a letter from you, & do not forget to tell me all about Henry. I have felt uneasy about him, but hope when you write that he will be well. I will not make any other suggestions as I shall expect you to give me all the news.

Now my dear one, I would like to write more, & feel that this is too shabby a letter to send my wife, but I am sure you will make allowances for it when I tell you that I have written it on a table within four feet of another table around which there are seven or eight noisy men playing cards. I write with a pencil because the boat shakes so much that I cannot write with a pen. I will have to ask you to excuse *all*. Oh how I would like to see you, if it were only for a few minutes this evening. We have now been separated longer than at any other time in our marriage, & it really seems like an *age* to me—but then I know my Emma loves me & thinks of me often and prays to our Heavenly Father that I may be spared to see her again. These thoughts cheer me & make me sensible of the fact that while I am blest with such a sweet loving wife, I ought to be the happiest man in the world.

Give my love to all—and believe me my dear one, your ever devoted & affectionate husband

W. Paisley

P.S. My belt got so heavy I had to take it off while on the Boat and deposit it with the clerk. Will put it on again when I get to Memphis. *Many kisses.*

William Paisley to Emma Butler Paisley in Tulip

[Feb. 28, 1867]

My dear one,

I don't think I can be satisfied just to hear from you once in five or six weeks. If you can plan write to me about the 18th or 20th of March & direct thus

W. Paisley
Care Anderson Gay & Bugher
Memphis, Tenn

& I will get it on my return

[no closing]

William Paisley to Emma Butler Paisley in Tulip

Cincinnati, O.
Mch 3rd 1867

My own sweet Emma:

How much more pleasantly could I have spent to day with you than here in the (to me) strange city of Cincinnati. I arrived here before sun up this morning & in consequence of its being Sunday, have to "lie void" until ½ past eight o'clock to night. And here I have been all day thinking of my dear one, and the long time that I will still have to be absent from her, and wishing that the long hours that detain me from my business & Emma would not creep away so slowly. I trust, however, that my time to day has not been spent without some profit. I attended church this morning at the 7th Presbyterian Church and, together with the sacrament of the Lord's Supper being administered, we had one of the best & most religious sermons I ever listened to, and I felt that it was *indeed good* to be there & that the presence of the Lord was with us.

I left Memphis at [half past three], and arrived at Louisville next evening at 1 o'clock. When I got to Memphis I was completely worn out with steam boats, & was very impatient to get on the cars. Could I have had you with me I would have preferred the boat, but they are too slow for a man in a hurry. I came from Memphis to Louisville in 21 hours, distance 376 miles, and now I wish, my dear one, that I could show you with my pen what I have seen since I left Memphis—the beautiful Mountain scenery of Kentucky—first the highly improved level country the cars passed through, then sailing along at the foot of high mountains, then through long tunnels as dark as Egypt & then almost flying around the mountains with the road cut out of the edge with the mountain rising up almost out of sight on one side & a deep precipice on the other with a beautiful valley beneath. Then the crowded depot at Louisville, with an innumerable mass of cabs and omnibuses and the porters & hackmen for different hotels & Rail Roads running after you, until you almost wonder whether you are in a city or a saw mill—then the city itself, with its towering churches, elegant residences & business houses & smoking factories. Then the crowds of fashionable Ladies with their long and tight waisted, small sleeved dresses on, with their hair pulled back over the slope of their head & fixed up with other hair, mohair &c in a bundle *something* less than a bale of cotton, then the men with short coats and high crowned silk hats that taper to a point and present some thing the appearance of a wooden churn with a brim to it, then the Elegant and Magnificent steamer the "Genl. Lytle" that I came from Louisville to this place on, with its Gilded Banjo work. Long row of tables adorned with fine silver ware & covered with every delicacy that you can imagine, surrounded with polite, white waiters that dance around to the tune of "double quick." Then Cincinnati and the fine granite church that I attended to day, its fine organ & splendid choir & crowded pews: but I will have to wait until I see you & in the mean time I will try and treasure up in my memory every thing I see of interest for the special benefit of my "little" Emma.

The weather has been very unpleasant ever since I left Little Rock. I don't think there has been a single day but what we have had either rain or snow. A very heavy snow fell in Louisville yesterday, & we had a heavy hail storm & sleet here this morning. The train I leave on is due in New York Tuesday next at 12 o'clock M. I hope to get ready to start back by the 18th, & sooner if I can. I can't help regretting that I started to New York. Capt. Simpson of St. Louis assured me that I could get goods in St Louis like I expect to buy in New York, & the Louisville merchants offered to sell me all the goods I wanted, on terms that were fully as good as I hope to be able to make in NY. I met Bill Nab & Asbury Smith in Louisville & would have written by them, but I found that I could get off sooner than at first expected. I would write more, my dear one, but it is now supper time & must eat supper—take off my Sunday clothes & get ready to start.

> With many kisses I am ever
> your loving husband
> W. Paisley

Love to all.

I have just written to your Pa & Henry sending them Bills—Please take care of *Mr. Doby's Bill.* Goodbye WP I wrote to Lewis from Memphis.

Emma Butler Paisley to William Paisley in New York

Tulip
March 5, 1867

My dear beloved one,

According to promise I will write tonight to my absent "husband," though all tell me they think it is of no use, for they think you will leave before this reaches New York; but nothing will be lost any way, and if you do receive it, it will afford you some satisfaction. After writing to you last Friday, I was very sick at my stomach [Emma is pregnant] and was lying down most of the day; but glad to say I have not been so sick since, though I am frequently annoyed with that most disagreeable of feelings.

I look for a letter tomorrow from you; I *do* hope I will not be disappointed. Pa was down to Princeton today and saw Col. Cameron, who told him that you left Little Rock last Sunday week. I was glad to hear that much, for I had not heard a word from you since you left Rockport. Annie received a letter from Charley, who mentioned that you met an old acquaintance from St. Louis. I am glad that you were so fortunate. Brother Henry and some of the others kill birds the last few days. I enjoy them *very* much. I am very anxious for Mr. Robertson to get his apples, for I do feel hungry for them. We are having very disagreeable weather now, which is the reason Mr. Clifton has not brought the apples. I am afraid the fruit will be injured, for ice has been on the trees for the last two days.

Willis brought me a letter last Sunday evening directed to you, or Miss Molly Paisley. I opened it, and found it was from Mr. Marshall, who said he was married, and had the prettiest baby you ever saw. He asked several questions, which brother Henry promised to find out, and said he would answer the letter for you if I would not.

Jimmie Cooper is still very bad off with his knee. I don't think he has been able to stand yet.

I would feel better about writing if I felt certain about its ever reaching you.

Negro Sarah is still here and we are very glad, for it would be cold for Alice to milk.

I must close for you know I am not a good hand to sit up late and it is now after nine o'clock. If I could only be with you I could talk a long while. You must pray often for your

Emma

March 6th

The hail seems to be tolerably deep this morning. I forgot to tell you that brother Henry and sister Mollie moved up in "our room" last Saturday; so our trunks and other articles had to be moved into the little room. We will not be here long after you get home, so it will not make a great deal of difference. My dear one, I *hope* it will not be as long as you expected before you return home. Sister Mary, Annie and others send love. Write immediately to your loving

Emma

P.S. Billy—If convenient, please purchase a "*Photographic Album*," a neat one but not very costly—say $5.00. If you can have the following inscribed in the proper place in gilt—"Presented to Mollie C. Butler by her husband." Success to you.

Yours truly.
H. A. B.

William Paisley to Emma Butler Paisley in Tulip

New York
March 13, 1867

When I look back to the 22nd of last month, the time we saw each other last and then think that I am here mingled with the crowd and bustle of New York City, so far separated from my dear one. It really seems like it has been an age since the morning when my heart, even in sadness, welled with the emotions of pride when I pressed my Emma to my bosom, felt that she was mine, and that the tears that trickled down her cheek so fast were the "overflowings" of her affections for me. But these thoughts are too sacred to put on paper, so I will try and interest you with something else.

I have been here now a week and one day, and I can tell you that I am thoroughly sick and tired of New York. On the way from Cincinnati I took cold and was quite unwell for several days after getting here, but I am quite well now, and for the last five days have been working very hard trying to get through with my purchases. Buying goods is very hard work, particularly when the buyer is limited and is compelled to wait after buying a bill, for the amount to be made out before he can purchase another.

I am trying to be very careful not to get anything that will not sell. I have finished buying dry goods, notions, clothing, boots and shoes, hardware, crockery and hats for Henry and myself. The bills I have now to buy are small and I hope to get through this week, but all my bills are to settle yet, as well as some other purchases that remain to be made, and it will be fully as much as I can do.

I would like to tell you something of this great city, but for my life I don't know where to commence, in fact I have seen but very little of it as yet, as I have only visited the portions of it where my business called me. You have often heard of the crowds that constantly throng Broadway. When the cab that I engaged (on arriving) to take me to the Astor House drove into Broadway, the first thought that I had was that there was something extraordinary taking place near-by, and that the people were all flocking to see it, and that the excitement would presently subside, but it has not abated yet, and until I became accustomed to it I found it hard to rid myself of the idea that there was something taking place that affected all alike, and that was the cause of the excitement.

Here we see every kind of people imaginable. At one minute on Broadway you are passed by the wealthy fop, and at the next you find yourself running against the suffering blind with a card pinned on his breast asking for alms, or the haggard old woman with her bag picking up the little pieces of cloth and paper that are thrown from the stores. Everything is excitement, and all seem to be struggling with all their might for the almighty dollar.

Monday 17th

You see my dear one that I commenced this four days ago, but just as I finished the first sheet I was stopped by some "would be" agreeable gentleman representing houses that were able to offer extraordinary inducements to Southern gentlemen who were visiting this city for the purpose of purchasing goods. And I have been prevented by drummers and other company since from finishing, but I have not returned any of their visits, and as I am nearly through buying now they have ceased to trouble me. I hoped to round up all our matters by Saturday night, but with all I could do I find that I have two other days' work ahead of me yet. I will try to do it in two, and I promise you I will lose no time in seeing sights. I have a few small bills to buy and all our accounts to settle. I have found no difficulty in getting what goods we want, and shall buy about five thousand dollars worth for Doby and Paisley, and about three thousand for H. B. and Co. I get six months on hats and only four months on all the rest, but the men I buy from tell me that they will not press us if we find it impossible to come on time. Goods are cheap and merchants are anxious to sell, but it is impossible for a man to get credit in first class houses unless he comes well recommended. Your Pa's old friends Garrett and Sherman Brothers have rendered me valuable service and introduced me to the best houses in the city. When Mr. Garrett read your Pa's letter, he remarked that he would sell "old man Butler goods if he didn't own a dollar in the world."

I bought our dry goods and notions from the house of Evans Gardner & Co. Mr. Evans is your Ma's cousin, and his house is doing a very large business. I have bought Miss Williamson's trunk and when I come will be able to show you the spring style of hats and bonnets. They are both very pretty I think, and look more like themselves than they have for some time. When I turned to "Sister Mollie's" memorandum the hat merchant picked out the "sweetest" little hat he had and wrote Coulter's name in it, and compelled me to take it without charge, but the hat was packed away in the box instead of being left out for my trunk as I intended, and you must tell Mrs. Butler that she must not be too severe when I come without it.

My time here has been spent as pleasantly as could be expected. I have met a great many acquaintances but have not had time to see much of them. Now, my dear one, I must close and that too feeling that my letter was not worth reading. I am feeling as well or rather my health is as good as ever, but I feel so jaded from bodily exercise and from loss of sleep that I am too stupid to write, but I hope to see you by the 3 or 4th of the next month at the furtherest, then I will be rested and we can talk much easier than I can write.

There is not an hour in the day, my precious one, but what I think of you, and wish that I could have you with me. You are uppermost in all my thoughts and my greatest temporal ambition is to make you happy and enjoy your love. Give my love to all, and believe me, Ever your devoted and affectionate husband

W. Paisley

P.S. If I start Tuesday I shall expect to get home [in] 13 or 14 days. I was 12 coming, and I shall not lose more than two or three days in N.C. Tell Henry that he can tell his customers that he has a "big" lot of Ladies Hats coming.

Yours &c
W. P.

Emma Butler Paisley to William Paisley in New York

Tulip
March 19th, 1867

My dear absent one,

I have received yours of 27th of Feb. and the one 3rd of March. Your letters afford me unspeakable joy and satisfaction, my dear one. If you do not hurry home you will find your wife toothless and bony, for I lost one of my teeth last week, and am somewhat thinner than when you left. Nothing serious is the matter, but I have lost my appetite almost entirely. I have been in bed most of the time for about a week. I am now seated in bed, which is the reason I am writing with a pencil, and a very poor one at that. I am still troubled with the disagreeable sickness I mentioned in my last letter. I suppose you have received both of my letters which I directed to New York. Brother Henry opens the mail now at Tulip, and as the stage came down today I thought maybe I would get a letter from you, but I was disappointed.

After writing the last sentence I was compelled to lie down, so if I write upside down, cross ways, and every other sort of fashion you can make allowances. I felt a little stronger yesterday, and regret now that I did not write then. You must not be uneasy, for it is very natural that I should be very weak after losing my appetite.

Emma Lipscomb [Billy's stepsister] was down to see me this evening. She will commence teaching school the first Monday in April at the same place your sister Mary taught last session. Your Ma was down to see me last Sunday evening. She told me to give her love to you when I wrote.

Pa has been complaining for the last few days. Brother Henry has had one chill since I last wrote you, but is now up and attending to business. He and sister Mollie have been very kind in making lemonade for me out of some Sugar of Lemon they got last summer. If you were here with me, I don't think I would be long in getting well.

Mr. Foster and Sallie staid with us Monday night on their way to Tenn. Bob Hunter has come up after Major Alexander's daughters, who will leave in a few days. He brought the news that Dr. Rhodes was buried last Wednesday.

Little Coulter is on the floor playing with the cat and saying "dad dad. dad." Sister Mollie says he wants to see you but that he would rather see his hat. I will have to wait till you come home, and then I can tell you every little thing of which I can think. Let me assure you again that nothing serious is the matter—I only feel too weak to write upright. But I must say I don't know what we would have done if Mr. Robertson had not been here to make fires for us during that cold weather, which lasted two weeks.

All send love. Pray for me, for I feel that I need your prayers. Remember me as ever

Your loving
Emma

Many kisses my dearest one.

William Paisley to Emma Butler Paisley in Tulip

Dobyville
April 29th 1867

My own sweet darling

You don't know how impatient I am to see you & have you with me again. Our goods have not yet come & I would have gone back to Tulip before now, but Mr. Doby looked for two wagons on Saturday and I had to stay. The wagons have not come & if you *will only be smart* you may see the first box of goods opened yet. Mr. Doby is waiting & I must close—I write to tell you to be sure & come from Arkadelphia by the lower bridge. The other is not safe—Remember to take the left hand this side of Mr. McDaniels & the left again this side of Mr. Murdocks, & then any body on the road can direct you to the Doby neighborhood.

Ever yours with much love & many kisses

W. Paisley

Emma Butler Paisley to William Paisley in Dobyville

Tulip
May 1st, 1867

My precious darling,

To look out on the beautiful sunshine, it seems there is nothing to prevent me from starting on my journey this morning, but day before yesterday Charley, Mr. Jim Looney and myself left Tulip at just seven o'clock, got along finely till just this side of Mr. Williams', we came to a road which I thought led into the bottoms, and directed Jim Looney to take it, as that was the way I thought Mr. Looney went. We had not proceeded very far till one of the mules mired and lay down, when Mrs. McAlister (I forgot to mention that she was going as far as Dr. McAlister's with us) and I got out and walked a little further on, to be certain whether we were in the right way or not. We found that I was mistaken, for we could proceed no farther: so we turned & walked on up to the house to wait till the waggon could be got out. After speaking to the family we enquired whether there was any gentleman about the place we could get to go and help them about the waggon. Mr. Death-ridge went, and we found out that this was only a road that had been used for hauling rails. It took them about an hour and a half, when we again started on our journey. I felt very badly for I was the one that was hurr[y]ing on and was the cause of our detention.

We reached Mr. Harris' when the sun was but an hour high. After finding it was impossible for us to get across the river, for it was still rising, we concluded to spend the night. The next morning after crossing *our* stopping place I began to think we would have no difficulty; but when we got within a mile and a half of town we found the bayou swimming from bank to bank. O! my dear one! I felt almost disheartened just to think that I had to go all the way back to Tulip. I never hated the thought of going to a place so bad in all my life. We came back and left some of the trunks at Mr. H.'s and got home last night a little after sun down. Almost the first thing I heard was that Mr. Looney and Martha Green were married that evening at four o'clock.

I must hasten on for Jimmie is waiting to carry the letter to the office. I don't know when I will start, but just as soon as I possibly can. I am *very* anxious to be with you, my dear one, but pa thinks he can't spare Charley till next week. I am all impatience to make a third trial when I think we will succeed. I haven't time to think of any news, but I *hope* I will see you in a few days when I can tell you every thing. I don't know whether this will reach you before I do, but I thought I would write a short letter any way. All are well. Much love and *many* kisses my dear one.

> Ever yours most affectionately
> Emma

Haven't time to look over and see what I have written. [Note in WMP's writing:] "From the sweetest and dearest creature in *this world*"

Mattie Phillips to Emma Butler Paisley at Tulip

> At Mr. Caldwell's
> Tuesday Morning, 4th of May [1867]

Dear Bremma,

Mr. Caldwell starts off tomorrow morning and will not arrive at Tulip until Saturday. So you see I cannot come with him, as I do not care to go around the circuit with him. I am sorry I can't come to see you, but I love you all the same. I staid up here last night. Mrs. C. gave me a fine treat of nice strawberries for supper. I suppose Aunt Mary has a great abundance of them. She has green peas, I suppose. They have had green peas and strawberries at Col. Whitaker's for nearly a week. I guess I will go there in a day or two; they have been after me once since peas came in, but I did not care to go that evening.

Brem I am so sorry you left, now that the weather has proved to be so fine. Today would have been so much prettier day for you to have gone up. The river is still high, falls very slowly. No boats have passed through.

I am nearly through with "Dick's Works" which I think I told you about reading. Then I expect to read "Travels in Egypt and the Holy Land," and "Five Years in China." Both belong to Mr. Caldwell. Tell cousin Mat that I like my Magazine much better this year than I did last.

Tell cousin Mollie C. to send her braid and floss along. I am anxious to work a pattern in one of the magazines that I think pretty. The slipper pattern she wished me to send her is in a magazine which is lent out. Will send it to her as soon as I get it home.

Bremma, don't forget to send my tooth-brush down by Mr. C. and I shall also expect a letter, Miss, or rather Madam, I suppose, a long one, too.

Kiss Aunt Mary for me and give my love to all.

> Truly your cousin
> M. Phillips

Mary Butler to Emma Butler Paisley in Dobyville

Tulip
June 5th, 1867

My dear Emma,

Your letter was received yesterday evening and I cannot better express my appreciation of it, than by replying immediately; in fact, I did feel complimented by getting yours first, whether I was deserving or not.

I have just sent off a letter to Helen McDaniel in reply to one I got from her husband not long since. He seems very much devoted to Helen, she has been very sick: for some time, her recovery doubtful—improving when he wrote, but then unable to move hand or foot without assistance; she expects to visit us as soon as able, for her health. They have lost a sweet little girl.

Well! Emma, the latest and most exciting news we have, is the marriage of Dr. Colburn and Mrs. McAlister: we must give them credit for one thing, and that is, keeping it such a secret; the Dr. came up late Friday evening (we saw him pass here) that was a week ago last Friday; Saturday, they fixed the time, and Sunday morning asked brother Hunter to marry them that evening at three o'clock. I must tell you how we first heard it. Mr. Robertson went up to the church and got the news from Willie Hunter; he hurried down, of course, greatly excited, and met us in the grove on our way to Sabbath school—asked if we had heard the news! We said no; he then told us to guess who was going to be married that evening: my first guess was correct. The much talked of net was worn on the occasion, and Mr. Robertson was very much hurt because he was not invited—threatens to make her pay for it. Miss Virgie, Kate, & Alice were at the church in the morning, and invited Capt. Cooper and Lucy Martin home with them. It is also reported that Bill Reid was invited, but they deny it: he didn't go.

Sammy Colburn preached here last Sunday—had a good congregation, the bride was out— dressed in her lilac colored poplin trimmed with black velvet and white shaker trimmed with green Becage: she failed to get a dress bonnet in Arkadelphia or Princeton, and I believe she has concluded to do without. Miss Virgie got a hat in Princeton trimmed with buff ribbon and a long tulle veil. She says it is much cheaper than those we had here. Ma is still weaving on her carpet. We cut off nineteen yards of it yesterday. I think it is going to look very well.

Charly had a chill this morning; says tell Miss Lizzie he hasn't had any before since she cured them for him, and hearing yesterday of her having so many beaux must have been the cause of their return.

We got a letter from brother Lewis last week, he was very well—had just been on a short visit to Kentucky.

Sister Mollie received a letter from her pa this morning. He has left New Orleans, will be here some time this month. He says Johnny will get through by the middle.

Several weeks ago we had a very nice little social party down at Mr. William Hunter's. They had a handed supper: all seemed to enjoy themselves more than usual: we are expecting one at Dr. Raimy's before long. Trade is dull at Tulip now; farmers are very busy in their crops.

Kate and Alice Colburn have dresses like your calico; it makes up very pretty.

Give my love to Mr. Paisley and tell him to write. Pa, Ma, and all send love to you both.

Coulter had another chill the other day. Annie speaks of writing to Lizzie Doby soon, give her my love. Write soon to your loving sister,

Mary

Henry Butler to William Paisley in Dobyville

Tulip Ark.
June 24, 1867

Dear Billy:

I write you in haste by Cousin Wm Kittrell, who leaves this morning for Dobyville. I received the Bed steads on yesterday for Mr. Doby. I have seen Mr. Bird in regard to the ware, and he agrees to let you have the Bill you want at 12½ cts, *provided* I will allow him to pay off what he is owing to G. Hughes in that way, which I promised to do. He will burn a kiln this week and I think I can send it over (together with the Bed steads) next week. I will send you a duplicate of the tinware purchased in P[ine] B[luff] if I can find it—also the Bill of your Powder & shot. The freight on my 2 kegs powder from N[ew]O[rleans] to C[amden] was five dollars. Johnnie made a mistake and failed to send me any shot.

Cousin Wm will give you the news pertaining to the family. Ma is yet suffering from a "bone felon." We have had Maj. Coulter with us for several days. He will be to see you about Saturday I suppose.

Trade is dull. I have remitted thirteen hundred & fifty dollars to New York purchased exchange in Little Rock. If you have any funds on hand, you had better get Wm Kittrell to take it if he will receipt you for it. I had to pay ½¢ premium for exchange, which will save you five dollars on the thousand. I don't know that Kittrell wishes any money. He is traveling to solicit custom for his house.

Cousin James Butler's mother is quite sick. Dr. Reamey thinks she is in a critical situation.

I will write you some day when I have more time. In the mean time would be glad to hear from you, and Emma, to whom give my love. Mollie sends her love to you both and says tell Emma, "Coulter can almost walk."

With my best wishes for your success and happiness, I am truly your friend and

Brother
H. A. Butler

Mrs. Emma Lipscomb to William Paisley in Dobyville

Tulip Dallas Cty
June 30th 1867

My Dear Son

Your very welcome as well as unexpected letter was received with pleasure. We were glad to here that you and Emma were well and so well pleased and I do hope you will continue to be pleased and prosper in business. You don't know how proud I was of the present you sent me. Say to Emma for me that I admire her taste very much. Maj Butler's family are all well at this time. Henry and Coulter have been sick but are now well. Mrs. Eveline Butler has been sick for some time and is still sick. I saw John pass after the doctor this morning. I have not herd how she is to day. Dr Colburn has been confined to his House and part of the time to bed, for the last three or four weeks. It is doubtful whether he will ever be able to preach again or not. Brother Hunter

Preached for us to day, and Mr Dixon the Presbyterian will preach for us next Sunday. Sim Williams has been at home for the last week. He will carry my letter to you. I hope he will pay you. He has paid Billy Cooper what he owed him. Your sister got the money you sent her by Billy Cooper. I have nothing to write.

Father [L. D. Lipscomb, Billy's stepfather] says he is much oblige for your good wishes and hopes he will realize them all. He got through laying by corn last week. This corn looks well. We have had a fine season. The last two days it has rained very hard, and at this time it is cloud[y] and threatning. Our cotton looks well. If no evil befalls it we hope to realize something Hansom. Father says if he does not make a comfortable living this year at Tulip, he intends to sell out and go where he can live with less labor. I hav no desire to leave Tulip. If we had enough of good land I never would.

Father and Emma had a gay time yesterday robbing bees, how I wish you & Emma was here to eat honey with me. Some of the Hives was very nice. Give my love to the Messers Dobye. Father and all the children join in love to you and Emma. You must write soon and often. I would like to fill out my sheet but have nothing of importance to write.

Your affectionate Mother
E. D. Lipscomb

P S Did you take one volum of the comentory and the Bible Dictionary. If so all is right I just want to know where they are.

E. D. L.

Mattie Phillips to Emma Butler Paisley in Dobyville

Cachemasso, Arkansas
July 16, 1867

My dear cousin,

I received your letter of July 3rd on the fifth, was very glad to hear from you. Had heard that your health was not very good. Cousin Charlie stopped here on his way home and told me so. Am glad that you are so well pleased with your home. I had heard that Mr. Paisley was selling out very rapidly, and that he had very cheap goods. Am sorry to learn that his health is not good. You will have so many watermelons that I guess he will get fat then. Aunt Eveline, after whom you enquire, is no better; we have all been down to see her; mother spent last week with her. Mother's private opinion is that she has the consumption. She is *very* thin, her voice is very much changed. When she has fever she is generally delirious, at other times quite rational. Her whole thought seems to be "Johnnie."

Cousin, I want to see you so much, can't you get Mr. Paisley to bring you over to see us this summer? We would all be so glad to see you.

Ellen was up at your Pa's a week or two ago—they were all very well there except little Coulter, he was teething. I suppose though you hear from there quite often. I have not been there since you left, and don't know when I shall. Not before fall or the last of the summer I suppose. I expect to go down to Camden the last of this week or the first of next, on a visit to Bettie Bridges. Will stay about two weeks. Her little baby is such a sweet little thing.

Our fishing is very fine now. We went down to-day and caught about twenty. The last time we caught twenty-six, just the children and I. I hope you have plenty of vegetables. Our garden is much better than usual. We will soon have tomatoes. I chop in there some myself.

I must close. They are waiting for me to send the letter to town. All the family send love to you and Mr. Paisley.

> Most affectionately
> Mattie

Sherman Bros. Hardware, N.Y., to Doby & Paisley, Dobyville

> New York
> July 22 1867

Mssrs Doby & Paisley

Gent.

We acknowledge your favor of 3 inst and note contents which are quite satisfactory. We only wish *all* our customers were equally thoughtful about their maturing paper. We regret the delay which occurred to your goods, but hope your sales will be liberal enough to warrant summer purchases or orders. We shall be glad to see you or hear from you.

> Yours truly
> Thomas Ruthen

Annie Butler to Emma Butler Paisley in Dobyville

> Tulip
> Aug 22nd, 1867

My ever dear sister:

I have been trying to write to you ever since my return home, but it seems that I never will *feel* like writing, so I concluded I would write contrary to feelings.

Brother Henry received a letter from Aunt Mary today, and enclosed found our photographs, which I was delighted to receive. She is now in Huntsville Ala. for her health, spent two weeks in Memphis. She is very anxious to leave the River, and I hope she will come to Tulip.

Ma and I were at Mrs. Lipscomb's yesterday evening and found them all well. Emma [Billy's sister] is weaving a carpet.

Brother Charlie and sister Mary left this morning for the District Meeting. Pa also went. I guess they will have quite a nice time.

I have just returned from eating watermelons. We have had the greatest plenty every day since I returned from Clark Co. We have a basket of nice peaches gathered every morning by Mr. Robertson, and have the nicest Indian peaches I most ever saw. It is a perfect treat to eat them. And while we are eating and enjoying ourselves, think not that you are forgotten, for I never see a basket of nice fruit, but what I say I wish so much Emma had some, but I fear when you come every thing will be gone.

Cora Reid reached home Saturday night a week ago. Johnnie and I called on her Monday morning, found her looking as pretty as ever and quite dignified. Kate Colburn remarked she "feared some of the boys around would have to be sent to the lunatic asylum since Miss Reid's return." She of course has called on her, and from actions I would judge she was using her utmost endeavors to captivate the lieutenant.

Brother George speaks of going on after goods for bro. Henry and cousin Jimmie Butler, but has not fully decided. The goods bro. Henry ordered will be here next week. Ma and sister Mollie have just gone to Tulip, the latter went to see her place, thinks she will move in Nov. Coulter had a chill this week, but is now well with the exception of a breaking out on his feet.

Tell Lizzie [Doby] I will answer her letter soon. I reckon it will not be long before you are with us, so I have written enough for the present. Present my regards to Mr. and Mrs. Doby and a kiss to the children. Also give my love to Miss Maggie. All send much love to you both. Write immediately if you do not come.

> Your affectionate sister
> Annie

How are Mr. Paisley's watermelons coming on? I hope they are flourishing. A kiss to him and yourself

> Annie

> 23rd

After finishing my letter yesterday evening bro. Henry received a note from pa, stating that they had broken down on Cypress Creek. One wheel was broken entirely down, and they sent for another. It seems they were crossing the bridge, and the mule commenced backing. I think pa was slightly hurt. We have not heard exactly how it was.

Brother Henry and cousin Jimmie have concluded to order all their goods. Excuse bad orthography. Write soon to your loving sister

> Annie Lou

Emma Butler Paisley to William Paisley in Dobyville

> At Home [Tulip]
> Sept. 23rd 1867

My dear precious darling,

Mr. Husbands is here and will leave directly after breakfast, but I must write a line or two to send by him. If I had only thought of his going I might have written you a letter. I expected to write today but had thought of no other way of sending it but by mail. Well to commence. Brother Henry has a fine daughter born last Saturday, weighs ten pounds. Bro H says you left a little too soon. Sister Mollie was doing very well till last night—she didn't sleep much and is not feeling well this morning. I have been very well since you left, and have enjoyed myself as much as could

90

be expected, being separated from my dearest one. If you *can* I don't know but you had better start a week sooner than you expected for ma seems to think I will be sick about the first of Sept. [i.e., October] I cannot tell exactly what time it will be, but I cannot bear the idea of your not being with me at that time. Your ma is still sick but was better yesterday evening. I would like to see her but reckon I can't, as it is such a public place. I will write again soon more at length.

Mr. H is ready to start, so I must close. Good bye.

Ever yours most lovingly,
Emma

William Paisley to Emma Butler Paisley in Tulip

Dobyville Ark
Sept 26th 1867

My own loving darling:

Your dear precious little missive of the 23rd inst. came to hand on the evening of the 24th—the day after it was written—and oh, what a delightful surprise it was to me to hear from you so soon! Mr. Doby went to town Tuesday and brought it out, and when he came into supper and handed it to me & I recognized the unmistakable traces of "*my*" *sweet little* fingers, could scarce realize that I had a letter from Emma. And although I had not had time to write the day before, I could not help reproaching myself for not having had a letter to you, ready so that I could have sent it to the office by Mr. D that morning.

My dear one, you can have no idea how lonely I am here without you. I reached home about 11 o'clock the day after leaving *you*, & was busy in the store until dinner was announced. When I went to the house, instead of walking into the room as usual, & having my precious one to meet me with her smiles & a kiss, I found it occupied by Miss Maggie, & I had to stand about the passage until Mrs. D called us to the *dining* room. While standing around & on starting out without you, the feeling of loneliness that came over me was oppressive and amounted almost to fear. Every thing about the place looked wrong & I could not help looking about to see what had become of you. And during the evening I caught myself standing in the store door gazing at your window, trying to catch a glimpse of you passing about or sitting at *your* place by the back door, but I was forced to realize the fact that I was alone, & nothing but the hope of being with you soon could make me at all contented. May God in His mercy grant us a long & useful life together, for life to me without you, I feel, would be a burden.

Billy Grier staid with me Friday night. Saturday I was very busy all day, sold about ninety dolls. worth. Sunday morning I went over the lesson with Miss May & Mr. D & went to Sunday school, but was soon called away to sell some shrouding for an old lady that died some fifteen miles below this. So I *saved missing* the lesson. Late in the evening I went over to Mrs. McGill's & spent the night with them—all were at home & Miss M as cheerful as usual, & had some of her nice fried chicken both meals. I told her how you had praised her as a chicken cook.

I am now very busy posting my books & getting every thing ready to turn over to Mr. Doby during my absence. When I got to Arkadelphia on my way home, I found a Bill of Clothing— we are looking for the other bills every day, all the goods are no doubt in Pine Bluff now. We will send wagons as soon as we hear from them. Mr. D. says he will stay in the store during my absence *provided* I can get some one to take his place in the field. Billy Grier has promised to attend to it for me, if he is in the neighborhood at the time, if I don't get him I will some one else.

After getting back here, I found that it would be impossible for me to stay from you longer than *two* weeks & I had determined to come over next Saturday week & return the following Monday, but since getting your letter I have determined to come over then and remain with you. Oh, how much I would like to be with you even tonight. Every day seems like a week, & from now until Saturday night week looks like an age. Some times I feel like complaining at the circumstances which compel us to be separated at a time above all others that I want to be with you, but when I think about it right I find that I have more to be thankful for than I have to complain of. Besides I see from your sweet little letter that you are cheerful & happy & I have nothing in the world to trouble me save being separated from you. You must remain sweet & cheerful my dear one, do not let any thing disturb you, particularly, my absence, for you know if there was any way for me to get off that I would be with you.

I believe I have no news of interest. Miss Maggie & Miss May McGill expect to go to Synod together. Mr. Smily McG will be their escort. Miss Lizzie seemed to be very sweet (in the eyes of the young men) sometime since, but I think she has about turned to Vinegar and looks sour now as a *crab* apple. Miss May says Capt. Steel seemed to be afraid of all the ladies Sunday, so much so that he didn't even speak to the married ones.

Oh, yes, I have neglected to say anything about the little stranger you spoke of. I had no idea of hearing of its advent so soon. I think I made my *escape* in *good time* don't you? Glad to hear that all passed off so well. Mr. Dyer spent Tuesday night with us (on his way to Rondo), & told me that Henry had a fine daughter, before Mr. D got in with your letter.

I think it probable that the goods will come about the time I will want to be with you, but you can expect me at the time I have mentioned (Saturday week) unless some accident happens. Should any*thing* my dear one, occur before that time, have me notified immediately & I will lose no time is seeing you. I can't bear the idea of being away from you, & trust that nothing will happen before I come. Give my love to all & believe me as ever your

> devoted husband
> Wm Paisley

P.S. I enclose the directions for making the yeast cakes which I suppose will be sufficiently explicit. Mrs. Doby promised to draw them off herself, but when I called for it she had not attended to it & I had to put it down as she gave it out to me.

I don't know when I will have an opportunity of having this mailed, but will give it to Dr. H and get him to send it by the first one passing. Be mighty sweet & accept much love & many kisses from the one who loves you above all others.

Emma Butler Paisley to William Paisley in Dobyville

> Tulip
> Sept. 27, 1867

My dear precious darling,

I wrote you on last Monday a short note and sent it by Mr. Husbands, who was going directly to Arkadelphia. I hope you have received it before this, for I judge you by myself in thinking that you will be glad to get even a few lines from me. I have commenced looking for a letter from you. I hope you reached Dobyville in safety and found everything in a prospering condition. I reckon your melons have about given out. Mr. Robertson has one more which he will bring down this evening. We still have a few peaches and plenty of apples—was compelled to gather the apples in order to save them from being stolen. The negroes commenced a meeting last Friday morning, which continued till last night. Every became worn out with the noise they kept up. Mr. Husbands' Quarterly meeting begins tonight—he spoke of bringing his wife over.

Brother Henry and sister Mollie speak of naming their baby Mary Albert. She keeps very well and grows fast. Coulter had a chill yesterday morning. Well, what do you think! Miss Virgie is really going to be married!! Come over and you can be a witness, as she expects the ceremony to be performed in the church. She is looking every day for Mr. Rice (her intended). Sister Mary, Fannie Pattillo, Fannie Wilson, Calie Barbee, Kate and Alice Colburn, John Smith, Dick Smith, Dr A. Kenedy, Charley, Johnny, and a gentleman who is coming with Mr. Rice are the waiters. Miss V. doesn't know what night she will be married till Mr. R's arrival, though. I expect it will be the first of next week, as Mr. Hunter leave[s] Wednesday, and I understand he is to perform the ceremony. Mrs. Colburn found it quite difficult in getting butter to make cakes but has succeeded at last in getting some—I don't know whether it was as much as she wanted or not.

Your ma is still sick—she thinks the fever is broken, and if she had any appetite, thinks she would be well soon. I sent her what sugar of lemon I had; so when you come over you had better get another box, as I may need it. I mentioned in my last note something about your coming over a week sooner than you expected—really, I don't know what to tell you as some doctors say nearly every young married woman is confined a week or two sooner than she expects.

Mr. Morrison has given out the idea of going over in Clark [County], and has concluded to move over to Camden in a few days. You will have to put up with this excuse of a letter, for I will have to close and send it up by Johnny. If I had had time I could have written you an interesting letter last Monday.

Give my love to Miss May, Mrs. Doby and the rest of my friends. All send love. Good bye my *sweet* one. Write soon to your most affectionate wife, Emma Paisley

Haven't time look over and correct mistakes.

Cousin Mat and Annie Phillips have come up to the meeting.

William Paisley to Emma Paisley in Tulip

Dobyville, Ark
Nov 6, 1867

Henry's kind note of the 30th ult was recd. night before last, my dear loving one—and it afforded me inexpressible pleasure & relief to hear for the first time since leaving you that you & our sweet little babe were & had been doing well [John Alexander Paisley, b. October 11, 1867]. My dear one, you can't imagine how anxious I have been about you & that precious little boy. Dr. Harris went to town Monday, and I was so much in hopes that I would get a letter by him from you that I hired Bob to go down after the mail after supper. He returned about ten o'clock bringing Henry's note, which relieved my uneasiness to a great extent, but I can't say that it satisfied me, for I had my heart set on one written by my darling herself. I am glad, however, that you did not write, for I know that you would have done so ere this could you have done it without *trouble*. I think if I could only get a long letter from you telling me *all* about how you are & about the little boy, that I could be better contented while I have to stay here without you. You don't know how lonesome and *restless* I am. When I left you, although I did not promise it, I hoped to be able to come to see you at least once before coming over after you, but I fear now that it will be impossible, and the thought of having to stay here nearly three weeks longer without you, almost sickens me. Last Saturday was the day I had fixed upon to come, but Mr. D had to attend to a law suit on that day & there was no one else to be had to attend to the store, and I couldn't come Sunday, because Tuesday was speaking day for the Candidates at South Fork Church & as Mr. D is a candidate, he had to be there, & had I started Sunday, could not have returned until Tuesday night. I am prevented this week by the *coming* of the goods & the election. We look for the goods Thursday night or Friday & the election comes off next Monday.

Every thing seems to interfere, while I am dying to be with you, my sweet Emma & little boy. In speaking of the trouble it causes me to stay away from you, I am not unmindful of the pleasure it would afford you to have *me with* you, but when thinking of it that way I can console my self with the thought that you are comfortable & happy with your dear Ma & sisters, & *last* but not *least* our sweet little baby.

Miss Maggie Williamson has been right sick for about a week but is considered some better, now. All the rest that you feel an interest in are well. It will be useless, my dear one, to tell you that I have written this in a great hurry. I did not know until a few minutes ago of an opportunity of sending to the office to day, but old Mr. Doby came up & I learned that Dr. Harris is going to town this evening, & I have had to write this to send down by Mr. D.

I have been unwell for several days, but hope to be well in a day or two. I have not been *sick* but only unwell with a "bad" cold, & *Home sick.* I have despaired of recovering from the latter complaint until I see you. I wrote you on the 27th & 29th last month and will write again soon. We have no fire in the store yet, or I would have written to you sooner than this after my last. Be Cheerful & happy my dear one, always remembering that I love you devotedly whether with you or not. May God bless & protect you & Little John is the prayer of your loving husband

> Wm Paisley

Love to all. Many kisses for you & the baby.

I dream about being with you & little John nearly every night. Last night I dreamed that he had grown large enough to sit on your lap & Eat out of his own hand & that his hair had grown long & curled. I wish you could tell me exactly how he looks now.

William Paisley to Emma Butler Paisley in Tulip

> Dobyville, Ark
> Nov 7 1867

My dear One:

I wrote you a hurried note yesterday which I sent to Arkadelphia to be mailed—by Dr. Harris but will write again to day, as I have an opportunity of sending a letter directly to you to morrow by a Mr. Doby of Pine Bluff—who is stopping to day with his *name sakes* & has promised me to spend to morrow night at your Pa's. Please ask your Pa to take care of him without charge.

I shall not apologize for writing *so often*, but could I have such an opportunity every day I should certainly avail my self of them all, (for as you said in your letter by Mr. Husband) I can judge you by my self & know that a letter from me every night—poorly written as all mine are—would not be *to you* an unwelcome visitor. Henry's note of the 30th ult which came last Monday night contained all that I have heard from you and our sweet little babe since I left. You can't imagine how uneasy and impatient I was to hear how you were doing, and although Henry's statement that you & our dear little boy were doing well relieved my uneasiness a great deal, I cannot help feeling some anxiety about your condition, my dear one, until I learn it from a letter written by *your own dear self*.

Henry said that you would write soon, & I am now impatiently awaiting Dr. Harris' return from Arkadelphia this evening, as I hope *certainly* to get a letter by him from you giving me all the perticulars. I find it utterly impossible for me to be contented away from you & our sweet little John, but I suppose I will have to *bear it* until I come to move you over. For the meantime, my dear one, you must be cheerful & contented, for you know that nothing but actual necessity could keep me away. We are looking for our goods (Dry Goods & Clothing) to night or to morrow morning and if I can only get a favorable letter this evening from you, I shall expect *it* together with the new goods to cure me of my spell of Home sickness. Our precious little baby will be four weeks old to morrow, & I hope to hear that you are well and going about the house.

I suppose George is with you now & that *all* will start for Conference in a day or two. What does George think of his little nephew? Tell him that he needn't be afraid of disparaging the rest of his kin by saying that our little boy *beats them all*. Tell sister Mary that she must not lose any time after Conference adjourns listening at sermons or speeches either, but that she must hurry Mr. Hunter home so that I can come over after you. You will no doubt be very lonesome when they all leave for Conference. Annie & Alice will be at school & you & your Ma will be alone, but you and her can visit together now, since you have got *to be old folks* & you must visit as many of your friends as you can & in that way pass off the time pleasantly.

I have not been visiting since I spent a night with Capt. Steele. I called at Mr. Strongs last Saturday a few minutes on business & saw Mrs. Felix and Albert Strong & Miss Sallie B. They all enquired about you & are anxious to see you & the *fine boy*. Miss Sallie says that she knows he is *bound* to be good looking & that she is going to wait for him.

Miss Maggie Williamson is still right sick. Mrs. Doby is uneasy about her but Mr. D think[s] there is nothing serious the matter with her. Miss May McGill was over to see her yesterday evening. I only spoke to Miss May as she was leaving. Miss Sallie McCullum is in the house now.

Our business continues to be as good as usual, though money is getting very scarce, and we are compelled to sell goods to some & wait with them until they can sell cotton.

The Election is now causing considerable excitement throughout the county. I wrote you that Mr. Davis & Mr. Jo Doby were the conservative candidates. There are two radicals running against them. Davis made a canvass of the entire county & made speeches at all the voting precincts. Mr. D. did not canvass the county, but made a speech at South Fork last Tuesday and is *out* now electioneering. One of the radical candidates has been traveling over the county making speeches declaring himself in favor of Negro Equality & Negro Suffrage & I believe confiscation. All the Negroes will go with the radicals.

You must excuse this badly written epistle & write me one *just* as long. You don't know *how* anxious I am to see you & that dear little boy. You must tell me all about how he looks & how much he has grown. Suppose you weigh him Saturday morning & see how much he has gained. Give my love to all, & believe me as ever your devoted & loving husband. Many kisses for you & the baby

Wm Paisley

Darling, If there is any thing you want specially out of the New Goods be sure & send me a memorandum & let me fill it & lay the goods aside. Yours &c

W. P.

Emma Butler Paisley to William Paisley in Dobyville

Home [Tulip]
Nov 9th, 1867

My *dear* One,

I have just finished reading your letter sent by Mr. Doby who got here a few minutes ago. Says he tried very hard to get here last night, but was compelled to stop at Mr. Thompson's.

We had weighed the baby this morning before receiving your letter. He weighed eleven pounds—less than I expected. Some guessed sixteen, fourteen, thirteen, twelve, and ten. All have a great deal of fun laughing at the way he primps up his little mouth (I believe you noticed it before leaving). He seems to be wakeful to-day. I had to stop a few minutes ago to get him asleep and since doing so, ma and I have taken a walk in the garden—the first time for me since I have been sick.

Darling, you don't know *how* much I *do* appreciate your loving letters. I am sorry I couldn't write sooner than last Tuesday, for I fear my letter was not in Arkadelphia while Dr. Harris was there and I *know* you will be *so* disappointed. Don't be uneasy about me, my dear one, for I am still improving. My back is weak yet, but think I will be strong in a few days.

Yes, all have gone to conference. Four preachers staid here last Thursday night on their way—one of them (Mr. Browning) preached. Ma was very much pleased with his sermon. What do you think? Annie received a card from Willis last Thursday, requesting her company to church. She sent him no reply, so he did not come. Cousin Jimmie took dinner with us yesterday. He is also on his way to conference. His baby weighed ten and a half—speak of naming him John Wesley—will be three weeks old next Tuesday. He came in to see me a few minutes—thought our baby was a fine boy. Brother George is of the same opinion (as well as every body else).

Those who have gone to conference will return in about two weeks. Mr. Hunter says I will have to wait on him if he is gone a month. I told him I would get some other conveyance if he staid too long. Brother Henry told me when he left to give his love to you when I wrote again.

Have received letters from Johnny since he left. He is in business with a Jew by the name of Levi—gets $1200 a year and boards at $35 per month. He thinks Louisville is a better place than New Orleans for a young man starting out in life.

Charley returned from his place since dinner, have not spoken to him yet. He and Jim (I believe) are fixing to go up to uncle Maurice Smith's to see Calie Barbee. Pa is attending the store during brother Henry's absence—says trade very dull.

Darling, I don't know of anything that I will need except the articles I mentioned to you during your stay with me. Don't forget the baby's hood and my nubia when you come over.

Fannie Macon is here, and will be in to see me before she leaves. *Very* sorry to hear of Miss Mag's illness, but hope she will soon recover. All are well and send love.

Little John thinks it will not require much candy to satisfy him, and besides his mama doesn't wish him to eat much, for fear it will make him sick, so he thinks his papa had better sell all but a few sticks, for he is afraid the temptation will be too great for him to resist if he sees much of it.

Remember me to Mrs. Doby and family. Many kisses from us both. May Heaven bless and protect you, my dear creature, is the prayer of your loving

Emma

Nov. 11th

Nothing new today. The baby seems to be rather troublesome. I reckon you had better lay aside a shaker [bonnet?]. I may want one. Good bye, my *dear sweet* one. Yours most affectionately

Emma

William Paisley to Emma Butler Paisley in Tulip

Dobyville, Ark.

Sunday night Nov 10, 1867

My dear loving wife:

Your long and interesting letter of the 5th bringing me the glad intelligence that you & our sweet little babe were doing well was received last night. Every line of your letter my dear one was laden with *love & sweetness* & oh, how it made my heart rejoice as I relieved them one by one of their precious burden, and swell with emotions of gratitude to our Heavenly Father, as they reminded me of the obligations I was under to Him for having blessed me with such a loving wife & sweet little child. And now let me tell you my dear one (though I would much prefer talking with you in person) that God in His Goodness has not limited me to the blessings above mentioned, but in addition to them He has recently filled my heart with a degree of love & joy that I never before experienced, and has enabled me to receive a *living* faith & other Christian graces in a manner that I had hitherto been a stranger to. When I see you I can talk to you more fully, & then we can rejoice together over what the Lord for Christ's sake has done for *us* in blessing me as He has. I am now *fully convinced* that it is our duty, *imperative* duty as well as privilege, to grow in grace, & that unless those of us who profess to be Christians do, we are in great danger of forfeiting our right to the title.

I was sadly disappointed when Dr. H (who returned from town Thursday night) came riding up Friday morning, & when I started out to meet him, told me that I needn't be walking so fast, that he had no letter from you. But had I known that you was kept from writing by our "little boy who has got to be such a *man*" that he wants to sit up by the fire with his "ma," I might have taken the disappointment more patiently, as *I am bound to acknowledge that you had* a good excuse for not writing, & I find it *impossible* to blame little John for had his *Pa* been there *he* would have done *just like him.* You must tell the little *man*, though, that he must not be too greedy of his Ma's time or affections either—that his *Pa* has the oldest claim & is not willing to more than *divide.* Glad to hear that he had got to resting better than he had for several days & that he seemed to be getting well of the hives. As to his not laughing—you can tell him that his *Pa* would think he was doing very smart if he could see him *laugh,* but that smart folks don't laugh as much as *silly* ones. So he is smart any way. Surprised to hear that sister M, Mr & Mrs Hunter got off so soon for conference. Hope they will be in as great a *hurry* about *getting back.*

Mr Grier (who brought your letter out) did not get here—on account of breaking a wheel—until last night about eight o'clock. Mr. D & my self sat up till nearly midnight opening & marking the goods. The Clothing & Dry Goods Came. We opened the former & all the Dry Goods but one box. We are very much pleased with all. The calicos & worsteds, as far as I could see at night, are beautiful, & show that Billy K acted fairly & displayed good taste. Miss Lizzie is delighted with her cloak. We have one pc of spotted flannel, *very pretty.* Wish you had seen it before buying. I shall select you some calicos & if you want any worsted drapes besides the dc Beige, or anything else, let me know.

The Election come[s] off at Dobyville to morrow & we will have a busy day, with new goods & all the voters, white and black, here at one time. I attended Sunday school and prayer meeting this morning. Miss Mary McG & Miss Sallie enquired very particularly about when you would return, & are anxious to get a look at our little *son.*

I am rejoiced to hear of little Mary's recovery & trust that her mother may soon show her appreciation of what the good Lord has done for her. What a trial it must have been to Mr. & Mrs. P to give up their little girl.

P.S. I send you Billy Kittrell's letter with this. I rec'd. Maj. C's letter with Henry's note, & am much obliged to the Maj for his congratulations, but think the "fine boy's" *MaMa* should have them all. Rcd Jim's letter with yours. Tell him if I don't answer it before I come that you'll attend to it then. *Glad to hear* from him. Write soon and often. I must now bid you good night, my *sweet one*, may God bless & protect you both

Your loving husband
W Paisley

Glad to hear George's health is good & hope to see him when I come over. Give my love to Ma when you see her. I am glad to know that she has recovered. Also give my love *specially* to *your* Ma & tell her I think that I can fully appreciate her goodness & kindness in attending to you & taking such good care of you & the little babe while I am away, but that I am afraid I can never be able to repay so much she has bestowed on you & him.

Miss May Wmson has been up nearly all day, but looking very thin. I thought last week, my dear one, up to the time I got your letter, that I would try & come to see you next Saturday & return Monday, but since learning that you are doing so well, I may conclude to put it off until the latter part of the next week, when I shall come to move you over. Mr. D. will be busy ginning, & if I make two trips so close together I will be hurried so that I would not be able to enjoy my self as much as to wait & take more time when I come after you. Continue to be sweet and cheerfull my dear one, & enjoy your self till I come. You dont know how much it relieve[d] me when I read your little Post Script telling me not to be uneasy about you, for I had troubled myself about it. Love to all and kisses for you & the baby.

Yours devotedly
Wm P

Nov. 11th 2 o'clock

Will send this by a man going to town to morrow. Election going on. The biggest crowd we have ever had at Dobyville, & have been very busy. Oh how much I would like to be with you & our dear little Babe to night. The dear little creature is just one month old, but it seems to me that he is really older, as it looks to me like it has been several months since I saw him & his sweet MaMa. Mrs. Doby, Miss May, & Billie all send their love. Little Maggie says tell Mrs. Paisley *howdy* & tell her to kiss her little baby for her.

There is a customer asking for something & I must stop.

> Ever your loving husband
> Wm Paisley

Emma Butler Paisley to William Paisley in Dobyville

> Home [Tulip]
> Nov. 15th, 1867

My dearest husband,

While the baby is asleep, I will write you once more before you come after me. I find no time to sew these days or visit either. If the baby continues as much trouble as he has been for the last few days, I think we would all soon be without clothes. But I can't blame the little creature, for the fleas are about to take possession of him. I found a very large one on his clothes yesterday, and last night about two o'clock, ma and I had to take him up, strip, and put some more clothes on him. Ma went up to see Mrs. Leiper and her fine daughter, who was born last Monday morning, exactly a month younger than our little boy, and weighed eight pounds. Ma says it is a very pretty baby. I think of going over to see her Saturday. Have not visited any but will try to go next week to a few places. Sister and sister Mollie spent yesterday with us. Little Mary doesn't seem to me as pretty as at first. You spoke of dreaming about the baby's hair being so long—I reckon he will have what little he has rubbed off, if he gets many more fleas on him.

I wish you could be with me to help nurse him. Another long week before I see you, but time doesn't drag near so heavily since I have little John to take care of. Several days ago while my back was weak I began to think if all children were as troublesome as our little boy—I did not know what to think.

Sister Mollie asked me to write and tell you to bring her a yard of that checked nansook like my white dress, also some bear-foot wool—said you could get it very plentifully near Mrs. Felix Strong's.

Well, what do you think? Charley went up to see Calie Barbee last Monday morning and didn't get home till four o'clock in the evening. Calie told him she would give an answer the next time she saw him, which will be the last of this or first of next week. Every one was surprised that he was so quick.

Mr Crawford and Mr. McNair have a meeting coming off here to-morrow week. We look for them to return from Conference to-day or to-morrow week. Darling, I wish you were here to enjoy the nice apples. I have two baked ones by me. I have been eating them raw, but the baby keeps so loose in his bowels have concluded to stop a few days and see if that is not the cause of it.

Mrs. Dyer and children have gone to Louisiana on a visit—in the meantime Mr. Dyer expects to go to Texas. Mr. Overby is putting up a store near uncle Maurice Smith's—he expects to sell all together for cash. Mrs. Tom Colburn has received a letter from Mrs. Rice telling how delighted she is &c. The letter gave Mrs. Colburn the blues. Says she reckons she envies her is the cause of it. The Dr. is not at home. I believe she thinks she gets on about as well without as with him.

The baby received a present the other day—a boquet from his grandma—said she would have come down to see him but had company. Maybe I will carry him up to see her this evening. Yesterday was the first time I put a dress on him. You ought to see how sweet he looks.

Love to Miss Mag and the other friends. All send love. The baby and I send many kisses to you my precious darling. Good bye. Always your loving wife

Emma

I hope we will have pretty weather when we move over. You mentioned on your last letter (last that I received) that you were unwell with cold—hope it has not proved to be anything serious.

George Butler to Emma Butler Paisley in Dobyville

Tulip Ark.
Jan 8th 1868

My dear Sister Emma,

"A happy New Year" to you and your "old man" and your John. I suppose "Billy" is not selling many goods this cold weather and these hard times. The ground is all covered with ice. Annie and I have been trying to have a snow balling exercise, but it is more ice than snow. Cousin Ellen Phillips is with Annie and Mary in their room. Cousin Ellen looks very well, I believe prettier than ever before. She will stay with us several days.

I have made one round on my circuit. Was received very kindly. Took dinner with a school mate of yours near Camden—Mrs. Elliott. She asked to be remembered to you. Enquired particularly about you. They are going to move down to her father's. Mr. Elliott has sold his place.

Miss Annie Watson was to have a party Tuesday night during Christmas. You remember there was a deep snow on the ground then. I was near by, but did not go, and left next morning for another part of my circuit. Some thought Miss Jinnie was to be married. Some thought it was Annie, and others thought Jim Watson was to be married to a Miss Bennett. Silas Drake was married on Christmas Eve, much against the wishes of his father, but there were no objections to the young lady he married. Joseph Littlejohn and his wife were at Dr. Drake's, expecting to go to Tennessee shortly.

I staid all night with brother Wheeler, whose daughters went to school at Tulip. They have been much afflicted. He moved to Texas during the war—lost two children out there—and his wife died after he returned. Miss Ellen Wheeler (sis. Mary thinks she was called Emma) is now very low with consumption. Not expecting to live many days. She is very patient. Ready to depart and be with her Saviour. Said she felt the comforts and joys of religion, but asked me to pray that her cup might be full to overflowing. Let *us* also be *ready* for the coming of the Lord.

There were not many gatherings of the young people around Tulip this Christmas. There was a storm party at Dr. Raimey's last Monday night. Brother Charles is down at his place. Jim Robertson is with him. Most of the young people around Tulip were invited to attend a party at Ben Holmes', and were anxious to attend. Mr. Johnson did all he could to prevent them from going and with good success. The Misses Doty were the only representative from Tulip. Sister Annie and Mary are glad now they did not go. The party was given by the young men of Princeton. There was considerable drinking and dancing. Brother Holmes was opposed to their dancing in his house, but could not well prevent it. They rented the room and said they would have the dance.

If you can put up with this scattering letter, I will not rewrite it.

Your brother George

Jan. 14th 1868

Last Saturday and Sunday was our first Quarterly meeting on my circuit: Held at Princeton. Weather was quite cold, snowing Sunday. Small attendance.

The ground is now covered with sleet. I gave Annie and Ellen a good snowballing this morning. I have just returned from brother Barcus' with Alice in the buggy. Brother Barcus has decided to quit his circuit and take a music class. He thinks the circuit will not pay him enough to support his family. He intends to locate next Conference. Very few preachers are now receiving enough to

101

support them. Brother Watson, the Presbyterian minister of Princeton, has taken charge of the female school at Prin. He preaches also at Tulip. He opened school with seven scholars.

I hope, Emma, that you will not neglect your Bible or any of the means of grace. Pray for me. May the Lord bless you and yours, and keep you both in the love of God.

> Your brother
> George

We look for John home soon. He was at Cairo 1st Jan. Bro Lewis said he would try to get him in business there. If he succeeds he will not come home now. All are well.

> G. E. B.

Annie Butler to Emma Butler Paisley in Dobyville

> Home
> Jan. 21st, 1868

My dear Sister,

Your long expected and most welcome letter was received this morning, which afforded much gratification to *every* member of the family. Ma was getting very anxious to hear from you all and especially little Johnnie.

We have had more bad weather this month that I ever saw in "Arkansas." Today the sun has been shining most of the time. Brother Johnnie reached home last Sunday morning. No one knew he was on the place before he opened our room door and stood like a statue not speaking a word. You can imagine how strange he looked at first sight, with his moustache and beard. He looks so much like bro. L—I think it quite an improvement. He walked all the way from L.R.—came thirty-eight miles in one day. Johnnie is now sitting by me writing, says tell you he can out-walk Weston. He speaks of writing to you soon. I could tell you some very amusing things about him which happened while in Cairo, but have not time. He left bro. Lewis very well and in high spirits, with the prospect of being made city attorney.

I am all alone excepting Johnny and Alice. Sister Mary and cousin Ellen are spending the night with sister Mollie. She is very comfortably situated—have a very neat dwelling. Cousin E. has been here several weeks.

I must confess we had no gay Christmas at Tulip. It is true there were several storm parties in the neighborhood, but I did not attend. Enjoyed myself very well at home, sister's, and sister M's.

Brother Charlie left home this morning to go to his *second home.* Received Mr. Paisley's letter before he left. He was very glad to get it. I would like very much to be at Mr. Greer's large sugar stew. I don't see where he gets so much sugar these "hard times." It is as much or more than we can do to get it to put in coffee and tea. I never heard of such times as these. Most every one is out of sugar, flour, molasses, without the prospect of getting any more soon. Pa and bro. Henry are making very little if not nothing in the store. Hard work is the only way of making a living and I think Johnnie is fully satisfied of that. He will farm at home this year. If sister Mary is sewing on any thing privately, she keeps me in the dark. Guess we will inform you in time to get here before anything remarkable transpires. Sister Mollie has written to Mrs. Dora Coulter, but has not received an answer yet. She got one from her cousin Cab, and he thinks Paul is delighted with his wife, happy as he could well be. Sister M. says his time is so taken up with her, he will never write to her again. Brother George wrote to you several days ago.

Aunt Lucy is still living with us, and also Puss and Pete. The former came in Sunday a week ago with the garment you lost in her hand, said Rose had put it in the bottom of her box and taken hers as yours was too small. I wish we could send it to you. Rose is considered a great rogue. Several have missed things taken by her. It is fortunate you did not get her.

All are well and send much love. Much love to bro. Billy and a kiss for the sweet baby. Love to Mr. Doby and family. Tell Lizzie I am looking for a letter from her every day and have been for some time. Mr. Leiper and Mr. Barcus will open a school here next month. The children will be taught at home. The prices are too high. I quituated Christmas.

I could write more, but have not the time nor space. Write very soon to your affectionate sis,

Annie

Emma Lipscomb to William Paisley in Dobyville

[Tulip]
February 4th 1868

Dear Brother

As Mr. Strong expects to return this way, I have concluded to write to you. We have bin anxiously awaiting a letter from you, although I dont know what right we had to expect one. I really feel ashamed of myself for so long a delay. I dont think there has bin a day past since you left that I haven't thought of and wished to see you all. I was sorry to hear you were all sick, but hope it resulted in nothing serious.

How have you stood the gloomy weather. I dont think I ever saw so much cloudy weather at one time before in my life. I dont feel like I could stand another such month. Last Sabbath was the first clear one we have had for preaching this year, and I enjoyed it so much, having a splendid sermon by Mr. Hunter. We don't hear but very little news except politics. Maj. Lea I believe expects to set up a grocery here soon. Mr. Lieper's school opened with 18 scholars the first of this month. Mr. Barcus has given up his circuit and taken the music department. Miss Mary Butler is teaching at home and Miss Wily, I heard, was going to teach on the Ridge. I really think Tulip will be famous for sending forth literature.

Mr. Sim Williams and Jimmie Butler have both come home to live. There is plenty of marrying all around in every direction, but none nearer than three miles. Sam Pryor to Miss Nun and Willis Green to Miss Man are the nearest.

Father and Willis have gone this week to the Bluff, and we are quite lonely now. Father has bin afflicted nearly ever since Christmas with a carbuncle over his right eye, but he has goten well without losing his sight. Sister Mary has bin sick every since she went back to the Bluff. Ma says she will write to you soon. Maj. Butler's and Mr. Henry's families are both well.

February 13th

As I failed to send this as I expected, I concluded to send it any how, as I haven't time to write another. Since I commenced this letter Mrs. Williams has been burnt out, lost a greateel of her household furniture.

We have Presbyterian preaching here twice a month now, by Mr. Watson. Give my love to Sister Emma, and many kisses for little John. I want to see him so much. Do come to see us soon. Excuse bad writing. Ma sends her love to all and espeshly to John. Write soon.

> Remember me as ever
> Emma

Henry Butler to William Paisley in Dobyville

> Tulip Ark
> Feby 7th 68

Dear Billy:

Why don't you write? Can it be possible your time is entirely occupied in *selling goods* and *taking* in *money*? If that be so let me know and I will come over, for it is distressingly dull over this way. There have been two days since the 1st of the year that I have taken in twenty-five dollars for goods, but those are exceptional cases. Five dollars and *one* or *two dollars* per day have been the ruling figures. I have collected about eight hundred dollars only. There will be much I won't collect at all, and much I will have to wait another year and maybe longer. You are in a better condition than I am since you didn't go so "heavy" on the credit system. Times look squawly indeed, with a "squawlier" prospect ahead. The "Rads" are playing a high hand, particularly in that junto *called* Congress. It seems they are determined to *utterly* ruin the country. I dont think there will be a vestige of the old government left in six months. However, it is useless to disturb ourselves about *that*.

No sickness in the neighborhood. Mollie and the babies are in fine health. Little Mary is *very* fat, weighs eighteen pounds. She has not been sick an *hour* since her recovery from the spell she had before you left. "Everybody" thinks her the best child ever seen. Coulter is less trouble now that he can run about. The greatest difficulty is to keep him in doors. He frequently gets out in the snow with his red top boots on.

We are pleasantly located in our little home, a good cook and good nurse. We have Margaret Pattillo (formerly with Mrs. John Pattillo) and Caroline. Mollie has a good deal of company, and takes great pride in "fixing up" things. We would like so much if you and Emma could come over to see us. I think Mollie would "put the Big pot in the little one." We have plenty of corn and meat and a bble [barrel] *of flour*. Haven't rec'd our groceries. They will be up "on the first rise." Our cooking stove is the "Charter Oak," with all the late improvements. It ought to be at the price—*Eighty dollars*.

Mollie sends her love and a bib pattern for nephew John, and regrets she hasn't one made nice enough to send him.

Let us hear from you. Our love to Emma.

> Affectionately
> Your brother
> H. A. B.

Sim Williams to William Paisley in Dobyville

Tulip Arkansas
Feby 27th 1868

Dearest Friend,

I say the dearest, because you may not know it, but you have been the best friend I ever had in my life. You have befriended me when I needed your friendship most. I received your letter on yesterday. I was absent when it came, but to save my life I do not know how to write to you. I know gratitude don't furnish a man a livelihood, nor does it pay a man's debts. You speak in your letter of having written to me last fall. At that time I was in Jefferson [County] and not at Richmond. That accounts for my not receiving it. I am very sorry that you think that I am so ungrateful: because you are kindly disposed that I have not complied with my promises to you. You say that I paid some other debts to men that had not shown more willingness to help me than you had. It is true that no one has ever showed as much willingness to aid me as you have, none; Billy. I sent mother last year at one time $75.00 and asked her to pay you for me $30.00 and Bill Cooper $20.00. As soon as Billy Cooper heard that Mr. Holmes had come (for he carried it to mother), he went over & wanted to know if I had sent him any money. It fretted mother and instead of paying him $20.00 as I had directed, she paid him $33.00, the amt. of my indebtedness, and you being away, she could not see you, and needing money she appropriated it to her use. There is one time I tried to pay you something. When I was at home last Summer I started from Richmond with $100.00. It took $20 of that to carry me home owing to the high water. After getting there, I thought that I would pay you something then. Mother was needing money, and Mr. W. W. Hunter asked me to pay him something if I possibly could, so I paid him and was compelled to give Mother the bal. If you had been at Tulip then I would have paid $50.00. It was not my intention to neglect you from it. I was defrauded out of $800.00 at Richmond by men making just such promises as I made you & I know how you feel.

You have a right to think me a d——— scoundrel or anything else & I could not blame you if you were to take the coat off my back & strip me entirely & sell my clothes. That is all in the world that I am worth. You say that you hope that I will "not ask or expect further indulgence." I can't ask you to wait longer, but I am telling you the truth when I tell you that I have only 15 cents to save my life. Very recently mother's house was burned, and we lost nearly everything we had, and I am compelled to move her away from here in order that she may live at all.

I have been to Montgomery County and secured a home for her, & intend to work this year & if what people tell me is true, I will make a great deal more than it will take to support us. If so you shall have the rest. *You shall.* I will leave in the morning, moving. I am sorry I shall not see you. I would like to see you and tell you all about my affairs. I could tell you better than write them. I will be more than glad to hear from you at any time.

Forgive me and write to me. My regards to your lady, & with my best wishes for your welfare & happiness, I bid you goodby.

Your friend
JoSim Williams

Tulip Evermore

Ma Butler to Emma Butler Paisley in Dobyville

April 3rd 1868

My Dear Daughter

We hear from you very seldom. I have been wishing to hear from you, trying to stir them up to write to you. It seems we might hear from each other [more] than we do, and Lewis, no one has written to him in some time. I know he think we might write and not wait for him, but you know who writes.

Yes it rained all day, to day the sun shines beautiful. Every thing looks fresh and florishing. Our garden looks beautiful with flowers—Jim takes great delight in fencing it. The vegetables looks well, cabbages set out, peas stuck, beans up, corn up, radishes large enough to eat. I must brag a little, you need not then. I have it from Mrs. C our strawberries bed looks delightful covered with blooms. Looks as if we shall have a good many. Now you must be sure and come when they get ripe and enjoy them with us. Won't it be fine?

We have over a hundred chicks. Your hen came off with 13, you will have some to start with. The children more interested raising chic than I ever saw them. I have 2 hens setting on turkey eggs.

Your Bro. Geo left this morning. It is so pleasant to have him with us so often. He wrote to you but would not send it. It would have been interesting to you. Molly spent to day with your sister. Geo W. [Hughes] gone to Benton, Mattie Phil[lips] staying with her. She is a smart girl. Said she would write to you as this is West's birthday.

Alice has gone to stay at her sister's to night, expected to go a-fishing to morrow. I did not know her voice was so much like yours. The other day was singing one of your pieces, I should have taken it for you if you had been here.

Now how is my little grandson? I want to see you all, especially little John. Tell him not to forget his GM. Mr. Roberson is waiting, I must bid you good by. Love etc. William, I shall expect you soon.

[no closing]

William Paisley to Emma Butler Paisley in Dobyville

[Arkadelphia
Apr. 15 1868]

My own loving darling

I have just got in (½ after one) after swimming several ugly sloughs & puddling through water until I got as wet as could be almost, up to my knees. We got through, however, without an accident, & find now that the boat will not leave before morning & that I will have to spend the night here. Oh! how much I would give just to be with my dear Emma & little John & spend it with them. I never fully appreciate the loving & precious society of you, my dear one, until I find myself deprived of it, but be assured that your unworthy husband always carries you with him in his heart & that his greatest delight is to dote on the treasure he possesses.

I will try & write you again from Camden. And now my dear one, let me ask you to be cheerful & happy during my absence. You now have our dear little John to keep you company, & my greatest desire is for you to be happy & contented, & I hope & pray that you may both be protected & spared to welcome your happy husband & father back home.

Many kisses and much love for you both, Affectionately yours as ever

W. Paisley

[On outside of folded letter:] No mail for us.

Darling, please put all my memorandums away, so that they will not be torn or lost. Good bye May God Bless you both

W. P.

William Paisley to Emma Butler Paisley in Dobyville

Camden, Arks
Sunday Morning Apl 19 1868

My own precious darling:

Had I written to you immediately after my arrival you might have gotten an interesting letter from me, but I have been detained here so long that I have taken a pretty severe *attack* of "*Home sick.*" So I can't promise any thing very interesting in this.

The Boat I came down from Arkadelphia on arrived here Friday evening about half hour by sun. My first business was to find whether Henry was in town, & the first man I asked told me that he was here. Henry was looking for me on the boat, & by the time we had got fairly tied up, I saw him coming down to the landing. We stopped at the hotel the first night, and after supper went around to call on Stephen and his lady. We were both very much pleased with Mrs. Winstead & think that Stephen has done well. We spent yesterday (which was a mighty long day to me) looking about town with our acquaintances & attending to what little business I had, and after supper went to the Presbyterian Church & heard a sermon by Mr. Dixon. Mr. McNair is also here, & he & Mr. D. intend carrying on a protracted meeting until time to go on to Presbytery, which meets at Mount Holly the last next week.

I forgot to mention that I took dinner yesterday at Mrs. Booker's, where I met Mrs. Ruth Harvey. (She & Mrs. Booker, you know, are sisters.) I never saw any one change as much as she has done since we knew her at Tulip. She then weighed one hundred & sixty pounds. *Now* she looks almost if not quite as thin as Ma did when she got up from her spell of sickness last fall. She and Mr. Harvey are boarding with Mrs. Booker. Mr. H is preaching on the Camden circuit. She asked a great deal about you & the baby & is very anxious to see John.

On my way down from Arkadelphia the boat stopped a few minutes at Montroy & learning from a man on the bank that Cousin Mat had come from Tulip the day before, I ran up to the house to see her for the purpose of enquiring about Henry. Mrs. Phillips, Cousins Ellen & Mat asked a great many questions about you & John, & made me promise to bring you to see them the next time we pass.

How much I wish I could have brought you with me to Arkadelphia & from there down on the boat to Mrs. Phillips. It would have been an easy matter for you then to get out to Tulip. However, I wrote to your Pa yesterday asking him if *it* was *possible* to hire a conveyance & start out after you as soon as the waters could be crossed. Oh my dear one, how much I wish I could be with you &

help you fix up for the trip. You don't know how it hurts me when I think about how I was forced to hurry off & leave you by your self. I don't like to think of your making the trip to Tulip without my being along to take care of you, & relieve you of all care and anxiety. I could also help you with little John & help you make the trip interesting to the precious little fellow. If your Pa can get a conveyance he will send some [one] over to accompany you, so you must not allow your self any trouble.

Now my dear one, let me ask you again to be cheerful & happy, whether you get to Tulip or not, & be assured that your husband will love & think of you & our dear little boy every moment while he is absent.

The boat we go down on is a very nice one & will leave this evening at five o'clock. I will write you as soon as we get to the city. When I left home I did not make any allowance for lost time, & thought it would be useless for me to ask you to write to me at New Orleans. In fact, I was so hurried I hardly thought of any thing. But I will say now, if you get this by the 25th (& have an opportunity of sending a letter to the office) write to me & direct care John Nixon & Co New Orleans. Time drags so heavily with me when I am separated from my sweet darlings, I don't think I can stand it not to hear from you till I get back to Camden. I feel now that it ought to be time for me to be starting back home, & can't help feeling impatient when I think of the long trip before me.

Reports from New Orleans in regard to the Dry Goods market are very unfavorable, but we have got this far & are determined to go on & do the best we can.

My dear one I have no doubt *much* but what you would think of it—but I will tell you, if you go over to Tulip do not ride over any of the bridges or run any risk of any kind.

It is now nearly time to go to church & I must close & I assure you, my dear one, that I do it with reluctance, for I feel that I could spend the entire day in talking to you (even if it is on paper) more pleasantly than I can in any other way. Henry sends his love & says he is anxious for you to get to Tulip to be with Mollie. Much love & many kisses for you & little John, that our Heavenly Father may bless & protect you both is the prayer of your devoted husband

W P

I would have written you by the "Star Pioneer" when she returned to Arkadelphia, but her oficers told me she would not leave until some time during the week, & I did not learn any better until late yesterday evening a short time before she started & I didn't have time. I wrote Mr. D[oby] a hurried note by her when it was so dark that I couldn't see the lines. Affectionately &c W. P.

William Paisley to Emma Butler Paisley in Dobyville

Camden Ark
Sunday evening ½ after 3 o'clock
Apl 19th 1868

My dear precious one

Henry & myself have just come down from the Hotel to get on the Boat, which will leave now in an hour or two, and although I wrote you this morning can not leave without writing you another *line.* I did not tell you this morning that I had been feeling a little unwell since my arrival here, but such has been the case. But I am feeling a great deal better this evening & hope to be all right in a few days. Getting wet the day I left you and being compelled to keep my clothes on till they got dry was the cause of my being indisposed.

We went to church this morning & heard a most excellent sermon from Mr. McNair. There was no preaching at the Methodist Church & I have not had a chance of seeing Rev. Mr. Browning yet. Now, darling, you can't guess who I saw at church this morning. It was Jimmie Watson & her husband. Jimmie was dressed out as fine as a queen—had on a new plaid silk—fine silk mantle & new blue silk velvet hat—in fact she was perfectly lost in finery, & it was apparent to any one that she was considerably embarrassed.

It is raining here very hard this evening & I am afraid the waters will get up again & keep you from getting to Tulip for some time yet. If you should be prevented my dear one, I hope you will try & be contented & happy, & I assure you that I will take you over & spend some time with you just as soon as I can after my return. Do not forget to write to me some time about the 30th of this month, and direct to me Care S Winstead & Co, Camden. Tell me all the news about yourself and our dear little boy. I hope you will get the letter I wrote this morning in time to write me in N. Orleans.

Now darling you must "consider the rest filled with love" for you & John, and believe me as ever your loving husband

Wm Paisley

William Paisley to Emma Butler Paisley in Tulip

New Orleans La
Apl 25 1868

My dear loving one

Maj Coulter & Henry are waiting on me to go around to examine a stock of goods, but I find a boat will be leaving for Camden this morning & I can't let the opportunity pass without writing you a short note. We had a long & tedious trip from Camden down, but the boats we traveled on were very fine and could I have only had my sweet Emma & little John along, would have enjoyed the trip finely. Henry & my self frequently talked about how nice it would be to have our families along, & determined that if possible would not take another trip without bringing them.

The most unpleasant thing [in] connection with my having to be away from you, my dear one, is that I don't know whether you & our sweet little John are spending a lonesome time at Dobyville or enjoying your self with our kind relatives & friends at Tulip. If I only knew that you was at Tulip, I think I should feel perfectly easy, but the thought of you having to remain over in Clark during my absence distresses me, & I can't help reproaching my self for allowing any thing to hurry me off in the manner I was. I find consolation, however, in the thought that I have a dear, sweet wife that will make allowances for what I could not help, & that she is assured that it would have been otherwise could I have made it so.

We arrived at the city steam boat landing last night before dusk & remained on the boat till the next (yesterday) morning. Before breakfast we drove around to Maj. Coulter's boarding house and did not have to wait long before the old Maj. came in & although he was greatly surprised at finding us there, was glad to see us & gave us a hearty welcome to the city.

We spent yesterday in looking around at some of the stocks, but have made no purchases as yet. We will buy Hardware, Drugs, & crockery today, & if there is a boat leaving the middle of next week we hope to be ready to start back by that time. We will get off by the last of the week at fartherest, & hope to be with my dear ones by the 6th or 7th of May. My dear one, you must excuse this hurried note. I started to write you last night, but I was so tired I could not write a letter good enough to send you, but when I found the boat would leave this morning I concluded to scribble you this, knowing that you would rather get it than none. Will risk sending this to Tulip, hoping that you are there before this.

May God bless you & our little boy is the prayer of your devoted husband

W Paisley

Many kisses & much love for you both Good Bye W. P.

William Paisley to Emma Butler Paisley in Tulip

New Orleans La
Apl 27th 1868

My dear loving one

I have been almost *run off my feet* to day, but I cannot lie down to rest without communing a short while with my sweet Emma & little John. Oh, how much would I give to quit the bustle & noise of this busy city & fly away & spend the night with my dear sweet ones. The want of sleep and rest would then be supplied by your precious society, & I would soon forget that I had been tired. But it is impossible to realize such a pleasure, so I am forced to try & content my[self] with the painful reality of having to remain here several days longer before I can even start homeward. I almost dread the trip home, for after getting started my impatience to clasp you & our sweet little John in my arms will make hours seem like days & days like weeks.

Well I must stop before filling my sheet & try to interest you by telling you what I have been doing since my arrival. Maj. Coulter, Henry, and my self went to hear Dr. Palmer yesterday morning, and were highly entertained & I trust benefited. His sermon was much shorter than I ever heard him preach before—it being only fifty minutes long, but he said enough in that time to afford us something to think about for a long while. My dear one, I have never been away from you on trips when I wished so much to have you with me as I have on this. The boats we came down on were magnificent steamers, & when I stepped aboard the large and splendid steamer "Vicksburg" (the boat we connected with at Trenton, about two hundred miles below Camden) my first impulse was a wish that I had my darlings with me, & every thing that I have seen interesting has caused the same wish to rise above every other thought & impression, & sometimes the wish prevents to such an extent as to almost render the enjoyment of the scenes unpleasant—if I can so speak—without you. Your imagination can furnish you with nothing like an idea of the many & varied scenes that meet the eye here, neither can I describe them. Yesterday morning on our way to church we passed by a large house in which there was a public show going on, with a brass band sitting just inside the windows discoursing music suited to the occasion. On our way back and within a very short distance of the church, we passed right by what is called a Pistol Gallery where there was a crowd of men shooting at targets with Pistols for prizes. Besides all this, it seemed that nearly every other store door was open & buying & selling goods was going on the same as it does on any week day.

At ½ past three o'clock we attended a Sunday School Celebration at the Carondolet Street Methodist Church, which was one of, if not the grandest sights I ever witnessed. All the Sunday Schools of the different Methodist Churches in the city joined in the celebration, and all together there must have been fifteen hundred or two thousand little Sunday School scholars present. The galleries were crowded with spectators, & the singing by the scholars was magnificent. Some of the larger boys delivered addresses & quite a number of little girls the size of Bettie & Maggie repeated sacred poems which were splendid. Just think of a little girl nine or ten years old mounting a rostrum in the presence of three or four thousand persons & repeating a long poem so that all could hear distinctly, & that too without seeming the least embarrassed. Oh how much I *wish* you could have been there. But the Maj., in whose office I am writing, is getting sleepy & I must hurry.

Sunday night Henry, Dr Ross of Union [County] (who is in the city) & my self went again to hear Dr. Palmer. To day we commenced purchasing, & have bought Hardware, Crockery & Woodenware. We hope to get off by Friday, & will do so if the boat does not disappoint us. When I get home, I can tell you all about my trip & while interesting you with its account, how happy I will be to know that I am again with my dear loving sweet wife & our little John. I can almost believe that the dear little fellow will rejoice with his mother & father & feel interested [in] what we will then talk about.

It was late before I could commence writing & I must now close, though I feel that I could write to you all night if I could only be where I would not disturb others. I hope that you are at Tulip & enjoying your self finely. Tell sister Mollie that I—no—that Henry is taking good care of me. I send you the hymns they used yesterday in the Celebration.

Many kisses for both. Ever your loving and *happy* husband

W. Paisley

Havent time to look over

William Paisley to Emma Butler Paisley at Tulip

Dobyville, Arks
May 14th 1868

My dear loving one:

Mr. Doby goes to Arkadelphia tomorrow & I will write this to send by him.

I am now seated in our old room, & a feeling of loneliness creeps over me whenever I look around, for I find it almost impossible for me to recognize a familiar feature about it. The Table on which I am writing has been moved to a new place since I left—one bed stead is gone—the trunks have all been moved—but the change which affects the appearance of things & myself— most seriously—is the absence of my dear Emma & our bright eyed little Boy—without you & John, my dear one, no place would feel like home to me & a palace with all its luxuries would be a dungeon.

After leaving you Tuesday morning, I tried to relieve myself of the unpleasant thought of having to come over here without you, by talking to—& hearing Jim talk, & by laughing at him whenever we would get to deep water. But notwithstanding my efforts the trip would loom up before me as a *monstrous blank*, & I felt that there was nothing ahead that was at all inviting. However, I will try and content myself until you can get over, & when we commence receiving goods I will have something more to do, and will not feel so lonesome.

I never saw roads in as bad condition as I found them between here and Tulip, & until there is a great deal of work done on them, it would be useless to try to get along with a conveyance of any kind. Several places between here & Arkadelphia I had to get down & lead my horse, it being impossible to ride over them with any degree of safety. All the bridges on the new route between Arkadelphia & the Turn Noire creek were washed away. The farmers in this neighborhood suffered some from the rains, but the damage—to them—is not near as serious as I expected to find it— & if the seasons in the future only suit—good crops may be expected.

You must try & make good use of your time at Tulip, & be ready to move over just as soon as the roads get passable & I can make arrangements to bring you over. Our goods had not reached Arkadelphia when I left there yesterday at one o'clock, but they were looking for the "Bluella" up, and I hope Mr. Doby will find them there to morrow. We will be compelled to pay one dollar per hundred to get them hauled from Arkadelphia on account of the wagons having to go out of their way.

I spent Tuesday night with Dr. Palmer—Mrs. had not returned but Miss Mary Helen was there, and told me when I left to give her love to you & tell you that you must come to see them the next time you pass through. Rev. Mr. Adams was kind enough to lend me a horse to ride home. I saw Mrs. Goodloe Pattillo on the street, & she told me that she expected to go to Tulip in about two weeks & that Mr. P would bring the conveyance back immediately. Should you be ready to come back then I would be glad if you could arrange it to come with him & I could meet you in Arkadelphia & bring you in a hack—but I want you to consult your own pleasure & write me what you think about it, & I will write you on the subject again.

It is now late & I must close this disconnected letter. Oh how much I want to be with you & little John. Hug and kiss the dear little fellow for his Pa, & tell him he must not forget me, & accept, my dear one, much love & many kisses from your loving husband

W Paisley

Mr. Browning closed a protracted meeting in Arkadelphia last week & had sixteen accessions to the church—nearly all of them were converted during the meeting.

Write soon & often—Give my love to all. I suppose you have heard of Mr. Ratcliff's death. How sad to think that he was called to go while away from home & family, but he was a good man & is now better off.

Yours &c
WP

William Paisley to Emma Butler Paisley in Tulip

Arkadelphia
May 17 1868

My dear one

Mr. Pattillo tells me that if he goes to Tulip he will not return immediately, so we can not make the arrangement I mentioned in letter, but will try to get off as soon as possible & come after you myself. How much I wish you was with me—I have just got in & find all our goods here, & must hurry back to start wagons after them. They arrived here yesterday. Little John's crib, buggy, chair & your chair are all safe.

Now, my dear one, let me ask you to be cheerful & happy. Do not entertain any ill feelings towards *any one*, but let us exercise a forgiving spirit & be happy ourselves.

Oh how I wish I could see you & little John. May God bless you

> Affectionately your husband,
> with many kisses for you both
> WP

Emma Butler Paisley to William Paisley in Dobyville

Tulip
May 22nd, 1868

My *dearest* loved one,

Since writing to you I have received both of your *loving* letters. To say that I was *glad* would not express half the amount of pleasure they afforded me. Surprised to hear that your goods were so long in getting to Arkadelphia. I know you must have had a *lonesome* time over at Dobyville without any thing scarcely to do, and more than that without your Emma and little John to *"bother"* you. I thought Martha would have been at home when you reached Dobyville—how have you made out without her services? I thought of what a lonesome time you were having last Sabbath, while I was here enjoying the happy privilege of attending church. I am glad you thought of reading some of my old letters by which to while away a few minutes of your time.

It is now before breakfast time, and little John is fast asleep, so I have come into the little room to converse with my dear absent husband, but I hear the prayer bell ringing.

Cousin Jimmy brought cousin Laura up last Wednesday, and he returned in the evening. You ought to see his *big* baby—three weeks younger than our boy, and weighs twenty-two pounds. Ma and I went up and had our photographs taken the other day, and to-day cousin Laura and I are going to take the *children* and try to have their picture taken. Sister is coming to spend the day so I must hurry and get through.

Cherries are ripe and plums soon will be. Alice gathered me a few strawberries which I ate at supper—all I have had since being over here with the exception of five or six I got in the garden one evening. Brother Henry and sister Mollie took supper with us Wednesday night. While here brother H remarked that his trip with you had endeared you more to him than since you and he were so intimate at the store. (an awkward expression) I hugged little John for you till I made him grunt—was that hard enough.

Ma (your ma) received a letter from Mary a few days ago—she was well—her school will be out in June. Brother George has not returned yet. His delay is caused by his having to visit his *sweetheart*. I will tell you more about it when I see you, which I hope will be soon. Cousin Laura sends best love. I forgot to mention that ma and sister Mary had received their albums, which are very pretty, but I like mine better.

Darling, you must excuse this letter. I would rewrite it but have not time. It is not worth sending, but I *know* you would rather get this than none.

All send love. Many kisses from your bright-eyed boy and loving

Emma

Be happy my dear one.

Lewis Butler to William Paisley in Dobyville

Cairo, Ill.
June 7th 1868

My dear Billy:

Notwithstanding the interest with which I recd your long letter to me, and my promise both to myself and to you through those at home that I would soon write, yet I have been grossly negligent now for several months. What construction you and Emma have placed upon this piece of carelessness I know not, but hope you know me well enough not to suppose for a moment that I really mean anything. Were I to be held to anything like a strict account to the law of etiquette, or whatever law it is that governs correspondence, I should long since have suffered its extreme penalty. But not to waste further time in apologizing, I will only beg your forgiveness and assure you that I am what I always professed to be, one of your truest, best friends, though encumbered with many of the frailties of human nature, one of which is the not always pursuing my own true happiness, for in that case I should ere this have had several letters from you.

It seems that I should write oftener than almost any of the family for being away among strangers to you all, in a strange place, about all I have to write is that I am well &c. My life is so uniform that the description of one day will almost do for a month. I am, as you know, City Attorney of Cairo. Well, the city attorney's business as expressed in the name is to attend to the legal business for the city. The greater part of that business pertains to the police court, where all offenders of city ordinance are tried & sentenced, the sentence in every case being a fine not exceeding one hundred dollars, which a man either pays in money or imprisonment at the rate of a dollar per day. We have two Police Magistrates, who are nothing more than justices of the peace, excepting that they have jurisdiction in cases arising under the ordinances of the city, and who hold court alternately every day. In these courts are tried all *scalliwags, all men who fall among thieves by the way side*, all men who are not expert drinkers of rum and such like disreputable characters, whether male or female, who either make their home in Cairo or have the good fortune to stop here. I am interested in these persons, of course, for whenever one of them is fined and has the money I get two & a half dollars. Now in these times, the number of those who fall into our hands who have the wherewithal is rather small, comparatively speaking—hence my office is not so lucrative as in former times and as I hope it will be at some future time. Yet it yields me a support, and with that I should now be satisfied. Of course there are many other duties incumbent on a city atty—and which do not thus bring him in contact with the characters I have mentioned. For in the multiplicity of regulations governing a city, frequently the best of men are found violating some of them. And moreover, all other legal business in which the city is interested in any court belongs to him. And yet his duties do not materially interfere with the ordinary practice which he would otherwise get, so that altogether it is a very desirable office. A good portion of my time I devote to reading and study, and this is a great advantage.

Business here continues dull. The Cairo & Vincennes R.R. which will give us a direct route through Cincinnati to N.Y. is in process of construction, & will be in running order in about one year. This we hope will make an improvement in our affairs. We also expect to have another road direct to St. Louis in a short time. These and other indications lead us to think that, notwithstanding dull times, our prospects are better than they ever were.

I am not married nor apparently any nearer that blissful state than when I saw you. I do not visit the young ladies often—am not in love nor *struck* with any one.

We take a great deal of stock in the Democratic party here, as you know. This state will be very close—had been heretofore largely Republican, but we hope to carry it for Pendleton or some other conservative. Oregon, as you have seen, went Democratic by a good majority—every part of the north appears to be changing—and the signs are favorable.

Tell Emma to write me and you write also giving me a full history of yourself and family. How is your little boy thriving? Kiss him for me—raise him up in the way he should go & when he gets to be an old man he will not depart from the error of his ways. You should always bear in mind this passage of Scripture. It will be a lamp unto your feet & a light unto your pathway by which you can see very plainly how you should raise him. Has he got that white eyelash of yours? My health is good—my habits regular, and altogether I am a better man than I ever was before. Having seen the "error of my ways" I have departed from them. Give me all the news, & I will answer promptly, and will have a better pen next time.

> Your affectionate brother
> Lewis P. Butler

Alexander Butler to Emma Butler Paisley in Dobyville

> Tulip
> 22nd June 1868

Dear Daughter

Yours of the 19th Inst is to hand. I had requested H A B to write you to come on to Arkadelphia to morrow week, and come over with James Pattillo and spend some time with us. The plums are ripe & apples, we will soon have peaches. We are done plowing now, and I can send you back without costing you so much as the last trip. If Billy can not come with you, he can come after a while and see you and go back. John will soon walk. You need not bring your nurse.

George expects to be married about the 9th of next month. He has just returned with Anna from Mr. Moores. We are all well. A letter from Lewis—he is well, no news.

You must come to stay some time. I have a hundred dollars for you or Billy when you come over. If Mr. P needs it, he can come over with you. Charles is up, starts home this morning.

Your affectionate
Alexr Butler

P S Mr. Pattillo says he does not [know] exactly the day, but some time about the last of next week. And there seems to be some uncertainty abot it, as he sent his carrige over to Sue, as I learn since writing the above.

Your Father

William Paisley to Emma Butler Paisley in Tulip

Dobyville, Ark
July 22nd 1868

My dear one:

Mr. Doby will go to town to morrow, & I will write you a short letter & must commence by telling you not to expect *much*, as I have been prevented from commencing my letter, on account of having company, until now it is nearly eleven o'clock. There is to be a grand Seymour & Blair Barbacue in Arkadelphia the 1st Saturday in August, & Capt Cloud is here to night on his way to Arkadelphia, where the managers will meet to morrow for the purpose of making the necessary arrangement. Mr. Doby & Capt C are both on the committee of managers. There is also a young man here from South Carolina by the name of Williamson, Mr. Doby's cousin, who is rooming with me to night, & since we came to our room has kept me until this late hour entertaining me with his war stories. He has come here with the intention of settling, and will probably live with Mr. Doby.

Well, I had a hot & tiresome ride from Tulip here & nothing but the prospect of seeing my dear one & little John could induce me to ride so far in a day again. I got here Monday night while they were at supper, & was almost too tired & hot to eat supper. After supper I came to our room & found every thing just as we left it, but I cannot make it feel like home while my Emma & little John are away. When I opened the door & saw the crib standing by the bed I involuntarily looked in to see John—but every thing that reminded me of you & him only made me realize more fully that I was alone & made me feel more lonely. But my dear one, I will try & be contented & happy, & console my self with the thought that you are with loved ones at home, where you can enjoy yourself & have a pleasant time.

It is useless to tell you how much I miss the "high living" I enjoyed while at Tulip. I have only eaten two peaches since I came over, & they were not fully ripe—but Mr. D's water melons are coming in now & I can do very well while they last. We cut one to day that weighed thirty-one & three quarter pounds, & there are a good many more very fine ones in his patch. *Our* vines are looking fine, & there are a great many young melons on them but the chickens are still troubling them & I have despaired of getting many melons. Mrs. Steward and her daughter Mrs. Jo McGill,

Old Mrs. McGill & Miss May dined here Tuesday, but I was busy in the store & only saw them at dinner. Miss May & her mother enquired for you as particularly as if you had been *kin folks*.

Mr. Husband's quarterly meeting will come off at South Fork next Saturday & Sunday. I shall go down provided I can get a horse. The members of Carolina Church met yesterday, & raised four hundred dollars to offer to one of the ministers that have written to them in relation to taking charge of the church. A copy of the Advocate came for us after we left. The Home Monthly for July has not come yet, wish I could send it to you when it comes, as you are anxious to see it in its new colour. *Nearly twelve* & my dear one, I must close this unsatisfactory note, hoping that you will make all due allowances.

Love to all the family *including* George and his fair one & many kisses & much love for you my darling.

Your devoted husband
W. Paisley

My dear one:

I can't close without asking my Emma to be cheerful & happy. Let us now forget the past, my dear one, & be happy for the future, & God will bless us if we do our duty. Oh, how proud & happy I shall be when I know that I have been the means of relieving your pure, sweet, mind of all unpleasant thoughts. May God give me grace & wisdom to make you as good a husband as you deserve. I would rather, my dear one, you would say nothing about the matter to any one, as it might do more harm than good. Let us try & forgive & forget, & have no unpleasant feeling for *any one*—May God bless & keep you both, is the prayer of your loving husband.

W. P.

Your Boiler is *all right*.

Henry Butler to William Paisley in Dobyville

Tulip Ark
Aug 21st 1868

Dear Billy:

Pa wishes me to write you in regard to some thoughts he has had since you left. Regrets not talking to you more fully while you was over in regard to your business. Pa thinks you would (and I agree with him) be doing yourself injustice to put yourself to much expense or trouble to find board elsewhere—or go to keeping house—inasmuch as it was part of the agreement that Mr. Doby should board you. Now I know *you* would prefer to be differently situated than what you are. Pa tells me that Mr. D. told you, or at least intimated, that he would like you to keep house or find some other place to board—he having a small house &c &c.

Now here is a suggestion made by Pa this evening, in which I heartily join should it be consumated—I trust you will not think it looks too much like dictating to you. It is only a *suggestion* any how. If it is not convenient for Mr. D. to board you, propose to sell out to him now—he taking the stock at cost and carriage—and make as *complete* a settlement with him as you can. Then *we three*—you, Pa, and myself, form a partnership and carry on the business at this place and Okolona. You take charge of the latter place under the style of "Wm Paisley & Co," and I at this place as H. A. Butler & Co. You put in as much as you can and I the same—and Pa as much capital as he can raise, one of us to purchase goods for the two places, and then each to receive one third of the profits. From what you tell me of Okolona and its probable future, I think it would be a good time to commence business there, and should *this* place prove unprofitable or grow worse than it is now, the whole capital could be invested in Okolona.

Now Billy, these thoughts were not conceived till an hour ago—and I am thus hasty in penning them because Goodloe Pattillo leaves here early to-morrow for Arkadelphia, and I wish him to carry the letter.

Emma and John are *well.* John missed his chill a few days ago, and I hope will not be troubled with them again. Em spent the day with us. We are having a good meeting at Tulip, some eight or ten conversions. Among the number is my beloved wife. I know you will join me in rejoicing and praising our Heavenly Father for His goodness. *Lem Pryor Smith* professed today at home, was a mourner last night, and seemed deeply in earnest. If I can find it convenient it is possible I may come over next week. You write me any how. There has been so much rain that Johnny has not saved his fodder. *Maybe* Emma will come over next week. I know you are *anxious* to see her.

Of course it is unnecessary to ask you to keep "entre nous" what I have written.

The meeting will last several nights. Rev. Andrew Hunter is with us. Bro George left this morning.

If Emma know of this opportunity to send a letter, no doubt she would write. I have sent my order for shoes to Currier Sherwood & Co.

> Yours truly and affectionately
> Henry A. Butler

William Paisley to Emma Butler Paisley in Tulip

> Dobyville, Arks
> Sunday Evening Aug. 23rd 1868

My dear Emma:

I wrote you two letters during the last week, one on Monday & the other Wed. The first I handed to old Mr. Clark as soon as it was finished & the 2nd I sent to Dr. Key. You can imagine my disappointment when old Mr. C. told me Thursday evening that he had seen no one passing up to that time & yesterday I heard that Dr. Key did not go & that your letter was still at his house. So I fear now that you will not hear from me at all. Oh my dearest one, how much your dear letter made me want to be with you to help take care of little John & to comfort you in your sickness, & since getting your letter I find it almost impossible to keep from starting to see you, but Mr. D expects to go to Hempstead [County] this week, & I shall say nothing about going unless I hear that you are worse.

My health has not been very good since I came over but I am better now & hope to be well soon. For the last three or four days I have been afflicted with a rising in the palm of my right hand, which is very painful. I now have it poulticed & my whole hand bundled up, & would think it impossible for me to use it if I were not writing to my sweet Emma. You will allow the condition of my hand to serve as an excuse for this badly written letter & for it being written with a pencil. Besides, I can't feel that you will get it, for I know of no one going to town the first of the week, & only write this evening to keep from missing an opportunity should one present itself.

Suppose from your letter that Wesley & his wife started from Tulip but have not heard of their getting home yet. Sorry that you have not been well enough to visit for I was in hopes you could spend some time with Mrs. Hughes as you did not stay with her much last spring.

I have not decided yet what time I shall start after goods. Tell Henry I will write to him when I find out more about it. Have made no arrangements yet about getting a Home. Dr. Harris still thinks of leaving his place. If he does, we can probably get his house. Well I must close. My dear one, be cheerful & happy & do not forget that your husband, although compelled to be absent from you, loves you devotedly & is anxious & impatient to see you again & to have you & little John with him. God bless you is the prayer of your devoted husband

W Paisley

Kiss little John for his pa, & tell him that he does not know how much it pains me to hear of his sickness.

Albert and Molly Butler to Emma Butler Paisley in Dobyville

Chocktaw Arks
August 25 1868

Dear Emma

Your favor of July 30 came to hand 23 in I was glad to hear from you and Bille. I am glad that you are doing so well. I hope you make a very large fortun and liv to be a good old age and en joy it. I reached home last Sunday night. Molley spent three weeks in Memphes and three or four in Huntsvell [Alabama]. Huntsvell is a very pleasant place and very helthy. Good water, fine crops, cotton and corn, wheat in that portion of the county. Molley's helth improved very much in Huntsvell. I would liked for he[r] to hav remained thar until Oct, but I could (not) prevail on her doing so. She is complanen every day since she got home. She is like you, cannot stay from her Husband. Thar is no crops in this naborhood. Thay were all destroyed by the caterpillar. My crop is not hurt yet, but I am looking every day for the worms to make thar apperance. If my young corn turns out well I will make corn enouf to do me. It was planted from 10 up to 20 of July. It is as big as my hed and looks like a cane brake. The cotton is late but doing well at present. I can not tell whither I will make expenses or not this year.

Molley joins me in lov to you and Billy. Nothing mo of intrest. I remain your nephew

A G Butler

Emmer you must excuse me as I am an invalid. I think [if] I could live on the mountains of Huntsville, I would get well. I did not have a pain while in Huntsville, go where I please and eat what I chuse. I cannot say that now. I did not expect to feel well coming home so soon. My Dr told me not to go home until past. My expenses was too great for our purse. Hearing that the cattle-piller was in the cotton we hastened home. I hope the cattlepiller will stay thar home.

You write about not having fruit. I recon it is a genl failure in fruit crops. I saw but few peaches, five cts for one, pears 25 for three, so you may guess I did not eat many. I would not eat fruit in Memphis for fear of taken the cholera.

The people complain of hard times. I tell you, when you see them dress in thar best, you would think that they never felt the war. Have you made you any gabrel drepes and goard skirts. I think that the gabrel will or would be appropriate to some *married ladies*, body and skirt all-together. They look nice with a belt for any one. Sacks are worn tight or loose any matter you fancy—like the dress or not. As for the bonnets, they cannot be called bonnets. Mr. Butler styles tham turtle shells, enough about fasion. Let me go back to Huntsville. We had church privileges there every night, quarterly meeting while I was thare. I did not feel much like I was at Shiloh Church. Good by, kiss Billy for me, I expect. Tell him to write to Mr. Butler. He will appreciate his letters.

[Molly Butler]

Emma Butler Paisley to William Paisley in Dobyville

Tulip
Aug 25th, 1868

My dearest one,

Language can't express my disappointment this morning, when I asked Mr. Robertson if he had a letter for me and he said no letter came for me. I looked a little Friday night; but fully expected one last night. I am fearful you are sick. I have been expecting to start for Clark tomorrow, but will be disappointed, for Johnny has not got through with his fodder yet. I have been drying some peaches, but if you could be here I would make a more rapid progress.

Little John seems to be over his chills. Ma says I must stay this week and be with her while I am weaning him. I dislike to wean the little fellow while he is so young but am compelled to do so. Little Mary has the thrush very badly and sister Mollie has it in her breast.

The meeting is still going on. Lem. Pryor Smith went to the altar one night last week and professed the next day at home. There seems to be a great deal of change in him. There are a great many at the altar every night. Mr. Doby went up last night for the first time. Well, I must tell you a piece of news. Miss Virgie has a little daughter. Brother George and sister Julia leave to-morrow for Arkadelphia. I dislike to see them start in that direction and leave me behind. I will send this note by them. I do hope I will hear from you to-morrow night. I have not heard a word since you left me.

Pray for me, my dear one. I hope you have enjoyed yourself religiously, for if you enjoy religion, I know you are happy. When we go to keeping house, I think then I can have a place to call Closet of prayer, for I am convinced that without secret prayer there is no real enjoyment of religion. Of course we can pray any where, but then I think it much better to have some quiet spot where we can retire alone, with no one but God to hear.

I received a note from Cousin Mat this week—she was then at Col. Whitaker's. All are well. Dow has got up again. Goodbye. Ever yours lovingly,

Emma

"Louie" Elliott to Emma Butler Paisley in Dobyville

Oakwood Farm
Aug. 28th 1868

Dear friend of my childhood;

Twas but a few days since that I was the happy recipient of your letter. I was glad to hear from you again, and to know you were so well and well pleased (may it ever be your lot to be so well blessed). I had often thought of writing to you, but did not know where to direct your letters, and kept waiting to hear. It so happened, the day before I received your letter, your cousin Mattie Phillips in company with her Sisterinlaw Mrs. Bridges and Mrs. Williams, stopped and took dinner with me, and spent the remainder of the day. They were "en rout" for Mr. Bridges's, only 2 miles from our house. Mattie came down to spend a few weeks, I was much pleased with her, having seen her but one other time before, twas through her I learned your where-abouts, and I had resolved to write the preceding week, when I received your letter the next day. For a few days I have not been very well, was quite sick 3 days ago, and now I find I am so nervous I can scarcely write a legible hand.

I reckon we are getting along as well as one could expect, husband has a splendid crop so far of both corn & cotton. And if you want nice watermelons and muskmelons, come down, we have a fine quantity of each. Before I was taken sick I was very busy making citron. I have made me 4 gallons of the nicest you ever eat or saw. (Oh I am a real busy body, and if you want me to prove to you, come down and see, or ask Mattie. I had rather you would come.) I have made other nice things, too (4 gal. of brandy peaches, and 3 gal of sweet pickles and ever so much jelly). I was drying "figs" and an old dog eat them all up, while in the sun, so I concluded not to try it any more, so I have a fine lot to preserve tomorrow. When I finish my pantry will be crowded.

And I add, you will be far happier when you have a home and can do the like yourself. I presume you are not adequate to the task at present. (excuse me).

Little Fannie grows some; is not very well now, is full of life and talks all the time. I have never got her picture yet. I feel right lonely to night, husband is hunting. He is a great hunter, delights in no other sport better, and he rarely goes with out bringing back the game. We have had fine times fishing this year, we were anxious to go while Ma surjouned with us but the day appointed I was not well and could not go or Mr. E. would not go without me, so she was disappointed.

I know no particular news which would interest you. Bro. Harvey is living in Camden, he intends practicing dentistry. *Mary Mc* (I learn is looking forward)

Respects to Mr. P.—love for yourself—write soon. I send the pictures. I will send mine some day—wish yours in return. Love to all inquiring friends.

J. A. Elliott

Please direct your letter thus, there are others of the family with my initials Mrs. L. C. Elliott

Henry Butler to William Paisley in Dobyville

Tulip Ark
Sep 8th 68

Dear Billy:

I was glad to learn from Jas Pryor that your hand was improving—*very* glad for I was quite anxious about it. I send herewith a letter rec'd by last mail—from L&S Henderson—You will perceive from the address that it has been out to *Texas*. I am sorry that it has been delayed so long as it appears. Henderson wishes Mr. Doby to commence business at once—that is, should he accede to the proposition. I trust Mr. Doby will feel that it will be to his interest to make the arrangement, for I would be pleased to see the house prospering and being represented by such an agent as Mr. Doby would make.

I am making out my memoranda for goods wanted this fall—and will send on my orders in a few days to New York. That is, if I don't hear from you in the meantime in regard to your going to Louisville. Although I am not needing many goods, I am almost persuaded to go on myself.

Ma has been sick but is going about now. Strange for ma to be sick. Capt. Lipscomb is determined to leave Tulip this fall if he can sell his place for *any thing*. I think he would take a wagon and two yoke of oxen for his real estate at Tulip. Loony leaves in about three weeks for Washington Co. Jim Pryor is going to Saline Co. to look at a place there. I am sorry I cannot report *any immigrants* to our county. The only purchase of land I have heard of is the Tunstall place. Russell and Henry Hall is to pay ten Bales Cotton for it in three payments. I shall at least be contented (or I shall try to be) till the political excitement is over.

I was glad you sent my umbrella by Pryor. I must say that I was not satisfied with my visit to your county. Of course you did all you could—and more than you ought—to make my stay pleasant. It *was* pleasant, but I wanted to see something of the country. I will be glad to hear from you as soon as possible.

Love to Emma and you

Yours truly
Henry A. Butler

William Paisley to Emma Butler Paisley in Dobyville

Arkadelphia
Sept 29 1868

My dearest one

You will doubtless be surprised to see from this that I am still in Arkadelphia. I waited last night for the stage going to Rockport to come in till ten or eleven o'clock, but no stage came & I went to bed, after getting the driver to promise to call for me if he should start during the night.

I shall start from here in about an hour on a wagon, and will not get off from Little Rock till

Saturday Morning. You can tell Mr. Doby, so he may tell when to start the wagons. Oh, how much I regret the delay, as it keeps me from you and John that much longer.

Mrs. Crawford has had an awful time, she was confined last Saturday morning but could not give birth but suffered intensely until yesterday. She had to be delivered by the doctors. She had twins but they were born dead. I understand she is doing very well this morning. I must close as I must now get my baggage to start. May God take care of and bless you both

> Affectionately,
> W. P.

Annie Butler to Emma Butler Paisley in Dobyville

> Tulip
> Sept 30th 1868

My dear sister Emma,

I have been thinking of writing to you for some time, but wanted to wait until I returned from the camp meeting near Benton, thinking I would have so much to tell you, but disappointment! Bro George, Sister, Sister Hunter, sister Mary, Andrew, Reavis and myself started last Wednesday, and on account of rain had to return home after traveling one day. Pete drove one of the wagons and had Rose for our cook. We were so well fixed, had our own provisions. We have had beautiful weather ever since it—camp meeting—began. Ma says she is going next time, says she won't turn back. I know you must have a lonely time now; wish I could be with you. Probably that would in some degree compensate for the absent *"One."* I guess John is walking a little, very glad to know his health is improving.

Asbury Smith was married to Mrs. Clark of Little Rock on the 15th inst. Sister Mollie, Sister Mary, and I got in the carriage and Pete drove us up to call on them. They did not return our call because of bad weather. I wish you could have seen her on Sunday. I never did see any one dressed so fine in my life, and Asbury was all attention and politeness. The first time, she married a widower with three children, he only lived two months. She is at least twenty-five years old. Carrie Williams is to be married to a Mr. Seay the first of next month. Sister Julia has been at home for the last month. Bro George said he would bring her *home* in a week or so—we miss her a great deal.

Mr. Watson began teaching a singing class last Saturday. I think he will make a splendid teacher. We were all very much pleased. He is so anxious to improve singing in the church. Mr. Robertson is very much displeased with Pa for charging him board. He left about two weeks ago to live at Mr. Pattillo's. He told Mr. Lee (the miller) that he was going to stick up a card "Beware the Butlers." Did you ever hear the like? He is also out with bro. Henry—He can't get enough money to go after his intended wife.

We have the peaches out in the sunshine; the worms are getting into them.

Mr. Looney left for Washington Co. this morning. Ma and sister Mollie went over to see them yesterday. Mr. Pryor speaks of moving near Benton. Bro. Henry will move to Mr. Tune's place soon.

Ma says how are you getting on by yourself—don't you get very lonesome? You will have to come over next Feb. before the rainy season begins. Does Martha want to come back to Tulip?

Ask her has she forgotten Wiley. Kate Colburn is boarding at sister's and teaches music for Mr. Leiper. I must close. Write very soon. Kiss John for me. All send much love.

Your loving sister

Annie

Overlook mistakes. Your church letter is here. I will send it. It was in the Post Office. I found it.

William Paisley to Emma Butler Paisley in Dobyville

Little Rock, Ark.
Oct 2nd 1868

My dearest one:

I arrived here yesterday evening about four o'clock—my trip was quite tedious as well as rough but I tried to exercise as much patience as possible—we were on the road two nights & the better parts of three days. At night I took lodging with the driver, and slept without shelter. Since my arrival here, I have attended to some little matters for other persons & am now waiting *very impatiently* for tomorrow (Saturday) morning to roll around, when I hope to get off on the train which connects with a boat at De Valls Bluff on White River—for St. Louis. You can't imagine, my dear one, how tired I am of the trip now. Could I have gone *right through* I could have enjoyed it all the time, but as it is I feel that it is nearly time for me to see my dear ones again & still I am hardly started on my journey. I hope, however, to have a pleasant time after I leave here.

Day before yesterday we stopped at twelve o'clock to feed at the old Reyburn place seven miles this side of Rockport, where Mr. Reyburn lived at the time his daughters boarded at your Pa's. Dr. Scull and his brother are living there now. The Dr. married Miss Jamie, & his brother married Miss Maggie. While the mules were eating, I went around to see Asbury Smith & found him & his bride in the store. I was introduced to Mrs. Smith & talked with her some time. She is a tolerably good looking lady, but I thought she would have to possess more attractions than I could see before I could have been induced to marry her, I mean if I wasn't. I can tell you more about them when I see you. Oh I must not forget to tell you that I met Leon Bullock in Arkadelphia, who told me that he saw Jim Robertson a few days before & that Jim had got out of the notion of getting married. The only reason he gave for changing was that he couldn't raise the funds, but I suppose there was something else.

Hope you have received letters from home before this. If so you know more about it than I do. Mr. Geo Lea of Princeton & Mr. Crow of Arkadelphia are here & will go on with me, which makes the prospects of my trip more promising for pleasure. My sheet is nearly out & I must close. There is no news of interest here. I will write every opportunity.

My hand is still stiff but nearly healed up, and has given me very little if any trouble since I left. Hope that you are right well and that little John has had no more chills. Tell him he must be able to run out & meet his Pa when he comes.

Excuse the writing & believe me as ever your loving husband

W. Paisley

Many kisses for both you and our little John.
I sent this by Mr. Mc Gill, who came in this morning with cotton.

William Paisley to Emma Butler Paisley in Dobyville

Little Rock, Ark.
Oct 2nd, 1868

My dear one—

I wrote you to day by Mr. McGill, but my room mates have gone out to night to attend the Lodge & I know of nothing that will afford me more pleasure than writing to my dear Emma. There is not much that I can write to interest you, but I know you will say *it is good* & interesting even if I do think otherwise.

After staying at Dobyville several months, Little Rock presents many *city sights* that look new, & keep me from getting tired as soon as I would in Arkadelphia where every thing is the same all the time. When I get to St Louis, Little Rock will seem as small as Arkadelphia does now. While walking up the street this evening, I couldn't help thinking about how much you could see here that would be new and interesting to you, & after getting to larger and finer cities you would feel (as I did when I first commenced traveling) that the whole world was crowded together in one place. Nothing, my dear one, would afford me more pleasure than to take you with me on such a trip & as I have frequently said before, I intend doing so just as soon as I possibly can.

I suppose you have heard of the death of Gen'l Hindman. He was shot through a window while sitting in his own house. It is not known who the assassin was, but the papers suppose that he was shot by some man that was under him during the war.

There is no other news of interest. I get off to morrow morning. Please say to Mr. Doby that he can start the wagons next Monday two weeks for the goods, & to send his orders to Jones McDowell & Co, as I intend shipping to their care. I will return as soon as I can, but cannot fix a time yet. You & little John must be contented & happy.

Please excuse this & believe me your loving husband

W Paisley

Emma Butler Paisley to William Paisley at Cairo, Ill.

Dobyville
Oct. 2nd 1868

My dearest one,

Feeling like writing tonight. I will commence my letter, and close to morrow or next day, so that you may have the latest news from us. I say news, though I don't know that any of importance have happened since you left, except that John has at last commenced walking a little, and I think by the time he is a year old he will walk tolerably well, that is, if he doesn't get sick again. Every one that sees him says he looks so much better than when I brought him over. I took him over with me and spent the day with Henry Harris—had a very pleasant time—this evening Miss Sallie called in (at Dr. Harris's) and spent a while with us at dinner. Mr. Williamson heard that she was expected (he has been staying at the Dr's helping about the houses that have been moved down at Mr. Doby's) so he comes over, fixes up ready to see her.

125

I understand that Mr. Grier and Lizzie have changed their time of marriage to the middle of November, or as soon as she can get ready.

Mrs. Doby is looking for her pa, Miss Jane and Miss Mag Monday night. The Dr. and Miss Jane are expected to go on to the Rock to attend Synod, and Miss Mag will stay here till they return. I will be glad to see Miss Mag and hope she will not get out of the notion of coming. Mrs. Doby and I called on Mrs. Burton the other evening—found them pleasant and comfortably fixed up. I want to go to Mr. McCallum's to morrow evening to see Effie, who has been sick a week with fever. Judge Coleman got off last Wednesday—expects to be gone two months or more. Mrs. Coleman will have a lonely time.

I was surprised to hear through Mr. Gilman that you did not leave on the stage, but would get on a waggon the next evening. It seems you have bad luck at commencement of your trips, but I hope you have prosperity at the close. If I had thought of it, I would have sent for a scrap book by you. It was two bunches instead of ten of blue braid that Henry sent for, but I suppose you will find a ready sale for the balance if she doesn't conclude to take all of it.

Dr. Harris expects to move all the houses from his place; so I don't see where we will find a suitable place for next year. But as *I am not a man*, I will not trouble my brains about such matters.

I don't know whether I will write home this week or not, as none have written to me since I left.

Sunday 4th

Mr. Grier told me this morning at the breakfast table that Mr. Gilman had a note at home for me, written from Arkadelphia by you. I did not know till then you had written. I was not at home the evening Mr. Gilman passed, and when he handed Mr. Doby the mail, neglected giving him the note, but told him you were still in Arkadelphia and would leave on a waggon that evening. I am very much obliged for the nice fruit you sent by Mr. Doby, and the note also. When I finish this letter I will have three ready to send to the office to morrow—one to cousin Mat, the other to Emma Lipscomb. I must be improving—what think you?

Well I reckon you are now, or have been, enjoying yourself with brother Lewis—having much to talk and ask about—how I wish to be with you—maybe I would find a place to slip in an occasional word.

Much love to brother L. I will close this letter and write again next week. Many kisses from little John and your always loving,

Emma

William Paisley to Emma Butler Paisley in Dobyville

Memphis
Oct. 5th 1868

My dear loving Emma:

I expected to make close connection here with the cars going to St Louis & found that I would not have time to write to you from this place, but our boat got in last night between 9 & 10 o'clock & we will remain here until past two this evening. I remained on the boat last night & came up to

126

the Hotel this morning for Breakfast. Mr. Geo Lee will go on to St Louis with me, so you need not be uneasy, for if any accident should happen to me I will have some [one] along to let you know.

I had a very pleasant time on the boat from De Valls Bluff—the boat we came on made the trip in the shortest time known since they have been running the river. Two boats running in opposition to each other started at the same time, & we had quite an interesting race for about twelve hours, when our boat out stripped the other & beat her to Memphis some two hours. We had quite a number of passengers, & among them a good many ladies both single & married. And Saturday night the *young folks* got up a dance which they seemed to enjoy hugely until near midnight. As a matter of course I did not participate in the dance, but I felt like if I *had* had some lady acquaintance along, it would have been some what of a temptation. Mr. Lee & myself have just finished examining the large stock of goods we so frequently see advertised in our Advocate, of Lowenstein & Co together with some others. Neither of us had any idea of purchasing here, but were merely looking for the purpose of seeing how prices here would compare with those where we are going.

My hand is almost entirely healed but still stiff. I am very anxious to hear from you & little John. When I think about the probability of either of you being sick I get right uneasy & at the same time blame my self, imagining any thing of the kind. My *dear dear* one, you must be mighty sweet & happy while I am away, & pray much to our heavenly Father for me. Hope little John is walking, but can hardly think that he is. I suppose you have done some visiting by this time. You must be sure & visit as much as you can conveniently.

By the by, it will do no good to talk about it, but I saw some of the finest oranges on the st this morning you ever saw. How much I wish I could send you some. I told Mr. Lee that if I could only see some one going back, I would fix you up a box. I tried to get some in Little Rock to send by Mr. McGill but couldn't find them.

They are now eating dinner & I must close. As soon as you get this, write to me care of Anthony House of Little Rock.

May God bless you, my dearest one, many kisses for you & John. Remember me to Messrs Doby & John & Billy

Affectionately &c
W Paisley

William Paisley to Emma Butler Paisley in Dobyville

St Louis
Oct. 9, 1868

My dearest Emma:

I started a letter to you late last night after getting off from the drummers, but was so tired & completely broke down that I had to stop & go to bed. I promised to write as soon as I got here but have been *drummed* almost to death, & really have not had time to myself to write a letter, so I hope you will excuse me. I left Memphis soon after finishing my letter & arrived here the next day about two o'clock. I fully expected when I left you to call and see Lewis on my way up, but I got to Cairo about two o'clock in the night & not knowing where to find him I got off the boat on to the cars & came right on.

I never saw such a crowded city as this is now. The State Fair came off here this week & it really looks like every body had come to attend it. When Mr. Lea and myself got here, it was as much as we could do to get a room in a Hotel, & they have been moving in ever since. We are stopping at the Southern Hotel (the finest it is said in the United States). There are now one thousand or twelve hundred persons stopping here, think of what a crowd! Two hundred are accomodated in the dining room at one time, & supper lasts from 7 till nine o'clock.

Last night the Democrats of St Louis had a grand Seymour & Blair torch-light procession. They marched through the streets in columns of fours, & every man had a little oil lamp fastened to the end of a stick which they carried on their shoulders. All had their badges &c & a brass band for every club. I do not know how many were in the procession but it is said there were over one hundred thousand persons on the street. The Democrats here talk very hopefully of the election of Seymour & Blair, but judging from what I have seen & heard—notwithstanding the demonstration last night, I fear that it is not at all Certain.

I have met a great many acquaintances here that I made in 1865, & among others a Mr. Jackson that was in the Medical Dept. with me at Charlotte—I have bought my Dry Goods, Hardware, Hats, & Shoes, & hope to complete my purchases & Start home by next Tuesday the 13th inst. Shall call to see Lewis on my return—Oh how anxious I am to be with you again—for the last two days I have been thinking so much about you & little John & from some cause have almost felt uneasy, fearing that you might be sick. My dear one, be sweet & happy while I am away, & do not get lonesome or sad. You know how much I love my *dear precious* little Emma, & I trust these separations that we have to endure now will enable us to live more independently after a while. May God bless & take care of you both is the prayer of your devoted husband

> Wm Paisley

All goods are cheaper than I expected, except shoes. They are high.

Many kisses for my Emma & many for our little John. Good night

I have taken the rag off my hand and it is a great deal better than when wrote last, though I can't shut it yet.

George Butler to sister Emma Butler Paisley in Dobyville

> Tulip
> Oct. 28th 1868

My dear Sister Emma

Julia says she reckons you will be surprised to receive a letter from me, and I reckon so too; but I have been owing you a letter for a long time. I got home today just before dinner. Found sister Mary and Annie busy preparing dinner, Ma and sister being at Dr. Colburn's. We received a letter from Billy written at Little Rock. I am glad to hear that he purchased his goods on such good terms. Hope he may succeed in selling them as well. Brother Henry thinks William bought cheaper than he did.

Brother H. & sister Mollie have moved into their new home. They are very well pleased with their place. Mollie especially is delighted with the exchange. Says she feels like a bird released from his cage. I suppose you know that he exchanged places with Mr. Tune.

Bro. H. received a letter from brother Barcus a short time since. His family have been sick nearly ever since they have been at Fayetteville, and consequently they are not very well satisfied with their home. Gen Nat Smith has gone to look at the northern part of the state and Mo. Mrs. Somerville thinks of going with him if he likes.

Mr. Leiper has about thirty scholars and his school is doing well. George H. is still at Little Rock. Johnnie is sowing wheat today. I stayed at Charles' last night. They are living pretty hard, but as well as bachelors could be expected to live. He has about three bales of cotton picked and about two more to be picked. His share will be about two and a half bales, and something over two hundred bushels corn. I think if he had a good wife it would add to the appearance and comfort of his place and increase his happiness.

I am glad to hear that John is doing so well. You must train him up to be a good boy. I feel sure you will do this. It will aid you much in doing so to have your own soul thoroughly and constantly imbued with the life and *power* of Godliness. Perhaps no light but that of Eternity can reveal the full extent of a mother's influence and the good she does if influenced by the Holy Spirit.

Remember me at a throne of grace. Love to William and John.

All join in love, and Julia especially sends her love. I wish I had time to write you a longer and better letter.

I will start to Conf. in about two weeks. Expect to carry Julia with me. They have paid me about one hundred dollars on my circuit and have promised to pay some more.

Our apples have been gathered and we are enjoying them very much. Ma & sister have just driven up from Dr. Colburn's. I must close. Will write again when I get back from Conf. Goodby.

The Lord bless my dear sister Emma.

> Affectionately your brother
> George

Mattie Butler Hughes to Emma Butler Paisley at Dobyville

> Tulip
> Nov. 3rd 1868

Dear Sister Emma,

I ought to have written you long ago. On your birthday, I wanted to write, but didn't find time, and while you were alone I thought I would surely write, but somehow I didn't feel in a writing mood. I haven't any one with me tonight, but the children. Walter and West are studying their lessons, and Reavis is in "Mamie's" bed asleep. I don't know how I could live without my little boys. I expect Billy told you he met with George in Little Rock. I hear from him every so often, but it is hard to be separated, though I try to bear it as patiently as I can, hoping the time will come, when we can live together.

Yesterday was brother George's birthday, and as he was at home, Ma prepared a nice dinner, and invited us over. We spent a very pleasant day together, wish you could have been with us, and last week we met to celebrate John's birthday.

Tomorrow I expect Brother Henry and Mollie to take dinner with me. Wish you were living near so I could have your company too. I suppose little John can run everywhere, wish I could see the dear little fellow. Mary is just beginning to step a little. She is as fleshy as ever. Coulter can talk right plain.

Mr. Nat Smith has bought near Fayetteville and expects to move this winter. I have heard that he was delighted with the country. I don't think Mr. Barcus is pleased. All of them have been sick, came very near losing Sammie. Says if he can't have his health, he will have to seek some other country.

Mr. Pryor expects to move to Saline County, this fall or winter. He started up today to sow wheat. Willie Hunter went up with him. Mr. Jim Toone has bought his place, so you see there will be several changes in our neighborhood. Charlie came up last Saturday, the first time he had been up, in five or six weeks. He is very busy picking cotton. John intends to farm with him next year.

We haven't heard from Bro. Lewis since Billy saw him. I am glad to hear that he is doing so well, do hope he will visit us next Summer.

Brother George and Julia expect to start to conference, the last of next week. Kate Colburn expects to go too. Her sister Alice will teach her music class while she is absent.

Ma and myself spent one day last week at Dr. Colburn's, he is suffering a great deal, can't even walk with crutches, Poor old man. I don't see how he can live through the winter. Have you made any arrangements about housekeeping? Has John quit having chills? Give my love to your "*other self*," and a kiss to John, and write soon to

> Your loving
> Sister M. W. Hughes

Mrs. E. D. Lipscomb to William Paisley in Dobyville

> Tulip
> November 6th 1868

My Dear Son,

Your very kind and urgent letter came to hand yesterday. We were taken by surprise as we had given out all idea of moving for the present As Father cant leave home at this time. We send Willis to let you know that we will go to Clark [County] provided you can get Mrs. Strang's place. Father wants you to procure the place for him, and pay the rent out of the crop. If not, on as reasonable terms as possible, as he is willing to rely on your judgment. Father would go himself, but has not got his winter clothing made and has some coats on hand that he is compelled to finish, and this morning two of our best cows are sick, one of them down. If you can get the place, send Willis back immediately, and we will begin to move right away, as we are all on the wing to go, as nothing would afford me more pleasure than to live where I could see you and Emma and dear little John some times. All join in love to you all.

Writen in haste

> Your Devoted Mother
> E. D. Lipscomb

Lewis Butler to Emma Butler Paisley in Dobyville

Cairo Ills.
Nov. 6th 1868

My Dear Sister:

You no doubt grow impatient at my delay in sending the photograph as promised. Having seen Billy, I thought he would be able to inform you more about me than I could write in many letters. He no doubt told you that he took the precaution before leaving to see that I had my negative taken & the pictures ordered.

Well, the election is over and Grant is President. I do not feel very bad over the result, for I believe he will do nearly what is right by you southern people, & you are the ones having much cause of complaint. Grant has heretofore been a Democrat, and if true to himself he will not be a Radical. We have carried our district, and elected our candidate for Congress—Col. Crebs—by about five hundred. Our county is Democratic by about the same majority. I hope, now that the election is over, business will revive. Unless it does I do not know what will become of us.

My health continues good. I have a serious intention of looking around for some one to love. I begin to fear old bachelorhood, a state I abhor, and the first young lady I fall in love with & can satisfy myself that we can be happy, I shall step off. We are having a good many marriages here— one of my acquaintances almost every month. Meanwhile, I do not see that I am making any advances in that direction, though the fact that I visit ladies oftener & *think more* and *more of myself* is a good sign—isn't it?

You must let the picture suffice for the balance of this letter, & take my promise that when I have something interesting I will write more. I enjoyed Billy's stay here very much, & wish you had acted upon the suggestion and accompanied him as far as here, so that I could have had a good old-fashioned talk with you while he was buying goods in St. Louis. Billy could hardly tell me about any body but you & Johnny whom I never saw (bless his little heart). Kiss him, that Johnny, for me & tell Billy to write me how he is doing &c.

Write to me often
Your affectionate brother
Lewis P. Butler

Henry Butler to William Paisley in Dobyville

Tulip
Nov 20th [1868]

Dear Billy:

I reached home last night about 7 o'clock and found all well and little Mary *walking all about the room.* I never saw such an improvement in a child in the way of walking in so short a time. I found Pa at my house with *the blues* terribly—Told Mollie before I came that he was in hopes I *would* purchase in Clark, for it looked like starvation here. This country *never did look so poor* as it does now, since I have an interest in better land. But the thought arises—maybe I am too fast—the trade *may* be *broken up*. Pa says "by all means write to Billy to close the trade *in writing forthwith*—the old man might die or get out of the notion." He thinks we ought to have entered into writing at the time. Billy, I hope you have already closed the purchase and taken the title bond. I think you ought either to have a witness to the fact (or expressed in writing) in regard to what we are to receive in the way of appurtenances such as fences, houses, gin stand & running gear. Of course, manage all so as not to give any offense to Mr. Hill.

I cannot ascertain what gold is worth here—in fact I know of none that can be had. Col. Maurice Smith (or Mrs. Barbee) no doubt has, but you know how hard it is to get any thing like a fair trade out of them. My sales to-day amt to about sixty five, but Pa has sold but little since I left.

Tell Emma I intended sending Coulter's Photograph in this, but came to the store and left it at the house.

Write to me immediately for I am anxious about our trade. I am much better please[d] with our purchase than when in Clark. The contract is *so striking*.

Mollie says she is much obliged for the Pine Apple and will keep it for her *"Christmas dinner."* Mollie joins me in love to you both.

> Affectionately
> Henry

Write to me freely about every thing.

The shoes for Mary are plenty large with thick wool hose, she could wear the 2's.

George Butler to Emma Butler Paisley in Dobyville

> Tulip
> Nov. 26th 1868

My dear sister Emma

According to promise, I proceed to write you a letter after returning home from Conference. Julia went with me and altogether we had a very pleasant time. We were the first to get to Warren, the only ones that got there on Saturday. Some came in on Monday and others on Tuesday. We staid at Maj. Bradley's Hotel. He is a cousin of John M. Bradley. He kept a good table. Brother Moores, Sammy & Catie staid at the same place. We made our own fires, made up our own beds, and fed our horses.

Conference was held in the Court house and preaching in the Methodist Church, the only church building in the town. There was a pretty full attendance of preachers, and a good many lay delegates, and many visitors, on Saturday and Sunday. The weather was quite cool and we had no fire in the church until Saturday. After that we had two stoves. Conference closed last Tuesday about twelve o'clock, and notwithstanding it was pouring down rain, the preachers were soon wending their way homeward. I got off a little after one o'clock and it continued to rain for some time after we left. We reached Edinburg, a small town fifteen miles from Warren, in time to get a good supper and very comfortable lodgings for the night. Bishop Pierce preached for us on Friday night and Sunday at eleven. McFerrin preached on Wednesday night and made a Missionary speech on Thursday night. I hardly need say that we had good preaching and an interesting time.

There are many things that I could tell you about Conference if I could be with you, which would occupy too much time to write. I am sent to Buenavista Circuit beyond Camden. Brother Caldwell returns to Tulip Circuit. Husbands to Arkadelphia District. Pope to Arkadelphia station. Steele returns to Washington. Brother Hunter is Bible agent. Sammy Colburn to Rockport Circuit, brother Holmes to Caddo. I think Clark circuit is to be supplied. The appointments will be published in the Ark. Christian Advocate next week I suppose.

Pa left home last Tuesday to go to Mississippi to see about the land which Uncle Albert wishes him to take in payment of debt. We expect him back the last of next week. I do not expect to be here when he returns. Julia and I expect to leave next Tuesday morning, if the weather is not too bad.

Brother Henry received a long letter from Sister Barcus. She writes like she is in good spirits. Brother Barcus was transfered to the Ark. Conf. and I suppose he will fill the station at Fayetteville, as I see from the appointment that it is left to be supplied. He had twenty scholars when I last heard from him.

This is Friday and I am trying to observe it as a day of fasting and prayer. I feel, Sister Emma, that I need more religion. I fear that I have not as much now as I had a year ago. My walk has not been as close with God as it should have been. I know that I am to blame if I do not continually have my heart filled with the love of God. Pray for me.

Sister Mollie and Brother Henry were over last evening, and sat until bed time. Jim Pryor expects to leave next month. I learn that Billy was over last week, so it useless for me to be writing any thing about the neighborhood. Sister Mary has received another letter from "Helen." She had twins some time since but they died. She is now in good spirits & good health.

But I will close. Write to me at Bell's Store, Columbia Co., Ark.

My love to Billy, & give John a kiss for me. May God bless you & yours. Continue to live for Eternity, and pray for your affectionate brother

G. E. Butler

P.S. Julia sends her love. G. E. B.

Henry Butler to William Paisley in Dobyville

Tulip
Dec 2d 68

Dear Billy

I am quite anxious to hear from you. I have written twice since I came home—one by mail and one by Mr. Orr—But have *heard nothing from you.* I hope to receive a letter tonight. I have engaged one hundred dollars in gold for you at 35 per ct. Let me hear from you at once in regard to it.

A gentleman from Selma Ala. (a Dr. Thompson) stopped with Mr. Jas Pattillo a night or two since, who owns about twelve hundred acres of land at or near Locust Hill (or Grove) six miles beyond Arkadelphia. His business out here was to countermand instructions sent a short time since to sell his land at $2 per acre. He was just in time—two hours later and the land would have been sold. He says he would not take ten thousand in cash for the land. This Dr. Thompson thinks land will be doubled in value in Clark in twelve months—that coincides with your opinion. I am anxious to hear from you to know for a certainty that *our trade is consumated.*

Pa has been to look at the land in Bolivar Co. Miss.—just returned. The land is not now cultivated, no fence around it and an encumbrance of fifteen hundred dollars on the place in the shape of taxes, lawyers fees &c. Pa thinks "it won't pay."

Mr. Wm Bird says he will be over to see Mr. Doby between this time and "the 1st of Jan" to fix up deeds &c. It is his intention to take the place he lives on.

Bro George wrote to Em and I suppose gave all the news as to conference appointments. I send you by this mail the last Confer. Bulletin containing the appointments in full. All well

> Yours
> Henry

Annie Butler to Emma Butler Paisley in Dobyville

> Tulip
> Dec. 9th 1868

My ever dear Sister,

Your letter which was received so long ago is still unanswered. I reckon you began to think I am going to do as I said, never write any more letters; but I have found out that won't do, for I do love to receive them, and the only way to get them is to write myself.

Brother Charlie came up last Saturday, and this morning he and Johnnie started with a wagon load of things for Mr. Pryor. He is to pay them $32. I was very sorry for them to leave. I fear they will have bad weather as it is very cloudy, and while eating supper it commenced snowing, but I think it has ceased, but no telling how it will be in the morning.

Johnnie will go down with bro. Charlie next week. They will farm together next year. I don't know what we will do without one of them. Johnnie has been trying to refix an old mattress, did not quite complete it before he left; but he says when he gets through with it, it will equal any spring mattress. He is trying to learn to do everything, is a pretty good hand on old shoes.

We killed our hogs last Monday. I think I will get fat now. One of them was stolen, and the others did not weigh quite as much as we expected, but I reckon it will be enough, as our family is small.

Bro. George and sister Julia left today a week ago for their circuit below Camden, fifteen miles from bro. Moores. I guess sister Julia will be at home most of the time. I have been expecting Fannie up every day this week, don't know when she will come, think likely I will get a letter tomorrow morning which will inform me. She made bro. George a present of a nice pair of jeans pants.

Mrs. Tom Colburn is looking for Mollie and Wilson McAlister to spend some time with her. Milton expects to take them to Mo. in the spring. I think she looks for the Dr. home Christmas. He has been gone more than six months. Sister Mollie gave Mr. & Mrs. Pryor a tea party last Friday night, and invited Kate and Alice, Sister Mary and I, and any of the other home folks that wished to go. Mrs. Colburn went without an invitation. Bro. Pope happened in the store that evening, and bro. Henry carried him over. You know I enjoyed myself. He is the same *good old friend*. He is stationed in Arkadelphia and promised to bring his family and spend the night with us when he returned. He expected to be here next Friday, but I don't think he will as the weather has been so cold.

Bro. Caldwell is our preacher again this year, and I think everyone is pleased with the appointment. He is an excellent man. I guess bro. Billy told you about the nice widower who spent a day and a night with us on his way to conference, and how he cut him out that night, left him to walk with the old people. You will have to teach him better if you don't want two or three old maid sisters.

I received a letter from Mary Barcus last week. They are delighted with their new home, and all have gotten well except Mrs. Barcus. Mary was serenaded by the young gents of Fayetteville a night or two before she wrote, said it was the prettiest music she ever heard. She said it was quite a gay place, dancing parties twice every week. Maj. A. has forty students and Mr. Barcus twenty. I suppose Lizzie is married, and will not have time to *think* of me now much less write. Present my congratulations to her and tell her not to forget every body but "One."

When are you coming over? Ma says come Christmas. We are all anxious to see you all, and especially John. Kiss the little fellow for me. Much love to bro. Billy and accept a full share for yourself. Excuse such a letter. I hope to see you *soon*, if not write. It is time for little folks to go to bed. So good night to you both.

Annie

I think Pa's trip to Mississippi improved him. He was not gone more than 2 weeks. Brought candy, nuts, cheese &c for Christmas.

Tulip Evermore

Emma Butler Paisley to William Paisley in Dobyville

Tulip
Jan. 17th 69

My dearest one,

This is Sabbath evening, and after being at home most of the day by myself, have concluded to spend a short while in conversing with my absent husband. This morning all went up and heard brother Caldwell, and this evening have gone to attend church meeting. Charley came home last evening and will leave in the morning. He is looking very well—did expect to spend the evening at *Dr. Colburn's* but having company for dinner has prevented. I believe he has decided to pay his *special* attention to Miss Kate at last. Johnny tells him that one of them has to get a wife that if he (Charley) does not, he will. They have no cook. Pompey Matlock came up one evening last week, and this morning rode up in his buggy and carried Annie to church. I don't pretend to say what his intentions are, but leave you to judge for yourself.

Well, what do you think! Mr. Caldwell found Jack Overton and Willie Hunter in the road between here and Princeton almost dead drunk. It was three o'clock Friday evening when he saw them, and staid with Willie (I believe Jack was able to get on his horse and ride home) till the stage came on at night, and had him put on and brought to his mother's. Imagine his mother's feelings at such a sight! There was an uproar at Dr. Tom Colburn's last week—the negro woman they have hired said something out of the way to little Tommy, which he reported to his father. Dr. Colburn went in to see her about it, when she spoke rather short to him, causing him to pick up a chair and was about to give her a lick when she screamed out, frightening Mrs. Colburn so that she picked up her baby, threw a shawl over her head and ran over to brother Hunter's and spent the day. I think she acted very imprudently to say the least of it. The woman left at the time, but has since come back, and I believe things have become somewhat quiet again. Little Tommy was sent down to his grandfather's.

John's nurse came last Wednesday—her name is Martha. John would look at her very hard when I would tell him that was Martha. He would not let her have much to do with him at first, but is getting to like her some better. The day you left, John, after taking a nap got to cutting up so that I could do nothing with him till I got a switch and used it, and ever since he has been a right good boy.

Monday morning

What a beautiful day we are having! how I would like to know how my dear one is spending his time! at the store of course—hope you have received your new goods before this time. Is my dearest one happy this lovely day, or is he brooding over the past? O darling! can't your Emma say one word to comfort your wounded spirit? I can only say the oft repeated words: "Be happy."

Little John is getting very well acquainted with home folks and is consequently much better satisfied than when you were here. The children are very much amused at the little fellow imitating the chicken, sheep, cat &c. He doesn't try to talk as much as he did before leaving Mr. Doby's, but is the most perfect mimic I ever saw.

Charley has just got off—said he had lots of word to send to you, and would write as soon as he got his house fixed so that he could write. Says he would like to see you very much. I have seen Ma [Billy's ma], father [Billy's stepfather], Emma, Ella, & Claud since you left. I have not been off the place, and don't know that I shall *very* soon unless I go to ma's or brother Henry's. Coulter and little Mary have been sick the last few days, but are getting better now. Where is Willis living? hope you have found some suitable place for him.

I have not written any letters since coming over, only a short one to cousin Mat last Saturday and sent it by Col. Whitaker's wagon. How are the neighbors in Clark getting on? Remember me to all who enquire after me. Write me the particulars of Miss Sallie's marriage if you have heard any.

Do write to Aunt Minerva if you can possibly find time, even if it causes you to write one letter less to me. I send you the only flower in bloom—in a few days there will be several others.

Good bye. May God bless my dear one. Write soon to your most loving,

Emma

William Paisley to Emma Butler Paisley in Tulip

Dobyville Ark.
Sunday night Jany 17th, 1869

My dearest one:

You doubtless looked for a note from me from Arkadelphia but when I give you an account of my day there, you will not be surprised at my not writing.

You know we got a late start from Tulip. Consequently it was after dark when we reached the river. The sun went down about the time we got to the slough where the mules refused to go in on our way over—which is about three & a half miles from Arkadelphia. When we got to the river it was about half an hour in the night, & I was fearful that we would have trouble in getting over, but as the Ferry man lived up on the hill (on the opposite side) in hearing distance, I hoped he would answer to our call although he had tied up for the night. So I "hollowed" as loud as I well could & was answered by some men camped over on the other side, who told me that the Ferry man had gone to church, but told them to tell me when I came to take the canoe & come over & get the Boat & ferry my self. I told them they had delivered the message to the wrong one, as I was not well enough acquainted with Boats to risk so much on the river at night. They then told me that the message was left for some one that had gone out to kill hogs. I continued to call for the Ferryman, knowing that his wife could hear me, & hopeing that she would send out & hunt her husband up, but no one came & there we were, without matches or fire & almost freezing with cold. After calling for about an hour we all got so cold we had to pull off our boots and wrap our feet up in blankets & straw to keep them from freezing. Willis & my self & Bob all got in the wagon together & were not very nice about getting close to each other. I got between Willis & Bob & I believe I fared better than they did as far as keeping warm was concerned. We all soon went fast asleep but I would wake occasionally & call for the Boat in order to let the Ferryman know (provided he had returned from church) that we were still expecting him. We remained there in the cold in that condition without fire or any thing to eat until eleven o'clock, & would have stayed there till morning, but Mr. Pattillo going home from his office heard us & came down & ferried us over. When we got up to his house it was midnight, but Mr. P made us a lot of hot coffee which we enjoyed hugely with a plate of biscuit & cheese by a nice hot fire. Had you and little John been with me I don't know what we would have done, as it is some distance from the river to a house & it would have been impossible to have stayed there without fire. It really seems that Mr. Pattillo will never tire of doing us favors. It was late when we got up the next morning & between nine and ten o'clock when we started from Arkadelphia & about sun down when we got home. Our goods have not yet reached Arkadelphia, & we have heard nothing from them.

I found every thing going here about the usual way. Mr. Doby killed hogs the day we got here, & we now have plenty of bones &c. Willis is still with me. I went to see Mr. McGill Thursday to see if I could get him in there, but they are undetermined yet as to what they will do & could not give him employment. Billy Grier is anxious to get him, provided it will suit Mrs. G to board him, & came up yesterday evening to see me about it, but I was away trying to collect an a/c when he came & did not see him. Willis seems to be very much changed & I am encouraged in the belief that he is determined to give up his follies & try to make something of himself.

Next Wednesday week is the day for Jno Williamson & Miss Sallie to get married & Mrs. Doby will look for Miss Mag & her Father then. I understand Miss Calie was invited for one of the Brides maids, but that she has notified Miss Sallie that she cannot attend. I have not heard whether they will invite many or not. They will have four attendants—each—but I have not learned who they will be. John told me yesterday that he thought of inviting a Mr. McClellan of Arkadelphia for one, suppose Dr. McCullum will be another. I told John that I should expect to be one.

The night we stayed in Arkadelphia (Tuesday) they had three marriages, one at the Methodist Church, Mr. Clark & Miss Singleton, one of them was a run away couple & were married at Dr. Rowlands. The parties were Miss Marberry and a Mr. Dale, Dr. Rowlands nephew. The other lady was a Miss Roper, but I have forgotten the man. The latter couple were married Wednesday morning before breakfast. It really seems that the girls made pretty good use of their privileges during Leap year—although they put off consummating their plans till the year was out. Mrs. Mat McGill is still in the neighborhood. I saw them all when I was over the other day. Miss Mag gave me as many apples as I could eat & made me fill my pockets—when I left I felt like telling Miss Mag that it was useless for me to bring any with me, as you & John were away, but I chanced to remember that I could eat them myself.

To day has been a long & lonesome one to me, & it troubles me to think that it is only the first of many that I will have to spend away from my dear ones. I am perfectly willing that you should always have the advantage in every thing, but I can't help thinking how much better off you are when we are separated now, by having dear little John with you. Bless the little fellow, how much I would like to see you & have a play with him to night. I cannot tell when I will be over, but you can depend on my coming as soon as possible. I want to try & come next Saturday week, but that is so near the time when I shall want to come over & stay that I may not get off. Do not look for me till you see me.

Have you secured a nurse yet? If not, please ask Henry to get you one as soon as possible & not to let the price keep him from hiring. Martha was here the Sunday we were away & Emily says offered to hire to Dick, but I don't suppose she was in earnest.

My dear one let me ask you to be sweet & cheerful while we are separated, remembering at all times that your husband loves you above anything in the world, & that we have a Heavenly Fathers assurance that he will withhold no good thing from us. I feel confident now that I will be with you unless you are sick this month, but should any thing happen, my dear one, do not fail to let me know immediately no matter what the cost—should you want any thing do not be backward in making your wants known. Suppose you are rooming with sister Mary. If not, get Henry to hire some one to cut you a supply of wood, & pile it up in the little room so that your girl can make your fire. Let me know all about it, & whether I can get you any thing here or not. You told me which dresses you wanted me to bring—but you had better write me about them, as I have forgotten which ones you said.

I found sister Mary's letter here when I came but will wait to bring it when I come, as you have heard the most of its contents. We expect our goods this week again, but it is not at all certain that they will come. I have bought one more Bale Cotton making in all nineteen.

Kiss our dear little John for his Pa, & dont let him forget me. Accept many kisses & much love for your self from

Your devoted husband
W. Paisley

Write soon and often. I shall expect a letter in a few days.

Yours
W P

Jan 18

Have just written Father & Henry a note, & send Willis to town to mail letters, to get the mail & ask about the goods.

My dear sweet one how much I love you this morning. Take good care of your self & our little boy. May God Bless you both. Good bye

Yours
W P

William Paisley to Emma Butler Paisley in Tulip

Dobyville, Arks
Sunday night, Jany 24th, 1869

My dear loving one:

Your precious sweet letter containing the little Flowers, tokens of your pure affection, was received last Friday morning. I ought to have gotten it Thursday evening, but Mr. Hill left it at Mr. Doby's, thinking that it was for him. Mr. Samuels told me that you had written, & when Mr. Hill came up Thursday evening without a letter, I felt that I couldn't be reconciled to the disappointment, but was relieved when it was handed me early Friday morning.

Oh Darling, you don't know how much good it does me to receive & read your dear *good* letters. I consider your last *one* of *your best*, & on reading it could but exclaim in my heart that my wife was the *best* woman in the world. I have just finished a long letter to Aunt Minerva. It was very precious in you to offer to get one letter less from me in order to get me to write to Aunt M., but I ought to have written to her long ago, and determined that you shan't lose any thing by it. How much I regret not writing to Uncle James regularly, so that you could have enjoyed the correspondence with me before he died. But it is too late now to regret, though I feel that I can never forgive myself for neglecting it.

139

Tickets have been sent out for Miss Sallie's wedding, which is to come off next Wednesday. Willis & myself are invited. My ticket came directed to Capt. Paisley. I told Mrs. Doby that I would cut it up because your name was left off. But John told me before he gave me the ticket that he and Miss S were both sorry you could not attend, & knowing that you would not be in the neighborhood caused them to write me alone. If I go I shall expect to enjoy myself, but would look forward to having a much more pleasant time if you could be with me. All the Doby's including Dr. H[arris] & Billy G[rier] & wives, Judge Coleman's family & the Clarks will all be there. I don't know whether there are any of the other neighbors invited or not. A Mr. Morrison, from Hempstead [County], Galley Coleman, & a Mr. McClellan from Arkadelphia are John's waiters. Miss May Williamson, Miss Humphreys, & Miss Effy are Miss Sallie's. Mrs. Doby will look for her Father & Miss Mag Tuesday.

Willis has not succeeded in getting a place yet. I shall try tomorrow & see what I can do for him. Several have talked of taking him, but do not like to hire any one they will have to board. Mr. Clark thought until yesterday evening that he would take him, but has concluded that he can work all his land with what force he has. I went over to our place yesterday evening to see what I could do towards improving it. I have spoken to a negro to clean me off a garden & have spoken to Mr. Gates to Pale it in & to build smoke house & kitchen. It is possible that I may not take the house of Dr. Harris. If I do I shall try & have it made more comfortable than it is at present. If I do not, I expect to have a little box house put up for us to live in. If I was only able, darling, to have a nice little cottage put up, I should feel a great deal better about it, but I know you will be satisfied when I do the best I can.

Willie Hunter & Jack Overton's getting drunk was really a sad affair & I am truly sorry to hear of their acting so badly. I know it must be heartrending to Mrs. Hunter to see her son acting so recklessly & I fear that such a trial to Mr. Hunter that it will injure or affect his usefulness. May God in his mercy give us wisdom & grace to enable us to show our dear little son the evils of such conduct, so that he may always abstain from such wickedness.

The other affair you mentioned surprised me considerably. I am really sorry that such a thing has occurred. We cannot tell who is to blame but it is an evidence that they don't get along very well. I agree with you in thinking that Mrs. C. acted imprudently in leaving home. Have you heard from Sister Mary yet? I have not. Tell sister Annie that two visits so close together look a little suspicious & that she can't blame me now if she doesn't do better than she did with the widower.

Send my best love to Charlie when you or any one write, & tell him that I would enjoy a long chat with him exceedingly. I have thought for some time that he would probably return to his first love. He of course must be his own judge, but my opinion is that she would make him a good wife, & I would rather see him marry her than Miss Calie. Charlie is, as you know, a favorite with me, & I am very anxious that he should do well.

Oh, Darling, how much I would like to see you tonight, & take little John on my knee while talking to my dear one. Today has been a long & tedious day to me, more so because I have been regretting that I didn't go to see you Saturday, but we are expecting several to settle soon & I did not like to say any thing about leaving. Besides, Mr. Doby has to go to town Monday to get his commission as magistrate.

You, my dear one, could say nothing more than what you said in your sweet letter. I still hope, my dear one, that all will yet be well, & that too when we see each other again. My only regret is my own folly, & if you will pray for me, our Heavenly Father will hear us & give us wisdom for the future. Be assured, my dear one, of your husband's love. It is for you that I live, & were it not for you & our little John, this world would be a desolate place to me. Write me as soon as you get this & let me know if you keep *right* well & happy. I will do all I can to get over between the 1st & 5 of Feby. If you would like for me to come sooner, let me know.

Tell John that his paw will see about his mama whipping him for crying after him when he comes over. Hope your nurse suits you. Let me know. Hoping to get another letter in a few days, I am as ever your devoted husband, with much love,

> W Paisley

Love to all

Excuse the hasty note by Mr. Samuel. I had no notice of his going till five minutes before he started, but thought I would send it any way.

> W. P.

William Paisley to Emma Butler Paisley in Tulip

> Dobyville
> Monday Morning [Jan. 25, 1869]

Mr. Doby goes to town this evening to get his commission as magistrate & expecting to meet Mr. Pattillo then with Dr. Williamson's carriage. I hope he will meet Mr. P., as he can take this to you sooner than it would go by mail. Oh! darling, I came near forgetting to tell you the main item of news. What do you reckon it is? You would not guess in a month, so I will tell you. We have a little *name sake* over at Mr. Newtons. Their baby is a little boy & they call him Florren Paisley. I give you the credit for the name, as there is no doubt that your visits had a good deal to do with our getting it. When I come over, I will bring some nice white goods & try & get some one to make him a nice little white dress like one of John's.

Well I must close. May God bless my darlings. This is too a beautiful day like the one mentioned in your letters, & I have commenced it with some good resolutions. May God help me to carry them out. Good bye.

> Your affectionate husband
> Wm Paisley

Many kisses for you both.

Lewis Butler to Emma Butler Paisley in Tulip

> Cairo, Ills
> Feb 20th, 1869

My Dear Sister Emma:

Yours of the 10th inst received this evening, and read with much pleasure. I have just returned from a political meeting held at our Court House, where we had several speeches on the subject of our local politics, the election for city officers being to take place next Tuesday. As you doubtless know, I am a candidate for reelection to the office of city atty, and if I live will certainly be successful. The office is not of much consequence, only as giving one some prominence and is very grateful to me, because I have already held it once & would be pleased to know that my official career has given satisfaction. I think it best to heed your advice, and not be hasty in taking the all-important step of linking my fortunes with those of one to be my companion for life in the most intimate of all relations, and yet I promise you that I intend trying during the course of the next year to find some one with whom I can be happy. At present I am foot-loose and fancy-free and heart whole, and it seems to me that I shall find trouble in suiting & being suited. At any rate I am far better prepared for assuming the responsibilities of married life than at any prior time, being more steady in my habits than you have ever seen me. I will endeavor to spend a few weeks at home this year, and would like for you and Billy to make it so that you could be there. I will inform you of the time when I will come time enough in advance.

I must write to Mr. Johnson—would have done so already but his sudden departure from Ky took me so much by surprise that I have neglected it. I had thought that my old sweetheart Mary Campbin was married long years ago—she waited long and I trust is happily married. Give my love to all and write often. Tell Ma that I shall certainly in my choice of a wife have reference to pleasing her as well as myself—for I know if I could suit her I should be apt to suit myself.

David Speed was here a few days ago, having been out from N.C. since Sept. last. He is hunting employment, out of money (I gave him ten dollars), and I am afraid not likely to succeed. He seemed to be endeavoring to look as barbarous & uncouth as possible—long and rough beard such as men used to wear in war times. I counseled him to cut off his beard & dress as well as possible, telling him that I believed it a good sound maxim for one to dress at least to the extent of his means, & I thought *then he was not* likely to be extravagant.

Yours affectionately

Lewis P. Butler

Since writing the foregoing I have been called on by Cousin William Kittrell on his way to Ark from Nashville, Tenn—in company with his sister Cousin Virginia Norris and a younger brother Jimmie, who has been attending school in Nashville. They are aboard of a Cumberland river boat, and expect this evening to take the "City of Alton" for Memphis. I have just returned from the boat where they are—left them because the boat is going to drop down the river several miles to take on corn. I found Cousin Virginia very friendly pleasant & glad to see me, as well as the boys. I never met any of them before, and am glad I have done so. They think of leaving Arkansas after this year and moving to Tenn—near Nashville. Aunt Polly Maureen was well when they left Nashville, and so were Cousin Wm Evans, James Maureen, & their families. All sent love, and extended a very cordial invitation for me to visit them at Nashville. I shall be pleased to do so, and as it is not a great ways may do so some time. Aunt Polly Maureen retains her health of body & mind, and cautioned Cousin V. to be sure to stop & see me.

It is only about one hundred & fifty miles from here to Nashville by river or rail—boats running constantly between there and here. They will leave this coming AM. I only see them again should their boat return before the "City of Alton" gets here from St. Louis. They send much love to you all. One of the girls, the youngest, remains in Nashville at William Evans'.

Affectionately

L. P. B.

I saw a letter from Henderson a few days ago, in which they said there was some talk of having a guardian appointed for [Aunt Pamela Wyche]. I suppose she is growing feeble-minded, but I should think the boys could manage to take care of her & her property without going into the Court. They are a queer set, those Wyches.

L. P. B.

Minerva Paisley to William Paisley in Dobyville

At Home [McLeansville, N.C.]
March 5, 1869

Dear Nephew and Niece,

I received your kind letter which afforded me much pleasure not only for the kind regard you manifested for myself and children, but for the love and esteem you have for my *dear* departed Husband. Every thing that can be said of his worth is gratifying to me. Dear Husband, I always thought I valued him, but feel now that I never appreciated his worth. No woman ever had a kinder husband. This he showed to the very last. While ever he could speak, my comfort was his constant care. The last thing he ever did was to fold me to his bosom and embrace me. This was just a few moments before he died. He was conscious to the very last, but I reckon you would like to know how long he was sick. The fall after you were here in the spring [1867] he had a bad spell, but seemed to recover from that, and I thought him as well as usual, but he seemed to have a presentiment that his time was short. I was passing by him during the Christmas holidays when he pulled me down on his lap and told me that he felt that he was not going to be with us much longer. I told him that I hoped he would be mistaken, but nothing could shake his opinion. He seemed tolerably well during the winter 'till sometime in the spring, when he had a hemorage of the lungs, after which it was a slow but steady decline—all that could be done for him was done, but nothing seemed to arrest the progress of the disease. He did not suffer much except from his cough, which was distressing at times. Everything that could be done to aid or comfort him was done.

His friends were not a few, and they showed the sincerity of their friendship when he needed it. We had to fan him day and night about a month before he died. It caused him to breathe easier. He slept a great deal of his time toward the last. His mind was perfectly free from doubt for months before death, talked as calmly about death as ever you heard him talk about any thing, made every arrangement for our comfort that he could, left every thing in my hands to go on just as we had done. We did not owe 5 dollars in the world. He had got a negro man to come and live on the place, I think he is a good fellow. I have a woman living in the kitchen who is a very good hand. Thus far we have got along very well. Johnny and Porter have been going to school all winter, but will have to stop now and work on the farm during the summer. I have been teaching Lacy and Annie myself. They done very well. We raised a good crop last year. Johnny and Porter are a great help to me. They are both large enough to plow. I hope they will be good boys and make useful men.

I feel that I have a great responsibility resting on me, but intend by the grace of God to do the very best I can, and I hope and pray that I may not be foolish to do as some widows do. I expect to have trials, but think I can live with my children as happy as I ever could live any other way, and besides, I don't feel that there is another person in this world in whom I could place the same confidence, or who could gain my affections as my dear Husband had. I know that I will have to spend many a lonesome hour, but as I told him, I will spend my lonesome hours in thinking of the many pleasant ones we had spent together. I was setting by him one day fanning him as he was dozing (for he sat up most of the time). He awoke and caught me weeping. He begged me not to do so, said it would not be a long separation, that he would only be in Heaven to meet me when I got there, said there would [be] a host there to meet me when I got there! O rapturous thought, that we will be again united in that world of Joy where our happiness will be complete.

You asked if he ever said anything about you. He seemed anxious to hear from you, but said he knew that you were engaged with your business. Said that he did hope you would make a useful man. Did you see his obituary and tokens of respect? If you did not, I can send them to you. He died very easy, just went to sleep. It was Sabbath evening of a communion at Alamance. Every respect that could be were shown to his remains. Mr. Tidball preached one of the most touching sermons that I ever heard. He appealed to the young men of the church to know who would take his place, said there was a fearful gap made in the front ranks and who would fill it? He preached from the text "whatsoever thy hand findeth to do, do it with thy might," Mr. Paisley's motto through life, given him by his good Mother. Dear Willie, you seem to be very happy. I am glad to see you so, but take care that this world does not occupy too much of your affections. I speak the language of experience when I say this. I think I have been taught the vanity of every thing in this world. How happy I was when I nursed my first babe, who has long since been taken from me I hope to a better world. Just half of our family I hope are safe in Heaven. What a strong magnet to draw those who are left behind.

Dear Willie I have written you a right long letter and I feel like I have not said half that I would like to say. Can't you come and see us some time again? If you ever go North, come this way if you can.

The children often talk of you. Lacy and Annie had you and your wife for visitors the other day in their play. They all send love to all, and say you must kiss your little boy for them, and tell him all about them when he is old enough, and you must both accept my love and best wishes and I want you to be sure to write to me. I must close by asking you again to write

Minerva W. Paisley

William Paisley to Emma Butler Paisley in Tulip

Dobyville, Arks
Mch 11th 1869

My dearest One:

I wrote you a hurried note last evening & after hearing that I would have an opportunity of sending to town tomorrow, thought I would write you a long letter, but I have now worked until it is so late & I am so sleepy & tired, that I will have to ask you to let me off with another note. You dont know how anxious I am about you, my dear one, as it has been impossible for me to hear from you since I left, though I shall expect a letter tomorrow evening. I can but feel that you are still up, although I know that the probabilities incline the other way. While the waters were so high, I feared that something might happen to my Emma & that she could not get me word, but I shall try & hope for the best, until I hear from you, & Oh how glad I would be to return & find you going about.

I cannot tell you when I will be over, but intend trying very hard to get off by Wednesday or Thursday next week. I have a great deal to do, but have been working till nearly midnight to get through. I am now sleeping in the store, & can work at night without being disturbed. I expect to make arrangement with the carpenter in a few days to build our house. He has my plan under consideration now, & will let me know in a few days what he will do the work for, & if we agree on the terms, will put in the bill for lumber right away. Wish I could see you to consult about the plan &c.

Mrs. McElhany is still *well*. Miss Mollie McCullum & Miss Effy were over this morning, & told me to give you their love. Mr. Orr has commenced his school & is talking of buying Mr. Culp's place. My dear one, you must really excuse me, but with all my efforts I find it almost impossible to keep awake. I am so tired and sleepy. What I have written is not worth sending but I will let it go. Be sweet and cheerful, my dear little one, & if possible do not get sick until I come. Kiss our dear little boy for his papa & tell him that he must be a good boy & not trouble his Ma.

May our Heavenly Father bless & protect you is the prayer of your loving husband

Wm Paisley

P.S. Darling I must have left a roll of money in the tray of your trunk. Please see that it is taken care of. There was $400.00 in the roll.

Yrs &c
W. P.

Emma Butler Paisley to William Paisley in Dobyville

Tulip
March 11, 1869

My dear *husband,*

Little John is just seventeen months old to-night. I reckon you have been thinking of it, and wondering if your Emma is sick while you are away. I wrote last Monday, but don't think the letter will reach you till the last of this week, if then. I write now, thinking if you do get it, it will afford you a great deal of satisfaction and if not, there will be nothing lost. Sister Mollie, cousin Mat, and the children spent to-day with us—you may know we had some noise. We have not heard any thing from sisters Mary and Annie since you left, but think we will hear something by to-morrow's mail. There was no mail Wednesday on account of high water. Sister did not get off till Wednesday morning—Mr. Johnson went up with her. Mr. George Lea passed through Tulip last Wednesday on his way to St Louis.

Well Burke's Weekly has come at last—that contains an answer to the long sought riddle—and the name is Stephen (Step-hen)—now is it not simple?

Dr. Coulter spent a day or so with sister Mollie the first of the week. He was just from New

Orleans—he recognized brother Henry on the boat, but did not think brother H knew him. Good night and pleasant dreams, I must prepare for bed and finish to-morrow if well enough.

Friday morning

What a lovely day! How is my dear one spending his time? I missed you last night in helping me look for the fleas that were biting little John. I found one but did not catch it.

I have not heard from you since you left, but shall look for a letter to-night. I expect this is the last time you will hear from me till you come over. How is your little name sake getting on? Mrs. Pattillo has named her baby "Mary Ella" after herself and sister.

I found a roll of money in my trunk the other day that I did not know was there. It has five hundred dollars marked on it. Have you needed it?

Good bye till I see you. May the good Lord bless you my dear one, and may we both be better Christians, is the prayer of your loving

Emma

William Paisley to Emma Butler Paisley in Tulip

Steamer "Liberty No 2"
12 Miles below Memphis
Friday Mch 26th, 1869

My dear loving Emma:

I wrote you a hurried & unsatisfactory note from Little Rock & did not think of writing again until I got to Memphis, thinking the Boat would get there "on time," which could give me some six or ten hours to spend in Memphis before the train would start to St. Louis. But we were detained a great deal on the trip taking on and unloading heavy freight, and it is now just two o'clock P.M. The train leaves for St Louis fifteen minutes before four so that we will not more than make the connection (if we do that). So I must scribble you another note with a pencil while the boat is in motion & shaking terribly, as I could not be satisfied to pass Memphis with out letting my dear little one—who is doubtless still in bed thinking of her absent husband—hear from me. Oh, how much I would give this evening to know how you & the dear little babies are getting on. You were all so well when I left that I can but think I have but little cause for uneasiness, but the fact of having to leave you in bed while our sweet little *Willie* was still so young makes me anxious. One thing, however, always consoles me when I am absent & that is that my darling is a little *woman* & will not disturb herself unnecessarily & that she will not get sick as long as she can help it.

As I wrote in my last note, we did not get to Little Rock Tuesday evening until after dark. My *business* there kept me up until nearly twelve o'clock, after having traveled all night the night before without sleep, & do not feel that I have yet entirely recovered my lost sleep & rest, though I am feeling very well & getting my sleep back both day & night, & hope to be fresh & vigorous by the time I get to St Louis. Mr. Young & Maj Smith have proved themselves to be very pleasant traveling companions, also the young man who is going to St Louis who I mentioned in my note.

My Boat is the same one that I traveled on last fall. Last night the young folks danced until 12 o'clock. Maj Smith participated while Mr. Young & myself acted as spectators. But I must ask some thing about our little John who I suppose is still partially separated from both his Ma & Pa. You don't know how badly I felt when I came by to tell that dear little fellow good bye & could hear him crying after me some time after getting out of the gate. I know that his grandma is just as good to him as we could possibly be, but it makes me feel sorry for him to think that with all his affection for his ma he is deprived of being with her *all* the time.

The passengers are now astir getting their baggage out, & I must close.

You must not suffer yourself to get lonesome, or think that you are troubling the loved ones at home because you have to be waited on, for I know they take pleasure in doing every thing you require.

Tell sisters Mary & Annie that we have quite a number of nice young men aboard, & that if they were only with me I think they could be better supplied with beaux than they were on the *Gov. Allen.*

With many kisses for my little Emma, John & Willie, I am as Ever

> Your loving husband
> Wm. Paisley

Love to all.

3 o'clock

We are now in sight & will be off in a few minutes. Will make connection by hurrying.

> Good bye
> WP

William Paisley to Emma Butler Paisley in Tulip

> [St. Louis]
> Sunday night Mch 28th 1869

My dear absent wife:

My old Charlotte friend, who accompanied me to church to night, has just left, & it is now after ten o'clock, but knowing my sweet little wife never tires getting letters from me no matter how hurried or uninteresting they might prove to others, I cannot retire satisfied until I write to her.

Our Boat arrived at Memphis just in time for us to get to the Depot before the train started to St Louis, so I lost no time, & got here yesterday evening at 2 o'clock.

I am stopping at the Planters House, which is a first Class Hotel & every thing as far as I have been able to see promises a pleasant & profitable stay in St. Louis.

Yesterday evening after changing my Linen, I went out & called on nearly all of my merchant friends—all of whom *as a matter of course* were very *happy* to meet me. I didn't have time to examine goods to any extent, but looked around enough to satisfy me that I had done well in coming here, & that I would be able to purchase goods on more reasonable terms than I had anticipated. The best Calicos—for instance—I can buy at 12 cts & the best yard wide Domestic at 16½ cts, & other staple goods in proportion.

This morning at half after ten o'clock I attended the Smithby [?] Methodist Church, & heard a most excellent religious Sermon by Rev. Wm Rush of the Mo. Conference. His text was the 15th ver of the 57th chap of Isaiah—thought the sermon did full justice to the beautiful text. To night I attend Dr. Brooks (Presbyterian) Church & had another first in the way of a Sermon. How much I wish we could enjoy such Heaven sent privileges every Sabbath at home. It seems to me that if we could, it would be much easier to live the life of a Christian. Those who can enjoy such privileges don't seem to appreciate them—as the Drinking & Gambling Saloons are all kept open here on Sunday, & on our way home from church we came by a 2nd or 3rd rate theater crowded with a noisy set, who seemed to be unmindful of the fact that there was a hereafter or any thing of the kind.

After Dinner to day I went with an acquaintance out to Lafayette Square, which is located in an elevated part of the city & from which you can get a view of a large portion of St Louis. There appeared to be about twelve or fifteen acres in the square, & all in a very fine state of improvement in the way of Shrubbery, Shade Trees, Grapes &c.

I was so hurried in Memphis that I did not have time to telegraph Lewis. Consequently, I did not see him as I came through Cairo at three o'clock at night. I will try & see him on my return.

Well it is late and I must try & get ready for work by morning. How are you & our dear little babies getting on. I could fill a whole sheet asking questions about you but that would neither be interesting to you or profitable to me if I cannot get an answer till I come. Could I only know that you are continuing to do well I would be perfectly satisfied to remain here as long as my business would require. I shall try however to be contented hoping for the best. May our Heavenly [Father] bless & protect you all is the prayer of

> Your devoted husband
> Wm. Paisley

Many kisses for you all. Tell John he must be a good little boy till his papa gets home.

Darling I must ask you to excuse this letter, which I have had to write suddenly & hurriedly, fearing that I might not have time tomorrow. You don't know how much I would like to see you, my dear sweet one. But you must not get impatient, as I shall hurry matters as much as possible. I am almost ready to say that I will leave here next Monday evening—but I may find it impossible to get off as soon as that.

> Yours affectionately & truly
> W. P.

Love to all

William Paisley to Emma Butler Paisley in Tulip

> St Louis Mo
> Apl 1st 1869

My dear precious one

It has just been ten days to night since I left my dear wife and little babies, & it really seems to me that it has been so many weeks. How, oh how, are my Emma & little ones getting on? You don't *know* how uneasy I get about you at times. The idea of leaving you in bed & having to be here harrassed with business & unable to hear from you is terrible. Still, I feel that I can trust that all is right & that you by this time feel as well as ever—although it is yet too soon for you to leave your room—and that little Willie is doing well—has doubtless learned how to cry by this time. As for our little John, he has been in good health so long, & is such a mischievous little saucy fellow, I can hardly feel that any thing would make him sick.

Well darling, I have been working hard all day & some at night, trying to get through with all my business in time to start home next Monday evening. If I succeed in getting off then, I will be with you next Saturday morning week, though do not be uneasy if I do not come then, as I may not get off & even if I do, I may miss a connection some where on the road, which would delay me one trip at least. I did not commence buying till Monday morning, & am now through with Dry Goods—Hats—Crockery—Hardware, Saddlery, Stationery & Drugs—all my bills are yet to settle, besides three or four more yet to buy. I have also filled some of my private orders, but am not through with them yet. I had to walk nearly a mile to-night (after it got too dark to buy goods) to get 14 sewing machine needles for Mrs. Judge Coleman. I bought ours and Charlie's furniture this morning, & with the lot got a nice high chair for John to sit in by his mama at the table. I also bought Miss Kate's & Alice's bonnets this morning.

Goods of every kind are cheaper than I expected to find them & I have been purchasing pretty freely, & will buy even more than I expected when I came. I get the best calicos at 12½ cents— Printed muslins (fast colors) for 15 cts. the best heavy Domestics for 16 cts. and some that is good—shirting width for 11 cents. You would doubtless laugh at me if you could see the quantity of La's [Ladies'] Hats I have bought—but we have never yet had enough in the spring and I determined that if we did not this time it would not be my fault.

I have bought Henry's Hats and wish I could bring them with me, but it will be impossible as I have so many other things to put in my trunk. Tell him I have bought more than he ordered, & that he can tell the young ladies if they will only wait he will be able to sell them the very latest style. I wish Henry had come with me, for I am satisfied if he was here he might invest two thousand dollars in goods that he could sell at a good profit.

I attended church last night, & heard another excellent sermon from Dr. Brooks. The night before I bought goods until eleven o'clock. I have not visited any of the places of amusement yet, & do not know that I will, as I understand they are nothing extra just at this time.

Last Monday night one of the largest fires occurred here that has been witnessed by the citizens for a long time. One of the steam Boats lying in front of the city took fire, & before they could get the others out of the way, seven (7) took fire & were burned to the water's edge. Nearly all the boats were loaded, & some ready to start out the next morning. Two lives were lost. The boats first commenced burning on the St. Louis side of the river, but they were cut loose from the wharf & four of them drifted against the opposite bank and were burned together. It was a beautiful night— but not to witness such destruction of property. While standing & looking on, I could but think how interesting & novel such a sight would be to my Emma if she could only witness it on her first trip *into the world*. While the fire was raging I reckon there must have been fifty thousand persons on the levee or street next the river, while it was light as day for some distance all around.

Well darling, I fear I have already taxed your patience so I must close, & I reckon it will be useless for me to write again before starting home. I am very anxious to get to Memphis to get your letter. I shall try & see Lewis on my return, but it will only be in passing—for if I do not get to Memphis in time to leave there (Memphis) Tuesday, I will be detained there until the next Saturday.

May God bless my dear little wife & babies is the prayer of their devoted husband & father

Wm Paisley

My dear one I really *hate* to stop at Lewis', but I have not seen him in so long, but it is now late & I must get to sleep. Be sweet & cheerful. With many kisses

> your loving husband
> W. P.

I thought I could find a paper to send you, giving an account of the fire, but can't lay my hands on one now. Good bye

> W. P.

William Paisley to Emma Butler Paisley in Tulip

> Dobyville
> Apl 16th 1869

My dear absent one:

You will no doubt be surprised when I tell you that I came all the way yesterday & arrived here last night between eight & nine o'clock. Just as I was leaving Arkadelphia, I fell in company with Mr. Carglo who told me that he intended going to Okolona before he slept, & I rode on with him. When night overtook us I was only six or seven miles from Dobyville (I can't call it home while my dear ones are away) & having good company, I concluded to come through & let the horses rest all day today.

Mr. Doby blew the light out to go to bed just as I rode up, but I called him out & he dressed, & after putting the horses up, prepared us something to eat. Miss Johnson went in Mrs. Doby's room & Mr. D, Geo. Doby & myself occupied our old room. I have before spoken of my feelings while being in the room without you & John, but I really don't think I ever missed you as much as I did last night. Every thing in the room has been changed, & I feel so painfully lonely in it without you that I *really* would rather sleep in the store than to occupy it without you.

Mr. Doby & myself are in here again tonight. I don't know what disposition they intend making of me. The bed has been moved from the store, and both lounges are now being occupied by two men who are ditching for Mr. Doby. I have been riding all day until nearly dark tonight, trying to get wagons to go after goods & as yet have only partially succeeded. Four or five are willing to go, but there seems to be something in the way of all that I saw getting off except two. I think two of the men I saw will get off Monday morning. Both have ox teams. Mr Clark says he will haul a load for us & will probably go Monday. Mr. McGill also thinks he can haul a load some time during the week. So I think the chances are pretty good for us to get as many as five wagons to start next week.

I found the bill of shoes—ordered from New York—here when I came (I mean the Bill, not Shoes) which—judging from the bill was filled very satisfactory—wish Henry could see it—think he would renew his orders on New York for goods of that kind in preference to purchasing in any other market. I now think that I will in the future buy all our Shoes from that house.

But enough about business connected with the store, & I must really ask you to pardon me for writing so much about it. Since I came over I have been so much engaged in trying to get our goods here, that I have not had time to make any arrangements for getting my dear ones with me.

I have been thinking, however, about how it would do to move into our little cabin until our house is finished. I have not had time to look for a boarding house, & think in fact that it would be almost useless to do so, but until I think about the matter more, I can't see how we could get along keeping house very well in that "one cabin," as we would have to use it as a smoke house, kitchen-dining room, sleeping room, every thing. Also besides, you would have to have either a nurse or a cook one, & with no other building we would have no place to keep any one.

I understand to day that my bill of lumber is all sawed, & I expect to have it hauled next week. Mr. Speaks (the carpenter) says he thinks he will soon finish the church, & that he will have our house ready for us in six weeks. I will have our provisions &c brought from Camden as soon as possible, & if we then think we can make out for a short time in our Cabin—which we can make a Palace if we are only contented & happy, I will either come or send after you. I am anxious to have you with me while the work is going on, for then we can consult together better how we want the work done, where the windows, doors &c should be, & where to place the kitchen. Oh, Darling, we will be so happy when we get to our own home with our own dear little children around us. It seems to me that we will then realize our responsibilities as parents & enjoy the relations we sustain to each other more than we have ever done—May our Heavenly Father grant that we may make all (with the guidance of His wisdom & grace) redown to His Glory. My dear one, I have been thinking much this evening (notwithstanding I have been so busy) of my dear sweet wife—how precious she is to me & of her many sweet qualities. You must be patient my dear one, & be assured that I will do all I can to have you with me as soon as I can.
Haven't time to look over
[No signature, though this seems to be the conclusion]

William Paisley to Emma Butler Paisley

Dobyville, Arks
Sunday night Apl 25th 69

My dear sweet one:

I was delighted this evening to get your precious letter of the 21st and can assure you, my dear one, that I had not thought of blaming you for not writing, although my failing to get a letter last Thursday made me quite uneasy and caused me to fear that my own one was sick—as you was not very well when I left. Billy Grier went to town last Thursday, & thinking you would not put off writing longer than Monday, and as the mail that leaves Tulip Monday night gets to Arkadelphia Thursday morning, I fully expected Billy would bring me a letter & about dusk I shut up and went down to old Mr. Doby's & could hardly realize it was so, when Billy told me that he had nothing for me. I spent the night with Billy, but did not see much of Mrs. Grier, only at the table. Her cook has left her again, & she has to do all her cooking & household work.

Friday evening I saw a young man going to town & asked him to bring the mail out. He returned yesterday & when he told me that he had no letter for me I felt I couldn't stand it any longer, & notwithstanding the fact that we were looking for two loads of goods every minute, had I consulted my feelings I would have started to Tulip immediately. This evening Jimmie Fairburn handed me your letter, which he brought out yesterday, and which relieved all my fears & anxiety.

I think your excuse for not writing is a very good one, & am glad that you could work on your quilt while you could get assistance from those who are willing to help. I know that you must have thought it very strange of me when you thought that *I* had not written by George Doby, as it would be hard for me to miss such an opportunity of writing something to my Emma.

When I wrote by George Doby I had not had time to mature any plans as to what we would do, but since thinking about the matter more, & I must say, since having to stay so long away from my dear one, I have concluded that we can all (including Ella [Lipscomb, his stepsister]) make out very comfortably in our little cabin for three or four weeks, and if you are perfectly willing to try it—as soon as I can get our furniture & provisions from Camden I will try & make some arrangements to get you over. I am very much afraid that it will be impossible to get any kind of conveyance & team here, but if it is not convenient for your Pa to let his wagon come, I must try & get some one, as I am not willing for us to live separated from each other as we have been for the last four months—much longer.

We commenced receiving goods yesterday & have other wagons out that will be coming in during the present week, and I will be very busy for some time to come, but if there is any chance whatever for me to get off, I want to be with you when you move, for I know better what my dear one needs than any body else, & think I can be of more service to you than any body else can—to say nothing of the pleasure of being with you—Another reason why I am anxious to come is that I would like for us to have our little Willie baptized as soon as we can & as it would be more pleasing to have it done at home, I would like to have it done before we move over, as there is no telling when we will get back again.

I am sorry that I cannot write more definitely about what I can do, but our provisions &c are still in Camden & I am not certain that I can get a wagon to go after them this week & it would not do for us to move until we get something to eat & sleep on. As soon as I find out more I will write.

Monday morning

Darling I got so sleepy last night that I couldn't finish my letter & now I only have a minute. Mr. Rush has come along going to town, & has promised to wait on me a minute, & fearing that I may not have another opportunity, I will close what I have written & send it on. We received two loads goods Saturday evening late & expect four more to day & another about Tuesday or Wednesday. We opened those recd Saturday night & have the most of them marked. Only a small proportion of the two loads were Dry Goods, one box Fcy Dry Goods & one box mostly filled with pants goods & a few Ladies Dress goods. No calicos yet.

Darling I am sorry that I can't write more, but you must take the will for the deed. I almost dread the present week's work, as we will be very busy, both opening & selling. Shan't read the letter—no more time. Be sweet & cheerful & kiss the babies for their papa & tell them they shan't stay away from him always.

And you, my dear one, must know how happy we will be when you see me. Will write again soon. Hoping to get another letter from you soon.

I am yours lovingly
W. Paisley

Love to all.

William Paisley to Emma Butler Paisley in Tulip

Dobyville, Ark
Apl 28th 1869

My dearest one

You have often heard me say that I was tired—but I don't know when I have been so completely *worn out* as I am to night, but as this is my birth day, I must say one word to my *dearer self* before I leave the store. Mr. D has just left to go to bed. We worked last night & the night before, trying to get the goods open & out of the way until 11 & 12 o'clock, & still every thing is in perfect confusion & we have not been able to even open some goods recd last Monday. Yet you never saw such a rush for goods. We never had any thing like it before. We rec'd some goods last Saturday & got the most of them open (2 loads) that night. Monday evening we got four more loads & have been run off our feet ever since. To day we had old man Doby, W. Doby, Mr. Patterson & myself all busy selling, & could not begin to wait on all who came to buy. I did not stop even a minute for Dinner, notwithstanding the fact that Mrs Doby had a *Ginny* (don't know how to spell it) & some other extras because I told her it was my birthday. We took in about eighty dollars cash. I have not had time to estimate the credit sales but think they amount to the neighborhood of four hundred dollars if not more. I would like very much for you to be here to see the new goods & to select such as you will need before they are picked over. If there is any thing at all that you will want please let me know immediately.

How much I want my dear ones with me. I could then have some relief from the busy scenes of the day by enjoying their sweet society. You don't know, my dear one, how poorly I get along without you. I can but feel that I am separated from my better self. And another thing. Our dear little Willie it seems, is getting to be a big little baby, while his papa is deprived of the pleasure of watching his little boy's infant innocence. How does our little mischievous little John get on. Does he even think of his papa now? Has he learned to talk yet? My dear one, I grow impatient & more restless when I think of all these things. You must be contented, as I have no doubt you are. As soon as I can possibly get our Bedsteads & Mattresses from Camden, I will make some arrangements to get you over. The Cabin will be very *comfortable* & nice I think, & if we meet with no further delays or disappointments, it will not be long before we can move into our new house. The Church can be finished in two weeks, & Mr. Speaks has employed more workmen & can finish our building in three or four weeks if not less time.

Darling, excuse my hurried notes. One word from you is always cheering to me & I will judge you by myself. Write often and believe me as ever yours in love

W. Paisley

Kiss the babies & Love to all.

William Paisley to Emma Butler Paisley in Tulip

Dobyville Arks
Apl. 29th 1869

My darling Emma:

Since writing last night I have summed up yesterday's sales & find that they amount to Five hundred & thirty one dollars & fifty cents, $531.50 including cash & credit. Don't you think that is doing pretty well for our little store, & that too with only part of our stock on hand & part of that not opened.

Today our sales have not been so large, but I think will foot up between two and three hundred dollars. Every thing we have goes off well with no complaints at all of prices. In fact the people buy like was a privilege to do so, & the only difficulty we have is in not being able to wait on all who come. Several had to leave this evening, because we did not have time to wait on them. We only have twelve (12) Ladies hats on hand to night. The Ladies fine dress goods both white & [colored] are going off rapidly. Will try & send you some samples in this if I have time in the morning. I think our sales this week will amount to $1500.00 if not more. Our crockery—Wooden and Tin ware, part of Grocery & hardware & Stationery bills, & our own furniture, bedding &c is still behind & as the waters are so high, I fear that we will be troubled to get them. One large six-ox wagon is now on the road some where, water bound. I shall send after our other goods as soon as I can get a wagon, & then I want you, my own one, to come *as soon as possible.*

Although it is extremely unpleasant for me to live as I am now doing, I don't know but what it is well enough for us that we did not commence keeping house just before moving the goods, for we would have no conveniences in our Cabin & it would give me a great deal of trouble for you to have to commence keeping house & have so much to do & be unable to help you. I have written to *Honorable* Mrs. Jett or Samuels (Colored) of Washington to hire me a cook, & am using every exertion in my power to get one, but the chances look very gloomy for the present. Could I only be with you as much as I would like, I believe I would not trouble myself about one—as I think with my assistance we could do every thing except washing & get along finely. Don't you think so? If you think you can get Martha & that she will be satisfied to come over & stay until you can go to Tulip I suspect you had better secure her, as she could be of good service in getting wood, cleaning up &c. Shall expect a long letter from you by the next passing from town. I would like now my self to come over next Saturday night to see my dear ones, but reckon there is no chance. My dear one be sweet & happy & love your *absent husband* a heap. Tell little John that he must not forget his papa, that he must be a good boy—May God bless you all is the prayer of loving husband

W. Paisley

Oh I like to forgot. In opening a case of shoes to day I found a little bundle in one of the boxes & on opening it found a nice little pair of No. 2 fancy baby shoes, with a piece of paper in one, on which the merchant stated that they were a present for the *little stranger.* Wouldn't fit in my letter. Wish you had them.

Yours affectionately with a kiss & reluctant good night.

W. Paisley

William Paisley to Emma Butler Paisley in Tulip

Dobyville Arks
May 3rd 1869

My own precious Emma

Your sweet little letter of 26th Apl. was handed me this evening and I was delighted to hear from my dear ones again & to know that although they are away from me, they are well & happy. Your letters always contain volumes, my dear one, even if they do not cover much paper, but my imagination could not help figuring out something of what my darling meant when she said she had a great deal to say to me if she only had time. My dear one, it is one of Heaven's best gifts to be loved by a dear sweet good woman as I am loved by my darling Emma & I feel that no man was ever blessed in that particular more than my dear wife's husband.

But we must not allow our affection for each other to lessen our love & adoration for our Heavenly Father, who endows us with such a Holy Faculty. For He is a jealous God & justly claims that our love & affection should centre on him & redown alone to his glory. I have thought at times that my love for you almost amounted to idolatry, but we are licensed by the Bible to love each another even as Christ loves the Church. So there is no danger of committing that sin so long as we do not allow our love for each other to interfere with that, for the Giver of all the Blessings we enjoy.

Your mentioning our dear little Wille & John makes me so anxious to see the precious little creatures again. I really think little Willie is a perfect Giant for his age. John did not weigh that much when he was three or four months old. He may have weighed that much to[o] but not more than that. Has John learned to talk yet? I am getting anxious to hear of his doing something in that way, though I take it for granted that he has made no improvement or you would have mentioned it. Tell him that he must learn to say something besides *No & Now* by the time his Papa comes.

I have not recovered entirely from the fatigue of last week yet, but we do not have to work at night now & I think a few good nights' sleep will make me all right again. You can form no idea of how much work we had to do. I have not counted up the sales of the week yet but think they will amount to at least eighteen hundred dollars & they may go to two thousand, if not over run it. One day we sold $530.50 & another $340.00 & I believe the other days will come up near three hundred each. Our calicos are now half gone & it doesn't seem to me that one fourth of our customers have been in yet.

Glad to hear that the Bride's Bonnet is at Tulip. She could not come out to church yesterday on account of the disappointment, & this morning She came down & bought one of our fine Hats—with the understanding, however, that she could return it any time during the present week—if we should hear that her bonnet was packed with Henry's goods. [No conclusion—possibly another page missing]

Emma Butler Paisley to William Paisley in Dobyville

Tulip
May 10th, 1869

My precious darling,

Let me commence by thanking you for your dear loving letters, which I received last Saturday morning. I did not write to you last week, thinking that you would certainly come after me. I reckon by this time you have every thing from Camden, so I will expect you this week. If you can possibly spare the time, I want *you* to come over yourself, for as you said in your letter I had rather have you with me than any one else.

Martha had a chill the other day—she says her mammy says she is not willing for her to go with me because it is too far from home. Martha's sister died last week, which is one cause I expect of her getting out of the notion of going with me. I don't want you to trouble yourself so much about getting some one to live with us, for I am willing to try doing without any one, since I have *you* for my husband. If you are contented and happy, I will feel perfectly satisfied. But I must talk about something else.

I attended church yesterday and heard a most excellent sermon from brother Hunter. His text is found in Malachi, last three verses of the third chapter. I wish so much you could have been here and we could have had our own little Willie baptized in the evening. Brother Hunter leaves tomorrow. I had rather have him to baptize little Willie than most anyone else—that is if you have no other choice. By the way have you decided on a name for him yet, and what is it? I went to church last Friday night and heard brother Caldwell—the first time I have been to preaching since I went with you to Okolona. I would have taken little John with me yesterday, had I been certain he would have behaved himself. Last night the little fellow waked and I had to take him up and whip him before he would hush crying. I reckon he must have been troubled with fleas, for I found several on his gown this morning. I believe I have not written you since we heard of the birth of sister Julia's baby—it is a little boy born 23rd April.

Ma sends her love, and says she is very glad to hear that you are doing so well in selling goods. She wants you to bring her over a pair of thread gloves, if you have any large enough and suitable for her.

I met with Mrs. Rainey one day last week at sister Mollie's. Her baby is nearly, if not quite, seven months old and has never been taken out of the house yet. I think there is no wonder they have such delicate looking children. Mrs. Cattie Young was down at her mother's a week or so ago—her health is still very delicate. Mrs. William Hunter is also in very bad health. Crisy and Tommy Coleman are now in the neighborhood. They were down with Kate and Alice Colburn to supper one night last week. Lem Smith and Pompey Matlock have both addressed Alice Colburn and both met with a discardal, but Pompey tells Alice he never undertook any thing in his life but he finally succeeded, so he is still going to see her. Annie told me this, but doesn't want it mentioned out of the family. Charley has given Kate an engagement ring, has the consent of her parents, and expects to marry between now and next November.

Have you had any strawberries? Ma had some yesterday for dinner. I wish you could have been here to enjoy them with us. And you did not have time to eat your birthday dinner—should have taken time any way, but it was just like you not to do so. If I ever have the honor of preparing you a birthday dinner if you don't come and get it *there will be a fuss in the family shure.*

Ma [Lipscomb] received a letter from sister Mary [Paisley Scott] last week—says her house will be finished in two months, when she and Charley will move into it. So I don't think she will beat me yet in getting to house keeping, that is, if we are not disappointed in our plans.

Has Mrs. Orr moved over to Clark? I heard someone say that she expected to go several weeks ago.

Sister Mary [Butler] received a letter from Miss Mary Cooper some three or four weeks ago stating that Mr. William Borden had sold out and was going North. Rebecca, Sallie, and Mr. Bray had already gone. I don't know who Rebecca is but it seems that she had disgraced herself, had a child and left it with her aunt, and she had gone with Bray and Sallie. If you remember, Sallie Borden married a Federal soldier and I think Bray is his name. It seems very strange that she should live with him if he has acted in that way. Miss Mary said it was well the family had left as they would not be countenanced by any one. Miss Mary stated that she supposed we had heard of the misfortune that had befallen the Borden family and then related what I have told you above. We were very much surprised to hear it—would like to know who Becca is—some think it is Sallie's sister; but I don't know whether she has a sister by that name or not.

Did you ever see such cool weather for May? It looks like we will have more rain soon, but I hope not much till I get over in Clark.

You ought to see John trying to walk over the rocks since I have pulled off his shoes. At first he could scarcely get about, but he does a little better now. He can't talk yet and has no more teeth that I know of. I thought he would have all his teeth before warm weather came again. Little Willie notices right smart now, and loves to be played with. I would like to see his little shoes but he will not need them before winter. All are well. Pa is out trying to hive some bees. Many kisses from little Willie, John, and

> Your loving
> Emma

I don't know that I will need any thing for myself, but if you have any thing suitable for making John aprons I wish you would lay it aside. Linen or cotton cheques will be more suitable than calico.

George Butler to Emma Butler Paisley in Dobyville

> Rural Home
> May 12th 1869

My dear Sister Emma

Your interesting and highly appreciated letter has been received and read with much interest by myself and others of the family. I wish I could write you an answer which would afford you as much interest and pleasure as I derived from yours. You must accept my congratulations in return, that you have become the mother of a second son. I feel sure that you will try to train him for Heaven. I believe this to be the end which every parent should constantly have in view, and by far the most important duty he owes his child. And the mother who gives birth to a goodly number of children and trains them for a happy immortality will have a bright crown of fadeless glory in the day of final retribution. She will then be repaid a hundred fold for all her sufferings and troubles in their behalf. Indeed, I do not think that woman can achieve a nobler mission than to

157

become the mother of immortal spirits stamped with the image of the great Creator, who shall sparkel as gems in her diadem when countless ages of eternity have rolled away. High and holy is the mission of the Christian Mother. If she is faithful to her trust, she will inherit a rich reward which shall increase throughout eternity.

From the very depths of my heart do I praise God for the inestimable blessing of Christian parents. God bless them in their declining years, and let their sun set in unclouded splendor to arise again with immortal glory in the resurrection morn. I expect to hail them happy on the plains of Heaven, and unite with them and you, my dear sister Emma, in shouting the praise of our great and glorious Redeemer.

We have named our little boy William Moores. He is a good baby. So says his Grandma Moores. He does very little yet but sleep and eat.

We have had a few strawberries this season. I had one nice mess. They are about all gone. The cut worms have been very bad in the gardens. Have almost destroyed the vegetables in some. Most of the fruit has been destroyed.

I am getting on moderately well on my circuit. Altogether I believe I like it better than Princeton Ct. It is not so large a circuit as Princeton Ct. I shall look for a letter from you when you get settled in your new home. Write me where it is and all about it. I think it quite doubtful about our getting to Hot Springs this summer. The quarterly meeting for this neighborhood is appointed to be held on the fifth Sunday in August, which was the time we expected to go. It is on brother Moore's circuit, and Julia and Sis Fannie would not like to be absent at that time. Besides we have no wagon that is suitable for such a trip.

Bro. Moores still expects to go to California next year if he can sell his place. If he goes, I will go too, but I do not much think we will get off next year.

Julia is going about again and is doing very well. She joins me in love to you and William and the babies. Kiss them both for me and write me something about your Willie in your next letter. What kind of eyes & hair has he? Our little Willie has dark grey eyes, I believe. We thought for a while they were black.

You go to housekeeping too late to have any garden, do you not? Hoping to receive a letter from you soon I remain—

Affectionately your brother,
George

Mrs. E. D. Lipscomb to Emma Butler Paisley in Dobyville

Tulip
June 3 1869

Dear Emma:

As I have a good opportunity to write, I thought I would send a sort of family letter, and write to all of you on one sheet.

We are all well at present. Husband's hand has gotten entirely well, and he is very proud to be able to work again. We have had fine rains for the last few days, and everything looks fine. I saw your Ma this morning. She told me they were all well. She gave me your letter to read. I was truly glad to here from you all, though I had herd from you since that letter was written. Mr. Orr called last Saturday morning, and sat with me some time. He told me all about you and Ella and the *Dear little boys*.

I am sorry to hear that you have the Whooping Cough in your neighborhood. Don't expose the children to it, and if it is in school, I don't think you ought to send Ella until the danger is past, as she has never had the Cough herself, and you have no Idea how much trouble it would give you; if they should take it, don't give them much medicine, as the Cough will have its course any how. I wish I was near enough to help you nurse those Dear little boys if they should take the Cough.

I had a letter from Mary yesterday. She says she will be out about the middle of July. I don't know how long she will stay; as she has been so long coming, I think I will try and keep her some time. She regrets so much not getting to see you and William and the Dear little boys. She says you treat her shabbily, that neither of you write to her.

Emma & Eliza [Lipscomb] send much love to you, say you must write to them. Emma is still teaching. You don't know what a cry she had when she came home and found out that you were all gone, and she did not get to see William.

I don't know any news that would interest you, as Tulip is a dull place. Kiss the Dear little boys for me. Tell John he must not forget grand Mamma. Write soon and often to your Mother

> E D Lipscomb

Dear William

Please to accept our warmest thanks for the bag of nice flour you sent by Ned. I don't know when I have had such a treat, and while I am on the subject of flour, I must say that I am glad to hear that you are such a good Cook. But I know with a little experience that Emma will soon beat you. Have you tryed to get Martha since you went back? Dick Littlefield told me that he saw Martha when he was in Clark, that she told him she thought she would go back and live with you, as she thought more of you and Emma than any boddy living. I think if you will try you can get her without much trouble. Ned was here at work yesterday. I asked him what I should write to you for him. He says he will go as soon as he gets through with Father's Work, but I don't much think he will, as it is a most too far from his old stamping ground, and he has taken up with a Negro woman in the Neighborhood. There is so little dependence in a freed man—If it does not rain any more today, Ned will get through here tomorrow, and I will try to persuade him to go, as he is a good hand if you can but get him to begin.

I want you to write to mamma often, and let me hear from your family and from Willis too, as I am always so glad to receive a letter from you.

Father and all join in love to you.

> Your devoted Mother
> E D Lipscomb

Dear Little Ella

I know you would feel slighted if I did not write you a few lines to let you know how we are getting on without you. Well, for the first few days, I couldn't help calling you when I wanted the table set or the churn churned, but I have quit that now, and have gotten used to doing without you.

I suppose you would like to know how every thing is going on, and what has happened since you left. Well, Jenny Lind has a calf, and they call him Rolly. Old High Comb and Carrie are both setting: Miss Boyd was in last Sunday, and made particular enquiry about you, Miss Lula Read also. Claud says he would like to see you, if you did pick at him when you was here. I don't know Dow's sentiment on the subject, but I reckon if his heart was sounded, he would like to have you here.

Ben and Elza Ann are still at Mrs. Wilson's. They never have been to Mr. Dyers'. Mr. Dyers met Elza Ann here last Tuesday evening for the first time since she was married. I don't know when I have witnessed a more affecting scene. He told her that she might come home, but he didn't tell her to bring Ben with her. Jim Toony and Ben have had a split, and what they will do, I can't tell. Ben speaks of going to Clark to try and get Brother Will to employ him, but I think he would find his wife in the way.

Emma and Eliza will both write to you soon. Eliza and I have a lonesome time all these long days. I want you to be a good girl and a smart girl, for I know Brother Will & Sister Emma will be kind to you. Father is still in the notion of going to Clark this Summer, and what would you think if you was to see Mamma coming too?

If you should take the whooping cough you must be prudent, and guard against cold or wet feet, be prudent and it will soon run its course. Kiss Dear little John for me many times, & Willie too. Tell them grand Ma does want to see them so much. You must be good and kind to Willis, poor, Dear wayward boy.

Write soon and often, and I will be prompt to write you. All join in love to you.

Your devoted mother E D Lipscomb

Now, I don't want you to laugh at my letter, but like good children, write to me.

Mary Butler to Emma Butler Paisley in Dobyville

Tulip
June 3rd 1869

Dear Emma—

I feel very little in the humor for writing this evening, but will make an effort any way, as Mr. Orr is going over tomorrow, and besides I promised to do better than heretofore about writing. Cousin Willie Kittle is visiting us; he came last Saturday—just from Sardis, Miss, where his brother is in business. I reckon he will remain with us some time. He expects to take his brother's place in the fall.

Pa and Ma are spending the day at Sister's. Brother George came up to see us last Monday, staid only one day and took Annie back with him. She was expecting to go down with pa—will be gone about two weeks, then pa will go for her.

The examination comes off the 16th-17th of this month. I have a great deal of work to do before that time—haven't made my linen yet. I embroidered the blue delain sack and sent it by Annie to Julia's baby. It looked very sweet. Ma sent two calicos and a white dress.

We received a letter from brother Lewis this morning. He says he is fully satisfied that he has met the lady who of all others has it in her power to make him happy and he has told her so. Her name is Jennie Bowman (I wish it had been some other name) she is pretty, intelligent, modest, sweet &c&c—eighteen or nineteen years of age, she is engaged in teaching in one of the schools in Cairo; her mother is a widow living near Springfield. I think they will probably marry next fall.

If so, he will bring her out to see us: He didn't say any thing about coming this summer to see us. His whole letter was a description of the young lady—He wishes it kept altogether within the family.

We had a very nice picnic down in the neighborhood of Mrs. Matlock's about three weeks ago. Annie and I went the evening before and spent the night with Mollie, most of the young folks from here were there—went down in wagons. Capt. Duffie—lawyer from Benton, was here at the time and carried Alice Colburn down in his buggy. Alice continues to be quite a belle. Charly can hardly get an opportunity of talking privately with Kate, there are so many young men there.

Pa expected you to keep the chairs which you rode home in, it seemed rather to disturb him because you didn't. Give my love to brother Billy, and kiss the sweet little children for me. Ma was very glad to get your letter, if she was at home would send some word. I have missed you and the children very much. I learn that Mrs. Maurice Smith has hired Martha. Write soon to your sister

> Mary

I send you some things that you left by Mr. Orr.

Henry Butler to William Paisley in Dobyville

Tulip Ark
June 4th 1869

Dear Billy:

Your two letters of recent date rec'd and your wishes attended to as far as possible. Mr. Orr will explain matters in regard to the Clifton letter. I sent it to Clifton the very day it was rec'd. In re-gard to Ned and Jacob—the latter is working in the neighborhood and I have not been able to communicate with him. Ned is just closing his engagement with Capt L., and says he will come over to work for you "as soon as he can." I don't rely much on that, for he is out of employment and says he has to go to Arkadelphia tomorrow "after his watches." Now why don't he go on to your place?

The fact is Ned dislikes to leave the vicinity of Tulip. There is a negro woman below here he *claims as his wife.* I have more confidence in Jacob, and think he would probably come over if his time is out. I will see him and do what I can. Bird is preparing to burn a kiln of ware and I will try and send you a load soon.

I am glad you have moved into your new home. However small the house may be it is Home—your "castle" and produces a feeling far different from any thing you have ever experienced. Doesn't it? I rejoice in your prospect for doing well, and hope your fondest anticipations may be more than realized.

Bro George paid us a flying visit this week. Carried Annie back with him. We have a cousin out from N.C., William Kittle, a steady good young man and wants employment—as clerk I believe. Lewis has been heard from, and I learn (for I haven't seen his letter yet) is *enamoured* with some young lady up near Cairo—which is in Ky, Ill, or Mo. I don't know.

My business is fair, am exercising more caution in crediting, as the crop prospect is not quite so favorable over this way—what is the prospect for cotton over your way? Hope *our tenants* (that sounds a little like the English *nobility*) are doing well, and will bring us in an income above the net payment on the land. I have just sent an order to Evans Gardner for some goods—my prints are all gone except a few remnants.

Mr. Orr is waiting so good bye. Success to you. Write me soon.

Yours &c
Henry A Butler

Annie Butler to Emma Butler Paisley in Dobyville

Tulip
July 21st, 1869

My Dear Sister,

Brother Charlie wrote to you by the last mail, but sister Mary says he gave you no news scarcely, so I will endeavor to give you a little more talk than he did, but we can all excuse him under the *circumstances.* His thoughts run on *one subject now.* I suppose he told you all about himself, and gave you a pressing invitation to come over in August. Cant you come? We would be so glad to see you all. I am expecting a nice time.

How do you like house keeping? We were very glad to hear you had Martha with you again. The weather is too warm to cook. I know it must have gone very hard with you to work such hot weather, but you had a kind husband to assist you, and I know he did his part. When we heard he had gone to Little Rock, I didn't know how in the world you would get along. He makes a good husband, but I can't say he makes a good brother-in-law. He would not come by to see us. Tell him never mind, I didn't like it one bit.

Ma says she often thinks of you when she has a cool drink of water, and wishes you could have it plentifully. We had both wells cleaned out today, so we have had but little fresh water, but it is some cooler today, so we didn't need it so much, and then we have water melons which answer the same purpose; we have had some very nice ones today.

Cousin Johnnie Butler brought cousin Laura, Flora, and the baby to see us yesterday evening. We were so glad to see them. Cousin Johnnie left this morning, the others will remain until Saturday. Cousin Jimmie will come up Friday. She and sister Mary are spending the day with sister Mollie, and are going to stay with sister to night and to morrow. Ma has gone over to spend the evening with them. Said she wanted to write when I wrote, but I told her she could write next week. Says she owes you and bro. Billy both a letter and says she intends paying it before long. Alice also speaks of writing soon.

I reckon you heard I had been to see bro. George and sister Julia, staid with them almost two weeks, enjoyed myself greatly, it is indeed a pleasant family. Bro. George and sister Julia seem to be very happy, and think they have one of the best, little Willie, in the world. I think he resembles sister Julia, but she and some others think he is like his Pa.

Returning home I went by to see the two bachelors, and spent a night with them. You have no idea how I enjoyed it. It was about four o'clock in the evening when Cousin Willie and I got there, and they were off in the field some distance. They looked for us at dinner, but bro. Charlie had given us out, but Johnnie said he knew I would come for it was just like me. So they put two chairs in the passage for us, thought they had their doors fastened securely, but I managed to get in and found my way all over the place. I found most every thing but the salt. I wanted to fix their butter up for them, but could find no salt. I had my own fun that evening sure. Brother Charlie looked like some old woman going around getting out supper. I laughed at him a good deal, but he thought I could not laugh *much longer*. What do you think of brother Louis? Were you not surprised? Soon one half the family will be married.

Mr. Johnson is preparing the parsonage for himself and bride, so I tell him, but he says I will be disappointed.

Maj. Smith and bride made their arrival about three weeks ago. Sally looks quite natural. I expected she would put on many airs, but was agreeably disappointed. I first met with her at our tableaux we had a night or two after they got home. The tableaux were gotten up by Cora Reid and Calie Barbee, for the purpose of having the grave yard paled in. We did'nt make more than $30, not enough to do much good. Mr. Leiper expects to have some more in Aug. for the purpose of repairing the school house.

I think Mr. Roberson has almost given up all hope of ever getting his Virginia sweetheart. There is still some talk of Ruth Smith and Bob Banks marrying. Alice Colburn is the *Belle* of *Tulip*. She has seven beaux, enough for one girl, don't you think? Pompey's visits were *very frequent*—before he left for Tenn. Capt. Duffy of Benton is the seventh, and his fate *was* that of the six, but *now* I think there is *some* hope for him. Alice is a very sweet girl, but I think rather young to marry, and I don't know that she will marry *very soon*, but it would not surprise me.

I have been looking all the week for Mr. Tannehill, Miss Mary Cooper, Eloise Jenkins, and Anna Colburn. Capt. Cooper said they were coming over. He has been home two weeks, will return to the bluff next Tuesday. Cousin Willie expects to go with him that far. I am looking for Bro Pope this or next week.

How are you all getting on? Write me every thing about you all. And Ella is delighted, so Mrs. Lipscomb was telling me. Much love to bro. Billy and a kiss for the children. Write very soon to

Your loving Sister
Annie Butler

Mrs. E. D. Lipscomb to Emma Butler Paisley in Dobyville

[Tulip]
July 23 1869

Dear Emma

Your very welcome letter was received in due time. You don't know how glad we all were to here from you all, and especially to here that those dear little Boys didnt have the hooping cough. I would have written sooner, but I have been sick for the last three weeks, confined to my bed most of the time, and before I was able to do any thing, Eliza was taken down and a few days after, Dow was taken sick. I sent for Emma. She came home last week and has been at home all of this week. We are all better now, and I think with prudence we will soon be well again. We are all up now. Well, Mary has been to see me. She came out the middle of June and stayed until the first of July. Mr. Scott came out after her. He didnt stay but one day. They are Housekeeping now. That was there hurry to get back to the Bluff. The[y] were so anxious to get Housekeeping. How I would like to peep in and see Mary in her own Home. I know Charlie will have everything convenient for her.

Well how does my dear little grandboys come on? You don't know how much I want to see them. Tell John he must not forget grandmama—though I did not get to see him with his pants on. I hope I will see him many a time in the future and have the pleasure of making him and Dear little Willie many a pair of pants. I don't know what kind of charm you passed over Ella. I had a letter from her last week. She says she don't never want to live at Tulip again. Well, I am glad she is so well pleased, but you must not let her go wild.

I am glad you have got Martha to live with you. I hope you will be able to keep her a long time. I think she is a good woman. The weather is so hot it would make you sick to have so much to do. How I wish I could send you a basket of Peaches. We have some that are good ripe now. I think of you all every day when we have peaches brought in, and wish you could have some too. And figs, I never saw so many on one tree in my life as my tree has this year. I don't know whether Husband will get to Clark or not. We have been so sick he will be all most afraid to leave home.

I send you Mary & Charlie's photograph. I will write to Mary for one for Ella. What do you think of my going to the Bluff this fall? Mrs. Roan has promised to take me down this fall, and I think Mary will go crazy if I don't go. If you all had your House built I wouldn't parley long which end of the road I would take as I could see so many more of my children by going to Clark.

Since I wrote the above Dow has had another chill. He is better this evening, though not able to sit up, he is clear of fever. Two of Sister's boys came over yesterday. It is the first time they have ever been over. I don't think there visit has done Dow much good, as it has been so hard to keep Dow from talking too much. The Rev. Mr. Lassen of the Princeton circuit preached for us today. He is a very fine Preacher.

Are you coming over this fall? We would be so glad to see you and the dear little ones, but I reckon you will find it hard to leave home as all Housekeepers do. I wish I had some thing of interest to write you, but I haven't, as every thing moves on about Tulip with the same dull monotony that it always does.

Have you got any Workmen to work on your house yet? I felt provoked when I heard the Workmen you had engaged failed to comply with there contract. I don't think there is much dependence to be placed in black or white.

Your Father's Family are all well, I think. Your cousin Willie Butler expects to leave some time soon. I think some of the girls ought to have set their caps for him, he is such a nice little fellow. I will write to William some time soon to pay him for his note he sent on Ella's envelope. You must write as often as you can, and I will try and be prompt.

All join in love to you all. Kiss the Dear little boys for grand mamma

> Your mother
> E. D. Lipscomb

William Paisley to Emma Butler Paisley in Tulip

> Little Rock, Arks.
> Sept. 14th, 1869

My dear Precious one:

We arrived here today about one o'clock fully determined, as we thought, to go on to New York, but since coming here we have concluded that it would be better—all things considered—to go to

St Louis & make our purchases. Our principal reason for changing our mind is this—I have already business acquaintances in St Louis, & think I will have no difficulty in getting all the credit I want there without trouble, & I can introduce Henry & Jim & they can get all they want. I believe we could get credit in New York for all we want, but we would have the unpleasant necessity of forming business acquaintances there, while I have them already in St Louis. I would have written by to day's mail but had some matters to attend to which kept me busy until late, & then we got to discussing the propriety of not going to New York, & could not decide the matter until it was too late to write by the mail that leaves in the morning. However, Mr. Lee of Princeton will go out on the stage in the morning & I will finish this & try to get the clerk to give it to him to leave at Tulip as he passes tomorrow night.

We had a very pleasurable time coming up. We travelled thirty-eight miles the first day, & camped out at night, & had quite a merry time around our camp fire. Henry & Jim occupied the wagon, & Billy & myself slept under a large tree near the fire & made out very well. As an evidence of it I slept soundly until time to get up this morning. We got up at four o'clock, fed the mules & made coffee, ate breakfast & were on the road by the time it was light enough to see how to travel. The most amusing thing that occurred happened the first day (yesterday) at dinner. We stopped to eat dinner & feed in front of a house & as we all thought it would be better to have coffee I went in & asked the lady if we could make it on her fire. She told me I could. After putting the kettle on the fire I asked her if she would lend me her coffee pot to make it in. She told me I was welcome to it, & brought out the blackest old coffee pot you ever saw. I regretted [to] have asked for it when I saw it, but I didn't know how to refuse taking it & determined that I would wash it out. I took it out on the front porch where I had a bucket of water & when I opened it, I found that it was literally plastered with old coffee grounds & dirt but I commenced washing it & continued the process until I thought it was clean, but when I went in the house I saw that the old lady was mad & she remarked in a short way that that pot had had nothing in it but coffee. I tried to smooth the matter over by telling her that I thought coffee was always better when made in a *clean* coffee pot. Henry & Billy & Jim laughed at me a good deal about it, but I preferred being laughed at to drinking coffee made in such a dirty vesel as that was.

Henry & Jim are both in bed, & I must close. You will have written to me to New York before you get this if it goes by mail, but you must write to me as directed on enclosed card, & Henry requests me to ask you to tell his wife to write at the same time & direct his letters to the same care that you send mine. He wrote to his wife this evening, but we then thought we would go to New York.

No more paper. Be sure & write. Kiss the dear little ones for their pa & accept much love for yourself—your devoted husband

W. Paisley

[Written on the back of the envelope]

My dear one

When I wrote last night, I expected to wake this morning at the time the stage would start for Tulip, but as usual I over slept my self & it will have to go by mail. We will go from here to DeVall's Bluff by rail, & from there to where the road is completed on the other end by stage & will get to Memphis to morrow morning.

We are all well this morning & in good spirits.

As ever your loving

W. P.

William Paisley to Emma Butler Paisley in Tulip

Memphis, Tenn.
Friday Sept. 16th 1869

My dearest one:

We arrived here this morning for breakfast, and will start to St. Louis this evening at 2 o'clock & without an accident, will reach there at ten o'clock to morrow morning. Our trip from Little Rock here was made in twenty-four hours, but I tell you the staging was pretty rough. There is a gap of about thirty miles between White River & St. Francis River that has to be travelled by stage—& that too over a pretty rough road—but by coming that way we saved at least a day & night, & that will fully pay us for all the jolts. When we left Little Rock, I did not feel fully satisfied about not going to New York, but my mind is perfectly easy on the subject now, & I am fully persuaded that it is to our interest to go to St. Louis. Henry & Jim & myself have been attending to some business since we got here, & it is now nearly time for us to start, so you must excuse me for writing hurriedly.

We called at the office of the Advocate & I renewed your subscription. Mr. Johnson, the Editor, was just starting to Nashville to attend Conference, & I handed him three dollars for Mr. Stark, & told him to be sure & tell him that I was to blame for his not getting the money sooner. Mr. Johnson is a very fine looking man, & as *jolly* as a boy.

Henry is now calling me, & says I won't have time to eat before it will be time to start. Good by my own one, wish I had time to write more but will write from St. Louis. Kiss the little ones.

Yrs. affectionately,
W. Paisley

Emma Butler Paisley to William Paisley

Tulip
Sept. 16th, 1869

My dearest one,

I was a little disappointed this morning that I did not get a letter, especially after hearing that sister Mollie got one, but I know you had some good reason for not writing, and not that you love me any less than brother Henry does his wife. Sister Mary received a letter from brother Lewis and aunt Mary—both well. Brother Lewis can write about nothing but Miss Jinnie, nor do I blame him. He is to be married next December, and will go immediately to keeping house. He doesn't think he can pay his promised visit till next summer.

The children both have taken a little cold since the change in the weather. If you slept in the wagon Monday night I am fearful that you are sick, for it turned so very cold. Little Willie has been rather fretful for the last few days, so I have not been able to get much sewing done.

I called on Mrs. Johnson last Tuesday evening—found her a very pleasant lady, though rather a sad countenance. On my way home stopped at the store and purchased a few articles which I am anxious to make up. Ma and pa have not got home yet, though we think they staid with brother Charley last night and will be at home about dinner time today. Cousin Ellen and Annie Phillips came up last Sunday, but expect to go home tomorrow.

Little John goes about saying "Pa's gone 'ork—pa's gone 'ork!" I think Willie had some fever last night caused from teething. I have just got him asleep—he misses his crib and I have no one to send after ma's. Darling, you must take care of yourself, and don't get sick while you are gone.

Friday morning

Cousin Ellen and Annie have just left. I feel very sorry for them. Cousin E. was in hopes pa would get here before she left so that he might tell her what to do. I think pa and ma are making a long stay. Little Willie had fever all night, but seems to be well this morning. I do hope he will not have a spell of sickness while you are gone.

Annie saw Miss Kate Moore with some cuff buttons that cost about a dollar and she is anxious to have some like them. They [are] washed over with gold, with a bar of coral across them. Of course she wont care if they are a little different from those she saw, but I merely mentioned this so that you can form an idea of what she wants.

Sister, sister Mollie and her children all came over yesterday evening, expecting to see ma and pa. Give my love to brother H. and Cousin J. but accept the largest portion for yourself. I will try and write you a better letter next time so you must excuse this. Always with much love your

Emma

Late in the evening.

Ma and pa have just got in and such a commotion you never heard.

William Paisley to Emma Paisley im Tulip

St Louis Mo
Sept. 19th 1869

My precious one:

I wrote you another very hurried note from Memphis & after finishing it, did not have time to eat a full dinner before it was time to get on the omnibus to go to the Rail Road Depot. So I hope you will excuse the entire note, & particularly the precipitant manner with which it was closed. We left Memphis at half past two o'clock Thursday evening & arrived here Friday (the next morning) at ten o'clock. The time from Memphis to St Louis has been made shorter since last spring by several hours—by opening a new route which crosses the Mississippi River at Columbus, Ky., thence all Rail to St. Louis by the St. Louis & Iron Mountain Rail Road. By this route we miss Cairo entirely, as Columbus is 20 miles below Cairo.

While in Memphis Henry telegraphed Lewis to meet "*us*" at Columbus. When we got within about twenty-five miles of Columbus, we met Lewis, who had come out to meet us on the train going to Memphis. It was ten o'clock at night when he got on our train, & we were all asleep (not thinking about seeing him until we got to Columbus) & were very agreeably surprised, when we were roused up & found Lewis standing over us. His coming out to meet us gave us some time to *talk*, & as he seemed to be more talkative *if possible* than ever before, you may know that the hour & a half we had with him passed off pleasantly & swiftly enough. His whole thought now seem to be wholly engrossed in the subject of getting married & as he has made arrangement to enter that happy state in December—he is hopefully looking forward to it as the threshold to fortune, happiness, & everything else that is good. But I have neglected to say that he was disappointed when he met Jim & myself with Henry instead of Henry's better half, Henry's telegram having caused him to expect to meet his family with him. We promised Lewis to try & return by way of Cairo & spend a short time with him, but I don't know now how that will be—as it will owe in great measure to the time we are detained here.

On our arrival here we stopped at the Planters House (the same I stopped at last spring) & are as comfortable as could be under the circumstances. Friday Evening & yesterday I spent in going around with Henry & Jim—introducing them to my acquaintances & looking through some of the stocks. We have made no purchases yet but expect to commence in the morning. From what we have seen, we are confirmed on the opinion that it was in our interest to come here instead of going to New York, to say nothing of the consideration of getting back so much sooner.

Hope your ma & pa returned safely and (without meaning to reflect on the good management of sisters Mary & Annie) that home looks more like home than it did without them. Give my love to all. Good night.

> Affectionately yours &c
> W. P.

William Paisley to Emma Butler Paisley in Tulip

> St. Louis Mo
> Sept 24 1869

My darling Emma:

It is now five minutes to 12 o'clock night, & you, my precious one, & the dear little boys are sleeping soundly—but I have just come in from the Dry Goods house, where we have all been hard at work trying to get our Goods bought, ready to ship by tomorrow evening. We do not expect to get every thing ready by that time, but there is a boat going out then, which proposes to take freight very low & we are trying to get the heaviest goods ready. How much I wish I was ready to start home, for it really seems like it has been a long time since I saw my dear ones, but I only write this to let you know that I am well.

I am very tired and must go to bed. Henry & Jim are both in bed but I had occasion to come out into the Hotel office after they retired & I felt that I could not sleep without writing you a line. We are all well and anxious to get back. We hope to start Monday evening next, & to be at Tulip by Monday or Wednesday, three weeks from the time we left. Have had no letters from home yet. You don't know how anxious I am to hear from my loving ones. May God bless & protect you all is the prayer of your

> devoted husband
> Wm Paisley

Love to all. Many kisses for you & the little ones.

> Saturday morning 25th

All well this morning. In a great hurry. Goodby.

> Yours affectionately
> W. Paisley

George Butler to Emma Butler Paisley at Dobyville

Tulip
Dec 22nd 1869

My dear Sister

I have been thinking for some time that I would write to you, and now I will write without further delay. I intended writing this evening, during the time I spent in pursuit of my mule (One of Bro. Moores'), which jumped out of the grove this evening soon after dinner and came up of its own accord after I had tried in vain to drive it back. There was no horse on the place, so I walked near eight miles in search for it, and thought I would renew the search tomorrow on horseback. Imagine my surprise to hear my mule braying up in the lot shortly after I had gotten home.

I have just written to Julia who is at her father's. Her brother expected to bring her over this week, but the weather is so cold that I do not look for them. The shoes which Billy presented to Julia fitted her very well, and are highly appreciated. She has been intending to write to you for some time, but had not done so before I left.

Our little Willie has five teeth. He had a spasm while we were returning from Conference. It was caused by teething. Did not appear to worst him much. His health has been very good with little exception. His mother thinks he is equal to any of the babies. You will not blame her much for that.

How do your boys come on? John will soon be able to run about on errands for Ma & Pa. The Good Lord bless them, and make them good boys, and may they grow up to be the joy and comfort of their parents and do much good in their day. You will not fail to seek grace from on high to aid you in discharging the duties of a Mother.

Have you heard that sisters Mattie and Mary are gone to Little Rock? Sister Mat expects to be absent two or three months. Will go on from L.R. to Clarksville. Sister Mary will return when pa can send for her, perhaps week after next.

There will be a supper given at Tulip next Tuesday night for the purpose of raising funds to help buy or pay for the Presbyterian Church. I hope there will be a handsome amount raised. We had a very pleasant time at Conference, but I reckon Annie wrote you about all that. I expect to leave for California next May, in company with brother Moores and family. Olin Moores intends to remain on his father's farm for a year or longer. There will be a new Conference organized in the Southern part of California next Nov., and we wish to be there and join when it organizes.

Love to William and kiss the Boys for me. May we so live that we will meet in Heaven.

Truly your brother
G. E. B.

Alice Butler to Emma Butler Paisley in Dobyville

Tulip
Jan. 24th 1870

Dear Sister Emma

Sister Julia received a letter from you about two or three weeks ago, says she will write soon. Christmas is all over, and how have you enjoyed yourself? It is the first, I believe, you ever spent away from home. We had a very nice time. I wish you could have been here Christmas day. It was rainy, but Ma killed her large turkey gobbler, and all of the family came over except Sister, and she had gone to spend her Christmas with Bro. George. She carried all of the children with her. Sister Mary also went as far as Little Rock, and staid about a month with Mrs. Fields. She had a very nice time.

But let me finish telling you about Christmas. Monday night the boys brought some skyrockets and Roman candles down, and such screaming and hollering you never heard.

Capt. Duffie and Miss Alice Colburn spent the day here last Saturday. I guess it will not be long before they are married. Cousin Mat and Alice [Phillips] came up yesterday, and would have left today if it had not been raining. I suppose you knew Annie [Phillips] was staying here until Sister came home. Bro. George speaks of keeping Walter with him, as he can make 30 or 40 dollars a month.

I wish you could see little Willie [William Moores Butler], he can pull up by a chair, and stood alone today for the first time. How is Willie & John getting on? I would like so much to see them.

We have hired Aunt Lucy again this year.

I received three nice birthday presents, a Lady's Companion from Sister Mary, a hymnbook & knife from Ma. Sister Julia also had a nice birthday dinner the next day.

It is getting late, and I must close. Love to all. Write soon.

Your affectionate
Sister Alice

Annie Butler to William Paisley in Dobyville

Tulip
Jan 24th 1870

Dear bro. Billy,

As Alice is writing to Emma, I have concluded to write you a short letter in reply to your and Emma's letters which were received sometime ago. I was very glad indeed to receive a few lines from you, the first time in my life.

Mr. Olin Moores, sister Julia [Moores Butler], Fannie [Moores], and two little sisters, reached here on Friday evening during Christmas, I was sorry they got here so late, our enjoyment was about over. Christmas day all the homefolks met here as usual, and we had the finest turkey I ever saw, it was so fat. The day was spent very pleasantly. Wish you and Emma could have been with us. Tuesday night we attended the Presbyterian supper, and had a real nice time. About two hundred persons attended, made $175 dollars.

Wednesday evening several of the boys concluded they must have a buggy ride, so they all came down to headquarters in order to start together. Willie Sample and Alice were in the van, then came Johnnie Colburn and Kate Coulter, next Johnnie, Kate Moore, Mr. Archer, and myself, leaving Mr. George Archer and Alice Colburn to bring up the rear. Oh, we had a most delightful ride; Went in three miles of Princeton. You just ought to have seen the men in Tulip running to the doors when they heard the buggies coming.

Alice and Annie Phillips are going to school to Mrs. Johnson, they are very much pleased with her teaching. Mr. Johnson teaches mathematics in the evening. They have ten scholars. Mr. Leiper opened school today with eleven pupils. I expect he will have a very good school, if the boys from a distance can get board. I have heard of several wanting to know if they could get board. Pa has promised to take Willie Sample if he returns.

We received a letter from bro. Louis a week or two ago, telling us he was married on the 15th of Dec. and was just as happy as he desired to be, and thought himself the luckiest of men to have become *her* husband. He said you and bro. Henry must come by and see him soon, as he is keeping house. I would like so much to visit *them*. Brother George and Mr. Moores are still in the notion of going to California, think of starting in May.

Johnnie came up to see us Saturday, left this morning. He expects to farm with bro. Charlie again this year. I wish he could stay at home, I miss him so much.

There is a great deal of sickness in the country at present. Dr. Reamy is riding most of the time. Pa's health has improved *very much*—all the family are well.

You hope next Christmas will dawn on Annie, somebody else. I am surprised that you should wish me so much unhappiness, but you may be gratified no telling, but I don't *love any one yet.* I am afraid to make the step.

Much love to Emma, and a kiss for the two children.

I neglected to tell you Lena Colburn was dead, have not heard the particulars of her death. I know the family will be very much distressed.

All send love.

Write soon to your sister

Annie L. B.

Mary Butler to Emma Butler Paisley in Dobyville

Tulip
Feb. 19th, 1870

My dear sister Emma,

I have been intending to write you ever since my return from Little Rock and give an account of my visit, but brother "Billy" has been here and no doubt has told you about it. I am glad you have moved into your new house, know you can appreciate it since being cramped up in one little room. I am very anxious to see you, and will endeavor to make you a visit as soon as I can.

Brother George left for his circuit this morning: this is the week he was wanting to take sister

Julia over to spend several days with you, as he could have more spare time, but he had no convenient way of going. I'm afraid they will be disappointed about getting to see you at all.

Have you heard of any Valentines? they are flying around here considerably: Annie went to Tulip this morning and brought down six—two for Alice, one for Annie Phillips, one for herself, and two for me. I suppose it is well enough to have something exciting going on to relieve the monotony of the times. Capt. Duffie has been down to see Alice Colburn. I believe they expect to marry the last of March or first of Apr. I have promised to bake the bride's cake. I went down to Dr. Colburn's and staid last Sunday night—had a very pleasant time. Charley and Kate were there. Mrs. Barbee and Mrs. Strong spent one night this week with me. I wouldn't be surprised if Mrs. B. is not thinking of marrying Mr. Barnett from the way she is fixing up. He was to see her just before Christmas. Sallie Barbee is carrying the day now with the boys—you know how it is when one starts? John Wilson, Pompey Matlock, and young Mr. Fuller from Princeton are among the number. Kalie and Cora are still in Little Rock. Mrs. Gantt and all expect to return next month.

We have been having some very pretty warm weather, and ma has commenced gardening some, but it has turned cold again and I fear every thing that was up is killed. Some of the peach trees are in full bloom.

I received a letter from Sister this week; she is enjoying good health and a pleasant time. We expect her home next week. Walter will remain with his pa.

Sister Julia has just been in, and says brother George told her this morning he would take her over to see you after the second Sunday in next month, if the weather is good and can get a conveyance, says she will answer your letter before long.

We have not heard any thing from brother Lewis lately. He keeps very quiet since he married. Annie has been anxiously expecting a letter from sister Jennie in answer to hers, which she wrote some time ago.

Mr. Holmes preached for us last Sunday. I think he has improved very much. Tomorrow is Mr. Watson's day. Give my love to Mrs. Lipscomb, the Capt. and all the family: we miss them here very much. I am looking for a letter from Mary [Paisley Scott] every mail.

We are all enjoying good health, for which we should feel very thankful. How is brother Billy? We felt uneasy about him when he left us: give him my love and tell him I would be glad to get a letter from him. Kiss the little children for me. All unite with me in sending much love.

Write very soon to your loving sister

Mary

Henry Butler to William Paisley in Dobyville

St. Louis
Mar 2nd, 1870

Dear Billy

Yours of the 14th inst to hand last evening. I sympathize with you in your disappointment in making collections, but it will all be right, only a little later than you would wish. I have been here one week yesterday, & have completed my purchases, save Woodware & the *many commands* of friends in the neighborhood such as "a spring Bonnet," a wagon, Bed stead &c &c. I shall close up on Tuesday—stop over a day with Lewis and one day with Foster, & then as fast as railroad & steam boats "to *hum*."

I have made satisfactory purchases, find Dry goods, Hats & Crockery & glass were *down* cheap, Shoes, Clothing, Hardware & Saddlery about as last fall—the latter a shade lower. I bought Standard prints at 10cts, Standard domsts 12½ for ⅞ & 15 cts for ¼. I am fearful there will be an advance in these goods before you reach the Market—there is already a tendency that way in the east. I dealt with *all* of our old friends except Crow McCreery & Co. & Filley. The former are *deficient in stock* and at *higher* prices—*decidedly so*. Filley & Co. is a good house, but I found one in Miller & Brothers on 4th st to suit me better. I bought staples of Chase & Cabot, who have a fine stock—somewhat better in every respect to Dodd, Brown & Co.

You will *not be here long* before you [are] *drumed* by some one from every house you ever heard of, and more besides. I have mentioned your coming to all your friends, & I must say that they manifest a high regard for you as a business man and gentleman, and I believe most of them *feel what they say*. I congratulate you on the stand you have taken. You need not trouble yourself about being a little behind in meeting your notes for fall purchases. Many are in the same condition. George Lea for one—who came as far as Little Rock and then *returned* for what cause is not known, though I learn he overstocked himself last fall and is still owing considerably.

I was much surprised on arriving here in going to the Register at the Planters to see the last names entered. "James N Butler & James A. Amis—Arks"—They got in from New Orleans one hour ahead of me, having come by *Boat* all the way. They report goods *very* high in N O (nothing new), and are delighted in making the exchange to this place. Cousin James finished his purchases & left on last Friday.

When you call on J. O. Ford & Co.—ask for Mr. Newton Ford, who you will be pleased with. You may *trust him* with safety and is as different from his old *gruff* brother as he can be.

I am not altogether pleased with the charges made at D. A. January & Co. I find I could have done better by looking around before making my purchases, & I would advise you to do so. In regard to Hotels, by all means put up at this house "Barnum." Here you will find Keyser (of J. H. W. & Co), Shopleigh (of A. F. S. & Co), Newsome (of D. A. & Co) and *many other* clever merchants. Nice beds—excellent table equal to the Planters. Much more quiet and one dollar a day less for Board.

Write me after you arrive here.

> Yours,
> H. A. B.

Mr. Petit of Chase & Cabot you will find a clever gentleman. Something of a Yankee but a clever one.

Julia Moores Butler to Emma Butler Paisley in Dobyville

> Tulip
> April 6th 1870

Dear Sister Emma,

Every week that I appoint to write to you, some one gets ahead of me, so I am going to write to day any way, and if you should happen to receive two letters in one week from home, 'twill not bore you very much to read them. I was so sorry that I could not go over with George to see you. As we have put off the trip to Ca several months longer, I still expect to see you in your own home. I hope Mr. P. will be at home when I go.

Bro Henry got back last week, laid in a larger stock of fancy and dress goods than ever before. Mollie, Annie, and Mr. Archer went up in [the] stage to meet him, got back about twelve o'clock and had a very nice ride. Bro. H. spent two days and one night with Lewis, he says he has a charming wife, and that they were so happy and time flew by so swiftly that they forgot to write.

Pa and Ma, Mollie and Bro. Henry, George and myself dined with Sister yesterday. We spoke of you, and wished you lived near enough to come over and spend the day too. Ma stayed all night, and Sister came home with her this morning—to get some work done on the machine. I hear Sister Mary stitching away now. She is delighted and it just suits her. I am so glad, for her sake more than any body else's, that Pa bought it. Ma says that she is going to learn to use it. Sister Mat says she has no desire whatever to have one. Mollie is still delighted with hers.

Mr. Parvin preached for us a week ago last Sunday. Isn't he a good man to come away here to Tulip to preach? He is coming back the last of May, as we all think to marry Alice Colburn and Capt Duffie. Both parties have taken a great fancy to him. Sammy C. came home Monday, he has to attend court in Princeton. Johnnie went with him and brought him home in Mr. Parvin's buggy. Kate & Charlie were up a few weeks ago. Kate is looking very thin, has not been well for several weeks.

Tell John "the man" is beginning to walk, and if they were together now they would have more scratching and hair pulling than a little. Moores is, if possible, ruder and noisier than ever, never still a moment, wants to be out of doors all the time. Ellen nurses him and he is very fond of her. Mattie is very quiet—and just as afraid of Moores as she can be.

Pa has just been summoned to go to Princeton on the Overton case. I do not know any of the particulars. Mr. Tannehill is to be at Princeton, and I expect will come up here. Johnnie Butler [Emma's cousin] was here Monday night; he expects to marry Laura Scott in a month or so. They will have six waiters, Annie, Johnnie, and Cousin Mat among the number. The rest are strangers. Sister Mat is very much pleased with Annie Phillips. I think she is a very estimable girl and rather my favorite of the sisters. Cousin Ellen seems to be having a very pleasant time at Princeton. All the sisters are pleasantly situated except the married one.

We are to have two days meeting up here next Saturday and Sunday, and the Sacrament on Sunday. Sammy Colburn, George, and Bro. Holmes will be here. By the way, we all like Bro. Holmes so much. He is not only a good preacher, but an excellent pastor, and so zealous to attend to all the duties of an itinerant preacher. He seems so much more cheerful than I ever knew him, his family I believe are comfortably situated on the Ouachita, he is being well paid and is very acceptable.

There is an artist here but he is a miserable artist, besides is a drunkard & gambler. Pa & Alice sat for their photographs but they were so indifferent that Pa would not take them, paid him three dollars for his trouble and let him keep the pictures.

I am making me a Water proof travelling cloak. Bro Henry got the patterns in St Louis. It comes almost to the bottom of my dress. Bro Henry got Mollie a dining table, oil cloth for it, and a colored cloth for supper and some colored breakfast napkins.

I have written enough gossip for one time, so must stop. Ma says don't kill all your chickens for any thing. Sister Mat sends love and says she wishes you could stay with her while Mr. Paisley was away after goods. Sister Mary says she would go over and stay with you if she had any way. I am getting very anxious to see them all at home and expect we will go over in a few weeks. Kiss the little boys for me, I wish I could see them. George left this morning to fill his last appointment on the Rock Port circuit will be back tomorrow, kindest regards to Mr. P.

> Yours truly
> Julia M. Butler

Mattie Hughes to Emma Butler Paisley in Dobyville

> Tulip
> Apr. 12th 1870

Dear Sister Emma,

I intended writing to you directly after getting home, but I believe some one from home, have written to you every week since. So I concluded I would wait awhile. Last Sunday when we got home from church, we were very much surprised to meet Billy at Pa's. It was so late in the season, we supposed he had gone on without coming by. I think he wrote to you yesterday evening, and I expect gave you an account of home affairs, also how much we regretted that you and the children couldn't come with him, and spend two or three weeks with us during his absence. I know you must feel lonely, wish you didn't live so far from the rest of us.

I was very much surprised to hear that Willie had only one tooth. I suppose by the time his pa gets back, you will have him walking. Is he as good and quiet as he used to be? has John learned to treat him any better? I read in one of your letters about John's straying off, and your starting out in search of him, and hadn't gone far till you met Mrs. Hill leading him home. I know you must have felt very uneasy, if you thought he was lost.

I heard Sarah was going to be married, how do you get on without her? Or did she get so trifling she wasn't much help. Annie Phillips is living with me now, and I am very much pleased with her. She is a good deal of company, and always ready and willing to assist me. She hears from her sister every few days. Cousin Mat [Phillips] is still at cousin Jimmie's with Alice. If she could be with you now, she would be so much company for you.

> Monday morning, April 18th

You see from the date of this letter, I commenced writing to you nearly a week ago, and here it is yet unfinished. I have just written a long letter to George, and will try to get this ready to send to the office to be mailed tonight. Sister Mary and Annie are busy getting ready for cousin Johnnie's wedding, which is to come off next Wednesday night. I suppose you knew that he was to be married to Miss Laura Scott. Annie, cousin Mat and Johnnie are three of the attendants. They expect to have a dining at cousin Jimmie's on Thursday, and I hear that Pa and Ma were invited, but I don't expect they will go.

Brother George, ma, and Julia went to Princeton yesterday, and heard bro. Cald[well]. Mr. Watson has engaged brother G. to teach for him, until his health improves. But I don't suppose he will teach but a short time, as they are still in the notion of going to Cal. this summer. Brother Henry has received his new goods, and has been selling a good many. I have been over several times, but haven't bought much. I believe the people around Tulip dress as much or more than they ever did.

175

I suppose you have heard of the Ransoms, living at Mr. Doby's place. One of the girls died very unexpectedly last week. Dr. Ramey was sent for the day before she died, but didn't think there was much the matter. I went over last Thursday morning to attend her burial. They were strangers here, but everyone seemed to show them a good deal of attention. The girl was about eighteen years old, and had never made a profession of religion. Ma and myself had called to see them about a week before, and she came in the room just as we were leaving. They seem to be very clever people, and the parents are members of the Methodist church.

We have been blessed with good preaching lately. Bro Hunter preached for us last Saturday week, and that night bro. Holmes. On Sunday at eleven brother George, and at night Sammy Colburn. I don't know of a community as highly favored as this, yet there are so many careless and unconcerned. And some of the young people act very badly at church. Yesterday Sammy Colburn preached, but I wasn't very well and didn't attend.

Did you ever see such cold weather this late in the Spring? I believe all of the fruit is killed, and a great many of the leaves and buds on the trees. Our trees were very full of apples, pears, and cherries, but now the fruit is black, and will fall of[f] in a day or two. Our garden is looking very well, owing to Mr. Robertson's care, not many of the vegetables were killed. The Irish potatoes are killed, but I reckon will come out again.

Ma has in her album quilt, and I was over there nearly two days last week quilting. I often think of you when we are together, and wish it was so that you could be with us.

Have you heard of any new cases of small pox in your neighborhood? Pa came in a few minutes ago, he is not well today, and is lying down on the little bed now. Says he suffered very much from headache yesterday. Annie P. is going to stay with Alice tonight, and ma sent me word that she would come and stay with me.

I expect you heard that I left Walter with his Pa. I miss him very much. It looks like there are so few of us, it is a pity we have to be separated. I spent a very pleasant time while I was with George, wish it had been so that I could have remained longer. The first week or two after I got home I felt very lonely. Julia has been staying with me some, and I expect her over this week. She has to bring Ellen to nurse her baby. He wants to be carried about all the time. You must write soon, and let me know how you are getting on while Billy is absent.

Remember me to Capt. Lipscomb and family. How are they pleased with Clark? West is going to school to Mr. Leiper, and Reavis to Mrs. Johnson. They seem to be very well pleased.

Kiss the children for their Aunt Mattie.

> Your loving sister,
> M. W. Hughes

William Paisley to Emma Butler Paisley in Dobyville

> St. Louis Mo.
> Apl. 20th 1870

My dear little one:

It is now eleven o'clock at night & I am mighty tired but will have to try to write you something, fearing that if I put if off I may not have time again before I start home. I have worked very hard to day buying Hardware & dry goods. Am not through yet with the latter Bill. I expected to devote my time to night after supper to writing to you & Mr. Doby, but one of my friends came around & insisted on my going with him around to hear the "Hay Makers." I was so tired that it was with reluctance that I consented, besides I wanted the time for writing—but after going was glad that I went. The entertainment is exhibited in a large Hall in the city & (as you will see from the enclosed Program) was gotten up for the benefit of a public Hospital in St. Louis. Those who take part in the performances are citizens of the place, & the entertainment was one of the most interesting I ever attended. How much I wished you could have been with me. I think there were at least fifteen hundred persons out & more there (particularly ladies) out who attend none but exhibitions of that kind.

But Darling, I only have this sheet of paper & that is most gone before I have asked any thing about your self & the dear little ones. I never felt more anxious to be with you & to hurry back than I do now, & have never more felt so lonesome on a trip of this kind before. I suppose it is owing in part to the fact that my having such good company in Henry & Jim last fall.

Goods are *very* low, that is, some kind of goods, & I expect to buy a large stock, more than I thought I would when I left. There is a boat here loading for Camden, & I hope to ship the most of the goods this week. Have not got your machine yet, but looked at them & will buy in time to ship on the Boat.

How do you get along by yourself? I am so anxious to hear from you. I recd a note from Dr. Harris this morning dated 13th, telling me that you were all well. It did me a heap of good. The Dr. wrote asking me to get him a Samuel Best shovel.

It was very cold here Saturday, & Sunday & snowed hard. The weather now is pleasant. Hope the garden is flourishing.

I have hardly had time to think of what we want ourselves. I have been so busy looking at & pricing goods. Wish I could get a letter from you telling me what to buy. Please give Mr. Doby all the items of news I have written, haven't time to write to night. May write him in the morning if I get up in time. I hope to get nearly (if not quite) through buying this week, so as to wind up & start home Monday or Tuesday. Do not look for me too soon but rest assured I will hurry all I can.

Love to father & Ma & all. Kiss the dear little ones for their Pa & tell little Willie that he must be walking by the time I come & must know me. Tell Jno Papa says he must be a good boy & papa's man.

As ever your devoted husband, with many kisses—

W. Paisley

Emma Butler Paisley to William Paisley

At Home
April 22nd, 1870

My dearest one,

I have just finished answering a long letter I received from Sister this morning mailed 18th. Old Mrs. Doby and Mrs. Harris passed by this morning on their way to Mr. Hill's. I saw them riding up, and thought, of course, they expected to spend the day with me, and must confess felt relieved when they said they had started to Mrs. Hill's and only stopped to give me the mail, but said they would spend the day with me after you got back. I felt very unwell last Tuesday and

Wednesday and was not able to do much, so I sent Ella over to Mrs. Hill's, to see if Miss Beckie could go and bring her sister Sue to stay with me till you get back. She came this evening and says she will stay till to-morrow week. I went over to the store this evening, took John with me and expected to spend a short while with Mrs. Doby, but John got into one of his contrary ways and I could do nothing with him till I gave him a little whipping, and he said he wanted to go home so I thought rather than have a fuss I would come with him.

Mr. Burton (the oldest one) and a young lady on the other side of Turnois [Terre Noire Creek] were married last night, and had a dining at Mrs. Burton's to-day. I understand that Dr. McCallum and Miss Humphries are to be married next Sunday evening week, and will go directly to Spoonville. I have not been to Mr. McCallum's but if I am well enough will go next week. Mr. Patterson planted some cucumber and tomato seed, but I believe I mentioned it in my last letter.

Pide's calf was turned out last night, and has not made his appearance yet. I am fearful something has happened to him. Miss Sue has just come back from the cow pen and says there is no cow nor calf either to be found. Ella fed the cow at dinner time, and I thought she would be satisfied to stay, but I forgot to have her watered, and I reckon that is what she has gone for.

Ma [Lipscomb] received a letter from Mary [Paisley Scott] yesterday, in which she mentioned that Dr. Jenkins is dead. Says she shall expect you to fulfill your promise to bring me and the children to stay with her, while you go after goods this fall. But I think she is looking most too far ahead—*don't you?* Mr. Scott has bought some land in the bottom below Pine Bluff. Mary says she reckons he will never leave Pine Bluff. Mr. Scott's Sister is very anxious for Mary to spend some time in Memphis with her. But Mary says she never would go without Mr. Scott.

Our water is not good but has to be strained before using it. You know how you use your fork in sopping biscuit in molasses. John tries to imitate you and says this is the way papa does. I wish you could see Willie walking—he can get up and walk all over the house. He will stay at his grand ma's to night, as I am trying to wean him.

I will close till I see you, which I hope will be last of next week. I am looking every day for a letter from Memphis. I forgot to mention that I sent by Mr. Doby last Wednesday for some oranges, but he could not find any in Arkadelphia. I tried to get John to send some message, but he is not quite large enough to understand what I mean. Many kisses from your loving,

Emma

Henry Butler to William Paisley in Dobyville

Tulip Ark
May 2d 1870

Dear Billy:

Yours written at Little Rock rec'd per last mail, with the articles sent down from Rockport all right. The balance in your favor on the purchases, $8.23, I have passed to your credit or rather D&P. You have pleased *every body* for whom you purchased articles—Ma, Pa, sisters, George, Dr. C., and all. Mollie thinks sister's Bonnet the prettiest she ever saw—says I "had better look out—they will think *you* can excel me in selecting goods to please &c." I make the acknowledgement *now,—and will turn over* to *you* all the *commands* I may hereafter receive. Glad to know of your safe return and no doubt satisfactory purchases. I have no doubt you did well in commencing with H. Bell & Son. There is another house I am not *entirely* satisfied with—J. H. Wear & Co. Somehow or other I am impressed with the idea that we can do better. What do you think? Now is the time (or better, just after receiving and marking the goods) to form an opinion. Please bear it in your mind.

Your letter from St. Louis also rec'd. Surprised at D. A. J. & Co presenting you the a/c for 3 Bbls flour. It is my firm conviction that *I sent them* the money which was handed me to pay for the flour *by Capt. Lipscomb*. Of one thing I *am* certain. I wrote them *a letter* ordering the 3 Bbls flour, and signed Doby & Paisley in the presence of your father. He told me that you was so very busy you did not have time to write. I have looked for a copy of my letter, but it seems I kept none of that—as is my custom. I know the money was paid me by your father. Please ask him if he saw me send off the money. I remember he was by (around the P. O. office) while I was writing.

You was fortunate in the matter of freights—and no doubt your goods will be in Camden before you get this. I have been selling very well. All my ladies hats gone except four or five, and nearly half of my Prints. Last Saturday week I sold four hundred & fifty dollars—one hundred cash. Smith & Hunter did not receive their goods in ten days after I did, and I felt the advantage. Pa rec'd a letter from L&S Henderson, saying they had written you at St. Louis offering to advance $7.50 per bale. Did you receive the letter before you left?

If I could possibly leave my business I would come over to see you and assist in marking selling &c. I know you will have a rush.

Excuse haste—written by twilight.

Love to Emma & the children. All well. Write if you can find time.

> Yours
> Henry

Annie Butler to William Paisley in Dobyville

> Tulip
> May 4th, 1870

Dear Brother Billy,

Your letter, with all the articles you purchased for us, were received last Saturday morning, and I must say we were all delighted with the things you bought and render *many many* thanks for your good selection. Sister's bonnet is the prettiest I ever saw, and she is *so much pleased* with it. I do wish I had sent for a hat by you, and if you have one you think would suit me please keep it for me. I got one here called the grachi, but I don't like it much. The last hat I got, you bought it & I never had one I liked better. I don't care about a very fine one. I expect you can suit me. Try it any way. Sister Julia wants to know if you have a bonnet that would suit her, and if so she wants it, and if not select her a hat. I don't mean to flatter you at all, but really you have *splendid* taste, at least *all* of us here think so.

Ma is pleased with her bonnet, but I tell her she don't think it is quite fine enough. It is just the very bonnet for her. Johnnie's chain is very pretty indeed, but I am sorry I did not send my hair and have one made. You did not mention bro. George, did you forget I sent for something for him? Sister Mary says she is *so much oblige* to you for the music, and will learn it soon to play for you. You will have to send Emma over with the things. I wish I could write you a long letter, but I am in a great hurry, as sister Mary and I want Johnnie to take us up to call on Cora Reid this evening.

Sister has been down to bro. Charlie's a week, and Johnnie brought her home this morning. I can't look at her bonnet without wanting it, and sister Mary also.

How did Emma and the children get on without you? I wish we could see you all, when are you coming? Kiss them all for me. Excuse mistakes and write soon to

Your sister
Annie Butler

Sister Julia says don't keep a bonnet or hat for her any longer than the first of June. She don't want it if she can't get it before then, says she is very much pleased with what you bought her.

Mary W. Butler to Emma & William Paisley in Dobyville

[Tulip
May 4, 1870]

My Dear Daughter,

Annie is writing to William. I will write you a few lines (to send with hers). I owe you both a letter and would like to pay my debts. Hope you can read it, have to write with a pencil, and but a few minutes to the mail leaves. Would like to use a pen. I feel like I would like to say a good word to you. It seems it has been a long time since I saw your sweet face. It has been a long time since I saw you and the children. How pleasant it would be if I could only stop in this beautiful day and see you, how much more so than writing. I feel for you, having all your work to do this warm weather.

Glad to hear of your Will's safe arrival. I know you missed him so much. Many thanks to him for my new bonnet. It is the very thing. Annie says she is going to tell him I think it not fine enough, but you need not listen to her.

We had a nice garden until the frost came. It is coming out some. Your papa takes great interest and works it. I was in the garden and got a few strawberries this eve.

I must not forget to tell you, I have seven little turkies, the sweetest little things. You all know I all ways delight in them. Chickens, I do not know how many, 80, I reckon. Had first chicken to fry today.

Now it is getting so dark I can hardly see. That reminds me of my shoes. I was more pleased to get them than any thing.

How is Cap. Lips. and family? Miss them so much. No one can fill his place. My love to them. Tell him we around here keep well. Tell him to remember us in his prayers.

Good by my darling

Your Mother

Annie Butler to Emma Butler Paisley in Dobyville

Tulip

June 1st, 1870

Dearest sister Emma,

Why in the world don't some of you write to us? We cannot hear a word from you. We are fearful you are sick. I wrote to bro. Billy several weeks ago, but haven't had a word in reply. Probably he never received my letter, but I hope he did.

Mr. Moores and wife and daughter, Lucia, reached here last Saturday evening. We had been looking for them, but had given them out, therefore it was a great surprise, but agreeable. I wish you could have seen sister Julia running to meet them! I don't think I ever saw a lady run faster in my life. She looked like she would knock everything down that came in her way. She came very near pushing bro. George out of the door, not quite. We enjoyed their visit so much, but it was too short; they left Tuesday morning, with bro. George and sister Julia with them. It seems very quiet here now.

I can't say at present either, for sister Mollie and Coulter have just come, but I must finish my letter before going in to see her. I can hear her talking very plainly, so much so, that I can scarcely help listening to hear what she has to say.

Brother George speaks of teaching the free school here, or in Princeton, in a few weeks. I reckon sister Julia will assist him if necessary. I don't know when they will start to Cal, probably September, if ever. Ma says she did want you here *so much* when Mrs. Moores was here. We are getting quite anxious to see you all.

Sister Mollie has just called to me, and says give my love to Emma, and tell her I am coming to see her this summer, unless something happens that she don't know of. Sister Julia was very anxious to visit you, but could not get a conveyance.

Moores and Mattie are walking all about. The former is the most restless little fellow you ever saw, the latter is very good and quiet. We have a great deal of sewing to do, but we have such a good machine that it won't take us very long to do it, if we all will work right hard.

Ma told me this evening that I did not have time to write, but I told her I was compelled to write *one letter*, and after I got that one written, she was willing for me to write to you. I think she just didn't want me to write *that one* [possibly to her sweetheart?]. I have a great deal to tell you, and I don't think sister Mary minds a few words for you, but don't fear any thing transpiring without giving you timely notice, no danger of that. Tell bro. Billy he guessed very well about me, and I wished afterwards I had told him everything, but there is plenty of time yet, for there is nothing definite.

Brother George has preached several good sermons for us, and Ma says one especially, which she wishes so much you could have heard, and held class meeting for us one evening. Bro. Moores preached two excellent sermons for us last Sunday. Mr. Crawford will preach for us next Sunday week. Mr. Watson hasn't preached for us in a long time. He is very sick, I think he has consumption.

Ma says is John any better. Says you must whip him and make him mind you.

We have been fishing several times and had a delightful time. We brought home about thirty the last time. You must excuse this scribble for it was written in a great hurry. Much love to all. Write very soon to

Annie

Brother Henry and I went down to cousin Jim Butler's not long since to see cousin Laura. She is very sick, and we heard yesterday no better.

Cousin Mat is at Sister's now. She will spend several weeks. Walter is on his way home, may get here this evening.

Johnnie and I expect to go to Camden the 22nd of June to attend Mr. Barcus' concert. Mary gave me a very cordial invitation.

Mr. Johnson and family speak of starting to Mo. in three or four weeks. I will miss Kate *so much*, as I have become very much attached to her. I don't know what I will do. But the best of friends have to part.

Ma had on her new bonnet Sunday and it looked so nice, so different from her old shaker. Sister's is beautiful. I am getting very anxious to hear whether I can get a hat from bro. Billy. I need it very much. If some of you don't write to us, I don't know what I will do with you all. Ma says did the earthquake shake you away? Don't get mad at me for scratching up my letter so. I have no time to correct mistakes, as it is getting late and I must send my letter to the office.

Pa speaks of going down to see bro. Charlie tomorrow. They are getting on very well, I believe. Capt. Duffie and Alice Colburn have concluded not to marry. I dont know whose fault it is.

Mary Butler to Emma Butler Paisley in Dobyville

Tulip
June 14th, 1870

Dear Emma:

I have only time to write you a few lines tonight—have been expecting to write you a long letter, but will have to wait for another time. I have been sick all the week, and do not feel well yet. We were very glad to get your letters by Mr. Patterson; the first we have had in a long time.

Brother George got here about an hour ago, and they are all in the parlor having music and enjoying conversation; sister Julia sent me some beautiful cape Jessamines which kept very fresh—look almost like they've just been gathered. Cousin Mat is also with us tonight.

I spent today at Sister's with her—also sister Mollie and the children. She has been here about four weeks—expects to leave tomorrow or next day to return to cousin Jimmie's: she sends you much love and is anxious to see you. Cousin Laura is still very sick—fearful she will not recover. I am anxious to go to see her. Annie has just been in, and says tell brother Billy she is very much obliged to him for the hat and cologne. I appreciate very highly the music he sent me—think it very pretty.

Ma says tell Mrs. Lipscomb she was glad to get her letter, and will answer before long or get some of us to write.

I have just been to prayers and now find it ten o'clock so I must hurry. It seems that Annie has been exciting your curiosity without gratifying it. I will leave her to tell all about herself. When you come over we will tell you everything which cannot be written.

I will look for my *Little Rock friend* down the first of next month. Mrs. Field has returned from conference enjoyed her visit very much. She now lives at the Cobb place about a mile this side of town. I have not heard anything from Helen since you left—think I'll have to write to her. Sallie Foster's health is very much improved: sister Mollie had a letter from her some time ago, she thinks her little girl is the sweetest in the world—which she has a right to think. I am expecting Miss Mary Cooper and her sister to come out the last of this month or first of next. Miss Virgie writes to some of the family [right] often. She enjoys fine health and seems to be getting on well.

Mr. Crawford is to hold a two day meeting here next Saturday and Sunday, beginning Friday night. Mr. Holmes preached Thursday night. Mr. Parvis preached for us last Tuesday night. Give my love to brother Billy and kiss the children. I am so anxious to see you all.

I have not answered Mary Scott's last letter—thought she intended visiting her mother this summer. Good night and pleasant dreams—

> Your ever loving sister
> Mary

Morning—Sister has come over to spend the day—wish so much you could be here too. She thinks of making another visit up above L. Rock soon.

I think you must enjoy fine health to be able to do so much hard work. Mrs. Leiper and Mrs. John Pattillo expect to have their babies baptized next Sunday.

Excuse this letter and write very soon to your loving sister

> Mary

Sister Julia has received your letter—we did not open it. I suppose Annie wrote you that Mollie Williams was married to a Mr. Bishop on the Ouachita.

Annie Butler to Emma Butler Paisley in Dobyville

> Tulip
> July 1st, 1870

Dear Sister Emma,

As Mr. Childs will start this morning for Clark, I will write you a short letter in reply to your very entertaining one. I was delighted to receive yours and bro. Billy's letters, but sorry I raised your curiosity so high about nothing of much consequence. I thought you knew me better than that. I expect to see you again before any thing *very important* takes place. The letter I spoke of writing that day was to Mr. Olin Moores, who they all call my sweetheart and maybe he is, but I just feel like I could'nt marry any one. He will be up soon, probably tonight. We are looking for bro. George and sister Julia today. I guess he will come with them.

Johnnie and I went to Camden last week, got there the evening of the 21st, and to our surprise found them all preparing for the concert, which we thought would be the 22nd as Mary had written me that day. Mr. Barcus met us, and seemed very glad to see us. He was fearful we wouldn't get there until the next day. We found them all looking very well, enjoyed myself very much at the concert, had some splendid music, formed several acquaintances, and was invited to the levee (a party given to the school girls). A great many were there, and we had a delightful time, met with three young gentlemen whose acquaintance I formed while at Mr. Moores. Had an introduction to Mollie Hunt's brother. I enjoyed my visit to Camden *very much*.

Mr. Holmes preached for us night before last, but previous to the sermon, Mr. Giles and Mrs. Jimmie Wilson were married, and of all the laughable marriages, you never saw one to equal this one. I don't really believe you could have gotten a pin between their shoulders, at any time after they were married. They sat together in the front bench and talked most of the time. Sister said she felt like getting off where she could not see them.

I received a letter from Kate Moore yesterday. They were then in Little Rock. She left Mr. Archer and Johnnie in the store, I tell them, shedding *bitter tears* over her departure, and I think there is more truth than poetry in it. Kate was a sweet girl. Alice Colburn spent one night this week with me. She and the Capt. have played quits. I liked my hat and cologne very much indeed. Several said my hat was the prettiest of the season. I think it very pretty, but Pa say[s] I look awful with it on, but that is not the fault of the hat but the wearer, which is quite important but can't be *hoped* as the negro says.

I am fearful bro. George will get off to California sooner than he expected, but I hope they will get over to see you before you leave. Alice would have written to you, but thought she couldn't get the letter written to send this morning.

Pa says you could have a cow if you could send for her. It is now time for breakfast so I can write but little more. Ma says she don't think her letter can be read, as it was written last night, and she couldn't see well, says you can read it if you can. I must ask you to excuse my writing with a pencil. It is something I *seldom* do if ever. My teacher taught me not to do it, but I have deviated this time.

All send a great deal of love. Write very soon to

Annie

William Paisley to Emma Butler Paisley in Tulip

Dobyville, Arks
July 28th 1870

My dear one:

John Doby has just come in, & says he is on his way to Princeton. His coming is quite unexpected, or I would have had a letter ready for him that would have been longer & more interesting than I can possibly make this in the little time I now have.

The evening I left you we got to Dr. Lantern's by traveling some time after dusk. There was no one at home but we *camped* & were very comfortable. The next morning we over slept ourselves, & did not get started until after five o'clock. Had you been with me, it would have been different. We reached Arkadelphia a little after 12 o'clock, stopped & fed at the mill this side & got home last night at ten o'clock. Had to drive from Ross's Lane home in the dark. You may know we had a dark time coming thro the bottom. When I got to the store, I knocked and called for Henry [Patterson] until I satisfied my self that he was not in the store. I then went over home & found him there. We then came back together to the store to take care of the goods, which Willis and myself left in the wagon standing in front of the store. I went over to the house this morning & found all right, but Darling, I am not right certain yet that I can go over there & stay by myself. It looks so lonesome without you & our precious little boys.

Henry says there was nothing disturbed during our absence except one water melon—the largest in the patch—but has no idea who took it. The vines look finely now & have a great many nice looking melons on them. A great many of the large tomatoes are now good ripe. The young cucumbers are looking fine & seem to be full of cucumbers. Those in the potato patch look well also.

We have not opened our goods, but think it likely we will soon, as the worms have now disappeared & the people think they are not hurt as bad as they had imagined. Our farm (tell Henry) escaped any thing like serious damage.

Messrs. Doby & Co. expected to start this morning, but Mrs. D. has been threatened with fever for several days & will not go now—might next week. Haven't time to write more, as he is hurrying me. Hope you will enjoy every moment of your time. How much I wish I could be with you. Kiss John & Willie for their pa, & tell Jno that he must mind his mama & be a good boy till papa comes.

My love to all & many kisses for my dear ones. Henry sends love to you & the children. Mr. Veazey has gone to Texas. Your devoted husband

Wm Paisley

Emma Butler Paisley to William Paisley in Dobyville

Tulip
Friday July 29th, 1870

My dearest one,

Since it has commenced raining, I think I can't spend my time better than in writing to one I love *so* much. The day you left I spent the night with Sister, and came back to brother Henry's next morning after breakfast, where I have been ever since except yesterday evening I went down *home* and staid till late. Ira came while I was there and said Charley, Kate and sister Mary were coming on, so I waited a while, and had not been back here long before I heard they had come. Brother Charley has traded off his buggy for an ambulance (or hack), a horse, and paid a hundred dollars difference. Pa thinks a few more such trades should break Charley up.

I only saw Annie a few minutes alone, and of course could not hear much in so short a while. She doesn't think she can marry before October and doesn't want to, even then. Never felt till his last visit that she could love him. As to sister Mary's beau, I don't know what to say, as she has not heard from him in some time, and he was expected at Pa's the first of July.

John has just come in to take a nap. I asked him if I must tell "pa he wanted to see him"—he said yes. The children miss you a great deal. I don't know what I would do without Sarah, for Willie had been very fretful but is getting better now. His actions are first bad and then good; and I expect he will continue to be delicate till cold weather sets in. The children have not been exposed to the whooping cough since you left.

Mr. Jimmy Jones was in the store, and paid brother Henry thirty five dollars that John Somerville borrowed from you.

I would like so much to know how you are getting on over in Clark separated from *your loved ones.* Do you stay at home and cook your own meals, or do you visit some other place about eating time? I know you must have a lonely time of it; but I hope you are enjoying yourself eating water melons. I have not seen any as nice as those we ate at Sister's. Love to your ma and family, and many kisses for your dear self. Will try and write you a better letter in a few days.

[no signature]

William Paisley to Emma Butler Paisley in Tulip

Dobyville, Arks
(night) Aug. 5th, 1870

My dearest one:

When Henry came over to supper, he told me that Tom expected to start to Tulip in the morning, & I have just come over to the store with him to avail my self of the opportunity of writing to my dear ones. I would have written my letter over at home (notwithstanding I cannot yet help feeling lonesome there by myself) but my last candle burnt out while we were at the table & as I had to come to the store any way, I thought I would write & let Tom have the letter tonight. The evening I left you I got to Dr. Lantern's about dark & staid all night with the Dr. Mrs. L (whom you will remember as the young lady we met at Mr. Morris') talks as loud as ever, & asked very particularly about you. My lodgings for the night were very comfortable, & the next morning I found a very nicely fried chicken on the table for breakfast—thought of you *in connection with the chicken* & did full justice to the dish for both of us. I got to the store Wednesday evening about dusk.

Mr. Doby & family left for Washington [Arkansas] Wednesday morning. I found Henry up at Mr. Doby's house getting supper, & remained with him until I got some thing to eat. The next morning I went down to Father's for breakfast & since then have been cooking for myself & eating at home. Henry is taking his meals with me, & I find it much more pleasant to have his company than to be entirely alone. Besides he is a great deal of help to me. Yesterday dinner was my first meal—I had fried Bacon, biscuit & tomatoes for dinner. Last night Henry communed with me, and we had biscuit, fried meat & tea. This morning we had the same except coffee in the place of tea & the addition of biscuit toast. We can't have much variety with the little time we have for cooking, but are doing very well so far as eating is concerned. The place still wears the same lonesome appearance, & will continue to do so until cheered by the presence of my dear wife & babies.

On my way out I stopped at Dr. Harris' to leave some mail & was shocked to hear from Mrs. Harris that Jno Williamson's baby was dead. It died last Friday & was buried Saturday at Mr. McCullum's. Old man McCullum is now sick, but from what I can hear suppose he is not seriously so. Mrs. Redwine's baby will be buried at the church to morrow. It was born dead last night.

While I was over at Tulip, some cows jumped into our patch, but Mr. George Gates happened to pass about the time they got in, & turned them out before they had time to do any damage. Henry then got Uncle Dick to go over & make the fence higher.

The night I got home I found a ripe water melon in the patch. Yesterday I pulled another & today got still another—all ripe & fine. I would like so much to have you to enjoy them with me as they are the first we have had grown on our own land; but I hope the pleasure you will derive from being with loved ones at home will more than make up for all that. I found a great many ripe cucumbers & tomatoes—some of the tomatoes are rotting on account of so much wet weather. The cucumber vines had so many yellow cucumbers on them that they seemed to have stopped bearing. I pulled off between thirty & forty very large ones this morning & as I have recd the sack of salt now, will commence putting away in brine as fast as the young ones come. The vines in the potato patch have commenced bearing & I think we will have no scarcity of pickles if the cucumbers will only save in brine.

I have a hand employed now to make rails, & hope to get the yard fenced before you get back. Have not seen Pide since I came but suppose she will be up soon. The tank is full-*to-the-top*.

I am now trying to make some reliable arrangement to have our garden paled. I am very anxious to have the yard & garden enclosed before you come, as nothing we can do will improve the appearance of the place as much, & I know you are tired living out doors. Crops are very promising now, tho some think they are suffering from the wet weather. There was a hard rain here day before yesterday & some to night.

Well darling, it really seems that I have written enough, unless I had *said more* but I do not feel like I am through & must run the risk of wearying you with a little more. You must excuse the style of my letter, as I did not know of the opportunity before supper & have had to hurry a little & *put down things* as they *come up*. Your letter of the 29th July did not reach me until this evening—I enquired at the office Wednesday, but heard nothing of it. I was glad to get it, & although I had seen you since it was written, the fact of its being from you prevented any thing else from destroying its interest.

I can't help feeling a little anxious about our little boys, particularly Willie. I don't think the whooping cough would hurt John much, but *Willie* has had such a hard time teething, I should feel uneasy about him if he should take it. I hope you will not allow the children to trouble you any more than you can help while they are well. We can't get to Tulip often, & I am anxious for you to enjoy the visit as much as possible.

Ma has recd three letters from Pine Bluff. Sister Mary, Mr. Scott & Emma—all telling her of her little grand daughter, whom they have named Lula Brunson. Ma wants to go over to see them as soon as she can do so conveniently, but I don't think she will get off before September or October. You must apologize to Mrs. Henry B. for my not taking the little buggy home after carrying Willie down in it. I did not think of it until I left. Now my dear one, I believe I am through, with the exception of a word for the children. Tell Jno & Willie that if their papa does think they are troublesome & bad some times, he misses them a great deal, & is mighty anxious for the time to come when he will have their mama & them with him again. Tell Jno that it made me feel very proud of him when he behaved so well when I left him, & that he must mind his mama & be kind to his little brother & be a good boy. Excuse this letter & write often. With many kisses for your dear self & little ones & love to all I am your devoted husband

Wm Paisley

I will send Henry a copy of the Arkadelphia Radical paper & write him a short note. If you can hear of an opportunity of getting a girl that you think will be of service, I think it would be well to get your pa or Henry to engage one to come home with you. Good night.

Affly
W.P.

William Paisley to Emma Butler Paisley in Tulip

Dobyville, Arks
Aug. 12th 1870

My own precious one

Day before yesterday evening I was feeling unusually lonely, & a little before sun down walked over home, & walked around there for a while, trying to decide in my mind where I would have the Garden—where the yard fence &c, but just before dark concluded I would make a cup of tea & eat supper. About half an hour after dark I got through in the kitchen, & was in the act of starting out of the door with candle in hand, when some one whose voice I didn't recognize spoke to me. I stepped out, and found it was Johnnie. The day before, Mrs. Johnson (Dr. Key's daughter) had died after being seriously sick for only about twenty-four hours. Mr. Johnson left home Monday morning—that evening she was attacked with inflamation of the brain & was not in her right mind any more until she died the next evening. Mr. J. got home Monday night, but his wife never knew of his return & was taken off without a parting word. After hearing of her death, under the circumstances I could not help thinking of it in connection with your absence & when I found that it was Johnnie who had called me, I was afraid to ask him about you & the children, & was greatly relieved when I found he was not the bearer of bad news. I feel that we cannot feel too thankful for the blessings that have been bestowed on us & our children in the way of health, but still I cannot help fearing—when I hear of so much sickness & death.

After John's arrival I had to go to work & cook supper for *him* as I had finished my last *cooked rations*. After supper we went into your room & talked (although Johnnie was tired) until near "the wee small hours" of the night. The next morning after breakfast we went up to our place & walked over the larger portion of it looking at the crops—all of which Johnnie pronounced very fine. We then returned to Misses Brown & Lawby's house & took dinner with them. Spent most of the evening at the store, & wound up the day by going down to Father's—looked at a portion of his crop, took supper with them, slept at home, & after breakfast this morning Johnnie left for Centre Point. Tom got in some time Wednesday night, but did not deliver your letter until yesterday morning, which I was delighted to get—The one Tom brought is the first and only one I have recd. from you since I saw you. I hope to get the one you speak of having written to morrow evening by the regular mail. I was surprised to hear that Ma & others had gone to the springs, as there was nothing said of the trip while I was at Tulip. It will no doubt be a pleasant trip to them all, particularly Ma, after having been so closely confined with so much company. Wish I could have been there to have taken you.

Mr. Doby returned from Washington [Arkansas] Monday evening. I have not learned any thing more definite as to what time Mrs. D. will return than that she expected to be gone about three weeks from the time she left home.

Miss Beckie Senyard left Mrs. Hill's a few days after you started to Tulip. Have not learned the cause. I saw Mrs. Hill a few days after my return from Tulip—the last time—& she said she had no idea that Miss Beckie was thinking about such a thing until about fifteen minutes before she left. Mrs. Hill said she was very anxious to see you & have a talk with you, & I thought intimated that she wanted to say something to you to prevent your employing Miss Beckie. I may however be wrong in that conjecture. I told Miss Beckie's brother the other day to tell his sister that I thought we would like to employ her after your return. Though if you hear of an opportunity of getting a good girl at Tulip, you had better avail yourself of it, as I have not heard from Miss B. whether she is willing to live with us or not.

I have made arrangements to have our garden paled by the 1st of next month, & have succeeded in getting about one thousand rails split. Don't you think I have done pretty well? Wish I could have all the work done before you get over, but all hands are now busy saving fodder, which will delay the work some.

Darling—After reading a *portion* of your letter—You don't know how anxious I felt to see my dear little one, & how sorry it made me feel, to think you had had your feelings hurt no matter whether the cause was real or imaginary. You need have no fears of my blaming you for childishness or any thing of that kind, for it takes your tender sensibilities, springing as they do out of a pure & gentle heart, to constitute my dear Emma, the loving & lovable sweet creature that she is. Though I hope that in the case you mention, the cause of your trouble if not wholy imaginary, there should be liberal allowance made for any show of impatience or seeming neglect on the part of home folks, as I have no doubt they have been greatly annoyed & had their patience overly tried with so much company as they have had for several weeks. I did not enjoy my stay at Tulip at all for the same cause that you noticed. There seemed to be so much bustle & confusion & care about others that I thought you rather over looked & that there was not as much done to make us feel easy at home as there should have been—But when I thought of the probable cause & not wanting you to notice it, I concluded not to say any thing about it—And now, my dear one, I hope that you will not trouble your self about the matter any more, & that you will not have cause again to *think* that you have cause for trouble. I must say, however, that I could not help experiencing a feeling of pride when I made what I considered to be a timely rebuke to this thing of always having others held up to us for examples in matters that we at least ought to be capable of managing for ourselves.

But this sheet is running out & I must write about something else. I have concluded to try & get off from here this day (Friday) week, to come over after you, & shall make my arrangements with a view of going to Pine Bluff the 1st of the next week & am anxious to go should there be nothing at that time to prevent. If I succeed in getting off then, you can look for me tomorrow Saturday week & if you know of nothing to prevent our trip to Pine Bluff & it suits you, try & have every thing ready to start the next Monday morning. I was rejoiced to hear from Johnnie (tho' [I] didn't know how much he knew about it) that the children were well & hearty & both getting fat. Tell dear little John that papa was mighty proud to get his message & that his papa loves him & knows that *he is* a good boy. Tell Will that he must not forget his "Bapa," & that they must both be good boys. I don't feel like stopping but some are waiting for me to get through & I must close. Ma & all send love & say although they did not see you often, they miss you a great deal. Write the 1st of next week & believe me as ever your devoted husband. With kisses for your precious self & children

> W. Paisley

I am getting on very well, tho mighty lonesome. Henry [Patterson] is now staying at Mr Doby's. I was up at Mr D's house a while ago, & found Mr D in the kitchen preparing some vegetables for dinner. He said he had been doing without something of the kind as long as he could stand it. Love to all.

> Affectionately
> W.P.

Tulip Evermore

Emma Butler Paisley to William Paisley in Dobyville

[Tulip]
Sunday night Aug. 14th,
1870

My much loved husband,

As it is too early and I don't feel much sleepy, I will try and commence a letter to you, thinking I will have a better time than if I put it off till tomorrow. It has been a long rainy day, consequently have been kept in the house most of the time. Yesterday we heard of the death of Mrs. Lucy Martin, and who was buried in Princeton this morning at ten o'clock. She went down on a visit and was taken sick. I understand she suffered a great deal and was entirely unconscious for several days before her death.

Our little children have not taken the whooping cough yet, but I reckon this week will certainly tell whether they will have it or not. I was in hopes I would get a letter by last night's mail, as I have not heard from you since Tom was over.

Ma and company returned from the Springs last Friday twelve o'clock—we were not looking for them before evening any way—all were perfectly delighted, but none, more so than Alice. Since writing the above I have come to the conclusion that it is hardly necessary for me to be writing, as you will probably start over this week and will not get the letter; but I will finish and send it to morrow any way, as I can't tell when you may come, as you did not know when you last wrote. Good night and pleasant dreams.

Monday evening

I have just finished reading a long and interesting letter from Olin Moores. He writes like he is in great distress, and begs Annie to be ready by first of Sept. at farthest. Annie expects him to visit her tomorrow, when they will come to some understanding about the matter. I wish you could be here to see him, as neither you nor I ever had that pleasure. I think from his letters that he loves sincerely, and I don't see why Annie doubts him for a moment—she is a strange creature any way.

Capt. Cooper has not made his arrival with his fair bride. I understand his mother has been making great preparations for receiving him and it will be a pity if he disappoints her. I have made only one visit since I last wrote, and that was the evening sister Mary and I went over to see sister Hunter. She had a great many curiosities to show us.

Willie has been entirely well for the last week or more, and consequently has been less trouble. Well, I have written all of interest that I can think of now so good bye.

Love to friends and relatives and many kisses for your dear loving self.

As ever your
Emma

William Paisley to Emma Butler Paisley in Dobyville

Little Rock, Ark.
Sept 6 1870

My dearest one:

I am in rather bad fix for writing, as you will presently see but cannot miss the opportunity of letting you hear from me at this place. As you are aware by this time when I got down to Billy's I found he had concluded to take his wife with him as far as Mr. Doby's & had arranged for me to go with him in the wagon to Arkadelphia—a change that I was very willing to make as I thought it more comfortable than riding a mule—though I feared that Billy could not make it in time with a wagon. We started from his house ¼ past 4 o'clock, & by driving fast reached Arkadelphia half or three quarters of an hour before the stage left; on starting I found that I was the only passenger, and rather dreaded the lone some ride, but obviated that in some measure by sitting outside with the driver until about ten o'clock, when I got inside & slept all I could with the jolts, until I got within Eight miles of Rockport. I concluded I would try it again with the driver, but it being right cool & as I felt very sleepy I soon concluded I would get inside & nod a while longer. The stage was jolting and rocking terribly over the rough road, but I lay down on the back seat & soon went fast asleep. When we got in two or three miles of Rockport (it was dark after moon down), the driver ran into a deep gully while driving fast, & the jerk being sudden, threw me off of the seat, & my head against the edge of the hack body. My left cheek bone near my left eye struck the edge & cut & bruised it right badly. I could do nothing but suffer the pain & hold my hdkf to stop the blood until I got to Rockport. When I arrived there, I found Henry & Jim [Butler] (who had gotten there several hours before me) & Henry put some turpentine that we got from the hotel keeper on the bruised part. We got to Rockport hour & a half or two hours before day, & by day light all under my eye had swelled considerably & the black blood settled under & around my eyes. It has been very sore all day & makes quite an ugly place, but hope it will be better soon, in fact it is feeling better tonight & I will do something for it to night. We will leave here, God willing, in the morning at 4 o'clock & reach St Louis Thursday night 11 o'clock. I think we can make the trip there & back in two weeks & a half. Henry told me of the death of Geo & Julia's dear little Moores, who died before they reached Sacremento City & had to be buried & left on the road. Oh how I feel for them in their sad loss—but I must close, as this is all the paper I have. Darling, let me remind you to be sure & get some of the confections & give to Willie & John particularly Willie. Little Moores, it is said, died of worm fever. Was delighted to meet Henry & Jim & know of nothing now to prevent my having a pleasant trip except my sore & ugly face & hope that will be well soon. Don't trouble your dear self about it.

The news has reached here of the capture of Napoleon and a large portion of the French Army by the Prussians. How unexpected & what a down fall to the proud boasting Emperor of France.

Excuse what I have written. Write your letter to Memphis & this place at least two days earlier than I directed, as I now expect to be back sooner than I expected. We go from here to Memphis by stage & rail.

Kiss the dear little ones for their pa. With much love from your devoted husband

W Paisley

William Paisley to Emma Butler Paisley in Dobyville

Humboldt, Tenn.
Thursday evening ¼ to 4 o'clock
Sept 8 1870

My dearest one

You will doubtless be surprised to hear from me at this place, but what was our misfortune this morning shall redown to your pleasure (*I say this without vanity*), for I know my Emma wouldn't object to getting a line from me every day. Hope you recd my letter from Little Rock. We left Little Rock Wednesday morning about Sun up, came to Devall's Bluff by Rail & there took a boat for Clarendon, & arrived at the latter place about eleven o'clock that morning. Then we took a stage for Brinkly, a point reached by the cars coming out from Memphis, & should have arrived at Brinkly at three o'clock, but the tongue broke out of the stage we were in, & besides causing us a good deal of trouble, delayed us considerably and we did not get to Memphis until half after eleven o'clock last night. Should have arrived there at eight. We took beds at the Hotel & slept about three hours & were called up this morning in time to start from Memphis by five o'clock & came out here (eighty miles) for breakfast.

Here we had to change cars for Columbus, Ky. Henry, Jim & myself went out & deposited our baggage on the train for Columbus, went into the Hotel to get breakfast, & when we came out again, our train had moved from where we had left it & before we knew anything of its starting, we found that it had gone & left us, & that too with all our baggage. You can imagine how we felt, but there was no remedy & we were doomed to lie over until five o'clock this evening. We telegraphed to the conductor of the train to take care of our baggage at Columbus until we called for it tonight.

Our stay here would have been very unpleasant indeed, but for the fact that old Mr. Transon, the man whom I traveled with last spring & who sent me that catalogue of fruit trees, lives near here & I proposed to H & J to [go] out to his place this morning to see his nursery, & when we got out there he compelled us to stay with him all day, so we got a nice dinner & had a very pleasant time indeed, so much so that we have just returned & I have but little time now for writing. I will tell you more about what we saw when I see you. We ought to have reached St Louis tonight at 11 o'clock. Will get there to morrow morning now if not detained again.

My face is much better now & I hope will soon be all right again. Excuse rush. Kiss the little ones for me & believe me as ever your devoted husband with many kisses

Wm Paisley

William Paisley to Emma Butler Paisley in Dobyville

St. Louis
Sept 12, 1870

My dear loving Emma,

Henry & Jim have gone to bed & I thought of retiring myself, but fearing that if I put off writing to night, that I might not have time again to write you in time for my letter to reach you before I come, has prompted me to sit up a little while to night to write to my dear one. We arrived here, as I told you in my last, Friday morning and did not do much, in fact nothing at all, toward making our regular purchases Friday & Saturday. Friday we felt fatigued all day from having travelled all night the night before, & Saturday being the general "closing up" day with the wholesale merchants, made it a bad day for us to commence.

I was not idle, however, but spent some of the time in making settlements with those we were indebted to, part in seeing some of our merchants & part in seeing after some of the private orders I have to fill for others. Mrs. Doby, you know, sent for a carpet & some furniture. I bought her carpet Saturday & looked at some furniture for her at two houses. Have not bought the furniture yet, but have selected it & will buy some time during this week & have it ready to ship by the boat that takes our goods. I had never before examined the fine furniture such as Sofas, Divans, Parlour Chairs, &c & could but almost covet the nice things in that line for ourselves, but hope we will be able to have such things after a while. All those to whom we are indebted treated me very well, & seemed to be perfectly willing to wait on us for what we are owing them until we collect the money.

Henry & myself commenced buying Dry Goods this evening. It will reach Pine Bluff before the other goods. Should Mr. D receive notice of its arrival he needn't take it for granted the other goods are there. Henry & myself met Mrs. Anderson at our Hotel to night—her husband is boarding here & Mrs. A came in from her mother's this evening.

H., J., & myself went to hear Dr. Campbell yesterday morning & Dr. Brooks last night, & heard two fine sermons. Hope you are getting along well at home & that none of you will be sick. Love to all at father's & to Henry. May God bless you & keep you all. Good night.

> Your loving husband
> W.P.

Tell Jno & Willie they must not forget their papa, that he thinks of them every day. Many kisses for you & the little ones. Haven't time to look over

Mattie Phillips to Emma Paisley in D'obyville

Princeton, Arks.
Dec. 6th, 1870

Dear cousin Emma,

I know you must think me neglectful. I am only paying you back in your own coin, though it has not been intentional. When I received your dear letter, I was so delighted to receive the enclosure that I answered your letter the same day, but I left the neighborhood and they neglected to send it to the office till it was too old to send. Since then I have no excuse save the old proverb "Procrastination is the thief of time."

When you wrote to me you had a white girl to assist you in doing your work. I hope you have been fortunate enough to hire some one ever since. Last summer I often thought of you, knowing you had your own work to do and wondered how you ever got through with your work, two little babes to nurse too. You know you were always slow. I felt like I wanted to help you. Annie wrote me last week that Aunt Mary has gone over to spend some time with you. I know how glad you are to have her with you.

I suppose cousin Annie has kept you posted in her affairs. Did you ever hear of so many ups and downs in your life? She sent me word last week that she had come to the conclusion to live an old maid.

When you can snatch another half hour from your multitudinous cares, please send me the photographs of your husband & children. I should especially like to have Mr. Paisley's. Your children I have seen so little of that they almost seem strangers to me. You can't think, even at this late day, how strange it seems to me that you should be a wife and mother.

I am obliged for the invitation to visit you, and while I should like to do so, I don't know when I can.

I write to cousin John Peoples by this mail to send for Alice and I the first week in January. He was up here last fall, and said any time we could go & would let him know, he would send after us to pay him a visit. He lives near Camden. Has one daughter grown. After that, I don't know where I shall go next. Love to Mr. Paisley.

Affectionately,
Mattie Phillips

Henry Butler to William Paisley in Dobyville

Tulip Ark
Jan'y 2 1870 [1871]

A *"happy new-year"*—to you and yours—I say this as no idle custom but heartfelt. May the year be a prosperous as well as happy one—I feel that *I* have been the *negligent one* this time—for one of us ought to have written ere this, if for nothing more than to *thank you* for accompanying us several miles on our route the morning we left, for it was a disagreeably cold rain—and then to leave home as you did with Emma in bed, the children needing attention—and your "help"?—"in a muff" & refusing to attend to them. I do hope I shall never see that *round one eye* glaring at me again. I don't think I could stand to have her look at me a month.

Well to our trip—I had a *hard day* of it after leaving you. On reaching the "Deseiper" I found it nearly bank full & had to place our baggage on the seats & in laps—for the water ran through the buggy—After crossing I had to rearrange the baggage, and took out ma's carpet bag & sat it on the ground—Started off and after traveling nearly to Mr. Murdock's home, found that it was left so I had to trudge back through the rain & mud after it, Margaret [the Butlers' cook] being ahead and out of call.

We ferried the river, being detained some time, & found we would be late reaching Mr. Bullocks—so trotted along as best we could through the mud & water till the right fore wheel suddenly fell into a short deep hole—when pop—(like a granite dish let fall on a stove) went *the spring*—broken in three pieces. However this did not detain us more than forty minutes. Getting an axe, I cut a piece of timber & wrapped the remaining pieces of springs securely, and reached Mr. Bullocks about an hour after dark—very tired—*wet* and *hungry*—We met a cordial welcome, and were soon *feeling good*, drinking hot coffee & sitting by warm fires in a lively group of young ladies. Mollie suffered some during the day's travel with neuralgia. We spent the Sabbath at Mr. B—and arrived home Monday evening—found all well, but *very* anxious concerning us—none more so than Pa.

I was much pleased with the manner in which my business was looked after in my absence—Could not see that I had lost any thing by my absence. My collections are slow. Have paid about $1500 on our fall purchases—but fear we will not be able to meet the notes at maturity—"Tom Reid" was in last week and proposed to receipt us on [our] note due Orr & L.—for a bill of goods for his fathers family. Although this would have been good against O & L—I refused his offer. I would rather miss the sale of a small (or even a large one) bill of goods than to see O & L lose that amount.

Last week was very quiet around Tulip. One party at Pa's—and one tonight at Mr. Wm Youngs—who has recently moved over to his new home—Dr. Reamy has purchased the Toone place near the Baptist church and is moving to-day—so we will be close neighbors. This causes us much gratification—securing him as our Physician for another year at least.

Charlie's wife is still confined to her room & most of the time in bed—About two weeks ago her life was despaired of, but it is now thought she will recover. Little Mattie has been right sick from teething—called Dr. R in once—but is convalescent. No other sickness in the neighborhood. We look for Johnny & sister down tomorrow.

Love to Emma & your Pa's family. We heard from you through John Doby last week—the only intelligence since we left you. Ma and Mollie expressed many thanks to you for accompanying us across the creek. I think they both have a higher appreciation of you since their visit to your house and witnessed the patience and kindness you exhibited under the many cares incident to the occasion. In this I agree with them.

Write to me soon, Billy, and *I will* not wait so long again to write you. I was in hopes you would write any how.

> Affectionately
> Your brother
> H.A.B.

I hope *your daughter* is growing & affords you *much comfort*.

[The Paisley's third child, Emma, born 30 November 1870.]

HOME AND AWAY: 1871–1887

Annie Butler to Emma Butler Paisley in Dobyville

Tulip, Arkansas
Jan. 26th, 1871

My Dear Sister Emma,

To show how much I appreciated your letter, which was received this morning, I reply imme-diately. I was indeed surprised, but delighted, to receive such a long letter from sister E. What a pleasure it would be to me to see the sweet little babe! I would like so much to spend a week or so with you. I think I could assist you a good deal in the culinary department, as I have learned to be a tolerably good cook, since Aunt Lucy left us; we get on finely. I had no idea we could do half as well. I am *very* glad to have it to do, at least for a while, feel like I am worth twice as much as I was a month ago. Aunt Lucy does our washing for us, & says she is coming back to live with us next summer. She seemed very sorry to leave us. She is living with her mother.

Mr. Cain got here day before yesterday, and it has been raining ever since until this morning. I think he is water bound for some time, but he says he don't care how long it rains, so we let him stay here. He and Pa went to Princeton this morning. Capt Cooper came out with him from P.B.

Mr. Leiper opened school last Monday with 40 scholars, a good commencement. I think he will have to employ an assistant. There are a good many boarders in the neighborhood, we have one. I was very sorry pa took any, but he is to assist Ira in getting wood and feeding, and pay $10 per month.

Margaret was married last Sunday, to Osbourn Lawson, so sister Mollie is without a cook. She will miss her a great deal. Florrie is boarding at bro. Henry's & assists sister Mollie very much. They speak of taking Willie Ransome to board.

Sister got home last Thursday. We were all delighted to see her at home once more. Sister Mary, Cousin Ellen & Annie Phillips and I spent that night with her. Cousin Ellen came up to spend a month, her time will be out next week. She is very lively & looks much better than I ever saw her, she is real fine looking. Cousin Mat has been having a gay time in Camden, attending parties & balls. She was at Cousin John Peoples' the last we heard from her. Alice didn't go with her.

I received a letter from Johnnie yesterday. He thought it likely they would suspend work for a while, owing to so much rain. Said he had a bad cold caused by wading through water. If they do stop work J will be at home soon.

Alice Colburn sent us word this morning we ought to come down to see the show. She had gotten Kate to take one step.

We hear from Cal. very often, sometimes every week. They are still pleased and bro. George says he expects to visit us in three years. Olin and Charlie Moores will start to Cal. just as soon as possible. The latter was up to see us week before last. He was quite pleasant, and we enjoyed his company very much. I don't know whether the former will visit us any more or not. Brother Lewis has moved to Murphysboro, Ill. They were getting on very well when we last heard from them.

Dr. Reamy is living at the Toone place, in the bottom, near brother Henry's. Dr. Smith has returned with his bride. She is only eighteen & very pretty. She must certainly have been anxious to marry. Mr. John Smith's sister came with them & will remain until summer. I like them both very well so far as my acquaintance extends.

Ma says tell bro. Billy she don't know what she would have done without the shoes he gave her, as they had such a wet time. Says she is glad you have gotten rid of your pest.

I received a letter from Cousin Sallie this week. She enquired what had become of you. She said the fire improved Henderson very much. I don't think Mr. Archer and Ella T will marry. I am certain there is nothing of the kind on hand at present. He has been teased about her a good deal, but if they *ever* marry a "mighty" change will have to come over him.

If I have neglected to answer any of your questions you must forgive me, for I sent your letter to sister to read & I may have forgotten some of your questions. What kind of eyes has the baby?

Much love & a kiss to all & especially the baby.

Your loving sister
Annie

Mattie Hughes to Emma Butler Paisley in Dobyville

Tulip
March 21st 1871

Dear Sister Emma,

Your welcome letter was received about a week ago, and ought to have been answered immediately. I wonder sometimes how you can ever find time to write, with three little children to take care of and most of your work to do. I know one of us (your sisters) ought to write to you every week, and not think of waiting to receive an answer; and I hope for the future we will do better. At least I'll try and be more punctual, than heretofore. Of course it gives us much pleasure to receive letters from you, and I wish that you could write every week. But I think you are much more excusable than we are.

Last evening brother and sister Hunter came over and spent the night, and today Ma, Mollie, and Mrs. Cooper came over and took dinner with them. At first I was a little troubled to know what to have for dinner, as everything is so scarce now. But with very little trouble, prepared a very good dinner, at least they seemed to enjoy it very much. I wish you could have been at Tulip, last Sunday, and heard brother Hunter preach one of his good sermons. It had been some time since I had heard him, and I felt that it was a great privilege to hear him again. His text was "Sirs, we would see Jesus." I felt much encouraged to press onward, and I intend, for the future, to try and live nearer to him than I have. You must pray for me and mine, my dear sister. It affected me very much to see Walter [her eldest son] go up, and partake of the sacrament. He has been a member of the church for some time, but I don't think he ever communed before. I am so anxious for him to be a zealous Christian.

Brother Henry left for St. Louis yesterday evening. He was writing to Billy when the stage drove up, and didn't have time to finish his letter. I rode over soon after dinner, and just got there in time to bid him goodbye. George [Hughes, her husband] was at home about a week ago, since he has been within a days' ride, he has been coming home nearly every week, and spending several days with me. He requested me to give his love to you and Billy, and to tell you that he expected to visit you in a week or two. I wish it was convenient for me to come over and stay with you while he is near you.

Mr. Robertson is still living with us, and will cultivate the garden, so you know I will have fine vegetables. He is paling brother Henry's front yard now, and as soon as he can get the lumber ready he will ceil our rooms. Walter, West, and Reavis are going to school to Mr. Leiper, and seem to be learning very well. I did wish so much that Mrs. Barcus was here to send Reavis to. I hated to send him where there are so many large boys.

Annie Phillips is staying at home, and I don't know how I could do without her, she is so much company for me. She has charge of the chickens this year, and takes a great deal of interest in them. She has about twenty-eight little ones, and we have had more eggs to use this Spring than ever before. Cousin Mat [Phillips] is teaching school near Camden, gets her board and $40.00 per month. Alice [Butler] is boarding at Mrs. Holmes in Princeton, and going to school.

It has been more than a month, since we heard from brother George and Julia. Pa received a letter from brother Lewis last week, and I think from the way he writes it is very doubtful about his visiting us next Summer. They call their babe "Jessie." I do wish they would come, for I am anxious to see them.

I am sorry you think you can't leave home this summer, I am very anxious to see your little girl. I expect we will have a great deal of fruit, and I know you would enjoy it so much. I reckon John feels like he is quite a man, to carry his brother Willie from home.

Kate went home with Charlie about a week ago. I do hope she will enjoy good health now, so that she can stay with him. They have an orphan girl, about 14 years old, and Kate thinks she will be a great deal of company, and help for her.

You must write whenever you can. My love to your "Hubby" and a kiss for the children.

Your Loving Sister
M.W. Hughes

Henry Butler to William Paisley at Dobyville

Tulip Ark
Apr 11th 1871

Dear Billy:

I reached home last Sunday evening, having come *via* Pine Bluff—leaving St. Louis on Thursday last. It would have been less expensive to have gone on to Little Rock and come down in the stage, but I made something over one day in time.

I wrote you just before leaving St. Louis—giving you items in regard to my purchases &c. I purchased saddlery of Myer, Bonnerman & Co on good terms. Altogether I now feel better satisfied with my purchases than any I have made since the war. I bought more goods than I thought I would, but do not see where I purchased too many. The amts purchased from the different parties are about as follows—

Crow McCreery & Co	1620
Orr & L (I had ordered before nearly $300 worth of shoes)	425
Wm Young & Co	415
Mellier	180
Cantwell & Short	110

E.A. Tilley	60
Myer Bonnerman & Co	200
Shapleigh	250
Brad. Rain. & Co	85
D.A.J. & Co.	480
	3825

and some other small bills, such as tin ware, furniture &c &c making in all about $4000. We are owing some $1100 in St. Louis, and I am disappointed in seeing how little was collected during my absence, not enough *to pay freights.* I am quite busy—as Warren [Archer, his partner] has been called to Little Rock as witness in the U.S. Court—had left before I returned.

We will receive one load of goods to-morrow, and I have given orders to four other wagons. Our Dry goods, clothing, groceries, drugs, & Queensware had arrived at Pine Bluff ahead of me—the residue will be there on Thursday. I am *quite* anxious to hear the result of your law-suit. I sympathize *deeply* with you—Hope you will come out without but *little more* trouble. I must congratulate you on the manner in which you have conducted the affair and *restraining* your feelings &c.

Try and come by—if you can without too much trouble or detention. I would so much like to talk with you.

Love to dear sister Emma and your *children*—

> Affectionately
> Your brother
> H.A. Butler

It seems to me there is something else I wanted to write you, but cannot think what it is.

Mary Butler to William Paisley in Dobyville

> Tulip Arkansas
> April 20th, 1871

Dear brother,

Think not because I've been so long replying to your letter that it was not appreciated, for I assure you it was, and I have time and again resolved to write, but alas for the frailty of human resolutions. Annie received Emma's letter not long since, and I suppose will answer before long. I hear Alice frequently reproaching herself for not having written, but she, like myself, is slow about writing.

Brother Henry has been at home now more than a week, and I think has received most of his goods. He did not visit brother Lewis while gone which was a disappointment to both. Yesterday brother Holmes and his wife spent the day with us, and we had quite a treat for dinner—strawberries and cream—now isn't it early for them! I think we will be blessed with an abundance of fruit this year, which can be well appreciated after being deprived of it, last. Asparagus, onions, lettuce, and radishes are the only vegetables we have had yet. It is almost impossible to remain indoors these beautiful bright days, everything without looks so cheering.

We are still doing our work and get on well with it, but prefer a servant, especially in warm

201

weather—aunt Lucy has promised to come the last of this month. Annie Phillips has just come over to do some sewing on the machine—making up some of the new goods, she says Sister is not very well—brought a letter over from brother George H.—He spoke of having visited you, and thinks you will have a nice home when you get it entirely fixed up. I would enjoy spending several weeks with you so much—but can't see how I am to get over there. By the way, you must be certain to come by to see us on your way to St. Louis—notwithstanding you said you were not coming until Annie gets married—you'll have to take that back, for there's no prospect of its coming off soon: and some of the rest of us *might* take a notion to marry, and would claim equal rights to your presence.

Cousin Jimmie Butler has just come in to see us—came up to see about his goods—the two cousin Lauras are not well. I suppose you have heard that Mat Phillips is teaching school down at Camden. I learn that she is getting to be very gay—attending dancing parties &c.

We received a letter from brother George not long since. He thinks he has found the garden spot of earth. Olin Moores and Mr. Greening had bought them a place and commenced farming.

Charley and Kate are down at their home. Kate's health is improving very rapidly. The old Dr. [Kate's father] and his wife speak of going to see them this week. I received a letter from our old friend Helen Pleasants not long since, her husband had been quite sick, but was recovering when she wrote. I also received one from Miss Mary Cooper. She wrote me about Emma's [Lipscomb] marriage. There are two contemplated marriages in this neighborhood—Sallie Barbee and John Wilson and Cora Reid and Mr. Dick Gantt.

I would like to write more but must get ready to go with Annie up to see the new goods—feel that I haven't written anything of interest, but hope to see you soon. I would like so much to see Emma & the children, especially the little stranger.

Kiss them all for me, and tell Emma to write soon and often.

As ever your sister
Mary

All well and send love.

Mary Butler to William Paisley in Dobyville

[Tulip]
Saturday Apr. 22nd 1871

Dear brother,

I wrote to you day before yesterday, which was before brother Henry received his new hats, and I now write again, to ask you a favor. The hat brother H. selected for me doesn't suit me, being made of pink crape and trimmed with so much pink: the hat is a pretty one costing seven dollars; if it had been white and only trimmed with pink I shouldn't have objected to it; he has [not] another that I like, and if it will not put you to *too* much trouble, please get me one, and I will be much obliged. I leave you to use your own good taste in the selection, only remember I have dark complexion. I hope you will decide to come by to see us, if you cannot write me immediately on the reception of this, that I may know you have received it; this will be the only opportunity I'll have of getting a hat and I don't see how I can do without one. Ma says this pink one will not do. If you should be gone, Emma can send this to you in a letter to St. Louis. I expect you will say "Women folks are hard to please." Well I agree with you. I think brother Henry has a very nice selection of goods. He says you must be certain to come by this way.

We are having some very cool weather now. Last night the beans and potatoe vines were killed, and I think there will be frost again tonight.

With much love I am as ever

> Your sister
> Mary B.

Alice says please get a piece of music for her. "Reply to no one to love" song. I don't know whether that is the exact title or not.

Annie Butler to William Paisley in Dobyville

[April 22, 1871]

Brother Billy,

Please get me a fan. I would prefer one that opens and shuts if they are used. I don't want a very costly one. What suits you will be apt to please me.

I am sorry to hear you are not coming to see us until I marry, for I have no idea of taking that important step soon if ever. But you will certainly come to see another sister married, and I think I will get to see you next fall at any rate. She is just going ahead—Look out—

I am writing at the store, and bro. Henry is waiting on me so Good bye, much love to all.

I remain your loving sister

> Annie

William Paisley to Emma Butler Paisley in Dobyville

> Camden, Ark.
> May 3rd, 1871

My dearest one—

I arrived here this Wednesday morning, after a rather tedious trip down the Ouachita on the little steamer "Bluella." We left Arkadelphia yesterday morning, & ought to have reached here the same evening, but the River being very full, our boat ran out on some timber & smashed up the wheel, which required some time to repair. Mr. McDaniel came down with me & I will have his company all the way down & as long as I remain in the city. The worst of all is, though, we missed connection here with the New Orleans boat, and will have to remain here until Friday or Saturday. I don't see how I can content myself or become reconciled to having to lie over near home so long—but will have to put up with it. If the waters were down I believe I would get on the stage &

run up to Tulip, but the River is two or three miles wide, besides other high waters between here & there.

While I am here I will try & see cousin Mat, though I have not been able as yet to learn any thing about her. The merchants here seem to think that I can do fully as well purchasing in N.O. as I could any where else. If I find that to be the case I will certainly buy there, but if I don't feel satisfied about the matter after looking, you needn't be surprised to hear of my going on to St. Louis. My anxiety to get back home as early as possible will be duly considered when I come to decide the matter.

Today is the day for the picnic. Wonder whether you are attending. Hope that you are and that you will have a nice time. I forgot to say any thing to you about it just before I left. I will buy a Barrel of Flour here & send it up by Boat to Mssrs Neely & Corden, Arkadelphia. Please ask Mr. Doby or Ben to send for it for you the 1st opportunity. I am afraid you will get out before you can get it.

Having only been here a short time I cannot write any news, but will write you again before I get off. The weather is beautiful now, & I anticipate a pleasant trip.

With many kisses for your dear self & little ones, I am your affectionate

Husband
Wm. Paisley

Emma Butler Paisley to William Paisley in New Orleans

At Home
May 7th, 1871

My dearest one,

I have just got through with dinner, and as the baby is still sleeping will commence my letter whether I finish it or not. Miss Beckie went home this morning (having heard previously that Sue had returned from Arkadelphia), and the little boys are out at play, so I am left alone.

Well! we all did go to the picnic and enjoyed ourselves better than I expected. You ought to have seen us start off. Miss Beckie (with the baby) and John went on ahead, leaving Willie and the basket of dinner for me to bring on the horse; coming back John got up behind, and Willie in my lap. I would not thought of riding, but the night before the picnic Willie was sick—vomiting and running off at his bowels, and I thought then that our trip would be broken up; but he seemed much better next morning so I concluded I would ride and carry him. We had quite a bountiful dinner—I mean after it was all spread on the table. It was quite cool all day, so *we* old folks with our babies remained in the school house most of the time by a fire.

I had Nettie [the dog] put up, but last Thursday evening, while Mr. Cordell and I were washing and examining the meat, she got out and came to the smoke house where we were, before we knew any thing about it. I felt afraid of her, and if she had bitten me it would have been certain death, but soon felt relief; for when I threw her some meat, she commenced eating and seems to be improving ever since. We have not tried to put her up again, for I don't believe any thing in the world is the matter but a very sore mouth. She is very poor, but I don't wonder at that, for it is with the greatest difficulty she eats or drinks. While in the coop she would neither eat nor drink and thought, I reckon, she was put up as a punishment for some crime she had committed. If you had not sent me word not to have her killed, I reckon she would now have been dead, and that too for being a mad dog—for Mr. Jordan had been reading some account of mad dogs, stating how any one could tell a mad dog &c. and as Nettie had so many symtoms mentioned I began to think she was mad and felt very much like having her shot.

I do hope she will soon entirely recover and relieve us from all anxiety.

I was truly glad to get your letter from Camden (as well as the flour and candy). We were entirely out of flour, but borrowed enough from ma to make light bread.

I received a letter from Johnny yesterday morning. He is now camped near Washington [Arkansas] and expects to remain about that place until the completion of the line. The baby has awaked, so I will have to quit for the present.

Wednesday

Last Monday we all walked over to Mr. Logan's and spent the day—found the road very rough for Willie, and had a good deal of trouble to get him along. We had a very pleasant time. I wouldn't be much surprised if Mrs. Harris came here to-day, since it rained very hard last night.

Mr. Cordell planted corn, Irish potatoes, and melons yesterday. All of the lumber has not been hauled yet, but Jim Snodgrass brought out part of a load to his father's last night, and promised to bring it over this morning. The carpenters say they can finish the house in two days after the lumber is brought. It is quite cool this morning and fire feels very comfortable.

Well, darling, I have written all I can think of at present—so I will bid you good bye. The children are all well. With much love and many kisses I am as ever your most loving

Emma P

William Paisley to Emma Butler Paisley in Dobyville

New Orleans
Friday night May 12th, 1871

My dear one,

You will no doubt censure me for not writing sooner when I tell you that I have now been in the city three days. I can't help reproaching my self, but really it seems that I haven't had time to write since I came. The Boat I came down on arrived here last Wednesday morning an hour or two before day. After daylight Mr. McDaniel & myself came up & stopped at the City Hotel, got our breakfast, & after eating I came around to Messrs. T & S Henderson's office, thinking I would write to you as soon as I could get through preliminaries, but Capt Sam Henderson, who does all the purchasing for T & S Henderson, soon got ready to start out on his regular round, & nothing would do but I must go with him & be introduced to his favorite merchants. There was then no chance for me to write that day, & since then I have been so busy examining goods & prices that I could not collect my thoughts sufficiently to write in the day, & until to night have had no facilities for writing at night. I felt very tired to night when I stopped work, but I found that some of Messrs Henderson's clerks would be in their office to night & after getting supper I came around determined I would not keep my little one—who is always glad to hear from me—waiting any longer.

Tulip Evermore

I had a very pleasant trip from Camden down. The Boat was one of the best I ever travelled on, & all the trip lacked of being the most pleasant one I ever made was not having you & the children with me. I could not help thinking about it all the way & told Mr McDaniel if I had to start again, I thought I would bring you even if times were hard. I have felt remarkably well ever since I started from Camden. Mr McD and myself remained at the Hotel until after supper the 1st day & then moved to a very nice private Boarding House that he had found during the day. Our fare is good & every thing very comfortable except being a little too much crowded.

Messrs T & S Henderson are just as kind as they can be, & although I never knew them personally, I feel almost like they were kin folks. They both think there is no better man living than your Pa. Capt Sam Henderson is a good deal younger than old Col. Maurice Smith, but I never saw two men more alike in their manners & way of talking than they are.

All the merchants here are hard pressed for money, & as anxious as they can be to sell me what goods I want. They have all learned that I intend paying the cash & you ought to see them running after me. I have been trying the Dry Goods market thoroughly, & think it probable that I will quit looking & commence buying to morrow. Nice dress goods are very scarce & nothing like the stocks that I have been accustomed to seeing in St. Louis. That, however, can be partly accounted for in this way—a great many of the fine dress goods we get are manufactured in France, & the late war having stopped all the Factories there, they are not to be had. I bought Men's Hats, Shoes, & Crockery to day. Have not bought any Ladies Hats yet. From what I have seen of goods in that line, I fear that I will not be able to get what I want. I have seen nothing yet that will at all suit sister Mary, but may find something yet. I don't think I will be able to find the kind of goods Miss Maggie Johnson wanted, but you needn't say any thing to her about it, as I may come across it. I have bought our carriage & think I have got just such a one as we need. I know you will think its the very thing. Hope Mr. Doby will find it convenient to send Ben down with the mules so I can bring it up.

Strawberries, Bananas, Plums & oranges are in great abundance here, & look mighty nice. I have not eaten many, though never see them without thinking of you & wishing you had some.

I regret now very much that I didn't ask you to write me here, as I would have had plenty of time to have received your letter after being detained in Camden as I was. How much I would give to know how you are all getting along. I hope Mr. Cordell & Miss Beckie are still with you, & that Mr. C is still pushing every thing forward. Tell him I want him to turn things around so that I will hardly know my own place when I get back. The weather has been remarkably cool ever since I came down & I am afraid we have had killing frost. I do hope the vegetables are not killed. Wonder what my darling is expecting me to bring her. I am going to try mighty hard to surprise you again, as I succeeded one time *last fall*.

It is now nearly 11 o'clock & I must close & try and get rested for a hard days work tomorrow. I hope to get through buying the middle of next week, but may not finish before the last of the week. Do not get uneasy about me. Tell John & Willie that I see a heap of pretty things they would like to have, but that Papa can't buy them all, but will try & bring them something. Tell little Emma that Papa thinks of her even if he is away & that she musn't forget him.

Wish I could write more, & that what I have written was more interesting—but will trust you to make allowances. May God bless & protect my dear ones. With much love & many kisses

Your devoted husband
W. Paisley

Wrote to Mr. D to night.

Julia Moores Butler to Emma Butler Paisley in Dobyville

Los Nietos
May 22nd 1871

My dear Emma—

George remarked a few mornings since—"I must write to Billy Paisley—Why don't you write to Emma." The answer I gave him is about the only excuse I can give you for not writing sooner. "I have been intending to write ever since I have been in Cal. but I don't know why I haven't." Once commence putting off any thing of the kind, and it is a hard matter to begin.

I have not written a letter for almost five months—the last I wrote was to Alice—in Jan—but I think I will do better hereafter. I assisted George in the school most of last session. That term closed about the middle of April. We had a very pleasant little examination at the close, the scholars did admirably, considering the short time spent in preparing. Two weeks ago the Dist Conference was held in this valley.

Friday the 5th inst we had a S.S. [Sunday School] celebration and picnic—several speeches—all very good, a nice dinner, and such good singing by the S.S. There was a large crowd out, although the day was somewhat unfavorable. These Californians beat any people to go you ever saw, very often go twelve miles to spend the day. To Los Angeles or Wilmington twelve miles and back by 2 o'clock is a common occurrence. The roads are level and the horses spirited, and in a good buggy or spring wagon travelling is a pleasure.

We have neither horses or buggy yet—we live in less than half a mile of the church—so that we can walk—and George hires his land cultivated. They are now planting it "sodding it in"—that is, plant the corn as they break up the ground. George thinks his is planted so deep that he will not have a good stand.

I like housekeeping first rate—get through with my work without any trouble. George does the milking, and we get our washing and ironing done for tuition—so I am relieved of the two greatest troubles. One cow gives more milk and butter than we can use. I make at least a half pound of butter daily. I succeed very well in raising chickens—bought 7 hens and a rooster, and ma gave me a hen and chickens—and now I have over a hundred in all, and have sold and eaten some. George kills the chickens and I pick and clean them. I am a slow and awkward hand.

Ma and all the family are getting on very well. Buddie [Olin Moores?] and Earle Greening have bought places. Charlie has rented—all doing very well, especially Buddie. He seems to understand managing better than the others.

George has commenced another session, has between thirty and forty scholars. He gets on very well teaching, but I believe he would rather be in a circuit. He is Supt. of our S.S. Twice a week we have singing—the singing master charges all the gentlemen two dollars each. The ladies and children go free. With the money he gets, he is going to purchase an organ and present it to the Sunday School. He teaches two months.

This neighborhood is improving rapidly—but the houses are very small, very few improvements. Los Angeles is a beautiful place—the ladies dress more after the styles of the North than we have been accustomed to—more flounces &c &c than you can imagine.

How is your baby? Who does she look like and what have you named her? Kiss all the children for me—Love to Mr. P. Write soon, and I assure you I will write oftener in the future. We live about a mile and a half from Ma's. I go over once or twice a week, but I spend most of the time alone. George sometimes comes home for his dinner.

J.M.B.

Lewis Butler to Mary Butler in Tulip

Murphysboro, Ill.
June 5th 1871

My Dear Sister Mary:

Your last letter was received some time ago. Our Circuit Court, which sits only once every six months, has been in session for almost a month, and it being my first term here, I felt that it was of unusual consequence to me that I should make a good appearance. I am satisfied I have succeeded even beyond my expectations. I was taken into several very important cases by a distinguished lawyer who now lives in St Louis, Col. Thos. G. Allen, but who used to live at Chester this state and practice in this county, and my efforts in those cases attracted pretty general attention and gained me considerable character as a lawyer. I have already a good and increasing business, and in a few years, if life & health continue, will be in a practice worth several thousands annually, and when that is the case I can afford to visit "home and kindred" without depriving myself of means necessary in the maintenance of my family. At present I could not undertake a trip "home" for the latter reason, and I know that will furnish all the apology necessary for me to make.

Jennie and Jessie are both well and happy. We have for the last two weeks had a servant girl, and as the weather will now be very warm, will continue during the summer to have one. Little Jessie I would so much like for you to see. She is the most perfect little cherub you ever saw— Acknowledged everywhere to be the prettiest baby any one ever saw, and the smile of intelligence and amiability which almost constantly lights up her countenance and sparkles in her large dark grey eyes is perfectly enchanting to behold. Jennie & myself frequently argue to ourselves that it is only parental fondness that sees such unusual beauty in her, but we always conclude that this is not the true solution, and that making all allowances for this, she is yet exceedingly lovely. She has scarcely been sick at all since she recovered from the *colic* to which she was subject during the early weeks of her babyhood. Yet we sometimes feel appalled at the thought of losing her. We will send her picture when we can get a good one taken.

Jennie is the sweetest and best of wives, all the heart could wish, and one day soon we hope you will all become acquainted with her. She would call me silly & foolish (in sport) if she knew I was writing so much about her and the baby, but I do not think I could write on a more interesting theme both to you & me.

Write soon again, and write one of [your] own long and interesting letters. Love to all.

Your affectionate brother
Lewis P. Butler

Annie Butler to Emma Butler Paisley in Dobyville

Tulip, Arkansas
June 23rd, 1871

My Dear Sister Emma,

It has been some time since your last letter was received, and really I feel badly for my long silence, but I have so many to write to I cannot write to one very often. It is getting too warm to write. We are having real summer weather now. We have a great deal to do before our District Conference meets, which will be the last of July; we are expecting a great crowd. Sister Mary and I spent last night at bro. Henry's, had a very pleasant time. He is improving his place rapidly, and it seems to me has every thing one could desire. His is now called the prettiest place on the Ridge.

Mr. Leiper's school will close in two weeks. He expects to have a little exhibition one night. Ira and Jimmy have gone up to the academy this evening to speak. Alice was too unwell to go. She isn't sick much, thinks she will be well tomorrow.

Have you had much fruit? We are just having plenty, we had a great many cherries, and now have plums, apricots, and apples, in abundance.

I had a letter from Fannie Moores about five weeks ago; the last we have heard from Cal. They all seem better pleased than ever. It must be a great country, but I believe I still prefer living in old Arkansas. I have heard nothing direct from ———— since he left, but think he is one of the best that ever did or ever will live, he has but *few* equals. "Blessings brighten as they take their flight." Johnnie told us about seeing you all, and especially you and bro. Billy making cakes. I am glad Eliza has married well, but she was right young. Tulip is the hardest place, I *reckon* in the world, to make a start in that direction, always talking but never acting. I think she will take a start this fall, if she don't I shall give her up, and think we will all live old maids together which I am bound to be, if—

Anna Colburn and Eloise Jenkins expect to visit us next month. I should dislike very much to be in a city now. Since I last wrote you, we have had two deaths in the neighborhood, Uncle Maurice Smith and Mrs. Ben Smith. They were both perfectly resigned to death. The latter left a baby six weeks old. Mrs. James Pattillo will raise it. The mother of thirteen children—how much they will miss her. Ma has come in and says how is Emma the 2nd getting on? and what do you think of bro. Lewis's great baby? I can't help but believe from his description, that it is the greatest baby now out. Mrs. Reamey has a little babe two or three days old—another little sister.

Aunt Lucy is with us and does finely. I think her baby improved her very much.

I am very much pleased with my fan, and render many thanks to bro. Billy for his trouble.

Mr. Archer, Annie Phillips, and I went over to Mr. Thompson's last Saturday night, expecting to attend the "foot washing" the next day, but were disappointed as it was deferred until the next meeting. We rode eleven miles horse back to see it & then disappointed, but we had a real nice time and enjoyed ourselves *very much*.

Much love to bro. Billy and a kiss to the children.

Your sister
Annie

Ma is saving seed for you, I mean fruit seed—how much I would like to see you all—Pardon my long delay in writing. I have *no sweetheart* at present. I am done with all until the right *one* comes. So Good-bye

Annie

William Paisley to Emma Butler Paisley in Dobyville

St. Louis, Mo.
Monday morning, Sept. 18th, 1871

My dearest one—

I wrote you from Memphis, & the next night at 11 o'clock found me in this city—started from Memphis Saturday morning, ½ past 4 o'clock & arrived here the same night at the time above mentioned—distance 347 miles. My entire trip was a very pleasant one, taking out the 1st night's staging.

On my arrival here I went to the Barnum house expecting to find Henry there, but was informed by the clerk that he was not there. I spent the night & Sunday morning after breakfast came up to the Planters, having been told that he was stopping here & learning the no. of his room sent my card up & was met in the Parlor by Mrs. B. She seemed delighted to see me. Henry had gone out to look for me at the other Hotel thinking that I might have gotten in the night before, but soon returned & we all had a happy meeting & a long social confab together, until it was time to go to church. I was sadly disappointed in not meeting Sister Annie, for I had expected to find her all full of life & reflecting every emotion of enjoyment (that I expected such a trip would afford her) from her bright eyes, but her stay here was so short that she did not even get to see much of the city, & I very much fear that her expectations were not realized. They all arrived here Friday night, & Saturday night went down to see Lewis (in Illinois). Henry & wife returned Monday, but Annie remained with Lewis' wife & will stay there until they start home. Mrs. B. seems to have enjoyed herself finely. Yesterday at 11 o'clock, we went out to hear Dr. Linn of the Methodist Church & at night went to hear Dr. Brooks. In the evening we walked out to Lafayette Park & strolled over its beautiful grounds, & all that marred my enjoyment was your absence. Could you have been along my enjoyment would have been complete.

Henry is about through purchasing, & expects to leave to morrow or next day. I shall feel very lonesome after they start, but more at home at my old Hotel than I would be at the Barnum. (I moved up yesterday.) Breakfast is now about ready & I must close, by asking you to excuse this, as I have only written that you might hear from me, & will write again soon. I have kept up my early rising ever since I left home & feel much better from it.

Lewis has sold out all his furniture & expects to move to St. Louis. Suppose tho that Annie has posted you about that.

With much love for your dear self & little ones

Your Affectionate & devoted husband
W.P.

Haven't time to look over.

Mattie Hughes to Emma Butler Paisley in Dobyville

Tulip
Dec. 11th 1871

Dear Sister,

I have been intending to write to you ever since I got home, but have postponed it from day to day, thinking I would feel more like writing some other time. I have been at home about four weeks, and have been quite busy most of the time. If you were near a post office we would write to you more frequently. When I sit down to write to you, I always think it will be two or three weeks before you will receive my letter or perhaps never get it. I think I sent my photograph to you last Spring, and you never received it. I know I wrote you a long letter, that you didn't receive. I would send you another picture, but didn't have one taken while I was in Little Rock.

I had a pleasant visit, and my health was good all the time. I weigh 124 pds. now, 8 pds. more than I ever did. I enjoyed conference very much, heard some excellent sermons, and spent every morning during the session in the conference room. We had so many visiting brethren, that it made conference more interesting than usual. Dr. Redford made a lengthy speech, and said a good many amazing things. This was his first visit to Arkansas, and I expect you saw in the "Western Methodist" how much pleased he was with Little Rock. Our next conference will be at Pine Bluff, and that will be your time to go. If I am at home, just come by and leave your children with me. I would take pleasure in keeping them for you. But it is a long time off, and none of us know what changes may take place, between now and then. It was some distance from where I was boarding to the Presbyterian church, and I didn't attend the Synod more than once. I would have gone on Sunday, but it was a rainy day. Some of their best preachers were absent, I think, at least Mr. Crawford was, and I think that he is one of the best.

I suppose you heard that Miss Cora Reid and Mr. Dick Gantt, were married. We were invited to the breakfast, and all seemed to enjoy themselves. I believe they had nearly every thing that is good, one table loaded with meats, and another with cakes and confectionaries. I suppose you heard some time ago, that Miss Sarah Martin and Bill Reid were to be married. "They say" his family have succeeded in breaking it up, and Mr. Gantt has given him some employment in Little Rock. It surprises me that she would think of marrying such a fellow.

I left Walter in Little Rock, and he has been home sick ever since. He is writing in the railroad office, I am anxious for him to come home and spend a week or two, but don't know when he can get off yet. George [Hughes] and John came by last week, but didn't spend but a day or two. I expect them again the last of this week. They are visiting every county in which the C. & F. company [Cairo & Fulton Railroad] own land, to have deeds recorded for the railroad company. They expect to get through about Christmas, and I am anxious to know what George will have to do next. Johnnie expects to visit *Centre Point* before he returns.

How do your little ones stand so much cold weather? Isn't it troublesome to keep them indoors? The snow here was over seven inches deep, the deepest I ever saw I think. West and Reavis enjoyed it very much. Andrew Hunter & Willie Bowman are staying with them now. I expect they will remain about a month, and then go to Saline to live. Brother Hunter and his wife have been staying at Pa's, but expect to leave for Little Rock next Friday. Alice thinks of going with them, to go to school.

Old aunt Anarchy is with me yet, but expects to leave soon. I don't know yet whether I'll have any one next year. I don't care much, for as long as I have Annie, we can do finely. Molly expects to do her work and is delighted. Says she is going to have every thing convenient, intends having her stove put in her dining room and will have it enlarged. May has been quite sick, from cold and fever, but she is up and running about again.

Charlie and Kate were up about two weeks ago, and expect to come up again and spend Christmas week. I wish you could be here to take Christmas dinner, Ma has had her "gobbler" up some time. My love to Billy, and a kiss for the children. Be sure and write soon to Your loving

Sister M.W. Hughes

Annie Butler to Emma Butler Paisley in Dobyville

Tulip Arkansas
Dec. 11th 1871

My Dear Sister Emma

Your note written to me was received this morning, and before writing any news I must ask forgiveness for *our negligence*, but I cannot say forgetfulness, for there is not a day that I do not think of and pray for sister Emma, her husband, and children. Now my dear Sister you must overlook our (I acknowledge) *great* fault and will endeavor in the future to be more punctual in performing our duty. I was thinking yesterday I ought by all means to write to you, but we have had so much company that it just seemed impossible to write to anyone. I have written very few letters recently. I have neglected other absent members of the family as much or more than I have you. My affection for you has not lessened, we all love you very much, and I hope you will not for *one moment* longer entertain such a thought that you are not cared for by the loved ones of home.

Brother Hunter & wife have been staying with us for several weeks, and are now in *our* room where I am endeavoring to write, while all are busily engaged in talking. I have to write all my letters in a crowd or go off in the cold, which I am fearful to do as I have already taken a very bad cold.

Miss Mary Cooper has returned from Ga., reached here at 10 o'clock at night on the 19th of Nov. on her way to Camden, and as I was invited to attend Mary Barcus's marriage on the morning of the 22nd, we got bro. Henry's buggy and Ira for our driver. We got to bro. Charlie's that night and the next evening reached Mr. Barcus's, where they all seemed delighted to see us. Lucy Bullock and Miss Sue Harris were also at the marriage; we were the bridesmaids. Mr. Tom Bullock & Mary were married at 7 o'clock on the morning of the 22nd, and we all started off in our buggies to Mr. Bullock's; we had a delightful ride and arrived at Mr. Bullock's about dark. A splendid supper had been prepared for us all, and all the young ladies in the neighborhood were invited, and some from Arkadelphia. I enjoyed the whole trip *so much*.

On the morning of the 28th we were all invited up to Maj. Reid's to see Cora & Mr. Dick Gantt married; a good many were invited. They had a magnificent breakfast. The table would have looked beautiful at night. Everything passed off well, and we had a real pleasant time. So you see I get to go to all the weddings if I don't get to go to my own. I will have to live single and enjoy myself, but I don't intend to live an old maid, that is if I can find one to suit me. I will give you ample time to get here—nothing in hand at present—and Sister Mary is making *no* progress in that direction.

From present appearances Johnnie will be the first one to marry. He went to *Centre Point* last week, and will return through here in a few days on his way to Little Rock. He expects to quit the R.R. next month. Brother Hunter has just told me to tell you howdy for him, he is the *same good man*, he certainly has few equals. Pa has been staying in the store since Mr. Archer left, but we heard lately that the latter was dissatisfied and wished to return to Tulip.

[no closing]

Mary Wyche Butler to Emma Butler Paisley in Dobyville

[Tulip]
[Dec. 11, 1871]

My Dear Daughter

You dont [know] how bad I felt when I got your letter, to think it had been so long since you had heard from any of us. It is too bad. I think it will not be the case again. You have waked us up now. Bro Hunter says you will get more letters now than you can answer.

We are busy preparing to go with Bro and sister Hunter to L R. They have been staying with us for a week. We have had a pleasant time with them. I feel it is a blessing [to] have a Preacher to pray with us. You know he is powerful in prayer. He carried sister Hunter and me to Hunter Chapel Sunday. He preached the funeral of Mrs. Thomas, Uncle Jimmie Williams' daughter, his text Job 19c 23vs. It may be the last time I shall hear him for a long time. Has no home here now. It is a great loss to us. He is one of the best men I ever saw. It is hard to give them up. The more I see of him the better I like him. They have gone to the old place tonight to stay with Bro Caldwell. I miss them so much.

I expect Annie will tell you all the news. I only write to let you know I have not forgotten you, you must know that if all the rest forget you, I never will. Daily do I remember you and yours at a Throne of grace. Do you the same for me. I am glad you wrote as you did. Write whenever you can.

How are the little ones getting on? Do they rember Grand ma? Wish I could send them something. My love to Cap Lipscomb and family. Wish you could be with us Christmas. You and William accept the love of your Mama   good night

Mary Butler to Emma Butler Paisley in Dobyville

Tulip, Arkansas
Feb. 5th 1872

Dear Emma,

I have been promising myself to write you for a long time and really must write tonight.

Well, Johnny begins to look a little "blue," as it has been raining all evening and still continues, and he will be compelled to start in the morning to reach Sevier [County] in time for that all important occasion. He regrets now that he didn't start this morning; however, he will make a desperate effort to be there at the appointed time. If the weather is favorable, we will look for him to return with our new sister the middle of next week. Pa says if you can come over at that time Dr Colburn will fix your teeth. I got on finely with mine, wouldn't be without them for anything. I was very much surprised to hear that you had never used yours.

Pa and Johnny went down to cousin Jimmie Butler's last week, found him quite unwell, his arm sprained and his throat so inflamed that he could scarcely speak above a whisper; the way the accident occurred was this—the children had been in the store, firing popcrackers and in their carelessness set the bed on fire, cousin Jim finding it out became alarmed, and in his hurry running out with the beds fell down and hurt his arm; pa was fearful that the blaze went down his throat and might prove to be serious: but we learn that he is now better.

Charley came up last Saturday night with his wagon for some sheep, left this morning. Kate didn't come with him. Johnny and I went down to see them not long since, and spent two days: they seem to be getting on very well: Kate has made her rag carpet and put it down: which is very comfortable. Sister went up to Little Rock week before last: we expect her home this week. Cousin Ellen has been staying with her sister Annie, she went home this morning. I will have to go and stay until Sister returns. Brother Henry and sister Mollie took dinner with us today, they have no cook now since Linda has married and left, but I don't think they will do without long; sister Mollie finds it too much for her.

Kate Coulter left last week, Capt. McKean came by for her. We have had only two letters from Alice since she left—says she has to study so hard, she can hardly find time to eat or sleep. She seems to be very much pleased. Annie was delighted with her trip. Tell Mr. Paisley she came home fully determined to marry after hearing his lecture on "old maids"; had never thought before of its being so bad here at Tulip; by the way, madam rumor has it, that Kate Cooper is to leave that list before very long, and from some indications we may judge it is true: however it is hardly worth while to write of such things until they actually take place, since there are so many slips. Mr. Carver from N. Ca is the name of the gentleman, with whom she got acquainted, while at Col. Whitaker's during Christmas. Mr. Archer was out to see us week before last and reported all our acquaintances down there well. He is not much pleased with Pine Bluff, but is doing well—gets a hundred dollars a month. John Martin Smith was married to Miss Bocage last week. Miss Sarah and Mrs Roane went down to the wedding.

Sister and I can't get over to see you this winter on account of bad roads: it seems hard for me to ever visit you though I hope to, some of these times. Annie left her black bow, which she wore on her hair, and wishes you to send it to Arkadelphia to the care of Mr. Neely, so that Johnny can get it in passing; that is, if you see no better opportunity of sending it.

214

I will send this letter to Arkadelphia by Johnny. He will soon be ready to start. All are well & unite with me in much love to you and Mr. P. Kiss the dear little ones for me, and write soon. With many wishes for a happy and prosperous new year, I am your loving sister

Mary

I forgot to tell you I received a letter from Helen, she speaks of visiting me in the summer. Her husband died last fall. Her sister Anna is married again to a Mr. Stuart.

William Paisley to Emma Butler Paisley in Dobyville

Camden, Ark.
Apl 9th 1872

My dearest one:

I suppose Mr. Jones informed you of my good luck in finding a Boat at Arkadelphia nearly ready to start to Camden. I hardly had time to attend to some little matters in Arkadelphia, but preferred letting them go to being detained several days. The River was so high that our Boat couldn't be managed in the night—so we had to tie up at dark & wait for day light—reached Camden this evening about 3 o'clock & found a Boat here, the "Marcella," which will start for New Orleans at 5 o'clock this evening. So you see that I am still in "Luck".

The clerk has just notified me to be ready, as the Boat will start in a short while &, as I have some business yet to look after, I will have to ask you to let me off with this short & hurried note. I was tired last night, went to bed early & got a *good* night's rest & to day feel first rate. You & sister Mary must keep in good spirits & have a good *Garden* when I get back. Hope that my good fortune may attend me throughout the trip, so that I will not be unnecessarily detained from my dear ones.

Your devoted husband, with much love for yourself sister M & children

Wm Paisley

Mr. Buchanan & Mr. Montgomery, Mr. Allen's uncle, are going down on same boat—very pleasant company

Annie Butler to Emma Butler Paisley in Dobyville

Tulip, Arkansas—
April 10th, 1872.

My Dear Sister Emma,

Your letter was received a short time since. We were very glad to hear from you all, & am surprised that S. Mary hasn't written again. I didn't know that you were indebted to me, but I would have written any way, for I won't be ceremonious with you. I suppose bro. Billy has gone for his goods before this.

Mr. James Pattillo left last Monday week, and is expected home tonight.

Tell S. Mary Mr. Minor has taken two dinners with us since she left. Yesterday Bro. George Hughes, sister, Annie, bro. Henry's family & Mr. Minor dined with us, and you just ought to have seen Annie [Phillips] & I entertaining the last mentioned. The day passed off quite pleasantly, and in the evening bro. Caldwell & wife rode over. Theresa Jones and I went down and spent the night with Alice Colburn. She had a lovely time while her Pa & Ma are at bro. C's. They expect to be there several weeks.

Last Saturday night Jimmie Pattillo came down, but hadn't been here but a short while before Bob & Dick Smith came. I felt quite strange to be the only young lady, to entertain three gentlemen but the time passed off very pleasantly, all seemed to be so lively & talkative. I believe Bob & Kate Cooper are now engaged, but don't know whether they will ever marry or not.

We have had several letters from Cal. Bro. George thinks it is the greatest country in the world. Sister Julia says she doubts whether a better one could be found this side of heaven, but as yet she has formed no attachment to the country or people. I don't think the ladies are pleased, & others had better take warning and remain in our beloved & native state.

Pa carried Sister Mollie & Coulter up to L. R. to meet bro. Henry. They seemed to enjoy the trip very much; spent a day and a night with Cora, said she seemed to be getting on so well, and perfectly happy.

Mr. William Reid is engaged to be married to a wealthy young lady in Little Rock. It is a great thing for some people that they are not *well* known *every where*. They look upon him as being something great.

I am so anxious to see S. Mary, hope it will not be much longer before she comes. Pa says he thinks it is very strange she doesn't write. Much love to S. Mary and the children. All send love. Write soon to

> Your loving sister
> Annie

P. S. If it is inconvenient for bro. Billy to bring S. Mary all the way, Pa can send to Arkadelphia, but I would like for him to come all the way. Ma says she misses Sister Mary more than she ever did, as we have so few in family. I don't think I can wait *patiently* very much longer. I expected to send this letter by bro. Caldwell, but he left the evening I wrote.

I think we will have a great many strawberries, as the bed is white with blooms. Wish you could have some of them. Ma says how many turkey eggs have you set, she has forty. We have about 50 chickens.

George Butler to William Paisley in Dobyville

[Spring 1872]

Mr. William Paisley

My dear brother—

I have been intending to write to you and Emma for a long time. And now I hardly know where to begin. There is so much that I might write about—and yet I reckon you have read our letters or some of them, and I do not wish to reiterate. I would like very much to hear from you—how are you getting on in business, in religion &c. When you write you must be sure to tell me something about bro. Lipscomb, your mother & all the family. What are the prospects of the country &c. Not that I have any thoughts of returning to Ark. to remain. I think I am settled for life in Cal. Here I expect to live and die. I would like to visit Ark. in a few years, and will try to do so if my parents live & I can spare the money to bear my expenses there and back. I say "if my parents live", for it would make me *too sad* to return in a short time if they should die. I hope however that this will not be.

Do you think that you are settled for life? I would not try to pursuade you to come to Cal. but I would like very much to have you all out here. All have not the same tastes. And you might be dissatisfied if you should come. I find some people here who came from Texas and wish to return, and a few from Ark. would like to go back. I should regret very much if any of my friends, through my influence, should move to Cal. and then wish to go back to Ark. And I wish them all to know that I will not be responsible if they come and are dissatisfied.

I think this country is one hundred pr. ct. better than Ark. I believe a farmer can make a great deal more money here in five years than he can in Ark. If he has the capital to operate with, he can make more in one year. Money here is worth 2½ pr. ct. int/ pr. month or thirty pr. ct. pr. annum. These are the lowest figures. This high pr. ct. is not owing to the scarcity of money, but to the superior advantages for investing capital.

Things grow in Cal. three or four times as fast as in Ark. What would you think of raising eight crops of hay on a piece of land in one year? Yet we do it here. The hay is equal to the clover of Virginia, if not superior. Nothing is better to make cows give milk, to fatten hogs and horses. The ground needs to be planted in clover only once in eight or ten years. My land yielded last year over eighty bushels of corn to the acre. Corn is now worth one dollar pr. bush. Fresh pork sells at eight cts. pr. lb. & bacon at 16 or 17 cts. It is very common for hogs to weigh two and three hundred lbs. before they are one year old. It costs very little to keep hogs and cows. Their food grows spontaneously all the year round. When a man gets a farm it is no trouble to support a family.

But I must stop. Good by—My love to your father's family

Affectionately yours G. E. Butler

Emma Butler Paisley to William Paisley

Dobyville
April 11th, 1872

My dearest one,

The day you left, Mrs. Jones came over and staid till evening—Of course we enjoyed her company very much. In the evening about three o'clock Mr. Jones came up for sister Mary and Miss Maggie to go to Okolona to the party—You may know they needed no persuasion to induce them to go but as soon as the arrangements were made they started off in the Jersey wagon. They had a right nice crowd, but only a plain supper, which they ate soon after getting there, and put on their finery afterwards. They got back the next day about twelve, but only stopped long enough for sister Mary to get out and come in, when Mr. J. (Mr. Arick having excused himself, stopped at home as they came back) went back and drove Miss Maggie around to Mr. Doby's and staid till after dinner.

Willis got very much offended at my putting his bed in the dining room. I *thought* he was very much pleased when I mentioned it to him, but he told Minerva he had a great notion to leave when I put his bed in the kitchen, and said he never slept in the kitchen before. I think he is doing very little good since you left, and is even more disagreeable than ever before. I know if you were at home you would have him to leave right away. I could mention several other little things, but I must leave this subject, for it is very unpleasant and frets me every time I think of it.

We all spent yesterday with Mrs. Jones—she prepared a *very* nice dinner. I understand that Dr. Williamson left this morning. I reckon the weather looked too unfavorable for him to stay longer—I would not be surprised if he got wet again, for it is thundering and raining some—he did not get over to see me. Mr. McGill sent some of the apples you engaged, which we enjoy very much. The horse has not been up since you drove her out of the yard Sunday. Mr. Jones, Mrs. Jones, sister Mary and I expect to go to the meeting Sunday at Mr. Hill's if it is a suitable day.

Monday 15th

The night after writing the above I had a very unpleasant dream about your scolding me for crying, and said you would break me from that yet. I was very glad to awake and find it all a dream. After spending a day and a half in looking for the horse, Willis succeeded in finding and bringing her home. Abraham Newton has been to haul a day and a half since you left, and I under-stand has come again to-day. They have not got the rails out of the new ground yet, and I am almost sorry when he comes for I think he and Willis have more of a frollick than work.

We had more rain Saturday, and Sunday morning it was still raining, so we had given out all idea of going up to Mr. Hill's to the meeting till some one said, "Miss Emma, Mr. Jones and Mrs. Jones are coming." So we concluded to get ready and go on with them—had a very muddy walk; but got there much better than we expected. Old Mrs. Duke was immersed in the branch back of Mr. Hill's but it was raining at the time, so only Mr. Jones and Willis went from here—the foot washing was put off till 3rd Sunday in May, so we were disappointed after all. Mrs Ross (the widow) spent Saturday night with us—she had been spending several days at Mr. (or Dr., I don't know which) Arnold's, and stopped out of the rain and as it continued to sprinkle, we persuaded her to stay all night, and Mr. Beatle (or some such name) went on, and one of the Ross boys brought a buggy down next morning for her. I had just got through putting away my little white pullet which we had taken out of the loft with eleven young chickens, and was consequently wet and dirty when she came. The hen has ten very pretty chickens, one having died the first night.

Last Friday evening sister Mary and I went down to call on old Mrs. Grier and Mrs. William Doby. Sister thinks Mrs. Doby is much more sociable than Mrs. Joe Doby. We found her up and improving slowly. We want to go to see Lizzie this evening, if we can get John's horse.

The children keep very well and bad as ever. John and Willie beg for the hatchet every now and then. Emma never thinks of crawling now. I am going to try to get some quilting frames and put my quilt in this week.

I believe I have written all—We miss you much. Very glad you got off from Arkadelphia and hope you had a pleasant trip down—haven't heard from you since Mr. Jones left you. We have not had any letters from Tulip. Your ma got a letter from Mary last week—she said she did wish you would come by Pine Bluff some times—think I shall write to her this week.

With much love and many kisses always your devoted wife,

Emma E. Paisley

218

William Paisley to Emma Butler Paisley in Dobyville

New Orleans
Apl 13th 1872

My dearest one,

I reached the city this morning about daylight & as Col. Goulding of the "Arkadelphia Standard" expects to start home this evening, I will write this hurried note to let you know that I have made the most dangerous portion of my trip without accident or trouble of any kind. We had rather a small crew of Passengers on the Boat from Camden—just enough to make it pleasant—and for the most part all were sober pleasant Gentlemen. Mr. Buchannan of Camden & Mr. Montgomery (brother to Mr. Ben Montgomery who died in Princeton) were my particular traveling companions, & I had quite a pleasant trip with them. Did not form any lady acquaintances, although there were several lady passengers.

One of the Ladies on the Boat was a Lady Merchant & on her way to the city to purchase her spring stock. She was good enough to her husband to take him along with her. I first thought when I heard her business that [it] would be mighty nice for a man's wife to attend to the store & let the man fix up things about home, but when I saw her husband looking so completely subjugated, I thought I would rather attend to the store a while longer than give up the *breeches*.

I am now writing in the Messrs Hendersons office—They were very glad to see me, and talked so nice about having sold our cotton without our orders that, instead of getting mad, I believe they put me in a good humor. I think them still clean, honest men & disposed to do any thing for us we asked. Cotton is firm today but no material advance. Merchants here can't bear the idea of my going to St. Louis, & are trying very hard to sell me goods. I feel that I have been away from you a long time & wish I was ready to start back, & look with dread on the long trip ahead of me.

Tell Mr. Doby that I could not arrange his insurance matters in Camden, but sent the amt. of premium to St. Louis to day.

It is now time for the boat to leave & I must close. Excuse haste &c. You and sister Mary must keep in good spirits & enjoy yourselves as much as *possible without me*. With much love & many kisses for yourself & little ones

Wm Paisley

Tell John & Willie they must be good boys & Pa will bring them something.

William Paisley to Emma Butler Paisley in Dobyville

New Orleans
Apl. 18th 1872

My dear Emma:

You will think it strange to find that I am still in New Orleans, but such is the case. I grew homesick before I got here, & dreaded the idea of having to prolong my trip by going to St. Louis, but for several days after getting here felt fully determined to go there to make our purchases.

Reaching here as I did on Saturday morning & not being able to do much that day, I would have been compelled to remain until Monday evening at best—which would have caused a loss of three days here & then two days more in to St. Louis, & *then* several weeks in getting our goods. All these things considered caused me to commence weighing what I considered advantages & disadvantages, & resulted in my concluding to remain & make my purchases here. I now think it was just such a decision *as you know* I am capable of making—*a very wise one*. The merchants here have large stocks that were purchased before the general advance in goods (which has taken place in the East within the last 60 days) & as it is getting late in the season, they are willing to make great concession in order to sell them for cash.

(¼ to 9 P M) I am now writing in the Messrs Henderson's office. Have been very busy all day and am quite tired, but could not put off writing any longer. Would have written you sooner, but did not have time in the day & had no facility for it at my room. Have bought Hardware, Crockery, Clothing, Shoes & Groceries, & expect to commence on Dry Goods (the most tedious bill) to morrow. I am very much pleased with my purchases so far, and think we will save several hundred dollars by buying in this market. I bought you a wardrobe & *myself* a Rocking Chair the other day. I shall expect an interest in the wardrobe but don't know how it will be about *dividing the chair*.

You will be surprised when I tell you who I found in the city this evening just before night— Johnny [Butler] & old Mr. Clardy. They are here buying goods, and say that I will have to assist them as they are both inexperienced, but I don't know how that will be yet—but am willing to render them any help that I can, provided it will not detain me or keep me from my own matters. Johnny is terribly homesick now, & mighty anxious to get back to see his wife—but I don't intend to let him keep me away from *mine*. I will telegraph to St. Louis for my letters, but fear they will not get here before I leave. So sorry.

Hope everything is getting along well in our garden and patches. Tell Willis to be sure & have the sweet potato ground prepared & the new ground broken up. Have him to keep every thing well worked in the garden.

Tell Mrs. Jones that I bought her a Singer Sewing Machine to day. I sent you a paper the other day & another yesterday. I attended the political meeting held at Lafayette Square—it was a great farce—Fred Douglas was expected to speak but did not.

Haven't time to write more—wish I had. Will try & be at home last next week. Much love & many kisses for all.

Your devoted
W. Paisley

Mary Butler to Emma Butler Paisley in Dobyville

Tulip May 17, 1872

Dear Emma

It has been a week today since I reached home. When we got to Arkadelphia, which was about eleven o'clock, found Ira impatiently waiting for me. He carried Mrs. Moore, Mrs. Pattillo's sister, over from here. Just about sundown we got here—found pa quite unwell, Jimmie in bed with fever and ma gone down to Charlie's (who, by the way, has a fine son about four weeks old named

Richard Colburn). You may know it looked lonesome here without ma. All thought I looked very much improved in health, but unfortunately I had to ride home in the rain without any top on the buggy and took cold, and I haven't felt well since; weighed the other day and according to these scales have fallen off five pounds.

Cousin Johnny came up yesterday and brought cousin Laura with her two little boys. She is very lively and so large and fleshy—inquired a great deal about you—sent her love, says you must be certain to come over this summer. She and Mrs. Daily went with cousin Jimmie down to New Orleans on a visit and enjoyed it so much. They went about the middle of March. I couldn't help but wish you could have gone down in company with them, as brother Billy didn't go any farther and I could have kept house for you. But what's the use of talking about that now. Perhaps you will go before very long. Cousin Laura left this morning, took Alice home on a visit.

Brother George and Sister got home last night—I rode over to see them this morning—took the album with me. Sister was so surprised and delighted with the present, said it was the very thing she wanted.

Monday 20th—I commenced this letter several days ago, but didn't finish it, as we could get a horse that evening to go call on Mrs. Bill Reid; we found her a nice looking lady, she expects to remain all summer. Mr. Young's mother and sister, Miss Ellen Young, have come up to stay some time. Annie and I went to call on her this evening. Brother George and Sister spent last Saturday night with us—both looking well. Alice and Florrie are getting on finely at school, but very anxious to come home. We had a letter from sister Julia last week—all were well, her little Mary is very delicate, and they have to be particular with her.

Brother Henry, sister Mollie, and Annie went down to Charlie's the first of last week, and pa and sister think of going this week. Then it will be my time next. Kate says we all show more respect to the baby than we did to her. It was brother H's first visit. Alice Colburn is going to travel with her father some. They expect to start to the Hot Springs this week.

I went to see Mary Durham last week, and was *astonished* to see how changed she was. I don't think it will be possible for her to recover her health, though she doesn't seem conscious of her situation, talks as if she expected to be well again.

Annie's cough is much better, her general health seems to be improving. She talks of going to Lockett's Springs this summer; Cousin Jimmie and the two cousin Lauras speak of going; those springs seem to be gaining notoriety.

I got here in time to enjoy several messes of nice strawberries. Ours were very large. I wished so much you could have been here too—all regretted that you couldn't come with me. I think it doubtful about brother Lewis visiting us this summer; but you must come anyway. I will get some patterns from sister and send you this week if I can. I be-[lieve] the polonaise is worn more than anything else. All think my dress beautiful. I reckon Annie will trim her buff linen with some of my cube trimming as there will be plenty of it. I think of putting it on without any fullness, however, don't know yet.

I hope brother Billy has more rest than when I was there, how is he? Brother Henry seems to have plenty of leisure. He talks of taking sister Mollie to cousin Jimmie's soon. I have not written to Mary Scott yet, but must do it soon.

Give my love to Mrs. Lipscomb and family. Tell her my flowers are blooming beautifully. I wish she could have some of them. Ma sends love to Mrs. Lipscomb, and says you must take care of that remedy in "Western Methodist" for piles and show it to her.

[no closing]

Mattie Hughes to Emma Butler Paisley in Dobyville

Tulip
July 5th, 1872

My Dear Sister,

I know you think we are very negligent, not writing to you more than we do. I have intended writing to you ever since I got home, to thank you for the nice album you sent me by sister Mary and to send you my photograph too. I have yours, but I want Billy's and the children, and when you get good ones, be sure and send them.

Miss Mary Durham died yesterday morning about two o'clock and was to be buried this morning at nine. She was perfectly willing to die, really seemed anxious. Spoke of the different persons she would know in heaven, and among them mentioned little "Moores." The night before she died ma and myself went around to see her, and her feet and hands were cold then, but I think she knew us, and seemed to try and talk but she was too weak. The family hated to give her up, especially Carrie, she will miss her so much. She scarcely left her bedside, you know they were devoted to each other. I didn't attend the burial, wasn't well enough. Annie Phillips sat up with the corpse last night, and is upstairs asleep now. The neighbors were very kind visiting her and sending her delicacies during her sickness. I have always thought there was more attention shown to the sick around Tulip than any other place I know of.

Alice and Florrie are at home now, got home last Thursday evening, in time to attend Mr. Leiper's exhibition. Mrs Feild came down with them, expecting to spend several weeks. Sister Mary and Annie are not very well. Both were bilious and had to take medicine. I think it agrees with sister Mary to stay in Clark. She seemed to improve so much when with you. Mrs. Feild says she is going to take her with her home.

Did you know Annie was expecting Olin by the 15th of this month? and he wants the marriage to come off just as soon after his return as possible. They have a great deal of sewing to do, have written to Little Rock for some articles she is compelled to have, and we are busy trying to get her ready. She says Olin is so far of[f], that it is uncertain about his getting here, so she wants it kept secret. She doesn't expect to have much of a wedding, but of course will expect all of the family to come.

I suppose you know that Maj. Coulter was here. I think he expects to spend two or three weeks here with Mollie, and then visit Paul and his other relatives. George and Walter were at home last week, and I expect one of them will come the last of this week. Charlie and Kate came up last week, and I think Kate expects to remain two or three weeks. They have a large and fine-looking boy, weighs 15 pds. Mrs. William Hunter has another daughter, and I heard it weighed ten pounds. I received a letter from Johnnie last week, he said they thought of visiting us this summer. We don't expect brother Lewis, maybe if they know of Annie's marriage they would come.

As I hope to see you soon I'll not write any more. My love to Billy and kiss the children. Write soon.

Your Loving Sister
M. W. Hughes

William Paisley to Emma Butler Paisley in Dobyville

Memphis Tenn
Thursday night Sept. 12th, 1872

My dearest one

I have neglected writing you longer this time than ever before, and told Mr. Doby this evening that you would think we were having a fine time sure enough and had forgotten home. But an hour never passes without my thinking of you, and I regret that I have not had an opportunity of writing sooner, but such has been the case. I would have written from Little Rock, but it was dark when we arrived there & after getting supper I concluded to purchase a bill of tobacco in Little Rock, and by the time I finished that, it was time to go to bed, as I did not get any sleep the night before of consequence & would have to get up early the next morning. There were no passengers from Arkadelphia to Rockport but Mr. D. and myself. Before we got to Rockport, the man driving our stage was arrested on suspicion of having robbed the mail a few nights before. He was allowed to drive us on to Rockport but the arrest detained us & we did not get there until day-light. Mr. Elder, who started from Arkadelphia the day before in a buggy, joined us at Rockport, and with him & others, we had a crowd all the way to Little Rock. Neither your Pa nor Mr. Pattillo met us—we supposed that your Pa had gone by Pine Bluff—but yesterday morning, when we started from Little Rock & had got on the Ferry Boat to go across the River to get on the cars, I looked over into another omnibus and saw your Pa, Johnny, Evaline, Alice, & Flora Hunter and Mrs. Pride [?]. They had come up the day before by private conveyance. The girls with your pa were going on to Clarksville [Tennessee]. After coming over the worst Railroad I ever saw yesterday, we arrived here a little after dark. The Girls were delighted with their trip, & I regretted so much that you were not with them to enjoy it too. Knowing that it would not benefit us any to get to St. Louis before Friday night, I got your Pa to consent to lie over here to-day & give Alice & Flora time to see the City, and I have spent a large portion of the time to day showing them around. We expect to leave in the morning about three o'clock, & get to St. Louis to morrow night. Your Pa will go to Clarksville & join us in St. Louis Saturday night.

Ex President Andrew Johnson spoke here last night. Mr. D & myself heard him. It was the finest speech I ever heard in my life & I think he is the greatest man in the nation. The trip fatigued me a great deal, but I got a good night's rest in Little Rock & again here last night, and feel all right again. Had rain in Little Rock Tuesday night. Hope you had it & will not suffer for water. Arkansaw River is very low, and the Rail Road is in such a bad fix I fear we will have trouble getting our goods home. Tell Mrs. Doby her old man is all right, & I do the best I can to keep him straight.

Your Pa & all send much love. The Girls are enjoying their trip hugely. With much [love] & many kisses for yourself & John, Willie, & Emma, I am your devoted husband

Wm Paisley

Excuse haste.

William Paisley to Emma Butler Paisley in Dobyville

St. Louis Mo
Tuesday night Sept 17th 1872

My dearest one:

Although I have been here since 10 o'clock Friday night I have not written to my dear Emma yet. On my way here, I thought one of the 1st things I would attend to after arriving here would be to write to you, but have, without being able to tell you how, put it off till this late day. Unless you could be with me, it is impossible for you to appreciate the difficulties that hinder me from writing—and really they seem to be increased more than usual in my way this trip. Your pa, Mr. Doby, Mr. Elder, Johnny, & myself are all rooming together, and when in our room at night, are crowded with drummers and other visitors. I thought it doubtful about my being able to write to night, and could not do so until the crowd left and all the rest went to bed. It is now late & I have been working hard all day, but could not think of going to bed another night without discharging the pleasant duty of talking a while with my dear wife.

Your Pa & Mr. Doby both being strangers here and depending on me to show them around, has given me a good deal of extra work & consequently have little time for any thing else. Mr. D., Mr. Elder, Johnny & myself separated from your Pa Friday morning at Humbolt (80 miles east of Memphis) and reached here Friday night. Your Pa took the Girls on to Clarksville, & arrived here Saturday night. Those of us that got in Friday spent Saturday in going around to the different houses we trade with, & yesterday morning all "hands" commenced buying.

I think Mr. Doby is getting a little tired of his trip and would like to start home to morrow if he could get off. Yesterday I noticed some little disposition on his part to hurry me up in my purchases, but I did not let on that I noticed it, as he has no idea how such things should be done. He has been going around with me, but has not bought any thing him self, and I am now fully satisfied that it would not have done at all for him to have come on by himself. *Don't mention what I have said*—& don't imagine from what I have said that it is at all unpleasant to me to have him with me, for he is as pleasant as ever, & seems to enjoy the trip finely. He no doubt feels awkward being along not doing any thing.

Wednesday Sept 18th

Beautiful Fall morning & I am feeling very well. Will ship home goods today. Mr. Doby will write this morning. Goodby

Yours
W.P.

Henry Butler to Emma Butler Paisley in Dobyville

Tulip Ark.
Sept 23rd 1872

My dear Sister Emma:

I write you a short note to inform you of an event—*a great event* which occurred at our house last night—the arrival of a stranger—a *boy-baby*—a regular *ten pounder*—so says Dr. Reamey, who tested his weight on a pair of scales a few minutes after arrival. Mother & babe doing well this morning.

I suppose Billy will get home by the time this reaches you. Have written him once or twice since his departure—but rec'd nothing.

> Affectionately your brother
> Henry

Tell Mrs. Lipscomb we thought of her last night—she was with us when Mattie was born. Love to Capt. L & family. Ask Billy to write.

Annie Butler Moores to Emma Butler Paisley in Dobyville

Tulip Arkansas
Oct. 21st, 1872

Dear Sister Emma,

Your letter was received last Saturday, we were all very glad to hear from you. I didn't intend being ceremonious with you this time, for I had set several days last week to write to you, but from some cause put it off until your letter came. Hope you will all have a nice time at your meeting and much good be accomplished.

Sister is now at Benton, been gone almost two weeks. Olin and I are keeping house for her during her absence, don't know when she will return home. The former *did* expect to go on the R.R. this week, but as yet there is no vacant place. Bro George said he knew he could find employment of some kind on the R.R. I am left all alone today. The [Hughes] children are at school, & Pa and Olin (I reckon) have gone over to the Jones place. He left here this morning with that intention.

I am getting on finely, but if Olin leaves I don't know what I am to do. I could have done without him very well the first week or two after we were married, for I didn't love him half so well as now; and my love seems to increase daily. I hope we may ever be happy, and I know if we both do our duty it could not be otherwise.

Annie Phillips is still with her sister Mat. I reckon she will get home this week. We hear from Alice often. She and Florrie seem to be very much pleased with their school.

Brother Charlie and Kate were up last week, they have a very sweet baby. Alice C[olburn] thinks there never was such another babe. Sister Mollie has *the large* baby, he grows rapidly. Sister M. is quite well, also bro. Henry & the children.

Sister Mary spent a day and night with me last week. Ma hasn't been over yet; she, Kate, Alice, Carrie, & the baby were coming over to spend one day last week, but I was a little ahead of them got down home as they were about starting. Mrs. H. Young has a son, also Mrs. Billy Cooper.

Tell bro Billy I was *very much* pleased with his selections, and render many thanks for his trouble. Sister Mary was also pleased with his purchases for her. I think she intends writing soon. Tell him to please send a bill of the things.

If Olin was here, I know he would join me in sending much love to you both. He was very much taken with bro. Billy. How are the children getting on? With much love to all I remain

                 Your loving sister
                 Annie

Let us hear from you as often as possible. Mr. Roberson has come in & says send his regards to you all.

Emma Butler Paisley to her parents in Tulip

                                [Dobyville, Ark.
                                Oct–Nov. 1872]

My dear ma and Pa,

I have been wanting to have a talk with you for a long while, and never knew how to get about it, knowing how opposed you would be to a mere mention of the subject. Indeed it is a sad trial for me to make, but feeling it to be my duty to my husband and children, I have concluded to write to you and ask your view about the matter—that is of joining the presbyterian church. You will know that I have been a dear lover of the Methodist church, and at one time thought I never would make any change in my church membership, but don't you think I ought to make the sacrifice if it would in any way promote my husband's happiness, and if his is increased, of course mine will be also. Let me assure you that I do not make *any* sacrifice of *principle* in the matter. If I should make the change I *do* hope you will not be offended.

My dear parents, lay aside all prejudice and go to our Heavenly Father in secret and ask his direction in the matter. I have made it a subject of prayer for several months. It is true you may say we have just passed through a Presbyterian meeting, and that has caused a change in my mind. We have had the meeting, it is true, but that has not caused me to make the change. As long as I have been married, I don't remember of a single member ever telling me I ought to join the Presbyterian church, but on the other hand how many of my Methodist friends have had a constant watch over me for fear that (I) might make a change.

Miss Nannie Bullock is the only one ever advised me to join the Presbyterian church and said the sooner I did it, it would be all the better. I told her I had thought of it, but knew your feelings in the matter, and consequently did not know how to approach you on the subject—she said sit down and write you a letter all about it. She said you ought not to have any objections, and you would not if you had the experiences she had had—said her advice to every one who belong to different denominations to go with her husband. She told her sister Bailey the first thing she did she must join the Presbyterian church as she had married a man of that denomination, and Mr.

Cass, who married her, gave her the same advice. Any body to understand the doctrines of the Presbyterian church will find that there is not such a vast difference as any one might imagine without understanding what is taught by the Confession of Faith. They believe in free Salvation as much as we do—I never heard a Methodist minister preach the doctrine any stronger than did last Monday.

Well, Presbytery has adjourned for the Synod to meet in Little Rock next Thursday night. I believe I heard every sermon but two, and most of them were as good as I ever heard. We had a very pleasant crowd to stay with us. Mr. Boyd his wife and two children and servant, Mr. Brawner most of the time, and one or two elders. Every thing passed off pleasantly, and I think every one was pleased. I had to get up very early so as to have breakfast over and for them to meet at the church by half past eight o'clock, and Monday morning had to meet at eight. I did not get to hear the morning preceedings, but went out to hear the eleven o'clock sermon and remained the ballance of the day, as we prepared dinner on the ground. It made me feel very lonely to see them all go off this morning, and more especially to see Mr. Paisley leave. He is the delegate from this church, and consequently had to go. Will be gone till Wednesday night

[remainder of letter missing]

Mary Wyche Butler to Emma Butler Paisley in Dobyville

Tulip
Nov 5, 1872

My Dear Child

I must confess your letter mad[e] me feel very very sad—the thought of your leaving the church of your choice, of your Parents, brothers & sisters, makes me sad indeed. How can I give you up when I think of the happy times you have had? How many times I seen you rejoicing in the love of God? It grieves me to think they are gone never to return. I fear you never can enjoy yourself in any other as you have in the church of your choice. How often have I thought of the time Bishop Marvin preached, how happy you looked. I never forgot how you looked. If I ever envied any one's feelings it was yours.

I requested Billy when you wer[e] going to be maried not to influence you to leave your church. If he could not sacrifice principle would he have you to do it? I didn't expect that of him. You should count the cost well before you leave one that may not have as much of form and fashion, but more of the power of Godliness. I feared at one time I should have this trial, had thought you were getting along so well would have trouble about it. I should not object to his having the children baptized in that church if he preferred.

I have loved the Presbyterian church next to the Methodist, but I think Nancy B had better regulate her own house hold before she begins with others. I heard the reason Mrs. Bullock did not join the Pres. Church she could not conscientiously make the confession of faith. I expect it would be the same with you. This is a personal matter. You have to stand for yourself.

I would like to see you first and have a talk wel I think you can enjoy the benefits of the church. I have been talking of going to conference, can't you go with me? Mr. Butler and Billy have had their trip. Now it is our time. What do you think of it? Then you could hear some of our best Preachers. You never hear any but very common ones.

I had gone to see Anna the day got your letter. I can't tel[l] how I felt almost lik[e] someone was ded. She is keeping house for your sister. Olin had gone to Benton Corner about getting work on the R.R. Martha came with him and visit. She was here this eve, looking very well. Olin expects to leave with her in the morning to be gone some time. He is having a fine time traveling on the cars, likes it so much. Anna will be the lonely one now. If you could only leave your little ones with her and go some yourself. Molly was here to spend a day last week. She has the finest boy I ever saw pretty black eyes named him George Story. Kate has a fine son, so has Mrs. Billy Cooper. Ruth lost hers like Mrs P did.

Your papa has come and says he has written to you. Pa expected to write this AM but will not now. I wrote it last night when he couldent see well. Mary has gone to see Anna

Love to all

Your Mama

Alice Butler to Emma Butler Paisley in Dobyville

C[larksville] F[emale] Academy
Tenn.
Jan 25th, 1873

Dear Sister Emma:—

I received a letter from Sister Annie yesterday, in which she said they would excuse me from writing *one* letter home, if I would write to you instead. However, it is not entirely through their suggestion that I am writing, for I had been thinking of it for some time, but it seemed that every Saturday would bring with it new duties, and you know this is the only day I have time to do any thing.

I suppose Sister Annie has told you of the different marriages, she says Mr. Ben Smith looks like a young man and Miss Anna Wilson much younger than she did before, she says, "you see what marriage does for people." I believe Col. Whittaker is now paying his attention to Miss Teressa and Bettie Smith, don't know which will carry the day, but I think either of them would be doing *but little* to take him.

Our school was half out last Friday a week ago, we had two young ladies to graduate at that time. They acquitted themselves *very well*, and left on the four o'clock train the next morning. It hardly seems that five months have passed away since we left home. Florrie and myself often speak of the pleasant trip we had coming. I don't know what we should have done had it not been for bro. Billy, who carried us around showing us every thing and treating us to candies, soday water, and every thing nice. We wished *so much* that you could have been with us.

I wish you could see Florrie sitting over here by me mending some old gloves that look like they might have come out of Noah's ark, but I think she will have them looking right respectable, before she is through with them. She says I am always very glad to get them when I want to sweep. We have six girls in our room, and we all get along very nicely together. I suppose you heard that Julia McGehee, a girl from below Pine Bluff, came soon after we got here. She is a cousin of Miss Sarah McGehee. She of course is among the number of our roommates we like her very much.

We attended a concert last week, held by the celebrated violinist Ole Bull. A splendid musician was with him who accompanied him on the piano. I don't know when I enjoyed any thing more. Several of the teachers as a matter of course, went with us.

I reckon John considers himself quite a man by this time. And Willie almost. Has little Emma fattened up much since she was at grandma's? I would like so much to see them, kiss each one for aunt Alice. Sister A spoke of brother Johnnie's paying them a visit, which she enjoyed so much. I wrote to Ma last Saturday. Reckon she has gotten it before now, but there is so much irregularity in the mail that we can't tell when they go or come. Florrie sends much love to you both.

Write very soon. Your affectionate

Little Sister

P.S. Tell bro. B. that we were not at all ashamed to own "our state" but were rather proud that we could say "we are from Arkansas."

A.P.B.

Mary Butler to Emma Butler Paisley in Dobyville

Tulip
Mar. 19th, 1873

Dear Emma,

This time last year I was with you assisting in gardening, hunting turkey nests &c. I suppose you are now very busily engaged the same way. Ma has planted all her early vegetables, and some of them are up. I have been busy getting my flowers worked. Ira and Jimmie assist me in the evening when they return from school. The early flowers are now blooming beautifully. I have not yet met with an opportunity of sending you any shrubbery.

Brother Henry left for St. Louis yesterday morning, and Annie is now staying with sister Mollie. Olin and brother George Hughes also went up as far as Benton. The latter has been at home nearly four weeks. He is in very bad health; suffering from indigestion—can't eat any thing but the very lightest diet—has fallen off very much, and thinks probably he'll have to give up his business entirely. I expect sister will remain at home now.

Maj. Coulter has been here and spent a month; he and Paul are going out to Texas to live, and wants brother H. to go there too. I don't know whether sister Jennie will return with brother H. or not. He will return by there: brother Lewis wrote not long since, but said nothing about it. Olin gets letters from Cal. very frequently. Annie wrote to sister Julia yesterday. Mrs. Moores' health has been bad for some time.

A letter came this morning to Alice from cousin Willie Kittle, he is now farming near Lewisburg in this state, and thinks his father will move there next fall—he visited home last Aug. Say his ma didn't have any of the children at home with her. Cousin Sallie is teaching school.

Well the much-talked-of marriages of Col. Whitaker and Mr. Harris came off at the appointed times, the 20th & 27th ult. The first took place at ten o'clock AM, the ceremony performed by brother Caldwell. We were all invited down, and also to a dining at the Col's next day. Only two young ladies from here went to the dining, Theresa and Alice Reid. Sarah Martin had thirty-two waiters; did you ever hear the like? not one in the neighborhood was left out. We formed a line as close as we could stand across the room from one corner to the other, the bride and groom standing out in the aisle. Some from every family in the neighborhood were invited, and when the ceremony was over we could scarcely turn around there was such a crowd. We were invited back again the next night, but I didn't go, as I knew it would be a dancing party. Mrs. Jones and Betty Somervell rode horse back all the way from Hempstead Co. to attend the wedding: they also had another dance the next night at Mr. Young's. Miss Berta Holmes was one of the waiters. She spent most of her time with me: cousin Ellen was also invited.

Mr. Harris left Monday and remained at home a week then returned to move over. Mrs. Smith will stay with Mrs. Roane and John M. Smith awhile before she goes over to live with Mr. Harris. They also keep Sallie Lea. Sallie Barbee was married some time last month at her aunt's in Tenn. to a Dr. Alexander, expects to visit her mother this summer. So you see there's three young ladies that have left Tulip recently to make their homes elsewhere. There's no telling who'll be next to marry. Candace Overton and Roby Dyer ran away and married not long ago.

Mr. John Doak has come out here to live. I believe he expects to farm with Mr. John Pattillo. Miss Fannie Smith's health doesn't seem to improve. I don't think she will ever be able to get back to N.C. She was to go this spring. Carrie Durham is teaching in Mr. Ben Smith's family.

We are well pleased with our preacher Mr. Biggs. I went to see his wife this week. They are living at the parsonage have two children. I have not heard from Mary Scott very lately—wrote to her this week.

How is Mrs. Lipscomb and Eliza and all getting on? My love to them, Mrs. Jones and all my friends.

When is brother Billy going for his goods? Cousin Jimmie is going to New Orleans. I heard brother H. complaining of brother B not answering his letters. I believe he has quit writing to every body. Give him my love and tell him not to be so taken up with his business as to forget us all. Are John and Willie learning any? Tell Minerva howdy for me. All unite with me in much love. Write me soon a long letter.

> As ever your loving sister
> Mary

Ma says tell you her mouth watered from some of that fine turkey you prepared for Johnny. Says she is going to try to raise a good many this year, and you must come over and eat some—has twelve eggs, three hens to raise from. How are you coming out with yours?

Annie Butler Moores to Emma Butler Paisley in Dobyville

> Home, Ark.
> April 4th, 1873

Dear Sister Emma,

Your letter was received, and read with *much pleasure* a few weeks ago. It had been some time since we had heard from you. I wish so much Olin & I could have visited you before now, but it has been impossible, as he has been busy on the R.R. He comes down right often to see me, left here last Wednesday. I do miss him so much.

Brother Henry has been after goods, and returned last Saturday evening, was absent almost two weeks. I staid with Sister Mollie while he was gone. I am now at my old home again. Bro. Henry, sister Mollie, the baby, Mattie, and sister Mary spent last Tuesday at Mrs. Matlock's, and while there bro. H. bought a wild turkey from some one, & invited us all over yesterday to dine with them. I enjoyed the dinner so much, and in the evening had some nice lemonade & cake.

Sister Mary went over to sister's this morning to assist her in baking cakes for West's birthday party tonight.

The little children are carrying the day around here since the old widowers married; they have had three or four parties. Brother Caldwell expects to start to Clark [County] tomorrow week. If he concludes to go in his buggy, sister Mary will go over & spend two weeks with you. Sister is very anxious to go with her, but I reckon she can't go.

Bro. Lewis still speaks of visiting us this summer. Bro. Henry didn't come by to see him. We hear from California about every week. Brother George and Sis Julia are very proud of their little Alexander. I hope he may be spared to them. I reckon Emma can talk right plain.

The weather is now quite warm, and every thing is beginning to look beautiful. The last cold spell injured the fruit, but I hope there is plenty left.

Ma is now running around generally, seeing after one thing & then another. She has had her last kettle of soap made today. There are few that could stand to walk as much as she does. Pa has been complaining for the last two or three days, but seems to feel better this evening; he & Ira are now in the garden.

Jimmie is almost ready to start to sister's, so I will have to close, as I want to send my letter off tonight, & the sun is almost down. I know Olin would join me in sending love to you all if he were here. I hope sister Mary can get to go to see you, then she can give you all the news. Pa & Ma send love to you all. Write very soon to

Your loving sister
Annie Moores

I send you sister Julia's letter, you can return it sometime.

William Paisley to Emma Butler Paisley in Dobyville

New Orleans
May 17th 1873
12 o'clock M

My dearest one,

I arrived here this morning at 10 o'clock, feeling quite well, and although I have not been here as yet long enough to collect my thoughts, will write, fearing that if I put it off until I get busy you will not hear from me until you get tired of waiting. I was the only through passenger on the boat from Arkadelphia to Camden & from there to New Orleans, & consequently had a quiet trip. Altogether tho, it was pleasant, as the officers of the boat were agreeable & attentive. The fare on the Boat was good, but I have exercised more care & prudence this trip in eating than ever before. The weather here is so very warm, and besides they have been troubled some in New Orleans with cholera morbus this season, to such an extent that the impression has gone out that they have cholera here, but since my arrival I have been assured in the office of Messrs Henderson that there are no grounds for that impression, save the cases of cholera morbus which is common here at this season of the year, when there are so many vegetables coming in. Do not be in the least uneasy about me, as I prefer waiting on our own garden for vegetables to running any risk in eating them here.

The country from the mouth of Red River to this place is now beautiful. The very finest kind of residences are in sight all the time, and the most luxuriant growth of shrubbery of every variety I ever saw & are in full bloom. The magnolias perfume the whole country. While in Red River I saw a very large Alegator swimming along by the Boat.

So far as I can see every thing here shows the effects of hard times—great political excitement and scarcity of money has had a depressing influence on business of every kind. I wrote you from Camden, and sent the note by Henry Winn. Have met with no acquaintances yet except in the office of T & S Henderson, where I am now writing. When you see Ben ask him to charge me with cash per Dr. Hamilton 15.00.

Suppose from news recd. at Camden that you have had a good deal of rain. Don't let the grass & weeds get ahead of you in the Garden & if it is dry enough & Minerva can spare the time, have the cabbage hoed, (ground loosened) every two or three days.

Can think of nothing more at present—will not remain longer than just time enough to attend to my business, as I am now impatient to be with you again. Tell Jno & Willie to be good boys & learn fast, & tell little Emma that papa hasn't forgotten her & that she must be a sweet little girl.

> With much love & many kisses your
> devoted husband
> Wm Paisley

PS   I forgot to tell you that I wrote to Messrs Dowell & Embry the morning I left, to know the fare from Little Rock to Baltimore for Mrs. Miller. If you get the answer you can send it to her

> W.P.

Henry Butler to William Paisley in Dobyville

> Tulip, Ark.
> June 23rd 1873

My dear Billy:

I reached home last week, and was prevented from coming *via* your house by the excessive rains falling about that time. I dreaded to encounter the creeks between you and Arkadelphia. As it was, I had some difficulty in getting through. Well! I did purchase land in Texas—bought in Hunt Co[unty] joining Fannin, unimproved open Prairie with some timber, enough for fire wood. I believe I have made a *splendid investment*, even if I should never live on the land. For the country is settling rapidly, and lands are certain to advance in price. I wish I could have come by to talk to you, for I have not time to write you my impressions of the country I visited—suffice it to say I believe the country from Red River County on the east, Montague on the west, with Tarrant & Dallas on the South, embraces the finest lands & most desirable farming country (as well as the *healthiest*) I *ever saw*. There are places in the heavy timber and on creeks I think sickly—but I am satisfied the open Prairie country I saw is much more healthy than right here at Tulip. I found my wife quite feeble, having been right sick the week previous to my return. Dr. R. thinks it was caused by the nursing of *our large baby*.

The rest are all well—except sister Annie. She was taken quite suddenly night before last, & suffered *intensely* the entire night. The child was dead when born.

I find a letter which I enclose from D[owell] & Emby relative to the Desk, and as the R Road will be completed to Arkadelphia in a few days, you can get it brought to that place on reasonable terms. I believe you proposed taking the desk yourself.

I would be glad to hear from you in regard to our land trade and if you purchase, how much funds could you let me have in *two* or *three* weeks? Can't you come over? We could fix up matters as well here as there. I am six months behind with my books, besides much other business to attend to. Write me soon.

Love to sister Emma & the children. Your frd & brother

> H.A. Butler

Mattie Butler Hughes to Emma Butler Paisley in Dobyville

Tulip
June 23rd 1873

Dear Sister Emma,

I had no idea so long a time would pass, without my writing to you. I know I ought to have written to you while Billy was absent, and fully intended doing so, but kept putting it off from day to day. I wish I could have been with you during Billy's absence, for I expect you were quite lonely. If we were living on the railroad, we could visit each other whenever we felt like it.

Papa expects to go to Malvern (the station opposite Rockport) today. I think he intends purchasing a lot there.

Brother Henry got home last Friday evening. He was from home nearly seven weeks. Mollie says she will never consent for him to go with her pa again. He is delighted with the country, but don't know when he will move. He bought a tract of land in Hunt Co., and thinks it is a good investment, if he should never move there, thought it would pay better than merchandizing. Says the taxes there are not near so much.

And now I must tell you about poor sister Annie. She was taken sick last Saturday and her baby wasn't born until five o'clock Sunday morning, and how it grieves me to tell you, that it was dead, and had been for an hour, before it was born. We felt so thankful that she got through safely, we couldn't grieve for the babe. It was a finelooking boy, weighed eight pounds, and if it could have lived, what a pleasure and comfort it would have been to her. Olin hated it very much, said he felt like a man who had suddenly been deprived of great possessions. And ma says she don't know what to do without it. Sister Annie was doing very well yesterday, but still had some fever. Dr. Raimy wants her kept very quiet, and not have much company for a few days. Ma says Annie suffered more than any one she ever saw, except Kate. But I hope, my dear sister Emma, you will not feel troubled and uneasy about yourself since hearing about it. For you know, with the first one suffers so much more. I hope it will be so that ma can come over to see you. I reckon she will write you something about it. She is very anxious to hear from you.

George [Hughes] is not at home now. He is riding over the country between Rockport and Hot Springs, preparatory to making the survey. I know he ought to be at home resting, for he is not well yet, and I feel anxious about him. Walter has been at home several weeks, and seems to be in fine health now. We intend sending him to school next fall. But don't know yet where we will send him. West is in Saline on a visit, went two weeks ago, with Ira, when he went to meet Alice. Alice is looking thin but her health seems to be good.

[no closing]

Mary Butler to Emma Butler Paisley in Dobyville

Tulip, Arkansas
Aug. 21st, 1873

My dear sister Emma:

I have written so few letters lately that it is almost a task now to write. I ought to have written you long ago, and cannot feel satisfied to put it off any longer. All hands are as busy as can be, taking down Pa's store to be carried up to Malvern; so you see instead of building up Tulip, we are tearing down; it makes us all feel sad, though it may be for the best: pa has the blues about it himself: Ma, Annie, and I, went up yesterday evening; nearly everything had been moved to the "old tavern" where they will be kept until the house is rebuilt at Malvern; brother Henry, Pa, and brother Olin will then go in together. The post office will be kept at Mr. Hunter's.

Mr. Alston came up yesterday to make arrangements about opening his school. He staid with us last night. I believe Mr. Tom Colburn has agreed to take his family to board for a while. They have four children. I do hope we can have large schools here again. Cousin Lewis Kittle has been to see us and spent several days. We enjoyed his stay with us, found him more pleasant than his brother Willie. Alice got a letter from him last night, written since his return to Miss. He went from here to Malvern and Arkadelphia, looking out a good business place. I expect he will come to this state. Cousin Willie is in Lewisburg.

Brother Lewis hasn't made his promised visit yet, and I don't expect he will get off this summer, though in his last letter he said he might possibly visit us soon.

Have you put up any fruit? we have dried some pears and apples, put up seventeen cans of pears, and peaches, and made some preserves. We have had a great many watermelons though very few peaches.

Sister and Alice talk of visiting you about the time of the District meeting at Okolona, which will be some time next month. Cousin Laura P. Butler was *very* sick last week, sent up for Dr. Reamy. Cousin Jimmy was at the Hot Springs for his health, but had to return. Brother H took sister Mollie and Sister down to see them last Sunday. I haven't heard from there since their return Monday evening. Mrs. Sample, her little daughter, and Frazier, passed through here two weeks ago on their way to Arkadelphia. They broke down three or four miles from here, and pa sent his buggy for them, so they were here two nights and a day getting the carriage mended. We were very much pleased with Mrs. Sample. She seemed to feel so thankful to Pa for his kindness. She didn't know how long they would remain in Arkadelphia. Annie P. had a letter from Cousin Ellen yesterday. She still seems to be very happy—has been on a visit to Little Rock.

Brother H. I think is still in the notion of going to Texas. He speaks of offering his place for sale. Ma sends much love and is anxious to know how your fine boy is getting on? *I* would like *so* much to see him. Does John and Willie want to see Jimmie? well they must make him the next visit. Little Emma! she must not be lost sight of in such a crowd of boys; she ought to be over here with her "aunt May" awhile. Love to brother Billy. I hope he'll get in a writing humor some time soon.

Now Emma, write soon to your ever loving sister Mary.

Love to Mrs. Lipscomb. Tell her she must be certain to go to Synod and come by to see us. Love to Eliza and all the other friends.

Annie is looking very well, she sends love and says maybe she'll get to see you when she goes to Malvern to live. Then she can go on the cars to Arkadelphia. She is busy preparing for house keeping, and Jimmie is to go too. Now won't we be lonely?

I got a letter from Mary Scott not long since. They were all well. Give my love to Mrs. Jones. Ma was so much pleased with her. Tell Minerva howdy ma says also for me.

Your sister
M.J.B.

Henry Butler to William Paisley in Dobyville

Tulip Ark
Sept 7th 1873

Dear Billy:

Truly glad was I to receive yours of the 3rd, which was not received till this morning—a long time out. The parties contracting to haul the old store house to Malvern will finish the job *this week* they say. The Counting room will be left, Dr. Reamey having purchased that with the lot & intends using it for his office. The moving of the store produced a sad feeling—it looked like the commencement of my "breaking up" at Tulip, besides it brought up the associations of the past, & I hated to see the old house torn down. Mr. Moores (Olin) is at [Malvern] having the house rebuilt and thinks they will have it ready in *three weeks at farthest* for the goods. I have never been to Malvern—expect to go up in a few days. Gus Cheatham is not with me now—left me one week ago, & is in Little Rock trying to get into business. He is a good boy—does very well for his experience.

In regard to our trip—I had settled on the 20th as the time of starting, owing to the fact the store house would not be ready for the goods sooner. I am sorry you have fixed the time of starting on the 16th, but if I find the store will be ready sooner than I now expect, I will certainly go up with you, for I desire as you say, one more trip together.

[no closing]

Mattie Hughes to Emma Paisley in Dobyville

Tulip
Dec. 7th, 1873

Dear Sister Emma,

I expect before this you have heard of the disaster [a tornado] at Malvern. Pa came down yester-day in the stage. He got some bad bruises, but nothing serious. He can't walk without his stick. I went over and staid with him last night. He feels so thankful he escaped as well as he did, says he can't grieve for what he lost. He is having the store rebuilt as fast as he can. George was sleeping with pa, but didn't get but one or two slight bruises. How thankful we ought to be that they were spared, for they made such a narrow escape. The hurricane didn't extend to Olin's. Brother Henry is nearly well, and wants to go up to Malvern the first of the week.

If Billy hasn't made arrangements to come or send for Alice and myself, I think we had better postpone our visit. We have had so much rain I know the road from Arkadelphia to your house must be very bad, and pa and ma seem to think we had better not go. But if I should get a letter from Billy saying that he will meet us, I will come for I don't want to disappoint you again. So if he hasn't started when you get this letter, we will wait until the weather is more pleasant. I know it will be putting him to a good deal of trouble anyway to send for us.

I am so anxious to see your baby and regretted so much, that you couldn't come down from Malvern and stay awhile with us. I asked Andrew Hunter which was the prettiest one of your children, and he said the little girl. Annie thought the baby was so sweet and pretty.

Did you get brother Lewis' letter containing Jessie's photograph? I was delighted with his wife, and when I see you I'll tell you all about my visit. Had you heard that Kate (George's sister) was dead? I went up to see her, and got there the day before her death. I brought her little girl, Alice, home with me. But I don't know how long we will keep her. Her mother gave her to Hattie before I went up.

You must excuse this badly written letter for I am sleepy, and my eyes are hurting me so much, I will close. My love to Billy and a kiss to the children. Write soon.

> Your affectionate
> Sister M.W. Hughes

Emma Eliza Butler in her late teens (circa 1860)

William McLean Paisley as a Confederate soldier

Alexander Butler

Mary Wyche Reavis Butler

Lorenzo Dow Lipscomb

Eliza Bradshaw Paisley Lipscomb

Emma Butler Paisley shortly after her marriage
(courtesy of Emma Hayley Hawkins)

William McLean Paisley, circa 1867

Emma Butler Paisley, circa 1884

William McLean Paisley, circa 1887

Mary Eliza Paisley,
daughter of William and Emma Paisley
(courtesy of Emma Hayley Hawkins)

Henry Lewis Paisley,
son of William and Emma Paisley
(courtesy of Emma Hayley Hawkins)

Mattie Butler Hughes
(courtesy of Emma Hayley Hawkins)

George Hughes
(courtesy of Mrs. Walter H. Allen)

Walter Hughes,
son of Mattie and George Hughes
(courtesy of Emma Hayley Hawkins)

West Hughes,
son of Mattie and George Hughes
(courtesy of Emma Hayley Hawkins)

Reavis Hughes,
son of Mattie and George Hughes
(courtesy of Emma Hayley Hawkins)

Henry Alexander Butler
(courtesy of Emma Hayley Hawkins)

Mary E. (Mollie) Coulter Butler
(courtesy of Emma Hayley Hawkins)

Coulter Butler,
son of Henry and Mollie Butler
(courtesy of Emma Hayley Hawkins)

Mary Albert (May) Butler,
daughter of Henry and Mollie Butler
(courtesy of Emma Hayley Hawkins)

Mattie Lee Butler,
daughter of Henry and Mollie Butler
(courtesy of Emma Hayley Hawkins)

Mary Jane Butler
(courtesy of Emma Hayley Hawkins)

Lewis Peter Butler
(courtesy of Emma Hayley Hawkins)

Jennie Bowman Butler, wearing a
"widow's brooch"
(courtesy of Emma Hayley Hawkins)

George Emory Butler
(courtesy of Emma Hayley Hawkins)

Charles Albert Butler
(courtesy of Mrs. Walter H. Allen)

John Reavis Butler
(courtesy of Emma Hayley Hawkins)

Anna Louise Butler
(courtesy of Emma Hayley Hawkins)

Olin G. Moores
(courtesy of Mrs. Walter H. Allen)

Wedding party of Annie Butler and Olin Moores (courtesy of Emma Hayley Hawkins)

Ira Wyche Butler

Alice Palmer Butler
(courtesy of Emma Hayley Hawkins)

James Oliver Butler
(courtesy of Emma Hayley Hawkins)

Paisley family in 1887 or 1888. Front row from left: James Ira, William McLean,
Lula Grier; back row from left: Mary Eliza, Martha Wyche, Emma, Henry Lewis

The cemetery at Tulip.
Pictured are the headstones of several members of the Butler family.

Henry Butler to William Paisley in Dobyville

Malvern, Ark.
Jany 12 1874

Dear Billy:

I was glad to hear from you—it has been so long since, we were getting quite anxious—

As to your failing to pay the note—it makes no difference *none whatever*—so you need not think I am impatient. *Butler & Moores* are needing funds badly—worse than D & P I think—but the amt you wish to pay me is a private affair, and I don't care to put into the concern. You can ship the cotton as you wish. You can ship to St. Louis without compressing. We are shipping to St. Louis and New York with instructions "*not* to be compressed." The freight is 20 cents per hundred pounds cheaper if compressed, but cotton loses more than the difference in weight—and is also detained & frequently exchanged.

I have *never* been so far behind in paying up. We are now owing some $3400 and have only about 50 B/C a head to pay with. We are still collecting, but 'tis hard work. We have had some "bad luck" if I may so speak—first I was sick some six weeks during the busiest part of the season. Then the *Hurricane* blew us away and the rain damaged our goods considerably. Then L & S Henderson suspended, owing us some $600, & Tucker some $175.00. All this with the "hard times" makes it *particularly hard* on us. *But* I never felt more *determined to succeed* and believe yet there is "a brighter day coming." I am *thankful* it is no worse, for we are blessed far more than we deserve.

I *had* promised Pa to stay at Tulip next week, but since you say you will make us a visit, I will try & get him to defer his trip till the week after. I will be *delighted* to see your face once more. I wish I could see *you* oftener.

Glad to hear little "Henry" is better. I want to see the youngsters very much—I am told it is *much the* best looking of any of your children. Wonder if there is any thing in a name.

Love to Emma—from whom we hear *so seldom*—but I know she has her hands full. Will you please present the small a/c inclosed & collect. Mr. G. requested that I should send it over.

In haste

Your Bro & frd
H.A. Butler

PS   R[ussell] R. C[arothers] wishes to know why he does not get an answer to his letter. We are *much* blessed with him.

Mail train is in & haven't time to look over.

Lewis Butler to Mary Wyche Butler in Tulip

Murphysboro, Ill.
Jan 18 1874

My Dear Mother:

It is night, and our little family, now numbering four, is all together in our sitting room. Jennie has the baby—a fine boy—whom we have not yet named, but to tell you of whose existence is the principal object of this letter—on her lap. Jessie now a large, healthy, noisy girl of three and a quarter years, is standing in her chair on the opposite side of the table while talking away and turning over the leaves of her new 1st reader, in which she has just said her lesson. The baby was born on the 29th of December, and is consequently three weeks old—about. He was a small baby like Jessie, but is now almost twice as large as when born. He is perfectly healthy and lively and thus far has been remarkably little trouble. His mother is very proud of him, and I think attends him more tenderly, if possible, and with more care than Jessie. But this may seem so to me because I have only had this one in my hands a time or two, whereas I was almost assiduous in my attentions to Jessie as Jennie herself was.

Those of the family who have visited us will imagine us living where we were when they were here, but we have moved and are now living in our own house, which we purchased and moved into about five or six weeks ago. There were but three rooms when we bought the place, but we had two others added on, and now have five very comfortable and neat rooms, all plastered and much neater and warmer than those in the house we left. Our landlord talked of raising our rent to twenty dollars per month—we had been paying sixteen—and as we bought the place where we now live for eleven hundred dollars, we concluded it would be much cheaper and better to move into it.

Just a week ago tonight I was at Poplar Bluffs Mo. on the Cairo and Fulton R.R., within about two hundred & fifty miles of you. I felt very much inclined to continue my trip, but I was not then prepared to make you a visit. Besides I want Jennie & Jessie to join me when I go, for I know you would rather see them, never having seen them, than me. I went to Poplar Bluffs on business.

> Love to all.
> Your affectionate son
> Lewis

George Butler to Mary Wyche Butler in Tulip

San Bernardino
Jan 28th 1874

My dear Mama,

I am all alone tonight. Julia with Aleck & her sister Lucia left last Monday for Los Nietos. They went in the buggy, accompanied by bro. Moores on horseback. It rained so much that we had no turnout at our Quarterly meeting. The Scarlet fever is prevailing in this place. Four or five children have died in the last few days. We do not wish Aleck to take it. He is nearly thirteen months old and has not a tooth. Were any of your children so backward? Aleck is in good health, crawls and pulls up by a chair and pushes it about, but does not stand alone yet.

Bro Moores has taken up a claim in a gold and silver mine about fifty miles from this place. It was discovered by a Methodist preacher on his district. It is uncertain whether the mine is worth any thing or not. Cox, the preacher who discovered it, thinks it is very valuable. They are digging up the rock in which the gold and silver exists in such small particles that you can hardly see them with the naked eye. Bro Moores still owes about $700.00 on his place. I would be glad if he could make at least enough to pay this. But if it is worth any thing it will doubtless pay much more.

I am sorry Charles could not get pay for his place & come out to this country next spring. However, it is all for the best. I still cherish the hope of coming back and seeing you all at some time, but I will have to wait until money becomes more plentiful. What a pleasure it would be to see my parents & brother & sisters once more! I hear from you all occasionally, it is true, but this is not the same as seeing you and conversing with you. I sometimes wonder if you do not think "George is forgetting us." "He is becoming weaned from us." No! No!! No!!! Every day, especially in prayer, do I think of my Parents, brothers, & sisters.

I hear so little of you, Mama, that I long to be with you again. I often think to myself that age is leaving its impress on you and Pa, and sometimes fear that you will be called away from time before I can get back to see you. Permit me, through this letter, once more before you go hence, to thank you, my dear parents, for all your kindness to me. May you reap a rich reward in Heaven, through the merits of Jesus our Savior. I often think of sister Mary. I have never forgotten our early associations. I hope her heart is fixed, that she has chosen that good part which shall never be taken from her.

Much love to all, including bro H's & sister Mat's families. Goodby. Your son

George

Please forward to Emma—G.E.B.

San Bernardino
Jan 28th 1874

My dear Sister Emma,

This is the third time I have commenced to write to you. About a year ago, I wrote about three pages, and a few months since, three of note paper, but never finished either. I am not certain about your post office, so I enclose this note in a letter to Ma. How are you and Billy getting on? I suppose you are still living where you were when I left, & have a considerable little family growing up around you. You will not neglect training up your little ones for Heaven. How do you get on with your house work with so many little ones? Four or five, which? Let's see, there is John, Willie, Lewis and ————. I don't know what the names of the others are. Write me about them all. I hear nothing from you unless it is when Ma makes you a visit. I hope you still enjoy the love of God and are growing in grace. Who preaches for you now?

I am not having much success in this place. Some of our members are pious and faithful, but others are very negligent of duty. May God bless you & yours. Good by.

Your brother
George

Alexander Butler to William Paisley in Dobyville

Tulip
31st March 1874

Dear son & daughter

I started to write you with ink, but found my hand so tremulous concluded to try the pencil. Well the sun is shining for a rarity. We are all in moderate health. Lewis' wife and chidlren are

253

with us. She expects Lewis to come down in two or three weeks. We are much pleased with her. We want you to come over and see us while L is here. She may spend the summer with us.

Charles was up last night. He left this morning. We will write again & will write to John when we know more certainly when L will come. I am sorry to learn that your baby is sore afflicted in its head. Hope he will soon recover. Tell John & Willy we want to see them.

Had you not better keep a small lot of goods until the end of the year to aid you in your collections? We will talk more about it when we see each other.

Kiss Emma & children for me. Some of the girls may write by Mr. Doby. Mrs Harris, Sarah Martin L, was buried yesterday.

Yours truly
Alxr Butler

Henry Butler to William Paisley in Dobyville

Malvern Ark
Apr 30 1874

Dear Billy

Yours of the 20th was rec'd at this place, having been forwarded by our good friends Orr & L. the day after I left the city. Many enquiries were made of you by our friends. Several seemed to think (Ely & other) you would probably do as you had on several occasions in the spring—make your purchases in New Orleans, & requested me to say to you, if you wanted any goods on order, to send them up, that they would sell *you* at *bottom* prices. I told old man *Harkadine* what you said about him—that if you wanted to borrow money, you would go to him & say "Here—Mr. Harkadine—I want to borrow $2,000.00 & believe I would get it." His reply was "yes—Paisley can get any thing he wants from this house."

Mr. Orr has the utmost confidence in you. I spent last Sunday week at his house, & never was treated with more genuine hospitality. He has an interesting family—lives well & I regard him *one of the best men* I *ever* knew. I purchased about $3200 worth of goods—paid every dollar down—besides the small balances we were owing on former purchases. We are owing some five hundred dollars in "home debts," but have that amount cash now on hand.

Some goods I found cheap. Prints—Standard 8½ & 9¢, St. Louis ¼ Shtg 10¢. I bought a good Brogan of Orr & L for 1.50. Crockery & Queensware is high, & I am persuaded we can do better in New Orleans except in glass ware.

Messrs Wilkins & Senter both called to see me several times, & invited me to see them. I made them a special visit—was treated *very* kindly & Mr. W. apologized for his seeming want of attention last fall. I have never doubted Senter & Cos being a No 1 house, yet I don't like them in all respects as well as some others. I was introduced by Mr. Orr to Alexander Dorman & Co, whom he recommends *very* highly, & I was quite favorably impressed with Mr. Alexander. J. H. Dowell & Co have done very well for us, but I don't like them well enough to continue with them another season.

As to the draft you sent on Senter & Co, I will hold it till you hear that all your cotton is sold, or till I hear from you, as I am not needing the money just now. You probably will hear from Senter & Co and can draw for the exact proceeds. Did you receive the Caddy Tobacco sent on per

254

your instructions to Doby & Paisley, Arkadelphia? If so how did it please you? I would like to hear from you as to your "future movements" in business—whether you expect to continue where you are or not.

I think I *must* make *some* change by next fall, & if *we* could so arrange matters as to form a business relation at Arkadelphia or elsewhere, it would please me much. One thing is in the way—*want of funds*, without which *nothing* can be done. When will you & Emma come over?

Brother Lewis was down to see me at St. L. He thinks of coming down in July. Court comes off soon, & it will be sacrificing a good deal to come sooner. He is doing well. Sister Jennie is well pleased with her visit, & has made all love her by her lovable manner & kind disposition &c. Can't you make a visit soon with sister Emma & the children? I have some idea of taking Mollie out to Texas on a visit this summer. I am more than ever convinced that *Arkansas* won't do for us to live in. Matters grow worse & worse. Love to Emma. Your brother

H.A.B.

Write soon.

Henry Butler to William Paisley in Dobyville

Malvern, Ark
May 28th 1874

Dear Billy

I have written you two letters since my return from St. Louis about one month since & have rec'd no reply. I would like so much to hear from you, how you are getting along—*how you feel* &c &c. Annie rec'd a letter from sister Emma some two weeks since & from that I inferred you had not rec'd my letter which I wrote just after my return from St.L. Maybe you have turned your attention to farming—*joined the Grange* and *lost interest* in merchants & merchandise! I received a letter from Senter & Co a few days since, giving net proceeds of your Co a/c at $250.29.

I still have your draft, thinking I would hold it till I heard from you, which I hope to do on my return home. My *oldest daughter* came up with [me] to spend a few days with her Aunt. May has been sick for a few days, & I thought the trip would benefit her. I will go down tomorrow. R.R.C. says *he will answer your very interesting* letter soon & is much obliged therefor.

Business dull. We are behind yet on cotton purchases, but only $30, & that will be covered by some sales made recently. Love to sister E.

Your brother
H. A. Butler

I would like to know something of your *future intentions*. You have always confided in me in such matters. I am *still unsettled*. This is a good point for business. Not very desirable to live at with family.

Annie Moores to Emma Butler Paisley

Malvern Ark
May 29th, 1874

Dear Sister Emma,

Your letter was received last week while I was at Tulip. I was there eight or nine days; the first time I have been down since sis Jennie came, but she spent a day & night with us, on her way down. Bro. Louis has been undecided when he would come until a few weeks ago, doesn't think now he will be here before the last of June or 1st of July. Sis Jennie seems to enjoy herself very much, but is getting quite anxious to see bro. Louis. She has two very sweet children. Jessie isn't so good as when she first came, has so many to humor her, but is much better now than the generality of children. She (sis J) & Ma spoke of going down to bro. Charlie's this week. Bro. Louis is anxious for her to go to Hot Springs, and bro. Henry said he would take her & Sister Mollie any time. Sis Jennie thinks it is getting most too warm, don't know whether they will go or not.

Miss Mary Cooper wrote to sister Mary to be ready to go with her to the Springs the first of June. She is anxious to go. Olin went with me to Tulip, & remained five days. He doesn't like for me to stay away from home long, as he then has no cook. He boards at the Hotel, and that is rather expensive for us. I enjoyed my visit *so much*, but don't reckon I will get to go again soon. Ma told me to tell Mr. Carrothers he must learn to cook, and stay here when I am gone. He told me to give his love to you, & said he thought it time he was going to see you, he seems to think a great deal of you & bro. Billy, said you must talk to Miss Smith for him.

Bro. Henry brought May up this week to spend several days with me. They returned home this morning. She has been having chills & sister M. thought probably a change would be beneficial to her. She looked much better to-day than when she came, enjoyed her visit very much.

Fannie Pattillo is visiting Calie Smith, came up last Tuesday, got here just in time to keep from getting wet, as a shower of rain fell about that time. She and Mr. John Pattillo remained with me about an hour, when the rain ceased. Mr. Carothers went over to see her yesterday evening, said she and Calie would be over to spend a day with me next week. He is very much pleased with Fannie, but I believe he falls in love with most all the young ladies. Bro. Henry doesn't think he makes a splendid clerk by any means, but of course you will say nothing about this. He is right young & will probably improve.

Our garden won't do very well this year. I only had peas twice, the vines are all dead. New ground doesn't suit them at all. I have had one good mess of Irish potatoes. The beans were looking so well but the rabbits have bit them down, they are so troublesome. Olin has killed three or four. It is getting very warm to cook, but so far I have gotten on very well, and hope I may be able to do it all summer, as I should dislike very much to be troubled with a cook.

I went down to see Theresa while at Tulip. Sister Mary & I spent a day with her, she seems to be getting on very well, does her own cooking, and is looking so well.

The third Mrs. Bailey was buried at Tulip last week. He has certainly been unfortunate. I heard Mary Scott had gone to Memphis to live. Is it so & why did they leave Pine Bluff? I am sorry Henry Louis' head still continues sore, he was such a sweet baby. Pa was complaining a good deal when I was at Tulip, but felt some better the morning I returned home, so he came with me. I drove most of the way. He felt quite well the day he went home. The ride improved him very much.

Olin has been saying all the time he was going over to see you this summer, but I don't know whether we can or not. Wish very much we could.

I suppose you heard Alice Ware had a fine daughter, weighed 12 lbs. She was in Little Rock with her father the last I heard of her. We still hear from Cal. Sister Julia sent us a splendid picture of herself & baby. When you have any more pictures taken be sure to send one to me, also the children. How is Capt. Lipscomb & family getting along—love to them. Fannie Moores expects to marry before long.

I had been thinking of writing to you several days before you wrote, for I know it must be a task for you to write many letters & do what you are compelled to do. I think you are entirely excusable, for I don't think I would do near so well as you if I were situated as you are.

Love to bro. Billy & a kiss for the children.

> Aff. sister
> Annie

Henry Butler to William Paisley in Dobyville

> Tulip Ark
> Aug 18th 1874

Dear Billy:

I have been delayed to write you on account of the discouraging prospect for crops in our section, but as the matter gets worse & *worse*, I think I had better write *now* before I "lose heart" *entirely* and can't write at all. After you left us, I sent to Little Rock for some millett, prepared the ground well and put it in nicely; a few days after we had a light shower—not enough to make it sprout—which is the only rain we have had. Mr. Howell informed me your crop looked well when he was over—that you had had a rain we didn't get. I feel glad that your crop is better than they are here. Some farms in this neighborhood will not make a bushel of corn to the acre—no[r] 200 lbs seed cotton. The failure is almost *complete*, & when I think of having debts out, the collection of which depends on such a showing, I feel like "pulling up stakes" and moving away from the debts—so that they would not give me further annoyance. You did a good thing last spring in going to the farm & not bringing goods to sell on a credit. I would have been better off to-day if I had kept out the money you paid me last summer & quit the business. We have about twelve thousand in notes & accounts and about four thousand in goods and if I could be assured of four thousand to my share of the business I would feel easier. The worst feature about the business is we are owing for the goods Pa bought of G. W. Hughes last winter while I was sick. We nevertheless have much to be thankful for when we think of our unworthiness. We *deserve nothing* of ourselves, and can *claim* nothing of ourselves. It is only through the Great Mediator that we can hope for any thing.

Dr. A Hunter was with us two weeks ago, and gave us several *excellent* sermons. How natural it is for us to look to a "Higher Source" for comfort when we have earthly hopes disappointed.

We—that is Mollie, sister Mary and myself—accompanied Brother Lewis & sister J. to Hot Springs, and then saw them on the cars for St. Louis. They left M[alvern] at 12—reached St. Louis at 5½ next morning and Murphysboro by dinner—So they were just twenty-four hours reaching home after leaving Malvern.

You doubtless have noticed an account of the arrest and closing up of Alexander, Dorman & Co for *heavy forgeries*. Mr. Orr introduced me to Mr. Alexander and endorsed him as a *good man*—said he had known him for years. It is only evidence that we *can* be mistaken as to the character of persons who we *think* we know well. Such a case as this redounds to the benefit (as it should) to old *established* houses—though it will operate somewhat against St. Louis as a cotton market. Farmers & merchants too will be more than ever inclined to sell their cotton themselves and receive the money *directly*. I think we will do business with Senter & Co., what *little* we will have. It will require eight or ten acres to make one bale on an *average*. Some farms will not make more than a bale to *twelve* or *fifteen*. The health of our vicinity is good—no sickness in the neighborhood.

I started out to write you a long letter, but I have been interrupted & have to close. Hope to receive a letter from you soon. I feel it would *do me good*. Love to sister Emma & the children.

Your brother
Henry

Mattie Hughes to Emma Butler Paisley in Dobyville

Tulip
Sept. 13th 1874

My Dear Sister,

It is Sunday evening, but I must write you a few lines, to send by Mr. Orr. He took dinner with us, at Pa's, today, and I am very much pleased with him. He preached a good sermon for us today, the first I have heard during the meeting. Our buggy is up at Malvern, and it is too far to walk often. Brother Henry left for St. Louis, last Tuesday, and George went with him as far as Little Rock. We expect them back tomorrow or next day. Did you know that brother Henry was about to build at Malvern, intending to move up there soon? I expect they will move up and occupy Olin's house, while Annie is with Ma. We expect her down in two or three weeks. I am very busy now, making clothes for Walter and West. They will leave about the 25th of this month. I will miss them so much, and how lonely we will be without them.

How is your health now? and how do the children do? I hope Emma and Henry are stout again. Pa and Ma are very well, and seem to be enjoying good health. Sister Mary and Jimmie are over at the district meeting, went over last Friday, and we expect them back tomorrow. If sister Mary was at home she would write to Mary Scott. Give my love to Mary [Scott], and tell her I wish she would come through Tulip, and spend a few days with us. It has been so long since I saw her. And Mrs. Lipscomb has gone to Pine Bluff to see Emma, quite a trip for her. I wish you could come and spend two or three weeks with us this fall. I was surprised to hear you weighed so little, only a hundred pounds. I hope you will improve this fall, and look like yourself once more.

We read a letter from brother Moores (Olin's father) last week. He says that brother George expects to visit next spring. I think he intends locating at conference.

Ma had a long affectionate letter from Lewis, and would send it to you if it was at home. They were very well, had commenced housekeeping. He says he would like to visit us again next Summer.

Alice is up at Malvern yet, and has been up there more than a month. Annie thinks she can't do without her. Ma says her—Alice's—next visit must be to you. Ma says tell Mary [Scott] she was hoping she would come by to see her, and sister Mary will regret it so much. Ma says she has been so lonely since bro. Lewis, Jennie, and the children left. So few at home now. Ma says she was glad to get your letter, and that you must come over and stay some.

Mollie expects to get one of Mrs. Grimes' daughters to do her work. Don't you think a good white girl would suit you? Ma says wouldn't you like to get one of Mrs. Grimes' daughters?

All send love to you and Billy. Write soon.

> Your Loving Sister
> M. W. Hughes

Alice Butler to Emma Butler Paisley in Dobyville

> Tulip Arkansas
> Nov. 5th 1874

Dear sister Emma:—

We have been so taken up with the *young stranger*, who came into our midst on the 21st day of Oct., that we have neglected to inform our absent brothers & sisters of this important arrival. The *Young Stranger* is a little boy just two weeks old yesterday and quite a fine looking little fellow— his mother (Mrs. Moores) is getting along finely, and has been doing well all the time.

Sister Annie and bro. Olin both are proud of their fine boy, and think that he has no predecessor to equal him. As there is no other baby here, I think we will make quite a "pet" of him. They have not decided yet what his name shall be, but think of naming him Edwin Butler, which I think is very pretty indeed. He has light hair (or rather auburn) and blue eyes, but is most too young to discern any favor.

I was very anxious to visit you at Presbytery, but thought perhaps you didn't want me to come then, as you said in Sister's letter that I must not come before that time. Miss Fannie Pattillo had expected to go, but Mr. Ben Smith was taken sick, and she was very much disappointed about it. She and her mother were over this morning to see sister Annie and the baby. Miss Fannie is looking as well as I ever saw her. She has fattened up so much since that last spell of sickness she had.

Sister Mollie seems to be delighted with Malvern. Were you not surprised to hear of their moving? We miss them a great deal. I have not been over to her old place but once since she left. It looks quite lonely. I guess bro. Henry will be ready to move into his own home in two or three weeks. Do you ever get letters from Cal.? Bro. George spoke of coming out next spring. I think we might get all the family together if he does. We received a letter from bro. Johnnie not long since, said his wife had been quite sick, but was much better then. It seems that we never know how to appreciate good health until we have gone through a spell of sickness.

We have received several letters from Walter and West since they left, seem to be perfectly delighted with the school, boarding house, and every thing else. They board with a private family, not very far from the University [of Virginia], and say they feel much at home.

Mrs. Morgan is now in sister Annie's room, came to call on Mr. Moores, Junior, & his mother.

She is a sister of Mr. Young's and such a nice lady, has been in the neighborhood about one month. Her husband has been dead some time I think. She has only one little boy. I suppose she divides her time with her brothers & sisters.

As I want this to be mailed tonight, will close. All send much love. Kiss all the children for me. Write soon.

> Your afft. sister
> Alice

Excuse mistakes, for I have been writing in a great hurry.

William Paisley to Emma Butler Paisley in Dobyville

> Malvern, Ark
> Monday Nov 9 [1874]

My dearest one:

I arrived here Saturday in time for dinner and found all well. Henry & family are living in Olin's house now, but will soon have their own house—a very nice & convenient building—completed. Their house is between Olin's & the store & on an adjoining lot to Olin's. Annie's baby is a few days over two weeks old. Both she & baby are doing well. Olin is a[t] Tulip, but will be up to day or to morrow.

Russell is looking well & seems to be perfectly satisfied, but anxious to make us a visit. Henry says he is very much pleased with him & is anxious to keep him another year, but your Pa wants Jimmie to stay in the store & they will probably not want both. Tell John & Willie [that] Coulter will come home with me & stay with them a while. Henry's wife is very cheerful, & seems to like her move very well.

I expected to go on yesterday & stop to see Aunt Ann, but the train reaches her Depot about night, & it being Sunday I concluded to give it out for the present. Henry's business seems to be good & every thing here looks prosperous. Three of the carpenters working on Henry's house are boarding with him. I will be at home, nothing preventing, Saturday night. Tell Ben to meet me at Curtis with a horse, as it will probably be impossible to drive the jersey thro at night. Mr. Doby will furnish one horse. Excuse blots as the pen won't hold ink. Will write again when I get to St. Louis. Be of good cheer & love your devoted husband

> W. Paisley

Kiss the children & tell them to be good.
Coulter can ride behind one of us from the Depot.

Henry Butler to William Paisley in Dobyville

Malvern Ark
Jany 4th 1875

Dear Billy:

A happy new year and many pleasant returns! How quickly the months pass away, and one year seems now like a month did "when we were boys." I reproach myself when I look back on the past year and see how poorly it has been spent, how much time passed unimproved.

Except colds, we have enjoyed good health this winter. Mollie has had a cough, which for two weeks gave us some trouble, but is now quite well. Annie's health is not good. You remember she had a cough before she married.

'Tis a discouraging "outlook" for us *unfortunate merchants*. Our collections are going to be so short as to compel us to ask indulgence of those we are owing. The people in many instances make use of the *hard times* as a *pretext*, and will not pay us what they could. Most of the cotton is in market, and we have collected only some two thousand dollars, most of which has gone towards keeping up our stock. Mr Hood has failed to pay anything on my place, and now wants to *cancel the trade*, says he does not want it &c. I have failed to collect the money for the place sold in Union [County]—in fact I have "the blues" badly. I don't regret building at this place, but it involved me more than I would like, and having failed to make collections for some individual debts causes me to feel embarrassed as I never did before. I think you *fortunate* in getting out of the business as you did.

Brother John is in about as bad a fix as we are. He is owing for debts contracted last spring, and is doing almost nothing in the way of business. But why dwell on *gloomy things*—it does no good. Will you please remind Mr. Doby about the am't due for Tobacco &c—we would like to receive the am't as soon as convenient. Or would you *prefer my writing* to him?

Russell is almost sick with cold, but as Dr. Reamey is his companion now, he will not suffer for want of attention. We feel fortunate indeed in having the Doctor to settle among us, for he *is a good physician*. For the present he takes his meals at my house & sleeps with Russell. Mr. Wm Carrothers was out last week—a nice man.

Love to Emma and the children.

Would like to hear from you soon. You neglected the Hat in making out your statement of amt bought for us in St Louis.

Your friend and Brother
Henry

Henry Butler to William Paisley in Dobyville

Malvern
Jany 23rd [1875]

Dear Billy:

I have commenced a letter to you twice but something has prevented my finishing, and to-night I cannot write but a short note. Hoping to have the pleasure of seeing you before long when we can have an "old fashioned talk" about all our "ups and downs"—though neither of us I believe have many "ups" now-a-days. I really sympathize with you in your trouble about farming—employing hands &c. It was *too bad* that you lost some of your meat after your painstaking. Hope you will not suffer as much loss as you anticipate.

We are collecting pretty well, find the *mortgage* a great help in getting in some old acts. We have shipped some 565 Bales, but have paid out considerable money and will lose at least one thousand dollars on cotton unless the price advances. We have some 300 Bales unsold. Have not "squared off" our debts as yet but feel that we are *almost* "out of the woods." I owe Adam & Wallace $500 for work on my Texas land. Do you keep up your Ins. policy? I am tempted to give mine up. I believe you took out a policy? am not certain.

I think as you do about a man following the business he is best acquainted with, & think as *you do* that I would make but a poor success as a farmer. Mollie says tho "tell Mr. Paisley I don't think you are *too old* to learn" says she is very sorry to hear about all those nice back bones & spare ribs spoiling—but hopes you will have better luck with *your beef*—says *she* could have given you a receipt for "corning" without your sending all the *way to St. Louis.* She has always succeeded finely in pickling beef. I have not succeeded in getting any good this winter.

Warren Archer takes charge of our business at Tulip. We furnish every thing—he to have one half the profits. Russell is over at Arkadelphia to-day—will remain with us, though he thinks of going home on a visit in a few months, I believe. All right well. Mollie has recovered from her attack of neuralgia. Try to come over to see me soon—as you promise—bring Emma with you if possible or some of the children anyhow.

I enclose statement as requested. Much obliged for your efforts to pay me as much as possible—though don't pay out too close. Love to Em & the children, in which Mollie joins.

Your brother
H.A.B.

Mattie Hughes to Emma Butler Paisley in Dobyville

Clarksville, Ark
Feb 5th 1875

Dear Sister Emma,

I expect you have heard, that George [Hughes] is engaged on the L.R. & Fort Smith Railway, and also that I am up here. It has been nearly a month since I left home. I left immediately after

Mr. Robertson's marriage. I don't know how long I'll remain up here, but expect to stay as long as it will be convenient to George's work. At present, they are only at work on the twenty miles, so as to finish that the first of May. But I expect the road will be finished to Fort Smith; and it is very probable that George will be engaged on it for some time. We broke up housekeeping for awhile, and left Mr. Robertson in charge of our house. But have it so arranged, that we can go back whenever we please.

Annie P. is in Arkadelphia, visiting her sister, and Reavis I left at his grandpa's. We are pleasantly situated here, have a comfortable room, carpeted and very well furnished, upstairs. I generally spend the forenoon in my room, but after dinner, I go down and sit with the family. I expect you wonder how I can be contented alone, and how I employ myself. But I get along finely, I write letters, read, or sew, just as I feel like.

The old gentleman, Judge Rose, is a cousin of Mrs. Durham's at Tulip. He seems to [be] very clever, and was in good circumstances before the war. He has been merchandising here, for thirty or forty years. But his soninlaw (Mr. Miller) is carrying on the business now.

This is a rough mountainous country, you can see hills or mountains in almost every direction. There is a great deal of stone here, the sidewalks are laid with it, and most of the chimneys and hearths are built of it.

There are only two churches here, Methodist and Cumberland Presbyterian. The former is a new church, was dedicated about a year ago. It is a very nice church, and will seat about four hundred persons. I have attended every Sunday, and one or two nights, since I have been here. The preachers are strangers to me, except Mr. Withers; I used to know him years ago. He said he was coming to see me, but hasn't been yet.

How are you getting on? And the children how are they doing? Is Billy engaged in farming this year?

I hear from Walter and West frequently. They are very much pleased and seem to be getting on finely. It has been eight or ten days since I heard from Tulip. Sister Mary is at Malvern, staying with Annie and Mollie. She expected to spend a couple of weeks there, and then Ma will go up and stay a week or two with Mollie.

I had a long letter from Jennie last week. Brother Lewis was absent attending court at Springfield, said he had been absent a good deal during the winter. They named their baby "Willard," she says he has improved a good deal, can walk and talk. But has only four teeth.

We are having a beautiful spell of weather now, though it is quite cold, and for several mornings we have had ice in our room. I hear of a good deal of sickness up here, mostly pneumonia, several have died.

Do you play croquet as much as ever? My love to Billy, and kiss the children for me. Is Emma as fond of babies as ever? Write soon.

> Your Affectionate
> Sister, M. W. Hughes

Alice Butler to Emma Butler Paisley in Dobyville

Tulip, Arkansas
Feb. 9th 1875

Dear sister Emma:—

Now this is fulfilling my promise nicely isn't it? but do not censure me too much, dear sister, for my seeming negligence, for I assure you that it was not voluntary.

After getting home from my visit to you, I received a letter from Florrie telling me to meet her at Mrs. Feild's in Little Rock Christmas, that the latter would certainly expect us. I had disappointed her once before, and thought it would be too bad not to go this time, so I began to fix right away, and off I started the next week to Little Rock, to spend my Christmas. We had a delightful time, although the weather was somewhat disagreeable.

I shall often look back with so much pleasure to the short week I spent with you & bro. B. Know that I could not have enjoyed myself more any where and don't think it will be long before I shall want to go again. How are all getting on now? we heard through Dr. Colburn that he had fixed your teeth for you, and said that you sent word that "you were all right now." I was so glad to hear that you had had them fixed, for I knew that you would appreciate them.

Ma has gone up to Malvern, don't know exactly when she will return, though I guess she will be gone several weeks. We miss her a great deal at home. Sister M. and I are still doing the work. We have had little Jim for two weeks, but his mammy wanted him to stay with her this week so we are without any one. He is getting right large, and is a great help about every little thing. Aunt Lucy has a baby. What has become of our croquet, do you ever play now? Tell Mr. John Carrothers not to let you beat, it would never do. Has he gained your friendship since we left?

Sister Mary just returned from Malvern last week, spent two weeks with them, says she intended writing to you while she was up there, and was very sorry she did not. I sent the picture you gave me of bro. B to bro. George & Louis, we received a letter from sister Jennie not long since, says she wants sister Mary to come up and spend the summer with them. Re[a]vis is staying with us. Annie P. is in Arkadelphia with her sisters, says that she is enjoying herself finely.

Give my love to the Doby girls when you see them *especially* Maggie. I liked them all so much. I don't know when I ever enjoyed a little party more than the one you gave us. We have not heard from brother Johnnie in some time. He doesn't write often. Pa wanted to know who I was writing to. I told him to you. He says give my best love to them.

Give my love to Ella & Mrs. Lipscomb. All unite with me in sending much love—kiss little Emma for me. Now do write soon, and a long letter to your ever true and devoted sister

Alice

Henry Butler to William and Emma Paisley in Dobyville

Malvern Ark
Feby 16th 1875

Dear Billy & Emma:

I have thought of you frequently of late and it occurred to me that we *ought* to *hear from* each other *oftener*. I confess *I* am a poor hand to write—have grown worse than formerly; now seldom write a letter unless it is on business. This is *not* as it should be—we owe it to each other to write sometimes.

We are in good health. You never saw Mollie *looking better*—her cheeks are *ruddy* & full— seems to be well pleased at our new home, though she has been out but little. Several ladies have called, and she is most pleased with two or three.

Ma is now with us, and will remain a week or two. She seems to enjoy her visit, and says she *likes* Malvern. Pa came up today, having tired of staying at home *without Ma* who has been up some ten days. We hear from Lewis but seldom.

I was at Tulip week before last, and it is really *distressing* to see that country, and learn how poorly supplied with provisions the people are. Mr. John Pattillo—for instance has *nothing*, and had been sick for weeks. His brother James, of course, is supplying him. I only cite this as an instance—numbers—white and black are *almost* & in many cases, *entirely* destitute. There will be much suffering.

Walter & West are *doing well* at the University of Va. Have made a fine impression on the Professors, who send the most flattering reports. We hear from Charlie & Kate occasionally. *They* are expecting Mrs. Colburn Sr. to spend *some weeks with them soon*!

I *did* think of putting off writing till *after* a *certain event* (to transpire *soon*) but I can write again. With a brother's love for you both I am affectionately your brother

Henry

P.S. Billy—in making out the a/c against "Doby & Paisley" I think I omitted the $4.00 you collected of John Green. Did I not? Please ask Mr. D—that is, if it should be charged to D & P. Business dull—money scarce no collections to speak of. Will be glad to serve you when I go to St. L.

Mary Butler to Emma Butler Paisley in Dobyville

Tulip Arkansas
Mar. 2nd, 1875

My Dear Sister:—

While at Malvern I fully intended writing to you, but put it off from time to time, until days have multiplied into weeks: so I've determined this morning to lay aside everything else, and write to *dear* Emma and Johnny. I censure myself for not having written to both of you sooner.

265

Alice received your letter last Friday. I got one from Sister at the same time. She speaks of coming home before long. I wish she would, for we miss her very much.

I suppose you know Mr. Robertson is living at her place, occupying the two rooms on the end of the gallery. He married Miss Rosa Garmany, a sister of Mrs. Hood: she weighs about 175 pounds, suits Mr. R. exactly: he says "not an angry passion has crossed my breast since the 7th day of Jan." I am glad he is so happily married. Alice and I went over to see them not long ago: we were also there the night they returned after being married, Sister and Annie P. fixed them up a nice supper, and we all had a pleasant time joking Mr. R. &c &c. Pa had promised him a turkey if he did marry (but had no idea he would), so the 18th of Jan. being his wife's birthday, we had the turkey, and fixed them up a real nice dinner, which they appreciated.

Mr. Ben Cooksey and Mr. Doak took dinner with us yesterday: Mr. D. says Theresa wants to come up this week, and will spend one night with me: he brags on his fine daughter. I fixed up a nice little boquet of flowers and sent it to Miss Mary Doak with my compliments. The white hyacinths are now in full bloom, also other early spring flowers.

Alice and I are getting on finely with everything, though we miss ma very much: she has been gone over three weeks, and I don't think pa can stand her absence much longer. He has been up and spent one week.

We are getting some eggs—have one hen setting—wish we could have *early* chickens, as well as vegetables. I have been gardening some: ma is getting impatient to come home to attend to it herself. Sister Annie and I are anxious to visit you before long—spoke of it when I was with her: and in her last letter said that I must come up when ma came home, and we would try to go. She is anxious to show you her sweet boy, which she pets a great deal.

Tell brother Billy I remember he told me not to visit him any more in the Spring, when eatables were so scarce, but I believe it will be too long to wait till summer: let us just eat to live.

I was surprised to hear that brother Henry had given such an account of the times around Tulip. I had heard nothing of it: of course it is an unusual year, but then I thought people were getting on better here than most of places, but perhaps I'm not so well posted. I feel *truly* thankful that we, thus far, have had an abundance.

I am much obliged to Mrs. Jones for her thoughtfulness of me: be sure to return my best love when you write. I fell much in love with her. I have been working some on my log cabin quilt lately. I have had it on hand so long that I'm anxious to finish it. I had a letter from Mary Scott some time ago which I must answer. Give my love to Mrs. Lipscomb, Ella, the Capt. and in fact *all* my friends. With much love for your own household, I am always your true and afft.

Sister Mary.

Cousin Jimmie Butler was to see us last week. Cousin Laura was improving some, can be put in a rocking chair to sit a short time. I do feel sorry for cousin J. His expenses have been very great. I expect you heard the baby died some time ago. Annie Phillips is now staying with her sister Alice, to help her nurse cousin Laura. We received a paper from Mo. not long since, containing the obituary of our old friend Mr. Johnson. He was resigned and talked of death with great composure.

This is Alice's week for cooking, so she is out now getting dinner. I was sorry your turnip salad was destroyed: we have some in the garden, which we all enjoy very much: it is so healthy to eat this time of the year.

We have just heard that sister Mollie has a daughter weighing ten pounds, and ma will come home Saturday.

Henry Butler to William Paisley in Dobyville

Malvern, Ark.
Mar 8th 1875

Dear Billy:

I wrote you over two weeks since (have rec'd no answer) and hinted at an expected *"event"*—well it has transpired, and it is *a daughter*—now one week old—and the only baby *I* ever thought was good looking—a *very young* baby I mean—Mother and child are in fine health—everything passed off right, for which I hope I am thankful.

Ma has returned to Tulip, having been *five weeks* at my house. Our anxiety and suspense was great but we were more than recompensed by *Ma's company*—which we enjoyed exceedingly—I have not been so much with my mother since I married & I feel that it has been for my benefit *spiritually*. Ma is so devoted as a Christian.

Sister is now with us for a few days & will visit Tulip before she returns to Clarksville. There is a party of Railroad men at Malvern, looking after the proposed branch to Hot Springs. The prospect is it will be built from this place during this and next year. I don't think that will affect the business of Malvern much either way. For a time it will cause much more money to be passing.

Our business holds up pretty well—we sell some goods for the *money*—but by far too many *on time*. That is the trouble, and how to keep our stock up through the season is *the* Question. I think of going to St. Louis shortly, and if I can serve you—command me *right away*. I would be glad to serve you.

Love to Emma.

Affectionately your brother
H.A.B.

I have never heard from Mr. Doby in reference to the debt of D&P—though I wrote him sending statement, and requested him to write—What do you think of his paying? Of course, I don't want you to speak to him about the matter. I merely ask your opinion of what you *suppose* he will do.

Henry Butler to William Paisley in Dobyville

Malvern, Ark
Apr 8th 1875
Thursday eve

Dear Billy,

Yours of 6th rec'd by this mornings train. Russell & myself have filled your order as best we could. The shoes for sister Emma are not such as I wanted to send—heels too high & narrow, but it is the best we have of the no. The Calf Brog. for yourself I send No. 6. Feel certain they are large enough, as *I* tried them on myself. We send 2¾ yds first rate Eng. Cassimere, which Ely charged me $.40 per yd.—in place of one pr. pants—didn't have the size & Russell thought his brother (or Mr. Cheatham) would be pleased with the Cassimere. I am glad to have the pleasure of selling the goods to you, and hope they will suit. The box will be sent over to-morrow, and you will find a few apples put in "to fill" which you will give to Emma & the children. If the box should remain long in Arkadelphia, you had better have it opened & the apples taken out.

Wish you *could* come over to see us. I would enjoy a night's talk with you *very much*. You are *perfectly* right—and I understand it properly—about not losing time from your plowing to meet Annie & others at Arkadelphia. They can come over at a more leisure time. Will you want the Scythes & Cradles?

What case do you refer to as the "old D & P case" which called you to Arkadelphia as a witness?

You have a heavy crop on hand. 35 acres in cotton will keep you stirring, I think. You will make money on your farm this year. You ought to, the way you are working.

Mollie & baby (and others) are quite well. The baby is small—but sprightly.

Love to Emma.

Write me & let me know how the goods suit you.

> Your brother
> H.A.B.

Annie Butler Moores to Emma Butler Paisley in Dobyville

Malvern Ark.
May 13th 1875

Dear Sister Emma,

Your letter should have been answered immediately, but I kept putting it off one day for another and this morning I have just concluded to let every thing alone until I answer your letter. I have just gotten Edwin to sleep, and have a quiet time. He is such a good baby, never has been any trouble, but a *great* pleasure. I guess the troublesome time is to come yet—but I don't intend to cross the bridge before I get to it.

Olin, Annie Phillips, and sister Alice have gone to the river to fish. They came up last Monday with Mr. Carothers, expects to return next Saturday. But Olin wrote to Pa yesterday that Alice would not be there. Ma wanted her to remain longer if she had any way to get back, said if I would come with her she could stay. Annie [Phillips] is compelled to return, as sister wants to make preparations to go to keeping house at Tulip for the summer. She expects Walter & West to spend their vacation at home. Sister, and Sister Mary spent several weeks with us. The former remained longer & kept house for sister Mollie several days, while she went down to Pa's. Said she never enjoyed herself more in her life. She and bro. Henry both seemed to have quite a nice time. They only carried George and the baby. The latter is a very sweet child, but I don't think she is as pretty as her other children at her age.

Bro. Henry has a set of croquet, and we have a nice time playing in the evenings, but it will be too warm this summer, as there is no shade, unless we play at night like you did. He also has Portrait Authors and Attitude which we play right often at night.

Olin received bro. Billy's letter, and we appreciated his writing just as he did, for it is an important time with farmers and I would[n't] have him neglect his work for any thing.

Dr. Reamy has moved his family up, and are living in sight of us. Mr. W. Hunter expects to commence building soon. Malvern is building up rapidly. Several dwelling houses are being built at present, and others contemplate building.

I have 38 little chickens, would have had more but bro. Henry's dog broke up two hens I had sitting. I still have Puss doing my work, but she has been complaining a week and I have to help her some. I do wish you lived near enough to visit us often, it would be so pleasant. Olin sent to St. Louis and got the baby a very nice little buggy with four wheels cost $11.75. He is so delighted with it. He is getting too heavy to carry any distance. He is sitting in his buggy now playing. He is very fond of rolling over on the floor, and could get about better if he had short dresses on. I have only one made.

Olin, Alice, Edwin, and I expect to ride over to the river tomorrow. There is said to be some very pretty scenery near Rockport, and any number of cedars.

Olin is having the stumps grubbed up in the yard to-day. It will be quite an improvement. All were well when we last heard from Cal. which was about two weeks ago. We don't hear from Johnnie very often, but when we last heard his wife's health was improving, and they spoke of visiting us this summer. Alice is looking thin, only weighs 101 lbs. and I 100 lbs. How much do you weigh?

A kiss from Edwin. If Olin were here he would join me in love to you all. Tell bro. Billy he needn't pity "poor Olin." Every thing seems to agree with him. He weighs 183 lbs. Write when you can.

> Your loving sister
> Annie Moores

> After dinner

Mr. Carothers is here now, playing with Edwin. Seems so fond of him. Sends love to you & says tell his bro. John to write to him.

> 14th

I couldn't get my letter mailed yesterday & Olin found out this morning that he would have to go to Princeton, so I guess we will all go to Tulip tomorrow.

Mattie Hughes to Emma Butler Paisley in Dobyville

> Tulip Arkansas
> June 11th 1875

Dear Sister Emma,

I expect you have heard before this that I am back at my old home keeping house. We have been here about three weeks, and I begin to feel at home, that is, as much so as I can without George and my boys. It seems strange to have another family living in the house, but we get along finely, and it is not so lonesome as it would be without them. I like Mrs. Robertson very well, and think she suits Mr. R. very well, that is, as well as any one would. Her youngest sister "Isla" lives with her. They occupy the two rooms at the west end of the gallery.

We will have an abundance of fruit this year, except peaches. Most of our peach trees are broken down. We had more cherries this year than we ever had before. I preserved nine pds. and pickled a small jar. While Sister Annie was down last week, she put up seven or eight pounds.

Edwin is very sweet, and a very good baby. He will sit on a pallet an hour at a time. The first of next month I expect Walter and West home to spend their vacation. Walter wasn't well during the last month, was threatened with Typhoid fever, and didn't attend lectures for a week. He says he feels very well now, and has a good appetite, but is looking very thin. I expect West has changed some, as he has grown a good deal. I am so anxious to see them, and begin to grow impatient as the time draws near for them to come.

I hope you can come over and spend two or three weeks with us, during the summer. I know you need rest and recreation. How do you stand the cooking since the weather got warm? I often wish that you were living nearer, so that I could help you about your sewing. I haven't had much to do lately, but when the boys come, I expect we will have a good deal to do for them. I have been expecting George home this week, and think he will surely come, or I'll get a letter from him today. He says he may spend most of the summer here.

All are well at Pa's, but sister Mary and Alice are looking very thin. Pa is trying to hire a cook during the summer. Alice expects Florrie to come and stay some with her, and Mrs. Feild and one of her sons also speak of coming. Ma has had a good many young turkeys, had as many as 40 a few days ago, but I think a fox killed four the other evening. How are you succeeding with your fowls? I am not trying to raise any, as I came here so late in the season. But Mr. Robertson has my chickens, and is to give me a part. We have some large enough for pies, and had one for dinner the other day.

[Final section of letter missing]

Walter J. Hughes to Alice Butler

Charlottesville Va
June 15th 1875

My dear Alice

Your letter fell to me (shall I say from heaven?) as one to make up that shower which refreshed me so, about the last of May. Such showers now have ceased to come. My "spirit," if I may so express it, is parched with a great drouth for the want of them.

Where in the wide world does that *so* much company come from that prevents you from writing to me as frequently as you would wish? There must be something grand going on at Tulip, or some great attraction that will draw such a continual stream of visitors as to make one entirely forget her relations when there is distance between. If I were at home I would not allow you to forget me, for you should see my countenance *very* frequently. But as it is I am forced to delay till your pleasure allows me to remind you that such a one as I am yet living. Living? Yes. But West says, "most dead though" he adds, "most dead in love." I think you will be surprised when you again see me. If what some of the students say about my looking so badly is true. But I must not raise your expectations too high.

West is looking "finely." He has improved in looks more than I have retrograded. Therefore if I was entirely unselfish, I should count that as a little gain and be proud of it. He tells me to say to you that he is now sitting in the window, throwing kisses at the young ladies as they pass, and they are thickly passing too.

Some of you will have to wait another year for my photograph. I know it will be very hard to do, but I only had half a doz. taken and they are all promised. This is the one I promised you. Take it and do with it what seemeth best to you. I think it would make a nice ornament in an album, but there may be others of you who differ from me. But that only shows the fault in their discernment. It cannot be attributed to any lack of elegance in the picture. For such perfection is rarely attained either by the artist or his subject. Again, I forget that my opinions may not be relished with the same pleasure by others.

In your next letter to Miss Florrie, return love for me, not that which she sent to me, no, lock that up and throw the key in the well till I come, but take some (a great deal) of mine which you have and send it, and when I return I will replace that and send some more. If you have any to spare, you may send some to Lily Kelly (by Pomp) [Pompey Matlock].

Don't be supprised at my having so much to spare, for West says I *live* in it here. A few days more than 2 weeks and I shall start for home.

Mamma will hear from me through this. As ever, I am yours with much love,

Walter J. Hughes

Annie Butler Moores to Emma Butler Paisley in Dobyville

Malvern Ark
June 16th 1875

Dear Sister Emma,

Your letter was gladly received last week, and I expected to answer immediately, but Dr. Colburn was here most of that week working on my teeth, and you know how unpleasant that is; a person doesn't feel fit for hardly any thing. He was here again this evening, expects to have his office at this place.

Malvern has improved *so much* since you were here.

Pa and Sister came up last Saturday, and returned home today, we enjoyed their visit very much. The latter came up to meet bro. George Hughes. He returned to Little Rock this evening. Walter & West will be at home in two or three weeks. Can't you come here & to Tulip while they are at home? Sister said she would be so glad if you could come over and spend several weeks. I have been down home twice since I last wrote you, and think I will make one more visit this summer in Sept. Pa told me to tell you that he *thought* of you very often, but he was getting so old he couldn't write much now.

I suppose you have heard that Johnnie was in Texas for his wife's health, which has been much worse than we ever knew of. Bro. Charlie said he would be up this week for groceries. I look for him to-night.

Olin had letters from his father and Lucia last week. They were all well and getting on finely.

17th

I didn't get to finish my letter yesterday so I will try to finish it off this evening. Bro. Caldwell will be here to spend to-night with us, & will preach for us. I want to go if I possibly can, for it

271

isn't very often I get to hear preaching. He came up to meet his daughter Anna, who is at school in Little Rock, and is expected on the train in the morning.

Our garden is doing very well this year, but we are needing rain now. Our Irish potatoes are splendid. Edwin is as sweet as ever, & gets about very well since I put short dresses on him. He hasn't a single tooth & will be eight months old the 21st of this month. Sister Mollie has put short dresses on her baby. She is a *very* good child. Carrie Durham's school is broken up. Dr. McCranie said he could not possibly pay her any longer. It has been about two weeks since it closed.

Ma had forty young turkeys but I think she has lost five or six. She never was as successful in raising them as she has been this year. She thought of coming up to see us soon, but says she don't believe she can leave her turkeys. I have about ninety chickens, have eaten only two.

Mr. Carothers says he is getting most too old to visit you now.

Reavis is spending several days here & at bro. Henry's. When he gets tired of the children up there, he comes down here & reads & plays with Edwin. The baby is so fond of him.

A kiss from Edwin to you all. Love to bro. Billy & the children. Don't the farmer get very warm & tired these hot days? Write soon to

> Your ever loving sister
> Annie Moores

Annie Butler Moores to Emma Butler Paisley in Dobyville

> Malvern Ark
> July 17th 1875

Dear Sister Emma,

We arrived safely a little after 1 o'clock, found Olin awaiting our return. Mr. Carothers said he (Olin) was about to start after us. Bro. Billy has told you about our ride to Curtis, what a time we had. I was fearful it would make him sick, he had to exert himself so much. Emma stood the trip finely. She, sister Mary, Alice Phillips, Mr. Carothers, & Coulter went down to Tulip last Wednesday. Mr. Carothers returned yesterday, in company with Ira. They brought me a note from sister Mary, in which she said "Little Emma misses Edwin so much that she hasn't been as well satisfied as she was at your house—wants to have me with her all the time. I think she will get over that after she gets acquainted with the others." She seemed to be delighted all the time she was here; never once said she wanted to go home. She didn't like to stay at bro. Henry's; *too many* children, I reckon. The first evening, sister Mary said she would spend the night up there, but when Emma saw Olin, Edwin, and I start off she came running, she seemed perfectly satisfied, but sister Mary came down after supper, & she wanted to go wherever she went. But sister Mary said she was always better satisfied here if she was with her. She is as little trouble as a child could be. I think she is *very good*. She intends to keep up with sister Mary. Edwin misses Emma so much. They seemed to love each other very much.

I saw Mr. Warren Archer a few days ago. He & several other young men are out on a pleasure excursion. They are fishing in the river, expect to return to this place this evening. Mr. Archer speaks of going to Tulip Monday. Mr. Hamlin is here a neighbor of Dr. Reamy's, don't know whether he will make this his home or not. I think he expects to make a lawyer. Walter & West got home at the time looked for. I know you don't have time to write, so tell bro. Billy he must write. Tell John & Willie they must be good boys, and then come to see aunt Annie.

Bro. Billy, how high did you say your cane was? Ira says sister Mary said she believed you said 20 ft. Mr. Carothers laughed at the idea. How is Mr. John C.? Give him my regards.

I would write more, but haven't time. Much love to all

> Your loving sister
> Annie Moores

Mary Wyche Butler to Emma Butler Paisley in Dobyville

> Tulip
> Aug 11 1875

My Dear Daughter,

I am sorry to have to tell you I can't come over. I expected it would be convenient for me to go, but I will have to put it off for another time. I feel sorry not to be with you. Hope you will do well. You will be in good hands. Give my love to Mrs. Lipscomb. Tell her she must take my place. She is such a good hand that I feel better satisfied about you. [Emma's fifth child was born Aug. 25, 1875.] I would like to see her and have a long talk with her.

You must come this fall if you can. If you can't, I must try and go to see you. We have fixed something for you. We would like to do more if we could.

We have had meeting on all the week. The preacher seem very hard. I enjoyed the prayer meeting yesterday morning very much. The meeting closes tonight. It is pouring down rain now. I reckon we can't have preaching tonight. I was in hope we could have preaching tonight. Mr. Profile seems more careless and indefinite than I ever saw him.

Walter has received a letter from his uncle Lewis. I haven't heard the news yet. We haven't heard from him in some time. I have just heard the letter. Very interesting and affectionate, says he is coming to see us next summer. You must come, & Geo expects to come. Now, that will be fine.

Emma [Paisley, her grand-daughter] has been as well satisfied as I ever saw, and she has been a little disordered in her bowels. I gave her some benal plant, then I will give her something to night. I gave her some paregoric last night. She is better this morning. I think she will soon be well. Has no fever. Little Emma has run in and said, "Grandma, I am most well now." You need not be uneasy about her.

Coulter has come and said who do you think took supper with them last night? Major Borden, on his way to Washington [Arkansas] to teach school. He says his pa, mama, and all the children are coming tomorrow.

Emma is getting fond of me. She has been going around with me, feeding the chicks. She is delighted with the young guiney. Sorry her ma haven't any. I gave her one to play with. She carried it about in her lap. I wish you could see my turkeys. I still have 26 half-grown. They look fine. I wanted to show them to William when he was here. I am affeard they will take the cholera.

Em so glad to see Coulter. She is fond of Jimmie and Walter. He slept here last night. Tonight Jimmie and West are invited to the children's party at Mr. Young. Em likes here better than it is anything.

Good by my dear daughter. The Lord bless you, you all. Amen. Like to be with you.

Mary Butler to Emma Butler Paisley in Dobyville

Tulip Arkansas
Aug 30 1875

My dear sister:—

Yours of the 16th inst written to Emma and myself, was received last week, and we felt so sorry that you were disappointed about ma's not coming over. Ma was really troubled for awhile, and felt greatly relieved when she got brother Billy's letter stating the birth of your little daughter, and that you and the babe were doing well. When I told Emma of her little sister said she wanted to go home. She has several times lately spoken of wanting to go home but she soon forgets it, and seems perfectly satisfied.

Mr. Howell said he would take Emma home when he went over, which will be next Saturday— that is, he leaves here then for Arka. but will remain there until the next Thursday, I believe, which will be too long for him to keep her there. Miss Mollie Howell expects to go with him.

Brother Olin and Annie came down Saturday and will remain until after our two days' meeting, which begins next Friday night. Emma says she is going to Malvern when her aunt Annie goes, then she is going home. She thinks, of course, she can get home from there, said one day she could go on the cars by herself. If she had some one to go with her from Malvern to Arkadelphia, it would be a good way for her to meet Mr. Howell there next Thursday week and go right on with him, which would save the trouble of sending for her. I hope you will not think, because I've written so much about her getting home, that we are at all anxious for her to go, for she is no trouble, and really I *don't* know how I can do without her. She is so much company and seems so much attached to me, that I shall hate very much for her to leave; says she has three homes and three ma's, aunt Mattie, aunt Mary, and yourself. I begin to feel almost that she belongs to me, and you will have to let her come back again. I think she has enjoyed her visit very much, and has been so well all the time.

Brother Henry and sister Mollie came as we expected, and spent a week. The children had a fine time together. I received a letter from Mary Scott a few days ago. She said I must come down to see her and bring Emma with me. I had written her to come up and stay some with me, but said it would be impossible for her to come.

I went down to see Charley and Kate last Monday, came back the next day, as we were so busy drying and putting up fruit—took them a dozen stone cans for putting up fruit which Mr. Byrd made. Aunt Lucy is now living with us again, but says *she can't* stay more than a month or two or until cotton opens—she is a splendid cook and does everything so well. The only drawback is her cross baby. Ma sends much love and say she thought perhaps she would come over and bring Emma, but don't know when she can come. Pa says he and ma must go over together and see you and then go on to see Johnny and attend conference, which will be the first of December at Greenville, twelve miles from Centre Point. Ma says tell you she is now mending the old dress you gave her. She always liked it so much, she wants to get one more wearing of it. Emma has just come to me to fix her doll and sends a kiss to you, Henry and little sister. She is so much amused playing with Edwin, loves a baby so much, she and Annie are busy playing with their dolls.

Ma sends love to Mrs. Lipscomb, says she mustn't be provoked about her not coming, as she got on so well without her, but she would have enjoyed being with her so much.

Maj. Borden passed through Malvern not long ago on his way to Washington to take the school which has been offered him there—he stopped to see Annie and brother Henry, thought Edwin a beautiful child, didn't see where he got his good looks from.

I am glad brother Billy is pleased with his shirts. I was afraid the sleeves would be too long, but they could be easily shortened by taking a tuck. I didn't feel exactly satisfied with them. If I can possibly find time, I will try to make two more. Jimmie is expecting to go to college, Randolph Macon, and we will have to sew a good deal for him and Ira. I don't know yet what he will do.

There is a camp meeting at Rock Spring the last of next week, and some of us are thinking of going. Mrs. Horton has invited us over. They are making great preparations.

Tell brother B he must write immediately as we are anxious to hear from you. Mrs. Leiper has a fine son, born last Sunday week. Fannie Macon is staying with her.

With much love from all I am your loving sister,

Mary

All out playing croquet but ma, Walter, and myself.
Walter and Jimmie are going to Malvern this morning.

Mattie Hughes to Emma Paisley in Dobyville

Malvern Arkansas
Oct. 15th 1875

My Dear Sister,

It has been nearly a week since I left Tulip. Papa came up with me, spent a day or two, and then returned home. Sister Mary came up last week, expecting to go on to brother Lewis', but had a spell of chills and fever, and hasn't gotten off yet. She was in bed when I came up last Saturday, but she is up now and improving every day. She is looking very thin, but I think a trip off would help her very much.

George went to Little Rock yesterday, but says he will have to go to St. Louis on business for the railroad soon, and will go with her to brother Lewis'. I don't know yet how long I'll be here, probably two or three weeks. George will have some running around to do for the railroad, but as soon as he can, we will go to Ozark, and I expect remain there all Winter and Spring. I had letters from the boys, yesterday, they were well, but Walter and Georgie had two or three chills after they left home. Jimmie and Georgie are at Randolph Macon, and seem to be well pleased. Say they have a pleasant boarding place, and seem to be getting along finely. Georgie is so young, that I couldn't feel willing for him to leave, but I hope it will be for the best. I was sorry it was so that you couldn't come over while they were at home.

Ma was very well when I left. But complains of feeling very lonely, only two of her children at home. So you know it seems lonely to her. When are you coming over? We have been very anxious to hear from you, was uneasy about Billy the day he left, with little Emma. Tell Emma we missed her very much, and that aunt Mattie wishes she had her for her little girl.

Sister Annie hasn't been very well lately, but has a good appetite and seems to be improving now. Edwin is not walking yet, can almost stand alone and is looking very well now. Brother Henry went to Tulip with Pa, had to go down to attend to some business. We expect him home today. Mollie's baby has been a little sick this week. I think she is teething. Miss Annie Yocum (a cousin of Mollie's) is teaching a small school here. Coulter, May, and Mattie are going. How is your little baby? Would like so much to see it. I know you have your hands full. Sister Mary and Annie send their love. Tell Emma "Aunt Mary" says, she missed her so much, and has been so anxious to hear from her since she got home.

Love and a kiss for the children. Write soon, and let me know how you are.

Your Loving Sister
M. W. Hughes

Henry Butler to William Paisley in Dobyville

Malvern Ark
Nov 5th 1875

Dear Billy:

I have been expecting to receive a letter from you for some time and have intended to write myself, but have put it off from time to time. I this evening read a letter from sister Emma written to "Sister"—a good lengthy letter. From what Emma writes, I am led to think you have written me lately on some business. *I have not rec'd any letter.*

I am surprised and quite sorry to hear of your feeble health. It seems strange to think of your being sick so much. But Emma writes that you had gone to the cotton field, and I hope you are rid of chills. Your anxiety to get your cotton picked properly causes you to expose yourself before you are well enough. *That* is one thing you ought to be careful about. *Your health*—we do not properly prize the blessing till it is too late, frequently.

We are getting in some cotton (have shipped over 100 bales), but it comes in slower than I expected. We have mortgages on cotton sufficient (with what we collect besides) to pay our debts, *I hope* but we are much deeper in debt than I ever expected to be, and will not feel comfortable till we can *see out*. I trust we will never have another year like the past.

Our place is improving. Some dozen houses have been built since you was here. W. H. Cooper, W. H. Hunter, & W. H. Smith are in business here—the former has bought a place & has his family with him. Mr. Hunter seems to be rather gloomy—is not doing as well as he expected at his new stand down on the R.R. *among the saloons*, where he is occupying his Tulip store house. Mr. Hunter did a good business when on the corner of *this street* in the way of bartering &c. Jo Reyburn is building a store house (small size) on this street & further out.

We are holding our trade pretty well, and have no cause to complain of our business, both as to selling & collections. We don't purchase cotton except in the way of trade or debts, and of course pay more than it is worth by ½ cent.

I am still well pleased with Senter & Co. They are clever men & good merchants. They advanced us $2000 during the summer to aid us in furnishing supplies to our customers and some $4000 since to meet some of our debts. We have shipped several hundred bushels wheat and over 4000 lbs Dried fruit. Have made some little money besides the trade on the fruit. But I *forget* you are at *present* a farmer & perhaps these things don't interest you as they once did.

I wish I could see you and have an *old fashioned* talk over "matters & things" generally. Hope to have that pleasure some time this winter.

As to our health—my family have enjoyed better health than for years. Mollie, myself or any of the children have [not] been sick abed in months. The children are rosy and growing fast. May is quite a large girl, looks strange even to me that I have a daughter so large.

Miss Annie Yocum from Union County and an own cousin of Mollies is teaching school for us, has but a small school, as the "free school" is being taught a short distance out of town by Mr. Robt. Thrasher. *Shame upon* us that we can't say we have a church in Malvern. We have spoken for a lot and some money subscribed to build, and hope we will succeed this winter.

Miss Mollie Howell spent last Monday night at my house, and I saw her on the cars Tuesday enroute home. She is quite a nice lady, and I hold Mr. Howell—her brother—in high esteem. He has preached for us once and gave us an *excellent* sermon.

Russell is very well, and getting along finely—laughs as loud as ever you [heard] him. He is a favorite with all, I believe. I sent him out into the country last week looking after the "lame ducks"—was absent eight days—but accomplished little. Don't think him a good collector, does finely behind the counter. We have Ira with us also, and find him quite serviceable at times. Some days we are over-run with business.

Mollie has been doing her house work, cooking &c for some time, three or four months. I think I have hired one to commence soon. She says she can—and does—sympathize with *Emma*. Can't you bring Emma over to see us after you get through the press of farm work? It would be so delightful to have you come.

Give my love to Em & the children. Russell sends his regards.

This is written at the store and quite hurriedly (as you perceive). If Mollie knew I was writing she would have *some words* for you, certain.

Do let me hear from you soon.

> Your brother,
> Henry A. Butler

Annie Butler Moores to Emma Butler Paisley in Dobyville

> Malvern Ark
> Dec. 9th, 1875

Dear Sister Emma,

Having just put Edwin to bed, I concluded to write you a short letter, as it has been some time since I last wrote you. Not since the birth of your little daughter, wish so much I could see her. How is she getting along and who does she favor? Is she a good baby? I think she ought to be, for I know you have your hands full even then.

Bro Henry read us an excellent letter from bro. Billy last Sunday week. Pa & Ma spent last Monday night with us on their way to Conference or bro. J.'s if he met them at Hope. They regretted so much that they couldn't go by to see you, but after the rain set in they concluded it would be too great an undertaking to go all the way by land, and I expect the roads are very bad. Ma said she regretted so much she couldn't see you. She was almost unwilling to go the trip any way, hated to leave home. Ira & Alice are there alone.

Olin and I went down to the depot yesterday with Sister. She went to Little Rock, & expected to go to Ozark next week. We will miss her so much, as she had been with us a good deal lately, and Edwin seemed to love her so much.

Sister Mary left here last Tuesday was a week, met with bro. George Hughes in Little Rock, and he went with her to bro. Louis'. Paid all her expenses, gave her a nice black cashmere dress; & also some money & I expect other things; said he would give her a hat if she needed it. He is just as kind to her as he could be. Said he wanted to see her fixed up real nice. Sister gave me a nice hat cost $8—also gave Sister Mollie one.

I am very busy every day making my black cashmere dress. It is quite an undertaking to make a nice dress. I neglected to say that sister Mary found Jessie in bed with fever, but hopes nothing serious.

Maj. Coulter is spending several days here, thinks of leaving Saturday. I went up this evening to have a game of croquet with him, but he had gone to the store, but Sister Mollie, Miss Annie Yocum & I had a nice game.

Christmas is almost here, wish it was so we could all be together, but the family are all getting too large to go about much. I think it is a good deal of trouble with one.

Ma gave sister Mollie & I a nice turkey for Christmas dinner, & we bought another, so we will have some turkeys if nothing else. Sister Mary left bro. Billy's shirts to be sent by ma, & as she didn't go we will have to send them to Arkadelphia. Good night & pleasant dreams.

> Your affectionate sister
> Annie Moores

Tell bro. Billy the next time I come to see him I think I shall bring Olin. Kiss the baby for me. Love to all. Write if you can.

Olin thinks I had better wait to send the shirts to Arkadelphia by Mr. R[ussell] C[arothers], to be carried to Dobyville by Mr. J[ohn] C[arothers]. I have Jim living [with] me. Puss is with Aunt Lucy.

Mattie Hughes to Emma Butler Paisley in Dobyville

Ozark, Arkansas
Dec. 16th 1875

Dear Sister Emma,

I kept postponing writing to you while at Malvern, thinking every week that I would leave for this place, and that I would write immediately after getting here. About two weeks ago, George went with sister Mary to brother Lewis'. As he telegraphed from St. Louis, they were expecting them, had an omnibus at the depot, and dinner waiting. They found all well, except Jessie, who had some fever, but was better when George left, the next day after dinner. Sister Mary stood the trip very well, and continued to improve.

While in St. Louis George went with her to Shaw's garden, and she was very much pleased, though she didn't spend as much time there as she would have liked. I should think it would take two or three days to see every thing.

It has been about a week since I left Malvern. I spent one day in Little Rock, and then came up here with George, who had just returned from St. Louis. We have a pleasant boarding place, and I think I'll have a pleasant time here during the winter. The cars are not running to this place yet, but we expect to have them here [by] the first of Feb. The family living here haven't any children, but have two or three young men, boarding here, who are clerking, for Mr. Fleeman (the gentleman with whom we are boarding).

This is rather a "romantic" looking place, on the Arkansas river, and mountains on two or three sides. You can't look out without seeing the river or mountains. Above and below here there are bluffs of rock, that will have to be cut down or blasted, before the road can be built. We went down in a skiff the other evening, opposite where they had been blasting. Thought of getting out, and trying to climb up to a cave about one hundred and fifty feet above us, but it looked so steep and rough, I concluded not to make the attempt.

Just before leaving Malvern, I saw pa and ma on their way to conference, or rather brother Johnnie's. I was very sorry they couldn't go by to see you, for I know you must have been badly disappointed. What beautiful weather we are having this week, looks almost like springtime. I was sorry I couldn't visit you while at Malvern, I would like to have spent a week or two with you, and helped you with your sewing, for I know you have your hands full.

I wish I could see the baby, I expect she is very sweet and interesting now. Is Emma as fond of babies as ever? I suppose John and Willie are going to school, and learning fast. And Henry is amusing himself, playing with Emma and the baby. Ask Emma if she has forgotten Aunt Mattie, and Uncle George, who was so fond of teasing her.

I hear from our boys every week, had a letter from West a few days ago, and expect one from Georgie tonight. They are enjoying fine health now, and seem to be well pleased. Jimmie and Georgie are boarding in a private family, and write as if they were getting along finely. George unites with me in love to you, Billy and the boys, and kisses for the little girls. Write soon. Your Loving Sister

M. W. Hughes

Henry Butler to William Paisley in Dobyville

Dec 26th 1875

Dear Billy:

I did think I would not write you till we were *out of debt* but that would be putting it off *so* long, you might think I was *never* going to write. I felt before your letter was received like sitting down & writing you a long letter detailing some of my troubles occasioned by being *so much in debt* in order to get your sympathy & advice, but then I thought it would be an infliction upon you, for *I know you* feel a concern in our welfare. We are not yet "out of the woods" by a great deal but it makes me shudder to think of the consequences if there had been *even* a *partial* failure in the crops this year—in that event one would have "gone by the board" irretrievably! As it is, we are going to be hard pressed to get through—if we do at all. I had to spend some money not only here in building &c, but in order to get my Texas land in condition to rent, had to contract a debt of $800—which is due 1st Jany. We have shipped something over 400 bales cotton, but have had to draw considerably for groceries &c to aid us in handling this cotton, besides some $3000 in cash. Most of our customers are coming up pretty well. James & Johnny Butler have delivered us 13 bales. Bro. Charles will let us have eight I reckon, & if I can collect some $800 from the Cummings, to whom I sold land, I will *begin* to feel a little easy.

You know it is not *my style* to go in debt. On moving to Malvern & while I was sick at Tulip, Pa bought a stock of G. W. Hughes, some $3000, then the house was blown away, goods damaged &c &c our trade increasing (*credit*) & at end of year all was out in hands of the people who, on account of failure in crops, had nothing to pay with &, *worse than that*, had nothing with which to make another crop. So you see what we did—*staked all* on the present crop, taking mortgages (on such as Bob Hunter) & furnishing some supplies in order to cover the old a/cts. The party above I considered one of the most doubtful—we have collected $135 & hold mortgages on wagon and horse for $25 more.

But this is getting to be an uncertain business—merchandising that is carried on as it has been for several years—times and circumstances change & I am *almost* persuaded that the day is past to make much money in this line. What *do you think*? We have been wonderfully blessed with health the past year, for which I think I feel duly thankful.

It made me feel sad to think of your being so sick and I did not know it. I certainly would have been to see you had I known it at the time. Hope you are enjoying your wonted health again. We are glad to hear of Emma's good health, & hope it will so continue. My wife enjoyed your letter very much & doubtless would have *many words* to send you if she was *awake*. You must excuse me for not writing more this time. I have *so much* to write you.

Would enjoy seeing you exceedingly. Hope yet to be in a condition to make you a visit. Will be over run with business for some time to come.

Love to sister Em—

> Your brother
> Henry

Happy Christmas to you and yours—

Henry Butler to William Paisley in Dobyville

Malvern Ark
Mar. 3d [1876]

Dear Billy:

Yours of *the 25th* was rec'd *to-day*—postmarked "Late Ark." I intended writing to you to-day anyhow for I wanted you to know of the change in *our business*.

Probably you remember my telling you *some time since* that I wanted to sever the partnership the first favorable opportunity. It seemed *that time* would never come up—but it *has been done* (whether to my advantage *time* will reveal), much to my relief, as far as my *feelings* at least. Olin and myself have gotten along finely—*not a single* jar occurring—but *you* understand me without my *particularizing*.

Pa came up over one week ago, & proposed taking an inventory of goods, which of course I agreed to, as that is something which ought to be done at least once a year. So hiring *Major Lea* & his son Nat—Pa & Olin took an a/c of stock, also a list of notes & a/cts due as well as those made this year. After approximating the cotton unsold—adding goods, debts due the firm, & deducting am't of indebtedness, the assets amounted to something over 16,000. The "Doubtful" & "Bad" debts (as classed by Olin and Pa—find I had very *little* to do with the matter) amted to some 1500. The Inventory of goods Malvern & Tulip amted to $6000.

I then made a proposition to Pa *through Olin* to give him $6500 for his interest (½), and just as Olin was going up to see him—I called him to say I was *anxious* to dissolve, & if Pa *refused to take that, I would*. To the first proposition Pa *indignantly* refused to listen, & told Olin *I was seeking to take advantage of him* &c &c. He sent Olin to say that he would *buy me out*—to which of course I agreed, as I was *honest* in making the offer. The next hour he told me he "had changed his mind—but the matter *had to be settled up*—that we would divide the goods & a/cts &c." To *this* I also agreed. But Olin and brother John (for *he* had come up on *that* day) talked with Pa, who agreed to take the offer made *if* I would give up *your* notes, Charlie's Johnnie's & one other—in all amounting to over two thousand dollars. This (turning over your notes) I disliked *very* much to do—but I was *so* anxious to be *quit* of the *unpleasant* affair that I consented. So Pa holds your notes—but with the understanding that unless it *suits you*, *nothing* shall be expected this winter.

Now Billy, I write to you as I would to *none other*—not even one of my *own* brothers, feeling that you can appreciate the *circumstances*. I have borne much during the past four years but I have talked—not even to you—but little. Olin acted in this matter in such a manner as to deserve my highest esteem. He told Pa very plainly that it was foolish in him to talk of my trying to take any advantage, that he could see nothing of the kind &c. Brother Johnny spoke in the same way—said I ought to excuse much (which I do) on account of Pa's growing old &c. It seems *so* strange that he should take up such notions. I feel yet that *I* have yielded much for the sake of peace & harmony.

Olin & Johnnie left to-day for the Mississippi farm—having agreed upon this some two weeks ago—to be gone several months. Sister Annie will live at Tulip, having gone down yesterday.

Warren Archer will go into business with me here, & will come up in a few days. I regard him as an excellent young man—of first rate business qualifications. I wish I could see you. I could talk better than write of all these things.

Tulip Evermore

You are correct about the Bal flour & Lard (amtg to 14.25), which was omitted in the a/c sent you, I hope it will be so that we can visit St. Louis to-gether—Keep me advised as to your matters.

You acted right & for the best in going into business on your "own hook"—I wish you every possible success. Glad your land will be cultivated. Love to sister E.—all well.

Truly your brother—

Henry

William Paisley to Emma Butler Paisley in Dobyville

St. Louis
Mch 25th 1876

My dear one

I wrote you a very hurried note from Malvern, & intended writing again immediately on my arrival here, but put it off. I reached here day before yesterday (Thursday) morning about six o'clock. It was snowing when I got here, & snowed & rained nearly all that day, & yesterday it was cold & rainy. I have done nothing yet in the way of buying goods & feel that I have done wrong in losing so much time, but I left home feeling that I was not ready to start, & had no time to collect my thoughts when at Tulip & Malvern. My friends have seemed glad to see me and offer to render me all the assistance I need. Still I feel a hesitancy & fear that is not pleasant. If the prospects were more promising I should feel very cheerful & bouyant but situated as I now am, a failure, so far as I can see, would be disastrous. Consequently I can but fear, as my failure would so materially affect my dear Emma & children. We can but trust to a kind Providence & do the best we can, and it is a great source of comfort to know that I have the prayers & hearty cooperation of my dear wife.

Was glad to get your letter by Mr. Doby. Wish I could get another before leaving. Cannot say when I will get through, but expect to commence buying to day & shall try & make as much haste as possible.

Mr. Doby & myself are rooming with Maj. Wilkins, & eating at the same hotel. He has bought several bills, & seems to be enjoying his trip & getting on very satisfactory to himself.

Haven't time to write more. Take good care of yourself & children, & believe me ever your devoted husband

Wm Paisley

Kiss the children & tell them to be good & mind ma all the time.

William Paisley to Emma Butler Paisley in Dobyville

St Louis Mo
Tuesday evening Mch 28, 1876

My dearest One

I regret exceedingly the delay which affords me an opportunity of sending you a letter that will in all probability reach you before I can. Mr. Doby expects to start in the morning for home, was about ready to go this morning but not quite. Had the weather been good I think I could have finished to day & gotten off with him, provided I could have worked. The trip to Tulip almost made me sick. In fact, the cold & exposure, all the way from home to St. Louis, was very severe, & for two days after reaching here I felt very little like business & done nothing but look around & make arrangements which were necessary. Saturday & Monday I worked & got along finely, & this morning till dinner, but was afraid to expose myself this evening & concluded to spend it in my room. Am not certain tho which would have been the best, the exposure or my impatience & anxiety to see my dear one & little ones. How in the world have you got along? I know the first snow was bad, & am in hopes the one that has been falling here for nearly 24 hours does not reach you, but doubt not you have bad weather, & no one to protect you & the bare footed children. It makes me shudder to think of it. Hope if you did not before, that you sent to the store & got a thick pr. shoes after getting my letter by Alex.

You must not let this make you uneasy. I think it likely that my sickness is nothing more than cold or dumb chills. Sunday evening about sun down, I felt a little unwell & was sensible of some fever. Took some pills that night & felt better the next day. This morning I felt symptoms of chill but did not have one, and about dinner had fever, have not been to bed & now 4 o'clock p.m. I have less fever. I fear that I have done wrong in writing what I have, but as you are the better part of my own self & not disposed to be foolish, I do not hesitate to tell you all, which you can rely on as true statement so far as I can tell. It may be very childish, but I feel so much bound up in you, my dear one, & our dear children, that the least ailment, either at home or abroad, brings you upper most in my thoughts & I feel at once like flying to you—but I will make you uneasy yet before I stop if I keep on. Mr. Doby has already been laughing at me.

My old friends here all seemed glad to see me and cheerfully tender their service to help me, but notwithstanding that, I feel that I have to be doubly cautious. Prints are very pretty & cheap. Lds Hats are prettier than I ever saw them. How much I would enjoy your being here to enjoy the many sights with me. The thought of being too poor to indulge such pleasure troubles me, but I can but feel that it is all right and that our Heavenly father would order it otherwise were it best for us—besides it is a comfort to know that I have the prayers of my dear one for grace to help in every time of need.

I hope to be at home either Friday or Saturday next. If not at home Friday night, please send one of the boys (Brewer or Deboise) with both mules to Gurdon early Saturday morning. If the waters are high they will not be able to get to Gurdon and if I can hear that they are up I shall stop at Arkadelphia. Let them go if possible, but do not be uneasy if they fail to meet me, as something may detain me. Hope you & the children have been well & gotten along better than I imagine. With many kisses for yourself & little ones, I am your devoted husband

Wm Paisley

Wednesday morning

Mr. Doby starts this morning. My fever wore off about dark last night. Slept well last night & feel very well this morning. Expect to take quinine to keep off chills & fever. With much love your husband

Wm P.

Mary Butler to Emma Butler Paisley in Dobyville

Murphysboro, Ill.
Apr. 6th, 1876

Dear sister Emma:—

I hope you will not attribute my long silence to any want of affection, for I assure you—I have time and again thought of writing to you since I've been here, but somehow time passes so rapidly that I can't get any thing done. They complain of me at home for not writing oftener, but they have been slow about writing too. I received a letter from Sister yesterday. I believe she expects to go to Tulip before very long.

It seems almost impossible that I've spent all winter here, and spring is here again!

I was surprised to hear that brother Billy was putting him up a store in front of his house: when is he coming for goods? Wish he could come with brother Henry, and we could all return together. I am expecting a letter every day stating the time of his coming; he speaks of bringing Coulter with him.

I have had a pleasant time since I've been here—found some pleasant acquaintances: we are all invited to take tea at Dr. Ford's tomorrow evening. I expect they'll prepare a nice supper. Last Friday night we attended an oyster supper, which was given for the benefit of the Lutheran Sunday school. They made almost sixty dollars. A supper and entertainment was given not long since, for the benefit of the poor widows and orphans. They made $105, which was doing remarkably well for this place.

Sister Jennie has just come in, and is sitting by darning Willard a pair of stockings. She says tell brother B. that he must bring you with him and make her a visit, and if *you* can't come he must come himself. Brother Lewis is down at his office; he goes almost every night and stays until about ten o'clock: this is court week, but brother L hasn't been very busy, as the time has been taken up with criminal cases.

Sister J. has been doing her own work all winter; of course I assist her about it. She is a very neat housekeeper, and I have been learning all I can from her. Have you had anyone to help you? With five children I think you have needed help. Sister J. uses the Singer machine and I like it very much; the only objection I have to it is, that it is heavier to turn than I like. Does yours work well now? Sister J. has an extra tension spring which she is going to send you.

How is my little Emma getting on? It is time she was coming to see Aunt Mary again. I feel as if she partly belonged to me since the time she stayed with me; kiss her for me. How is my name sake little Mary? I'm anxious to see her. I think it time you were making us a visit.

Tell brother B I was astonished to hear the cause of his hurrying off so that morning with the children, and didn't like it a bit—think if I was expecting a visitor, he ought to have staid to see him.

Jessie enjoys good health and is growing fast—is a smart child but a great tease some times. Willard has a more amiable disposition. He has a remarkable talent for singing and can say almost anything he wants to.

It is now bed time, the others have all retired. Good night. With much love for all, your afft sister

Mary

I suppose you are as much posted in regard to news at home as I am. I was distressed when I heard of pa's affliction some time ago: our parents are growing old and can't be with us many years longer; it makes me sad to think of it.

How is Capt Lipscomb and family? Is Ella still with them? Give them my love. I am owing Mary Scott a letter—must certainly write to her before long. Write me very soon.

Jimmie Butler to Emma Butler Paisley in Dobyville

Ashland, Va.
April 16th 1876

Dear Sister;

No doubt this letter will rather surprise you, yet I guess you have often thought that I ought to write to you. I think myself that I ought to have written several months ago, but I always was a poor hand at writing letters. But I will assure you that it was not for the want of love to you, that has caused me to delay writing so long.

Well, we have been here now for about four months, and are very well pleased. Although I don't seem to be getting along as well as I ought to in my studies, yet I don't see that the fault lies in the College, for I don't think that I would be any better pleased any where. We have a very nice reading room here that was gotten up by the two Literary Societies after we came here. It is kept very well furnished with papers and magazines. The members of the two Societies can have the use of it without paying anything, and as I am a member of one of them, I can go in whenever I find time. I very seldom find time to go in during the week. I generally go in and read some on Sunday evenings. The two Literary Societies are named after Washington and Franklin. I joined the Washington. The Wash. gave a public debate last Friday night between four of its members, who were appointed for that purpose, but owing to the rain there were few ladies there. The Frank. will give a public debate next Friday night.

We have some very good preaching here. Dr. Duncan, the president of the College is a splendid preacher. He preached a funeral sermon this evening. He has not been preaching as often this session as he did last. He has been going around collecting money for the College, and has succeeded very well. They have commenced putting up a new building for the College, which will add very much to it. They are building it out of brick.

Sister Annie wrote to me that brother Billy had commenced merchandising again at Dobyville. I was very glad to hear it, for I think that suits him much better than farming.

It is now time for me to close this letter. Much love to all. Write soon to your devoted brother

J. O. Butler

Annie Butler Moores to Emma Butler Paisley in Dobyville

Tulip Arkansas
April 20th 1876

Dear Sister Emma,

Your very interesting letter was received yesterday evening and read with great pleasure. I was also glad to get a note from bro. Billy. I was very sorry to hear you had all been sick, colds seem to be very common. I have had one for nearly two weeks, felt very badly last Sunday.

Yes, I have returned to the old homestead to live a while, and am much better satisfied here than I could any where else with out Olin. It is better for husband & wife to be together if they possibly can, for we have but a short while to live here, & surely they ought to enjoy that short time in each other's company. I think Olin will be here next month, though he didn't know exactly when he could get off now, as Johnnie had to leave. He hadn't heard from his wife since he had been there until a few weeks ago, said she had been confined to her bed ever since he left, so he left immediately for home. Olin said he hated so much to give him up, never was associated with one he loved more. Olin says he had much rather manage a farm than to sell goods, so I don't know what we will do, or where we will live.

I received a very good letter from Jimmie yesterday evening. Alice also received one from him, he writes very often. I get a letter from Sister every week or two. It won't be long before she comes home. I wrote to her this week that Pa would go to Malvern after Sister Mary next week & she could come at the same time. She expects to come next month any way. We will be so glad to see them, as they have been gone so long.

Edwin can't talk much, but I wish you could see him playing croquet. It would astonish you to see how well he can knock the balls, & with one hand, exactly as we do. I don't think he ever misses a day, playing with his balls. We play almost every day, and I would dislike to be where I couldn't get to play as I love it so much & it is such good exercise. I think you can do more than any of your sisters, but I don't doubt that we could all do more than we think for; yet I don't be-lieve I could attend to *five* children & do all my own work, without feeling tired *all* the time. I would never expect to visit, write, or to see any pleasure outside of my family—I hope I may never have that much to do.

Ma & I went to Mr. James Pattillo's & bro Caldwell's yesterday evening, had a very pleasant time. Mrs. Goodloe Pattillo is looking so badly. She will live at Capt. Lipscomb's old place. Reckon she will move there today. I cannot send my letter off today so I will wait & add a little more tomorrow or next day.

21st

I cannot write more as Ma & I are going down to bro. Charlie's. We are nearly ready to start. Much love to all. Write soon to your ever loving sister   Annie Moores

Henry Butler to William Paisley in Dobyville

Malvern Ark
May 5th [1876]

Dear Billy,

I have been home from St. Louis over one week—Have been looking for a letter to hear how you "opened out" your stock—and about your sales &c—

I heard on yesterday that you had *written to Pa*, & that you had been right sick after getting home, but had made a better commencement than you expected. This I am glad to learn & trust you will do better & *better*, which I think will be the case. I bought a good stock of goods (about $3500) & from our old friends. I looked at shoes at Dreas, Rainwater & Co, but bought of O & L. D R & Co's stock I thought was *not* first rate—a good many *old* goods, though Maj R gave me some *low* prices & seemed to be quite anxious to sell. He told me he would sell me if he did "not make five dollars on the bill." Mr Orr spoke to me of not selling you & expressed his regrets— said it was on account of his speaking to you *freely* & candidly as he always has done—that he had the *utmost confidence* in you paying every dollar you contract. Mssr Senter & Co are *friends indeed*—and offer to do more for me than I could expect. We are short on our cotton a/c considerably. Notwithstanding this, they told me to go ahead & purchase what goods we needed, & any amounts we could not have extended till after the cotton cash began to move—draw on them & settle now. "Old Man" Wilkins told me he considered me "one of his family" and would have to take care of me—I like them *very much*—and will do *my best* to merit their confidence.

Our business is very good, take in some money every day, & I only have to *pick my customers* to sell *all* the goods I wish on time. This I am endeavoring to do—taking mortgages &c. If I had the *capital*, I could sell $50,000.00 worth of goods a year & it would not be necessary to make bad debts either—I could sell ¾ of the goods needed around Princeton, Tulip, & all through the country.

We have been making some money on cotton since the change in the firm—shipped eleven bales yesterday—3 to-day & pick up a little every day or two—Guggenheim & Smith & Dr K are not buying—& Mssr Hunter & Cooper are *very tame*. G & S—are endeavoring to compromise at 25¢ on the dollar—but their creditors don't seem inclined to come to their terms—I learn their indebtedness is some $16000.00.

I spoke to Senter & Co about furnishing Olin & Johnny, but they *declined* to take them—did not want business on the river &c. Olin has spent some $900 for mules, plows &c, and now wants $800—to pay taxes ($400.-for this alone) & furnish hands with Bacon &c. I think Olin has *considerable "cheek"*—("Subrosa")

I hope your health is good now, & think you will enjoy much better health than last year.

Write me *fully* about your business &c.

Give my love to sister Emma—tis fortunate she enjoys such fine health.

Affectionately
Your brother
Henry

Annie Moores to Emma Butler Paisley in Dobyville

Malvern Arkansas
July 4th 1876

Dear Sister Emma,

Almost every one is at the Barbecue today except myself. I have quite a quiet time, Edwin is asleep, and Olin went down home yesterday after a cow. I don't reckon it will be very long before he will be at home, as it is almost 12 o'clock. I felt like I would enjoy being at home answering my letters more than being in a crowd.

Ira and Alice have been up several days. They are at the barbecue, I reckon the latter will be here in a short while, as she expects to leave on the train today & it is now 12 o'clock. She received a telegram from sister this morning, telling her to come into L.R. today. She expects to go on to Van Buren & spend several weeks, & then bro. George & Sister will go on to Va & Centennial. Sister Mary went into L.R. yesterday. She expects to return here the latter part of the week.

Mr. Archer and Alice have just come and gone down to the depot. They will be in time, as I haven't heard the train come. It has been over two hours and I haven't heard the cars yet. Olin has gotten home, & he & Edwin are lying down on a pallet. All are well down home.

Mr. Cooper is quite sick, not expected to live long. Fannie & Sue Pattillo expected to be up here today, but wouldn't leave as they were needed to sit up with Mrs. Cooper. Good many came up from Tulip.

Olin and I get along finely in our quiet little home, we have had very little company since we returned. We don't mind doing our own work at all, rather do it than not. Edwin isn't as much trouble as I expected he would be. He has been more fretful for the last day or two, but I know he isn't well. I had a letter from Fannie Kerns a short time since. They were all well and seemed to be enjoying themselves. I see Alice Robertson right often, she is looking so well, and seems to be happy. I see a good many of the Tulip people right often. Brother Henry and all his family are at the barbecue. I expect they will have quite a crowd. I see them all returning from the barbecue.

I am very glad you are going to visit Tulip this summer, hope you will all be well, and have a pleasanter time than you did the last time you were at home. I am anxious to see little Mary. Do you expect to come by Malvern?

I was very glad to hear bro. Billy's health had improved, I felt right uneasy about him when I received your first letter. I hope he is doing a good business.

I had a letter from Jimmie a few days ago. I believe he expects to remain at the College until Sister gets there.

Olin unites with me in love to you all. Write whenever you can to

Your loving sister
Annie Moores

William Paisley to Emma Butler Paisley in Tulip

Dobyville, Ark
Aug. 17th 1876

My own dear Emma—

I wrote to you yesterday morning, and sent the letter to town by Mr Orr, who went to day. Have nothing of special interest now, but there is a man at Mr Bailey's, a relation of his with a drove of horses taking them from Texas to Miss, & will start from here in the morning by way of Tulip, and I write this hurried note to send by him. It is now nearly time for me to close up & go home to supper, but I am looking for Mr. Orr back every minute & hope to get a letter from you by him.

The Baptists are having a protracted meeting at South Fork that has been going on nearly a week. I thought some of going down to night, but can't leave home very [well] without it being known. Mr Gus Wills is conducting the meeting, and I feel more anxious to go on that account, as he is a great friend of mine & I have never heard him preach yet.

Mrs. Little & Bob came over to day & bought about forty dollars worth of goods from me, partly on time. Trade as a general thing is still dull, & I have quite a lonesome time both here & at home and am getting very anxious to have you & the children with me again, but I don't want you to imagine that I want you to shorten your visit on my acct., for I want you to remain as long as you think you ought & desire. After the 1st day or two by myself I got along very well, & have not been at all lowspirited, but have done as well I rekon as any one could under the circumstances.

I entirely forgot to get your buttons in Malvern. Did not think of them till after I returned home and picked up the note you wrote me before you left, asking me to send you some for your dress. Sorry I forgot them. You will see that I commenced without having any thing to write & will have to excuse this. I only send it because I know it will be to you better than nothing.

Hoping that you and the children are having a pleasant time, I am as ever your loving husband

Wm Paisley

William Paisley to Emma Butler Paisley in Tulip

Dobyville Ark
Saturday Aug 19th 1876

My own loving Emma:

Your sweet letter of the 17th inst. came last night, and received this morning, and although there is little prospect of my being able to send this to the office before next week, I cannot refrain from answering yours immediately. Nothing affords me such pleasure when I am separated from you as do your frank loving letters: they are both meat & drink to my soul, and never fail to arouse fresh the pleasant emotions which your love & devotion first called into action.

Sorry to hear that you had been unwell & threatened with a chill, but glad that you escaped without being seriously sick. The symptoms show that there is something wrong with your system, and you must be very cautious and take some medicine if necessary, and try and prevent having chills & fever. You say that you found my prediction would be fulfilled. I have been trying but cannot now call to mind what that was. You are fortunate in having an opportunity of having your teeth fixed. Dr. Colburn will now doubtless let politics alone & betake him self to his profession and I want him to fix your teeth so you will not be troubled with them, even if it would require additional cost.

Hope you got off on yesterday to Charlie's. I feel disappointed & regret that I could not go with you. The arrangement you have made in regard to coming home suits me very well. I am exceedingly anxious to have you with me, and week after next looks like a long ways in the future when viewed in connection with your absence, but I wanted you to fix the time yourself, and as it will suit better for you to go to Malvern with Sister Mary & Annie, & give you another week at home, I resign myself very cheerfully to the balance of the lonesome time I shall have to spend without you.

The protracted meeting commences at Okolona to day and will probably be continued through next week. If continued, I don't know whether I can get Ben toward the last of the week or not. If I can get him I will try & get to Tulip next Saturday with the mules, and go with you to Malvern & come on home with you. I can get Scott to come with me, & let him bring the carriage back. If not detained, he could leave Tulip Monday & get home in time to meet us at the RR by the time we would want to leave Malvern, provided we would not have to use our time in getting to Malvern. Ben does not seem to care about being confined in the store, & has got girls on the brain to such an extent I am not at all certain that I can get him, & should I fail, of course it will be impossible for me to do more than meet you at the Depot. In that event I will write to Henry and inform you through him where to come.

Tell John & Willie I am glad to hear that they are good boys & disposed to make themselves useful, and that they must not disobey their grandpa in any way. Tell Emma & Henry I know they will be good & mind their ma. Tell Ma that I am not inclined to be sensitive as to the looks of our children, but that her saying little Mary resembles Mr. Holmes is putting my sensibilities to a pretty severe test, but it is said ugly babies make pretty grown people and if your ma is correct, we are pretty certain of one pretty daughter, provided Mary lives.

Mr. White was in this morning, & says his wife was right sick last night, something like Cholera Morbus. Little Annie is still troubled with her eyes & some kind of skin disease, and looks badly. Willis has been sick several days since he got here, but is up again. Ma was complaining more last night & is quite feeble. Old Mr. Doby had the Dr. with him last night again but is up this morning. I am sorry to hear that your Pa is not so well. It makes me sad to think that we all probably in a short while will have to give up our parents. They are now showing unmistakeable evidences of decline, & those to whom we are most indebted for what we are, & who have done & cared most for us will soon be call[ed] upon to exchange time for eternity, and my prayer is that they may, when called, enter upon that Rest which remaineth for the people of God, & then it will not be long before we who are younger will be called to follow them. Would that we could realize these truths more fully.

Recd. a letter from Mr. Jones yesterday says he is anxious to come back to Dobyville, & thinks now they will come next winter. Wants to know if I can fix him off in any way.

Bettie & Maggie & Walter Adams are invited to Willie Johnson's marriage, which will take place in Washington next Wednesday. I don't know whether they will go or not. Mr. Carothers here to day, Saturday, and wishes to be remembered. He would have like very much to have gone to the Bluff with you if he could have left his school.

(Evening)

Have been right busy to day. Am selling a few goods now on a credit. Recd. a letter from Senter & Co. yesterday telling me they would assist me in getting up my full stock. I feel in very good spirits as to my business prospects now. Hope Olin & Johnnie will do well in their new enterprise. Walter Adams has just come in—says he will go to town Monday, & I will close this & give it to him now, as I may not have another opportunity of seeing him. Wish I could have gotten it off this evening. You could have gotten it Monday. With much love,

> Your devoted husband
> Wm. Paisley

George Butler to Emma Butler Paisley in Dobyville

> San Luis Obispo Cal
> Sept. 13th 1876

My own dear sister Emma,

Your interesting and highly appreciated letter was received before I left home more than two weeks ago. I am off on my district, more than two hundred miles from Los Nietos. It will be three weeks yet before I expect to get back. I am resting today between two Quarterly Meetings, and will improve the opportunity to write to my much loved sister. I have not written to you in a long time, but I have never ceased to cherish your memory with brotherly affection.

Indeed, I did write a long letter or a part of one to you soon after I heard of your having joined the Presbyterian church, but I believe I never sent it. However there was not in that letter, and never has been in my mind, any thing of censure for the course that you took. I have always had the greatest confidence in the sincerity and depth of your piety, and the genuineness of your religious experience, and I doubted not but that in the change of church relations you were actuated by the finest motives & did what you thought would be, & *I trust will be* for the happiness & eternal well being of yourself and family.

I have no doubt but that the most & perhaps all of us in this life attach entirely too much importance to the points in which Christians differ. I am glad to know that Christians are coming nearer together & that in this centennial year, we see Methodists, Presbyterians, Baptists, & Episcopalians working harmoniously in the same revival meeting.

But I did not design to go off on this subject when I took up my pen. I feel a deep interest in your welfare & that of Billy and the children, especially your eternal well being. I hope that together you will so live and train up your children that they may be brought into the fold of Christ and rise up in the last day and call you blessed. There is hardly a position in life more responsible than that of the mother. She writes the first lesson upon the infant mind; and by the grace of God, she may train up her child for a blissful immortality. Two of our little babes have been taken from us. Before they had known sin they were taken to the land of the blessed through the merits of Christ, and now they are ties to bind us to Heaven. The two we have left we have dedicated to God & are trying to train them up in the way they should go.

I left Julia and the children well. She has a little girl about ten years old staying with her while

I am gone. A good meeting closed at Los Nietos just before I left. About twenty professed conversion and joined the church. A good camp meeting was going on about twenty miles distant. There were ten or twelve preachers present. One a brother of Bishop Kavanaugh.

The School at Los Nietos is doing well. Bro. Riddick, the teacher, is also an excellent preacher, very few better. He has planted out the ten acres of school land in orange trees, which are growing beautifully. His wife is an excellent lady & teaches music. One or two other teachers assist in the school.

Julia makes one or two hundred dollars on her chickens this year. Her mother will make three hundred, I reckon. We had some fine grapes about one inch in diameter getting ripe when I left home. Some peaches and apples. Have you an orchard on your place? I have about sixty orange trees & about as many walnut trees doing well. The latter will bear in a year or two.

My love to Billy and the children. The Lord bless you all. Good by—

> Your affectionate
> brother George

William Paisley to Emma Paisley in Dobyville

> St Louis Mo
> Saturday night
> Sept 23 1876

My dearest one

I came up to my room soon after eating supper for the purpose of writing to you, having neglected to do so until now, & although it has not seemed convenient till now, I cannot help feeling like blaming myself for putting it off so long.

I do not like to write or send letters written with a pencil, & will say by way of explanation for this, that after coming to my room, I could not find a pen, & have had to resort to the pencil from necessity. I am rooming with Maj. Wilkins again, & taking my meals at a Restaurant.

The train was an hour behind time the morning we left Malvern, & when we got to Newport we were about two hours behind time, which threw us considerably in the night. But there was a hack at the Depot going over to Jacksonport, and we had no difficulty in getting out to Aunt Ann's. When we drove up to her Hotel, all had gone to bed. The Negro boy who was sleeping in the office called Aunt Ann up, & she came out & gave us quite a warm reception.

She is indeed a very remarkable woman. Her Hotel is a very fine building, elegantly furnished & conducted in the very best manner. She sees to every thing herself, but does it with so much ease that she has the appearance of having nothing to do but entertain her company. Her only daughter (Mrs. Gill) is a widow & quite a nice, intelligent lady.

I spent Thursday with Aunt Ann & left her house Thursday evening about 4 o'clock, expecting to leave Newport at 6 o'clock, but the train was again more than 2 hours behind time and it was after dark when I got off. I reached here yesterday morning for breakfast. Have commenced buying dry goods, but have not quite finished that bill yet. Hope to get through so as to be home Friday or Saturday morning, but cannot tell how that will be yet.

Forgot to mention that we found sister Mary [Paisley Scott] at Malvern but she had recd. a letter from Charlie [Scott] telling her to come home, & she left us at Little Rock.

Expected to write you a long letter, but just [as] I commenced this, Maj. Wilkins brought in another of his friends who is staying with him, & I had to stop till he went to bed. It is now after 1 o'clock.

My friends here seem perfectly willing to do all they can for me. I took dinner today with Mr. Ely.

Hope you are all well. Tell Jno & Willie to keep plenty wood & feed every thing well. With much love & many kisses for you all.

Your affectionate husband
Wm Paisley

Annie Moores to Emma Butler Paisley in Dobyville

Tulip, Arkansas
Oct. 4th 1876

Dear Sister Emma,

I don't know whether I owe you a letter or not, but I will write any way. I have just hurried through with a letter to Olin, so that I could have time to write to you to-night. Ma is so very anxious that the letter should go off to-night, or rather in the morning, so that you can get it this week.

Sister Mary and I spent nearly three weeks with Johnnie, had a very pleasant time, went buggy riding twice nearly every day, except the week we were at camp meeting. We all enjoyed the camp meeting very much. I didn't get to hear much preaching, as Edwin was sick most of the time. He had fever three evenings after I got home, but he is well now. I think it was caused from teething. I haven't nursed him for two days and a night, not near as much trouble to wean as I thought he would be. It was so gradual he hardly knew it. Ma says she thinks he is very easy to wean.

When we came from Johnnie's we lost our trunk, but fortunately found it in a week or two. It was put off at Witherspoon. Brother Henry was just about to bring suit, but concluded first to write to the P.M. at that place, as he heard it was put off there. We were rejoiced to see the trunk.

Kellie's health is much improved, but lacks a good deal of being well. Johnnie & Olin think of going in business together at Centre Point. Olin mentioned being on the train with Mrs. Lipscomb & bro. Billy—I reckon the latter is at home, or will be when you receive this letter.

We received a letter from Sister last week from Centennial. They were all having a fine time. Walter & West were going with bro. G. & Sister by Niagara Falls & other places. Jimmie and Reavis had to return to their school as it opened sooner than W[alter] & W[est]'s. We received a letter from Jimmie this week. He was then at College. Said they had a splendid time at Centennial. They all seem to be enjoying such good health. We look for bro. G. & Sister next week.

Pa, Ma, Alice, Annie Phillips & Ira attended the camp meeting on Ouachita. Ma said she heard some splendid sermons, preached by Sandy Winfield, Mr. Evans & others. All seemed to enjoy themselves very much. Annie P. went over to Arkadelphia to spend a week or two. She met with her sweetheart. Sister Mollie had another severe attack of neuralgia a few weeks ago, but was well when bro. Henry wrote. Brother Charlie went up to Malvern last Saturday, expected to be back Monday and he hasn't come yet.

Alice received a very interesting letter from Florrie Hunter this evening. Said there was a good deal of sickness, said she & her pa were the only ones that kept well. Mrs. Caldwell sent for Ma about a week ago to come & stay with her. She spent two nights with her. She got better & ma came home, look for her to send again any time. I suppose you have heard Mrs. Robertson had a fine son, nearly a month old. Mr. R. says he can almost crow now. Ma & sister Mary went over to see Mrs. Hall this evening. She has been confined to her bed for some time. Hope she is a little better.

We received a letter from bro. George & Olin's pa last week. They were all well, but bro. George had had a right severe hurt, by a wild horse he had in his buggy. Ma has been sitting in here with me. She was so anxious for me to write to you that I think she feels a great deal better since the letter is written. Pa says tell bro. Billy to buy him $9 worth of county scrip.

It is bed time, so I must close, with much love to bro. Billy & the children from all. Ever your loving sister

Annie Moores

J. W. Gilmer to William Paisley in Dobyville

Gilmer's Store, N.C.
October 27, 1876

Dear cousin,

I received a letter from you about a month since, which should have been answered long since, but I have delayed principally for the reason that I hoped I would be able to find a suitable young man to send you, & one that I could reckommend, but so far have failed. There is only one I know of that would likely go, & I know but little about him, tho I think likely he might do well enough. His name is Mclean, a son of Unkle Thomas Mclean of Grayham, Alamance Co., N.C. He has a steady father, & so far as I know his boys are sober, industrious boys, & have farmed some, tho not raised entirely on a farm—and altho they are my relations, I know but little about them, as they have been brought up in a different county some twenty miles from me. I understand one of his boys would be glad to get such a position. You can write to their father, Thomas G. Mclean, Grayham, N.C. I know of no other young men that would likely accept your offer.

This leaves myself & family well. I have four sons and one daughter. Henry, my oldest, is married and living near Mcleansville. Mary Anne, my daughter, is married to a Mr. Phipps, has two sons & a daughter. Robt, my second son, is going on 23 years, and is still with me helping on the farm. John, my third son, is going on 20 & is now at Davidson College, entered last Sept. Charly, my youngest, was 12 last July, so you see my family are nearly all grown up. Aunt Minerva Paisley's family are well, & getting along very well. Her boys are very nice young men & all of them members of the Presbyterian church. Porter, her second son, is preparing for the ministry. He entered college at the same time my son did. My son also has the ministry in view. I forgot to say to you that Thomas Mclean is a Presbyterian, & his boys have had Presbyterian training.

Nancy, my wife, wishes to be remembered to you. We would all be glad to see you once more here in your native country.

The history of Alamance church that our Pastor prepared was not published, and was not intended for publication. Crany Presbytery assigned him this duty as they have to different ministers, that is, to get up a kind of a historical sketch of the different churches in the Presbytery, to be read before that body & then filed away with the papers of Presbytery.

Your friends here are generally well. We are hoping to elect our conservative ticket throughout the state the 7th of Nov & carrying the state by a handsome majority for Tilden and Hendren. We have got desperately tired of radical rule (I take it for granted that you are a conservative Democrat).

I will stop writing by asking you to write to me. I would like to keep up a correspondence with you.

Your cousin most affectionately

J. W. Gilmer

P.S. I received both your letters. The first was forwarded to my brother, but sent back to me in a short time.

Mattie Hughes to Emma Butler Paisley in Dobyville

Tulip, Ark.
Nov. 1, 1876

Dear Sister Emma,

I have been intending to write to you ever since I returned home, but have postponed it from day to day until now about three weeks have passed, since my return. I fully intended writing to you while in Virginia, but my time was so much occupied with "the boys," and other things, that I wrote very few letters. I spent a month very pleasantly with the boys, and the family with whom we were boarding did every thing to make our stay pleasant.

And the Centennial, what must I tell you about that? It far exceeded my expectations, and if I were with you, I could tell you many interesting things, but when it comes to writing, I don't know where to commence. I saw many things that would amuse and interest your Emma. And among them was a doll standing before a mirror, trying to powder her face. No doubt you have read a good deal about the Centennial (that is if you ever find time, with so many little ones.)

I have had several letters from "the boys," and they seem to be getting on finely. When I left, Walter wasn't feeling very well, but he writes now that he is in firstrate health and that he had gained five pounds, since school commenced. Jimmie is in splendid health, and weighed 145 pounds during vacation. West is in good health too, but not near so fleshy as Jimmie. Reavis has grown a good deal, about as tall as I am. Don't it seem strange, to think that all three of our boys are nearly grown? Walter will be twenty-one the 12 of Dec. I intended bringing you their photographs, but none of them had any but West. I'll get you one of his, and will send you one of Walter and Reavis, as soon as they have some taken.

George went up to Fort Smith last week, but returned to Little Rock a few days ago. I expect him this evening, but he will have only a few days to spend with me, as he will have to go to Tale-quah, Indian nation, next week, but says he will be gone only a few days.

Olin and Annie left for Malvern yesterday, on their way to Centre Point. Edwin has the whoop-ing cough, and has been having chills for two weeks. He had fever the day before they left, and wasn't well enough to go, but they had written to Johnnie to meet them at Hope. Olin had been having chills, too, and was looking badly. Ma says she is so glad that you came over, and staid as long as you did, and thinks, it is owing to your visit, that your little ones have kept well.

Mrs. Caldwell has another little girl, nearly two weeks old. I believe every one felt disap-pointed, and especially the family, for there were so many girls there already. And Mrs. Dr. Smith has a boy, when I expect a girl would have pleased them. Mrs. Hare is quite sick, and Ma spent night before last, and most of yesterday with her.

Did you hear of Mr. Tom Bullock's death? Wasn't it sad? Poor Mary, left a widow so young, with three little children, and one born after the death of its father. You know they expected to move to Texas during the winter and I suppose now, her father will come for [her].

Sister Mary and Annie went to see Theresa Doak a few evenings ago, found her very well, and her children in fine health. She is coming up the last of the week, and expects to spend Saturday night here. Miss Loula Gantt and Mr. Martin were married about two weeks since. I wish you could see the marriage notice in the "Arkadelphia Standard" of last week. It was written by Pom-pey Matlock.

Annie P[hillips] expects to be married some time this month, to a Mr. Alford living near Curtis station, I think. I hope Annie will do well, for I think a good deal of her. I have never seen the young man, but he is expected the last of this week. Alice will come over with him, and remain until after the marriage. They expect to marry in the morning, and leave for Arkadelphia.

All send love. Pa and ma are in good health now, and the rest are well. Pa says tell Billy, to send that scrip to brother Henry at Malvern. He is wanting it to pay taxes. No late news from brother George or Lewis. My love to Billy, and a kiss for the children. Write soon,

> Your Loving Sister
> M. W. Hughes

Annie Moores to Emma Paisley in Dobyville

> Centre Point, Ark
> Dec. 5th 1876

Dear Sister Emma:—

Every day I think about writing to you, but put it off to do a little more work, but tonight I have put knitting aside, determined to answer your letter which was gladly received while at Tulip. For a month or two Edwin was sick, and I didn't get time to do any thing but nurse him. He got very thin, had chills, whooping cough, jaundice and teething all combined went right hard with him. It has been about two weeks since he had his last chill, and he is getting right fat and stout again. I am very glad he had the whooping cough. He still coughs, but it doesn't hurt him much. I have a negro girl living with me she seems to be very good, but is *so careless*. If Olin didn't have to go to Miss. I don't know that I would keep her, but Edwin is fond of playing with her, & we only pay her $2 per month. I wrote for Alice to come over and stay with me while Olin is gone, but haven't heard from her. Have had only one letter from home since she came over. Olin will be gone during Christmas and I hate it so much. Don't see how I will get along without him, and Edwin will miss him so much.

Johnnie and Olin are doing well. We have never regretted our move. For the present I like living here very well. We have a comfortable house, four fire places, and pay $100 rent per year. Kellie is complaining today. Edwin & I went over to see her this evening—she is a great deal better than she has been for years, but her throat is the great trouble now. If that could be cured I think she might get well. I never saw a more devoted mother than she has, and she is just as kind to me as she can be.

Olin received a letter from bro. Henry this evening, he said sister Mollie, Annie & George were at Pa's spending several days. I expect they went down to Annie Phillips' marriage.

I received a letter from Jimmie last week. He sent me his photograph. I reckon they have written you from home that bro. George expected to visit us this spring or summer. I want to be with him as much as possible while he is here.

Olin wants to have prayers, so I will have to close for tonight. A pleasant night to you & bro. Billy.

Last night after we had gotten to bed I was a little frightened at hearing several men walking up on the front porch, but I was soon relieved when the music commenced.

We have more church privileges here than when at Malvern, preaching three Sundays in the month.

The people around here doesn't seem to visit much, at least no one has been to see me expect Mr. Clardy's [Johnnie's father-in-law] family. It suits me exactly, for I haven't time to visit much. Olin & I walk over to see Johnnie & Kellie every Sunday evening. How is bro. Billy getting on in his business? Have you got a nice turkey for Christmas? We haven't gotten one yet but it is time we had him up fattening.

How are all the children getting on? Write me as soon as you can, for I am anxious to hear from you all. Olin joins me in love to you all.

Ever your loving sister
Annie B. Moores

I received a letter from Fannie Kerns several weeks ago. She sent me the photograph of her little girl, which is very sweet looking.

7th

Edwin had a slight chill yesterday evening.

Mary Butler to Emma Butler Paisley in Dobyville

Tulip Arkansas
Dec. 6th 1876

Dear Emma:—

It has been some time since anyone has written you a letter, and I believe I owe you a letter. Have been talking of writing for a long [time], and must not postpone it any longer. This morning

297

at half past 8 o'clock Annie P[hillips] was married by brother Caldwell, and very soon after left for her new home. Every thing passed off nicely. Sister Mollie had been with us a week, and bro. Henry came day before yesterday to take her home: she had Nannie and George with her. Alice Phillips came over last Monday week, with her sister Ellen's little baby. It did look so pitiful to see the poor motherless child. She is just a year old, and of course a great deal of trouble to Alice.

We made a large silver cake and iced it, which was placed on the centretable immediately after the ceremony, which after being sliced all were invited to partake: it was as nice as any cake we ever made. I wish you had some of it. Mr. Allford and the young man with him staid last night at Mr. Robertson's, and he and his wife and her sister came over with them this morning. Kate Caldwell, Katie Bird and Mr. Ellis from Arkadelphia were here; so you see we had the parlor about full—all left this morning; so after a storm there's a calm tonight.

Brother G[eorge] H[ughes] has been with us nearly three weeks. He spends his time with us when he is unemployed—will have to go to Little Rock next week. They occupy the front room; sister put her parlor carpet down up there, which makes it much more comfortable. I am glad they will be with us this winter.

I received a letter from Mary Scott not long since, all well she said. Ella was going home, so I suppose she is there now. Has Mrs. Lipscomb improved any in health? Did you know that Miss Mary Cooper was married? I received a long letter from her a few days ago; she is living in Chester, Ill., not very far from brother Lewis, and says I must come up there again and make her a visit. She was married the 18th of Oct. at the Centennial; her sister and some others were there to witness it. She married the gentleman who addressed her ten years ago. He afterwards married and was left a widower with two little boys, five and two years of age. Her husband is teaching school. His name is Rohrbaugh.

7th

Brother George has just come in, and says give his love; he is waiting to take the letter to the office, so I will have to hurry. Alice is now writing to brother Olin. She expects to go over and stay with Annie while Olin is down on the river; will start over Monday week. I don't expect any of us will attend conference, as we have no invitation and learn they will be much crowded. Mary Scott is anxious for me to visit her and I would like to go down and spend Christmas. It will be very quiet here. We are expecting Charlie and Kate this week. Kate is going up to stay with her mother several weeks. Ma, Pa, and all send much love. You must excuse this hasty letter. I will write you more next time.

> Very Afftly. your sister,
> Mary

Love to bro. Billy & kisses for the children.

We got a letter from brother George [Butler] not long since; he has located, with a view to visiting us some time next year. Now won't we be delighted to see him—will have to have a reunion of all the children.

John M. Carothers to William Paisley in Dobyville

Marion Junction Ala.
Jan. 1st 1877

Dear Friend

As this is the first opportunity I have had for letter writing, I will spend the first hour writing to you. I reached home without accident, Friday night after I left Ark., found all the family at home and anxiously looking for me. Sister was getting rather impatient for me to get there, as her arrangements were made to leave home the next Wednesday, & she thought I ought to have spent more time with her. She was married and did leave us last week, leaving Pa & Ma almost heart broken. She being the only daughter will be missed more than any other one.

The weather has been extremely cold & raining most of the time, so that I got to see but few of my old friends, but they kept me pretty busy telling tales on you Arkansas folks, so that I had barely time to write two short notes. Willie and myself left home this morning for the "Junction" in a snowstorm, found no one at the Depot to meet us, thinking that we had more sense than to come out. Worked our way to the school room & found no one there. Will commence tomorrow if the snow is not too deep. Phebe will stay with Ma, for a month or six weeks. Pa will then move his little family to "Valley Creek Parsonage" six or seven miles from Selma. He regrets very much leaving his present home, where he has been so pleasantly situated for the last six years and where the people seem to love him so much, but he thinks it is his duty to do it for more reasons than one. Some of his people have asked Mr. Wilson (Sister's man) if he would come here when Pa left, but I don't believe he wants to leave his Miss. home. It would be very pleasant indeed for all of us to have him so near to us but he & Pa, like all other "poor preachers" think "duty before pleasure."

Pa & Ma have changed very little since I left home. Pa's whiskers are a little more grey, but no other change, and we have several times had a good laugh together, as I told you we would. Jimmie, the oldest one at home, is nearly as large as Russell—was in a drug store last year, getting as much as I was, & at the same time having a good trade, but the poor fellow's health failed and Pa had to make him quit. He has a terrible cough, and we fear that he will never be well again. The two little boys are at school learning very well, and large enough to help some at home, so that Pa can very easily support his family on his salary & if he were not a preacher, might save something.

But you have heard enough of the "Carothers tribe" for once, & I am not able to give you one item of news, concerning the political, financial, moral, or religious condition of the country, have been housed up all the time. Will try to write a more interesting letter next time.

I want you to write soon and give me all the Dobyville news. I haven't heard a word from there since I left, and I have some friends there that I would love to hear from, & none more than you & Mrs. P. I shall never cease to feel grateful to you both for your kindness to me. I know you will never write to any one that would appreciate a letter from you more than I, knowing as I do your aversion to writing. So please write soon.

Your sincere friend
J. M. Carothers

Ma and Pa, Willie and wife asked me to send their love to you & Mrs. P. when I would write. Remember me to all enquiring friends. Tell Ben [Logan] I'll write to him in a few days. Much love to Mrs. P. and the children from me.

Jimmie Butler to Emma Butler Paisley in Dobyville

Ashland Va.
Jan. 2nd 1877

Dear Sister:—

Your very welcome letter was received some time ago, and I intended writing sooner, but have been very busy of late on account of the approach of the examinations, which will begin on the last Thursday in this month. I will be right busy until they are over. Time seems to pass away faster this session than I ever knew it before. Nearly half of this session has past by, and it does not seem that I have been from home more than three or four months, yet is has been fifteen.

I look forward to this summer with a great deal of pleasure for then, if Providence allows, we can all be together; for if brother George comes home from California, I guess all the rest of the family will be with him at home. Brother Lewis expects to go home sometime this summer. I hope we can all be at home at the same time: for I know of nothing that would please Ma better than to have us all together at the same time.

We are having a very cold winter in Va., much colder than it is in Arkansas. Ice and snow together have been on the ground for nearly a month. It snowed most all day yesterday, and the snow today is about seven or eight inches deep. I am getting anxious to see dry land once more. I expect John and Willie would be delighted to see this snow, and I once liked it; but I believe that the interest that I once had for it has departed. Tell John and Willie not to forget their uncle Jimmie, that it may be that he will see them this summer, and tell them to raise me plenty of watermelons, for perhaps I will help them eat them when I come home.

The young ladies around Ashland are quite industrious. They have been working for about three years, so as to raise enough money to build a new church. They have made about five hundred dollars. They were to have had a new year's feast last night, but it had to be put off until after the snow melts.

I wrote to Pa last night but could not mail it because the snow has blocked up the rail-road track. I must now close. Love to brother Billy and the children. Write when you can to your loving brother,

J. O. Butler

William Paisley to Emma Butler Paisley in Dobyville

Pine Bluff Arks
Jany 15 1877

My dear Emma:

You no doubt think the time long to hear from me & through me from Sister Mary. Ma has too doubtless suffered much anxiety & uneasiness, but the delay has been almost unavoidable on my part. I arrived here Saturday evening at 3 o'clock. Heard nothing definite from Sis, until I got within a few miles of town when I met Mr. Wm Lipscomb, who told me that he had heard she was alive & better. When I reached here I found her very sick, but the Dr told me she had taken a turn for the better & without another backset would get well. Her Lady friends have been very attentive & kind & neither she *nor Charlie* [Scott] have wanted for attention.

It is sad to be here. I can hardly suppress the feeling that Death is still lurking about the place, eagerly watching for more prey—but at the same time I feel much relief in the thought that it is no worse than it is.

The circumstances surrounding Charlie's death are very sad & distressing. Sister Mary was first taken with pneumonia & very sick for several days—the Dr succeeded in getting the disease checked & she was getting better, when Charlie took the disease in the most violent form. Charlie was attacked last Sunday 2 weeks, and Sister Mary got up and exposed herself too much, and in a few days relapsed & on the following Saturday was so bad she had to be moved to another room, where she could hear Charlie's dying groans but could not see him, & never saw him more after being taken from the room. Charlie died Tuesday.

Dr Brunson tried to tell her that Charlie was dead, but was so overcome that he could not. She however knew what had taken place & at that time no one had any thought but that she would soon follow. The Dr kept her under the influence of opiates for several days, & they say she was not able to appreciate her situation.

Since she has commenced improving, they have commenced leaving off that treatment. She bears the affliction rather better than I expected, but at times her grief seems irrespressible. When she gets up & sees so many things that will remind her of Charlie, I fear it will be worse.

The most distressing thought to me connected with his death is that we have nothing to cause us to think that he was at all prepared. He was a noble, kind hearted man, but I fear wholly neglected the most important duty of life, & it is awful to think of being called into Eternity with [out] being prepared.

His family have enough to make them comfortable I think, provided it is properly managed. I don't think he has any thing to his credit on his salary, but from what I can learn is not in debt, & his Town property & land in the country is unencumbered.

I cannot say when I can leave but will do so as early as possible. Tell Ben to push things in the store, *not* to make any accts. that will have to run over, & be very careful about any. Tell him to look after Mr. Townsend. As ever your loving husband

Wm. Paisley

Please send this to ma as I may not have time to write to her. I will telegraph to you this evening at Gurdon if I can. The office was closed yesterday, & this morning. The wires were down.

W.P.

[On separate sheet marked *Private Private*:]

Write me immediately on receipt of this and direct Care M M Dodds & Co. Sister Mary will probably expect to read your letter so it would be better not to allude to any thing I have written about Charlie that would be unpleasant to her. Charlie lived fully up to his income, & has nothing at all to his credit in the store. Consequently Sister Mary has no money to pay current expenses. I have thought some of proposing to her to sell her house & lot here, & land in the country all of which would bring $3500.00 or $4000.00 & to come out & live with us, & let me use the money in my business, but I have not mentioned it to her yet, & will not until I think it safe to talk to her about such things. Besides, I don't know how that would suit you, & unless it would, I could not think of making it. Please write me fully what you think of it on separate paper from your letter.

Lula is staying with a neighbor. She does not seem to realize her loss as much as I expected she would.

Tell Mr. Boyce to do all he can about getting hands, & try & be sure that every arrangement he makes is a good one, & not to allow an impatience to get hands lead him to make unprofitable arrangements. He can be judge of what kind of work to be doing. Should any of you get sick so as to require my attention, send to Gurdon and telegraph me here care of Joseph Dodd. Take good care of yourself & children. With love to all your loving husband.

W.P.

Emma & her baby are here & all very well.

Alice Butler to Emma Butler Paisley in Dobyville

Centre Point Arks
Jan. 25th 1877

Dear sister Emma:—

I have been thinking of writing to you ever since I came over here, but haven't done so, and I guess tonight is as favorable a time as I will have. Sister Annie received your letter several days ago. We were glad indeed to hear from you, but sorry to learn of the death of Mr Scott, and continued illness of Miss Mary. I hope she will yet be spared, for what would poor little Lula do without her mother!

Sister Kellie's health is better now than it has been, though I don't think she is feeling so well today. We see bro. Johnnie almost every day; since bro. Olin left he feels like he has to take care of us.

I must tell you how much we were frightened here one night while sister A was sick. All were asleep (or in bed) except myself, and I was just ready to get in, when I chanced to look at the window and saw some one standing there, I drew the curtain back a little and the object vanished. Sister A was right smartly frightened, and wanted us to go for bro. Johnson (they live very near) but said if the kitchen door was locked she wouldn't mind it, for we knew almost his object was to steal. So I woke up the girl she has hired, and went down and locked up the house. I don't think you would have been afraid, but sister A says she never could have done it in the world.

Did you ever see so much *snow snow*. Yesterday was a beautiful day but now it is sleeting and snowing again, going on the second month now of snowy weather. I have had very little chance for visiting since I came to this place, but like Centre Point better than I expected. There is more life about the place than Tulip. I am not certain yet when I will go home, but guess it will be some time the last of next month.

Edwin can talk right plain, and is very sweet sometimes, but being the only child of course he is somewhat spoiled.

Write soon to yours

Lovingly
Alice

Annie Moores to Emma Butler Paisley in Dobyville

Centre Point Arks
Feb. 22nd, 1877

Dear Sister Emma:—

Your letter was received in due time, and would have been answered sooner, but Alice said she wanted to write to you so I concluded to wait a while, but have delayed replying longer than I expected.

Olin walked over to Mr. Clardy's tonight to see Capt. Coulter & Johnnie, said he wouldn't be gone longer than an hour, so it won't be long before he returns. Edwin is asleep, so I am all alone. I never was as glad to see Olin as I was the last time he returned from Miss. He was exposed so much, and hearing of so much sickness & so many deaths that I was quite uneasy about him. I feel like I don't want him to leave me again to be gone so long. I was sick for two or three weeks, don't know what I would have done without Alice. Olin came by Tulip, & Ira came over with him in the buggy and Alice returned with him. She had made up her mind to stay several months longer. I was so sorry they sent for her. Olin wrote for sister Mary to come and stay with us a while, but we haven't heard from her. It made me so sad to hear of Mr. Scott's & Pompey's death. Have been anxious to hear from Mary, but think she must be well or we would hear from her.

I hope Emma's arm is well. It was too bad to have it broken. I reckon Henry has gotten well before this. Does bro. Billy feel right well? Olin's health is better than it has been for a long time, & Edwin is as fat and rosy as he can be. He is getting so he can help me about somethings, & is a great deal of company for me. He talks very plain and a great deal.

Kellie has been sick for two weeks, has suffered a great deal, has something like gravel. I fear she will never be entirely well again. Olin has just returned, & says she is not feeling so well tonight. I can't finish my letter tonight, as it is bed-time. Good night to you both.

23rd

I went over to see Kellie this evening. She seemed to feel better, but she suffers more at night; said she got right blue some times. I go over most every evening.

We are getting on very well, and I like living here as well or better than I expected. We have preaching regularly twice a month by two good preachers. Mr. Matthews is on this circuit & is much beloved. Dr. Custer lives here & preaches once a month. I have taken Edwin to church twice, and he behaved very nicely. It won't be long before the parsonage is finished.

303

John Somerville is living here and teaches school, has 39 scholars. I have been to see his wife twice. She seems to be a very nice lady, looks some older than I expected, has three children. Annie Somerville has been spending some time with her, but went home a few days ago.

Do you expect to visit home this summer? Bro George still thinks of coming.

Fannie Kerns has another little girl. Cal. is a great country for children. I had a dream some time ago that you & I wanted Ma to visit us at the same time.

Do you ever hear from Mr. Russell Carothers? the last I heard he was traveling for his health.

I have four hens sitting. One will come off in a few days. How many have you? Eggs are selling here at 8 & 10 cts. Don't think we ate as many before in my life. We have them twice a day, all of us are fond of them. How is bro. Billy getting on in the store?

Olin unites with me in love to you all.

Remember me to Capt. Lipscomb & family, & also Mrs. Jones. How is Mrs. Lipscomb's health now?

Write soon to

Your loving sister
Annie B. Moores

Mary Butler to Emma Butler Paisley in Dobyville

Tulip Arkansas
Feb 26th 1877

My dear sister:—

Your letter was received some time ago, to which I should have replied sooner. Your last I believe was written to Sister, and she has been speaking of writing. I wrote to Mary Scott as soon as I heard through your letter that she was getting well, but haven't received a reply yet.

I suppose you have heard that brother Lewis is now living in St. Louis: he hadn't moved his family, but I expect they are there by this time.

Ma and sister went to Malvern not long since, and spent a week very pleasantly—almost in the notion of going there to live. Sister Mollie wants sister to rent a place and live there while "the boys" are spending their vacations, however, I don't think brother George has any idea of doing it. I expect we will have them all with us this summer—hope we will have an abundance of fruit. Mr. Leiper expects to move to Malvern this week; he will take charge of the school there. The church from Rockport has been moved, and is being built in front of brother Olin's old place, which will for the present be used as church and school house. I learn that Mr. Ben Smith is going to move up to Mr. Leiper's place. His health is very bad; it is believed that he has consumption. Carrie Durham is teaching school here and I suppose he will send some of his children to her.

Mrs. Strong (Mary Pryor) and Lucy Jones spent last week visiting in the neighborhood. Mary spent a day and night with us: she is looking so much better than when I saw her over at your house: her health is so much improved. I had a letter from Annie P[hillips] a few days ago. Her sister Alice was married to Mr. Sid Hall on the 22nd: he has been loving her for five years: he is a son of David Hall's. I've heard he is a nice, steady young man. Alice expects to keep cousin

Ellen's baby. I suppose Maj Thompson is very dissipated, consequently no account. Lou Baugh expects to go to Ill. to see Mr. Wancey's parents and will probably live with them.

We have been having some beautiful weather this month, and I suppose you have been busy in your garden; Ma has planted some seeds. I think this spring will be earlier than usual. I have been working my flowers. They are blooming now very pretty in the garden.

Aunt Lucy is living with us again, and is delighted to get back, says we'll have to drive her off if she ever leaves. Ira has hired Jim to work for him. We pay aunt Lucy four dollars a month. She has two children; and four for Jim. I really think it is cheaper than keeping a girl and paying for washing scouring &c &c.

I am writing in Ira's little office and have just been up to the house. Mrs. Cooper has just come and as usual full of talk; she is as fleshy as I ever saw her. Jim and Bud Cooper are both at home; the former does not expect to return to the river. I got a letter from brother Olin not long since insisting on my coming over to stay with them; it seems they are anxious to keep one of us with them all the time, as it has not been very long since Alice got home. I wrote them it was not convenient for me to leave home now, but would like to go later in the spring. Brother George has been with us all winter, goes to Little Rock occasionally. He is better satisfied here than I thought he could be.

With much love for you all, I am afftly,

> your sister,
> Mary

Write soon

I don't think Pa has succeeded yet in getting any hands for brother Billy, though he has spoken to some about it. I got a letter from bro George not long since; he still speaks of visiting us. They have another little boy and asked us to send them a name for him—sent me his, sister Julia's and Aleck's photographs, which I think are very good.

All send love.

Mrs. Emma Lipscomb to Emma Butler Paisley in St. Louis

> Clark [County]
> March 13th [1877]

Dear Emma

I received your more than welcome letter to day, and I am so glad you have gone on to St Louis, as you may never have another as good an opportunity. I know you will be glad to hear that the children are all well. Not one of them has whimpered for you since you left. Dear little Mary is just as good as she can be, and not one bit of trouble. The children are all good. I mention Mary in particular, as you seem to think she might give me trouble. I had to read your letter several times that all might hear. All of them send much love to Pa and Ma. I hope you will enjoy your trip and have many things to tell when you get home. I haven't a doubt but what you will feel far a way from home in the big city. Things are going on at home about like they were when you left. The children did'nt have any company, Willie's Birth day. Mrs Orr wouldn't let her children come, as you was not at home. Mrs Patterson came to see me last Thursday evening. Father comes up right oftan and sits from five to ten minits. Ella came up last Friday evening. Mr Joe Doby and his wife have gone to Washington [Arkansas]. Mrs Doby's Mother is not expected to live. The Rhoda mule was right sick this morning for a while, which made Mr Boyce look blue for a while. She is well to night. I dont know of any thing new in the neighborhood that would interest you.

One of Dick Stit's little girls was burned to death yesterday.

I will close. The children are all asleep. It is Henry's night to sleep with GrandMa.

Much love for yourself and William

> Your Mother
> E D Lipscomb

Ben Logan to William Paisley in St. Louis

> Dobyville Arks
> March 19th 1877

Dear Sir

I received your letter from Little Rock yesterday. I was glad to hear that Mrs. Paisley was going with you to St. Louis, as I think it will be a pleasant trip for her. I don't think she could have had a better time to go, as she has left her children in good hands. They are getting along fine. They dont seem to care. They mind their grandma better than they do their Ma.

Mary never has cryed for her Ma yet. We ask her where ma is and she points the way you started. I don't have much to do since you left. Every body is at work. We haven't had rain enough to stop the plows since you left. Boyce finished plowing his place last week. He is planting corn to day. He has got another hand, he hired him the day you left. I dont know how you and him will make it when Court comes on. It is Nat Clark he has got. I thought it would be well enough to take him, and by the time court comes on, maybe you can get some body in his place if you don't get to keep him. I asked him if him and McCallum had went in to writing and he said that they hadnt. He said that was what him and McCallum fell out about.

I got sales for two Bales Cotton yesterday. One of them was the Bale that I bought. Made $1.11, one dollar and eleven cents on it, after loss of 10 lbs.

I haven't had a chance to send for the goods that you ordered before you left, and don't know when I will have. I haven't collected any since you left—I have got twenty five dollars that I have got for goods since you left.

One of old Dick Stitt's children got burned to deth Saturday. She was working around the fire, her and a little boy, and her dress caught fire, and the little boy ran to tell his pa, and before he got there, her clothes was burned off. She lived about six hours.

Well I will cease as this will be enough to tire you.

> Yours Truly
> B. V. Logan

Mrs. Paisley, you must keep Mr. P straight.

William Paisley to Emma Butler Paisley in Murphysboro

St Louis
Tuesday Mch 21, 1877

My dearest one:

I only have a minute to write. Am feeling much better than when you left.

Senter & Co. will extend me such accommodations as I recd. & the wholesale merchants seem really anxious to accommodate me. I commenced buying yesterday Evening, & will hurry through as fast as prudence will allow.

Olin is rooming with me in the same room you left—came in yesterday morning.

Hope you arrived at Sister Jennie's safely & that you & she will enjoy the visit. I miss you greatly. It is hardly necessary to caution you, but I will say that I think it will be best for you to say as little to sister Jennie as possible about the trouble between Henry & Olin & c. I learn from Olin that she has been talked to a good deal about that & other matters—and the more I hear of it the more rejoiced I am that we know so little about it.

Shall expect you Saturday. Haven't seen Lewis since yesterday morning. Love to all, & much for your dear self.

Yours devotedly
Wm. Paisley

Emma Butler Paisley to her four children in Dobyville

Murphysboro, Ill
March 22nd, 1877

My dearest children,

No doubt you think it a long time for your mama to be away from home. Well, it seems long to me, for I never was away from you much. I will not have time to write to each of you separate, but will write one letter to all of you, and you can get grandma to read it to you. I am now at Uncle Lewis's, but he is in St. Louis and will not move aunt Jennie, cousin Jessie and cousin Willard in two or three weeks yet. Uncle Lewis will come here to-morrow or next day, and stay till he gets ready to move his family.

I wrote to grandma while in Little Rock, which I reckon she has received several days ago. I left your pa in St. Louis to buy his goods while I am staying with your aunt Jennie. I don't know when he will get through buying, but I reckon the first of next week.

While in the City we occupied a room on the third floor in Barnum's Hotel—a very nice, comfortable place, and only four dollars a day for both of us. I don't know whether your pa will stay at the same place or not.

There are a great many wonderful sights in St. Louis. The day before I left, brother Lewis hired a buggy and took me out to Shaw's Garden. There are no flowers blooming in the garden this early, but there are some beautiful ones in the hot houses. I thought of Mrs. Orr while walking in the garden, and thought how delighted she would be. Now my dear little children, you must be good and kind to each other, and do what grand ma tells you. I hope none of you will get sick while pa and ma are gone, but be as little trouble to grand ma as possible, for it is very kind for her to stay with you all. Good bye and a kiss for all of you. Love to Grand ma. Regards to Mr. Boyce and Ben.

> Always your loving
> Mama

Dear little Mary, mama is coming home soon. God bless you all. I will be so glad to see you.

Lewis Butler to William Paisley in Dobyville

> St Louis
> April 16, 1877

Dear Billie:

Enclosed I send my receipts for Mrs Scott's policy and premium receipts. I returned last week from attending court at Murphysboro and brought my family with me. We are now in our new home here, and fast getting things in shape for comfort. We reached here Tuesday night, and stopped at Mrs. Davis' on Walnut between 5th & 6th, and Jennie and myself were aroused by the screams of the people and noise of the engines at the burning of the Southern Hotel, which was in close proximity to where we were sleeping. We dressed and went on the street and saw the horrible sight. The papers have already apprised you fully concerning it.

We are all very well, and think we shall be satisfied with our new home.

If you and Emma could have only waited till we got fixed, we could have made Emma's visit much more enjoyable. Tell Emma that when our trains met between here and Murphysboro the day she came up, it was impossible for me to see her which I regretted very much. The trains were off of time, ours being very much delayed, and it was snowing hard, and they did not come close enough together for me to get off.

Love to all. Let me hear from you soon.

> Yours affectionately
> L. P. Butler

Alice Butler to Emma Butler Paisley in Dobyville

> Tulip Arkansas
> May 4th 1877

My dear Sister:—

I have been thinking for some time that I would answer your good letter, received some time ago. I regretted very much that we could not see more of you and bro. B. as you passed through Malvern; one day seemed like such a short time, and we felt like we had hardly seen you.

We made quite a lengthy stay. I was there two weeks, and sister M. spent about a month, though she remained, thinking probably she would go on to Centre Point, and at last concluded not to go. Sister had a letter from sister Annie a short time since. She had been having chills and was not right well at the time. I suppose you knew bro. Johnnie was in Texas with his wife, and the last we heard she had improved very much. I hope she will get entirely well. Cousin Laura's visit to St. Louis seemed to do her a great deal of good, as we heard since her return, that she had walked a little. She will certainly know how to appreciate health if she ever does get well.

This has been a rainy day so far. I do hope we will not have another spell as we had in April; such weather is very bad on the little chickens. We have had more than a hundred, but I guess not over ninety now. Ma has six little turkeys, just come off yesterday. She lost her best turkey hen a month or two ago and it grieved her very much. We suppose something caught her. I don't know what she would do without some turkeys to raise, calls them her little babies.

Mr. Ben Smith died on the 1st day of May. He had been sick for some time, but it was very unexpected to us all. We were all gathered down on Tulip creek having a May party, and all of his daughters except Fannie, the oldest, were also with us. We had partaken of a splendid basket dinner, and were sitting around in groups, enjoying ourselves as usual on such occasions, when one of the boys came riding up at full speed and said his father was dying. The girls were greatly distressed, and hurried home as quickly as possible, but did not get there before he died. So our May party turned out to be a sad one after all. Dr. Cooper had told us a few days before that he was liable to die at any moment. I hardly know what was the matter with him but some say it was consumption.

I have just received a long and interesting letter from sister Annie while I was writing. Bro. George [Hughes] came in and handed it to me. She said she had just gotten a long letter from you. It seems like it is hard for her to break the chills, though she said she had been improving some the last few days. I reckon bro. Olin is kept very busy while bro. J. is absent. We also had a letter from bro. George [Butler] not long since, says he is making preparations to come to see us in July or August. I think sister Julia would come with him if the children were a little larger. Their baby is named George, and they say it is very much like Ma.

Ma has a splendid garden this year, has had peas and Irish potatoes once, which I suppose is doing better than almost any one else. Reckon we will have plenty of fruit. We have had several games of croquet this evening, although it is quite damp. Bro. G. is still very fond of playing, and we play some almost every day.

Oh! I forgot to tell you that I saw Miss Emma Borden while at Malvern, she and Miss Nellie Lawson spent a week there together, the former was looking very natural, enquired about you, and said she would like so much to see you.

Does little Emma suffer any from the arm that was broken? We have been looking for a letter from you. Sister wrote to you about two weeks ago.

Are Bessie and Maggie Doby both at home now? The boys will be coming home about the last of June or 1st of July, we had a letter from Jimmie a few days ago, sent one of his photographs which is much better than the one he sent some time ago. I must close. All send much love.

> Lovingly
> Alice

Give my love to Ella and Mrs. Lipscomb.
Pa says he will come over to see you as soon as the roads get better, if he can find a wagon

going from Arkadelphia. We heard from bro. Charley & sister Kate a few days ago, said both of the children had been right sick but had gotten well.

Do you hear from Mrs. Scott? Sister M. hasn't heard in a long time.

A.B.

Some one broke into Mr. John Hughes' store a few days ago, and broke open his safe, taking out a large amount of money. His own losses were about $1200 dollars, and several others had their money deposited in there for safe keeping. Bro. George thought at first that he had lost about 500 in scrip, but found out they didn't take that. No clue has been found out as to who the parties were.

Mrs. Barnett's little girl was very badly bitten by a dog, we noticed an account of it in the *Gazette* said both sides of her face was badly torn and her nose bitten. Her name is Mattie and she was about 6 years old. I believe you have seen her.

A.B.

Annie Moores to Emma Butler Paisley in Dobyville

Centre Point, Arks
May 7th, 1877

Dear Sister Emma:—

Your letter was received a little more than a week ago, and read with much interest; glad you gave me the history of your trip and especially was I glad to know you had a pleasant time and enjoyed your stay with sis Jennie. Last Wednesday Mrs. Matthews, Edwin, & I went over to see Mrs. Somerville & baby: and while there Edwin was taken sick had fever, and it lasted all night: he isn't well yet and has a *very* bad cold, it makes him fretful and wants me to nurse him a good deal, but I made him a pallet & told him to lie down until I could write to aunt Emma. He was so little trouble to me before he got sick.

I received a letter from sister Mary last Friday, telling us they had a letter from bro. George saying he would be out in June or July. We would like very much to get over in June, but don't know yet when Johnnie and Kellie will get back. Johnnie said he thought they would be back the 1st of June, but Kellie thinks she would get well sooner by staying until July, and her mother is going to write to her to stay. They are very much pleased with their boarding place, pay $50 per month. Johnnie said he spent his time in reading and playing croquet—several men are boarding there who have nothing to do. Johnnie's health has improved as well as Kellie's.

We have a weekly paper published here. Our Sunday School is flourishing, 70 members. Olin is superintendent. Mr. John Somerville teaches the Bible class. He united with the church last Sunday.

Our camp meeting commences on Friday before the second Sunday in Sept. Ma said she would come over to see us then.

Well, haven't we had rain and cool weather. I have on my winter clothing yet. It has now been a little over two weeks since I had my last chill, and I have felt very well since & have a splendid appetite. This evening, I feel a little more drowsy than usual & don't feel quite so well, but I hope the chills are not going to return.

310

Edwin has gone fast to sleep on his pallet; I would rather be sick myself than see him sick. It is something unusual for him to go to sleep twice the same day. He feels so badly.

I hope Henry and Mary have gotten well, if I get sick again I think I shall have to go over & stay a while with you.

Will you have much fruit this year? A good deal of it is killed in some places. I was in hopes we would have plenty to put up in cans, for it is so nice to have during winter & spring. I reckon you have a good garden.

How is bro. Billy getting on in his business now, and has he entirely recovered his health? Olin has a very bad cold, but I believe he has gotten rid of the chills.

Love to bro. Billy and the children, also Capt. Lipscomb & family. Edwin is awake & wants to know where mama is, so I reckon I will have to take the little fellow a while as he is feeling so unwell. Write soon to your ever loving sister

Annie B. Moores

Mary Butler to Emma Butler Paisley in Dobyville

Tulip Arkansas
June 11th, 1877

My dear sister Emma,

It has been a long time since I've written to you but I will not now consume time in making excuses. You know I'm a poor letter writer any way.

Last Friday week, Ma and I went down to visit brother Charly, and attend quarterly meeting—had a pleasant time and heard some good sermons preached by Mr. Jewell, the presiding elder. Kate prepared extensively for the occasion, had fresh beef, mutton, ham, chickens, guinea, cakes, pies &c. We carried them a bucket full of nice ripe cherries which were very acceptable. I wish you lived near so that we could send you some, for I believe you have no cherries on your place, and we've had more than we ever had before—sent sister Mollie some.

Maj. Coulter has been at Malvern now more than a month; we expected he and sister Mollie would come down to see us, but the Maj. said he was too feeble to come. He expects to take Coulter to Texas with him just as soon as he gets well of the measles; the children up there all have it, and so far hasn't given them a great deal of trouble: is so much better for them to have it while young.

We are very busy now preparing for the return of brother George and the boys—have a workman here today who has put in a south window in the old office, and doing other little jobs. Sister will have a bureau and some bedsteads brought over from her place, so when we get it fixed, the old room will be very comfortable. The letter Brother Billy wrote ma was received, and much appreciated, and ma thought the reception of it had been acknowledged long since, says she regrets it when she thought so much of it too.

Ma says if it is inconvenient for you to come, she will try to get over to see you with brother George: we have heard nothing very late from him; he may come unexpectedly: just think of it; he has been gone about seven years! won't every thing look strange at the old homestead?

Brother G[eorge] H[ughes] has just returned from Tulip with the mail but brought no letters, only a note from sister Mollie thanking him for the cherries which he sent. They have five cases of the measles, and George and Nannie are troublesome.

311

Tuesday 12th

Ma says she is going to try to put you and Annie up a *little* jar of cherries if she can get them. Our chickens have commenced dying with cholera; the turkey gobbler died last week and ma thinks her "baby turkeys" will not be in the way of her coming over to see you this summer; she has only five. We were expecting to have a feast of chickens this year as we had so many, but I'm fearful we will be disappointed. We are having plenty of vegetables now.

Ma has just been in sending many messages, sends love, and says she did want to write some to you herself. All send love.

How is brother B. getting on with his business? He might write occasionally—my love to him and all other friends—glad that Mrs. Lipscomb's health has improved.

Write soon to your loving sister

Mary

Kisses for the children. Excuse this letter.

Ira Butler to Emma Butler Paisley in Dobyville

Tulip Ark.
July 17th 1877

Dear Sister Emma

This will be my first letter I have ever written to you, and hope you will not attribute my negligence to a want of love: for I assure you it is not the case. Bro Charlie came up yesterday, & left his family all well. He came expecting to go up to Malvern after Mrs. Colburn; but found her at Tulip with her sister. They are going to return this morning. Bro. C. is looking quite thin and badly. He has worked very hard this year, says it will take him two weeks to finish his cotton. I am pleased to say that I am through with my crop until harvest time, and am now enjoying the sweets of shade. Alice & myself expect to visit you this summer, & expect to have a nice time. I am in hopes that the Misses Doby will be at home.

Pa received a letter from bro. O and Sister Annie. They enjoyed their visit with you very much. Bro. O said he could have spent several days longer very pleasantly.

Pa received a letter some time ago from bro. George. They expected to be at St. Louis on 15th of this month. We will look for him down from Malvern to morrow. West & Georgie carried the buggy up this morning. They are going to Benton from Malvern, to spend a while with their uncle John. You and bro. Billy must come over this Summer. I am sorry I did not write by the last mail to let you know when he was coming. We are getting anxious to see him. Have you a Croquet Set now and do you play? We have two sets up, but I have played a very few times this year; but will play oftener now since I have layed my crop by. Walter went to Malvern last Friday to attend Mr. Leiper's commencement, which came off last Friday night. We are having plenty of ripe apples & peaches now.

I have a good crop this year, as good I think as I have ever seen grown on the hills. You must not let the Misses D. go away before Alice and myself make our visit. I am quite anxious to form their acquaintance. We can't tell yet when we will come over, but it will be some time after bro. G

312

comes. Give my love to bro. Billy & the children, & reserve a portion for your-self & write soon & a long letter to your devoted brother.

Ira

P.S. July 18

Bro George & his son Ellick [Alec] is at Malvern, & will come down home this evening.

Ira

Henry Butler to William Paisley in St. Louis

Malvern Arkansas
Sep 25th 1877

My dear Billy—

Breckinridge Hitchcock & Co is the firm I wished you to pay the $100—#214 N. Commercial. We are owing them $116.05, & if entirely convenient pay the whole, & I will meet you the morning you come down. Write & let me know any how what morning you will pass. Would be so glad for you to stop off—but under the circumstances can hardly expect it.

If it "comes in the way," please say to our friends that I will either be up soon, or make arrangements to pay just as soon as cotton moves sufficiently to justify our drawing. I would be glad if you would say this to Mr. Orr any how. We are owing O & L more than any others, & I feel about it (or them) as *you once did.*

Our prospects for trade & collections are good & we are *determined* to sell less on credit—"lop off" many [names] from our books. I am not keeping up our stock as well as our trade demands, just from the fact I dislike to *strain* our credit. This operates for the present somewhat against our business.

Warren [Archer, his partner] has never put in any capital as yet (nothing to amount to much, say $500), and our expenses have been heavy for building, clerk hire, &c &c. We have sold goods enough this year on a credit & even the cash (including the cotton trade) has been fair. To the 1st of this month our sales have been—Credit 13714
Cash   9579

Much of the cash went into last year's business, being cotton paid on old debts. We have several thousand owing us—*much* cannot be counted on—as you know.

If we had the means (out of debt, of course, to start on) we could do a business of fifty thousand dollars here and pick our customers in this, Dallas, & Grant counties. I wish *you* was with me here in business—I know we could make money.

But excuse me, I was just letting my pen indite my thoughts, without reflecting that you had business on your hand.

Let me hear from you. All well—Do hope your health will improve on your trip—sorry to see you looking feeble.

Your true friend & bro.
H.A.B.

Emma Butler Paisley to William Paisley in St. Louis

Home
Sept 25th 1877

My dearest one,

I was very glad indeed to receive your first note from Gurdon. I feel a good deal better than I did yesterday—have not got over the diarrhea. Felt very lonely last night but not at all uneasy. I was almost sorry I let you go yesterday, as about twelve o'clock I thought I would have to send for the doctor and ma, but after I got over it was glad you got off, as you will get back a day sooner than if you had waited till today. Well I reckon you are in the City—looking around before this. Now let me say, don't hurry through so as to neglect any matters to which you wish to attend. Of course I want you to get back as soon as possible, but I don't much think I will be sick before next month.

John brought Ella a note from Dr. Bently as he returned from school, but she hadn't much time to answer as the wagon was ready to start. Of course I know none of the contents of either, but Ella was looking quite sad.

Dow drove the wagon down to Mr. Grier's and was after dark getting back. It was well he went, for Mr. Boyce had some cotton to weigh and the mules to look after, which kept him out till after supper. The hands are ginning Mr. Burton's cotton today, and getting on very well, Mr. Boyce thinks.

Good bye. Will send this over and see if Mr. B. has gone. Hope I will get a letter to-morrow or next day. In haste, always your loving   Emma

William Paisley to Emma Butler Paisley in Dobyville

St. Louis
Sept 28th 1877

My dear sweet one:

Your precious letter of the 25 & 26th inst. was received this morning & I assure you afforded me much pleasure and relief. I am so much in hopes that you will hold out until I get home. Your telling me to remain until I got through with my business did me a great deal of good, for it is a great relief to me to know that even if any thing should happen, you will not injure yourself in any way from imaginary fear or trouble on account of my absence. I can but exclaim, "who has got such a wife as I have?"

I have been hard at work today, & gotten along very well. My greatest trouble is that I cannot keep from buying too many goods. Tell Ben to keep the customers stirred up, and insist on their bringing in cotton as soon as possible, as I will need the collections as fast as they can be made.

I cannot see far enough yet to tell whether I can get off before Tuesday or not but will do all I can tomorrow Saturday and get through if I possibly can. There is so much for me to do yet I fear I will not be able to make it, & should I fail I can hardly expect to finish before some time in the day Monday & consequently not start home till Tuesday morning. Will come just as soon as I can, but don't be uneasy should it be Wednesday before I see you. Excuse pencil, as there is no pen & ink in the room.

I am alone to night & feel quite lonely. With much love & many kisses

Your devoted husband
Wm Paisley

Mattie Hughes to Emma Butler Paisley in Dobyville

Tulip Arkansas
Nov. 7, 1877

Dear Sister Emma,

Your letter to Ma, also the trimming for "Mattie Wyche's" dress was received several days ago: I'll make the dress next week, and send it over by mail. I wrote George [Hughes] about "my little namesake," [Emma's sixth child, born 17 October 1877] and he says she ought to be a good baby. Mrs. Goodloe Pattillo says you ought to name it "Mattie Hughes," and that I ought to go over now and get it and raise it as my own baby. But that would be impossible, for it makes no difference how many a parent has, they never have one to give away.

I had the pleasure of receiving a letter from Walter last Friday, mailed at Plymouth, England, on the 17th of Oct. He was thirteen days going from N.Y. Walter says for nine days he didn't see the sun, except for a few minutes, that he found the Ocean rougher than he expected, and couldn't take the pleasant promenades on deck that he thought he would. But says he suffered very little from seasickness. There were two other young men on the same vessel going to Germany. One from St. Louis, going to Leipsic, where Walter expects to spend most of his time. You don't know how thankful I felt to know that he was safely across the ocean.

Nov. 9

I expected to send this letter by the last mail, but didn't get it ready in time. Ma is very well, and delighted to be at home, and we are equally as well pleased to have her here. As usual she is going around all the time, doing first one thing and then another. Pa is complaining some today, but as a general thing he is very hearty, and enjoys good health. He was very lonely without mamma, and will never be willing for her to be away from him so long again. I was very glad she was with you during your confinement, for I know it gave you so much pleasure to have her with you.

We get letters from "the boys" in Virginia every week. They are getting on very well. West says he is studying more this session than he ever did. Jimmie and Reavis went to Washington city three or four weeks ago, and say they had a splendid time. They went with an excursion party, and the round trip only cost them two dollars. Went one night, spent a day there, and returned to Ashland the next night, completely worn out.

Ira left home about ten days ago, intending to go to Centre Point and Dobyville. We would have expected him home before now, but we have had so much rain, I expect he has been water bound. I know sister Mary will want to return with him, but as he went horseback, there will be no way for her to come. We have been expecting brother Charlie to come by, with some cotton on his way

315

to Malvern, but owing to so much bad weather, I reckon he thought it best to stay at home. Cotton has been selling so well at Pine Bluff he may have carried his there.

Pa killed a large beef yesterday, and this morning sent a quarter to brother Henry. I know he will appreciate it, for they have to pay a high price for what they get. George is at Little Rock now, but I expect will be at home in a few days. At one time we thought of going to St. Louis, to spend the winter and board with brother Lewis, but now I don't much think we will go. Sister Jennie seemed anxious for me to come, and so was brother L. But it would cost so much more there than here, for I would have to spend so much more for dress. I have never thought that I would like to live in a city as large as St. Louis, especially since George would have nothing to do there. I had a letter from aunt Betsy a few days ago. Her youngest daughter Bessie, was married in Oct.

We received a letter from Jimmie this evening. He and Reavis spent one day at the fair in Richmond. I suppose the whole school went, as he said they formed ranks, and gave three cheers for the President, as he passed by them. The President took off his hat and made them a polite bow.

I had a letter from Annie Allford today. She has named her baby Mary Alice. Says she wants to come over during the Winter to see us. Ma often speaks of your garden, how well it looked. She has a plenty of new Irish potatoes, as large as hen eggs, and have had butter beans and tomatoes until the frost killed them. Pa hasn't finished digging his sweet potatoes, and thinks they will be injured by the cold and rain. Alice didn't go to the fair, wasn't feeling very well at that time, though her health seems to be much better now.

I am glad you have such a good girl to do your work, and hope you can keep her some time.

My love to Billy and the children, also to Mrs. Lipscomb. Write whenever you can. Don't you think Mattie Reavis is prettier than Mattie Wyche? You know Reavis was Ma's maiden name.

Your Loving Sister
M. W. Hughes

Ma says you must be particular about taking cold, going from the house to the dining room. Says she wishes you had some of her strawberry plants that she has to throw away.

Ira Butler to Billy Paisley in Dobyville

At Home
Dec. 3rd 1877

Dear Bro Billy

Your letter of the 29th was received last Friday and read with much pleasure. I had nearly decided before receiving your letter to commence business at Tulip, but after a mature consultation and deliberation, concluded it would be better for me to clerk for you. I can't leave until after the 6th Dec. Mr. Timberlick was over to see me last week, in regard to making a payment on the note I hold against him. He is to come up the 6th and pay me four hundred dollars then, if he can raise that amount, and if he could not he is to pay the other hundred by the first of Jan. If Providence permits, I will leave home on the 7th for Malvern, and will be at Gurdon Saturday morning. I am in hopes that I will find your wagon at the depot, as I might find it difficult to hire a horse. I want to get there by Sat. so that I will be prepared to commence business Monday morning in good earnest.

Pa and sister Matt thought of going up to Malvern tomorrow, but Pa received a letter from bro. Lewis yesterday stating that he had a very bad cough, and was fearful he might have the consumption. He has called on several prominent physicians in St. Louis. They say his lungs are not affected, but call it the congestion of the lungs. They advise him to go to a milder climate. Bro Lewis thinks of bringing his family to board at Pa's until he can find a place, unless there is a change for the better soon. He said that he had not thought much about it until about a week ago, while sister Jennie & Jessie were off at preaching, he began coughing very badly & expectorating a dark mucous substance. Dr. Johnson, one of his physicians, says it may be caused from a spell of sickness he had while at Murphysboro. I am in hopes it will all pass off without any injury.

Hoping to see you soon I am Yours truly

> Ira

Excuse mistakes, as I haven't time to look over my letter.

Alice Butler to Emma Butler Paisley in Dobyville

> Tulip
> Dec 6th 1877

Dear sister Emma:—

I have been thinking for a long time that I would write to you, and expected once or twice to make you a visit, but failed to do either, so will write a few lines to send by Ira.

I reckon I will have to wait now till Spring to make you a visit, as it is so unpleasant traveling about in such cold weather. It seems strange to think that Ira is going to leave us to be gone so long; don't see how we are going to get on without him. You must take good care of him and don't let him fall in love too quick (if he is not already in), for I think he is quite susceptible. He is out now making his *last farewell* calls to some young ladies.

The little bundle we send by him are some things made for Henry and Emma, the pants made by sister Mary, the coat *cut* by Ma and made by Sister & myself, and the drawers made by Sister for little Emma—sorry we haven't time to make something for little Mary. How is the dear little Mattie Wyche (suppose that is her name) getting on? all send a kiss to her and would like to make her acquaintance.

We had a letter from sister Annie not very long since, they were all well—says she has put pants on Edwin, and he is not willing to wear dresses any more. Suppose you received the little dress which Sister sent some time ago.

All unite in sending much love. Let us hear from you. Ira can tell you all about the letters we have had from Walter, and how much delighted he is away over in Germany.

> Afftly
> Alice

Annie Moores to Emma Paisley in Dobyville

Centre Point Ark.
Dec. 14th, 1877

Dear Sister Emma,

Until bro. Billy's letter to Johnnie & Olin was received I thought I had written to you since the birth of your little daughter. As he said nothing about hearing from us, I got to thinking & inquiring about it, and found I hadn't written. I had the letter in my mind enough to have written it several times. Well, the little girl is getting to be a big girl. I would like so much to see her, especially since she is called the prettiest & smartest one yet. I hope she is as little trouble as a child could be, for you certainly have your hands full. And you have Ira with you. I am so glad he has gotten in business and I wouldn't be surprised if he found him a wife before a great while. How things change around.

I reckon you have heard bro. Lewis has gone to Southern Cal. for his health. It is sad to think of his health failing, I do hope he may recover. Sis Jennie & the children will soon be at Pa's. I would like so much to see them. I know she must feel sad.

Work has commenced on our house. We will have five rooms, but will move in as soon as two are finished. It is between Mr. Clardy's & the school house. Ira remembers the place. Oranges, apples, nuts, and candies have gotten in for Christmas, & we have two turkeys up fattening. Your family is getting so large that it will soon take two small turkeys at one meal for you all to get enough. Olin is kept so busy while Johnnie is gone that he has no time for writing. He is drawing off accounts now.

Mr. Matthews returned from Conference this evening, we are all delighted to have him for our preacher another year. The death of Bishop Marvin was so unexpected & sad. He will be greatly missed. Just at the prime of life & so useful.

I will close for tonight. I have just finished a letter of five pages to Alice, so it is bed time.

16th

I didn't get time to finish my letter Saturday, so it won't get off now before Tuesday. I received a letter from Sister yesterday, said she knew we would be so anxious to hear from bro. Lewis. His physician thought if he could get to Southern Cal. without getting worse he could be cured. Bro. George Hughes wrote us a letter telling us of his real condition. It is certainly distressing to us. Sister is at Malvern.

Have you a cook, and how are you getting on? My health is very good but still have a cough. Olin has had only one spell of Asthma since he got home. His health seems to be tolerably good, and Edwin is as fat as a pig, and looks right large in coat, pants, and boots.

Olin joins me in love to you all. Ira of course included; tell him to write to us, and let us know how he is getting on.

Write whenever you can to

Your loving sister
Annie Moores

Mary Butler to Emma Butler Paisley in Dobyville

Tulip, Arkansas
Dec. 17th 1877

Dear sister Emma:—

Your interesting letter to Sister was received this evening, which we opened and read, as she is at Malvern, and will send it to her in the morning. I have been talking of writing to you for a long, long time, and must not put it off another day; I regretted that I couldn't visit you on my return from Centre Point; if Ira had gone for me in the buggy, I would have visited you.

Brother Lewis left for Los Angeles Cal. last Tuesday; he has had beautiful weather for travelling, and I hope is there by this time; the physicians advised him to go there. Brother George Hughes went up a week before he left to assist him in his business matters, and is still with sister Jennie, helping her to dispose of her furniture &c. They will be here the last of this or the first of next week. Brother L. has written and also telegraphed to his family that he was getting on well so far, and no worse for travelling. I have written to brother George Emory [Butler] to go to see him if possible; it would be convenient to him if he was living at his old home, but he is sent on another district two hundred miles away—he rented his home to Joe Moores.

Sister will remain at Malvern and come down with sis Jennie; she gets letters almost every day and sends them down to us. I have been very busy trying to get the little room fixed for sister J.— think she would prefer that, as it is more private than mine.

Ma says she is glad to hear you are having such good prayer meetings—thinks Ira will enjoy them and be benefitted. In Sister's note yesterday, she was writing about attending at Malvern and what bad behavior they had there among the young people.

Tuesday

I didn't get any letter off by the mail this morning, so it will not leave here now before Thursday: Just one week till Christmas, all the little children are looking forward with anxiety for the time to hang up their stockings, and you have six—quite a number in your household. I am anxious to see the little stranger.

Wednesday 19th

Brother Caldwell preached a good sermon last Sunday "God is our refuge and strength a very present help in trouble." Ma and pa thought it suited them exactly. Brother Hunter spend last Thursday night with us, and brother Caldwell and his wife came and sat till bed time; we enjoyed their company so much. Pa and Alice went down to bro. Charley's yesterday and returned today: they expected to spend Christmas with us, but Alice Ware thinks of staying with them; she has been in L Rock visiting her mother. Mr. Ware has gone up for her; they expect to spend a few days in this neighborhood, so we look for them tomorrow. Willis Green, who was a widower with six children was married not long since to Miss Rebecca Holmes, an older sister of Miss Fannie's. Miss Archer Hays is to be married on the 26th to a gentleman from Texas—said to be a nice man—and rumor also says Mack Adams and Miss Mattie Amos are to be married soon: they seem to be in the marrying notion about Princeton. There is to be a supper and tableaux there next Friday night for the benefit of the Presbyterian church, or rather to finish paying for an organ. I

319

don't think Alice and I will hardly go down, as Ira is not here to go with us, though Kavanaugh said if they went we could go with them—fifty cents admission fee.

Mr. Davis is our circuit preacher, and Mr. Johnson presiding elder. Mr. Ware on Malvern circuit. Alice received Ira's interesting letter this morning and will answer soon. Mr. Jewell is to be married soon to Mrs. Daneau, a widow with one daughter living not very far from Pine Bluff. She is said to be an excellent lady. He is stationed at Monticello. Kate Cooper went to Malvern Monday with Bob Smith to stay a few days—perhaps they will marry yet some time. I went for the mail this evening and, as the weather was so pretty, concluded to go to see Carrie Durham, as I heard she was not well. Miss Catherine is still confined to the bed, the rest were well. Tell Ira Sue Pattillo got home last night—enjoyed her visit very much, so Jimmie told me this evening.

Ma says she would like to have some of your nice cabbages you spoke of. All send much love. My love to Ira, bro. Billy and all. Write soon to your ever loving sister

Mary

Mattie Hughes to Emma Butler Paisley in Dobyville

Tulip Arkansas
Jan. 16, 1878

Dear Sister Emma,

Your letter was received some time ago, while I was at Malvern, ought to have been answered sooner, but for the last few weeks I have been rather negligent about writing. And you know the longer one postpones answering a letter, the less they feel like writing.

George and Jennie got to Malvern on the morning of the 30 of Dec., got there about 5 o'clock. We knew they were coming, so we were up and had good fires ready to welcome them. We spent that day there, and came to Tulip the next day with papa, who had been there a day or two, waiting for them to come from St. Louis. George and Jennie failed to dispose of the furniture and household goods, so they had them brought to Malvern, and will sell them there for the most that they can get. Jennie had very nice furniture, and it is a pity to have to sell it at such a sacrifice. But if brother Lewis can regain his health, we will not grieve about the loss. We feel much more hopeful about him, than we did a week ago.

By the last mail pa received a postal from bro. Moores, written on the 3 informing us that bro. L. was better. Jennie also received a letter from bro. Lewis dated a day later, in which he said he had felt better for several days, though his cough and expectoration continued about the same. He has a good appetite, usually eats for breakfast several pieces of fried chicken, a couple of soft boiled eggs, some toast or bread, and two glasses of sweet milk, a hearty meal for an invalid isn't it? His digestion too, is very good, and his bowels regular. We feel so thankful to know that he is with kind and loving friends, who do all they can to make him comfortable. They take him out riding every day, when the weather is pleasant. In a letter to pa, bro. Moores writes, that he has been very lowspirited ever since he was there, until a day or two before he wrote, he appeared more cheerful. At one time he thought of returning, and was about making arrangements to leave there on the 2 of this month. But the family there told him they could not see that he had declined, and that two weeks were too short a time to see what the climate would do for him. We are so glad they advised him to stay, for if he had started he might have died on the way. Jennie or one of the family write to him by every mail.

I wish you could see the children, they are as sweet and interesting as any children I ever saw, and not much trouble. Both of them are very fond of singing, and can sing several songs, such as "I want to be an angel," "The beautiful river," "Put me in my little bed," &c. Willard is very fond of pa, and occasionally pa puts him on "Romeo," and then he is delighted, for he was never on a horse until he came here. They see something new and surprising every day, came running in a few days ago delighted, had found two little lambs, and Grandpa had given one to Jessie and the other to Willard.

George, Jennie, and Alice went to Malvern yesterday, Jennie to clean up her furniture, and get some things that she wanted. We expect George and Jennie the last of the week, but Alice will remain up there two or three weeks. Last night Willard missed his Ma, and cried some, but during the day he is as happy as ever.

You mentioned receiving a nice cloak as a birthday present. While at Malvern, a box was sent by express to "Mrs. M. E. Butler," containing two very nice cloaks, one for her (a present from

George) and the other for me. I knew of their coming, but hadn't told Mollie, so she was very much surprised on opening the box. Said she had been wanting one so much, but didn't want to buy one.

We get a letter from the boys every week, have had three from Walter, within the last ten days. He continues pleased with Germany, and says he is making some progress, learning the language. His last letter came in sixteen days, just the same length of time that it took one of Annie's late letters to get here from Centre Point.

Enclosed you will find one of Reavis pictures, taken since he returned to College. What has become of Ira? I think it has been more than a month since he has written to any one here. The last we heard from him, he had cut his hand quite badly. I think you wrote about it to Alice. Tell him Pa wants to know how he came out with Mr. Timberlake, and if he got his money from Johnnie & Olin. Says he must write to him occasionally.

Pa hasn't succeeded in hiring a boy yet, though he hires one occasionally to cut wood and bring it up. Aunt Lucy and family are keeping house at Mr. Hunter's old place near Tulip. Jim came the other day, and said he would hire, for 75 cts a day! Patsy, the cook that Mollie had last year, is here, has agreed to stay a month or two. After that I don't know who we will get. You mentioned having weekly prayer meetings, at private houses. A good place during the winter, and I expect you all will derive much benefit from them, though I don't expect you can attend often on account of your baby. At Malvern they have them at the church every Sunday night, but unless they have better behavior than they did when I attended, they will not accomplish much good.

Mrs. Nat. G. Smith has moved to her old home, and it is said that Mrs. Roane will live there with her. The house must be in a dilapidated condition, for it has [been] inhabited by negroes for the last two years, and I don't think they did any repairing.

There are several families from Michigan in the neighborhood. One of them bought the old Billy Smith place, paid $320.00 for it. So you see the old waste places around Tulip are being reoccupied, and it is probable that the country will improve. I haven't seen Mr. Robertson since he moved to his own home. I don't believe he feels very friendly towards us since we sold our home. I am anxious to see you, for as you say it has been a long time. Just think you have two children that I have never seen! Would like so much to visit you, and will try and come over next Summer. All send love to you, Ira and Billy. Write soon.

Your Loving
Sister M. W. Hughes

P.S. Tell Ira that George Henry Archer and Alice Mathews are to be married this week, and that Mr. Mack Adams and Miss Amiss of Princeton were married last week. Another letter from bro. L. He thinks he is better.

Thinking you would like to read one of Walter's letters, I send you one we received some time ago. I know Ira would like to read it. Tell him to take good care of it, and Ma says send it back. She wants Charlie and Kate to read it.

Annie Moores to Emma Butler Paisley in Dobyville

Centre Point, Ark.
Feb. 17th, 1878

Dear Sister Emma,

Your letter was received about two weeks ago. At that time it had been five weeks since I had heard from Tulip. Previous to that time I had been hearing almost every week, but there was something wrong with the mails. Since that time I have gotten three letters, the last was received night before last from sister Mary bearing the sad news of brother Lewis' increased illness, and sister Jennie had gone to him. It did make me feel so *very* sad, but since reflecting I hope it isn't as bad as I at first thought. I felt almost like he was dead. I pray that he may yet be spared, if consistent with divine will. If not, that he may be prepared to meet death in peace, and have a home in heaven. I do feel so much for sister Jennie & the dear children. It will be so sad if he does die unprepared. We could all bear it so much better if we knew he was ready. I know that he has many prayers ascending for him night and day, and I cannot feel that all will be lost. I know that almost every breath with our dear mother is a prayer in his behalf. I trust that all will be well. I reckon some one has written you all about him from home.

We had Quarterly meeting here yesterday & today week, the weather was quite cold, but we had a right good meeting, had several excellent sermons from our presiding elder with whom we are all pleased. We wouldn't care to exchange our *two* preachers for *any*, we are satisfied. We had a very interesting and good time Sunday evening in our love feast. I always feel benefited by such meetings. Our church is being repaired, but not ready for use. We worship in the school house for the present, which is quite convenient to us. It is nearer than Mr. McClardy's. I will finish in the morning.

We haven't enough lumber to complete our house, but have the promise of some more Tuesday. We are very anxious to have it finished. We have our room, cook room & pantry in use.

We told Mr. Atkins we could feed him, but not sleep him. He dined with us twice. If nothing prevents, we will have a room ready for him the next time he comes around. He is very much pleased with our country. Mr. Orr said he was going to try to get you to come over this summer. I hope you will. Brother Billy might bring you over to spend a few days or a week, as I reckon he won't keep so busy all the time. Glad Ira is pleased and getting on so well. He must be feeling rich, bought him a gold watch and chain, or probably he is thinking about marrying. I hadn't heard Miss Fannie Bullock was married until I received your letter, and haven't heard any thing more about it. Did Bessie Doby marry well?

Today is such a pretty day that it looks like spring time & gardening. I expect you have commenced, but we haven't the lumber to pale a garden. Olin bought me White's machine, & I like it very much. Johnnie wants to get Kellie one like it. Sister Mary was much pleased with it.

Kellie has been confined to her bed a good deal lately, but is better. The Dr. said she was threatened with a miscarriage.

18th

This is another lovely day. It is Olin's birthday. Edwin has gone to the store with his pa. He isn't so much opposed to kissing as when you saw him. He is the proudest little fellow you ever saw of his new suit I made him for Quarterly meeting, trimmed in brass buttons.

I would like so much to see your baby. Love to bro. Billy, Ira, & the children, and write when you have time to.

> Your loving sister
> Annie Moores

Johnnie came by and eat dinner with us & then carried Kellie a glass of boiled custard & cake.

Mattie Hughes to Emma Butler Paisley in Dobyville

> Tulip Arkansas
> Feb. 19. 1878

Dear Sister Emma,

Yesterday we received the sad intelligence of the death of our dear bro. Lewis. Brother George sent a dispatch to brother Henry, stating that he died last Saturday morning at six o'clock, and that his remains were in a metallic case. Jennie will get there today, three days after his death!

We have received two postals from her, one from St. Louis and the other from Omaha. Said she was getting on well, felt hopeful and encouraged, as she hadn't received a dispatch. How much I do feel for her, will not hear of his death until she reaches Los Angeles! where I suppose brother George will meet her, and tell the sad tidings.

Yesterday we received a letter from Lucia Moores to Jennie, written on the 9, in which she said bro. L. was no worse, but very weak and got her to write for him, thinking it might weary him to write. Said he was not confined to his bed at all, and might be altogether better before she received that letter. She wrote that brother George had just gotten there, and she thought his coming would cheer him. The letter was written just two days before they dispatched for Jennie, and just a week before he died.

I know it was a great consolation to have bro. George with him. We are so anxious to hear the particulars of his death, and think brother George will write us, but it will be a week or more before we can get a letter from there.

> [no closing]

Ira Butler to Billy Paisley in Dobyville

> Tulip Ark.
> Feb 27th 1878

Dear Bro Billy

I was very much distressed when I reached the depot at Malvern, when Billy Cooper informed me of the death of Bro Lewis. I found Bro. Henry & Sister Mollie very much grieved, and on reaching home found grief pictured on the faces of all. It seems hard for me to realize that Bro. Lewis is dead & that I will never see him again in this life. When I think on the past it seems but a short time since he was at home, looking so stout & healthy & now he is dead. Oh; how sad a thing it is to die, & yet we will all have to die soon or late, and we should strive to make our calling & election shure, so that we will be prepared for the change. Pa received a letter from Bro. Moores written after his death, Giving an account of his death. He thought he was prepared to die.

I found Mr. Kirkendorfer still at Pa's, and wants to go into the Tomb Stone business, and we have been talking about going in that business right away. But since I have been with him several days am afraid he will be a very disagreeable one to be in business with. He has gone to Little Rock to see about making arrangements for some lots, but I have about concluded not to go in with him, but don't know for certain until he returns.

I wish now that I was back clerking for you, but it is too late to wish that so I will have to do the best I can for myself. I reckon I will go in business at Tulip, if I don't go into the tomb stone business. Have thought of going in business at Princeton & Malvern, but reckon I will go in at Tulip for the present, as I would have Pa to give me some assistance. Don't know how I will get my stock of goods. I will want my money, and would like to get it as soon as you can let me have it. How would it suit you to buy me a stock of goods when you go on to St. Louis this Spring? If you will buy the stock of goods for me I will be willing to bear half your expenses for the trip. Write me as soon as possible to let me know whether you will go this Spring, & what time you want to get off. If I go in at Tulip, would like to get them as soon as possible.

I sold my County Scrip this morning to Bro. George for two hundred and forty dollars. Did not make any thing on it. Have written to J. R. Butler & Co. for the amt. they owe me. I will have about eleven hundred and fifty dollars if I can get what Bro. J & Bro. O are owing me, but think I can get enough from Pa to make out the fifteen hundred dollars. If I conclude to sell goods at Tulip and you go on after goods this Spring & will buy my stock for me, it will not be necessary for you to send me a draft for the amt you are owing me.

Love to all. Write soon to your loving bro

Ira W. B.

You can take 90¢ from the amt I am owing you for the hymnbook.

Alice Butler to Emma Butler Paisley in Dobyville

Tulip Arkansas
Feb. 27th 1878

Dear sister Emma:—

Sister has written you the sad tidings of our dear brother's death. Although he has now been dead over a week, we can scarcely realize it even yet, being so far away from us all. We received a letter from bro. Moores by the last mail giving the particulars of his death, and oh what a comfort his letter was to us all! even though it opened afresh the wound so lately inflicted; it bore the happy news that our dear brother had passed away from earth, but only to enter a far brighter world where sickness and sorrow can never come. We all felt deeply grieved that we would never be permitted to look on that manly form, now cold in death; but oh! the thought of his not being prepared, was almost more than we could bear! especially Ma who seemed that she would almost give way under the burden.

Bro. Moores said, "I talked to him several times about his salvation, and told him that he must look to the Lord to make the medicine effectual to his cure, but if he should not get well, we would, friends and relatives all soon follow;" said he told him he must look to the Lord for help, and he responded "Yes." I will write you just what he said. "At family prayers a few nights ago, I prayed he might know he had a home in Heaven and he responded "Amen" so as to be heard all over the house, and when I prayed for his wife his response was again "Amen." Said he had been reading good religious books and papers. Bro. George has written and talked to him several times about his salvation, and he did not fear but what he would be saved; bro Moores said, "I have good grounds to believe he has entered into rest."

They did not sit up with him but two nights before he died, said he gradually grew weaker and weaker; bro George was by his bedside all the while, and it was such a comfort to bro. Louis to have him with him. Bro. Moores' letter was written on the same day he died; he said he seemed to rest better than usual that night until midnight, when he became restless; at half past five he went to his bedside and bro. George said he thought he was dying; and just a few minutes before six he breathed his last, without a struggle, not even seeming to draw a shorter breath. He said, "Thus passed away Louis P. Butler. A noble man never complained; but endured his severe sickness as a good soldier of Jesus Christ." Said they all felt it a mournful pleasure to wait on him, and do him all the good that was in their power.

Poor sister Jennie, how will she stand it, if we, as sisters, brothers, and *parents*, feel that only religion can comfort us in such an affliction, how much greater the loss which she sustains.

May our Heavenly Father who "doth not afflict any but for their good," comfort her heart in this hour of trial. Bro. Henry had a postal from her written from Ogden, and she was very hopeful then, when our dear brother had been dead several hours. Oh what a shock to her! When bro. Moores's letter was written, he said she would get there in three or four days, and they had placed his remains in a metallic coffin (the bringing out of which from Los Angeles and sealing it up cost $125.00) where he would be kept until she arrived, that she might bury him there or bring him to Ark. as she liked. Bro. G. would stay until she got there, and then hurry home as he had left his family all alone.

Ma says she appreciated the nice cabbage which you sent her so much, says you were so thoughtful. She hasn't done any thing in her garden yet, but has been getting ready. Ma says she thinks Willard is the best child she ever saw, so much like his Papa, and they both feel doubly dear to her now—they have gotten on very well since their Mama left. Little Willard is trimming off some sassafras root. Ma says she would like to send you some, as you were always so fond of it. No one here is very fond of it.

All unite in sending much love. I believe Ira has written to bro. Billy.

A.B.

Ira Butler to Emma Butler Paisley in Dobyville

Tulip, Ark.
March 17th, 1878

Dear Sister Emma

Your very highly appreciated letter has been received, and read with a great deal of interest. Have concluded to stay and work on the farm for Pa for three months at $10.00 a month, provided I can't find any thing else to do that is more profitable.

Bro G. received a letter to day from Sister Jennie. It was written the next day after she arrived at California. She was detained on the way by a wash out in the road, and did not get to California until ten days after Bro. L's death. She was detained only a day's ride from Cal & while there, she telegraphed to know how bro. L. was & received telegram that he was buried Tuesday, about seven days before she arrived there.

She speaks something of remaining in Cal. if she can get her children out there. Says she won't have money enough to raise her children like she would want to raise them. Says that Bro. George & Mr. Moores says she can put her money out on good security at 2 per cent a month, and there is a good many more ways that she can make money. She asks the advice of the family. We had been expecting her for some time.

How did Bro. Billy come out on selling his cattle?

And how are all the young ladies getting on? Write soon to your loving bro.

> Ira

Have written a very poor letter but will have to let it do this time.

> I. W. B.

Mary Butler to Emma Butler Paisley in Dobyville

> Tulip Arkansas
> Mar. 23rd 1878

Dear sister Emma:—

Your letter to me was received some time ago, which I have been promising myself to answer for a long time, but as others were writing concluded to wait. Pa and Ma appreciated the good letter you wrote them not long since, and also one from Jimmie received by last mail, writing of a great revival going on at college and a great many of the students had been converted—said he had never before been fully satisfied about his own conversion, but now he knew he was a Christian, and wanted us all to pray earnestly for Reavis' conversion, as he had reasons for believing that he has serious thoughts on the subject. Oh what a great thing if he could be converted, for he has never manifested any concern about the matter. Let us pray with faith, earnestly for him, as all things are possible with God.

Our first quarterly meeting was held at this place last Saturday and Sunday: we are very much pleased with Mr. Johnson, our presiding elder; he is such an excellent man; he brought his daughter, Maggie, with him who is a very nice girl: they have gone to Princeton, where the next quarterly meeting begins tomorrow. Pa thinks of going down and taking Alice, if he feels well enough; he has been feeble for several days. Our congregations here were larger than we have had in a long time, the weather being pleasant, and so many new comers in the neighborhood. Mrs. Goodloe Pattillo looked for Fannie Bullock, but she didn't come. You see she is not married yet, as you heard some time ago.

We received a letter from brother George by last mail written to pa and ma the 8th of this month, soon after getting back to his family. He was six days making the trip by stage, he remained one day after sister Jennie got there, which I suppose you have already heard took her a week longer than we expected to get there. We have the second letter from her, and still she thinks of making

327

that her home—says she can board for $30.00 a month, herself and children, at a place a mile from bro. Moores near a good country school.

Brother George [Hughes] has promised to take the children out to her after awhile, if she concludes to remain: we will hate very much to have them go so far away from us, for we have become much devoted to them and sis Jennie too: she is an energetic business woman and will live wherever she thinks she can do best; regardless of ease or pleasure. She can make $75.00 a month by loaning her money at 2 per cent, which I think she expects to do, when she gets it all together; which I think will be something over five thousand dollars.

You have already heard of dear little Jessie's misfortune, which will add fresh grief to her mother, who has scarcely heard of it yet: her fingers didn't grow together as we hoped, but the one next to the forefinger is still on but looks very dark, we still have some hope that it may be growing, as it has been three weeks since the accident happened. Jessie feels very well—is hearty and as fond of play as ever—hasn't suffered much pain since the first night. Willard keeps well all the time and is an excellent child, so happy and gay both of them: they can never realize their great loss.

Brother George's account of our dear brother's last moments causes tears of sorrow to flow afresh. The evening before he died he told bro George he would like to talk to him but couldn't—he was too weak and his voice nearly gone, he couldn't then speak above a whisper.

I received an excellent letter from Miss Hattie Bowman, sister Jennie's sister, she seemed to love bro. Lewis as an own brother, she writes—"Oh when I think how noble, how good, how fitted to adorn the world and benefit mankind by the example of his pure unselfish life, and his many virtues which shone brightest in the family circle, I cannot refrain from asking why, oh why must such as one be called away in the full glory of his manhood?" I may write something more after hearing from the mail this evening.

Pa has returned with the mail but no letters but one for Sister from bro. George [Hughes]—he went up to Little Rock last week, which is the first time he has been away in a long, long time, said he had written a long letter to sister Jennie and endeavored to cheer her all he could. Both of her letters were written to him principally on business.

Bro Charly and Kate were up to see us two weeks ago. Ma is writing some to put in my letter which she will have to do very hurriedly, as we will have to send letters up this evening to get them mailed. We write and receive a great many letters. I believe we had eight or ten by last mail.

Much love to bro. Billy. Does he expect to go to St. Louis soon? I am real anxious to see all of you. Love to Capt. Lipscomb and family.

Affectionately your sister
Mary

Write soon. Ira received bro. B's letter with card for which he is obliged. Bro Henry has been sick for several days but is now better.

Ma wants to know how it is that you raise such fine cabbage. What kind of seed and what time you plant them? Ira has just come, and sends his love, and will send you his likeness soon. Ma says that she feels that the quarterly meeting did her a great deal of good, says how are all the children, doesn't remember the red spot on the baby's neck.

Mary Wyche Butler to Emma Butler Paisley in Dobyville

Tulip
March 23, 1878

My dear Daughter,

I was glad to get your letter. It was a good one and did me good to read it. We also got one from Annie the same time. I do like to hear from the dear children. I am very sorry Ira left you. He was so well satisfied & getting on so well. I think he has been sorry ever since. He will feel the difference, working this hard poor land. Sorry his pa wrote any thing to him about Kirkendorfer. We haven't seen or heard of him in 2 or 3 weeks.

We were rejoiced to get such a good letter from James. I wish you could read it. It cheers us so much. I sent it to Henry. He seemed to be troubled about his condition, not feeling as he wished. They had a meeting there. I was in hopes it would do him good to read J's letter, as it did us so much good. Henry has been sick.

A glorious revival going on at Ashland. About half the students profest religion. James says he is no longer on doubtful ground about his conversion. He is rejoicing in the love of God. He is much concerned for Reavis, says we must all pray for his conversion. I have been praying for him. Oh, wouldn't it be a blessing to have him converted? I would be so rejoiced. It might have some effect on his papa.

We also received one from George [Butler] about his being with his Bro. L. It seemed I could see them. He says he wished to talk to him, but could not. He was with him to the last. I think it was the saddest night Geo ever experienced. It starts our grief afresh, to think that none of us could be with him. I do hope and trust it is well with him. We should not grieve. Wish you could see the dear little darlings. Willard is the best child I ever saw, so much like his papa.

Good night, my dear. Love to all. Your Pa sends love to you, Billy P &c

[no signature]

Alice Butler to Emma Butler Paisley in Dobyville

Tulip Arkansas
April 10th 1878

Dear sister Emma:—

Your letter was received some time last week, and as no one has written to you lately, I will answer mine this morning. I have been wanting to write bro. Billy a letter for some time, in order to vindicate my self, or rather sister Mollie's and my statement in regard to Miss Nannie Bullock, whom he has doubtless heard has not changed her name yet. He well remembers the little quarrel we had at Malvern about the above-mentioned lady; and in fact *ladies* in general. Just say to him that I was very much pleased when I heard that Miss Nannie had returned without marrying any Texas gentleman; and I think he had better hold his tongue the next time and wait until he knows a thing, before he talks about ladies going on a "bumming" expedition.

We had a letter from Jimmie a few days ago, he says their examinations will be over by the fourth of June, and that he and Reavis did not care to stay to the commencement exercises; so it will not be long now before they will be coming home. I think Tulip will be right lively this summer, for we have heard of several who think of making visits. Mrs. King from the river we heard was anxious to rent a place, so they could spend the summer out here. Mrs. Nat Smith is delighted to get back to her own home again, and in fact the whole family are pleased; Mattie Roane and Sallie are both grown now, and the former is quite pretty. Mrs. Roane has changed a good deal, looks considerably broken.

We had a letter from sister Jennie by the last mail; she still thinks of making California her home, at least a few years, and is anxious for us to send the children as soon as possible; she wrote that there was a minister and his wife coming out to attend the General Conference in Georgia in May and would return in June, and if they could not come any sooner, she could make arrangements for them to come out at that time. Don't know what she intends doing yet, but she said she would go to housekeeping as soon as the children came; was still boarding with Mrs. Moores. We will miss the children so much, now that we have become attached to them, and hate to give them up. Ma says she doesn't know how she will get on without Willard. She thinks he has a disposition so much like bro. Louis. We were surprised that you had never heard how the accident happened to Jessie. One day while out playing she chanced to find our oat cutter and began to turn it, putting some straw in at the same time with her left hand, and instantly ground off the ends of three fingers; It frightened us all very much and we sent for Dr. Cooper as soon as possible who sewed the ends back but they did not grow. They are healing up now and will, we think, soon be well, though her hand will be somewhat disfigured; she commenced school again last Monday a week ago.

I have one music pupil now—Candas Green, who has been taking lessons little more than a month; she learns very well, though it will be a little confining to me, as I will be compelled to stay at home more closely than ever. I am glad to hear that you are pleased with your new teacher. Tell bro. Billy I would like to go over. All unite in sending much love.

> Affectionately,
> Alice

I reckon sister Mary wrote you about the great revival they had at Ashland among the students. I am glad Jimmie seems to enjoy himself so much religiously.

You spoke of wanting us to send you some patterns; but we have none at all that you would like, want to get some to make up our spring and summer dresses. Ira says he will write to bro. Billy soon.

> A.B.

Emma Butler Paisley to William Paisley in St. Louis

> Home
> April 21st, 1878

My dearest one,

It is now nearly twelve o'clock, and as I have got Mattie asleep will try and write a while before they get back from church.

Mr. Patterson hauled the corn Friday morning, and would have set out some potato slips that evening, but the mules got out, so he and Mr. Jenkins had to look them up. They got out again this morning, and I don't know whether they will succeed in finding them so easily, as they went to Mr. Boyce's and he put them up.

I have not called on Fannie, but expect to do so this week if Mattie keeps well enough. I lost several of my little chickens night before last in that very hard rain and hail. The weather has not turned cool yet, but think we will have more rain as it is very cloudy.

Mr. Jenkins told me about the mule throwing you in going to Gurdon—it is a great wonder it didn't hurt you. I received your few lines from Arkadelphia and will look for a letter about Tuesday or Wednesday.

Mr. Brown Hall was up yesterday evening for the mule, but did not come in—he stopped at the store, and Ben said he seemed very cool toward him, on account of believing Ben had something to do with a valentine he received. I believe he left in good humor after Ben assured him he nor Miss Julia had any thing to do with it, and told him who sent it.

Mrs. Grier is down with Lizzie so I do not know whether she will stay any with me while you are gone or not. I had some trouble to get Willie to go to Sabbath school this morning—hope he will come home in a more pleasant humor.

After supper: Mr. Tidball is ready to go over to the store, so I will close and send it over, thinking some one may go to town before breakfast. Good bye my dear one; may God bless and take care of you.

Always your loving,
Emma

William Paisley to Emma Butler Paisley in Dobyville

St. Louis
Apl 22 1878

My dearest one,

I ought to have written you yesterday, but have been feeling so drowsy & sleepy since I left home, that I have not felt like writing. I went to hear Dr. Brooks preach yesterday morning but had some trouble keeping awake during the service. Yesterday being Easter Sunday was a big day in the Catholic & Episcopal churches here, but I did not attend, as I have long since concluded that it was wrong to attend a church where we cannot engage in the worship.

Think I have fully made up my mind to make a change in my commission house. I am now waiting in the office of the firm at the head of this letter to see old Mr. Kirtland to see what arrangements I can make with them. I may not do any better, but don't feel that I would [be] as satisfied to remain with Senter & Co.

Tell Ben if he has not yet used the blank drafts I left with him on Senter & Co—*not* to do so under any circumstances & that if he has used them to write me immediately. Should any one call on him he can tell them to wait until I return. I had quite a lonesome trip coming up. There are very few merchants in market now. Henry was up a week or ten days ago—Nothing more of interest now.

With much love to all I remain

Your devoted husband
Wm Paisley

William Paisley to Emma Butler Paisley in Dobyville

St. Louis, Mo.
Apl 22 1878   Evening

My dearest one

You will think me crazy but am not more so than usual—This morning I wrote you from the office of Kirtland Humphries & Mitchell, thinking then I would be certain to give them my com. business. This evening after talking with Senter & Co., & telling them of what I had to complain of, I think I may continue my business with them. Am at a loss to know what to do for the best & have not fully decided yet, but will try & determine for the best so far as I am able to judge. Don't say any thing about the letter this morning—that is—what I said about changing houses. Am anxious to be at home with you all, but will hardly get off before 1st part of week.

Yours devotedly
W. Paisley

Emma Paisley to William Paisley in St. Louis

Home
April 23rd, 1878

My dearest one,

I wrote to you last Sunday but don't know that the letter has left the store—it was still there this morning. Henry brought me your postal card this evening as he returned from carrying the teacher his dinner. Was glad to hear that you reached St. Louis in safety—shall look for you home Saturday unless you write differently. Dr. Doby was over a while yesterday evening, but thought Mattie did not need medicine—she has had no fever since Sunday night, but is fretful. Mr. Grier was over this evening for Dun, but he had followed the wagon off after corn. By the way, Lizzie has another daughter, born Sunday night. We had a very hard rain last night, and I had twenty or thirty chickens drowned, found fifteen dead in one coop. Had some potatoes set out yesterday evening and some okra, pepper, and nutmeg melons planted.

I don't know that I can get my photograph to you in time, but it will not make much difference, as I may get a better one taken. I have received no letters since you left, but sent off one last week to sister Mary, and have one to Alice ready to send off. I am looking for one from sister

Annie every day. The rain last night kept Ben and Mr. Tidball from coming over to supper, so they had to make out on a little snack at the store.

Every thing in the garden is growing very fast—think we can get a mess of peas tomorrow.

Well I will close. Hoping to see you very soon I remain your ever devoted,

Emma

J. Porter Paisley to William Paisley in Dobyville

Davidson College, N.C.
May 1878

My dear Cousin Will,

It gives me great pleasure to write to you & thus communicate the thanks I am not permitted to express "viva voce," for the very gratefully received token of your kind feeling for, & your interest in, your cousin Porter. I am of the opinion that your generous nature could not have found a more fit object upon which to bestow presents, & especially one like yours. I was just on the point of going to Charlotte to invest in a suit of clothes, when I received your letter. And I am sure you have my deepest feelings of gratitude for your kindness. Either Charley T[idball] must have given you a very accurate description of my size & figure, or else you made an excellent guess at to the same, for you could not have fitted me better. I have received many congratulations on my generous cousin in Ark. I was also much gratified to hear how much pleased you were with my friend Charley Tidball. I hope he will prove an excellent teacher, for he has the ability to make a first class teacher. I believe he is a novice in the business, however, & suppose it will take him sometime to get used to the work of teaching. He's the son of an extraordinary man. I think old Alamance is peculiarly blessed with good preaching.

Cousin, I would be delighted to see you & wife & *all* those six children of yours. I know they are lively little pieces if they are any thing like their Pa used to be, when I last saw him. Nothing used to do me so much pleasure, as to get you & bro. Will together. Those, I imagine, were happy days with you too. And then too, my Father was alive, & it seems that if it had not been for war, that destroyer of nations, our happiness might have been complete—but all too fleeting were the days of my Father's life. The death of that son, who was, I have no doubt, the dearest of us all to his heart, hastened his own. But thanks to an all wise Providence, we were left with a dear Mother, who has acted her part well, & now she & the rest of the family are living in harmony, & are getting along very well.

Cousin, I reckon Chas. has told you something of my success in college. I am first man in my class, & am a very hard student. I have been teaching this year, & thus make enough to board myself. I have to be very economical in my habits in order to get money enough to get along here. I don't ask my mother for help at all now, except clothing & such things as that. So you see I am taking practical lessons in economy, at the same time that I am trying to procure an education. I expect to go to Seminary after I get through here, i.e. after 2 more years here. Tell Charley I heartily congratulate him on his success, & to write to me.

Cousin, I would be glad to hear from you at any time, & will take pleasure in answering your letters. Hoping you will accept the thanks I have expressed for your kindness, & that I may be allowed to see you some time in the future, I remain your cousin

Jas. P. Paisley

P.S. I would have written sooner, but the suit did not get here until some days after I rec. your letter, & I wanted to tell you how it fitted.

Porter

Ira Butler to Emma Butler Paisley in Dobyville

Tulip, Ark.
May 19th 1878

Dear Sister Emma

I fully intended answering your letter sooner, & commenced one to you some time ago but did not finish it.

There is nothing particularly interesting to write abought. Sis Annie is now with us. Bro. O brought her over in the buggy. Bro. O left for Centre Point last Thursday. He thought of going by and stay all night with you, but did not know for certain when he left.

I went fishing yesterday on the creek and had a rather bad time. After I heard it thunder and quit fishing and went to get my horse to ride home, but when I got to the place where I had hitched him, no horse was to be found, and I had to walk home about three miles and most of the way in pouring down rain. I got completely saturated before I got home. I had the horse tied in Dr. Smith's feel. I went down to Dr. Smith's this morning to see if he had seen any thing of him, and found him in his stables. He had brought him out of the feel. I caught a tolerably good mess of fish. Caught one very nice trout, the rest were perch, cat, & jack.

I was somewhat supprised to hear of Boyce marriage. I thought it was Miss Burton he was waiting on in place of Miss Rollins. Who do you think will be the next to marry at Dobyville? How is Ben Logan & Miss Julia Orr coming on matrimonially speaking. Who is waiting on Miss Maggie Doby now? Dr. Ross was over at Centre Point sometime ago, looking for a situation to practice medicine, & he told bro O that he thought Miss Maggie was engaged to a young man in Mo. Write me all about the Dobyville young ladies. You wrote in one of your letters that Miss Mamie Doby & Miss Lila Adams were going to School. When will they have their vacation? What prospect would there be for you to store away Jimmie Pattillo and my-self for a few days this Summer? Jimmie wants to get acquainted with the Dobyville young ladies. We thought of coming over after we lay our crops by.

20th

Jessie and Willard will start for California some time in June. We think we have two chances of sending the children to Ca.—either by Mr. Law or Mr. Smith. Both expect to start for California about the same time. Would rather send them by the former if his wife returns with him. Mr. Smith expects to go on the freight train, and Mr. Law on the passenger. Would be on the road much less time than Mr. Smith.

A rogue has broken into Pa corn crib twice lately. The last time was last night. He tore off one of the slats off the crib inside the shuck house. This morning as I was going out to work, I noticed a track. I hollowed to Pa, who was sitting on the front porch, that I had found the rogue track. He & bro. G. came out then, & we proceeded on the trail & came to the fence by the church, and found the shucks & cobs of several ears of corn where the hogs had eaten. We then followed on the trail through Mrs. Hattie Pattillo's feel & Mr. Davis's in the direction of old uncle Joe's. While bro. G. & myself was trying to make out a track down by the fence, Pa called bro George in the direction of Joe's cabbin, & we went up there & found old Joe sitting up in bed, & Pa measuring his foot to see if it corresponded with the foot we had been tracing & found that it did in every particular. Pa then asked him where was his corn that he had stolen, had to ask him several times before he would acknowledge it, but finally said it was out in the crib. We went out there & found one bushel & a half shelled corn. He had shelled & shucked it that night & was sleep when Pa went in his house. He denighed of ever making but the one trip, but it was the same track the first time as the last. He offered to pay Pa for the corn if he would not say any thing about it. Pa said he started him back with the corn, but felt so sorry for him that he told him to carry it back, & get Mr. Davis to write him an order for that & some more. He is working for Mr. D.

We have a right good Sunday School now. Have 44 members. Still have our Singing every Sunday evening, but will change it to morning after Sunday School, excepting when we have preaching. Then we will have it in the eve.

Am glad bro. B. did not lose any more on Cot than he did. Think he did pretty well to come out as well as he did. Give my love to bro. B & B[en Logan] & tell the latter that I will try & write to him soon. It looks as if he is not going to write.

With much love for yourself & all, I am as ever your devoted bro.

Ira

Write to me soon. Excuse mistakes & bad writing

Ira

Mattie Hughes to Emma Butler Paisley in Dobyville

Tulip, Arkansas
May 31, 1878

Dear Emma,

I feel that we have [been] too negligent about writing to you for the last month or so. Since the weather has gotten warm I have felt very little like writing, haven't written but few letters to the boys.

If Georgie comes home as soon as he expected, when he last wrote, he will get here about the 10 of June. Said he would be through with his examinations about the 5 of June, and he didn't care to stay until after Commencement, as they were not going to have any good orators. I think Jimmie intends remaining, and Georgie may conclude to stay also, though he said he wouldn't mind coming home alone. It will be the last of June or the first of July before West is through. Walter has decided to spend another year in Germany. His health is very good now, and he continues well pleased.

Annie and the baby are very well, and have been all the time. Every morning directly after breakfast, I wash and dress the little "fellow," then he goes to sleep and doesn't awake more than two or three times during the day, and only once or twice during the night. Edwin didn't much like him at first, but now he is very fond of him. Olin says Ma must name him, that he never expects to name one. We have thought of several names, but haven't decided on any. Ma says it will be time enough to name him when he is a month old. He is not as good looking as Edwin was, though he is too young to know how he will look. I think his eyes will be blue. Olin got here on Friday, and the baby was born on Thursday morning, 23 inst. He was surprised and glad too, that it was over, and Annie getting on so well. He thinks of returning to Centre Point next week.

We haven't had a letter from Jennie very lately, but heard from her through bro. Moores, in a letter to Olin. He says she is reviewing her studies with the expectation of teaching school. They think a great deal of her, and say that no two people were ever waited on with more pleasure than she and brother Lewis. The children will leave for California in three weeks. George will take them to St. Louis, and from there a Mr. Smith and his wife will take charge of them to Downey City. They haven't any children, and have promised to take as good [care] of them as if they were their own. Jennie is to pay them for their trouble. We will miss the children so much, but we are anxious for them to go, for they ought to be with their mother.

We heard from Charlie and Kate last week, all well, but very busy.

For the last two weeks we have been feasting on dewberries. Ma has made about a gallon of wine, and preserved about the same. Olin also gathered some to preserve for Annie. I expect you have visited the patch, an old field just east of the house. I have been out there several times, and never saw as many before. We had very few cherries, only got enough to make two pies. We have but few good plums. I have been wanting to visit our old home, to get some, but it is rather far to walk.

The young people of the neighborhood are trying to get up some kind of an exhibition, consisting of dialogues and tableaus. They met here a few evenings ago to arrange matters. They want some one to take the lead, and I expect Mrs. Roane will have to come and take charge of affairs. She is the most suitable person I know of.

We are having some nice vegetables, fine Irish potatoes, beans, beets &c. I expect you have a fine garden, for I think you generally have an abundance of vegetables.

Ma has about 15 young turkeys, 11 of them nearly two months old, and doing finely. She has a great many young chickens. They commenced dying with the cholera, but Ma began feeding with dough mixed with water in which smart weed had been boiled, and it seemed to cure them.

All send love, I may add more after the mail comes. You must write whenever you can. George sends love, also remember us to Capt. Lipscomb and family.

> Your Devoted
> Sister

Kiss my namesake. I wish I could see her.

Mary Butler to Emma Butler Paisley in Dobyville

Tulip, Arkansas
June 24th 1878

Dear sister Emma:—

I believe I am owing you a letter so I must write this evening; yours to ma was received a few days ago which was a long time getting here.

Last Thursday dear little Willard and Jessie started for their long journey to California; pa, ma, and sister went up to Malvern with them, and brother George who had been in Little Rock several days, came out that morning to go on to St. Louis with them, where the arrangement was made for Mr. Smith to take them out to his house in Warrenton about fifty miles from St. Louis: they left Malvern about five o'clock Friday evening, the train being behind time. Mr. Smith and his wife will start with them for Cal. tomorrow. It was a great trial to part with the dear children, having been with us more than four months since their mother left; we felt as if they belonged to our household, and it seems very lonely here now without them, so many things to remind us of them. I told sister the other day I didn't think I could love an own child any more than I did Willard, he was so sweet and interesting. I generally attended to all his wants, and Alice to Jessie, and they loved all of us dearly and would have been satisfied to have lived with us always. Edwin misses Willard very much, and stays in the house nearly all the time since he left.

Sister Annie has not gained strength and improved as fast as she ought, doesn't feel as well as she did two weeks ago. She took a pill of bluemass [a mercury compound] this evening and will take another tonight. The baby is growing and improving rapidly—don't know who he favors. I believe the naming of him has been left to ma, and she has talked of naming him William Lewis, though I don't think it has been fully determined. Annie looks for bro. Olin the last of this week and thinks of returning home the next week.

We received a letter from bro. Moores last Friday. He said sister Jennie was studying very hard to be examined, so as to get a certificate for teaching school.

You must excuse this blot, for Edwin has upset the ink on it. Ma and sister have gone out this evening to see Mrs. Greybill's sick child. Alice and I were at Malvern week before last; a company of us went on the Ouachita fishing and had a pleasant time, but caught no fish. West got there in time to be one of the party and enjoyed it. He is looking thin, his health hasn't been good but has improved some since getting home. Reavis came first. We expect Jimmie this week. He remained till after Commencement, so they come one at a time. We didn't get a letter from Walter last week, and sister fears he may be sick.

You seem to take great interest in croquet to be playing by firelight: the game has died out with us, haven't played this year.

Tuesday 25th

Received a letter from Walter. He is very well. Ira and Jim Pattillo speak of going to Arka[del-phia] about the 4th of July and then going to see you. The night ma was gone to Malvern something caught five of her large sized young turkeys, which left only five. Ma says tell you she has very fine cabbages now heading up—sends her love and was glad to get your letter.

Sister got a letter from bro G yesterday written from St. Louis about the children, and oh, how it grieved us to hear that they cried as if their little hearts would break when he parted from them, leaving them in the hands of strangers. Bro G said he liked the looks of Mr. Smith, he is a cousin of bishop Marvin's. I think the children will be satisfied when they get acquainted with them.

Write soon to your sister

Mary

Mattie Hughes to Emma Butler Paisley in Dobyville

Tulip Arkansas
Aug. 13, 1878

Dear Sister Emma,

It has been some time since I wrote to you, though I think you have been hearing from us every few weeks. Since the weather has been so warm I have written very few letters, haven't written to Walter for nearly a month, but will try and write to him today. George or one of the boys have written to him every week.

Have you heard that sister Annie is quite sick, threatened with typhoid fever. She has been confined to her bed about two weeks, and we feel very anxious and uneasy about her. Sister Mary left for Malvern last Saturday, expecting to go over there, just as soon as she could hear from them. Since she left we had a letter from Johnnie, saying that he or Ira might come over this week for Ma or sister Mary. I hope they received sister Mary's letter telling them to meet her at Fulton, before they started over. If they should send here, I expect Ma will go over. We may hear something more this evening, if we do I'll write you. In Olin's last letter, written on the 6th inst, he said the doctor thought she would have to wean the baby.

Alice is at Collegeville now on a visit to Florrie Hunter, but I expect she will return the last of this week. Jimmie went up with her, and we look for him back today. When Alice left, she thought she might make a visit to you before returning home. As sister Mary is away, Ma thinks she had better come home and stay awhile first.

We were glad to see Mr. Logan and Julia Orr over, and hope they had a pleasant visit. I suppose they gave you a full account of the "Exhibition."

When are you going to make us a visit? There are so few here now, that it has seemed lonely for the past week. Just think, I am the only child at home. Ma suffers a great deal from the heat, said it was one o'clock last night before she could get to sleep. Papa hasn't been very well, feels weak and badly most of the time. But he will keep going, attending to something, and frequently comes in almost exhausted.

We had a long letter from bro. George [Butler] by the last mail. As it was written to sister Mary we sent it to her yesterday. He wrote about going fishing in the Ocean, said he took Aleck with him one day, and of course he was delighted. He is on a poor circuit and doesn't expect to get much pay. Says if Pa and Ma live five or six years longer, he expects to make us another visit, will bring his family and remain some time.

It has been about two weeks since we had a letter from Jennie. She writes much more cheerfully, since she has the children with her. She and most of bro. Moores family went to the beach and went in bathing, said the children screamed so she had to take them out. But they were delighted to stand at the water's edge, and let the waves wash over their bare feet.

Have you had much fruit this year? We have had very few peaches and scarcely any that were good. None to dry and haven't canned or preserved any yet, want to try and get some from Mr. Green's. West and Reavis gathered all the pears this morning. They were rather mellow, but will make very good preserves. We have on a kettle full stewing now, and will have about eight pds more that we will preserve whole. Ma has had more cabbages than she ever had before, but the nicest ones are all gone.

We had a letter from Walter this evening written July 30th. His health is very good, and he seems to be well pleased. He expected to leave about the 10 of this month for Switzerland, where he expects to spend a month or six weeks, make a walking tour over the country. George is here now, and has been all Summer. His health is very good. He and the boys weighed today, his weight was 140, Reavis 129, and West 110. West hasn't been very well, but I hope his health is improving, for he seems to feel better for the last few days.

All send love to you, Billy, and the children. Kiss my little namesake. I am anxious to see her. Write soon, and let us know when you are coming over. Your Loving "Sister"

M. W. Hughes

Jimmie hasn't come, nor have we heard from Annie today. As they didn't write, she must be better.

Did you know that Kellie had a little baby some time ago? She suffered a great deal, and when the baby was born, it was dead. She has been confined to her bed ever since, some times better, and at others worse.

Aug. 14

Ira came last night, got here about 8 o'clock. Annie is some better. She has taken a great deal of medicine, and is very weak. She continues to have fever. We will write to sister Mary by today's mail, to meet Ira at Arkadelphia Friday morning. Ma has the heat so badly she can't go.

Alice Butler to Emma Butler Paisley in Dobyville

Tulip Arkansas
Oct. 1st 1878

Dear sister Emma:—

It has been my intention to write to you some time since and when your last (written I believe to Sister) was recd. I thought I would reply immediately, but met with some hindrance at the time, and so it has been put off until now.

We were very much surprised to hear that Bro. B. had sold out his stock of goods, and sorry that his health has not been good of late; like a good many others who generally *look well*, he does not get as much sympathy as some. Would like very much to have seen John while at Malvern, I know he has grown a great deal. When are you coming to see us? I thought you would get over some time during the summer or fall. The boys, all except Jimmie, have left us. We miss them so much and will be still more lonely when he goes. He has agreed to clerk for bro. Henry, and will probably go up to Malvern the last of this week.

Had letters from Ira and sister Annie a few days ago; the latter is improving slowly, but is anxious

339

that Ma should come over and stay awhile with her. Ira said some one would bring the buggy over for her some time this week, and I suppose, as sister Mary has gotten well, she will come home in the buggy. I think they had quite a time of it, waiting on so many. All seemed to get sick at once. We felt very uneasy about sister Annie for a while, though I hope now that she will continue to improve and soon be well again; it seems that she is not able to sit up but very little—know she must have enjoyed your visit very much—I have been thinking of going over myself, but can't well leave home now, as my music pupil has commenced taking lessons again—have anticipated all the summer making you a visit, but could not get off.

Jimmie, Reavis, and myself went over to the Rock Springs camp meeting; had a delightful time and a good meeting, though there were more conversions on Monday after we left than there had been any previous day. We expected Mr. Sandy Winfield would be there, but he failed to come; his brother was there and preached some good sermons. Bro. Pope expects to transfer to the Georgia Conference before long, and of which I was very sorry to hear, for the Conference will miss him greatly. I have an invitation to attend the Conference, which is held at Hot Springs in Nov. Don't know yet whether I can go or not. Sister Mollie thinks of going.

Isn't it dreadful to think of the yellow fever sufferers and to think it continues without much abatement. I suppose you heard that Dr. Doby and another gentleman from Arkadelphia went to Memphis as volunteers; the last papers we received stated that Dr. Doby had been stricken and could not live. He was such a promising physician. I know his death will be much lamented. [Apparently he did survive, for he is mentioned in later letters.]   Afftly—

Alice

Mattie Hughes to Emma Butler Paisley in Dobyville

Tulip Arkansas
Oct. 7, 1878

Dear Sister Emma,

We were very sorry to hear, from Billy's letter to Pa, that little Mattie had been so sick. I hope she has entirely recovered, and that it will not be long until you can bring her to see us. I have been very anxious to make you a visit, wanted to go on from Malvern when the boys left, but we had no way of getting the buggy and horses to Tulip, and Pa was needing the horses to haul in his corn. If you and Annie were only living on a railroad, I could visit you occasionally. I was sorry to hear that your cook had left and that you hadn't been able to succeed in getting another.

We had a letter from sister Mary last week, and she wrote us that Annie's cook aunt Louisa had left and Olin hadn't been able to get any one else. If Ira comes over this week, I expect Mamma will return with him, to spend a few weeks with Annie, as she seems so anxious for her to come over. We want to get Clarissa to go too, to do the work, as it seems impossible to get any one over there. Annie was improving, sitting up and walking about her room.

Jimmie left early this morning for Malvern, where he expects to clerk for "Butler and Archer." He was the last one of the boys, and it will seem very lonely here without him or Ira, especially when Ma leaves.

We received a letter from Georgie by the last mail. They arrived at the University a day before the school opened, ready to begin their studies for another year. West's health improved a good deal during the last month, and he had commenced increasing some in weight. If he will continue to be prudent in his diet, and take sufficient exercise, he will be all right. Georgie was in fine health, and full of life and mischief. We get letters from Walter very regularly. His health has been very good and he has enjoyed his walking tour over Switzerland very much.

Alice and Mrs. Colburn went to bro. Charlie's last Friday, and we expect them to return today. They went alone in the Dr.'s buggy. Papa and Mamma are in very good health now; pa is feeling much better than he did a few weeks ago. George [Hughes] is here now and has been all summer. He sends love to you and Billy, and says he is anxious to make you a visit, but don't know when we can come. You must come whenever you can.

Alice was saying a few days ago, that she wanted to visit "sister Emma" and spend two or three weeks with her, but she had commenced giving Candace Green music lessons, and doesn't know when she can leave home. Her health is not good yet, though we think she is improving. We were weighed a few days ago, her weight 96, and mine 129.

James Pattillo left today for St. Louis to purchase goods. I expect bro. Henry returned this morning. Is Mr. Tidball boarding with you? and what has become of Mr. Logan? Love to all.

Your sister
M. W. Hughes

Have you nice cabbages like you had last fall? Ma hasn't any now, but some collards for winter. We haven't any apples to put up for winter.

Mary Butler to Emma Butler Paisley in Dobyville

Tulip Arkansas
Dec. 7th 1878

Dear sister Emma:—

It has been a long time since I've written to you. I don't know whether I'm owing you a letter or not, but it has been my intention to write you ever since your visit to Centre Point, where I received such kind attentions from you while sick, which were I know cheerfully bestowed by a kind and loving sister's hands: they were laughing at me to-day about having made my "will," and the only one I left anything to was you.

Sister made quite an extended visit after she left you, going to Little Rock to the fair, conference &c &c. I went up to Malvern and kept house for sister Mollie while she attended Conference. She and sister went in on Thursday, and returned Tuesday having had a most delightful time. Brother Henry and bro. Pope went together early Wednesday morning. The latter returned next day, having left his family at Malvern on their way to Georgia, to which conference he has transferred on account of bad health here. Cousin Laura Scott with her baby came on the same train, and staid with sister Mollie, so she had quite a company that night. Fannie Caldwell was also there, beside bro George, sister, and myself. Mrs. Pope's mother was with her, besides the three children. Sister had a special invitation to stay at Mr. John Kimball's, who is an old friend of brother George's. Brother Henry and sister Mollie were at the Avenue Hotel free of charge.

A large number of preachers and their wives spent the night at Malvern on their return, so sister Mollie was again crowded. There were more visitors at conference this year than usual, as a great many were anxious to see the Hot Springs. Mrs. Colburn went from here first to see her sister in Little Rock, and then went with Sammie out to conference. Bro George, sister, and I returned from Malvern last Wednesday. Pa went up in the buggy for us.

You remember the night it turned so cold and we had a little snow? That night Mrs. Gantt's residence was entirely destroyed by fire, and almost every thing she had: they did'nt wake till two o'clock and the top of the house was then falling in. Mrs. G and two children, Cora and Ned, were the only ones there, except two negro children. It must have been very alarming to be aroused by fire that time of night, and no one to help save anything. Lem Prior Smith and some negroes got there, but too late to do any good; it is thought to have been caused by some ashes taken up that evening and put on the steps; though I've heard that Mrs. G thinks that some one set it on fire. Dr. Robinson sent them down twenty dollars of clothing next day, and telegraphed to Tommy Martin of the misfortune. I suppose he will help them some. I havn't heard where Mrs. G intends living, but met her going to Malvern the day we came down. I was very sorry when I heard of the accident: such places can never be rebuilt in our country. It ought to make us more careful about fire when we hear of these things. I was at Malvern at the time and thought, just suppose I had heard that our home and every thing had been swept away so suddenly; what a shock it would have been! and yet we have had some narrow escapes.

Have you heard of brother Henry's misfortune? Not long since a thief raised the dining room window, went into his room and took his watch and seven dollars in money out of his pants pocket, and he knew nothing of it till morning; also got something out of the safe to eat. I suppose he will never find any clue to the robbers. I was careful to have every thing securely fastened while I was there, and had Jimmie to sleep at the house. A great many tramps are constantly calling for something to eat—one night [one] came in just after the young men had left, and there was no one in the room but the children and myself. I got him some bread and meat as quickly as possible, and sent him off. They are certainly a great nuisance to the country.

Sunday 8th

This has been a rainy dreary Sabbath day—no preaching, though it was Mr. Davis' appointment. He is our preacher for next year.

Brother Olin expects to leave in the morning for St. Louis; he and pa have concluded to see what they can do in the way of selling goods here at Tulip. I suppose the busines will be small, but that will be better than doing nothing. Annie has improved a good deal since she came over, but still unable to lift the baby or do anything scarcely: they will board with us this winter. I hope her health will soon be restored. I expect bro. G. and sister will also be with us most of the time; so you see our family will not be so very small.

Sister enjoyed her visit to you, said you spoke of coming to see us Christmas. I do hope you can come, for it has been a long time since you were here, and I think you and bro. Billy would enjoy getting away from the cares and duties of home for a while, as all of us do some times. We can't promise you any great enjoyment—outside of being with relatives and friends, for Christmas of late years has been a dull time with us: if the weather should be pleasant we might have some games of croquet. Be sure to come, and we will endeavor to make your visit pleasant.

I wish you could get acquainted with cousin Johnny from Va. he is very pleasant, and was anxious to visit you and bro. Johnny before he went to the river; he left nearly two weeks ago—expected to board at Mr. John Pryor's in Arkansas City.

We hear from sister's boys frequently. They seem to be getting on well. I believe Walter wants to remain another year in Germany; he writes as if he had fallen in love with a beautiful American girl out there, but we think he only wants to tease his mama.

We have heard nothing from Cal. in a long time. From the papers I notice bro. George is sent back to the same place he was last year.

Charlie is still selling ware. He was at Mr. Welch's last week for a load, but didn't come to see us, as it was out of his way; he and his family, I think keep well. A letter from Ira by last mail, he seems to be getting on finely. I suppose you hear from him.

I have written eight pages and it is now bed-time. Love to bro. Billy and the children. All send love. Annie is not feeling so well tonight—has pain in left lung. Kate Caldwell is to be married to Mr. Ryland the 19th of this month. She has invited Alice and I to be present on the occasion, although I believe it is a secret yet. Little William Lewis [Moores] is a sweet baby, and is growing and learning rapidly. He sits on the floor and minds himself a good deal. Ma said she wanted to send some word to you. Write soon to your ever loving sister

Mary

P.S. Ma says you must come to see us whenever you can, she was glad to get home again after her long visit to Centre Point though she had a pleasant time.

Mattie Hughes to Emma Paisley in Dobyville

Tulip Arkansas
Jan. 21, 1879

Dear Sister Emma,

Your letter was gladly received and read with much pleasure, a few days ago. We were very anxious to hear from you, felt a little uneasy about you, after having so much cold disagreeable weather. Colds have been prevailing everywhere we hear from. All of the family here have been nearly sick from cold. At Malvern they have been suffering a good deal, and Jennie writes us that in her neighborhood, two thirds of the people were sick from cold. Sister Mary has been quite sick for eight or ten days, confined to her bed most of the time, for the last two days, she hasn't sit up but very little. We hardly know what is the matter with her, though I think she has had some fever most of the time.

I commenced writing this morning, thinking I would have time to write you a long letter, but was interrupted by company. Mrs. Colburn came first, then Hallie Pattillo, and after she left Miss Ellen Young came and spent some time. Now brother Charlie is here, and it is after supper, so I can't write you as long a letter as I expected.

Sister Mary has felt tolerable well today, and Dr. Sims, who called to see her this evening, says she is free of fever, and thinks if she hasn't any fever tonight or tomorrow, she will soon be well. We were very uneasy about her for two or three days. She hasn't been well since Christmas, lost her appetite, and I think had fever some time before she took her bed. She is very poor, about as thin as any one I ever saw. She has very little appetite, and hasn't taken any solid food for four or five days. I think now with careful attention she will soon be well.

Kate [Charlie's wife] has a little girl two weeks old, named "Alice Palmer." Her mother is with her, and she is doing very well.

I had a long letter from Jennie a few days ago. I don't think she is much pleased with California, she says there are a great many dissatisfied people there, a good many out of employment, and can't get anything to do. She advises brother Charlie never to come to California. She sent the children's photographs, and they are excellent, wish you could see them. By the mail today I received a letter from Julia and brother George [Butler]. They were sent back to Guadaloupe, and live in the same house they did last year.

Annie has improved a good deal since she has been here. She has a cold now, and coughs more than she did some time ago. The baby hasn't been very well. He has had a very bad cold, and teething too, makes him more fretful than usual. He was very good, not much trouble until he took this cold, would sit on the floor and amuse himself a good part of the day. Pa and Ma have been very well, and Alice has been in better health than she was last Summer.

Ma sends her love to old Mrs. Greer. She wants to know how she fixes up rice so nicely for sick people. She told her once, but she has forgotten how it was. Did you know that Olin Smith was dead? he was buried in the graveyard here last week. The weather was so bad that none of [us] went to the burial.

They have been doing very well at the "new store," some days take in as much as $25 in cash.

George [Hughes] is in Little Rock now, went up last week. I expect he will return home in a few days. The boys were very well when we heard from them a few days ago. Did you read that letter of Mr. Howell's written to his mother just two weeks before he died? It was published in the "Observer," and one of the best letters I ever read. How comforting to a mother to have such a son!

I will stop now and add a few lines tomorrow, to let you know how sister Mary is.

Wednesday morning, 22 Jan.

Sister Mary slept well last night, is clear of fever and we hope now, that she will soon be well. How is little Mattie? Is she gaining in flesh?

Pa bought brother Henry's old place from Mr. Davis, paid five hundred dollars for it. Olin and Annie thought of going over there to keep house, but I believe now they have concluded to board here this year, that is, until Annie gets entirely well.

We heard not long since that Mary Scott [Billy's sister] was thinking of going to Malvern to live, thought she might make something there by keeping boarders.

All send love to you Billy and the children. Write whenever you can, with or without a pencil.

Your Affectionate
Sister M. W. Hughes

Ira Butler to Emma Paisley in Dobyville

Centre Point, Ark.
Feb 10th, 1879

Dear Sister Emma,

I am very anxious to hear from you & Bro. Billie. Has been a long time since I have heard from you. I have been thinking of writing to you or Bro. Billy for a long time, and commenced a letter to you but never completed it. This truly has been a severe winter. Don't think I ever experienced such a severe one before.

There is a good deal of pneumonia and colds in the country now. I have had a very severe cold and was fearful that I would have pneumonia, but have nearly recovered from my cold. Bro. Johnnie was confined to his bed several days with cold and fever. Came near having pneumonia and would, if he had not taken a course of medicine. He was able to be at the store today, but was feeling weak. Hope you and the rest of the family enjoy good health.

Our quarterly meeting came off last Saturday and Sunday a week ago. Had some very good sermons from our Presiding Elder, bro. McGloflin. It would have been pleasanter sitting if we had had stoves. We have sent for a stove for the church, and it is now at the depot at Fulton. Jones & Bro made our church a present of a chandolier.

Our church would compare favorably with a city church, if it was painted and had blinds for the windows and a nice bell in the belfry, but the work that has been put on it, has not all been paid for. There is some talk of having a supper to finish paying for it. Something of the kind would take well at Centre Point, as it would be new to the most of the people.

How is bro. Billy succeeding in collecting his debts? Hope he has succeeded well. How is Ben and Miss Julia getting on in regard to a matrimonial sense? I thought in the Summer that probably they would have married before now. How is Boswell getting on merchandising? Is Mr. Tidball still teaching school? Who is going to see Misses Mary and Maggie Doby? Write me about the

Dobyville girls, who has married and who is going to marry &c. I have written to two young ladies asking them to correspond with me, but haven't received answers yet. You are acquainted with one of the two, but the other you never met, and I never met her but once, & only saw her for about ten minutes. I was very much pleased for the acquaintance I had with her. Won't tell you now their names.

Bro Johnnie & myself are getting on very well merchandizing. Lost some on cotton in the early part of the season, but will make up what we lost if cotton continues as it is now. Have shipped about two hundred and fifty bales this season. Most of our cotton is on shipment.

It is now getting late so I will close for this time. Love to all. Write soon and a long letter to your loving brother

Ira W. Butler

Mary Butler to Emma Butler Paisley in Dobyville

Tulip Arkansas
Mar. 17th 1879

Dear sister Emma:—

Your letter to me was received long since, and I must try to answer though I've gotten entirely out of the way of letter writing since I've been sick. This will be only the second letter I've written since Christmas: the other was in reply to one received from sister Julia.

After recovering from the spell of fever, Alice and I both commenced having chills at the same time, which served us very badly; and it is hard to break them. I think I had one yesterday, but kept it off today; quinine affects my head so that I'm trying "Ayers ague cure." Alice went home with bro. Charly last Friday week to see if a change wouldn't be beneficial, we haven't heard from her since the first day after getting there. She was then feeling very well: both of us are looking extremely thin.

I am greatly obliged to bro. Billy for his kindness in offering to come over for me, and think the change would improve me more than anything else; but it would be expecting *too* much for him to come during such a busy season. I wish I was with you without the trouble of getting there. I haven't been to church or any where in the neighborhood since Christmas—have never been to see Annie since she has been housekeeping, she left here three weeks ago—bought bro. Henry's old place. Her health I think is improving. She was with us all day yesterday, staid with me while the others went to church. Wednesday will be sister's birthday, and Annie has a large turkey gobbler to kill, so she wants us all to come over there and take dinner. I hope I'll not have a chill before that time, as I am anxious to go.

Bro. George went to Little Rock last week. He expects to go to St. Louis, and will purchase our organ for the church. I expect he will be home again next week.

Sister has gone to see Mrs. Cooper this evening. Her health is not good, and her mind is impaired; she has been very sad ever since Kate married, and seems to be growing worse. She thinks she can't live many days and feels that she will be lost. I feel very sorry for her. She is afraid to stay by herself even the shortest time in the day. Dr. Cooper and Howell are the only ones at home. She had a white woman living with her, but she left Saturday—said she couldn't stand Mrs. Cooper. Ma and sister went up that evening and carried them their supper, as Mrs. C. is not able to do the cooking. Mr. Fraser, a cousin of Ma's who was a member of the legislature, got acquainted with bro. George, and promised to make us a visit, but he wrote by last mail that he would have to hurry home to see his wife and little ones—sent his photograph to sister. He lives in the northern part of this state. His parents you know live in Ala. I am sorry he didn't come to see us.

Mrs. Maria Baird from N.Ca. is here now visiting her parents after an absence of twenty years. Ma and Sister called on her last week. She has her youngest child with her, a little girl five years old. They expect to remain until May—she has six children.

Mrs. Ed Gantt is staying at her father's. She and Cora, I've heard, wanted to get a school somewhere.

Mrs. Dick Gantt is living at Dr. Robinson's place and takes boarders. Dr. R. and Alice board with her.

Haven't those families been broken up rapidly in a few years? I've heard that Cora was very sad since the death of Mr. Gantt.

Johnny writes us that he expects to bring Kellie to see us this summer. He seems delighted at the great improvement of her health. She is now able to walk to the store. Ira seems to be getting on very well. He still talks about trying to get him a wife.

Sister had a long letter from sister Jennie not long since. She seems better pleased with Cal. Her health has improved, and the children's too. Jessie is learning fast—she has written several letters back to Alice and myself. I must answer hers as soon as I finish this. It came while I was very sick. How is Emma getting on learning? Tell her it is time she was beginning to write to me. And John and Willie are getting to be large boys and a great deal of help.

Jimmie stays at Malvern, closely attending to business, never comes down, but writes occasionally.

Our family seems small since Annie left, only four at present. Ma has some vegetables up, though I think our garden will be backward. Much love to bro. Billy and the children. Write soon.

Lovingly your sister

Mary

Excuse writing

Wednesday 19th—

This is a beautiful day, and I am feeling well. Went to see Mrs. Cooper yesterday evening. She was looking better and more cheerful. Receive letters from sister's boys every week—one from Walter yesterday. Bro. George thinks of going with West to Europe this summer if he gets through at the University—will take sister if she wants to go. Reavis will spend vacation with us.

All send love.

Lovingly your sister
Mary

Annie received an excellent letter from Mr. Matthews. His wife died in Jan. & he is much grieved.

Annie Moores to Emma Butler Paisley in Dobyville

Tulip Arkansas
May 6th 1879

Dear Sister Emma,

Your letter was received last week, and I am determined I won't be so long replying as before. It surprises me that you find time to write as often as you do. I am glad to know you expect to visit us this summer. We looked for Johnnie and Kellie last week, as two men came from over there said they would be over that week. We felt disappointed as we were expecting them every day— Annie P. Allford wrote she, her father, and sister-in-law, would be over this week if nothing happened to prevent, but it rained last week and commenced again Sunday, and has been raining most ever since, until this evening. It is still cloudy but some cooler. It has rained a good deal, but I don't know whether the waters will be up enough to prevent her coming this week or not.

Jimmie came down last Saturday week, to take Alice to Malvern on Monday, and brother Henry brought her home last Saturday. I think she has improved some. It seems hard for sister Mary to get rid of the chills, she looks as well if not better than Alice. Nannie came with her pa [Henry] & they returned Monday. Bro. Henry & Jimmie got down in time to enjoy the strawberries. We have had a nice time eating them, but they are most gone. Ma told me to send Ellen down this evening to gather some for me if it didn't rain. I go down once or twice a week. The gardens at this place have almost been destroyed by the cut-worms. I never knew them so destructive before. It will be poor living without gardens. Every thing is very scarce now in the eating line. We have had some May cherries, but the birds eat them almost as fast as they ripen. I think we will have plenty of plums.

The organ creates a good deal of excitement among the young people. Mr. Davis preached for us last Sunday, and that was the first time it has been used a preaching. It is a very nice organ, cost $95 dollars.

Alice has to do the playing & Sue Pattillo doesn't want her to be absent a single Sunday, because the organ could be used. I received a good letter from Mr. Matthews last Saturday. He is coming over to see us in June, and will preach for us on the 4th Sunday, if not providentially hindered.

Mrs. Guggenheim died last Thursday. She gave birth to a seven months child on Sunday. She left two little ones to be motherless in this world. She said she didn't know what to do with them, but told her husband to keep them at home. I suppose she had no near relative she felt willing to leave them with. I don't know whether she felt prepared to go or not. How important it is to be ready at any time for life is so uncertain. Olin had a good long letter from his pa last week. He always urges us to live for eternity, and that is of more importance than all things else.

Ellen has had the baby and Edwin off ever since I have been writing, but they have come, and I will have to let Ellen go down home & gather strawberries. Olin brought over a dozen oranges, and it would do you go[od] to see Edwin & Lewis eat them. I am glad the children got on so well with the measles. Olin unites with me in love to you & bro. Billy & the children.

Write when you can.

Affectionately sister
Annie Moores

I heard you had a P.O. now at Dobyville, but not being certain will direct as I have been. Love to Capt. Lipscomb & family when you see them.

Mary Butler to Emma Butler Paisley in Dobyville

Tulip Ark
July 21st, 1879

Dear sister Emma:

It has been some time since the reception of your letter, which I should have replied to long ago, but somehow I have gotten out of the way of writing letters since the warm weather set in, and now I'm in debt to all my correspondents and must begin to answer or I'll not get any more letters soon. Received one from Mary Scott a month ago, and was surprised to learn that she hadn't heard from any of you in so long.

Mrs. Rohrbough (Miss Mary Cooper) still continues to write me long interesting letters, and seems as much interested to hear from all of her old friends as ever, and always sends love to every member of our family. She always speaks affectionately of her two little boys, aged eight and five. Miss Laura spent the winter with her—doesn't it seem strange that Miss Mary is married to a Methodist minister and living in a parsonage? They also teach school.

I enjoyed my visit to Malvern. No doubt Alice told you I had gone up to attend the exhibitions and a "fish fry" over on the river five miles from town. Went in the buggy with brother Henry and sister Mollie. It was the first time I ever saw any one seining—it was a curiosity to see the large fish they caught. The river bank was lined with crowds of people eager to see. Five young ladies from Tulip and two from Arkadelphia were there—all seemed to enjoy themselves, and regretted that Sue and Alice couldn't be there, though they didn't seem to have any regrets about it—and said they couldn't have enjoyed it more than they did their Dobyville visit—they were all perfectly delighted.

I suppose you are now expecting brother H. and sister Mollie to visit you, as we heard they were going over. May [Henry's daughter] is still with us, and seems to enjoy herself, though after Coulter and Mattie went home she seemed to be lonely, and for the first time said something about going home. May has just come in, and sends love to you and also to her mama if she is there. West can tell you all the news.

We are looking for Mrs. Feild, Florrie Hunter, Mattie Hughes and her brother George tomorrow week, as they have written they will be here then. I don't know how long they will remain.

And now, what about your visit? We are all anxious to have you come, and want you to have as pleasant a time as possible. I know you would enjoy it much more to be here when there are none but the home folks, so I write you about these others coming so that you can use your own pleasure about the time of coming.

We will be disappointed if you don't come to see us some time this summer or fall. The weather has been very warm, but I hope it will be pleasanter now that we have had a good rain. All send much love.

349

Excuse this, as I have written very hurriedly, and it is time now for me to see about supper. Alice is not feeling well today.

Write soon to your loving sister

Mary

Mary Butler to Emma Butler Paisley in Dobyville

Tulip Arkansas
Nov. 2nd, 1879

Dear sister Emma:—

When I reached Malvern I found brother Henry awaiting me. I spent a pleasant night with them, and left for home on the stage next morning. Jimmie was looking a little thin from the spell of fever he had, but said he was feeling very well again. Nannie had a chill that day. Mrs. Williams came to see me while there, and is looking natural though some older.

I was astonished when I got to Malvern to learn that Annie had a daughter several days old, born last Friday week, the 24th of Oct. It was unexpected, and the Dr. didn't get there in time. Ma and old Mrs. Wilson and Viney, the white girl, were the only ones there. Sister and Alice being away, I was needed at home very much, as ma had to be with Annie, and pa and Ira were here alone. You can imagine how lonely it looked to me when I got here Thursday evening and found no one at home. I went immediately over to Annie's, where I found ma, and had a pleasant time talking with them—found Annie and the baby both doing well; it is a very small child, weighed seven pounds. No name has yet been decided on. Pa came by in the evening, and I came home leaving ma with Annie, and after supper pa and Ira had to go out to look after some fire that was getting near his fence, and didn't get back till 8 o'clock, so I was left entirely alone. Bro Olin came down late Friday night and will go back tomorrow morning.

William Lewis is more trouble than the baby. We kept him here last night. I took him to sleep with me and he kept me awake all night. Ma has him in her room tonight. I hope he will not be so troublesome tonight. He is almost sick with a cold, and Annie was afraid he was taking whooping cough.

I was glad I got home when I did, as the flowers were suffering for attention, and the weather turned so cold I had to take them in; they are looking very pretty blooming in the hall. Old Mrs. Matlock is very sick—not expected to live. Dr. Reamy was to see her yesterday. Ma and I expect to go to see her in the morning, though I learn that company is not allowed in her room.

Mr. Davis preached for us today, his last sermon for this year—gave out an appointment for Sammy Colburn the first Sunday in Dec. He will be on his way to Conference. I met all my old friends, and they expressed themselves as being very glad to see me back again. Mrs. Goodloe Pattillo was not well enough to be at church today. Kate Cooper was at her mother's today and went by to see Annie this eve. I have curiosity to see her baby. I saw Mr. and Mrs. Robertson at church today both looking very sad, but the sermon was comforting to them.

I got letters from Sister and Alice while at Malvern. They are all improving, and I expect will be home in a week or so. Ma and pa keep well. They enjoyed those nice apples I brought.

It is getting late and I must go to bed. All send love and are anxious to hear from you. I would like to have been with Mary [Scott] while she is with you, but it was best that I came home. Have you still got "aunt" Sylvia with you?

Love to all. I know the children are having a nice time with Lula. Write soon

Afftly your sis
Mary

Mary Butler to Emma Butler Paisley in Dobyville

Tulip Arks
Dec. 9th 1879

Dear sister Emma:—

I will write a short letter tonight to send by Mr. Nesbitt tomorrow; he tells us you are all well, and that Mary Scott is still with you. I am glad she is, for I know she will assist you so much.

We first heard of our new niece through Mr. Jack Doby last Wednesday night. He told West at our choir meeting, and on our return home we were surprised to hear of it—glad to learn you are feeling so well. [Lula Grier Paisley was born in November 1879.]

Mr. Lem Smith and Lola Garmany were married this morning at ten o'clock at Mr. Dunlap's, no one invited from here but Ira and West. The ceremony was performed by bro. Caldwell, after which they all went to dine at Mrs. Smith's. Brother Caldwell left for Conference immediately after marrying them, and took ma with him. They expected to go only twenty miles this evening. Brother Hunter and his wife staid with us last Saturday night and Sunday. It was like old times to have them with us. Bro. H. preached one of his good sermons for us Sunday at eleven. In the evening they went to Princeton.

Annie improves very slowly, not able to sit up much, and is very thin. She requested the united prayers of the church for her recovery, which was announced by bro. Hunter publicly last Sunday. I do wish she could get well and stout again.

Ma hated to leave on Annie's account, but there were so many of us to attend to her, and we can write and let her know how she is. I believe she is as low as she was as Centre Point. The baby, whose name is Mary, is growing fast, but seems to have colic every night. Sister and I take it time about staying in the room with Annie to attend the baby and wait on her. William Lewis sleeps in his cradle in ma's room. I don't know how he will get on without his grandma. I hear him now waking and I'm afraid pa will not get to sleep much. Coulter came down this evening in the wagon with Ira. He says they are fixing to have Christmas trees at Malvern. I know John and Willie would enjoy seeing them: do they still talk of going there Christmas? Jim Reid and Sallie Lea are to be married on the 18th of this month. They are to have twelve couples of waiters. You see they are beginning to marry around Tulip again.

I wrote to bro. Billy about having sent the book to Arkadelphia which I promised—hope he has received it. I think he will do well merchandising at Dobyville.

I am so hurried every time I write you, I will have to close now and see about Annie and the baby. Sister has gone to bed, as she slept so little last night.

351

West speaks of going to Dobyville with Mr. J. Doby when he returns from Pine Bluff, though he is not fully determined—his health has been improving lately. A letter from Walter this evening. Love to Mary and bro. B and the children. Write soon, or get Mary to write for you.

Lovingly your sister
Mary

William Paisley to Emma Butler Paisley in Dobyville

St. Louis
Dec. 17th 1879

My dearest one,

I have been thinking until to night that I would certainly get through in time to get home Saturday, but in order to do so I would have to leave here early Friday morning, so that I would have all my work to finish up tomorrow. I will probably not come home till Tuesday, as I feel that it is not right to take in Sunday when it can be avoided. Should I not come Saturday, ask Mr. Hall to be sure and get a wagon to go to Gurdon Tuesday, as I think there will be goods there by that time, and I can come home on it. If he can get any one to do so without extra charge, would like for them to go to Gurdon Monday evening & stay all night & return Tuesday morning.

There are not many merchants here buying goods, but the stores are crowded with people buying Christmas things. The toy & funny goods houses particularly are doing a big business. It has been quite cold here & the wind on the streets is very cutting. Ice is flowing down the River in large quantities, but the river has not frozen over here yet.

I am very impatient to get home, and feel that I have been away a long time. Wish the children could be here to see the many Christmas toys on exhibition. Tell Jno & Willie that I have bought their boots & that they are very nice ones. Have not bought your & sister Mary's shoes yet, but will try & find something good for you. Have been working hard in order to get goods shipped & to get thro by Friday. Consequently have not taken time to pick up little things. Cotton is reported a little better to day.

With much love to all, I am as ever your devoted husband

W. Paisley

William Paisley to Emma Butler Paisley in Dobyville

Senter & Co.
St. Louis, Mo.
Apl 2nd 1880

My dearest one

I reached here on time this morning, & now only have a few minutes to write in order to get this off in time for you to get it by tomorrow's mail.

Expected to write you from Malvern, but found so many to talk to & so much to talk about, did not have time.

Saw Annie Wednesday evening & yesterday morning. She is looking exceedingly thin, & I might say in one sense very badly, but still she looks bright & seems to keep in very good spirits—thinks the oxygen treatment is benefiting her. I can but hope she will recover. Henry's business is in terrible fix. An inventory of all the assets of B & Archer shows that the concern is not worth as much as when they commenced business 4 years ago, & that it is owing nearly as much as the assets amt. to. Haven't time to write more about it. Don't know what is to become of Henry & his family.

I unexpectedly met Mr. Burke—the Prescott preacher—on the train yesterday. He is called to Mo. to see his mother, who is not expected to live. Can't say when I will get through. My cold seems to be some better, but not well yet. Slept tolerably well last night, but feel a little stewed this morning. It rained on us very hard all the way from Little Rock to St. Louis. Will write again soon. If you get this Saturday, write me the first of the week care Senter & Co.

With much love for you all

Your devoted husband
W.P.

William Paisley to Emma Butler Paisley in Dobyville

St. Louis
Apl 8th 1880

My own dear one:

I went down to Senter & Co. office this morning & was handed your letter of the 4th. After learning from it that you had written to me care of Orr & Lindsley, I hurried to their house & found that one too, so I was made doubly happy by the reception of two of your dear precious letters at once. I might have gotten your first several days since, but I bought my shoes Saturday, & had been so busy I had not been back till this morning. I don't think your letters were ever more gladly welcomed, although they are always prized as something peculiarly *precious* by me.

The prospect of losing smartly on the Doby lot of cotton has made me rather low spirited all week. And your letters made me forget all that. You did right in telling me your troubles, & you

353

need never imagine, my dear one, that you will *trouble* me in the sense you fear by imparting such things. It would trouble me to think that I could not share them with you. I thought of you all day while at work, & have determined that if Sister Mary [Scott] can't see that her ways are not agreeable, I shall feel it my duty to inform her. I cannot bear much longer to have my dear one constantly annoyed in *her own house & home*, but as I hope to have the pleasure of seeing you very soon after you get this I will not say more now. I am nearly through, but found this evening that I could not finish up in time to start home in the morning. I hope to get off Saturday morning, which will cause me to get home again on Sunday, but it seems unavoidable.

You will please send Walter down early Sunday morning with a horse for me—he can ride Jim & get a horse from Mr. Jones for me to ride. If Charlie Wingfield can leave the store, I would like for him to go down Saturday evening, so that I could come right on home, & that would require less Sunday work. If too late for him to come all the way, he might go as far as Mr. Huffmans & take an early start from there.

I have bought a right full stock, & had no difficulty in getting all the credit I want. The Styles are very pretty this spring & goods, with few exceptions, not as high as I expected. Feel that this is a poor letter to send for the *two* such good ones rec'd from you, but it is late & I am tired & must close. As Ever your devoted husband

Wm Paisley

Be sure & keep this out of the way or destroy it.

Yrs.
W.P.

Tell Mr. Hall I expect to get his horse to morrow, also to have wagons ready to go to Gurdon Monday morning.

W.P.

Mattie Hughes to Emma Butler Paisley in Dobyville

Malvern Arkansas
May 17th 1880

Dear Sister Emma,

I'll write you a few lines this morning to let you know Annie's condition. Several days ago her bowels commenced running off, and it has been very difficult to get them checked. It has been twelve hours now since she had an action, and we think she is feeling some better. She rested tolerably well last night, and relished her tea and light bread for breakfast. She hasn't had any appetite lately, is weaker and thinner than I ever saw her. We thought she was as poor as she could be before, but now we can see that she looks much worse. She complains of great thirst and dryness of the mouth, thought she had fever yesterday, as her pulse was over a hundred, but Dr. Reamy didn't think she had any. Ma came up Saturday, said it almost shocked her, to see her looking so much worse. I was very glad she came. If Annie improves she will take her to Tulip, for we think a change will be beneficial.

The baby is very good and not much trouble, goes to sleep about eight, and generally sleeps until four or five, without any tea through the night. Alice is at Hot Springs, went over there about ten days ago. She is trying the baths, to see if they will do her any good. She will remain there awhile, and then go to Mountain Valley Springs. George bought Annie some of the Mountain Valley water, and for three weeks she didn't take a dose of laudanum or anything to check her bowels. I think if she had some more fresh from the springs, it might do her good.

George came up from Gurdon last Saturday, but returned this morning. Says he will be getting so far from the railroad, he can't come back next Saturday. We had letters from the boys a few days ago. West continues to improve, and Walter's health is good. Georgie will be at home about the 26th of June, but it will be Aug. or Sep. before Walter gets here, and then he expects to remain only a few weeks, before going to Harvard law school. All were well at bro. Henry's except Nannie. She had a chill yesterday. All were well at Tulip when Ma left. You heard of the death of bro. Charlie's baby, didn't you? It died several weeks ago.

Love to all. Write soon.

> Your sister
> M. W. Hughes

> After dinner.

Annie continues to feel pretty well.

Jimmie Butler to Emma Butler Paisley in Dobyville

> Malvern Ark.
> May 30, 1880

Dear Sister:

Doubtless you will be surprised to receive a letter from me, as it is so very seldom that I write. I will write you a few lines to let you know sister Annie's condition, as I know you are very anxious to hear.

For the last month I think she has been growing weaker, until now it seems wonderful that she can live. I know you would be surprised to see how thin she is. She is thinner than I ever saw her before. She has had no appetite for about two weeks, and it seems even what little she does eat disagrees with her. We are very uneasy about her and unless there is a decided change for the better soon we fear she will never recover. None of the Doctors understand her case. Drs. Reamy and Robertson both have tried her case, but neither one seems to have benefited her in the least. They cannot tell what keeps her in bed. She has been using the compound oxygen, and it seems to have entirely restored her left lung. Yesterday she had a right high fever and was vomiting and had these night sweats which prevented her from sleeping. She has had fever again today which is very weakening. She also has what you might call fainting spells every few days. Whenever she has one, without some stimulant it does not seem that she could live. She had one of these spells today at dinner time.

She has been praying for a blessing for several days, and today while she was so weak she got very happy. I was in the room observing her at the time. I was praying that she might be restored to health, and was astonished when I looked up to see her with her eyes stretched wide and laughing. I never saw a happier person in my life. Her face looked angelic, and she spoke and praised God as if she was inspired. I do wish you could have been present. She wished several times that all the family could be present to see how happy she was, especially ma. Sister Annie had been praying for several days that she might have a blessing and had resolved not to close her eyes in sleep until she did have one. She had been doubting whether she was prepared to die; but says she is ready now to go at any time. She was very weak when she commenced shouting and this almost exhausted her. She said she did not care how much worse it made her feel, just so she could remain happy.

We wrote to ma that she was growing worse, and that she had better come up. We look for her up this evening or tomorrow. If sister Annie should happen to die without Ma being present, she would never get over it. We hope and pray that sister Annie may yet be restored to health.

This leaves no one at home but pa, ma, and Ira. When Ira brought sister Mary up, there was no one there but pa. I guess that was fewer than there ever was in that house before.

I haven't time to look over my letter, as I wish to write to brother Johnnie. Love to brother Billie and the children.

> Your devoted brother
> Jas. O. Butler

Mary Butler to Emma Butler Paisley in Dobyville

> Tulip Ark
> July 2nd 1880

Dear sister Emma:—

I know you feel great anxiety to hear from home, especially since Annie is here with us. I feel badly that I havn't written you much sooner, but have had so many letters to write and so much to do, that you ought to excuse me. The friend I told you expected to visit me [the Rev. George Matthews], came week before last and spent four days very pleasantly: we talked over matters and things generally.

I hardly know what to say about dear sister Annie. She improves sometimes for a while, and then gets worse again; night before last she rested well; last night, she scarcely slept any and this morning she was very weak and low. She feels better this evening; said she felt so peaceful and happy in religion. When I went in her room I noticed her countenance beamed with joy. She is scarcely able now to help herself any—have to lift her and put her in the rocking chair to make her bed. She spoke of how much she enjoyed having you with her at Malvern. I'm fearful she will not be spared to us a great while longer; she is very thin, and doesn't seem to improve permanently at all. The thought of giving her up is indeed painful; all we can do, is submit all into the hands of the Lord praying for resignation to His will: we know not what is best.

The baby has been very sick, teething. Sister [Mattie] was uneasy about her, and she is still sick, though some better. I expect Sister will come down with her next week. I am anxious to see them, Walter especially, he has been there two weeks, and Reavis has come too. I don't know when they will come down. Bro. George is still out on the survey and hasn't seen them yet, unless they went out to Gurdon today, as they had some idea of going.

Alice is still at Mountain Valley Springs. She doesn't write home often—thinks she is improving some, but hasn't gained in weight from last accounts. I do wish she could get well, and come home, she is away so much. I have just finished a long letter of ten pages to bro. George Emory [Butler]. It has been some time since we have heard from him. Sister Mollie has been troubled with asthma lately, though I think she as well [as] the children have also been sick. Kate and the children have been here a week. She is looking thin and complaining all the time. She went over to her aunt Becca's this morning. It is right bad to have so many children here together while Annie is sick. I don't find any time scarcely for sewing. Mrs. Feild speaks of coming down when Alice comes. She can assist me in waiting on Annie. I see Ira just driving in with the wagon. He has taken some young ladies out to Mr. Green's to attend the closing exercises of Cora Gantt's school.

Saturday 3rd

We were much surprised to see bro. George late yesterday evening. He came up on a buggy from Camden, expecting to find sister and Walter here, and was much disappointed. He thinks of going to Malvern this morning in the mail buggy. Annie didn't rest well last night, but looks bright and seems to be feeling tolerably well.

I haven't time to write any more. All unite with me in much love to you all.

Lovingly sister
Mary

Write soon.
Mrs. Jones has a daughter.

Henry Butler to Emma Butler Paisley in Dobyville

Malvern, Ark.
July 27th, 1880

My Dear Sister:

Mollie & myself returned from Tulip on yesterday, where on the day before we consigned to the tomb the body of our dear sister Annie. On Saturday evening last, just as the sun was setting, her spirit winged its flight to that *sun bright* clime where God's dear children dwell in unalloyed bliss.

Mollie left Tulip Saturday morning with much reluctance, though Ma & others thought Annie would probably live for several days. Mollie had not been gone but an hour when sister Annie told them she was dying—thought it was about three o'clock when it was evident that she would not live but a few hours. George R. Hughes came up that night, and we left early Sunday morning, reaching Tulip Sunday morning about ten.

I suppose you *already knew* that sister Annie was prepared for the *awful* change. She "died in the faith," triumphantly! She talked much of dying and although a few weeks ago she did not *seem altogether* satisfied, yet before she was taken to Tulip, *every cloud* was banished, and she ever afterward felt and *knew* that her Savior was altogether reconciled. She died *very easy*, & apparently without a pain or struggle. Ma says she never saw any one die so easy—just like one falling asleep. Her *only* concern was about her children, particularly the babe—but when she was told that Sister would take the babe, she seemed relieved of every care. This was some time before she died. Ma takes her death calmly & with Christian resignation (so does Olin), though before she died Ma said it seemed *very* hard to *give her up*. It does look almost wrong to wish her back. I was so glad Mollie could be with Annie several days before she left us.

There was no minister in the neighborhood on Sunday, and Mr. James Pattillo conducted the service at the grave.

Your *excellent* letter was read to Annie & she appreciated it greatly—was perfectly *conscious* to the last. Your letter was highly prized by Ma & all. You, Johnnie, Charles, & Brother George were the only children not present.

May we all live so as to be prepared when the *summons shall come to us*! There we will meet our dear sweet sister, in a world where disappointments never come—where no farewells are ever said.

Love to Billy.

> Your devoted Brother
> Henry

Mary Butler to Emma Butler Paisley in Dobyville

> Tulip Ark
> July 29th 1880

Dear sister Emma:—

You have no doubt already heard the very sad news of the death of our dear sister Annie through brother Henry, as I think he promised to write after getting home.

She breathed her last without a groan or struggle, just before the setting of the sun Saturday evening, while we were all around her bedside, watching and hoping she would revive and speak one more word, but she continued in a stupor from the opium she had taken; she told us that morning she was dying, and said all was right. A light has indeed gone from our household, and we have every assurance that she is in heaven freed from all sorrow and pain. Our loss is her eternal gain. She was indeed a dear sweet sister; so patient and uncomplaining through all her sickness: she was always afraid of our doing too much for her, and didn't want us to sit up with her. The baby was baptized by bro. Caldwell in her room Thursday before she died—named Annie Mary. I believe it was the same evening that your letter was received and read to her; she remarked what a good letter, and said she would like so much to see you.

Two other letters came for her the evening she died, one from Lucia Moores, and the other from Jimmie. It was too late for her to hear them. I wish I could see you and talk about our dear sister.

Mrs. G. Pattillo, both the Mrs. Colburn's and Mrs. Caldwell were here when she died and prepared her for the grave. She was dressed in black cashmere, with white lace necktie & looked very neat and natural. Oh, dear Emma, how consoling it is to know that she was so well prepared and resigned. We cannot grieve as those who have no hope, for we all have to die at some time, and we have another link and strong tie to bind us to heaven. God grant that our afflictions may work for our eternal good, and at last when our time comes, we may be ready to meet the loved ones gone before. The time she was so happy at Malvern, you remember she said she felt like she could lean her head on Jesus' breast, and breathe her life out sweetly there. So it was when she died, her head reclining to one side calmly, softly breathing her life out sweetly there. She told us she thought she would die easy—didn't cough or expectorate any that day, nor suffering any pain.

She was buried Sunday evening not long before sunset—all the ministers being away, we got Mr. James Pattillo to sing and pray. Bro. Olin bears her death with a great deal of fortitude. He went to Malvern Tuesday. The children are with us. I hardly know what arrangements he will make about housekeeping. Sister has charge of the baby and will remain here this summer, as brother George is away so much. Reavis is here now; we haven't seen Walter yet: he is out with his pa and it will be a week or two, I think, before they can be here. West was in England when he wrote, but expected to return to Paris.

My friend Mr. Matthews left here this morning, came Monday night. This is his last visit before we are to be married, which if nothing prevents will take place the 8th of Sept. which is only about five weeks off. Of course I shall want all my brothers and sisters, that can, to be present on that all-important occasion: expect now to spend several days after at home & probably make a visit to Malvern before going to Magnolia, which will be my future home for a while. It is hard for me to realize that I am to leave my pleasant home and loved ones to go out into the world among strangers. Yet I feel it to be the path of duty, and think I shall be happy with one who will be good and kind, and I have every assurance he loves me devotedly, and has unlimited confidence in me, and I have the same in him. I wish you and bro Billy were acquainted with him—feel sure you would like him. He was a good kind husband to his wife, and they were very happy together. Annie boarded with them for awhile at Centre Point, and had every opportunity for observation, and I knew them there, too, and had already formed a high estimate of Mr. M. as a Christian gentleman. He has two sons, George and Herbert. George is with Mr. Hays in Prescott going to school, and Herbert is in Magnolia going to school. 13 years old. I anticipate no trouble with them.

It will keep me very hard at work to get ready, for I have made no preparation scarcely. Brother Hunter is my choice to perform the ceremony; and I want him to come if possible. I expect Mrs. Feild will be here some time next month, and remain until I'm married. She has promised to help me get ready.

Alice is looking some better than when she left, though her health is not restored yet. Sister Kate is here spending the day. She has been staying at her aunt Becca's: promised to stay at bro. Caldwell's with the children during their absence at district conference. She expects to visit her sister Alice at Centre Point the 6th of next month. Read a letter from bro. Charley. He is doing some better in his business.

Ma sends much love, and says you must write to her and pray for her in this our affliction.

Let us strive earnestly to be better Christians and do more good while we live.

My love to Mary, brother Billy and the children.

> Lovingly your sister
> Mary

Under the circumstances we think it best to have a quiet marriage. I would like to have all my particular friends. Tell Mary she had better answer my letter before I change my name.

William Paisley to Emma Butler Paisley in Tulip

Dobyville Clark Co. Arks
Sept. 7th 1880

My dearest one:

I might put off writing a day or two, but if I do not avail my self of the opportunity to day I will not have a chance to send a letter by mail this week that would be likely to reach you. I cannot give you any news of interest from home, for I hardly feel like I had been there since you left.

Yesterday was a very busy day, the turn out of whites & blacks being more general than I ever saw it. All the Negroes & some of the whites voted the Greenback Slate Ticket, & the Negroes voted for their own color for Township officers. Churchill, the Democratic Candidate for Governor, only beat Burks the Greenbacker, 2 votes at this precinct—175 for amendment & 6 against it. The white candidates for Justices of the Peace & Constable beat the Negro candidates 25 or 30 votes.

The vote for or against whiskey license was carried for license by 20 votes—would not be surprised now if we have whiskey retailed here within the next two years.

The judges & clerks were in the store until about 2 o'clock this morning counting the votes. I went home about 8 o'clock & got supper and returned to the store, & did not go home until 1 o'clock. Mr. Hall is sick in bed this morning, complaining a good deal. Mariah is at the house helping there.

Fletcher returned yesterday evening & reported that you got started from Gurdon all right. This is a pleasant day for your ride to Tulip, and I do hope you will have a pleasant time. Tell sister Mary that I regret very much not being able to come over to see her "off," but that she needn't allow my not being there cause her to put off the marriage. My best wishes will attend her.

I felt quite lonely last night after going home, and bolted the front door securely before going to bed.

Haven't any thing more to write. You will give my love to all the home folks, and believe me as ever your devoted husband

Wm Paisley

Mr. Hall has called in the Dr. Am afraid he will be right sick. Mr. Smiley McGill has been very sick, but is reported better.

William Paisley to Emma Butler Paisley in Dobyville

St. Louis
Sept 23rd, 1880

My dearest one

While waiting for a salesman who has gone to dinner, I will drop you a few lines. Have been right busy since my arrival, have bought Dry Goods, Drugs, Books & Stationery, Hats & Tob., and have gotten along so well that I hope to get through buying this week, but may not be able to wind up before Monday evening. Should this be the case, I will not reach home before Wednesday morning. Should I not come before then, please send a horse for me very early Wednesday morning.

Walter Hughes & his brother returned here from Colorado Tuesday morning, & are still in the city. Walter will go from here to Harvard College. My old friend Mr. Johnson, of the firm of Wilson & Johnson died a week or two ago. Maj. Wilkins seems to be in bad health, but is still attending to business. I am rooming with him as usual. Mr. Weir is still here, but expects to get off Sunday morning. I am anxious to be back at home, & will come as soon as possible. Wish I could have gotten here one day earlier.

I have been feeling quite well & I believe in better spirits than usual when here buying goods. The salesman has returned, & I must close. With much love as ever your devoted husband

>Wm Paisley

Mattie Hughes to Emma Butler Paisley in Dobyville

>Malvern, Arkansas
>Oct. 10, 1880

Dear Sister Emma,

Enclosed you will find Walter's photograph, that I promised to send you some time ago. He is at Harvard law school now, had just matriculated when we heard from him, so I don't know how he will be pleased. West is in Switzerland yet, climbing mountains and growing stout, he writes. Georgie is back at the Unviersity; it was so long after he left here before we heard from him, that I got uneasy about him, and had his pa to telegraph to know if he had reached the University. I wouldn't have felt so uneasy, but he was to have stopped in St. Louis, and I didn't know but what he had been foully dealt with there.

Alice is in Austin, Texas. Pa went with her and remained there several days, and returned to Tulip last Thursday. He was very much pleased with Dr. Wooten, and thinks Alice may be greatly benefitted by going to him. Such a pity she didn't go to him two or three years ago. You know Johnnie was anxious for Annie to try him, says Kellie would have been dead long ago, if she hadn't consulted him. Sister Mary is at Tulip now, got there last Tuesday, and will remain about a week longer. I expect to go down tomorrow. The baby and nurse are here with me. The baby didn't take the whooping cough. She has been very well until now. She has cold which makes her fretful. Every one says she is like Olin, I do wish she favored Annie. Maybe she will grow more like her as she grows older.

Brother Henry returned from St. Louis last Thursday. His catarrh is much better. Mollie and the children are very well, all at Sunday school now.

I would write more, but it is time to get ready for church. Love to all and a kiss for the babies.

>Your Sister
>M. W. Hughes

Minerva Paisley to William Paisley in Dobyville

[McLeansville, N.C.]
Oct. 13th 1880

My dearest Nephew

As Annie is writing to Mary, I will try to write you a short letter, though I am not able to sit up. I have had chills for a few days and I feel weak and nervous. I have been wanting to write you for some time to express my gratitude for your noble kindness to my dear boy.

He and all of us appreciated your generosity very much, and hope that you may be blessed temporally and spiritually, and enjoy the consolation of having helped one who will return your kindness by ever being thankful, and will consider you one of his best friends. Dear Will, how much I wish you could see all the children. They are all about grown now, so different from what they were when you saw them last. My hope and prayer is that they may all be useful wherever their lots may be cast. Porter is at Oxford N.C. teaching, as he could not get through college without having to borrow some money, but he can easily pay back now. Lacy is with him. Porter says he is doing well, and is a general favorite in school. I wish so much you could see Lacy. I think he is more like you than any one else. I think [he] will be just your size, and is very much like you in disposition.

Oh! how thoughts of your last visit crowd into my mind—how many sad changes since—I have given all of my home management into John's hands, who I think will make a good farmer, if he has health, which seems to be good now. My health is unusually good for one of my age. I was sorry to hear of the death of your dear mother. Tis a sad thing to see a mother die.

I must close at present, as I do not feel able to write much. Give my best love to your wife and children. But dear Will, do write to me. You can't imagine how glad I would be to get a letter from you. Tell all about your children, and whatever you think would interest me. Goodbye, and may God bless you and yours, is the prayer of your aunt

Minerva P.

Mary Butler Matthews to Emma Butler Paisley in Dobyville

Tulip Arks
Oct. 14th, 1880

Dear sister Emma:—

You see from my letter I am at home now on a visit; we came a week ago, found only ma and the two children [Annie's children Edwin and William], and you can imagine how lonely it seemed; pa had gone to Texas with Alice, and Sister and the baby at Malvern, Ira at the store. Mr. Matthews had to leave next day to attend his quarterly meeting, and will not be here before next Monday or Tuesday, which seems a long time; no one else can fill the vacancy caused by his absence, as you know full well from past experiences—have had two letters. I can truly say, from short experience, that I am happily married. Not an unkind thought or feeling has ever passed between us, and I feel assured never will: our love for each other is such, that it is the pleasure of each to make the other happy and the utmost confidence exists between us. I anticipate no trouble with the two boys. They respect and recognize me as a mother.

I received an affectionate letter from George [Matthews] just before leaving Magnolia; he is still in Prescott and Herbert is with us, going to school to Mr. Eagleton; he has over a hundred pupils: he and his wife called to see me, and I was much pleased with them; in fact I am well pleased with my new home and the acquaintances I have formed. We board with Mr. John Baker—have two comfortable rooms with fire places; they have only one child, a little boy about six years old, and three other boarders besides our family. They have splendid fare all the time, and my appetite has been such as to do it full justice; the greatest trouble is eating too much, though I have been improving all the time: the change of place and water always seems to benefit my health. You remember how I improved while with you.

We were unfortunate in losing our fine buggy horse after we had gone about fourteen miles from Magnolia; she was taken sick with colic from eating too much new corn, and in half an hour from the time we discovered anything was the matter, she was dead; of course it was a great loss to us and a source of grief too, as we had become attached to our faithful Fannie, and her death was so unexpected. Before she could be unhitched, she fell and broke one of the shaves right in the road. I don't know what we would have done if it hadn't been for our friend Mr. Todd. You remember he married Collie Chester. We happened to be near his house just about dinner time. I went in and talked with Mrs. Todd while Mr. M. and Mr. Todd were doctoring the horse, but before anything could be done she was dead. Mr. Todd did everything in his power, and loaned us one of his mules without any charge—for which we felt very grateful.

Mr. Matthews is now riding Romeo, and pa says we can use him to the buggy until we can get one.

The loss of our horse made us late at night getting to Camden, where the quarterly meeting was to be held the next day. I found some pleasant acquaintances in Camden. We didn't leave there until half past ten, and reached home Tuesday for dinner; the mule was very different from driving a horse, so slow and hard to get along.

Your letter was received since I came, and ma appreciated getting it. I did too, had been thinking of writing to you while at Magnolia. The children have never taken the whooping cough, and are all well. Sister came down with the sweet little baby last Monday. I was indeed glad to see them. It makes home look more cheerful. Pa returned the day after I got here—left Alice in good spirits about her recovery, as the Dr. thinks he can relieve her. She expects to remain there a month.

We received a letter from brother Charlie few days ago. He is now in business, expects to commence hauling before long. I was sorry I couldn't get to see Johnny when he was here. He staid only a short time, got here for dinner and left the next morning. I want to visit him some of these times, and also make you a visit. I would enjoy it very much and can leave home conveniently while boarding, that is, when the roads are good—that will be the trouble in the winter season. I expect to attend conference in Prescott, which will be the 24th of Nov. Hope to meet with Mrs. Logan, Jennie Hatley and Annie Thompson—wish I could meet with some of you. I saw Sue Pattillo and Miss Shives yesterday. Sue had a pleasant time at Presbytery and told me about meeting with Mary [Scott] there. Give her my love, and tell her to meet me at Conference. I would be so glad to see her, and think she has treated me badly in not writing to me. Pa saw Emma Harding [Billy's half-sister] and the children when they got on the train, thought they were looking very well.

Mrs. Howel and her sister are visiting at Mr. Pattillo's; ma and I called to see them. They expect to go to Arkadelphia this week. Mrs. H. is in bad health and is going to be under Dr.

Dale's treatment. I believe we have had company every day since I came home. Mrs. Gantt and her mother and Mrs. G. Pattillo spent the day Saturday, and Mrs. Colburn spent the day Thursday. Sunday evening Mr. Young and wife came to see me. They have good many relatives in Magnolia.

I expect you think I was in a hurry getting back to my old home. I came now because it was the most convenient time before conference, and will have to give Mr. Matthews all the credit for being here, as I had never been home sick or said any thing about coming, although I am delighted to see them all and be with them again.

Friday 15th

I have written you a long letter and must send it to be mailed. We received another letter from Alice yesterday, she seems to be getting on very well, but couldn't write much on account of her eyes; the Dr. had cauterized the pimple that had been growing on the lid. I do hope she will come home in a fair way to get entirely well. Ma has just been in, and says tell you she did appreciate your letter so much, and if I hadn't been here would have tried to answer it herself. Says she enjoyed Lorenzo's [Billy's half-brother] company so much the night he spent here, sends regards to Capt. Lipscomb.

Love to bro. Billy, Mary, and the children

Affectionately your sister
Mary J. Matthews

I expect to leave for Magnolia next Wednesday, and will expect a letter from you soon direct to Magnolia, Columbia Co.

There is to be a circus in Tulip next Thursday; pa and Mr. Young have agreed to take care of a good many that night. I am glad to get away before such a crowd comes, and think it is too bad that such people should take all the money out of the country. Sister and I expect to go visiting to spend the days. I have many visits to return before I leave.

Alice Butler to Emma Butler Paisley in Dobyville

Tulip Arkansas
Dec. 10th 1880

Dear Sister Emma:—

I have been thinking of writing to you for some time, but I had no idea I would leave Austin without writing you a letter, but kept putting it off from time to time, and have now been at home almost a week.

Pa said he appreciated your letter, which was received a few days since, very much and is glad to hear that you are doing so well in business. Says tell Capt. Lipscomb to come over and make him a visit, and he thinks he would do well to settle at Malvern.

I was in Texas two months exactly, and my health has improved very much; all my friends tell me that they can see quite a decided change. Austin is quite a pretty town, located on the Colorado river, and the climate is mild and pleasant. The country around Austin is mountainous, which makes it a health locality, and the surrounding scenery is just as pretty as can be. I tell the home folks that I have fallen in love with Texas. Formed some very pleasant acquaintances while there.

The people generally are very social, and there is a good deal of hospitality. I boarded with Mrs. Nichols, a widow lady who kept a private boarding house, and was very pleasantly situated. Her house was generally full and she had about twenty-five boarders most of the time, with quite a number being day boarders. I think there are very few physicians like Dr. Wooten, and if I had a hundred patients would send them all to him—he said he would send me back to Arkansas as an advertisement. Am still under his treatment but he thought I could do as well at home now as under his immediate care. He thinks by careful attention that my health will be fully established in a few months. He is now down at New Orleans attending the medical convention there.

I left Austin last Tuesday a week ago, but did not reach Malvern until Thursday—the train did not make connection at Texarkana, and consequently I had to stop and spend the night there. I got along finely, however, and don't think it is as bad to travel alone as I had imagined.

Had the pleasure of bro. Henry's company from Prescott, which was quite a surprise to me. He had gone down the day before to see brother Caldwell, who was taken very sick during Conference, and they thought for a while that he could not live; however, he improved much faster than they expected, and reached home this evening. They telegraphed for his wife, who went to town with brother Henry, so she was there to return with him. The physician thought he was running a risk to leave when he did. Sister and myself went around a little while this evening, but he was sleeping the whole time we were there. They thought he was doing very well.

We also stopped by to see Miss Fannie and Sue. They still have Mrs. Howell's two children with them, and she is in Arkadelphia and improving under the treatment of Dr. Doby. They think it will not be long before she is able to have the children with her. I hope she will be entirely restored.

You have doubtless heard that sister Mollie's health has been bad for the last six weeks. She had not been out of the house when I passed through for almost that length of time, and still had a right bad cough though she was looking tolerably well.

All are well here, and the children get along finely. Sister has become very much attached to the little baby who is almost old enough to walk, has two teeth through.

Ma says tell Capt Lipscomb that brother Johnnie is very anxious that he should come to Centre Point, and thought he could do a good business there. All unite in sending much love, and want to hear from you often.

Affectionately
Alice

Cousin Johnnie Butler from Arkansas City wrote us a few days ago that he would be up to spend the Christmas with us. We want to have a little party when he comes. They are going to have a Christmas tree at Malvern, and Ma wants to go up and take Edwin. They also expect Maj. Coulter.

Mattie Hughes to Emma Butler Paisley in Dobyville

Dear Sister Emma,

Your letter to Alice was received about ten days ago, and we were glad to hear that you were all well. We have had so much cold snowy weather, hard on any one, especially children, almost impossible to keep them from taking cold. The children here have had bad colds, for a few days we feared Edwin would have pneumonia, but he is about well now.

A few days since Pa heard of the death of his only sister, aunt Eliza Doves, which has made him feel very sad. She died from pneumonia on the 3 of December, wasn't sick but six days, had high fever all the time. She said very little about dying, but uncle Joseph said, her life was sufficient evidence. Just before she died, she said there were many mansions prepared in heaven, and one was for her. She was an excellent woman, and I dearly loved her.

Cousin Johnnie Butler from Arkansas City was here during Christmas and spent nearly a week with us. He is very lively, and we all enjoyed his visit; says if he doesn't go to Virginia, he will visit us again next Summer. He has never seen you and Johnnie, he spoke of that while he was here and said he would like to see you.

Charlie and Olin, besides sister Mary and bro. Matthews, were here to eat Christmas dinner, and although it was quite cold, we had a pleasant time together. Charlie had been down to his farm collecting rents, and making arrangements to rent it for another year. Kate says unless he builds in Little Rock, she thinks they had better come down here to live. She has been giving music lessons, and has made enough money to buy herself and children's winter clothing. It does seem strange that Charlie should stay in Little Rock without some regular employment. He has a wagon and team and has done some hauling, but that is disagreeable work, especially in a city.

Sister Mary and bro. Matthews spent about three weeks with us, and while they were here they went to Malvern and staid two or three days. The weather was so cold they couldn't visit but little. Mollie's health is better now, and she is surely well of the cough she had. She is expecting her father to visit her, as soon as the weather moderates. Pa and Ma are very well, Alice's health is much better than it was before she went to Texas, but I don't know that she has improved much lately. She is so much more cheerful, and looks much better. Ira has commenced business for himself, bought out Pa and Olin, and thinks he will do very well.

One of the Halls has opened a saloon in Tulip, and I expect they will sell a great deal of whiskey, as it is the only place in the county where it can be sold. Pretty bad for Tulip, isn't it?

Mrs. Howel is at Mr. Pattillo's now, but expects to return to Arkadelphia, before going home. Her children have been at Mr. Pattillo's all the time. She thinks her health will be much better. I expect she has as much confidence in Dr. Dale as Alice has in Dr. Wooten.

George is here now, and has been for the last month. The weather has been too bad for him to get away. He has been reading a good deal, and seems to be con[ten]ted, but he has to go to Little Rock very soon, and may leave in a few days. Georgie has the measles, but thought he would be well in a few days. Though when he wrote last, he thought he had taken a little cold, and wasn't feeling quite as well. I will feel uneasy about him for some time. I have dreaded the measles for West and Georgie ever since they left home. It would have been so much better if they could have had it while they were little boys. I think all of yours have had it. Walter and West were very well when we last heard from them.

Can your baby walk yet? Little Annie can stand alone, but will not venture to step without assistance. Sometimes I'll stand her against the wall, and she will stand there for some time, holding up her little hands, looking so happy. George notices her a good deal, she will reach out her hands for him to put her in her crib every night. She says some words very plainly, but she hasn't but two teeth yet.

Olin has been talking of going to California on a visit, but I believe he has about given it out, for the present, anyhow.

I suppose Mary and Lula are with you yet. Give them my love, also Billy and the children. Write whenever you can.

Your Loving Sister
M. W. Hughes

Ma says, be sure and give "Emma" my love. Wish you could have taken Christmas dinner with us, it has been so long since you did. Let us hear from you soon.

Your Sister

Mary Butler Matthews to Emma Butler Paisley in Dobyville

Magnolia, Ark.
Feb. 11th 1881

Dear Sister Emma:—

It is too bad that I have not yet replied to your good letter written so long ago; my conscience will not let me rest satisfied to let it remain longer unanswered, whether I'm in the humor for writing or not.

Mr. Matthews has just left for his quarterly meeting, and I feel uneasy about him as we have had so much rain. I fear the creeks will be swimming. I would like very much to have gone with him if the roads had been good, for there is to be the dedication of a beautiful new church at Mt. Vernon Sunday.

I received a letter from Ira this morning, said the baby was not very well, thought she was teething. Alice had gone to Malvern to spend about two weeks—expects also to visit Lizzie Crouch while there.

Sister Kate has a little girl born last Sunday; brother Charlie thinks of going to Tulip to live, if his place there has not been rented.

We spent three weeks pleasantly at Tulip and Malvern during the Christmas holidays, although the weather was extremely cold. On our return, visited cousin John Peebles' family, living three miles from Camden. We had a pleasant time, and they seemed to appreciate our visit; they have a grown daughter who is an interesting young lady. She spoke of visiting Alice this spring or summer. We staid during the quarterly meeting in Camden at Dr. Brown's, which is a pleasant family to visit.

We are comfortably fixed at our new boarding place, though the room is too small to arrange things to my entire satisfaction. There are six other boarders besides our family. Herbert will start to school Monday. He is almost well of the whooping cough. George is living fourteen miles from us at Dr. Hardison's, who is a nice family: he gets ten dollars a month besides his board: he is to assist in doing any kind of work about the place; the Dr. wanted some one about the place to be with his family during his absence.

If the roads are good and weather pleasant, we will perhaps visit home again the last of March or first of Apr. Another quarterly meeting at that time six miles beyond Camden, which will be just on the way: we can only stay a few days at home: visit them again some time during the summer.

I received a long interesting letter from sister this week, she said she had heard that brother Billy had been sick. I hope he has entirely recovered. My love to him, and tell him I want him to become acquainted with my good, kind, affectionate husband. I know he would like him. He has been suffering several days with a rising on the back of his neck. I have been trying to get it well before he had to leave, but it is still a bad place.

It is turning very cold, has the appearance of snow: we use a stove in our room, which makes it comfortable when we have a good fire: though I believe I prefer a fireplace, can keep my feet warm better.

I suppose Mary is still with you. Give her my love, also Lula, Emma, and all the children. How is the baby getting on? Kiss her for me. Don't wait as I have done, but write soon to your ever loving sister. Mr. M. was here would send love.

Mary J. Matthews

William Paisley to Emma Butler Paisley in Dobyville

St Louis, Mo.
Apl 15 1881

My dearest one

I am here comfortably situated, Rooming & Sleeping with Johnnie whom I met at Little Rock. Kelly is staying with Kate & Charlie while John is here. They both stopped at Malvern a day or two. Kelly's health is pretty good. Your ma & pa were at Malvern visiting, but left the day I passed.

I have done but little as yet buying. My loss on cotton will be very heavy. Nearly every merchant I have met is in the same fix with my self. That, however, is cold comfort. The whole sale merchants are kindly disposed, and I can get all the accommodations I want. The only difficulty I have lies within my own fears, as usual. The commission merchants think cotton will be no better. I expect to have mine sold while here &, as the saying is, "pocket the loss."

Please have as much gardening done as you can. I can't say when I will be home, but will write again soon. I have been sleeping like a log all night since my arrival. Got but little sleep the night I came.

Mollie & Maj Coulter expect to go to Eureka Springs this week.

Haven't time to write more. Take care of Father as much as you can. With much love for your dear self & children.

Your devoted husband
Wm. Paisley

William Paisley to daughter Emma Paisley in Dobyville

St. Louis
Apl 18th 1881

My dear little girl

You have been so anxious to get a letter, papa thought he would write you a short one.

I have just written to mama, but could not say as much to her as I wanted to. The men in the room are talking so much I can't write. I have been very busy for several days buying goods, and feel very tired at night. Have bought a great many goods & some very pretty ones. Have not bought your hat yet, but will do so before I come. Tell Henry I will try to get his ball.

I went out to Mr. Senter's yesterday & saw several little girls about your size. They looked like they would like to get out in the country &, could they do so, they would see—to them—as many strange sights as you would in this great city.

You must all be good & smart children & help mama all you can.

With much love for you all I am your loving

Papa
Wm. Paisley

Alice Butler to Emma Butler Paisley in Dobyville

Tulip Arkansas
May 19th 1881

Dear sister Emma:—

I should have written to you before now, and hope you will pardon delay on my part. It seems that I never get time to answer half the letters that I wish, and yet I cannot see that I am kept so very busy either.

I have a music class now consisting of seven pupils, and it is true that it takes up a good deal of my time, am kept pretty busy until noon every other day. Two days I have only two lessons to give. Began about the middle of March, and I think as a whole my class are progressing very well. Sue is taking, and has improved very much—she is very fond of music, and has learned to play several pieces—Helen is still taking, and Virgie Colburn is among the number.

Miss Fannie Pattillo has gone on with her Father to attend the [Methodist] General Assembly, which was to meet at Staunton, Va. They left last Monday. She expects to visit her relatives in N.C., and will be gone about a month—her father will return after the meeting adjourns. Sue says they are very lonely now. They have Mrs. Dr. Smith's little girl with them; she (Mrs. Smith) went on to visit her relatives in Tenn.

We (Ira & self) attended a picnic yesterday down on the creek near Maurice Smith's, which was given by the creek girls. Every body seemed to enjoy the day, and we had a nice dinner prepared. There are two young ladies at Mrs. Matlock's—Lena Allen and her cousin Miss Grey, and also a family living near by the name of Carlton; they are from Georgia, and seem to be very clever

369

people; there are two young ladies in the family, and so they all clubbed together and fixed up a very nice dinner—also had a set of croquet with which we amused ourselves.

I suppose Sister has written to you since she has been at Malvern keeping house for sister Mollie. She spoke of it some time ago. Sister has not been very well for the last week or two—says the baby is improving all the time. She has only two front teeth, and has cut one jaw tooth. Did you ever hear of such a thing?

Reavis is still in the store at Malvern, and seems to like merchandising. Brother George [Hughes] has accepted the position of chief engineer on the road from Pine Bluff to New Orleans, and sister says he will be busy most of the summer; says he wants her to go to Little Rock and stay awhile. She will.do as soon as sister Mollie returns. She will send the baby down here. Sister M[ollie] is improving, and expects to come home in about two weeks. I think her Father has improved also, and he is very much pleased with the [Eureka] Springs. Sister M. wrote a very interesting piece in the last *Meteor*. I suppose you do not take the paper.

Cousin Jimmie's son Johnnie spent last night with us. His little brother, the baby, died last Saturday, which we were very much surprised to hear. Cousin J wrote us some time ago that he was quite sick, but he had about recovered from the spell, and was taken suddenly with a spasm from which he died. I know they are all so much distressed. They telegraphed for Flora and she reached Arka. Sunday.

Had a long letter from Jimmie [Butler] day before yesterday. He is very much pleased in St. Louis, and getting on finely with bookkeeping, says he will be able to get through by the middle of next month. He is delighted that Mr Crouch & family are there, and says Lizzie is so much company for him. He and Mr. Charlie Adams have a room very near to where they are boarding.

Ira is getting on very well with his store here, and takes a great deal of interest in it. He hasn't been feeling very well for the last few days.

Ma and Pa both keep well, also the children. William [Moores] has grown a good deal and thinks he is almost a man, since he has learned to ride horseback.

We have a new cousin at Princeton who is teaching school there, Mr. Tillett from N.C. He came up to see us a few weeks ago, and spent Saturday & Sunday. We are all delighted with him, and so glad to have him near enough to visit us. He has not had charge of the school but a few weeks, and we had not heard before he got here that he was going to take the school. He is just from the University of Chapel Hill, and is quite an intelligent young man. Jimmie went to school with his brother at Randolph Macon College.

Heard from sister Mary not long since. She was just preparing to visit Mrs. Powel, about seventeen miles from Magnolia, while Bro. M. was attending his appointments; said she would spend a week, as she had a very pressing invitation to do so.

Did you have any strawberries this year? We had several good messes and would have had more, had there not been so much rain. Ma has had peas and a few Irish potatoes, but her garden is backward. She has a good many chickens, about fifty or sixty, but I expect you can beat that.

Suppose you have heard of sister Jennie's marriage & we have her husband's picture and also his little boy. They are both fine looking. A good many think he resembles bro. Lewis.

Ma had a letter from cousin Betsy Kittrell a few days ago. She writes that she wants to make us a visit some time this summer. Ma met Capt. Lipscomb at Malvern, and was glad to see him looking so well and natural. Ma says can't you come to see us this summer?

Will now close. All unite in sending love. Let us hear from you soon.

Lovingly
Alice

All send love.

Ma has seventeen young turkeys. Pa sends love, and says he would like to know what bro. Billie lost on cotton.

Mary Matthews to Emma Butler Paisley in Dobyville

Magnolia Arkansas
May 20th 1881

Dear Sister Emma:—

In looking at the date of your letter, I'm surprised to find so much time has elapsed since its reception: time flies rapidly—Just think of it, over eight months since I was married, and it seems such a short while; nothing has occurred to mar my happiness and I have been as free from all care and trouble as it is our lot to be in this life.

I have been travelling a good deal with Mr. Matthews, and meet with many old friends and form pleasant new acquaintances—just returned this week from Mr. Powell's, where I spent more than a week very pleasantly, while Mr. M. attended two quarterly meetings not far from there. He never takes me to places where we can't be accommodated. Mrs. Powell insisted on my making her a visit, as she is quite lonely, just the two old people there, besides a servant girl. They have just moved into a nice new house and are well fixed. Mrs. P. would have me to play on the piano for her, so I practiced more than I have since I married. My health has been better this spring than usual, which I attribute to travelling, which you know always did agree with me.

Mr. M. left this morning, Friday, and will return Monday. I will have to stay at home now and get ready for a long trip which we contemplate taking next month—want to visit you and Johnny before going to Tulip to spend nearly two weeks—will visit bro Johnny first—expect to leave here on the seventh of June and will probably be at your house the 13th or 14th, or it may be 15th, can't tell exactly yet. I anticipate a pleasant time, and hope nothing will prevent our going; it is the only spare time Mr. M. will have from his work.

Do you hear from home often? I received a letter from Sister which on my return I found awaiting me—it was written the 4th, and I think got here the day I left. I have not answered it yet. I suppose you know she is at Malvern keeping house for sister Mollie, while she is on a visit to Eureka Springs with her father, also Sandy Winfield all there for their health—expected to be gone six weeks. I got the "Malvern Meteor" and read an account of their trip written by bro. Winfield.

I was surprised to hear of Mary [Paisley Scott]'s being married. Present my love and congratulations. I did think I would write soon after getting your letter for it was certainly appreciated. I know you havn't the time and opportunity for writing that I have, consequently I censure myself for not writing sooner. Love to bro. Billy, and tell him Mrs. Orr has excellent taste, and he must improve his looks all he can before we get there, for I don't want him to feel *too* badly.

Have you many chickens and a good garden this year? Mrs. Couch has potatoes, peas, beets, beans large enough to eat. I enjoy the vegetables very much.

Herbert has returned from school, says his teacher is sick. He is a good deal of care, pray for me.

I hav'nt written home in some time since Sister left—don't hear from them often. I suppose Alice's music pupils take up a good deal of her time.

Tell Emma she is getting large enough to write, and I would be glad to get a letter from her, also John and Willie. Love to all the children and friends. I enjoy getting letters so much—please don't wait long before writing.

Lovingly your sister
M. J. Matthews

Mary Matthews to Emma Butler Paisley in Dobyville

Magnolia, Ark.
Aug. 8th 1881

Dear sister Emma:—

I have been wanting to write to you ever since my return from Tulip, but the weather has been so extremely warm that I haven't felt like writing to anyone; and besides, I've been from home most of the time. We returned from District conference last Tuesday, which convened in Eldorado; notwithstanding the heat and dust, we had a pleasant time, and I hope also a profitable meeting; our home was at Mr. Schuler's, which is a nice pleasant place to visit, and by the way we went to see our old friend "Phena Finley" and it would almost make you cry to see how changed she is. I told you about having heard of her face being disfigured from being burnt; it was even worse than I expected, she has to wear goggles over her eyes or at least put them on when in company: she sent me a special word to come to see her and I was glad I went, although it made me sad to see her so afflicted; she inquired about you particularly and many questions about Tulip and other friends. She told me she hadn't been to church in four years. I was surprised to see her there Sunday night, said she came just to see me once more. I think I shall spend a night with her some time in passing down that way. She has six children. I wish you could find time to write to her just to assure her of your continued love & remembrance. I know it would be highly appreciated. Her husband, Mr. Jamison, seems to be a kind, clever man, though I understand he drinks.

Mr. Smeade, who boards here, came with his bride last Friday night. He married Anna Chester, William Chester's oldest child. She seems to be a nice good girl, looks young, about 18 or 19 years old, a member of the church. They attended Sunday school with me yesterday, and of course the bride was the observed of all observers. Mrs. Couch has no room for them, so she promised to board them only two weeks. Mr. Matthews left for his meeting near Falcon Friday evening—will return tomorrow. I would have gone with him, but the weather was so warm and dry; besides I had some sewing to do.

I have thought much about you this hot weather, and wished you could be relieved from cooking; don't know how you manage to keep up under it—hav'nt heard anything from you or Johnny since we visited you. On our return, Mr. M. took Herbert to Tulip; he is clerking for Ira, and says he likes it better than he expected. You remember we were talking of pa and ma leaving the old homestead. I don't think now they have any idea of leaving. This is pa's birthday, and I wanted to write to him, so you must excuse me for not writing more. Mr. M. was much pleased with his visit to you, and requested me to send love and messages for him. He formed a high estimate of brother Billy, and desires to extend his acquaintance with him. Love to him and all the children, and let us hear from you soon.

Lovingly your sister
Mary

I was much surprised to hear of the death of Mrs. Davis so soon after her visit with us to Tulip.

Mattie Hughes to Emma Butler Paisley in Dobyville

Little Rock Ark.
Aug. 15, 1881

Dear Sister Emma,

It has been a long time since I wrote or received a letter from you. I really feel badly for not having written to you before now. I have gotten so much out of the habit of writing letters, that it is a task to write. I feel so unsettled, first in one place then another. It seems to me if I could feel settled, I could do everything better than I do. This way of living has never suited me, but I try to be content. I have been most of the time for the last two months, and if the weather hadn't been so very warm, I could have had a pleasant time.

Walter came the last of June, and with the exception of two weeks we spent together at Tulip, he has been here. He has been assisting his pa some in the railroad office. Reavis has been in the survey between Monticello and Warren. He has quit now, and expects to go to Tulip some time this week to rest awhile, before returning to the University of Va. The weather was so very warm, I felt uneasy about him while he was on the survey. But he stood it very well, and seems to be in fine health. Walter is quite thin, has lost fifteen or sixteen pounds since he came home. West is in good health now, or was on the 25th of July. I don't know when he will return home. George [her husband] has stood the heat very well, and keeps quite fleshy. He is very busy most of the time, and I think he will be engaged on this road for some time.

I had a letter from Alice a few days ago, all were well. She and Ma have been taking care of the baby since I have been here. I hated to leave her very much, but know she is better off there, than she would be here. If she was old enough to do without a nurse, I would like to have her with me all the time. She has eight or ten teeth and talks quite plainly.

How have you been, and have your children kept well? There has been a good deal of sickness here amongst the children.

I saw Charlie last night, he was very well, but said the baby was sick. They are keeping house, living very near Mrs. Colburn. How are the crops in your county? Nearly everywhere we hear from they are ruined. I expect merchants as well as farmers have the "blues."

What was the name of that book belonging to Mr. Doby, that bro Lewis had? Since the books have been sent to them we can get it. I want to write to Jennie soon, and will ask her to send it by mail. We have never had but one letter from her since she was married, but Alice wrote me she had a letter from Jessie a few days ago. I think Jennie is happily married, wish I could see her and the dear children.

I was sorry to hear of the death of Mrs. Davis. How greatly she will be missed, especially by her husband and children.

We are rooming at Mrs. Cates, but taking our meals with Mrs. Brisbin, who lives near. Love to Billy & the children.

Your sister
M. W. Hughes

Do write soon. Direct to Mrs. G. W. Hughes and I will be sure to get it.

Alice Butler to Emma Butler Paisley in Dobyville

Tulip, Ark.
Aug. 24th, 1881

Dear Sister Emma:—

The children, together with Walter and Jimmie, have just gotten off to Malvern, and I will now write you a few lines, for I know you are anxious to hear about them. They seemed to enjoy their little stay very much indeed, and we were very glad to have them with us. Emma has grown so much and is so very fleshy. I think she would weigh about as much as I do. Edwin was delighted with Henry, and said he didn't want him to leave at all. They are so near the same size, and were so much company for each other. I hope they will enjoy their visit to Malvern.

I was glad to make the acquaintance of Miss Hall as they passed through on their way to Dobyville, and was very much pleased with her, would have written a note by them but didn't have time. Lula has grown so much I don't think I would have known her. Mr. Hall and Adams looked very natural, no change in them since our trip to Dobyville.

Walter, Jimmie, and Reavis came down last week, and also Mr. Johnnie Steele, who left yesterday. We have enjoyed their visit so much. All left except Reavis, who will probably spend the rest of his vacation with us. I suppose you knew Sister was in Little Rock with brother George. I don't know when she will return, as bro. G's business will hold him there for some time.

We have the baby [Annie Mary Moores] with us, and she is growing very fast, can talk as plain as William [her brother] now.

Ma says she was very glad to get your note and felt like replying to it immediately; says she has enjoyed the children's visit very much.

Ira and I think something of going over to Centre Point to attend the camp meeting, which begins on the 12th of Sept. If so, we will either go or come by to see you and brother B. Heard from sister Mary a few days ago. She was not very well, but not sick enough to be in bed. They will be over to see us the last of Sept. His son Herbert is here clerking for Ira and seems to make a very good clerk. He is not quite fifteen and is a very nice boy. We had a revival here a week or two ago and he, together with several others, professed religion and joined the church. There were twelve conversions and we had a good meeting. Brother Winfield from Malvern came down to assist Mr. Atchley. I like him so much, think he is a good preacher.

We had a sociable here last night, just to have all the boys and girls together before Walter and Jimmie left. It was a supperless one, but everyone seemed to enjoy it just as well, expected to have had it the night before, but the rain prevented. We were more anxious to have it then, for cousin Gus Tillett and Mr. Steele were both home. Cousin Gus had been up to Hot Springs, and spent the night and day with us on his return. He dismissed his school at Princeton for a week, but was compelled to be back today. All send much love. Let us hear from you soon.

Alice

Mary Butler Matthews to Emma Paisley in Dobyville

Magnolia, Ark.
Oct. 17th 1881

Dear Sister Emma:—

Your much appreciated letter was received some time ago, which I concluded to postpone answering until our return from Tulip, which was about two weeks ago. We were gone three weeks, but only spent two days and a half at home—reached there Tuesday for dinner, and left Friday morning on our way to Hampton, to attend quarterly meeting. Cousin John Peebles lives three miles from Camden. We were agreeably surprised to meet Jimmie and Alice there—having come down to make them a visit, also to meet us and attend our meeting in Camden. They enjoyed it very much, and we all had a pleasant time together. Cousin Sue Peebles is a nice young lady. She went with Jimmie into town and called on some of the young ladies, thus making it pleasant for him.

Ira and Alice were planning a visit to Centre Point. Herbert wrote us they started the following Monday after we left. Alice expected on their return to take the train at Arkadelphia, go to Malvern, and from there to Little Rock to attend the Fair which opens today. I suppose she is now there. Kate wrote her a pressing invitation to come.

I received a letter from Sister a few days ago, said she expected to spend two or three weeks at Tulip after the Fair. I missed her while at home very much. It has been about seven months since I've seen her. "The Baby" has improved so much. She talks very plain and is so interesting and affectionate. Sister is very anxious to see her.

Pa and ma were looking very well. I feel thankful that their precious lives are still spared, and hope we may have them with us many years yet. I notice in the Los Angeles Conference that G. E. Butler located at his own request. I haven't seen a letter from him in a long time. Don't know why he has located unless he intends visiting us again next year. I really must write to him soon. Mr. Matthews left last Thursday for his quarterly meeting. He enjoys excellent health—look for him this evening. The weather continues warm and dry; how are you making out for water?

Time passes very rapidly, seemingly more so since I've been in the itinerancy; another Conference year will soon be here, and where our home will be we know not: if the weather is not too bad, and no Providential hindrance, I expect to attend Conference, which convenes in Pine Bluff the 14th of Dec.

Much love to Bro. Billy and the children, also Mary [Paisley] when you see her. How is she getting on? Mr. M. would also send love if at home.

I have written a poor letter. Hope to hear from you soon.

Lovingly your sister
Mary

Tulip Evermore

Mary Wyche Butler to Emma Butler Paisley in Dobyville

[Tulip
Nov. 1881]

My Dear Daughter

I am so much concerned about you since hearing of your sickness. I sayed as soon as I got William's letter, I expect Emma is sick. I wish I could have been with you. Wish you lived near us where could see you often. I was thinking what Alice told me, you was doing all your work. It was to much for you. I am afraid you can't stand so much. You have a hard time, with so many children and Boarders too. It is too much for you. I hope you will get over it.

The children keep well. The Baby as fat as a pig, talk very plain. Will has on pants and thinks he is a man. Says he can't get cold with pants on. Edwin goes to school and is learning well. Tell Henry Edwin liked him better than any Boy he ever was with. Wish he could be with him again. I could give you a turkey if you were near me. I raised 12, have 16.

I begin to feel that my children will soon all leave me. I wish some of them could live near us. I shall want to hear from you soon. I hope you will soon get well. Tell the Boys I have some of the Walnuts yet, and they are as good as ever. Lord bless you and yours, restore your health.

May I see you soon.

Goodby, your mama

Hoping to see you soon

Alice Butler to Emma Butler Paisley in Dobyville

Tulip, Ark.
Nov. 20th 1881

Dear sister Emma:—

We were very much distressed to hear of your sickness through a letter from brother Billy a day or two since; glad, however, to know that you had improved, and hope you will have no further trouble. We will still feel uneasy about you until we hear again. Wish Ma could have been with you, for I know it would have been a great deal of comfort to you. Ira was over at Centre Point last week and sister Kellie was quite sick. They thought she had a congestive chill; she was a little better when he left, but we haven't heard since and feel a little uneasy about her.

I have been wanting to write to you ever since I came from Little Rock, but we have had a good deal of company, and I have had very little time for writing. Sister came down with me, but left again for L.R. last Tuesday. She has not heard of your sickness, but I will write her a few lines tomorrow. Am sorry that you are so far away, for some of us would like to be with you to wait on you.

I spent about ten days in L.R. and had a very pleasant time, indeed enjoyed the Fair very much. May and Coulter also went in to the Fair, which was quite a treat to them. Brother Charlie was living in a rented house, but very well fixed up. He has commenced to build on his lots since

I left. His lots there was a good investment, and it is a pity he had not bought more, instead of buying a place here. They have a very sweet little girl baby about eight months old, who is a great pet with them all. Colburn and Sammie are going to school and learning fast.

Well, now about myself &c. We have appointed the 20th of Dec. for our marriage, just a month from today exactly and I feel that the time is rapidly approaching. You must make haste and get well, and be able to come over on that occasion. We don't expect to have many outside of home-folks, and it will not be a grand affair. I acted as bride's maid on last Thursday evening for Fannie Caldwell, who was married to Mr. Arin. I never met him before, and am therefore unable to say whether she has done much in marrying him. He is a widower with three children, and lives about eight miles from Arkadelphia. They had a very nice supper prepared, and the table looked as pretty as any I have seen in a long while. Miss Fannie P. made the bride's cake which was very nice indeed. There were six couples to wait on her. Jimmie, Ira, and self were among the number, also cousin Gus Tillett. The others were Mr. Pattillo, Mr. Wilfong (our Preacher), and Jimmie Smith—the ladies, Misses Bethenia Roane, Mary Smith, Sue and Hellen Patillo and Anna Caldwell, of course. It was quite a pleasant little company, and all seemed to enjoy it. They had very few except the waiters. Mr. Atchley performed the ceremony.

Little Annie has grown to be very fleshy and can talk right plain. Ma put pants on William today, and he thinks he is a man. Edwin goes to school to Mr. Wilfong and learns fast. With much love for all and a kiss for the baby—I am affectionately

Alice

Sister M. and brother Matthews will be here the first of Dec. on their way to Con. Had a letter from them not long since. Tell bro. B. we were glad to get his letter, and hope to hear from you again soon, and that you will be entirely well. Pa, Ma, and Ira all send love.

Minerva Paisley to William Paisley in Dobyville

Mcleansville [N.C.]
Nov. 24th 1881

My dear Nephew:

I received your long interesting letter, and am sorry it has lain so long unanswered. I thought when I read it I would answer it in a few days, but we know but very little what is ahead of us. A few days after received it I met with a painful accident, which has been the cause of my not writing sooner. I went out into the orchard to gather some apples, and fell and broke one bone of my left arm just above the wrist. It was very painful at first, but is well now, but my fingers are still stiff. But reckon they will all come right some of these days.

Will, you can only imagine how glad we all were to hear from you, and to get such a long and exceedingly interesting letter was simply a treat. It seemed to bring back much of the past vividly to my mind, and that is one of my greatest pleasures. To think of the many, many happy hours and days spent with loved ones is a source of neverending pleasure to me. I sometimes feel that the spirits of loved ones are hovering over me, bidding me not to be discouraged, for the trials of earth will soon end, and if we are faithful in the discharge of our duties, Heaven will be our home through an endless eternity. Surely this ought to stimulate us amidst our daily trials. I have had a great deal of care, as you well know, since my dear husband's death, but I have much to be thankful for. I have had excellent health, never have had a single Dr. bill for myself until this accident, and never had much sickness in the family. My children were obedient and kind, and we have been happy.

The only thing that caused us sorrow was having to be separated, which could not be avoided, and I am certainly thankful that I had the nerve to give Porter and Lacy up—for I think it is better for them. I think John is perfectly satisfied to be a farmer, and you know I am glad to have one of them to stay with me. Jno. is a kind, affectionate boy, and has a cheerful healthy companion with a sweet disposition I think will take care of me. Porter's health has not been very firm hitherto, but I think it is improving, and hope he may be spared to fill some useful station in life, which I think he will do. He has not given up the Ministry, but seems to shrink from the responsibilities of so high and holy a calling. I hope he will be guided by an over-ruling Providence in the path of duty. Lacy has his mind on being a M.D., and if resolution, energy and quick motion are any advantages, he has that much to recommend him. Porter is highly pleased with his situation at D.C. [Davidson College]. Says he lives near the fountain head of knowledge, from which he can draw at leisure. He has more than half of his time to devote to his own improvement, and says he studies about as hard as any student he has. Porter loves study. It is his delight. He says the farther he goes, the more he sees ahead that he wants to know, and feels that he knows comparatively nothing.

But I am afraid you will think me an egotist, so I will quit writing about my children. But I must tell you something about Annie. She is grown. I suppose from what you told about Mariannie, I think she is about her size. She is a stout, healthy girl, and a great comfort to me. She has a pretty voice and is fond of music. As to her casting shy glances at the boys, some of them commence that so soon that I put a stop to it. But she has been flying around for some time she says having a good time, but I tell her to let it stop there for some time yet.

I will now try to tell you something about your acquaintances you made while here. Mr. Jos. Gilmer's family are still the same as you knew except Miss Jane, who I told you married Will Wharton. She has one of the smartest little boys I ever saw, has but one. Eli married, and is merchandising in Winston, N.C. He is doing well. Mary Rankin is living near Greensboro. Married Jerrie Wharton, has four children. Callie Stewart married a Mr. Glass and is living over on Alamance, and is just as pretty as ever, has four children. Miss Sue Rankin, sister of Mary, married Mr. Will Rankin and is living between our house and the depot. I believe every girl, so far as I know, is married that you knew while you were here.

I was about to forget to tell you about the Rankin girls, that is the William Rankin of Greensboro. They are all dead but one. She—Maggie—is in New York living with her brother-in-law, a Mr. Cummings. The other three married and lived only a short time—two of them married Cummings and died, leaving one child apiece. The other married Col. Graves of Mt. Airy.

Mr. Joseph Gilmer's family are all living and doing well. One of his sons, Henry, is sheriff of Guilford Co. and one (John) is a graduate of Davidson College, and is a worthy young man, speaks of studying for the ministry. Charlie Tidball is teaching in Graham, N.C. Mr. Tidball sends his kindest regards to you and family.

I don't remember whether I ever told you about the new churches at Bethel and Alamance. They are very pretty. We attend one about as much as the other. We certainly have great privileges here, the best of preaching every Sunday.

But I haven't told you anything about the drought. We surely had the longest drought that I ever saw. Jno. says the roots of the corn were never wet from time it was planted, until it was pulled. You may know there was not much made on up-land. There was scarcely any. Jno had low ground, and made about ½ crop. I think this will be a hard year with some people. I think we will have plenty to do us, but very little to spare. And another calamity that befell us in this country—the tobacco was all frostbitten. All together will necessarily make this a hard year, but we did not suffer from scarcity of water, as you said you did, though it began to get scarce before it rained. I hope you have had plenty before this. We have had abundance for the last few weeks.

I thought I was done telling you about the children, but I was about to forget to tell you about Jno's little boy (you know I have the dignity of a Grandma). He is a sweet little fellow, just beginning to walk. His name is James Percy. He is a real pet. You will think he is smart when I tell you he walked when he was just eight months and ½ old. He is beginning to talk, is not 10 months yet. He reminds me so much of his uncle Lacy, has the same go-ahead disposition. Jno. and Bessie are proud of him. He is a great deal of company for me. His ma has taken him visiting today, and it seems as if there was nobody at home.

Well, I guess I have written enough for once. I hope we will do better at writing hereafter. I forgot to tell you how glad we were to get your group [picture]. You certainly have a great deal to live for. I hope and pray that you and your wife's life may be spared to train your dear little children, and that they may live to be a blessing to the world and a comfort to you in old age.

All join in love to you and family. Write soon

from your loving Aunt Minerva

P.S. Tell Mariannie [Billy's sister] that I think she ought to write to me or her name sake, and will look for a letter from her soon. P.S. I forgot to tell you that Mr. and Mrs. Gilmore wanted me to send you their best love. And Mrs. James Wharton and family were here yesterday, and wished to be remembered in kindest wishes to you. Mrs. J. says she well remembers the night you and her got up to kiss in our parlor, and Mr. Paisley and myself held the candle to see it well done. No more but ever remain

your affectionate aunt

Mary Matthews to Emma Butler Paisley in Dobyville

Tulip Ark.
[Dec.] 9th, 1881

Dear Sister Emma:—

We reached home night before last after dark, and was much surprised to find pa quite sick with something like pneumonia, though Dr. Cooper says it is not really pneumonia. Ma was gone to Malvern, and Alice being here alone, felt greatly relieved when we got here—ma returned yesterday: I do hope pa will not have such a severe spell as he had before. He is resting quietly today, has a blister on his left side which has been paining him some—he seems to be doing very well at present, if he doesn't get worse. It seems hard to get the blister to draw.

Mr. M. will leave tomorrow for Con. I have decided to remain at home, look for Sister tomorrow. Alice is busy getting ready to be married on the 21st, which will be just after Conference closes: if pa continues very sick she may marry in the day very quietly. Can't tell about that yet; bro. Olin will be down tomorrow to talk it all over. My opinion is that Pa will not be up by that time—he is so weak now, though I sincerely hope he will. I don't think he is dangerously sick at present. Sister Mollie has been sick with asthma again, was improving when ma left.

I was sorry to learn of Mary's and Lula's illness. Alice and ma received your letters, but haven't time now to reply. I have taken cold and suffering with toothache, which makes me feel almost sick, so you must excuse this short letter. As you think of coming, can talk to you better than I can write.

Mr. Matthews sends his regards to bro. Billy, and says he will be very glad to see you. All send love. This letter will not go off today so I will add a little more in the morning.

Saturday 10th

Brother Atchley and Mr. M. left for Conference in the buggy together this morning. Pa rested very well last night. It is hard to tell whether he is any better or not.

Monday 12th

Pa didn't rest very well last night, but seems to be resting quietly this morning. I hope he is some better, though it is hard to tell. He changes sometimes so soon. I don't think it will be possible to have company on the 21st, but you of course must come to see pa: ma says come—will be glad to see you. Pa is very weak, and sometimes his mind seems to be wandering. Alice says she may have to postpone her marriage if he continues so sick.

All send love. Write soon. Ira is waiting to carry up my letter, so I must close.

Afftly your sister
Mary

Henry Butler to William Paisley at Dobyville

Tulip
Dec 14th 1881

I have just come down with Dr. Reamy to see Pa. He is *dangerously sick*. Has Pneumonia and his condition is *alarming*. Sister Mattie and Jimmie are here—also found sister Mary here.

Your brother & friend
H. A. Butler

George Butler to Mary Wyche Butler in Tulip

Downey, Cal.
Dec. 28, 1881

My own dear Mama,

Yesterday brought me the sad intelligence of the death of Papa. Sad in some respects, yet in others joyful. I feel like I have been deprived of one of the truest of parents. I believe no father ever lived who was more devoted to the welfare of his children than Alexander Butler. He was deeply concerned for their Spiritual as well as temporal well-being. His children owe him a debt of gratitude which they can never cancel. I have a thousand times praised God for the gift of such parents as He blessed me with. But Pa now rests from his labors. He has finished his work. *He did it well. Praise God.* I told Julia that if I had done my work as well as pa has his, I would be willing to die. I am trying to do my whole duty.

I have thought of you often of late. Have been thinking of making you a visit next fall. I would like to go to see you all now, but I can not. How I would enjoy a long talk with you. Can you not come out with Olin in Feb.? I think you would enjoy a trip out here, and it would do you good. You could attend some of our holiness meetings in our large tent or tabernacle, and I think they would do you more good than attending the General Conference. You would not see so many "big" preachers or hear such *intellectual* sermons, but you would see & feel more of the pentecostal power.

The delegate from the Los Angeles Conference, T. R. Curtis, is opposed to the Holiness work. The pastor of this place, bro. Grove, not yet ordained elder, tries to overthrow the Wesleyan view of Sanctification, & has forbidden the Holiness band from holding any more meetings in the church building. But the work moves on. Meetings are held in private houses, school houses, &c. Last Sunday at a School house about five miles away one professed conversion and another entire Sanctification.

Today, Jimmie wrote, Alice is to be married. I hope she & Olin may both be wholly consecrated to God. My all is on the Altar that Sanctifieth the gift. Heb. 13: 10 & Mat. 23: 19

[no closing]

Alice Butler to Emma Butler Paisley in Dobyville

Tulip, Arks.
Dec. 29th, 1881

Dear sister Emma:—

Your letter to Ma and also bro. Billy's were received several days ago, and read with due appreciation. We were glad to know that you were so much better, and able to write yourself, for we felt uneasy about you, and were fearful you might have a serious spell of sickness.

Yes, our hearts have been filled with sorrow such as is known only to those who have lost a beloved Father. Truly we sorrow not as those who have no hope beyond the grave, but it is hard to realize that we shall never on earth see that beloved face and enjoy his society. The pleasures of earth seem fewer when we recognize the fact, and we see the necessity of living for eternity, when we expect to meet those who have gone before. I regret that you could not be here to administer to him in his last moments. It would have been a great satisfaction to you, but as you say, Providence ordered it otherwise, and we must bow to his will.

I have always feared that he might have a return of the pneumonia since the first attack. His sickness was short, but he was taken severely at first, and we felt uneasy about him all the while. He did not speak of any of the children that were absent except brother Charlie, and he knew we were looking for him. We were so much afraid of disturbing his mind, or making him worse, that we kept him very quiet—am sorry we did not talk more to him. He expressed himself as being prepared to go, and told me at one time that he was so happy, to cover him up. Don't think I ever saw an infant breathe more gently than he did for several hours before he died—just like he was falling asleep. Heaven seems brighter now, and I feel more like striving to get there than ever before. We have several links to bind us there.

Brother Johnnie came over on Monday after he died, though he had not heard it until he reached Malvern, said he could have stood it better if he could have seen him in his last illness. Our dear Mamma—the burden falls heavier on her than all else; let us strive to cheer and make her life brighter, for she is all that we have now. She bears it much better than I felt she would.

Of course we had to change the time of our marriage; have appointed the 10th of Jan. Can't you come over? Ma says she would be glad to see you but you must not run any risk in coming over, should the weather be bad &c. We will have a very quiet marriage, and but little company. Brother Hunter will perform the ceremony at half past seven o'clock, and we will leave the next morning for Malvern. May God bless and take care of you, my sister, and may his grace sustain us in this hour of affliction. All send much love.

Your affectionate sister
Alice

Ma received a very sad letter from brother Charlie yesterday—says he doesn't see how he can stand to meet her without Pa at the old home.

Mattie Butler Hughes to Emma Butler Paisley in Dobyville

Little Rock, Arkansas
Jan. 15, 1882

Dear Sister Emma,

I returned here last Thursday, after an absence of four weeks, found George at the depot waiting for me. Alice was married Tuesday night. No one but the family except Sue and Jimmie Pattillo. Brother Hunter went down to marry them, and everything passed off well, but it was a sad wedding, Ma says the saddest she ever witnessed.

Poor little Edwin could hardly stand it. As soon as the ceremony was over he began to cry; and cried for some time. I expect he was thinking of his dear mamma. He loves Alice dearly, but didn't want her to take his Ma's place, told someone he could never call her "Ma." Of course Alice had rather he would call her aunt, as he has always done. The two youngest children will remain at Tulip, for awhile, anyway. Ma will keep William, and Sister Mary will attend to the baby, while I am here.

The baby is very sweet and talks very plain, says her name is "Annie Mary." She loves me better than she does anyone, and always says she is "Battie's girl." I expect she will become fond of sister Mary, and sister Mary will become very much attached to her; she is very affectionate in her disposition, and I wish I could keep her. If we were keeping house, I don't think I could give her up. It would be inconvenient and expensive to have her here, for we would be compelled to have a nurse. We have a room at Mrs. Cates' and take our meals with Mrs. Dick Gantt, who is keeping a boarding house on the same block. Mrs. Cates and sons board there too. In wet weather it is disagreeable, for we have no pavement, and it is quite a muddy walk, always have to wear overshoes.

Our dear old home at Tulip is sad and lonely now, since dear papa is gone. It will never be the same again. Dear Mamma bears her great loss with Christian fortitude, and seems more cheerful than I thought she would. The Sunday before I left we visited pa's grave together, the first time Ma had been there since the burial. She was very much affected, knelt by the grave, wept and prayed aloud for some time. I am so glad that sister Mary and bro. Matthews will be with Ma. She couldn't have remained there without someone.

I regretted so much that you were sick and couldn't be with pa during his last illness. For awhile we felt uneasy about you, and were greatly relieved when we heard you were convalescent. You ought to be very careful, and try to keep a cook if it is possible. I don't know who Ma will get for a cook. Aunt Lucy is living near, and will come anytime she wants her, but doesn't want to hire to cook regularly. Annie (Allen's girl) was there when I left, but she expected to go and live with Alice. I haven't heard yet what day Alice left; it rained so much Thursday, I don't think she came up. She has a nice home at Malvern, everything so nice and convenient.

I saw brother Charlie a few minutes yesterday, said Kate and the children were well. They have moved to the new home, but I don't see how Charlie can live here without some employment. He has had nothing to do for the last two months. I saw Florrie yesterday. She looks very happy, and Mrs. Feild is delighted to have a daughter. She ought to be, for there are few such girls as Florrie.

Our boys were well when we heard from them, and making good progress in their studies. George is in good health, and desires to be remembered to you and Billy. Love to the children, and a kiss for the baby and Mattie.

Your Devoted Sister
M. W. Hughes

William Paisley to Emma Butler Paisley in Dobyville

Malvern, Ark.
Jany 25th, 1882

My dearest one:

I was just a little too late for the train when I reached Gurdon yesterday, and between 2 & 3 o'clock I took a freight train which reached here a little after dark. I went directly to Henry's & found them ready to go into supper. All are well. Henry & I talked until 12 o'clock, & I slept well the remainder of the night. Henry seems to be doing very well in his business and will evidently get [along] all right.

Alice has been keeping to herself since her [marriage]. I went by to see her a while ago, found her pleasant, but thought I could detect an undercurrent of sadness. I have felt so much opposed to the marriage that I guess I was not able to make my self as pleasant as I ought to have been.

Old Mrs. Nat Smith and Mrs. Durham are both dead. Ira & Jimmie Pattillo are both here, & report all well at Tulip. I may lay over here until tomorrow. Don't feel that I have time, but feel like I need a little rest & change.

Tell Charlie & the children to keep every thing straight until I get back. How I wish we could live here or some where else, where there would be some pleasure to mix with work.

With much love to all,

Your devoted husband
W. Paisley

Mary Matthews to Emma Butler Paisley in Dobyville

Tulip Ark.
Feb. 7th 1882

Dear Sister Emma:—

You must excuse me for not replying to your letter sooner. I had forgotten I was owing you a letter until I came across your last a day or two ago.

I suppose you have already heard the particulars of Alice's marriage, which passed off quietly on the 10th ult. Tuesday night. Brother Hunter and Jimmie came down together in a buggy. You remember it was a very rainy day. Jimmie and Sue Pattillo were the only ones invited outside the family. Sister left for Little Rock next day. Alice remained and left next day in the rain, though she didn't get wet and found a nice fire and every thing in readiness when she reached her new home. Jimmie was expecting them, and had been over and made a fire.

Cousin Sue Peebles was here several weeks, and was anxious to remain until after the marriage, but her mother was sick and sent for her the week before. It was well she went when she did, as we have had so much bad weather ever since. I expect the road to Camden is now *very* bad.

Bro Charlie has been down to see after his farm—spent several days with us. He talked of writing to you while here but didn't find time; he left yesterday. Ma troubles a good deal about bro. C. not having any employment, which of course makes him dissatisfied, and he is so anxious to get out of debt. I am sorry he has to have so much trouble. He is such a good Christian—he would be much happier living in the country.

A long letter from Uncle Kittle to Pa was received not long since. I have replied to it, and Ma wrote some to aunt Betsy.

Mr. Matthews and I went up yesterday evening and planted some white hyacinths around pa's grave. They are blooming beautifully now. The weather has been so bad that we couldn't attend to the graves, and found them in a bad condition. The cows had trampled them and Annie's had sunk in. Ira and Mr. M. went up this morning and fenced around them and fixed them up.

Cousin Martha Fraser's husband died not long since, over eighty years old; his son who is editor of "Clinton Banner" lives in this state—send us his paper, which contained the obituary of his Father.

We have Annie Hawkins to do our work, and aunt Lucy does the washing and ironing. Ma was saying she wished you had a good girl like Annie to help you.

We have William and Annie here with us. They play together and are a great deal of company for each other. I take care of the baby. She sleeps in her crib by my bed. She is one of the sweetest and smartest children I ever saw, talks so plain and is so nice about everything—seems to [be] natural with her.

How is your little girl getting on? You must come to see us when the weather gets pleasant. Mr. M. sends his love to you, and says he would be so glad to see you, also bro Billy.

Mr. M. is now at work in the garden. He is fond of gardening, and ma says she is well fixed to have him with her. George is busy getting ready for farming. Herbert is clerking for bro. Henry, and seems well satisfied.

I suppose you have heard of the death of old Mrs. Durham and Mrs. Nat Smith? All the old people of Tulip are rapidly passing away. Ma feels sad and lonely at times. We all miss our dear Pa more than words can express. Ma sends a great deal of love and is anxious to see you. Much love to all and a large [share] for your dear self.

> Lovingly your sister,
> Mary

Mary Matthews to Emma Butler Paisley in Dobyville

Tulip Ark.
Mar. 8th 1882

Dear sister Emma:

Your letters to Ira and myself were received not long since. I suppose ere this you have heard of the great failure in business at Malvern. Although it was so greatly feared by papa, yet when it did come, it was a great shock to us. Ma has been greatly troubled about it and I have too. I don't think pa could hardly have survived it; he had been doing business forty years and never had to make an assignment, and as Sister remarked, his name is dishonored in being connected with the firm. Bro. Olin thinks he can soon make his way up again, but I don't think he will find it so easy. If he was the only one damaged it would not make so much difference; but to think of ma being left a widow with every thing swept away just from bad management and not taking pa's advice: don't suppose now I'll ever get what Pa intended me to have. It was his desire that all the children should share equally.

Mr. Emerson was made assignee, and Jimmie is clerking for him. He has been very busy drawing off accounts and fixing up the books &c—hasn't been to see us in a long time; the rain prevented for awhile, and then he had to go on for goods, don't know whether he has returned or not. We were glad to hear that bro. Billy returned all right from St. Louis, and hope he will be successful in business.

Alice came down week before last, and spent more than a week with us, left last Saturday. She doesn't seem much troubled about business matters. She and I visited most of the neighbors while she was here.

Mr. Wilfong, the teacher who is boarding here, will leave next week to attend school. He is preparing for the ministry—an excellent young man. We will miss him very much. The Presbyterian minister Mr. Moore, who now lives in Princeton, is expected to move up here and take the school. Don't know yet at what place he will live or board: they have two children.

Did you ever see so much rain? it is now raining and cold without. The farmers will be put back, and it is impossible to do much in the garden, though we have planted most of the vegetables. Mr. Matthews is very fond of gardening and is a great help to ma. Ma says he doesn't leave anything for her to do—he will get ahead of bro Billy, she says tell him. He is now busy in the garden.

Mar. 14th

Jimmie came down Friday and left this morning. We enjoyed his visit very much. A letter from bro. Billy he brought down with him, which we were glad to see—also one from Johnny and Charlie. All well.

Sociables seem to be the rage now—have one in the neighborhood every week or two. Friday night one at Judge Green's. They fixed up a real nice supper, and all seemed to enjoy themselves. About sixty there. Mrs. G. enjoyed it. There is to be one tonight—Mr. Banks, for the benefit of young Dr. Allie Banks, who is visiting them.

Mr. Wilfong left Monday. Mr. Moore is renting a part of Mrs. John Pattillo's house. He was to commence his school today. Mr. David Phillips and Miss Barbee are to be married tomorrow night. Mr. M. is to perform the ceremony.

We hear from Sister every week. Don't know when she can come down. I still have charge of the baby and Ma has William. The baby is very sweet and talks very plain. She loves "Mamie" very much, but never forgets her "Battie."

Love to bro. Billy and the children and yourself

Affectionately your sister
M. J. Matthews

P.S. The walnuts you brought ma how long has it been? she has some of them yet which we were eating yesterday.

Ma sends much love. Write soon. Ma sends you bro G.'s letter take care of it and return it some time.

"Capt." L. D. Lipscomb to William Paisley in Dobyville

Pittsburg, Texas
March the 14th, 1882

Dere William,

It is with plesure that I read youre kind Letters, and it affords me a great deal of Satsfaction to here from home, as I call it, for I have no abiding Place, no foot of land Do I posess, no cottige in this wilderness, a wayfaring man.

We have one of the best Prechers here I ever hird. I think one Mr. Stan is [to] take him on[e] sermon with another. I met Dr. Grier, a Presteterian minister here, some time ago. He preachers here one Sunday in the month. He told me [he] new Mr. Howerson. I think he said he was in college with him. He lives at mount Plesant.

You say money is scace. We dont need much in this World. Just that we can Eat and ware. Naked we came into the world, and we wont carry eny thing out of it.

[conclusion missing]

Mattie Hughes to Emma Paisley in Dobyville

Monticello, Arkansas
April 19, 1882

Dear Sister Emma,

I know I ought to have written to you long ago, and censure myself for not having done so. We are staying for a while at Monticello, have been here about a week, expect to return to Little Rock, some time next week. We are boarding at Dr. Robertson's. His wife went to school at Tulip, about the time the war broke out. He[r] name was Sallie McGehee, says she remembers you and Annie very well. I can't remember her, though she says she was to see me, at the McNeil place, two or three times, went with you or Annie. She remembers so well the fine plums that we had there.

It is a very pleasant place, they have a nice home, a beautiful grove of forest trees in front, a summer house covered with vines in one corner of the yard, which looks very pretty as the honeysuckles are in full bloom. She has three children, only one at home, the other two are at school, about twelve miles from here.

Sammie Colburn is boarding here, and tomorrow we expect to go to Hamburg, he to lecture there, on his travels, and I to visit Cousin Betsy Kittrell's family. Cousin Betsy is not there now. She is in Nashville visiting her brother.

I received a letter from cousin Maggie Dean, soon after getting here urging me to make her a visit. I'll not stay but a day or two, will come back Saturday.

Ma is thinking of going to General Conference. If she does it will be so pleasant to be there with Cousin Betsy. Jimmie expects to go with Ma. If they do go, no doubt they will have a pleasant time.

I am sorry you haven't been able to make Ma a visit. We will have to try and meet there during the summer.

Night before last we received three letters, one from each of the boys, and I was so glad to get them. West had just recovered from an attack of measles, and we were unusually anxious to hear from him. When he was taken sick he was in Bologna, Italy. As soon as he was able he left there and he went to Montreux on Lake Geneva, where he thought he could recuperate more rapidly. Said he had spent an hour and a half that day, rowing on the Lake, and enjoyed it very much. Walter is in fine health and writes very cheerfully; he thinks of spending the vacation in New England and Canada. Georgie's last examination will be on the 20 of June, and then he expects to leave for Arkansas.

Since the Readjusters have control, they are having some trouble at the University. They are talking of turning out the old professors, and putting new ones in their places; if they do, the University will be ruined.

All were well when I heard from Malvern and Tulip. Alice has William and the baby with her. Sister Mary carried them up about two weeks ago. I wish it was so that I could keep little Annie, but living like I am, I could not train her properly. I shall always have a tender feeling for her, and she seems to love me so much. But I have been away from her so long I fear she will forget me.

Brother Charlie has a right nice home in Little Rock, but he has no employment. Now they are talking of renting a larger house near the business part of town, where they can keep boarders, and make a living in that way. Mrs. Colburn, Johnnie, and Jessie will board with them.

How is your health, and how are the children getting on? I know they have grown a good deal since I saw them.

George is out on railroad, where they are at work, or he would send love. Love to Billy and the children. Write soon.

Your Sister
M. W. Hughes

Jimmie Butler to Emma Butler Paisley in Dobyville

Tulip Ark.
April 23rd, 1882

Dear Sister,

You either owe me a letter or I owe you one, I know not which! but I do know that neither of us have much to exult over, for it has been a long time since either of us have written. I received a letter from brother Billy some time ago, and am ashamed of not having answered it sooner. It does not matter to which one of you I address this letter, he can claim as much of it as yourself, as you are both one.

I came down home last Tuesday, and, of course, have been having a splendid time, both at home and abroad among the girls. Time has passed so rapidly since I came down that I can scarcely see where the days have gone or what they have brought except pleasure.

Ma and myself are eagerly anticipating a trip to Nashville [Tennessee] the 1st of May to attend the General Conference, which meets there on the 3rd. I wrote to Wm Evans not long ago, telling him that ma and myself expected to attend the Conference. He replied to the letter, and very kindly invited us to make our home with him while we were in Nashville. Cousin Betsy Kittrell will be there, which will make it exceedingly pleasant to ma; for they are as Jonathan and David were to each other.

It was some time before ma would fully consent to go, but she is fully decided now, and has very near made all necessary preparations. She will go up to Malvern about next Thursday, and we will start for Nashville about the 1st of May. I may go up to Malvern tomorrow or next day, as I have some business to attend to before going to Nashville. I have been exceedingly anxious for ma to make this trip, as the change will doubtless be of great benefit to her as well as exceedingly pleasant. I shall do all in my power to see that she has a good time. Ma thinks it an immense trip for her to take as old as she is, but I think it will strengthen both soul and body. Brother Henry, Johnnie, Ira, Sister and myself have agreed to bear her expenses. Ira received your letter Friday, and we were glad to hear from you. I will stir Alice up when I return, and get her to answer your letter. If you answer my letter shortly, direct to Nashville care of Wm Evans, and I will give you a Conference letter.

Ma is very much blessed in having brother Matthews and sister Mary with her. Bro. M. is so much help to her in keeping up a garden. He is very industrious and has a good garden.

As today is Sunday I will omit business. All are well and send love. Let me hear from you. We will probably be in Nashville two weeks or more.

Your devoted brother,
Jimmie

[Enclosed in same letter was the following one from Johnnie from Centre Point, April 3rd, 1882]

389

Johnnie Butler to Jimmie Butler in Tulip

Centre Point
Apr. 3rd 1882

Dear Brother

I recd yours 21st few days since. I am gratified that I should have written anything that would add one comfort to our dear Ma while she seems to be called to pass through many sorrows. I do feel exceedingly anxious that nothing should be left undone by us that would be of any pleasure or profit to her in any way. And after we have done all in our power, it is nothing in return for the great love that she has bestowed upon us.

Your "plan" I endorse heartily with a small check of $20, made payable to Bro Henry, who will cash it for you. Ma should not miss the trip for anything, and you go with her will be splendid, for I know our dear Ma will so much enjoy having her *Baby* boy along with her. In case you think this mite is not my share, notify me at once and I will double it.

By all means prevail on Ma's going. It will be the greatest help in the world to her, both soul and body, and I would not have her miss for ten times the little cost of the trip.

Much obliged to Olin for the letter from bro. Moores. The letter contains good counsel, and suits many of us. Though you are mistaken about my having left home on Sunday when I went to St. Louis. Though I did travel on the RR on Sunday, I have very seldom in life left home, in making a trip, on the Sabbath. I do oppose the practice and think we as a nation are too slack in the observance of the Sabbath on this very point. But sometimes it is unavoidable.

Glad to hear that Ira is doing well in his business. Hope he will succeed. I would like to know a little about your business. How are you getting on with your Texas girl? I have no doubt but that she is *splendid*. Kellie has not been very well lately, but able to be up all the while.

We have a young preacher here who says he is kin to us. Ask brother Henry how we are related to the Hutchinsons. His name is Johnson, but I believe his mother was a Hutchinson. He is from Ga., here last winter, and a very clever young Methodist preacher.

Kellie joins me in love to bro. Henry & family, Olin, Alice and all. Write to me often, Jimmie. I love to have letters from you.

Your Brother

Sister Emma:

Ma requested me to enclose this letter that I received from bro. Johnnie some time since. She says you must come over to see her soon after her return from Conference, so that she can relate the incidents of the trip while fresh in her memory. She almost regrets to leave home on account of her turkeys. She has five young turkeys and about 40 eggs setting. Sister Mary promises to look after the turkeys.

Jimmie

Jimmie Butler to Emma Butler Paisley in Dobyville

Nashville, Tenn.
May 11th, 1882

My Dear Sister:

Your much appreciated letter was received a day or two ago, and we were very glad to hear from you. Instead of leaving Malvern on the 1st of May, we left on the 29th of April, and staid in Little Rock until the evening of the 1st. So you see, we did not have the pleasure of traveling with brother Billy; but we were so fortunate as to meet him when the train came in from Malvern, and talked with him a short while. We were very glad to find him looking so well, bearing the burden of *forty years* upon his shoulders. I had not thought of his being *so ancient* until he told us.

We left Little Rock at about 3 PM, and arrived in Nashville about 9 o'clock the next morning. We made a safe and very pleasant trip. The train was filled with delegates and visitors, several of whom we knew. This made our trip more pleasant. I had the good luck to meet two young ladies on the train who insured me a magnificent time. Ma stood the trip as well as any young lady could. We had no trouble in finding our relatives, and they have given us a most hearty welcome. Their kindness surpasses anything that we had hoped for, and will not soon be forgotten by us. We have made our home with cousin Wm Evans, though we occasionally eat with some of our other relatives.

I find our relatives are more numerous than I expected. Cousin Wm Evans has two married daughters and two unmarried sons. Cousin James Manire has two sons. Cousin Wm lost his wife last January, which fact has caused him sadness ever since. He is one of the best men that I ever met. He is quite wealthy, but knows how to use his money for good purposes. He gave a thousand dollars toward building the Publishing House and about three thousand to help rebuild the McKendree church. He is very charitable to the poor.

Cousin James is also a splendid man, and has one of the best ladies for a wife that I ever met. She is a great worker in the missionary cause, and is known all over the United States. She and Cousin James live in a hotel at present, but are having them a very fine residence built. They also have plenty of money, and are very liberal to the church.

Ma and myself took supper with cousin Maggie Fall, one of cousin Wm's daughters, night before last. She·has the finest residence of any of them and lives in grander style. I suppose their residence, fitted up, must have cost them $25,000. Cousin Wm gave about $12,000 toward building it. Ma says she does not know how she will content herself at home after living in the midst of such splendor. We both will doubtless have to be toned down considerably.

We are having a splendid time attending Conference, hearing preaching and sight seeing. We will probably remain here something over a week longer, and then it will be difficult to tear ourselves away. Ma goes by the name of Polly among all our relatives here; they had all longed to see "cousin Polly." Aunt Polly lived with cousin Wm until her death. Ma now occupies her room.

The conference is getting on very well. The election of Bishops will very probably take place tomorrow. Two fraternity delegates spoke last night, and made splendid speeches. Missionary addresses are to be delivered tonight at McKendree church. This is considered the finest church in the South, and has the finest organ. Ma says she never saw such an immense organ before; sounds to her "like thunder." The church was dedicated by Bishop Paine last Sunday, and a splendid sermon was preached by Dr. Messick of Louisville.

Ma keeps perfectly well, and seems to enjoy herself beyond our highest expectations. She has been greatly cheered, and I think the trip will add many days to her life, at least I hope so. She enjoys being with Cousin Betsy so much. Cousin Betsy will return to Arkansas with us when we go. I wish she could go to Tulip, but I expect she will hasten on to Hamburg. Ma and cousin Betsy would both send love and some messages if they knew that I was writing to you. It is just after dinner, and I suppose they are taking a nap.

I suppose ere this reaches you bro. Billy will have returned. Much love to you both and the children. Write to me soon.

> Your loving brother,
> James O. Butler

Ira Butler to Emma Butler Paisley in Dobyville

> Tulip Ark.
> May 23rd 1882

Dear Sister Emma:

Jimmie & Ma has not arrived yet. Received a letter from the former Saturday: thought they would start for home about the first or middle of this week. Said they would spend a day or two at Little Rock. I am in hopes they will get home this week. They seem to have had a trip of uninterrupted pleasure. Sister Matt expects to return with them.

We are going to have a big Presbyterian meeting commencing next Thursday night. Mr. Monroe & another preacher will assist Mr. Moore in carrying on the meeting. Some are making a good deal of preparations for the occasion. Miss Sue [Pattillo] says every thing dates to the meeting at their house. We can have plenty vegetables now, such as potatoes, snap beans, beets, squash, & onions. Have corn silks but no roast ears. Have plenty cabbage heading up nicely & a fine prospect in way of all vegetables. Bro Matthews is a good gardener. How are your prospects for something to eat in the way of vegetables? I planted a nice little water mellon patch a few days ago. Bro. M. has a good many up with several leaves, but they are not doing well on account of so much rain & cold weather.

Summer is most here, but the weather fails to indicate her arrival. Heard of several who said there was frost this morning, but I think certainly they must have over reached the truth. This & last are years that will long be remembered. After a long torrid drouth had swepted over the country, laying waiste its beautiful crops, was followed by hail, storms & floods, which has reduced the people in some places almost to starvation.

Business with me is very dull. Have 5 mortgage customers who I am running, & two or three who are not mortgaged. This constitutes my credit business this year which is quite small, & I am rejoiced that it is so. While I won't make a great deel this year, neither will my losses be great, since I haven't put the goods out.

Coulter came down yesterday. Bro. Olin employed him to assist in driving the cattle he has bought to Malvern. They are starting up with them now. Alice is coming down to stay awhile when Ma comes.

Write me about the Dobyville young ladies, but I believe they have nearly all married. Who has Bro. Billie with him now in the store? Write often to yours affectionately

                    Ira

Love to all the family.

Mattie Hughes to Emma Paisley in Dobyville

Tulip Arkansas
June 12th 1882

Dear Sister Emma,

Here I am again at the dear old home, after an absence of nearly five months. Every thing looks natural, and it seems like old times for sister Mary to be here, but oh, how much I do miss dear papa, hadn't realized how much I would miss him until I came down. It just seems like he ought to be sitting on the front porch, where he staid most of the time during warm weather. If I miss him so much, how much more must dear Mamma, and how lonely she must feel at times. I know she felt sad returning home, thinking he wouldn't be here to welcome her. We visited his grave yesterday, by the side of dear Annie, and I thought of the happy meeting, when father and daughter met never to be separated.

Ma and Jimmie had a delightful time at the General Conference; had such a pleasant home at Cousin William Evans'. Cousin Betsy Kittrell, his sister, was with her, and they did enjoy being together so much. You must come over soon, and she will tell you all about her visit.

I left L.R. nearly three weeks ago, spent nearly two weeks at Malvern, and expect to remain here a week or two, and then I'll return to L.R. to stay until Georgie returns, which will be about the first of July. If George could be here, or visit me occasionally, I would remain here all Summer, for Tulip is the best place to stay during warm weather.

Walter is not coming home during his vacation, thinks now he will go over and join West, and return with him next fall. West is in Paris now, expects to remain there until the first of July, then make a pedestrian tour over part of Switzerland, and then he thinks his health will be fully restored, before returning to America.

If you want to enjoy vegetables you ought to be here now, have all kinds and as fine as I ever saw. Bro Matthews has attended to the garden, and takes so much interest in it, I don't know how Ma could have done without him, and sister Mary too. You know she is a good house keeper, and took such good care of every thing while Ma was gone. Nearly all of the young turkeys died, but you know how much cold and rainy weather we had, and how bad it is for young turkeys; she has only three. The hens are laying again, and she says she is going to try and raise some now.

All were well at Malvern. Alice has all three of the children, and gets on finely with them. Little Annie is so good and sweet, I wanted to bring her, to stay with me while I was here, but we would have had to bring William too, and we had no good way of bringing them. I do feel so much for Annie, wish I was settled so that I could keep her always. I don't mind the trouble of caring for her, I would be willing to deny myself of a great deal for her sake. She feels dearer to me than any other child. She is very fond of Alice, but if I could be with her, I believe she would love me best, for I think I love her most, Alice says I do. I have prayed about her, and have tried to commit it all into the hands of the Lord.

I wish I could see you and all of your children, I know they have grown a great deal since I saw them. May [Henry's daughter] begins to look like a young lady. Bro. Henry will soon have two grown daughters, and one son, Coulter, is about as tall as his pa.

We are having warm weather, and I know farmers are glad to see it, as well as merchants. Love to Billy and the children.

Your Sister
M. W. Hughes

13th

Ma says you must come as soon as you can. She thought of writing to you, but don't feel like it this morning. Says she appreciated your letter so much, she sends love. I expect to go to Malvern the last of this week. Direct to L.R.

William Paisley to Emma Paisley at Tulip

Dobyville Ark
June 21st 1882

My dear one,

I wrote you a postal last Saturday morning, & directed it to you at Malvern, but the Post master at Gurdon sent it back to this office by the mail Saturday evening. Since then there has been no chance of sending letters to the R.R. I am anxious to know how you got along on the train with the children, & whether you had any difficulty in getting from Malvern to Tulip.

Emma made us a very good cook, & seemed to get along very well keeping house. The day you left she cooked dinner & had all in good time & every thing nicely cooked. Saturday she cooked the Sunday meat & had vegetables for dinner, but I thought she would get tired of doing so much & having spoken to Mr. Powell about the old col[ored] woman at his house, I sent Willie down to see her, & she consented to come up & stay until you return. She came Saturday evening & does very well. She is 70 or 75 years old, but gets about very well, & seems to be nice about every thing. I tell her we shall want her the balance of the year, but she has not told me whether she will stay.

It is thought that Mrs. Adams has lost her mind. Mr. A. brought her up to Mrs. Doby's the evening before you left, I believe, and while at Mrs. D's she acted very strangely. Mr. Adams took her home & sent for Mrs. Rush. Sunday morning Walter said she was more quiet, but Monday morning Mrs. Rush passed going back home, and reported that she was no better, and that her mother seemed to be entirely deranged. It may be that she had taken too much exercise, being so weak, & that she will recover, but this I think hardly probable, as she has been sick so long.

I took Emma & Henry to Okolona Sunday. Mr. Davies preached. We took dinner at Dr. McGill's, & came home about five o'clock. Read a long letter from Mr. Tidball, Saturday. He thinks of paying us a visit this summer, as his school will soon be out. He is teaching in Mississippi. We had a fine rain Monday morning, and every thing in the garden & field is growing finely. We now have plenty of fine white head cabbage & will soon have ripe Tomatoes. Eddie Harris came home Saturday.

I have written this hurriedly but believe have given all the news. Shall have to close or be too late for the mail. Wish I could be with you at Tulip, but as I cannot, hope you will have a pleasant time, & that the care of so many of the children will not interfere with your enjoyment. With best love to all, I remain your affectionate husband

Wm Paisley

Shall expect to hear from you by every mail

Henry and Emma Paisley to Emma Butler Paisley in Tulip

Dobyville Ark
June 22th 1882

My dear mamma

I though[t] that I would write to you. Pa has got a cook. She appears to be a very good' one. Pa says she is. She milks and I keep off the calves. She is a colored woman. The pepper is growing very fast. Papa had some for dinner. All the vegetables are growing very fast. I hope that all are well. We are all well. Is Aunt Allice at Tulip, and is Edwin there? I hope that you got there time to see Aunt Mary. Well I will close this short letter, sending much love to all. Write soon to your child

Henry L. Paisley
[9 years old]

Dobyville Ark
June 22nd 1882

My dear Mamma

I thought I would write to you, having nothing to do now. I would like to see you and the children. I am getting along very well by myself. Aunt Winny come to wash yesterday. I am very much pleased with my cook. Is Aunt Allice at Tulip now and the children? If she is, kiss both of the babes for me. That is, Lula and Annie. How is the babe getting along? Papa got a letter from you yesterday. I went to see Eddie Farris Monday. They are all well. Mrs. Addams is very low the last time I heard. Well I will close this short letter. We are all well, and I hope you are the same. Write soon to child

Emma Paisley
[11 years old]

William Paisley to Emma Butler Paisley in Tulip

Dobyville Ark
June 22nd 1882

My dear one:

Your very welcome letter was recd. yesterday (Wednesday) evening, and we were all delighted to hear from you and the little ones. You were fortunate in meeting with Ira & getting him to take part of the children, as you speak of going down on the mail Buggy instead of hack. The buggy would not have furnished room for all. Mr. Outlaw told me that you barely had time to get on the train at Gurdon, which made me uneasy, fearing that the children were probably frightened, & that Mattie particularly would have a spell of the "jerks." It must have been tiresome to have to hold Lula all the way to Malvern.

I had to meet Mr. Hall & Esyn Cheatham at Lindsey McGill's this evening, having been appointed by a school meeting as a committee to select a site for a (free) school house. Spent nearly all the evening at Mr. McGill's, & while there feasted on Peaches, Apples & Plums. Some where on Billy Grier's land is the most central place in the District for a school house, but in deeding his land to his wife & children so as to keep it from his creditors, he has got it in such shape that it cannot be deeded to the School District for school purposes, or to anyone until his *unborn* children become of age. So we did not locate it there, & failing to agree on any other site, we did nothing but eat fruit & talk about matters & things in general.

On my return home I came by and stopped to see Mrs. Adams. Walter met me, & on going in I found Mrs. Adams up & going about in the dining room. Walter told her I was in the room and wanted to see her. She came out immediately, walking briskly, & spoke to me calling my name— asked about you in a way that indicated that she knew you were away, but soon commenced talking at random. Mr. Adams who had been lying down in Mrs. A's room came in, and Mrs. Adams asked about you again. Mr. Adams told her that you had gone to Tulip. Mrs. A said yes, she knew that, & that you did not come to see her. I had some very mellow apples in my pockets which I gave her, & she ate two of them, the 1st of any thing she had eaten for a day or two. While eating the apples she was sitting in a rocking chair which she kept constantly in motion, at the same time patting the floor with her feet, & nervously picking at the chair & her clothing with her hands, & occasionally talking & laughing in an irrational way. It is indeed sad very sad to see her. Yesterday she lay in a stupor all day but without sleep, & slept none last night. To day she has been going about & seemingly as active & strong as if she had not been sick. I did not stay long, probably 30 minutes. When I left she did not seem to know me. Mr. Adams appears to bear it all with his usual composure, but it is plain to be seen that the affliction is weighing him down & almost crushing him. He is certainly an extraordinary man, and rich in grace. Mrs. Adams may continue in this condition some time, but I would not be surprised to hear of her going down any time.

Mr. Hall says Sis is improving under Dr. Dale's treatment & that they are all better this week than they have been for a long time. We are getting along much better than I had any idea we could without you. Still we miss you & the little children much. Henry appears more lonesome than either of the other children, & I believe still thinks more of his ma than of any one else. John & Willie have been busy in the field, & expect to commence plowing in the sand field to morrow while Mr. Womack hoes the cotton.

Old aunt Caroline has proved herself to be an excellent old darkey, and I could not have gotten any one better suited for the place. She is kind to the children & at the same time talks to them like she expected them to respect her authority. Emma went over to see Eddie one evening, & with that exception has not been away & seems contented. She & Henry have been gathering beans & peas.

The pole beans have commenced to bear & in a few days I think I can gather a bushel or two a day. I made some brine this morning, & put up a large tin pan full of cucumbers, a great many of the cabbages are heading nicely—some okra about ready for use—full grown pods on the pepper. Tomatoes ready to ripen with many melons half grown, & water melons forming, so you see we are having vegetables in abundance. The fruits on two more peach trees are now ripening, as are the plums at the back of the garden—but I must stop or you will be wanting to come home before your visit is out.

It was hard for me to see how we would get along by ourselves, but I am glad now that you went when you did, for we are getting on comfortably, so much so that you need give yourself no uneasiness about us & thereby deduct from the pleasure of your visit. It is now late & I will stop & wish again Good night

Morning 23rd 1882

I found Bob Rawlins is going to Gurdon this morning, & I will finish this hurriedly to send by him. Have just come over after hoeing a while & gathering vegetables for dinner. We are all well. The morning is beautiful, & vegetation both in Garden & field is growing rapidly & has a charming effect on all. Let me know when you wish to come home & write me immediately. Should you prefer remaining until Monday week, do so and I will try & meet you in Malvern & escort you home. I would like to come to Tulip, but cannot spare the time now. Bob is ready & I must close.

With much love for all & a kiss for yourself & the little girls.

> Your affectionate husband
> Wm Paisley

William Paisley to Emma Butler Paisley in Tulip

> Dobyville Ark
> June 23rd 1882

My dear Emma:

I reckon it is hardly necessary for me to apologize for writing so often. This is a beautiful night, the moon making it almost as light as day, while the Katie Dids are filling the pleasant night breezes—which are refreshing after such a hot day—with their music. For some reason, I know not what, I feel more lonely than any time since you left. All have retired but me, but this in not unusual, as I am always the last, so that it must be due to the fact that I wrote you last night and as that is the nearest substitute I can have during your absence of talking with you in person, it causes me to miss you to night. Every thing here is going on as smoothly as could be desired without you. Our old cook does finely, and I believe improves every day. She is pleasant and agreeable with the children, and all of them like her. She seems to take a pride in trying to see how nice she can have every thing and her cooking, particularly in preparing vegetables, is first rate. To day she had Cabbage, Beans, Irish potatoes cooked in two ways (I mean the latter), cucumbers & onions. After dinner to day, I got Mr. Womack to plow the water melons and while it was very hot, I went out and hoed them until I was completely exhausted. After resting a while, I rode out to see one of my customers' crop. John & Willie plowed until dinner, but I think they were very willing to give it up at dinner time. Emma did some ironing this morning, while Henry served as general lackey boy for all.

We had a very hard rain Monday morning, & the ground in some places is full heavy to plow yet. Hill lands were badly washed—my own fully as bad, I think, as it was the 9th of May, but further than this there was no damage of consequence to the crop.

I had a very interesting letter from Henry with yours last Wednesday. He wrote as if he expected to find you with *two* or *three* babies that could not walk. How much I would like to have been with you at Malvern & to be with you at the old home, but as you say, there is one who would be constantly missed, which would cause a feeling of sadness which other associations—no matter how pleasant—would fail to remove.

I am glad that you stopped to see Mrs. Wm. Doby. Mr. Doby & Miss Mamie have both spoken of it, & seemed much gratified that you did so. I have not heard from her for several days. Mr. Orr went to Prescott for Sallie this morning and expects to return to morrow.

Well it is now late and I must close, but will say again that you need give yourself no uneasiness about us, for we are doing *mighty* well & should every thing continue as now could not be more comfortably arranged for sparing you.

Hope sister Mary & Mr. Matthews are both at home. I think if I had the time I could enjoy being with him very much, even if he does out look me. With best love to all I remain as ever your devoted husband

Wm. Paisley

I found to day that our tomatoes are turning out about ripe, but as the gardens are so much earlier at Tulip, suppose they have been using them for some time.

W.P.

William Paisley to Emma Butler Paisley in Tulip

Dobyville Ark.
June 27th 1882

My dear one:

I am feeling a little tired & stupid to night, but as it may be the last opportunity I will have of getting a letter off in time to reach you before you will start from Tulip I will try to write. All are in bed but me. This evening I had to walk down to Mr. Adams' old place to see about selecting a location for a school house—worked a good deal in the garden to day, & as it has been the warmest day that we have had, it is not strange that I should feel fatigued.

Charlie has gone to night to call on Miss Sallie Orr, who came home Saturday by way of Prescott. I have not seen her yet. Mr. Tidball is at Mr. Wm Doby's—came Saturday. I did not know he was in the neighborhood until he came in church Sunday morning. Spoke to him at church, but have not seen him since. Suppose he cannot be away from Miss Mamie long enough to come to see me. He is looking very natural, cannot see that he has changed a particle. Mrs. Jones seemed to think he and Miss M would marry in a short time—but I hardly think they will. I heard a few days since that Mrs. Davies is the mother of a fine daughter.

The children are having a great deal of trouble from fleas at the office. John and Henry have just come in and say they cannot sleep. I suppose they are brought in from the lot. The children are all doing remarkably well. John & Willie have been taking it time about plowing & hoeing. Henry goes with them, & has made a regular hand with the hoe. Emma & old aunt Caroline get on finely together, & both seem contented. Altogether we have gotten along finely considering your absence, but we are getting tired of doing without you & the little girls, & think the time long to have you with us again. After passing thro Sunday, I regretted not writing you to come the last of the week, but it will suit me better to meet you in Malvern Monday night & come home with you Tuesday, than to be away Friday or Saturday.

Mr. Hall & Lula took dinner with us Sunday. After Mr. Hall left, I walked up to Mrs. McGill's. Mrs. Patterson has had her teeth extracted with a view of having a new set.

Tell Ma that I regret exceedingly not being able to be with you at Tulip, for nothing could afford me more pleasure, but it was impossible.

Give my best love to all and believe me as ever your devoted husband

Wm Paisley

Your letter of the 23rd came Saturday. Hope to hear from you again to morrow. We have a great many nice apples now suitable for drying. Peaches will be hard to get.

W.P.

Morning 28 1882

We are well this morning. Jno, Willie, & Henry are going to Esyn Cheatham's this morning where they expect to meet Lula & all go a-fishing. Charlie wants to go to Prescott this evening to make arrangements with them to board Katie, his sister, to go to school. He is doing this to keep her from getting married to young Jim Sloan.

Yours
W.P.

William Paisley to Emma Butler Paisley in Tulip

Dobyville, Arkansas
June 28th 1882

My dearest one

Your letter of the 26th & 27th came this evening, together with one for Emma & Henry, and we are all delighted to hear from you again, & that you are enjoying your rest & visit so much. Could we always be so fortunately situated in the way of help, you might go much oftener than you do, and I heartily wish you could have more frequent recreation. Sorry you are troubled with cold but hope you will soon be well. Charlie goes to Prescott to morrow, & I will send this by him to be mailed. He does not want any to know the object of his trip.

When we went into the dining room today, Emma & old aunt Caroline were standing at the head of the table, and it was plain to be seen that something was "up." Aunt Caroline with her hand over her mouth said "Dis is mighty poor dinner, haint it!" Emma was trying to keep her face straight, & directly aunt Caroline uncovered the side table and handed out some biscuits, stewed apples & some nice peach & Huckleberry pies, which were very nice, & a pleasant surprise, as I had not authorized any thing in the way of dessert since you left. Emma and the old cook seemed to enjoy the surprise as much as we did the eating.

Mrs. Adams is no better though Walter reports her more quiet today. Mr. Tidball was up a short time this evening, but I was not with him alone. He promises to come up to see me this week & stay until we get tired of him.

John & Willie & Henry returned about night from fishing with their usual success, and tired & broken down. I expect to meet you at Malvern Monday, start home Tuesday morning. Should any thing prevent my getting off, you had better come down on the Tuesday evening train to Gurdon, and I will meet you there. I don't know of any thing now to prevent my getting off, & will be sure to come if I can, but mention this as an alternative should I fail.

With best love to all

> your ever devoted husband
> Wm Paisley

Emma Paisley to Emma Butler Paisley in Malvern

> Dobyville Ark
> June 28th 1882

My dear Mamma

I was very glad to get a letter from you I rcd it with pleasure. I was very sorry to hear that you took cold. I wish that I could see you and the children, I get right lonesome sometimes, and I go off to play by my self. Henry get lonesome to and goe to the field and help John and Willie hoe that is the reason that I go out doors and play by my self but I soon get tired of playing by my self, and I go and take a nap of sleep but my naps are very long. The cook looks for me but she cant hardly once she find [me] in the other room behind the curtain. Miss Sallie Orr has got back and Mr. Tidball, and Mrs. Baley. Eppie goes to school again. Well, I will close, sending much love. Write soon to your daughter

> Emma Paisley
> [Age 11 years]

John A. Paisley to Emma Butler Paisley in Malvern

Dobyville Clark Co Ark
June 30 [1882]

Dear ma,

I have been wanting to write to you ever since you left but I haven't had time. I have been ploughing this week. Henry and Emma received your letter. Pa has been working in the garden very hard. It come very near making him sick one day, when he was working the watter melons. We will get through laying by our corn next week if it don't rain. It is about time to go to work. All are well. We are getting along very well, but I will be glad when you get home. I will close. If you have time to write, you can write.

from your
son J. A. Paisley
[Age 15 years]

Henry L. Paisley to Emma Butler Paisley in Malvern

Dobyville Ark
June 28th 1882

My Dear Ma

I thought that I would write to you once more. We all are well. I was sorry to here that Grandma was sick. I hope that she will get well in a few days. Mr. Tidball has come in this state. I think that he will come to dinner here to day. I wish that I could see you and the Baby so bad. I hope that none of you all are sick. If you see Edwin in Malvern tell him to write to me. It seems to me like you have been gone two months. Has Mary and Mattie got a sweet hearts in Tulip or Malvern? You must come soon. They have not decided yet where they are going to have the free school at. Give my love to all, so I will close this short letter. Excuse such hen scratching.

H. L. P. [age 9 years]

Mattie Hughes to Emma Butler Paisley in Dobyville

Little Rock, Arkansas
Sept. 24th 1882

Dear Sister Emma,

I ought to have written to you some time ago. If I don't write this evening, it may be some time before I can write, as we expect to leave for Boston tomorrow, to be gone several weeks, and I know I'll not feel much like writing, while we are travelling around. Georgie left last Thursday,

401

and I expect he got to Cambridge today. He is going there to take the law course, so he will be there one year with Walter. We expected to leave when he did, but George had to go to Warren first, and didn't get back until last night.

Walter and West were to leave Glasgow on the 15th Sep, and I suppose they will get to Boston about the time we will. They have spent most of the Summer in Holland and Scotland, and have had a pleasant time. West's health is much better, and he expects to commence the study of medicine, soon after getting over. He hasn't decided whether he will attend lectures in New York or Philadelphia. If in the former he will be near Walter and Georgie.

Jimmie came in today, and expects to obtain a situation here. He has had an offer to clerk for Quinn bro's., and if he can't do better, he will begin there tomorrow. I expect he will board at bro. Charlie's. Will if they have a room for him. He tells me that Ma and Ira have gone to Hamburg, will return the latter part of next week.

Alice is having a pleasant time in California, and thinks her digestion is better. She has been to see Sister Jennie, and spent a week or ten days with her. Says the children haven't changed much, that Jessie is very pretty now. I haven't had any letter from her, but hope to get one soon, as I wrote to her a few days ago. She met with a warm welcome from all the relatives, will spend most of the time at bro. Moores, as bro. George has so little room. I do hope she will have a pleasant time, and come back improved in health.

All well at bro. Charlie's. Saw Kate at church today. They have about 14 boarders now, and I suppose they are getting on very well, though I think bro. Charlie would be better satisfied on a farm.

How are your children getting on? and what is the prospect for a good crop of cotton in your county? George sends love, to you and Billy, write soon to

> Your Devoted Sister
> M. W. Hughes

Mary Matthews to Emma Butler Paisley in Dobyville

Tulip, Ark.
Oct 5th 1882

Dear Sister Emma:—

You begin to think it is time you were hearing from home again, and so it is. Ma received and appreciated your letter written her on her birthday, also one from Sister at the same time. They came during her absence. She and Ira had gone on another trip to Hamburg, getting there Friday the 22nd. They had quite a pleasant time, returned the following Thursday, making it a little over a week that they were gone.

Our protracted meeting commenced last Saturday and is still continued. No conversions yet and only one penitent at the altar. Bro. Caldwell and Mr. Moore are assisting Mr. Matthews. It may close tonight as Mr. M. will have to leave to attend another meeting: this place seems harder to move religiously than almost any other on the circuit: though the church will no doubt be revived and strengthened, sinners faithfully warned, whether they accept salvation or not.

Several late letters read from Alice. Ira received a good long one from her last night. She is having a pleasant time, enjoyed her visit to sister Jennie and the children; visited bro. Lewis' grave while there; after her return to Downey, she attended the campmeeting which continued about three weeks. They had a glorious time religiously, and Alice felt that she had been greatly blessed. We were much surprised from Alice's last letter to learn that she was going on a pleasure trip to Humboldt beyond San Francisco, will be out on the Pacific ocean out of sight of land 13 days. She seemed delighted and not the least afraid. Thinks it will be beneficial to her health. Mariah Moores is going too, free of charge, as they were well acquainted with the Captain and his family who are their friends, said they would be on the trip 30 days. Bro. Olin had written her to start home the 6th of next month, but she hadn't received the letter before starting on this trip. Ira's letter was written on board the schooner dated Sept. 30th. It will be a long time now before we can hear from her again.

I suppose you have heard that Jimmie is clerking for Quin Brothers in Little Rock, and boarding with bro. Charlie, who has thirteen other boarders and expecting more. We have had only one letter from Jimmie. He was well pleased so far, and thought it would be improving to him to be in a large city establishment—said he was as green there as when he first commenced business at Malvern. Mr. Matthews went to Malvern last week and brought me the shoes, for which I am much obliged. They are charged to bro. Billy as requested. Tell John that Ira got his ring the day he left—Jim went after it and got it from the girl he loaned it to.

Glad you are having so many late vegetables, for they help out and are fine to have now. Our late cabbage didn't do any good. The early ones have just given out. We are having an abundance of turnip greens, sweet potatoes, peas and have young Irish potatoes. The turkey hen that was setting while you were here has only five turkeys. They are growing rapidly. Something caught 3 of them not long since, after considering them entirely out of danger, have eight we raised this year.

There has been more sickness around here than usual. Mrs. Wm Young's baby died this morning, caused I suppose from teething. He has had chronic diarrhea for several months. His family have been sick a great deal. Old uncle Jim, the black smith, died not long ago. He is much missed, was a good honest negro, which can be said of so few of them.

Ma sends much love and will try to visit you if possible. Mr. M. and Ira also unite with me in love to you all.

Affectionately your sister,
Mary

Write when you can.

Sister has gone to meet her boys at Boston. Expects to make us another visit when she returns, which will be in two or three weeks.

Mary Wyche Butler to Emma Butler Paisley in Dobyville

Tulip
Oct. 31, 1882

My Dear Daughter:

This is your birthday. I have thought of you all day, felt like I wanted to write to you. You and your sister remembered me and wrote to me on that day. You have not such a pretty day as mine. I was in Hamburg. I told Mary she must write to you today. I hope you are feeling well.

403

I was reading my little lesson book today. Your verse was so suitable, so consoling, I want you to read it. 41st Chap. 10 verse of Isaiah. May the Lord bless you and strengthen you, uphold you with the right hand of righteousness, is my prayer. You are 38, I am 68. What do you think of that?

Next Thursday will be your Bro. Geo[rge's] birthday. He has written me 2 letters, seem very happy. We hear from Alice right often. She has had a fine time, seems to be improving, though she was very sick on the ocean. Mariah Moores was with her. I wish she could stay all winter. I expect she will come some time next month.

I suppose you have heard that Jimmie has gone to L.R. I went to Malvern to see him last week, is very well pleased, has to work night and day. Says he never knew what it was before.

Our quarterly meeting next Sat. and Sun. I can go over any time next week, as Geo [Matthews] goes in a buggy. I don't know what my little boy [William, Annie's son] will do without me. No one can take my place with him.

Mrs. Cooper has been right sick, had them sitting up with her, is better.

My love to William & all the children. Good night, all. Dear one, hopeing to see you soon.

Your mother

Mattie Hughes to Mary Wyche Butler in Dobyville

Tulip Arkansas
Nov. 11th 1882

My Dear Mamma,

Knowing how anxious you are to hear from home, I'll write you a short letter this morning. I hope you reached Billy's safely and found all well. I think you must have spent the night in Gurdon, as it must have been too late, for you to have gone that night. William has been a good boy most of the time since you left, has been sleeping in your bed with Ira, and gets on finely. The day you left he fretted a little once or twice, said he wanted Mamma to come back. Now he seems to be contented, doesn't say anything about your coming.

Jessie has been down twice, spent one day, and yesterday he came after dinner. I believe he frightens the children, for last night Annie awoke two or three times, said dog would catch her, said Jessie said so.

Bro Matthews left for one of his appointments yesterday, and will not get back until Monday. Today week, he and Sister Mary expect to leave for conference. I hope it will turn cold before he leaves, so he can kill one the of hogs, for I want to eat some fresh pork, and then we will have some good lard.

I think George may come down next week. I hope he will come before Sister Mary leaves. He sent me a letter from West. He keeps well, and is delighted with the study of medicine. Said some time ago, [he] saw an announcement in the *Gazette*, that Dr. Winfield was to lecture on the "Valley of Dry Bones," thought he chose a nice subject, said he didn't find them dry in the sense of un-interesting, he had become very much interested in them.

Mrs. Cooper is getting on very well. I called to see her once, and Sister Mary stopped to see her day before yesterday. We haven't had any visitors since you left, except Sue Pattillo and Helen. Mrs. William Pattillo's youngest son, Willie, came yesterday. They had been expecting him several days, thought he would come on Mr. Pattillo's birthday, last Wednesday. They prepared a nice dinner and invited near relatives, I heard they had a turkey, but didn't hear where they got it. He was 70 years old and looks so cheerful and happy.

Today the contest over the wagon is to come off, at Tulip. Ira wrote for Maj Duffie to come up; he said he ought to have Olin here, so Ira wrote for him to come. He didn't hear whether he would come or not. I expect Maj Duffie will come here to dinner.

Sister Mary sends love, and says you musn't feel uneasy, that every thing is going on all right. She asked William what he wanted me to tell you, said tell you to come home as quick as you could. Annie is very sweet, and says so many smart things; said when she "got as big as Battie, she would put on spectacles, and write letters too."

Much love to Emma and the children. I am glad you are with them, though I am denied the pleasure of your company. Ira had a postal from Charlie the other day, said he thought he might come down this week or next; on his way to the farm, I expect, to see about his rents. George says Jimmie is looking well, had bought him a new suit of clothes (ready made), and they fit him well. Get Emma or Billy to write, so we can hear from you all.

> Your Loving Daughter
> [Mattie]

(Haven't heard from Alice)

Ira Butler to Mary Wyche Butler in Dobyville

> Tulip Ark
> Nov 14th 1882

Dear Mama:

Bro Billie's letter to Sister Mary, bringing the glad news of another Grand child [named Annie Orr] was gladly received. Am glad Sis Emma is getting on so well. Haven't time to write but a short note this morning.

Bro. M. killed the beef & a hog yesterday, and we had bones for breakfast and they did eat splendidly. The only trouble about it was that there was hardly enough cooked. Sis Mary is not as good judge of our appetites as you are. Bro. M. says he would have killed all of them if you had been here.

William sleeps with me in your bed & is getting on finely. He cried some the day you left, and asks when you are comming home very often. He wants to go to Malvern to come back with you. Little Annie knows all of her letters, and is getting on finely with Battie. Received a letter from Jimmie yesterday. He is getting on well.

There is nothing new. We miss you a great deal. Am sorry that I haven't time to write more. Love to all.

> Your loving Son
> Ira

Mary Matthews to Emma Butler Paisley in Dobyville

Tulip Ark
Feb. 15th 1883

Dear Sister Emma:—

I have been thinking of writing to you for some time. Ma was glad to get Emma's letter, which was received a few days ago—glad to see that she can write so well.

Haven't we had a long spell of snow and freezing weather? George had him a sleigh made, and took some of the girls sleigh riding; you would have been amused to see Ma riding all around in the grove. It was so nice and smooth. I also got on and rode up to Mrs. G. Pattillo's. Went in to see her while Helen took a ride: we very seldom have snow suitable for sleighing.

The weather has turned warm again, and it is time now to be gardening. Mr. Matthews did plant some seeds yesterday. George has plowed a part of the yard and grove to be sown in grass—having the trees topped today, which seems to be hard work. There will be a great deal of cleaning up to do when they get through.

Ira has bought out the old stock of goods from Orr and Lindsley, and I expect gets a good bargain. They at first refused to take seven hundred cash which Ira offered, but have since telegraphed that he could have them at that price. Ira went up this morning to see about having them packed and hauled. I expect he will have his store well filled. Ira is doing a very good, safe business, really saving more than he could in a large place. He buys up horses, cattle, corn &c and sells at a good profit. That is, he takes these in payment of debts.

Herbert is here with us this year. Came down expecting to go to school to Mr. Moore, but he has decided to quit teaching, so Herbert will assist George about farming this spring; he has been attending to the store for Ira during his absence. I understand Miss Ellen Young and Miss Carrie both expect to teach, so you see Tulip can afford two schools. I regret that we can't keep a large school with a male teacher.

Mr. Matthews expects to carry Ma to Malvern next Tuesday if the weather is favorable; she will remain with Alice some time. Sister thinks she will come down and bring little Annie to stay awhile with me, that is, if bro. George gets well enough to return to LR and attend to business; he was still there when she wrote last Saturday. The bad weather made against his improvement—couldn't ride out or exercise enough.

Ma and I went up to see Mrs. Robertson this evening. She has a little girl two weeks old. Mrs. Dunlap, her sister, is staying with her. Ruth Banks also has a boy born yesterday, Valentine's Day. I saw Mr. Banks in Tulip this evening. He seems very proud of it. They have felt some uneasiness about Ruth for several weeks.

Ma received a good letter from Jimmie this evening. He is getting on very well.

Mr. Matthews unites with me in much love to you, Bro. Billy and the children. We would like *so* much to make you a visit some time this coming summer.

I suppose you have heard of the death of Mattie Holmes. She was taken sick Friday and died Monday. Bro. Holmes wrote for Mr. Matthews to come down and preach her funeral, also desired ma and myself to come. We went. The services were conducted at the parsonage. The people of Princeton seemed very kind. Oh, it was so sad to see the bereaved husband and six motherless children, the baby, a little girl named Mattie, five months old. She died the 29th of January of congestion. Bro. Holmes staid with us Thursday night before she was taken sick—said she spoke of coming with him to spend several days, but concluded the weather was too damp. Her health has been bad for a long time, and at Conference when appointed to Princeton circuit, they thought it would be impossible to go on account of her health. I don't know what bro. Holmes will do with the children. He spoke of sending the three daughters to his sister, Mrs. Hays, of Prescott.

It was also very sad about the death of Bro. Keith's wife at Malvern. They had rented bro. Henry's vacant house which was nicely fixed up for them, had been living there I think about a week, when Mrs. Keith (who was quite young) was taken sick Friday and died Monday. She was left a child about a year old I think.

It is now bed time, but Ma may have some message to send in the morning. Good night!

Afftly
sister Mary

[In pencil, "Ma's" handwriting]

Dear little Emma,

I write a few lines on your Aunt M letter. I was sory to hear you had sprained your ankle. I hope it is well. How is your papa getting along and do he still sit up so late? Tell him he had better sleep in the night work in the day.

Mattie Hughes to Emma Butler Paisley at Dobyville

Malvern, Arkansas
March 10th, 1883

Dear Sister Emma,

It has been a long time since we wrote to each other, but I believe you wrote the last letter, and I deserve censure for not writing to you long ago. I know your time is fully occupied with your children and housekeeping, but you have always been prompt in answering letters. Ma received a letter from you last week, and I have read several letters from your children. Was surprised to read such a good letter, from Henry to Edwin, didn't know he could write so well.

Alice has a little boy born on the 5th, weighed 6½ pds, she got through finely, wasn't sick more than an hour and a half; if Dr. Reamy hadn't been so near, he couldn't have gotten there in time. The night before, Ma had staid at bro. Henry's, but said she wouldn't leave her any more, for she felt uneasy. Alice [has] been very well, and the baby just as little trouble as one could be. Annie is delighted with it, calls it her baby.

Ma is very well, and I suppose will stay with Alice, until the baby is three or four weeks old; don't know yet what they will name it. Bro. Henry and Mollie went to Little Rock last Wednesday and returned yesterday. They had a pleasant visit, Mollie met a good many old acquaintances, and bro. H. attended to some business. They slept in our room at Mrs. Cates' and took most of their meals with Mrs. Gantt, took dinner with Kate.

Bro. Charlie was from home, had gone to see bro. Johnnie, went over to look at the country where David Coulter is living. Johnnie has bought a place over there, and is very anxious for Charlie to buy near him. I don't know what he will do. He stopped by here on his return, but hadn't decided what he would do. Said he was anxious to stop and see you. If you had only lived nearer the railroad, he would have stopped over. Ira was up from Tulip yesterday, all well and getting along finely, Clarissa is doing the work, and so far they are pleased with her.

George is feeling very badly today, couldn't sleep last night, took Dover's powders, and bromide of potassium, but they didn't have a good effect. He has been growing worse for the last two weeks, feels greatly discouraged, doesn't know what to do. I have been trying to get him to go to Eureka Springs, but he doesn't believe it will do any good. For awhile he improved, gained several pounds, and thought he would soon be in his usual health. Sleeplessness is his greatest trouble, but I believe that is caused by torpid liver.

We are staying at bro. Henry's now, but don't know how long we will remain, may go to Tulip soon.

The boys were well when we heard from them, haven't heard from them this week, and George is getting uneasy.

Kate Cooper has a little boy about two weeks old. Did you know that Jennie had a boy? Maria Moores wrote Alice about it, but didn't say how old it was.

Maj Smith has been very low with pneumonia, but he is slowly recovering. Mr. Doak and family have come back from Miss. and just as poor as they can be. He has been seen drunk several times since he came.

Love to Billy and the children, would like so much to see you all. Write whenever you can.

Your Loving Sister,
M. W. Hughes

Mary Matthews to Emma Butler Paisley in Dobyville

Tulip Ark.
Mar. 20th 1883

Dear Sister Emma:—

Your good letter was received some time ago, and it is time I was replying, for if I judge you by myself, it is always a pleasure to get them as often as possible. I suppose you hear from them all at Malvern. Ma is still there. Haven't heard from her for several days. I wrote to her to know when she wanted us to send for her, expected a letter this evening, but was disappointed. Alice's little boy is now over two weeks old, but I've never heard what name has been selected. Sister and bro. G. are still at Malvern. Mrs. Young, who returned from there yesterday, told me this evening they talked of coming down here soon.

This is a very busy time now with farmers. Mr. Matthews works hard all the time when he is at home. I have no trouble about gardening, for he plants all the seed and works the vegetables &c. The early vegetables are growing very nicely now, but this cold weather will check them some. We had a heavy frost last night. We are still using sweet potatoes made last year which kept finely. Our kraut kept well too, which has been enjoyed all winter: together with peas, turnips, parsnips, and now turnip greens, we have made out to have some variety. I have only opened one can of peaches, which I had for supper last night.

Dr. Allie Banks, his sister Mollie (who is in the neighborhood visiting) and Helen Pattillo took tea with us and sat till bedtime; we had some good music and a pleasant time. Mr. Banks brought his daughter Mollie with him to attend Fannie Macon's wedding, which took place at Mr. Lieper's about two weeks ago. She married a widower by the named of Lybrand with six children. They live at Sheridan in Grant Co. Miss Mollie is a lively, pleasant young lady, favors her mother. It looked like old times to see Mr. Banks in the pulpit at Tulip. He is looking very natural, though of course older and is hard of hearing. Preached four or five sermons—doesn't confine himself to his notes like he used to.

Clara Cooper with her wonderful baby is down on a visit. She has been here two weeks. The baby is troubled with something like tetter or some bad eruption of the skin. Dr. Cooper is trying his skill in curing him and, by the way, they were making great preparations up there to have a party to night, had baked the cake, killed turkey and kid, and wrote to Malvern for Howel and two musicians. But it seems all this was going on without Dr. Cooper's knowledge or approval, so this morning he told them they shouldn't have any party there, and wrote a note to Mrs. Roane, for she was the chief manager, and I suppose was preparing to have a dance. Dr. Cooper said as poor a Christian as he was, he was'nt going to submit to any such thing being carried on his house; so it was all broken up, and I suppose the young people were disappointed. I haven't heard whether Howel and the musicians came or not—if so, I suppose they can enjoy the good things prepared.

Ira received a letter from Jimmie a few days ago. He is now book-keeping for Quinn Bro. and likes it—has more leisure time than before, but didn't know how much his wages would be increased. Says he doesn't believe he can save anything in L R, and yet he doesn't spend foolishly. Bro. Charlie had been over to see Johnnie and look at the farm, but returned as undecided as ever. I wish he could settle on some good farm, but the trouble is getting some place that will suit Kate. You know she is not of a very contented disposition any way.

I have written out my sheet and must close. Love to Bro. Billy and the children. Mr. M. also sends love.

I have about twenty young chickens and 18 turkey eggs. Five more hens sitting.

Write soon to your sister   Mary

Mattie Hughes to Emma Butler Paisley in Dobyville

Malvern Arkansas
June 8th 1883

Dear Sister Emma,

I know you will be suprised to hear that we are again at Malvern, have been here about a week. George took a severe cold, had fever for a day or so, and thought he would do better here than at Little Rock. His digestion was bad before, but since he has had this cold it is worse than ever. I think he has improved some, would have done better if we hadn't had so much rainy weather. He has been riding horseback a good deal, and that is good exercise for him. If he doesn't get worse, we will return to Little Rock the first of next week.

We have been staying with Alice, but came to bro. Henry's yesterday, as he and Mollie had to leave for Texas, to visit Maj Coulter, who is in very feeble health. They received a letter from Paul Coulter, the day before they left, saying that he continued to grow weaker, and he thought they had better come. If he is able to travel, they will bring him here. Brother Henry had expected to go in a few days any way, wanted to see about his farm there, and get the Maj to return with him. Mollie felt very anxious about him, and I think she had cause to be.

Alice is very well. Edwin has recovered from the measles, but Annie Mary is sick with it now, was badly broken out this morning, but she is not confined to the bed. Said she wanted me to stay with her until she got well. I hated to leave her, for Alice has so much on her hands, I fear she will take cold. The baby is very sweet and pretty, has black eyes and hair, and some one remarked the other day, just like the Butlers. I can see that he favors bro. Henry & George. I did want little Annie to favor her Mother so much.

Sue Pattillo spent two nights with Alice, as she returned from her visit to Mrs. Ben Logan, intended staying longer, but her brother came sooner than she expected. Says she enjoyed her visit to Julia so much. Last night bro. Caldwell and Anna staid with Alice. Anna had been on a visit to Fannie, who lives near Hot Springs, and taught a three-months school while she was there.

The children here are very busy preparing for a concert, that Miss Nannie Strong has tonight. May takes a prominent part in it. Nannie sings one song. We had letters from our boys today. All three of them will be here in about three weeks. I expect Reavis will come in two weeks, thought he would leave on the 18th. If we are in Little Rock they will stop there.

The carpenters are busy at work, have finished the dining room, kitchen, and bathroom, are busy now on the main building, haven't troubled the old parlor and dining room, will have the other nearly completed, before they trouble that. When it is completed Mollie will have a large house, ten rooms, I think.

9th

Received a letter from bro Henry this morning, they arrived at Maj Coulter's the same day they left here (Thursday), got there at supper time, and had the pleasure of seeing the Maj. sitting at the table eating. They will return home the first of next week, bring the Maj. with them, get here Tuesday or Wednesday. All well at Tulip. Had a letter from sister Mary day before yesterday. Edwin went down with bro. Caldwell. Love to Billy and the children, a kiss for the baby.

Your Sister
M. W. Hughes

Glad to hear that your children are becoming religious while they are young. Henry must be an uncommonly smart child. I would like so much to see you all. Hope I will during the Summer. George sends love. I enclose you one of the programs of the concert they had last night.

Jimmie Butler to Billy Paisley in Dobyville

Tulip, Ark, August 16th, 1883

Dear Brother Billy:

Your letter was forwarded to me by brother Henry last Monday, and I should have replied immediately, but I have been in doubt for the last few days as to what arrangement I should make for the fall. When I left Little Rock, I fully expected to go in business at some place this fall with Ira, but I have since concluded it will be best for me to sell my property at Malvern first. I think I can sell it this fall, and, for this reason, I would prefer being in Malvern where I shall have an opportunity to see after it. I would prefer not to make any permanent engagement for the year, as I may find sale for my property this winter, and would then wish to go into business for myself. When I was at Malvern last, brother Henry made me an offer of $50 per month and board me during the busy season, and said he would be glad to have me all the year. I expect now to begin with him the first or fifteenth of September. I could get at least a thousand dollars a year in Little Rock, but expenses are so enormous there that I could not save much even at that salary. I certainly appreciate your kind offer, and I wish that circumstances were such that I could accept, for I assure you it would be a pleasure to live with you and sister Emma. Ma has some notes and accounts that I want to collect this fall, and this business, in addition to my own, can be much better attended to in Malvern.

I have a strong notion of going to Texas when I wish to start in business. If I could get a start out there in some growing town, I am confident that I could succeed much better than in Ark. I might do better in Malvern for the first year or two, but I am satisfied I could succeed better in a few years in Texas.

Ira has succeeded very well here, and I am not sure but what he would do better here than any where else. He has not been doing a large business, but it has been a safe one. He had managed much better than I feared he would. He is a good collector, and very careful to whom he sells on time.

I came down to Tulip on the sixth of this month, and I do not think I ever had a better time in life than I have had since coming home. There are nine of us boys together, and were ten until Andrew Hunter left us last Monday. We do nothing but play, *eat* and sleep. I used to think that your family were pretty good at eating, but you are nowhere compared with us. It took several days for the cooks to find out how much they had to cook. I have gained six pounds, Gus [Tillett] seven and the others in nearly the same proportion. We play lawn tennis, marbles, quoits and various other games besides hunting, and target shooting.

I would like so much to make you a visit this summer but I haven't a good way of coming and only a short time to stay at home, and for these reasons I am afraid I cannot come.

All keep well at home and in fine spirits. Ma looks about as well as she has for the past ten years, and but little older. Bro. George Hughes and family are here and will remain until Sept.

Cousin Gus (as you doubtless know) is a charming fellow. He is thinking of staying at Princeton another year. The people there almost worship him. They offer him $600 for the nine months and he thinks he can probably get $70. per month. He does not like the idea of staying at Princeton and longs for Texas, but thinks it will probably be to his advantage to make the sacrifice for a short time. He fully expects to return to Texas.

I hope sister Emma and the children are well. Much love to you all. Let me hear from you often.

> Your loving brother,
> J. O. Butler

Mattie Hughes to Emma Butler Paisley in Dobyville

Malvern, Arkansas
Sept. 4th 1883

Dear Sister Emma,

I fully intended writing to you from Tulip, but there were so many of us together it was almost impossible to write a letter. While I was there, I finished a little dress for Mattie, and sent it to her by mail. Hope she received it and that it fit her. I had no little girl of her size to try it on, so I had to make it without knowing how it would do. We came from Tulip last Friday. George went to Little Rock Sunday evening. Walter left last night. West, Reavis and myself will remain here a week or two before going in. Jimmie came up with us, and commenced with bro Henry the first of the month.

We had a pleasant time at the dear old home, the boys amused themselves with various games, playing marbles, pitching dollars, lawn tennis &c. They had three or four sociables while we were there, which they all seemed to enjoy very much. The night before we left, they had one on the creek, at George Smith's, and when the boys got home day was breaking; so the boys didn't get more than two hours sleep, and we had a late start for Malvern.

We left Ma and sister Mary very well, said they would feel lonely after we got off. But no doubt it was a relief to sister Mary, for she had her hands full while we were there. She had a plenty of help, aunt Lucy, Clarissa and Annie, but just as we left the cook was taken sick, and I don't know whether they have any one now or not. Clarissa was wanting to quit anyhow. George Matthews was quite sick the last week we were there, but was able to be up when we left.

I am staying with Alice. She is very well, has left her baby with me, and gone out to do a little shopping. She has a very sweet baby. Cousin Betsy Kittrell, who was up here a week or two ago, says it is just like Ma, and ought to be called "Reavis." He is lying on a pallet now, and Annie is playing with him, has black eyes and looks very different from the other children. I did want Annie to have black eyes and look like her mother, so much. I don't think Annie is very well. She slept with me last night and was very restless every noise frightened her; & this morning she looks pale.

This is sister Annie's birthday. I have been thinking of her all morning. How is your little Annie? wish I could see her, and all the children. I do wish you lived where we could visit you. Have you commenced building yet? They haven't gotten through at bro. Henry's yet. I believe it will be a month or six weeks before they finish everything, have been at work there nearly four months, will have a nice house when it is finished. Mollie has a cook now, had been without one all Summer.

Coulter was all ready, and expected to leave for Fayetteville, last night, but had some fever, and concluded to remain here until he felt well. They thought he might have a spell of fever, and of course it would be better for him to be at home. His cousin Edgar Kinsworthy, came by expecting him to go with him. Edwin started to school this morning to Miss Emma. Mattie, George and Nannie are going.

Much love to Billy and the children, hope you all are well. Write soon. Your Loving Sister

Mattie Hughes

Ira Butler to Emma Butler Paisley in Dobyville

Tulip Ark
Sept 13 1883

Dear Sister Emma:

I dont know how we stand on the Letter Business, whether I am debtor or creditor. To settle the dispute & avoid all hard feelings I will write—We are having quite an extensive drouth, and every thing is beginning to feel the effects of the parching sun. It has been about five weeks since we have had a rain. The cotton crop is cut off at least a half. Am afraid some of my customers will come up short. One thing I am thankful for, and that is that I am not in debt for any goods. I have the promise of 2 or 3 bales of cotton this week. I am in hopes you havn't had as severe drouth as we. And also that your crops are better.

I have no one to stay in the store with me now. Consequently, am kept right closely confined. Herbert is going to school to Cousin Gus. Have employed George Matlock for 3 months, to commence first Oct. Cousin Gus is getting good wages at Princeton. They pay him 70 dollars per month, and also to the amt of 15 dollars per month for outside patronage in case they attend.

He says he is going to return to Texas in the Spring and carry Jimmy and myself with him & I would not be surprised at his success. Ask Bro. Billie what he thinks of Texas as a business point in comparison with Arkansas. Don't know whether I can sell, but think I can, to Bob Banks. He talks like he will buy me out. If we get off, we will try and come to see you before that time. Had a pleasant time with the boys this summer. Was with them a good portion of the time, & joined in their sports and plays. Walter brought a set of Lawn Tennis, which we enjoyed hugely. Jimmie and I made a break in our circle by making Cousin Sue Peebles a visit. When we returned, Gus and Georgie were at Malvern. I did not get to see Geor. any more. We had a very pleasant visit, & I formed the acquaintance of several of Camden's nicest young ladies. We got down to Cousin John's Thursday Eve. & left Monday.

We look for Alice down next week. Brother M[atthews] will go up, & she will return with him. Sister Matt was at M. when last heard from. All well & getting on tolerably well. A young man by name of Wasdon is teaching our public school. He boards with Bro. M. Reckon you have heard of Miss Sue Bullock's death, also Miss Berta Holmes.

Write soon to your

Loving Bro.
Ira

413

Mary Matthews to Emma Paisley in Dobyville

Tulip, Ark.
Oct. 8 1883

Dear sister Emma:

Your letter was received several days ago. Very glad to hear from you. The one you wrote Ma was sent up to her. She went home with Alice on Monday after her birthday Saturday. I wrote you about Alice and the children spending a week with us, or I believe it was before she came I wrote. Ma is still at Malvern—expects to visit Little Rock with Jimmie before coming home.

I received an interesting letter from Sister about the same time I received yours. West and Reavis were in New York. Walter is practicing law in L.R. I miss Ma and William very much, especially when Mr. Matthews is away. He left Saturday to hold a protracted meeting. Will be gone several days. I get Ira to sleep in Ma's room, as I would be entirely alone in this large house. George Matlock is clerking for Ira and boards here. He and George Matthews and Mr. Wadson are in the offices. We regret that Mr. Moore and family will have to leave. They have been talking of going to Va. but I think it is doubtful about their leaving the state. Mr. Moore has gone to Warren, and I wouldn't be surprised if it wasn't to look out a situation there. Mrs. Colburn and I went up to see Mrs. Moore Friday. She has a young daughter ten days old. We met with Mrs. Amis and Mrs. William Lea there from Princeton. Virgie Colburn left for school at Warrensburg Mo. last Tuesday, in company with Jimmie Pattillo as far as St. Louis; she will board with her aunt Virgie. Mrs. C of course visited her sister Virgie. Said her health was not good, she was looking thin.

Mr. Young's family left a week ago for Malvern. He is here himself looking after things. Miss Ellen is also here, waiting until they can get a room built for her. She will visit around among her friends. I want her to come and stay some with me. I like her very much. Mr. Matthews baptized the two youngest children of Mrs. Y's on Saturday of the Quarterly meeting.

Rev. Josephus Anderson is expected down tomorrow. His son has been in the neighborhood about two weeks, and has secured a school in Rock Spring neighborhood: he is much pleased with this community, and talks of buying a place for his father, who is in bad health. I do hope that some good citizens will come in and occupy the places of those that leave. This young Mr. Anderson is boarding at Bro. Caldwell's, and having a fine time riding the young ladies around. He brought Phoonie Roane to prayer meeting Wednesday night, and I met him a few evenings ago sailing out with Anna Caldwell. I don't know whether the rumor is true or not about Sue and George Smith's marrying. You know they will have to leave the state if they marry. I have heard there was some opposition on both sides, on account of their being so nearly relative.

Dr. Cooper has been sick for some time and is still sick, though I don't suppose he is at all dangerous, has had no physician. When George Matthews was sick last summer he had Dr. Simmons. We have fortunately not needed any physician only that time in our family.

I suppose bro. Billy has returned and is now receiving his new goods. I sent by bro. Henry for a cloak and dress. Want to attend conference, if I can get any one to take care of things here. I have been thinking I would get to see you there, also Johnny and his wife.

It is now nearly mail time, and I will have to go and carry up my letter. Write soon and often. Love to bro. Billy and the children and friends.

Lovingly your sister
Mary

Alice Moores to Emma Paisley in Dobyville

Malvern, Ark.
Oct. 15 1883

Dear Sister Emma:

I have been wanting to write to you for quite a while, but it seems a bad matter for me to get started to writing letters.

I heard that you thought something of coming to Conference, and I have been wanting to write especially to tell you to be sure to come. Brother Johnnie and sister Kellie say they will be here, and I expect most all the family will be here at that time, so you and brother B. must come over. We expect to entertain two preachers besides the members of our own family, and that is about all we can accommodate. I haven't made any preparation in regard to it yet, but it is high time, for it is not much over a month off now. We are having a glorious meeting here now, and every one seems to be interested; quite a number have professed religion, and I don't know how many accessions to the church. There were twelve united last night. May and Mattie Butler were both at the altar this morning, but are not yet fully satisfied. Malvern has been called a very hard place, and I do hope the whole town will be fully awakened, and that the meeting may continue to grow in interest, until every one may be made to feel the need of true religion. I am satisfied that this is the one thing needful, and above all things else wish to make sure work of heaven. Let your prayers ascend in behalf of Malvern.

Ma has been up spending two or three weeks, but went to L.R. last Saturday; she took William with her, as he had never been on the cars and was anxious to go.

Ira also came up from Tulip Sunday, and went into L.R. Monday. We look for them back tomorrow. I went down and spent a week at Tulip, and was there on Ma's birthday. As I had no way of coming back except on the mail hack, she and I came back together in the buggy.

You just ought to see our fine boy, Olin Alexander. He will soon be eight months old, is fleshy like his papa, but they all say he is a Butler, since he has black eyes. Is just beginning to crawl a little, has always been very healthy. How does your little Annie come on? Is she still so delicate? She is a good deal older than Aleck, but Olin was telling me that she was quite as small.

Edwin has started to the graded school. They have something over two hundred pupils. I think he is very well pleased—tell Henry he must answer his last letter.

Annie has not been quite so well for the last month, she is still inclined to awaken every night with scary dreams. I think she must be wormy.

I hope you will write to me soon, and make your arrangements to attend Conference. Love to all and a kiss for the baby.

I can hear my baby now up in the kitchen, not crying, but trying to make some one hear and listen to him. I have an old woman now for cook and her daughter about thirteen; we pay her five dollars per month to do the work, leaving out the washing and ironing. She was anxious to keep her girl to help her, so I can have her to help me a good deal and attend to the baby.

Lovingly,
Alice

Mary Matthews to Emma and Billy Paisley in Dobyville

Tulip, Ark.
Oct. 23, 1883

Dear Brother & Sister:

Your letters to Ma and Ira came at the same time, and not having heard of the illness of your dear little babe (one that I had hoped to see), it was indeed a sad surprise to hear of her death. The first one of your little household band that has entered Heaven, which is another link added to the chain that binds you to heaven, and calls off your affections from earthly things, and fixes them more firmly on things above; while we grieve at the departure of these loved ones and feel so keenly their absence, yet they have only preceded us to that Heavenly land, where they are "safe in the arms of Jesus" to await our coming, which will not be long.

I regret that none of us could be with you in this hour of trial, for I think it is some comfort to have loved ones with us, who can mingle their tears of sorrow and sympathy at such times; but you can go to our Heavenly Father, who alone, can pour in the oil of consolation. I am glad that you can submissively say, "The will of the Lord be done."

Mamma is still at Malvern, returned from Little Rock last Thursday, and expected to return home Friday with Ira, but was prevented by the rain. I sent your letters up to her yesterday by bro. McKinnon. We will send for her this week, if the weather is not too bad; it is so cold and cloudy today.

I suppose you have heard of the revival they have had at Malvern? good many of the young people have professed religion and joined the church. May and Mattie among the number; the last I heard May was not satisfied of her conversion, though earnestly seeking. Mr. Matthews was there and preached the night they joined the church. Mr. Moore preaches for us Friday night, Saturday, and Sunday, which I suppose will be his last appointment—I regret to see them leave.

Mr. Matthews unites with me in warmest love, and be assured dear Sister and Brother, you have our prayers and sympathy in this painful bereavement. Love to the children. Write soon.

Very affectionately your sister
Mary J. Matthews

Mary Wyche Butler to Emma Paisley in Dobyville

Oct. 30, 1883

My Dear Daughter,

And this is your birthday, how soon it follows after mine. Beautiful bright day, may you be spared to see many more.

So with our lives we are swiftly passing. Soon we will be gone the way of all the earth & may we be also ready when our time comes, ready for our soul's bright home in Heaven. Let us give all diligence to make our calling and election sure.

416

I feel more than ever determined, by the grace of God and his assistance, to run the Christian race so that I may obtain eternal life. I read yours and William's letters while at Ma[lvern] containing the death of your little babe, your dear little Annie. I can feel and sympath[ize] with you in this your first bereavement. You have another tie binding you to heaven. It is sad to lose our loved ones here, but the thought of meeting them in Heaven should cheer us and cause us to rejoice. You know your little one is safe in the arms of Jesus. May our affections be weaned from earthly things and placed on Heavenly things. Where our treasure is, there will our heart be also.

We had a fine meeting at Malvern such I never saw before. It was delightful to see so many converted and joined the church. I can't tell how many Sunday night, 30 I think. It was a beautiful sight to see so many young ones coming in. Bro. Math was so rejoiced, filled with gratitude to our Heavenly Farther.

They have several preachers to assist him, Dr. Bard from Hot Springs preached 2 or 3 times, fine sermons. Dr. Anderson preached one of the sweetest sermons I ever listened to. His text was seek the Lord and his strength, seek his face. I stayed until the meeting closed Tuesday night. I went to Little Rock Saturday and stayed until Thursday. Herd Bro. Purlman. The church seemed very cold and dead. I caried Will with me. He had a fine time with Charley's children, saw a gred deal. Martha came to see me after we had a letter from her. Said they were having some good meetings there, had quad meeting and Prayer meeting at 11 o'clock. Said they had a shout, the first one ever in the new church. She is very much stirred up. She enjoyed Prayer meeting, said Charley looked happy. She said she intended to be more devoted than she had been. Said if she only had her husband and children to go with her, says we must all Pray for them, that they may be brought in. Mrs. McKenon has been praying for him ever since he was sick at Mal. She seemed to feel so much for him. I think she is one of the best women, one of the best Christians I ever knew. I would like for you to know her. She has a meek and sweet spirit. Geo H remarked she had the meekest look of any one he ever saw. I think the revival at Mal was brought on by her Prayers. It is a treat to be with her. I shall be glad to see you at con[ference]. You must come if you can. My love to William and the children. Tell my little Henry I have a book for him.

Your Mother

Alice got a letter from Julia. Says Geo is having a room built for me—must I go?
Alice has one of the finest looking babys you ever saw. Look like Geo.

Jimmie Butler to Emma Paisley in Dobyville

Malvern, Ark.
Feb. 1, 1884

Dear Sister Emma:

Ma and Ira not long since ordered a monument for pa's grave. It is to be a real nice one and will cost $115.00. I have made a proposition that his ten children pay $10.00 each toward paying for it, and that ma pay the larger part, which will be $15.00. Brother Henry acquiesced in the plan, and thinks it would be a pleasant thought in after years connected with our pa's memory. The monument will be here very soon. Are you willing to give the $10.00? I heard from home a day or two ago, and can report all well.

Coulter has not returned to Fayetteville since he came home Christmas. He has not been well this winter, and is sick now. He bruised his hand not long since, and it has swollen badly. This has caused him to have fever. I doubt whether he will return to school this session.

Tell Bro. Billy that Ira and I concluded that when we moved, it will be to a better town than Gurdon. We expect to go to Texas this spring, and see what we think of that state. Love to all.

Your bro.
Jimmie

Mary Matthews to Mattie Hughes, forwarded to Emma Paisley in Dobyville

Tulip, Ark.
Feb. 22, 1884

My Dear Sister:

Your letter to Ira was received yesterday. Always so glad to hear from you, and I know you are anxious to hear from us, especially if you heard of the accident that happened to mamma last Sunday evening. And oh, how thankful I feel that it is no worse, for I was terribly alarmed.

We have a cow that has to be tied when she is milked, and Jim went off Sunday morning, leaving her tied up in the shed. Ma and I went up there and untied the rope, but left it hanging on her horn. In the evening we were just ready to go over to Bro. Caldwell's to see the afflicted family, when I went to the lot and discovered the cow lying down in the fence corner apparently very near dead. I called to ma and told her I thought the cow was nearly dead. She came, and we soon found the rope was hitched to a log and she was choking to death. I came to the house for a knife as quickly as I could, and ma cut the rope from her throat, but her horn was buried in the ground so that she still couldn't get up. I started off then as fast as I could, to go and get some one to come and get her up. Ma staid there and took a stick and pryed her horn out and called to me. The cow bounced up immediately and ran after ma, knocking her down.

I was some distance off, and when I saw the cow and ma on the ground, you can better imagine than I can describe my feelings, fearing that she was almost killed, and not a person on the place but myself to do anything or go for any one. I was greatly relieved when I saw that she was able to get up and walk to the house, still fearing it might be a serious hurt. After getting to the house and rubbing with camphor and liniment and knowing there was no immediate danger, I went out beyond the big gate and called Clarissa. They seemed to know from the way I called something was the matter and came immediately. I sent up for Mrs. Cooper, and Miss Pattie came without delay; very soon after Mrs. C. and Mrs. Grimes. George had gone for his pa to conduct the funeral exercises of our dear friend Anna C[aldwell], and Ira was at Malvern. I was agreeably surprised and greatly relieved to see Mr. Matthews soon after supper.

Miss Pattie staid all night, and we fixed wheat bran poultices to put on ma's right side, which hurt her more than anywhere else; that seemed to relieve her a great deal. Her face was also bruised, but is about well. The only place about her body that I could find was hurt was a bruised place on her back near the right side. Ma is getting on as well as she could, and I hope in a few days she will be well again. Ira told Dr. Grimes to come by and see ma. He has just been here and thinks after examination there is no cause for uneasiness. She is sitting by, reading the St Louis Advocate. I have been thus particular writing you every little thing, knowing you would like to hear.

It is so sad about the death of Anna, which has cast a gloom over the community; her parents didn't get to see her until she was unconscious only at short intervals; this makes their grief still greater, and then they reproach themselves for letting her leave home [in] such dreadful weather. She was very uncomfortably situated at the place she boarded, occupied a shed room without fire, which it seems to me would have been enough to have killed any one. She walked two miles through the damp bad weather to her school. She was complaining a week before she gave up. Mr. M. held funeral services in the church Monday at 11 o'clock. There was a larger attendance than I've seen in a long while, and it seemed that almost everyone wept and sympathized deeply with the family, whose grief seemed uncontrollable. Mrs. Caldwell has been sick ever since and I have been anxious to go to see her, haven't heard from her today. A great many of the neighbors have been to see ma.

Cousin Gus dismissed his school this week on account of measles. He is in my room now writing. He went to Malvern Tuesday and returned yesterday, thinks very likely his school will have to suspend another week. Bro. Atchley is just getting over the measles, and I suppose all of his family will have it.

Herbert is here assisting George about his work. I love to have him here, especially when his pa is gone. He always looks after everything. Ira is now selling out at cost, and has a good many customers. He has not decided yet what he will do. All the neighbors express regrets at his leaving.

I was much surprised yesterday to receive a letter from Miss Mary Cooper after a silence of more than two years. She is living in Jonesboro Ill., not more than twenty miles from Murphysboro. Ma says don't you think Ira and Jimmie had better continue in business here? Ira seems to be doing so well and is in such fine health, he may regret the move. What does bro. George think of it? Ma expected to go to Malvern soon after Mariah came out, and will go if she gets well enough, expected to meet with you there. She is much concerned about Edwin and the children, expects trouble herself unnecessarily. Ma had a letter written to Helen before she was hurt, but expected to rewrite it, and I thought I would write too, but it seems I haven't felt like it or had time. Alice wrote a note to ma by cousin Gus, said her baby was not very well. She didn't say anything about Edwin. Ma wants to know if you didn't enjoy reading about Bishop Pierce's golden wedding?

Cousin Gus brought me the frame and glass, and he fixed it up and put it in the parlor. We haven't heard anything from the lost turkeys, still have three hens, a gobbler, got from Mrs. Jim Toone.

23rd. Ma rested finely last night, and says she feels more encouraged about getting well soon, enjoyed her breakfast. We had fried partridges. Ma has been sick so little that confinement goes harder with her; in a week, at least, I think she will be entirely well.

The Presbyterians have a two days' meeting beginning today. I am so glad to see such a beautiful bright morning. It makes every one feel better. Tell brother George I expect he will have to come down and stay with us to get well. Love to him and the boys. I haven't time to write any more. Ma sends love to all. Write soon.

Very affectionately your sister

Mary

When Walter returned from Malvern, he told me that Edwin was looking very badly, and that sore on his leg hadn't healed. That was why Ma was troubled about him. Jimmie said Dr. Reamy was treating the sore, and it was much better. It was hurt last Summer. Walter said Edwin and William too looked badly.

Emma, I send this letter so that you can read all about the accident that happened to Mamma, also about the death of Anna C. I have just written a long letter to Ma, haven't time to write to you for it is about dinner. If sister Mary hasn't written to you, I know you will be glad to get her letter. Jimmie came in last Saturday, but returned Sunday night. All well at Malvern. George has been feeling very well this week. Walter is at Benton, attending court.

Love to all

Sister.

Jimmie Butler to Emma Paisley in Dobyville

Malvern, Ark.

March 1, 1884

My Dear Sister:

Your letter containing the $10.00 was received some time since, but I have not had time to write until now. The monument is at the depot now, and we want to have it sent to Tulip the first of next week.

My time is out now with brother Henry. I shall probably remain here about two weeks to get my matters arranged, and then I expect to go to Tulip and remain until Ira and I get ready to *skip*. We want to leave in a month or two.

Miss Maria Moores arrived last night. I went up to see her this morning. She gives a glowing account of California. She brought a lot of oranges and English walnuts with her, and says the orange trees are now loaded with ripe fruit. The oranges she brought had just been gathered and are certainly large and sweet. She says bro. George is getting on finely. His fruit will make him a support. He has built him a very good house, which cost him about one thousand dollars.

Maria is not pretty, but is quite sociable and attractive. She will probably remain in Ark. several months. I hope you will get to meet with her.

Ma came near being seriously hurt not long since by a ferocious cow that brother Matthews has at home. She was butted down twice by this cow, but, being close to her, did not hurt her very badly. She was in bed several days, but is about well now. We were quite uneasy about her for a while.

Coulter left last week for Fayetteville where he will remain for the next three months. He was a little afraid to go, but concluded that he ought to use all the time that he possibly could at school while young.

Alice's baby has been unwell of late and has fallen off considerably. He is not sick in bed, but looks badly and is fretful.

I was in Little Rock last Sunday and saw sister and bro. Charlie. Both are well.

Love to bro. Billy and the children. Let me hear from you.

Your brother
Jimmie

Mary Matthews to Emma Paisley in Dobyville

Tulip, Ark.
Mar. 12, 1884

Dear Sister Emma:

Your letter received about ten days ago, and I felt that I ought to write you immediately to relieve your mind of all fears in regard to Ma. I think she has entirely recovered from the hurt, which I am thankful to say was nothing serious; she went with Ira to Malvern Monday, stood the trip well except being a little tired as Jimmie writes. We expected Ira home tonight, but he failed to get here. I suppose he wanted to see more of Maria Moores or some other young lady up there.

I regret his not coming or Jimmie one, as we are having trouble in getting the monument down from Malvern, which has been there a week. Jimmie got Jackson, a colored man, to start with it yesterday but before getting many miles he concluded it was too heavy, and took off a part of it, leaving it on the way. I fear it may get broken or injured. I learn the Negro was drunk that brought it, also in company with others that were drinking, and one was stabbed, don't know whether it will prove fatal or not. Mr. Early, the agent from whom we bought the monument, has been here two days waiting to put it up. I think he will leave tomorrow, as he can't afford to lose so much time. I regret this very much, as I was anxious for him to fix it all right himself. Ira or Jimmie ought to have come down with the monument; the part that got here late last night was brought with Jimmie's wagon and mules.

I don't know how long mama will be gone, all of this month I expect; she was very anxious to see Maria and hear from Cal. I miss her very much especially when Mr. Matthews is away.

Mrs. Sallie Lea's little girl, ten months old, died yesterday from measles, and was buried this evening; they take it very hard, have another child very sick, a boy six years old, the Drs. think his recovery doubtful. Miss Pattie Yarbrough went with me to see them this morning. The baby was a beautiful corpse, so large and fleshy, the only daughter they had. Mrs. Roane also seems greatly distressed.

I think Miss Pattie has come to make her home with Mrs. C. I think it suits so well, as Mrs. Cooper has none of her children with her and was so lonely. She is in excellent health now, seems stouter than Dr. Cooper. I like Miss Pattie, think she is a good Christian woman and will be an advantage to Mrs. Cooper.

421

Ma received another letter from Helen Pleasants in reply to one she and I wrote—says she will probably visit us this summer.

Mr. M. has planted some early vegetables which are up, peas just beginning to come up. He has fixed a hot bed for cabbages, took the sash off of one side of my flower pit for covering. He is always busy at work when at home.

I was sorry to hear of a piece of needle being in Lula's arm, hope you can get it out. Sister Mollie is suffering with a severe attack of asthma, the worst she has had since her visit to Eureka.

Mr. M. joins me in love to you all. I am always so glad to hear from you. Write soon to your loving sister.

> Good night
> Mary

Mary Matthews to Emma Paisley in Dobyville

Tulip, Ark.
May 4, 1884

Dear Sister Emma:

You must really pardon me for waiting so long to reply to your letter. I had no idea it had been so long until I noticed the date of it. Today is Sunday, but for fear of not getting a letter off to you in tomorrow's mail, I will write if it is only a short one. Bro. Atchley preached a good sermon this morning—"Remember thy Creator in the days of thy youth&c"—wish more of the young people could have heard it: it suited all classes. The congregation was small owing to the wet weather.

Did you ever see so much rain? The farmers are prevented from doing anything. Cousin Gus Tillett is with us now on his way to Texas. He had to close his school before the term was out, on account of rheumatism, with which he has been suffering for some time. He seems to be better now.

We are expecting Jimmie and Maria Moores tomorrow or next day. Ira also went up to Benton as a delegate to attend the Sunday School Convention, which met the first day of May. Cousin Gus thinks of going tomorrow, and will return with them. He goes to carry the horse and buggy, expected to go Saturday but the rain prevented.

We have been having strawberries, but the rains have damaged them very much. I think we would have had a great many, and may yet if the rains cease. Ma, I think, will write some to you. She enjoyed her visit to Malvern and Little Rock: she was there during the sickness and death of Sammie Colburn, which was a sad time. He is much missed not only by his own family but the church also. I was so glad to have mamma at home again, for I missed her *so* much. We have a good garden, can have peas this week and potatoes too I think.

Mr. Matthews is well pleased with Princeton circuit. He left Friday—preached in Princeton today. That is, if he could get there yesterday. Herbert is assisting George about farming. We would like to make you a visit some time this summer if we can; the District meeting is to be held in Okolona. The time has not yet been appointed, and it may be that we can come then. I haven't been from home any this year. In about two weeks Mr. M. preaches again at Sardis. I want to go with him to visit cousin Jimmie Butler's family.

We received a letter from Sister a few days ago. She seems to keep well, but bro. George was not feeling so well. He only weighs 121 pounds, less I believe than he has ever weighed. Sister wants him to quit business and go to Malvern to rest. Walter is well pleased at Malvern.

Cousin Gus sends much love, and will write to you in a few days. He thinks now that he can't stop to see you on his way to Texas.

Much love to Bro Billy and the children. Write soon to your loving sister.

Mary

Mary Wyche Butler to Emma Paisley in Dobyville

[Tulip, Ark.
May 4, 1884]

My Dear Daughter

I have been wishing to write to you for some time ever since I got home, but have put it off, until I feel I must write to you. I have so much I wish to tell you. I got back on the 7 of April, now it is the 4 of May. How swiftly time flies. I s[t]aid 2 weeks in Mal and then went to L Rock with Martha & James & staid 12 days. Had a pleasant though a sad time. Bro. Sammie Colburn was taken sick and died while I was there. It was very unexpected. He came home Sun from his apointment very tired, said he had preached hard that day. He did not feel well, but was up until Tues. He sent for the Dr. They thought he would soon get over it. He [died] the next Tues 4 oc in the eve the 1st of April. It was hard for him to be reconciled to leave then. At first he felt he had so much to wish to live, for he was getting on so well with his Paper and Books. Opened his new Book store, prospering in his work. He felt sory to leave his family & friends, but when the Dr. told him he could not live, he seemed surprised. Thought he was getting better. Bro Jewel prayed with him often, and Dr. Welch, Dr. Harvey, his Mother & myself. He got reconciled, said he was ready to go, not afraid. He was trusting in his saviour. I feel gred deal for his Mother. It is the greatest affliction she ever had & his Brothers & sisters. Mr. Ware and Alice [Colburn] got there just after he died. I thought of the happy meeting with his father.

Charlie was moving when I left, in a large brick house. They have a fine boy name George. They were looking for you to come. I got acquainted with a good many, spent one day with Mrs. Ausbury Smith, one with our daughter and several nights with Mrs. Feild. Saw Flora and her fine boy, one of the best & smartest I ever saw. She is now in Camden with her mother & father. Your sister came every day. We went to see Sally Vaughn. She was delighted to see me. She is looking well, fine looking children, 3 boys & 2 girls & I think she was so glad to hear from you. Sent much love to you. She had rather see [you] than anybody. Says if you ever come to L Rock, must be sure to come to see her. She never will forget you. She says she think of you often. She had her horse hitched to the bug when we got there to ride. She would have us to ride home in it. Her son drove. I was glad we went to see her. She liked to talk of old times when she went to school. Said she would be delighted to see you & talk of old times. I was pleased with her, did not see her husband. They seem to be getting on well. I saw Patsy & Sally, told Sally you wanted her. She is very anxious to see you. She thinks as much of [Jimmie] as ever. Gave him a fine book. Patsy still loves Charley, says he is her heart's delight. She is well fixed. She lifted me up when she saw me.

We have a fine garden now, have peas. We are looking for James to bring Maria down tomorrow.

Ira gone to Benton convention. I have a turkey setting, 40 eggs seting. Can't you come to see us this summer.

Love to all

Bro [Jewell] preached Wed eve. It was sad & impressive. Should be ready, we know not how soon we may have to go. I want to send you some pictures have of Ira, better than the one you have. I can send them another time.

Jimmie Butler to Emma Paisley in Dobyville

Malvern, Ark.
May 15, 1884

Dear Sister Emma:

I believe you are owing me a letter, but I have some news to write you, and guess I had better not wait any longer. To be brief, I will state that I am engaged to be married on the 12th of June. Who do you suppose is to be the unfortunate one? I don't suppose you ever saw her, but her name is Maria Moores. I claimed her for my sweetheart about fourteen years ago, and I have always believed since then that for me to love her, she would only need to be seen, and thus it was. She is as pure and noble as can be. It is useless for me to attempt to picture her *good qualities*, and I in my blindness, have not been able to see her bad ones, if she has any.

> "She is modest, but not bashful,
>   free and easy, but not bold,
> Like an apple, ripe and mellow
>   not too young and not too old."

Can't you and bro. Billy come over and see your baby brother marry? You ought to make us a visit any way, and you would never be more welcome than then.

I took Miss Maria to Tulip last week, and spent five days there. Gus Tillett and Ira were there, and we had a most delightful time. All of us, including Ma, came up to Malvern last Monday. Ma will return to Tulip some time next week. Alice and Miss Maria went to Little Rock yesterday, and will be there until next week. Ma is keeping house for Alice while she is off. Ma and Sister Mary will come up to my marriage. Sister will also be here. You would get to meet quite a number of the home folks if you were to come. I guess Miss Maria and I will board with Alice when we marry, as Sister Mollie always turns her boys off when they marry.

Ira and I will not start in business together before fall. We have not fully decided where we shall settle yet.

Gus Tillett expects to go to Abilene, Texas, in about a week. That is to be his future home. He will write us full particulars in regard to that place, and we may decide to go there. All are well. With love to all I am

Your loving brother
J. O. Butler

424

Mary Matthews to Emma Paisley in Dobyville

Tulip, Ark.
May [24], 1884

Dear Sister Emma:

Your letter was received a few days ago. Very glad to hear from you. Ma went to Malvern last Monday week to keep house for Alice, while she and Maria went to Little Rock to make a visit and do some shopping. I suppose Jimmie has written you that he and Maria are to be married the 12th of June? He said while here he was going to write you about it. It is quite a surprise that they have fixed up things so hurriedly: they enjoyed their visit here very much, could be together here more than at Malvern. It makes me feel sad to think of our youngest brother marrying. Maria loves him devotedly, and I hope she will make him a good wife. I don't know yet whether I can go to the marriage or not. Would like very much to be there. Ira went up for mama yesterday, but today is William's birthday and she will not come before tomorrow (Saturday). I did expect to go with Mr. Matthews to the quarterly meeting, but it has rained so much I expect I'll have to give it out. Bro. McKinnon and his brother from Ga. got here to dinner, and are still here—going on to the meeting twelve miles from here at "Macedonia," Capt. Winstead's church.

I have just received letters from Sister, Ma and Alice. They are all well. Alice says they had a pleasant time in L.R. She took the baby and Annie with her. Annie staid with Sister while there. They went in Thursday and returned Monday. I have just learned from bro. McKinnon that the District meeting at Okolona will commence on Monday night, the 23rd of June. Bishop Hargrove is expected to preside; he is to attend the next annual Conference in L R next fall. I do hope nothing will prevent my making you a visit at that time. We would like to stay a day or two with you before the meeting commenced, spend Sunday at least. Mr. M. will get to see you any way.

Mr. John Holmes and Miss Emma Van-M were married last Sunday evening at 2 o'clock, which was a surprise to all.

Bro. Henry's George is now with us. He has been here little over a week, seems to be enjoying himself shooting birds &c. I think Edwin expects to come down with Ma. Ira has sent for him a buggy, and expected it to be there when he went up, and will bring ma home in it. Cousin Gus and Ira made a short trip to Hot Springs. I think he [Gus] and Maj Coulter left Malvern together for Texas last week or first of this.

I expect you have seen Frank Tidball's soap advertised. I sent on and got a trial cake, followed strictly the directions and was much pleased with it—think it would suit you as it is a saving of water, labor and fuel. If I didn't have some one to do my washing, I would be sure to get that soap. I will bring or send you the directions.

Ma has 23 little turkeys and another hen setting on 14 eggs. I don't know [how] many chickens I have. Had one fried for breakfast and two for dinner. Our earliest peas have nearly given out. Irish potatoes very fine; we had good many strawberries, and next year will have raspberries. We have the earliest garden in the neighborhood. I don't know where we will be next year—would like to see you and bro. Billy, and have a long talk about family matters &c. Mr. M. is anxious to make you a visit. He sends love.

I wish you could come to see us. Maybe you can come this summer or early fall. With much love for you all

I am affectionately your sister
Mary

I don't much think ma will get here before next week. George Matthews has just returned, and says Ira's buggy hadn't come this morning.

24th. Ma, Ira, and little Annie came last night at half past 9 o'clock. She sends love and a picture of Jimmie. It is not one taken lately.

Ira Butler to Emma Paisley in Dobyville

Tulip, Ark.
July 11, 1884

My Dear Sister Emma:

I send you one of my pictures that I had taken some time ago. I start Monday for Malvern, where I will remain a day or two, & then skip for Abilene, Texas. Expect to be gone two or three months. However, can't tell how long I will remain until I get there & see how I will be pleased. Gus is still delighted with Abilene & the surrounding country.

Tell Bro. B. that he had better wind up his Business this Fall & shoot for Abilene, as he is not settled anyways at Dobyville. Jimmie Pattillo will go up with me as far as Malvern, enroute to Hot Springs. He expects to remain there several weeks. He wants to try the virtues of its waters for the tetter.

Walter is getting on pretty well in law at Malvern. He acquitted himself very well. There was a large crowd of people at Barbecue—supposed to have been two thousand. Every thing passed off quietly & peacefully. No drunkards, no fights.

George Matthews left last Sunday Eve for Magnolia where he expects to canvass the county for fall orders for the Laconte [Company]. I called on Miss Fannie Pattillo last night, & had a very pleasant evening. She has been on a trip to Fordyce. Said she had a delightful trip; was very well pleased with the place. All getting on very well at Tulip.

Hope to get a letter from you soon. Direct your letter to Abilene, Taylor Co., Tex. Am not feeling much in the humor of writing this morning. Excuse all mistakes & write soon to your Loving Bro.

Ira

I will be so anxious to get letters from all the Loved Ones. As I will be so far from them & all acquaintances.

Love to all
Ira

P.S. Sister M. has just come to my office to make up my bed & told me that she carried you one of my pictures. I won't send you another yet. Will let you wait until I get married. Ma says Sister Matt wants to make you a visit this summer if she can. Think it will be doubtful about her having that pleasure, as she won't have a way.

Alice Moores to Emma Paisley in Dobyville

Tulip, Ark.
July 27, 1884

Dear Sister Emma,

I have been thinking of writing to you for a long time, and when I came to Tulip told Ma that I must write while here. A few days ago she received your letter, and we were glad to hear from you and to know that you were all well. I came down last Friday was a week ago, and have spent a delightful time at the old home, where it is always pleasant to visit. I was to have gone home last Friday or Saturday, but Ma prevailed on me to remain until Monday when I will return. Annie and the baby came with me, and Edwin and William came on a wagon last Tuesday, so we are all here except Olin, who was out canvassing during my absence. He is running for clerk, which I suppose you were aware of.

Jimmie and Maria are keeping house for me, so I don't feel at all uneasy about affairs at home. It is very pleasant to have them with us, and I shall regret very much when they leave us for Texas. Was very sorry that you could not be at their marriage; was anxious for you to meet Maria, whom I already loved as a sister and have no doubt but what you would be pleased with her.

Just before leaving Malvern, I read a note from you to sister Mollie about the children coming over on a visit. I don't know when they will return (that is bro. H. & family) but you can send the children on, as we would be glad to see them at our house. Edwin has always thought a great deal of Henry, and would be delighted to see him.

I was surprised to hear you had been trying to do your washing. Ma says she thinks that is most *too much* for your small hands says you ought to have "Frank Tidball's soap" which would not hurt the hands so badly.

I have put me up a jar of apple preserves since I came down, which are very nice. Ma has some very nice grapes, wish you could enjoy some of them. They are going away very fast, the birds are so bad after them. Mrs. Pattillo sent me over a bucket of plums a few days ago. They were very fine, and we enjoyed them very much. We have to pay for all the fruit we get at Malvern, so I enjoy it very much.

Ma says she enjoys fine health now, and felt especially well yesterday. I am so glad that she keeps well and can get about so much. Health is the greatest blessing one can have, and we ought to appreciate it. I feel so sorry for Mr. Durham's family. Miss Carrie is hardly able to be up, and has a very bad cough, and poor Miss Catherine Rose has never been able to leave her bed since the fall she got, & feels that death would be a welcome visitor. Jessie Boyd has been doing the cooking for them, together with what the neighbors send in.

Cora Gantt (now Mrs. Banks) is here on a visit. She is staying with Mrs. Bob Banks. Sister is keeping house for Sister Mollie while they are gone, so she can't come down now until sometime in Aug. She is anxious to be at Tulip now, as it seems cooler down here. I went out this morning to hear Mr. Moore preach. The congregation seems smaller every year.

Ma had a letter from Ira last week. He seems to be pleased at Abilene and wanted to go into some kind of business right away.

Aleck is walking and can talk a little, he is not so fleshy as he was, but seems to feel very well;

427

we think he is a great boy, and as a general thing is very little trouble to me. I can leave him at any time with Ma or sister Mary. Haven't time to write more. All send love.

Afftly
Alice

Mattie Hughes to Emma Paisley in Dobyville

Malvern, Arkansas
July 28, 1884

Dear Sister Emma,

Ever since I came here, two weeks ago, I have been intending to write to you. Brother Henry, Mollie, Mattie, George, and Nannie left for Sevier Co. nearly a week ago. Coulter went as far as Hope. After leaving home he felt sick, had some fever, his tongue was badly coated, so they thought he had better return home and take medicine, fearing he might have a spell of fever. Dr. Reamy gave him a large dose of calomel, and for a day or two he took quinine, and since he has been feeling very well.

May and I get on finely with the housekeeping. We have a cook so we have very little trouble. Mollie thought she would be gone about two weeks, and after her return I'll make my visit to Tulip, expect to spend three or four weeks there.

George left L.R. a day or two before I did, joined West, at Parkside, in Penn, where he spent two weeks. Left there a week ago for New York, spent a day or two there, when they took steamer for Halifax in Nova Scotia. They sailed on the 23d, and it would take them two days and nights to make the voyage. George thought a sea voyage might be beneficial, and he wanted to get where it was cool and pleasant. I fear he will be too far north for sea bathing, but if so, he can very easily come south. He was well pleased in Penn, the thermometer was 60 of mornings, and about 69 in the evening; and it was a beautiful mountainous country where they were.

I do hope the trip will be beneficial; I was very anxious for him to go, wanted to leave earlier than he did. Until he left for Halifax I received letters from him every other day. He didn't think he had made any decided improvement, but had been feeling very well; he was quite thin, didn't weigh more than 115 pds. West will be with him all Summer. His health is very good now. Reavis is at work in the Gazette office in Little Rock. I hated to leave him there, but he is anxious to be employed during the Summers; he will return to Harvard Law School, the last of Sept. Walter is here. He is in good health, and well pleased with his business. He likes Malvern and has such a pleasant home, at bro Henry's. Alice and the children are down at Tulip, have been there about 10 days. We expect her back today. Jimmie and Maria have been keeping house and getting on finely. Olin has been out electioneering. He came in Saturday, very sanguine of his election, and so are all of the candidates, I believe.

We had a delightful rain last night, I think it rained quite hard for two hours.

Ira is in Abilene, Texas. Jimmie had a long letter from him yesterday. He thinks he can do well there, has bought a stock of goods, but says it will cost a good deal to live there. He has to pay $5.00 a week for day board, and five or six a month for a room. Water is quite scarce, have to buy all they use. He is anxious for Jimmie to go out there, as soon as he can. I think Maria dreads going, and of course had rather go on to Cal. I like her very much, and I think she will make Jimmie a good wife.

How are your children? I heard that Emma and Henry were coming here, would like to see them, and the rest of the children. Sorry you can't make a visit to Tulip. I want to visit you during the Summer or Fall. Much love to Billy and the children, a kiss for Mattie & Lula. Your Sister

M. W. H.

Walter Hughes to his Aunt Emma Paisley in Dobyville

Malvern, Ark.
Aug. 23, 1884

My dear Aunt Emma:

I have, since meeting here your two boys John & Willie, been wanting to write you a short letter, if only to tell you how pleased we all were with those boys. I have passed nearly all my life as a looker-on among strangers, without being engaged actively in any of the business of life. That is, perhaps, my misfortune, but it has made me rather contemplative, silent and rather inclined to keep my feelings to myself. I will break that habit now, because I think it will perhaps give you some pleasure to hear some good words of your children. I was glad that they came while I was here. It had been long since I had seen them and from the many stories I had heard of them when younger, I was not prepared to see such polished and polite young men. I liked them very much. I have heard others speak of them the same way. They give promise of being for you a source of pride in the future. Emma and Henry have received a welcome from us all that was heart-felt. These visits renew family ties and are always enjoyable on that ground.

Uncle Henry and Aunt Molly were at Tulip to the birthday dinner of Aunt Mollie. They have come back delighted with their visit. When they returned, they found a full house awaiting them, where they expected to find a deserted hall. I had gone over to Sheridan to Court, and having finished my business there, returned earlier than expected. The following morning, two young ladies from Hot Springs brought a letter directed to Uncle Henry signed "your old friend D. Samuels," asking him to take care of his daughters and see that they got a way to go down to their uncle's in Dallas Co. Jimmie took them to the house, & he and George came back to the store puffing and sweating with the heat. George exclaimed, "Whew! Business! Two more for the Butler House!" Then Coulter, standing in the front of the store, called George, saying "Yonder come Emma and Henry." George went up to the House with them. While he was gone we got a telegram from Major Coulter saying that he, in company with Mrs. Stevens, would be in Malvern that night. About three o'clock, Uncle Henry and Aunt Mollie came from Tulip, and at eleven o'clock at night Major Coulter & Mrs. Stevens came in from the south. So our house is full again, though it was roomy & new—but we are not crowded now. The ladies from Hot Springs are gone, & Mrs. Stevens is gone over in the country among her relatives.

Mamma is at Tulip now. I look for her at Malvern in two weeks. I heard that she was going over to see you, but nothing of that lately. Love to Uncle Billie & the family.

Your Nephew
Walter J. Hughes

429

Ira Butler to Emma Paisley in Dobyville

Abilene, Texas
Oct. 5, 1884

My Dear Sister Emma:

I have been walking so much this morning that I don't feel like attending preaching this morning. We are somewhat inconveniently located for attending service. We are three quarters of a mile from the nearest church, which is Methodist. Gus is the only member of our household who will attend today.

I am very sorry to have to write that our very dear Bro. Jimmie is pretty sick. He was taken sick Saturday night was a week ago. He has what the Dr. terms Slow Intermittent Fever. He is feeling much better this morning than last night. He is generally clear of fever of mornings. Dr. Alexander, who married Miss Sallie Barbee, is attending him. We are so much in hopes we can keep him from going into typhoid fever. The Dr. seems to think he is getting on as well as could be expected. I went to see the Dr. this morning and he made a prescription for him, and he will call to see him this eve. Really, I felt uneasy about Jimmie yesterday Eve. He seems to be getting on so much better this morning. If we can just keep his fever down, he will begin to improve. Gus examined his pulse this morning and thinks he has no fever.

If Jimmie hadn't been sick I would have spent to day with the Loved ones at home. I know Ma will be very uneasy about Jimmie until she hears he is well. I am very hopeful, and think it won't be a great while before he will be up again. Am afraid it will interfere very materily with my collections at Tulip. I may make some arrangements and go to Tulip before Jimmie recovers.

Oh Yes! Ma let you into my secret did she? Guess I will have to own up. I was surprised when you wrote that you had never met Miss F. We have been engaged for several months. We think of marying some time next month. Haven't set the date yet, owing to my unsettled business at Tulip. I think Miss F. and I will suit for pardners very well. Wish we could come over and let you be your own judge in the matter. I don't know the nature of our marriage: whether there will be any parade or show.

I will have to close for this time. Write soon to your loving Bro.

Ira

Sunday Eve. Jimmie is feeling a good deal better this Eve. Write Soon. Love to all. Your Bro. Ira

I am very much oblige for the compliment. [Emma's 9th child: James *Ira* Paisley]. No doubt but what he will grow to be a very large man in every sense of the word. I. W. B.

Jimmie Butler to his Mother in Tulip

Abilene, Texas
Oct. 25, 1884

My dear Ma:

I believe it has been about one week since I wrote to you. I thought of writing to you a few days ago, but concluded to wait until Ira had reached home, as I knew he would be anxious to hear from Abilene. I suppose he had the delightful pleasure of meeting with you all yesterday evening. It seems like a long, long time since I saw you, and I have wished time and again that I could have the pleasure that Ira is to experience in being with you all. We are confidently expecting you to return with Ira, so as to go on out to California with us.

Brother Charlie passed through here last Thursday morning. He came up to our store, but none of us were there. He left word with the man who keeps next door that he had been to our store. He had written to me that he expected to pass through on Tuesday morning, and Ira went down to meet him; but, as is usual with him, he was behind time. He left word that he would have come out to our residence, but he only had twenty minutes to stop over, and could not come, as we live so far from the depot. I should have liked very much to have seen him. I shall write to him in a few days. I wish that Maria and I could have gone on with him. If it had not been for my sicknes, I guess Ira would have been back from Tulip by this time.

I received a long letter yesterday written by brother Olin and Alice. Bro. O. is very anxious to sell his place, and leave for California. I think we will get a majority of the family out there before long, and then I guess you would be willing to live out there, wouldn't you? I would never be satisfied to make this my home, for I don't believe it would suit you, and I would never live where I could not have you come and visit me or live with me. I want to get to a place where I can make my permanent home, and then get me a place of my own as soon as possible. It may take me a long time to get a home of my own, but when I do, it will be one that will always be worth something.

I am very glad that brother Charlie has at last gone to Cal, for I think that country will suit him. He wrote that sister Kate was more in the notion of going to Cal. than she had ever been, and was hurrying him off. Brother C. O. Steel expects to go to California in about two weeks. It is now after twelve o'clock and it [final page missing].

Jimmie Butler

Mary W. Butler to daughter Emma Paisley in Dobyville

Tulip, Ark.
Oct. 30, [1884]

My Dear Daughter,

As this is your B D I must write you a few lines, though I have so much to do, I hardly know which to do first. I am trying to get ready for a visit to Cal. Had you heard of it? It seems a great undertaking for me at this time of life, almost more than I can stand. How can I leave you all to go so far?

I got letter from James yes[terday]. He says I must be sure to go with Ira, when he leave. He expects to get married some time next month & go right on to Abilene. I feel that he feels that James has gotten well. Was very uneasy about him at one time. He now high up for Cal & Charles is there by this time. The day you was writing to Ira he was here writing to James. He hasn't seen your letter.

My dear Emma, the Lord Bless you on this day, help you to serve the Lord faithfully.

I will have to carry the letter to be mailed. I have a great deal I would like to say to you & Billy. I am pleased with the names of your Baby, think it very suitable. May the Lord Bless you all and prosper you in all things for this life, and for the life to come.

Much love to Billy and all the children & neighbors, old Mrs. Grier. good by My Dear Daughter. I feel like I have the best children in the world. I see a long letter from John. Your loving   Mother

May we all make an unbroken family in Heaven. Let us give all diligence to make our calling & election sure. We have been blessed with health. We should be very thankful. The Lord be with all, wherever we may be. Pray for your mother. Good by.

[Invitation to the marriage of Ira and Fannie Smith]

1884

Mrs. R. M. Smith
At Home
Wednesday Evening Nov. 19th
At 7 O'Clock
Ira W. Butler   Fannie J. Smith

Henry Butler to William Paisley in Dobyville

Malvern, Ark.
Dec. 4, 1884

Dear Billy,

I appreciate your congratulations, because I know you felt what you said on your Postal. If it had not been for some rubber hose belonging to the Rail Road, my store would have gone, & even as it was things looked so badly I thought I was gone at one time, & moved out some $2,000 worth of clothing, dress goods, & flannels. I have collected $30 from Ins Co for damage in removing the goods, & will get something for repainting my front. I had but little Ins., only $2,000, several policies having been cancelled within the past two months. I cannot get any more without paying 8%. This is terrible, but I must have some more at any rate.

Well, I saw Ira & his wife and my dear mother off for Texas this morning at 2-30. Ira came up yesterday. Richard Smith goes with Ira to stay in the store—a good looking boy. Ira done well in marrying—*beat Jimmie badly*. His wife is a superior woman in every *respect*. Ma will remain at Abilene 'till Jimmie is ready to start to Cala which will be a week or two I suppose.

All well. Love to Em & the children.

Your brother,
Henry

Mary Matthews to Emma Paisley in Dobyville

Tulip, Ark.
Dec. 14, 1884

Dear Sister Emma:

Your letter came the day after our return from Conference, and I wanted to write you immediately, but have been quite busy about our meat &c&c.

There is so much to write you that I hardly know where to begin. Will answer some of your questions in regard to Ira's marriage. Very few besides relatives were invited. There were 12 waiters, that is, six couples. Maurice and James Smith, Jimmie Pattillo, Kavanaugh, Walter & George Matthews. Mary and Willie Smith, Lena Allen, Fannie Pattillo, Helen, and May Butler. They had a very nice supper prepared, and all seemed to enjoy themselves. Mr. Matthews performed the ceremony. Sister also came down with Walter, May, and Mattie, and Ma went to Malvern with them next day, Thursday. Mattie staid with us till Monday, when we went up on our way to Con. Ira didn't leave next day after his marriage, as he at first expected. His business compelled him to remain about two weeks. He and Fannie spent Saturday and Sunday with us before we left for Conference; we enjoyed having them with us so much. Both seemed happy together, and I hope they will always be so. Fannie's health is not good since the spell she had. She looks pale and thin, had a chill or two since they were married. Probably the change of place may prove beneficial.

We returned from Con Tuesday, the 2nd, and expected Ira and Fannie to be with us that night at Malvern. Sister Mollie fixed a very nice supper for them and looked for them till dark, but Fannie was sick and they didn't go until next day. We met them on the road, talked a short while, and bade them goodbye. I spent the night at Alice's with Ma, felt sad to part with her. She was getting impatient to go on, as she had waited so much longer than expected. Fannie wrote to bro. Henry immediately after getting to Abilene that Ma stood the trip finely. That was on the 5th. I haven't heard whether they have left for Cal. or not, but suppose they have, as Jimmie and Maria were anxious to go on. Bro. Charlie writes that he is delighted with the country, and thinks he will be perfectly happy if Kate will only be satisfied; he had made an offer for some land near Downey.

We had a pleasant time at Con. Spent a part of the time with Mrs. Feild, and part with Mrs. John Hughes, so that we could be more with Sister and bro. George. Bro. G has a horse, and rides a good deal every day for his health: he looks thin and badly—had a letter from Sister a few days ago. Said he had taken cold, and she felt uneasy about him. Didn't think he could stand a spell of sickness. She said "If he would only accept Christ and be resigned to the will of the God, what comfort and consolation it would give me and how much happier he would be. You must pray for us." I do feel so much for Sister as well as bro. George, and we must pray for them that his afflictions may lead him to Christ. Ma was very much concerned about him before she left.

Mr. Matthews is appointed to New Edinburgh circuit, which is much farther from home. The P.E. [Presiding Elder] didn't inform the bishop how we were situated, &c or he would not have made this appointment. It is impossible, as you know for us to leave here at present.

Mr. Green and Herbert are in business here, together having bought Ira out; they are doing very well. We brought Annie Mary home with us. I expect to keep her with me this winter. She will be a great deal of company for me, especially when Mr. M is away.

I have a white girl living with me Mary Studer. Her parents live at Benton. Sister Mollie kept her three weeks, and thinks she is a good girl, but not fast enough to get through with her work. I am glad to get her, as I need some white person here with me while Ma is gone. We were determined not to keep Clarissa and feed so many, if we could possibly do any better, though she was a better cook than any I can get. The girl I have came from Switzerland about six years ago. She is about 24 years old. She can speak and write English.

We killed 9 hogs. Will have more than enough meat to do us. Haven't made any souse and stuffed sausage yet. I miss Ma very much. She would enjoy the fresh meat so much. Mary never eats any kind of meat, not even chicken or turkey, yet she is large and fleshy.

Annie says tell Lula she must come and stay with her some. Alice wrote that they were going to have a Christmas tree, and Annie ought to come up to see it, but I hardly think she can go. We will have a quiet time here.

Love to Bro. Billy. Several at L. Rock spoke of meeting him, and enjoyed his company so much. Love for yourself and the children. Mr. Matthews also sends his regards. Write soon and often.

Afftly, your sister
M. J. Matthews

Mattie Hughes to Emma Paisley in Dobyville

Little Rock, Ark.
Dec. 28, 1884

Dear Sister Emma,

It has been some time since I wrote or received a letter from you. I have thought of you often, and during the Christmas holidays I have wondered how you were, and if the children were having a nice time. Of course Santa Claus made them a visit; for they are good children and ought to be treated well by old Santa. It hasn't seemed like Christmas. If I had been where there were little children, no doubt it would have seemed more like it. I love to see children happy, and I believe every one ought to do all they could to make them so, especially during Christmas time.

I haven't heard from Mamma since the day after she got to Downey. Jimmie wrote me a postal on the 16th, telling me of their safe arrival. I have been expecting a letter for several days, have written to bro Charlie, Jimmie and Ma, wrote to her on Christmas day. Nobody will enjoy the fine fruit more than Ma.

I suppose you have heard that Alice has a little girl, born on the 16th. She was doing well, had "aunt Maria," a good colored woman, with her. Annie was at Tulip with Sister Mary, went with her when she returned from Conference.

Yesterday we heard of the death of Cora Gantt (Mrs. Dr. Banks). She died at Tulip on the 25th, the day after the birth of her baby. The baby was dead, and they were to be buried in the same coffin Saturday morning. Mrs. Reid and Mrs. Gantt seemed much distressed. Her sister Loula Martin, didn't go down, couldn't leave her children. Her husband went as far as Malvern, but on account of the ice he couldn't go down. Cora was very much beloved.

George has been getting on better lately. He keeps a horse and rides every day, when the weather will admit of it. He is eating some more and I think he surely will begin to increase some in weight. West wrote us that he was getting on very well. He is trying Lager beer and thinks it agrees with him; says for five days he gained a pound a day. I expect he is at Cambridge with Reavis, and will spend about a week with him. I hope they are having a good time, had'nt been together for more than a year. Walter doesn't come in often. I haven't seen him since I went out to attend Ira's wedding.

I haven't heard directly from Ira since he got to Abilene. We are very much pleased with his wife; and they wrote me that they were charmed with her at Malvern. Maj. Coulter was so much pleased with her that he wrote to her, soon after she got to Abilene. All I fear is that she may be delicate. They say she hasn't been very well since she had measles.

We are having an abundance of rain, and I expect we will have an overflow. It is pouring down now, about as hard as I ever saw it.

I enjoyed Billy's visit, and did [wish] that we were keeping house so that we could have entertained him. How is your baby? and what do you call him, George or Charlie?

I was at bro Charlie's about a week ago. All were well. I suppose Kate intends going to California next Spring, though I think it is doubtful. I don't believe she will be willing to go without her mother. She says she is getting on well, making expenses. Brother John's family are very well pleased living in Little Rock. We go there very often, frequently go there from supper and stay until bedtime. But now it is a muddy walk, and I'll not go for several days, unless the ground freezes.

Write me about your children, if they are going to school, and how they are doing. George sends love, kiss the little ones for aunt Mattie.

Your Loving Sister
M. W. Hughes

435

Minerva Paisley to Emma and William Paisley in Dobyville

Mcleansville (N.C.)
Jan. 6, 1885

My Dear Nephew and Niece,

It has been a long time since I heard from you, and I will take this morning to talk awhile with you. I think of you often, and heartily wish that we could hear from you oftener. But I will excuse you on the ground of having a large family to care and provide for. I know something of your cares, having passed through the same. Well, Will, that little Mary Annie is married. Don't it seem impossible! to think that about 19 or 18 years have passed by since you were here, and she was just a child! She was married the 30 of Dec. at 8 o'clock P.M. to a Mr. Hendricks who lives near Greensboro. I think she has married a nice little fellow, and one who I hope will take care of her. So you see all of the children are married but Lacy, and you will hear from him some of these days. He and Porter are teaching down in South Carolina. Both have good classical schools and are doing well. John is left on the farm, and I hope will do well. He is a tobacco raiser, has been right successful for the last few years. Our family now numbers four: Jno and Bessie, James Percy, and myself. You may know that it was a sore trial to give Annie up. She was not only my child, my only daughter, but my companion and bedfellow. So you see there were so many ties to break. I felt like one of the strong ties that bound me to earth was breaking. But I try to console myself with the thought that it was for her good, and I ought to be satisfied. Mr. Tidball married them, and I think had one of the prettiest ceremonies I have heard. There have been and going to be more people married this Xmas than I ever heard of.

I reckon you are busy trying to educate and train your loved ones. I hope you may have the unspeakable pleasure of seeing them all do well. If they do you will feel rewarded for all your toils and cares. How much I wish I could see you all! The memory of you brings back so much of the precious past.

How is Marianna getting on? I would like so much to hear from her. Tell her to please write to me. I will write to her if she will write to me. I expect to have leisure now that I have all my children provided for, and if I can be any help or comfort to you, I will gladly do so. You both and your families come very near to me, you know. There are so few relatives of my dear Husband left, all of whom are dear to me. Him whose memory is still as fresh and dear to me as it was the *sad sad day* that I had to consign his precious remains to the silent grave.

Now I am going to look for an answer soon, and shall keep on looking 'till I get one. Please just set down and answer at once, and let me see how quick your answer can come. I wish you could see Annie and her Husband. It was said by several that they were a nice little couple, Annie weighs 120, he 132. They took a little bridal trip down to S.C. to see some of his relatives, will be back the 8th, to see one of his brothers married on the 8th. Heard from Annie, said they were having a splendid time.

Now, Will, I will close by once more asking you to write. All join in love to you and your family, and give the same to Mary and family.

From your devoted Aunt
Minerva P.

P.S. Give my love to Charlie T[idball] and wife.

Mary Matthews to Emma Paisley in Dobyville

Tulip, Ark.
Feb. 13, 1885

Dear Sister Emma:

Your letter received about two weeks ago. I intended replying immediately, in fact was just thinking of writing to find out what was the matter when yours came. I made a short visit to Malvern to see Alice and the little newcomer; was there only two nights and one day, expected to bring Annie back with me, but Alice was not willing for her to come. I felt so sorry for Annie. She was so anxious to come almost cried, and told Alice she had plenty of children without her. I was anxious to keep her all winter.

Alice has her hands full with the young baby and Aleck. She has a colored girl doing her work. She likes her better than the white one she had, though she is slow and has to be told how and what to do. The Swiss girl I have is doing very well. She loves to scour wash and iron—cooks tolerably well. I don't think she is a first-rate milker, at least we get very little milk from three cows. It may be the cold weather has something to do with it.

Mr. Matthews has to be away more than ever before; he left this evening. Told me to give much love to you and bro. Billy for him. He will return Monday, and if the weather is pleasant will do some gardening. We haven't planted any thing yet.

I had a letter from Ira a few days ago. He had a severe cold and cough, and Fannie was not well. Colds have been severe all through the country and a good deal of pneumonia. George and Herbert [Matthews] have very bad coughs, and I have not been well for a week or two until now. I am feeling better.

I have been expecting a letter from Cal. for some time, but disappointed. Ma, Charlie, and Jimmie are delighted with the country, but haven't heard of their getting into any business. Jimmie says he never appreciated his poverty so much before, seeing so much he would like to buy; but it is impossible for them to live on sight-seeing &c. Ira acted wisely, to remain where he already had a good business. I am looking for a letter from Sister every day. When she last wrote she said bro. George was out of business, and talked of going on a visit to Cal., but it was very uncertain.

It is not thought that Miss Carrie Durham can possibly live longer than a month. Mr. Matthews went with me while at home to see her, and she asked him to read and pray with them. She is fully aware of her condition, made her "will" several weeks ago. When Mr. M. asked her if she could trust the Saviour she replied yes, she was trying to be resigned. Bro. Atchley has also been to see her and prayed with her.

Mr. Durham's health is very bad. Some think he will die now before Miss Carrie. Mrs. Boyd is staying with them, and although blind gets about very well; there lies poor Miss Catherine in another bed helpless; she always seems patient. Did you ever know of such an afflicted family? How thankful we should feel for the many blessings bestowed on us. I hope we do rightly appreciate them and strive to become better Christians every day.

We also went to see Ruth Banks. She has been quite sick from cold but is getting better. The children have the whooping cough, and others are taking it.

Do you ever hear from Johnny? Mr. M. wrote to him this morning. He is very slow about writing, also sent our photos. We had them taken while at Conference. Will send them to you, as I don't think you have a good one of mine. I think Mr. M.'s is good, except his hair looks too white. Love to bro. Billy and the children and a share for yourself.

Herbert and Judge Green are getting on very well in business here. Write to me soon.

Afftly your sister
M. J. Matthews

14th

Last evening got letters from Alice and bro. Henry. Alice had heard from Ma dated 2nd, all were well. She sometimes gets a little "homesick," and wishes to be back. Mrs. Dick Gantt expects to be married in March. I was surprised to hear bro. Billy had gone to St. Louis. Alice wrote for me to try to get Annie Hawkins, Allen's daughter for her. I suppose her girl wants to leave.

Mary Wyche Butler to Emma and William Paisley in Dobyville

Downey, Cal.
Feb. 14, 1885

My Dear Daughter Emma and William

I feel that I must write to you. I have been expecting to hear from you ever sence I cam. Ch[arlie] said he had written to you. I thought I would wait until he got your letter. I have heard from all the others. I feel anxious to hear from you, how you are getting on.

I have been [here] all most 2 months. We got here the 15 of Dec. We stopped with Ira, Fannie one week, had a pleasant time. The wind was the worst there. It rained a good deal while we were there. They seem to be pleased with Texas. Fanny hasn't been very well, having chills. Gus [Tillett] is with them, much pleased.

I had a good time coming, didn't get as tired as I expected. It has been so long now, I hardly feel like writing about my trip, have written it so often. I enjoyed the scenery very much. The mountains were beautiful grand. We got to Laws Angeles . . . Mon morning, sitting in the Depot, waiting for the train to take us to Downey, had eaten breakfast. Geo[rge] & Cha[rlie] came in. Geo look over there, saw me. He came, said "Ma is that you?" He was surprise to find us there. He could hear when we would get there. They were so delighted to see us as we were to see them. We got on the street car, went to see Jennie & children. We stayed until after dinner, took the cars for Dow[ney]. James and the children looking well, glad to see us. I have been to see them, staid 2 weeks. I found Julia looking very much as she did. Has 5 children, good looking. The youngest 3 years, Julia, the next is 5, pretty girl, reminded me of Anna, her size, Alex 12, Lou 10, Geo 8.

I brought a feather bed. Well, I am glad I did have it now to sleep on. It is cool enough for fire every morn. Charley makes me a fire. We had frost last week. It was right cold. It seems you are having cold weather in Ark. I see letters today from your sisters Mat and Mary. Cha got one from Kate saying it was as cold as any. They have had a good deal of snow. Your sister [Mattie] said she had a letter from you. She is troubled about Geo [Hughes, her husband]. Says he is very thin, weighs less than her, is sometimes hopeful then despondent. Says they will stay there until the cold weather is over, then go somewhere for health. I think he ought to try this climate. It is so pleasant, like spring. I feel so much for him. If he was only professed, it would not be so bad.

You must pray for him. It is the principal duty with us all to be ready for the soul's brighter home in heaven. May we all be prepared when the time comes for us to go. It can't be long with some of us.

Every thing looks green, pretty. The trees with oranges close to the house look tempting. They are ripe now. I enjoy them so much. They live in most too much style for me.

I expect to go to see Jennie next Thurs. She has been looking for me again. I have one letter from her and Jessie, insisting on my coming. I staid with them 2 weeks not long ago. She drove me out to your Br. Lewis' grave. She has it fenced up nicely, fine monument, cost 500. She take pleasure having it fixed up. He was very kind. The children was so glad to see me. They care me all over good many times. It is a beautiful city. They were glad having me.

I was pleased with Mr. Wicks [Jenny's second husband]. He is a good man, remins me of your Bro L. He is so kind & pleasant, has prayers with his family at night. She has been blessed with 2 good husbands. They have a little boy 2 years old, nice little fellow, live in style, every thing they want. They have so many oranges they hardly know what to do with them. Now don't you wish you had some. I do—My paper is full. I haven't written hardly anything. Haven't told you of the great Pac Ocean.

[no signature]

Mary W. Butler to daughter Emma Paisley in Dobyville

Norwalk, Calif.
[Dec. 1884–Feb. 1885]

I must hurry up and get my letter of this [place]. I went with Geo, sat and stood until noon to one of his meetings. Had good time, got to see good many people, was very much pleased with them. They are so kind, and seem to love each other. So nice.

We staid with a very pleasant family name Hugens. They seem so glad to see us. They have a pretty place, have a fine artesian well, the prettiest geese. Said they have 2 hundred young chicks, half of them large as Partr. The prettiest ducks I ever saw, Pekin. They are so well fixed for raising them, plenty of water for them to swim. They make a living on chickens.

The next night staid with Mr. Davis, good people. They want to sell their place, get a smaller one. He was talking of renting to Chas. There are plenty places, but they ask so much for them. I wish he could get him a suitable one. There is one close to Geo I think it would suit him better than any. They ask 3000.

He is now canvassing with his book, got 12 sold. It is rather dull business. They make more on chicks' eggs than any thing. They get 40 or 50 eggs a day, sell 15 or 16 doz a week. I think it is the easiest way to make money of any.

I haven't said anything of my trips to the ocean. I have been twice. It is a grand sight. I never could imagine how it looked. I came and I was on the beach to see it together for the first time. I felt impressed with the power of the Almighty more than I ever did, to see the tide coming in— white as snow. I never could look at it enough. I feel thankful that I was permitted to see it.

Wonder how Alice gets on with her 2 babes? Would to see how James Ira [Paisley] getting on. You must write soon. Julia and Geo send love to you and Billy, much love to all the children. I suppose you hear from Ira, Fannie.

Love from Grand MaMa

439

Mary Matthews to Emma Paisley in Dobyville

Tulip, Ark.
Mar. 4, 1885

Dear Sister Emma:

Your letter was received a few days ago, and I was glad to hear from you. It is with sadness that I write you of the death of little Aleck Moores. He was taken sick Saturday evening, but was not thought to be much sick. Sister had been with Alice all day, and went over to spend the night at bro. Henry's, but Alice sent her word she had rather she would come back, as Aleck was not well, so she went back, and thinking nothing serious was the matter, they all went to bed. But by ten o'clock, Alice got uneasy and called for Sister to come in. By 12 o'clock they found he was having a spasm and sent for Dr. Reamey, and in one hour he was dead. It was such a shock to Alice that she felt like she couldn't stand it, couldn't shed a tear all day Sunday. Said it was the darkest day of her life, and was constantly praying for Grace to bear the affliction. Monday she gave vent to tears which was a relief.

Bro. Olin was down at Hamburg. They dispatched for him, but Tuesday morning he hadn't arrived, and it was not thought prudent to keep the corpse out any longer. Bro. Henry and Sister came down in a carriage with it. Alice felt too badly to come with her little baby. They went back this morning. The casket was opened at the grave, and we looked through the glass at the body of the sweet little angel—had not even then changed much. What an affliction it is to the parents. How much I feel for them. You can indeed sympathize with them having passed through a like affliction.

Edwin was greatly distressed and called on Dr. Reamey to know if he couldn't do something to save his little brother. He didn't want him to die, said he had rather die for him. That was very affecting. Sister had Aleck in her lap while he was dying. It was a fortunate thing she was with Alice. When Bro. Henry and Sister Mollie got there, he was dead; never recovered from the spasm—passed into Heaven without a groan or struggle.

It will be a great surprise to Ma when she hears it. I expect she will feel like coming home. I got a letter from her written the 5th of Feb. Since that I've seen a letter from Bro. Charlie written the 22nd. Ma had gone to stay some with sister Jennie, which is her second visit. She said in her letter she sometimes felt homesick thinking it would be so long before she could see us all.

You spoke of making soap. I made my first effort at it last week, but didn't succeed very well with the soft soap. Made beautiful hard soap with concentrated lye.

Some of our earliest vegetables are coming up. I will be glad when we can have vegetables to eat.

Miss Carrie [Durham] died the 14th, the same day I sent off my last letter to you. Mrs. Boyd and Hattie take it time about staying at Mr. Durham's.

Bro. George [Hughes] is now trying the virtue of Mountain Valley Springs. If he improves and concludes to remain some time there, Sister will go over and stay with him.

Mr. Matthews unites with me in love to you all. It is now bed time. Good night!

Afftly your sister
M. J. Matthews

Alice Moores to Emma Paisley in Dobyville

Malvern, Ark.
Mch. 26, 1885

My Dear Sister:

Your letter was received some time ago, bringing with it a sister's love and sympathy. Yes, death has entered our household and taken from us our darling little Aleck, and we have been left to drain the cup of sorrow to its very dregs! Our hearts were bound up in that of the child, and the strings are bleeding and torn, yet, we must not murmur at our Father's will, for "He doeth all things well" and "doth not afflict any but for their good." You, my dear sister, have felt its touch in the loss of your little one, which was always delicate, but ours so full of life, with health blooming on his cheeks, thus to be taken, was a shock from which my nerves have not yet recovered. God does give me strength and grace to say "Thy will be done," but oh! the gloom and sadness still lingers about our little circle, for the merry voice is now hushed, and like a bird has he flown to the realms of light, where there is no night. God grant that this affliction may work out for our good, which I do not doubt, if we only trust him. We sorrow not as those who have no hope, for if faithful we shall meet on that sun bright clime. What a strong tie to bind us there—and there will be no more parting there. Yes, you and I have a cherub there, which makes Heaven seem dearer still.

Our little baby keeps well and is growing fast. Annie is very fond of playing with her. Edwin and William are going to school again, the former commenced another letter to Henry, but don't think he ever finished it. Olin got home last night. He doesn't expect to travel any more now for about two months, of which I am glad, for I do miss him so much. He spoke of traveling on the cars with Bro. Billy a short time since.

I suppose you have heard that Bro. George H[ughes] and Sister are now in Cal. I received a letter from the latter since they arrived. They are very much pleased, and think Bro. G's health will improve; Sister says he has been very cheerful; they are staying with Olin's Father, as Bro. George [Butler] has Ma and Bro. Charlie with him. The last we heard bro. G had gone to "Fulton Wells" about five miles from there, and he was going to stay up there awhile and try the water, which is very strongly impregnated with sulphur.

I thought I would finish on the half sheet, but will add a few lines more. Sister thinks Cal. a delightful country; said they would go to Los Angeles to visit sister Jennie soon. Ma had just returned from there and had a pleasant visit. Bro. Charlie is delighted, and expects to rent a place near there. I don't know when his family expects to move. Jimmie also seems to be pleased, but hasn't yet decided where he will locate.

I will close. Much love to all and write whenever you can. Olin joins in love—

Affectly your sister
Alice

Mattie Hughes to Emma Paisley in Dobyville

Downey, California
March 27, 1885

Dear Sister Emma,

I know you were surprised when you heard that we had left for California; but no more so than I was, when I received a telegram from George, while he was at Mountain Valley Springs, telling me to get ready for California. He spent more than two weeks there, didn't improve any, and concluded he would try a change of climate; which we all were anxious for him to do. We left Malvern Saturday morning (the 14th) at two o'clock, and got to Downey at 4 o'clock Tuesday afternoon (the 17th of March) making a quick and pleasant trip. Charlie and Jimmie met us at the depot, took us to bro Moores, where Ma was anxiously awaiting us. Brother George was from home, attending a meeting at Pomona, some distance from here, but came home the next day.

George is boarding at Fulton Wells, about five miles from here, and I am staying with Ma at bro George's. I don't know how long we will remain here. If George is not benefited at the Wells (the water is strong of sulphur), we will try some other place. He comes over very often, about every other day, was here yesterday, and spent several hours. I don't know that he has improved any, but he is more cheerful, and looks better than he did when we left Arkansas. He sees so much new and interesting that his mind is diverted from himself.

This is a pretty country, the orange trees look beautiful, full of fruit and flowers, but I believe it would soon get to be monotonous, and one would get tired of it. Two or three days ago we went to Fulton Wells, Brother George, Julia, Ma, and myself; we spent an hour or so there, then we went to the Hawkins Place, quite near, where there is a beautiful garden or park. So many lovely flowers, growing in such profusion, plants that are rare and tender with us. While we were there George had the gardener to gather some strawberries. We brought them here, and had them for dinner the next day. They were very good, for we had such nice sweet cream to eat with them.

Brother George and Charlie are busy today, irrigating, had to be out until nine o'clock last night, getting the ditches ready. A few days ago brother George sold a beef, just two years old, for $30.00 to a butcher from Los Angeles. He came out here and dressed it, George said it was the nicest beef he ever saw. Ma cleaned and prepared the tripe, has just put it on to boil and it looks so white and nice. They usually throw it away here. I don't think the children here ever tasted any.

Every body here do their own work. The men do the washing and milking. There are China men near, who take in washing. I put mine out this week. I don't know how they will be done up, ought to be done nicely, for you know they excel in laundrying.

I don't think this is a good place for making money. You can live well if you have a small farm, for you raise nearly everything at home. Oranges are very cheap, hardly get a cent a piece for them. Brother George hasn't very many, but has a good many English walnut trees, and I believe they are worth more; he has sold all of his last year's crop. When I have been here longer, and have seen more of the country, I can have a better idea of it.

I haven't been to Los Angeles yet, saw Jennie and Jessie at the depot, while we were waiting for the train to leave for Downey. If George begins to improve, I want to spend some time with Jennie. Ma is very well, and all send love, or would, if they knew I was writing. Remembrance to Billy & the children. Write soon.

Your Sister
M. W. Hughes

We have had letters from our boys. Reavis had a bad cold, and we feel anxious about him. West was in good health. Reav says he will never take the California fever, and under no circumstances would he come here to live; says Arkansas is good enough for him. I hope your baby is better.

M.

Mary Matthews to Emma Paisley in Dobyville

Tulip, Ark.
Apri. 20, 1885

Dear sister Emma:

Your letter was received some time ago, and should have been answered sooner but my time has been so occupied during the day looking after chickens, turkeys, flowers, &c that I have put off writing until I've gotten behind with my correspondence. The nights are too short for writing. I received a letter from Sister last Friday. She and bro. George were visiting sister Jennie. Her little boy Percy had just broken out with measles, the rest all well. Bro George has not improved, in fact lost 3 lbs in weight. Sometimes he gets greatly discouraged and thinks he will never get well. Says he will not try mineral waters any more, thinks it has been a disadvantage. Brother G's ill health mars Sister's enjoyment very much. Jimmie wrote me some time ago that she sometimes looked sad on that account. They have no doubt written you of our new nephew named Walter Hughes. It (is) said to be very much like Jimmie. He says it is very hard to realize that Ma's baby is now the father of a son himself, but says, "I guess I will realize it after pacing the floor a few nights with baby in one hand and paregoric bottle in the other." Maria and the baby were getting on finely. I was much astonished to hear through your letter that Mary Strong had a little girl.

I received a good letter from sister Fannie not long since which I must answer. She was getting better, she thought, but I've heard through a letter to Fannie Pattillo that she had a chill. I greatly fear she will never be stout. It is said she has never been well since she had measles. Her sister Mary is still with her, and has joined the church since going there. Fannie seemed much rejoiced.

I look for Mr. Matthews home today. He has been gone over ten days, which seems a long time. He wrote me from New Edinburgh that the community there were greatly shocked by the news that the Rev. Lumley, Baptist minister who left for his appointment over Saline river on Friday, was in all probability drowned. His mule was found hitched near the river, all his heavy clothing hanging on a tree, and tracks and signs indicating he attempted to cross on a temporary raft pulling over by the ferry boat rope, the boat being on the other side and the ferry man absent: it is supposed the current cut the raft out from under him: diligent search had been made, but up to the time of Mr. M.'s writing no tidings of his being found. His poor wife was so shocked at the first news brought that it was feared she would die, but had somewhat recovered. Mr. M. knows of my uneasiness about him and assures me that he will run no risk in crossing swimming waters. He has had bitter experience in that regard, a promising son just grown was drowned in Red river, and his only brother and his wife's brother drowned in Virginia.

We are enjoying the early vegetables now, mustard, lettuce, onions, radishes and asparagus, which is finer than usual, as the bed was so well manured and salted. Think we will have an abundance of strawberries. The bed is white with blooms, will also have raspberries. The promise seems to be fine for plenty of fruit. My chickens have not been doing well, though I get more eggs

443

than I ever did. Some hens left their nest and others didn't hatch, I think because the eggs I saved were chilled by the cold weather. Perhaps they will do better now. I have two turkey hens sitting, had one to die on her nest, but fortunately had another just ready to set to put on the eggs. Think there is another wanting to set which I must have brought up, have 23 eggs. I would like to raise 25 or 30. They are great deal of trouble. How are you getting on with your fowls, garden &c.

I forgot to tell you I made my soap this year for the first time myself and succeeded finely. The cake soap I made with concentrated lye, which is very white though it shrinks a great deal. Miss Pattie Yarbrough left for Malvern this morning. She is going to keep house for Mrs. Billy Cooper while they attend the Exposition. By going on the excursion train next Friday, the round trip only costs 9 dollars. I sent Alice a nice mess of asparagus, and Annie a beautiful bouquet of tulips and snowdrops. I will miss Miss Pattie a great deal. She comes to see me oftener than anyone else. She is an excellent woman—takes great interest in church and Sunday school. She has a large class of boys and girls. She is very different in disposition from Mrs. Cooper, so unselfish and thoughtul of others. She and I visited poor Miss Catherine not long ago, and promised to go and read some to her. I carried her some mustard ready cooked. She seemed so thankful and enjoyed it. Her appetite keeps good. She sometimes gets low spirited thinking, should Mr. Durham die, what would become of her. We that are able to get about and have our sight can't fully appreciate her condition, nor feel as thankful as we should for our blessings.

Mr. Matthews reached home safely between 1 and 2 o'clock, reports they found the body of the minister just where they thought he crossed the river. He sends love to you all. Mrs. John Pattillo came to see me a few days ago, said she expected to leave for Dobyville Wednesday. I am much obliged for your kind invitation to attend Presbytery, but it is impossible for me to leave home at present—I would enjoy the visit very much.

Love to bro. Billy and the children, also any friend that enquires about me.

> Lovingly
> sister Mary

Alice Moores to Emma Paisley in Dobyville

> Malvern, Ark.
> June 15, 1885

Dear Sister Emma:

Your letter was received several days ago, and I will reply this evening—I received a postal from Ira this morning, saying that this wife was quite sick again. I was in hopes that her health had greatly improved, but it seems that she is still subject to those spells. Ira seemed to think she was dangerously ill, but said she was a little better when he wrote.

I suppose you have heard that Cousin Gus [Tillett] and Mary Smith [Fannie's sister] were married last Thursday; tomorrow was the day appointed, but they received intelligence of Fannie's illness, and so had to hurry up matters—they married about one o'clock in the afternoon and reached Malvern after dark, then left for Texas on the two o'clock train that night. I didn't get to see them at all, as they spent the night at bro. Henry's. Cousin Gus was here and spent nearly a week when he first came back from Texas, and told us all about his anticipated marriage. It would have been a great surprise, had Ira not written it to me in his last letter.

Mr. Jimmie Pattillo's marriage surprised every one; he passed here just a few minutes ago with his bride. They have been over to visit her relatives in Arkadelphia and came in on the afternoon train. I have not met his wife since she was quite a small girl—I remember stopping there once when on my way to visit you, with Miss Alice Dale, and bro. Billy met us there. I have heard that she is a very nice young lady. She taught school near Tulip, where I suppose he first met her.

Annie is down at Tulip with sister Mary, has been gone about a month. I miss her very much, and have written sister Mary to send her up, but she feels so lonely that she is anxious to keep her a while longer. I may go down myself the first of July and spend a week. Olin will begin drumming again at that time, so I can leave home better.

By the way, Edwin and William are anxious to visit Henry at that time, and if it is convenient to meet them, would like to know so that I can have them ready. I should like very much to visit you and want to do so when Olin can have a little spare time. He is always busy, has been staying in the store with Mr. McCray. Can't you come over to see us some time this summer? I think you and bro. B both might leave, now that you have a good cook who can take care of every thing.

The Sunday School Convention meets here on the 18th. I suppose there will be a good many preachers in town; we will have two with us—Lizzie Crouch is also coming up on Thursday to make us a visit. Sister Mary may come up, but I can't tell. She has written me nothing about it. Hope you will write as soon as you can and let me know about Edwin and William making their visit.

We hear from Cal right often. Ma and Sister both wrote us interesting letters last week. I am glad to know that bro G's health is so much improved, he had gained nine pounds in ten days, Sister wrote us, which is wonderful. Ma says she gets homesick sometimes and wishes she was back again; it has been six months since she left. Jimmie and Maria were going to house keeping in a few days when they wrote; they are very proud of their fine boy, which is said to favor Jimmie.

I must close and write a few lines to Ira, have never answered his last letter. Much love to all and write soon.

> Ever your loving sister
> Alice Moores

Mattie Hughes to Emma Paisley in Dobyville

> Downey, California
> June 25, 1885

Dear Sister Emma,

I hope you will forgive me for not having written to you before now. I have had a good many letters to write, and for the last two or three weeks I have been going around a good deal. Last week we had a delightful trip. We hired a horse and buggy, and visited some of the most interesting places in Southern California—among the number Riverside, which is considered the garden spot, or most highly improved portion of Southern California. It is settled primarily by people from New York and New England, people of wealth and culture, who have spared no expense to beautify and improve their homes. There are some of the prettiest avenues I ever saw, and all kept in nice order. On Magnolia Avenue, which is the principal one, there are some as fine residences

445

as you would find anywhere. On the same avenue we noticed a very nice church and parsonage near. Where we spent the night we enquired, and found that it was a Presbyterian church (O.S.).

We also saw a very fine school building built by the state. In riding through this country, one will see many fine school houses, built for the public schools. No excuse in this country for one not to be very well educated. Near brother George, there is a good school—three of his children go. They have an exhibition there the last of this week, and we are going to see how the children do.

We spent yesterday at bro. George's—there was quite a number besides us, Mrs. Moores, her youngest daughter Edna, Maria and her baby, Fannie and two of her children. It reminded me of the old times at Tulip, when so many of us would meet at the old home. I missed Mamma very much. She is in Los Angeles visiting sister Jennie, who came out here about eight days ago and took her in to spend some time with her.

Jimmie and Maria are keeping house in Downey, about half a mile from her father's, where we are boarding. George and myself are going to take dinner with them today. They have rented a cottage of five or six rooms, and are very comfortably fixed. Their baby (Walter Hughes) is growing fast, and beginning to notice a good deal.

I saw Charlie a little while yesterday—he has a wagon and team, and for the last two months he has been quite busy, gathering and selling oranges and other fruits. Brother George has a good many apricots, and [Charlie] is selling them now, one half for the other. I think he is doing very well. He expects his family out here next month. He hasn't bought a place yet. I think he intends renting for awhile. I fear that Kate will be very much dissatisfied out here, away from all of her people.

George is improving rapidly—weighs 128 pds.—and when we came out here his weight was 108 and four weeks afterwards he weighed 104. He is in fine spirits, and thinks of returning to Arkansas about the last of Sept. I weigh 143, six pounds more than I did when we came here, and then I weighed more than I ever did before. I hope you all have kept well.

I suppose you have heard of the sickness of Ira's wife. When we heard from her last she was quite sick, couldn't retain any nourishment on her stomach. We feel very anxious about her.

I suppose Reavis is at Malvern. He finished the law course at Harvard and also took the degree of Master of Arts, which was a surprise to us, considering how much he had been sick. After spending a week or two at Malvern, he will enter Judge Rose's office in Little Rock. I don't much like the idea of his remaining in L.R. during the Summer, fearing he may get sick.

West is in New York city yet—though I don't suppose he will remain there during the Summer. He graduated about the middle of May, and wants to practice medicine during the Summer and Fall, so that he can make his expenses. The first of December he will enter New York City Hospital, where he expects to remain for 18 months.

Ma is not looking very well, and I hope she will improve while she is in Los Angeles. George says she eats so many oranges they keep her thin. It will be a great trial for her to part with Jimmie, to leave him so far, thinking she may never see him again.

Much love to all of your family—George would send some message if he was present. Write me when you can, for I am anxious to hear from you.

Your Devoted Sister
M. W. Hughes

[On the back of this sheet]

Dear Emma,

Tell Billy I congratulate him on the fine crop prospects in Arkansas, which I learn from the papers. I hope he will make the most out of the prosperous condition of the country. I see it is hot, hot, hot where you are. Such weather, though, is necessary for cotton. Here for instance, this morning the thermometer was 53, and at 11 AM it rose to 78. That is the warmest part of the day—a cool breeze springs up from the ocean at that time of day which makes it pleasant until night, when it gets quite cool again. Hope you will keep well. Love to all your family.

> Your Bro.
> G. W. H.

I do not expect to return to Arkansas until I weigh more than Nannie. I am gaining on her fast.

Alice Moores to Emma Paisley in Dobyville

> Malvern, Ark.
> June 30, 1885

Dear Sister Emma:

Your letter was received a few days ago and I will reply this morning. Edwin and William are very anxious for me to let you know the time when they think of starting. If nothing prevents, they can leave home on the 9th, which I believe is next Thursday week. They can stay a week or ten days, provided they give you no trouble. I was sorry to hear your baby was not well, and that you were without a cook again just at the time that you most need her, for the weather is getting so warm. Of course, if the baby should be much sick, I would not want Edwin and William to make their visit at this time. If everything is not convenient you must let us know.

Mattie and Nannie are going to Tulip the last of this week, and I will not go down until they return, so I can't tell yet when I will make my visit. Olin expects to start on the road next Monday, and will probably be gone two weeks.

Annie had a pleasant [visit] with sister Mary—she came up with Mr. Green last Friday. I think she has fattened up some. Our little baby grows fast and keeps very well, she is so much pleasure to me. She has blue eyes, but her complexion is not very fair, don't know who she favors. She is just beginning to sit alone well. I put short dresses on her about two weeks ago. She will be seven months old the 16th of July.

I had a letter from Ma and Sister not long since. Ma is getting a little homesick. I am getting very anxious to see Ma, she has been gone so long.

Olin has come from the store with some chickens (we have not raised any this year), so I will close my letter and send it back by him. I have not bathed the baby yet, as she has been asleep since breakfast.

I forgot to mention any thing about making dresses. You wanted to know in your letter before, so I suppose you have made yours up. I have a lawn made with short basque, and the skirt is full in the back with tucks more than an inch wide; the front has a narrow ruffle on the bottom, and that extends to the tucked widths. Also have an apron overskirt in front; they are using flounces a good deal also. Almost any way is stylish. I don't care much for such things any—though of course we want to look decent and not odd.

Write when you can. Love to all

Alice

I didn't see Cousin Gus as he passed back on his way to Texas; they married unexpectedly at one o'clock, came up that same eve & left for Texas that night. Mary was anxious to be with Fannie while so ill. We haven't heard in a day or so, but the last we heard she was slowly improving, though cousin Gus said it would be at least a month or more before she could possibly get well. I feel so sorry for Ira. Fannie and Mary both are sweet girls.

A.

Ira Butler to Emma Paisley in Dobyville

Abilene, Tex.
July 8, 1885

My Dear Sister Emma:

It is with a sad heart that I attempt to write you. My Darling Fannie died last Monday at Ten o'clock. Oh how sad I do feel. No one knows but those who have passed through the same ordeal. Although our union had been only about seven months, nothing but death could have separated us. Our hearts were as closely knit together as hearts ever get to be, at least for the time of our marriage. Our love grew as time passes. Oh! how mysterious are the ways of Providence. When we think we are just fixed for happiness in this world, some calamity comes upon us and we are made to feel most awfully its pains. My Darling died after long and severe illness last Monday at ten o'clock. She was not rashional at her death, but a few hours before she talked with me some on the subject of death. Could only make out a few words that were uttered. She said she was in the hands of The Lord, and that it was all right. She said God Bless us all.

She was buried in the cemetery here last Tuesday. Cousin Gus thought there was the largest procession attended her burial services than any he had seen at Abilene. She made friends faster than any one I ever knew. Don't guess she ever had an enemy. I have lost a jewel of the rarest order. Sometimes it seems to me that it is more than I can bear. Pray for me my dear sister, that I may devote my life more fully to the service of my Master. Heaven is all that is worth living for.

My prayer is that we may all form an unbroken family in Heaven without the loss of one. My Darling had been sick about seven weeks. Several times during this time, she and I were right happy in the love of the Lord.

Cousin Gus, Sister Mary & Rick are well. With love from all to all I am your devoted Bro

Ira

Chas. Wingfield to William Paisley in Dobyville

Prescott, Ark.
Aug. 5, 1885

Capt Wm Paisley
Dobyville
Dear Sir:

I heard a few days ago that you had returned from N. Carolina. I feel anxious to see you, to hear you tell about your trip and the pleasure I know you had while gone. Can't you and Mrs. P. come over and spend a while with us before the meeting closes.

The grandest work is going on here that I ever saw or nearly ever heard of. There has been up to this time about 125 conv. And some of the hardest cases I ever saw. A few I will mention: N. Richmond, Fade Barnes, Mr. Gee, Luke Steele, J. K. Hamilton, Lee Cloud. These persons I mention you probably are not personally acquainted with, or not more than Mr. Richmond at least, though all are past middle life, and some of the worst that Prescott affords. Mr. R. got up this morning before a crowd of not less than 1000 people and gave a good talk, asking his associates in the life that he had been living to change. Also led the congregation in prayer, praying a tuching and well worded prayer. All seem to be deeply interest, old white headed men ask continually the prayers of the church.

The town is closed and every body goes to church. I don't think there will be a man, woman, or child but what will be greatly improved that attend the meeting. The saloon men go, and seem to be tuched at what he says. I wish you could have heard his sermon this morning. It was directed to the saloon keeper.

I think he is the most wonderful man I ever saw. He certainly has an almighty power with him. You doubtless have heard of his coming. He is an evangelist from Tenn. He was borned in Arkansaw, Yell Co. He will be here till Monday any how, and I think by that time the Town will be converted if the interest is kept up that now exist.

Will close, with kindest regards to all,

I am as ever
Chas Wingfield

Alice Moores to Emma Paisley in Dobyville

Malvern, Ark.
Aug. 6, 1885

Dear Sister Emma:

I have been wanting to write to you, and ought to have done so soon after the children came back, but the weather has been too warm to write or do any thing almost. William was sick last week and had right high fever, but is now beginning to look like himself again, though he is still pale. I wanted to write you a few lines in Edwin's letter to Henry, but he had sealed it before I knew he had written. They both enjoyed their visit so much, and I am so much obliged for the care which you took of them—was glad you kept them a few days longer, for they seemed to enjoy it so much.

Olin is now up on the Fort Smith road, and I look for him back Saturday, feel right lonely when he is gone. I have been anxious to hear how bro. Billy enjoyed his trip &c. You must write me about it. No doubt he enjoyed it very much.

The baby doesn't seem to feel very well. She had some fever a day or two ago, and has taken cold in some way. She has one tooth through, and it may be teething that makes her feel badly. There is a good deal of sickness in Malvern, and I have heard of several deaths.

I received a long and interesting letter from Sister yesterday. She says bro. Charlie's wife is better pleased than she expected to be, and spoke of their all going to a quilting at bro. George's, said there were sixteen children there all belonging to the family or connection. Bro George [Hughes] now weighs 142 lb and she weighs 145. That is pretty good—bro G. said he didn't want to come back until he caught up with Sister—if he continues to improve as he has done, he will soon pass 145 lb.

Ma was with them. I shall be so glad when she returns. I expect they will come about the first of Sept. Reavis is here now attending court. I haven't seen him since he came out this time, but he was looking well when he was here about a month ago. His health has not been very good since he went to L.R. He went to some Springs and spent a week or two. Mattie Butler has returned from Tulip—she spent some time with sister Mary. The latter has a rising on her hand which has given her some trouble.

Love to all. Write soon.

> Afftly
> Alice M.

D. Lacy Paisley to William Paisley in Dobyville

> Bennettsville, S.C.
> Sep. 6, 1885

My Dearest Cousin:

This is Saturday night, and we have been teaching one week. Our schools started off very well, and we think we will do well. My boys seem to like their new teacher very well. I do hope we will get on well. Teaching is just as pleasant as it can be, when the scholars seem to be interested and are good. I do love to see them get on well. A man can do a great work in the school room. He has so much to do with forming his pupil's character, and you know this is not only for this world but for the next. God grant that my influence may never be for the worse.

We are all boarding with Cap. Dudley. It is a nice place. Lou and I furnish our own room, and it is very cozy. I want to keep house, but we would have to pay $150 rent to start with. This would leave us about $13 per month to live on, so we think that it is cheaper to board for a while at least.

All of the teachers are here, and they are very pleasant, I assure you. One of the young ladies is now sitting by me writing at my desk. I wish you were doing business in Bennettsville, and could send your children to our schools. I think we could brighten up their ideas, and at the same time set them an example of push. I am very much pleased with the looks of things here. Every thing is pushing. This is a good time of the year. Cotton is coming in right briskly.

Lou has not been one bit homesick yet. I have just got one of the best little wives that is going, if not the best.

Give our love to your wife and children every one of them. 'Tho we do not know them, yet they are yours and we love them. Now old fellow, I am going to write to you once in a while, and if you can, I would be glad to have you do the same. If not, I will not think hard. So good by, with much love and wishes for your prosperity in this world, and for a happy meeting in the world to come.

Your cousin
D. L. Paisley

Porter [Lacy's brother] sends love.

Mary Matthews to Emma Paisley in Dobyville

Tulip, Ark.
Sept. 20, 1885

Dear Sister Emma:

You must pardon my long delay in replying to your letter, will try to be more punctual. I had a serious time with my finger and hand, was fearful at one time I wouldn't have the use of my forefinger, but it is nearly well again. I have been prevented from writing so long that I'm behind with my correspondents—have had so much to do, drying fruit &c that I haven't felt like writing. I am still unable to do much sewing. Will be very busy this week preparing for our quarterly and protracted meeting, which begins next Saturday. I was in hopes Ma would be here by that time. Haven't heard any very late news. Sister wrote they would leave for home the 24th of this month. Now won't it be delightful to have ma safely back again after such a long trip. I have been alone and missed her so much.

Mr. Matthews is away more than half the time, only stays a day or two and has to ride so far. He left Friday and will not return before Monday week. These long rides horseback fatigue him very much. I feel very thankful that we have all been spared and no serious sickness. I suppose you heard that Mrs. Ben Smith (Annie Wilson) lost her little Bennie soon after the death of Ira's wife [nee Fannie Smith], and now Sam Smith's little boy died a few days, with diptheria; one affliction seems to follow another.

Received a letter from Ira few days ago. He has had a nice monument put on Fannie's grave, cost $100 dollars. He wrote that cousin Gus was suffering with rhumatism. He (cousin G) wrote me not long since of the nice presents his family presented his wife. His father sent $50.00 dollars, and left it with her to select. She sent to New York and got complete set of table ware— very beautiful about 96 pieces. His brother Charlie gave her a set of solid silver tea spoons & half doz. large steel ivory handled knives. His brother Wilbur, fruit and cake stand, and his sister Nettie, silver card receiver. Said he gave her himself, which was the best he could do, but then went on to write me about making a nice walnut wardrobe for her such as he would have to pay $60.00 for. Worked on it six weeks, mornings and evenings after leaving business. He has great mechanical genius.

451

21st

This is a beautiful morning after so much cloudy weather. I have a great deal to do. Want to sun Ma's beds, and have her room nicely scoured and put in order. I have one of Milley's girls living with me, 12 years old. She is a great deal of help. Alice has her sister that is older.

Wish I had time to write more but must write to Mr. Matthews—want yours to go in the mail this morning.

Excuse haste and the blot. Do you ever hear from Johnny? It seems he has forgotten us all. Much love to bro. Billy and the children, and a large share for your dear self.

Afftly your sister
M. J. Matthews

Write me soon: when are coming to see us?

Ira Butler to Mary W. Butler in Tulip

Abilene, Texas
Oct 2nd, 85

My Dear Mama:

I noticed from the Malvern News that you all were to have arrived at Malvern before now. Wish very much I could see and be with you to enjoy your sweet conversation and hear of your long visit. I am in hopes I can come out to see and be with you a while this Fall or Winter, but I see no opportunity as yet. I don't know that I can get my business in such a shape as to leave. I would have to employ some one to take charge of my business, and I don't know of any one in whom I could trust my business. If I should leave, don't believe I could do so until after the first or the last of next month. Would like so much if I had been able to have been with you a while & other loved ones in California. Hope you all had a safe and pleasant trip home. I was very sorry you could not come by.

Gus and Sister M[ary, Gus's wife] also were disappointed, when we heard you were going a different route. Gus continues to suffer with rheumatism, at times very much. I'm fearful he never will recover entirely. He has been working very hard for the last week on a residence he has bought. We expect to move into it next Monday. Gus has done considerable work and done it very well. The house was very much dilapidated, and will be a homely structure even when the work is completed, but it will beat paying high rents. He gets the property right cheap. It is a story and a half house with four rooms, two above and two below. My room will be above, at the north end of the building.

Rich has been complaining with his back for the last two days of evening. He has taken medicine tonight. Am in hopes he is not going to be sick. Sister M has been puny for some time, but I think she is getting her strength back and health. I have enjoyed splendid health all summer, although I am right thin. Believe I weigh as little as I ever did. I only weighed one hundred & seventeen pounds. I generally commence to improve before or by this time. I am guilty of the same thing here as at Tulip: will eat too much trash in the store. Rich says that is the reason why his head aches of evenings. I am going to try and controll myself better.

Gus and Sis M are getting on very well. They are both very anxious to move to their own place.

I am having some more pictures taken of My Dear Fannie, and will send you one some time if you haven't any. As soon as I am able and can have the work done, I want to send off and have her picture enlarged. Thought of having the work done here & had made arrangement with the Artist, but was afraid he could not do the work as well, and on as good material as I could get abroad. It is now bed time, so I will close.

Love to all at home, and write when you can to Your Loving Son   Ira

Mattie Hughes to Emma Paisley in Dobyville

Malvern, Ark.
Oct. 5, 1885

Dear Sister Emma:

We arrived here safely Friday morning, Oct 2nd and found all well. Brother Henry, Walter, Reavis, and Olin met us at the depot. As Alice was expecting Ma, she went on with Olin, and we stopped at bro. Henry's. We had a long trip—were on the way eight days. Had to stay in Kansas City 24 hours, and then 8 hours in Hoxie. Ma stood the trip very well, and didn't seem to be very tired when she got here. She is delighted to get back to Arkansas, and so are we.

George and Reavis left for Little Rock today, but I'll remain here a few days longer. I don't know where we will live. I am anxious to keep house, now that we can have Reavis with us, but I think George had rather board. I have had a great desire to have a home, where I could entertain friends and relatives, but I doubt if I ever have one. George seems to think he will have to leave every Summer, and says there would be no use in our having a home.

Harry May is carrying on a protracted meeting, and a great deal of interest is manifested. He is a strange man, and sometimes acts very much like a clown—says a great many funny things, and at first you wouldn't like him. You would feel disgusted. But he attracts people—they will go to hear him, and I believe he will do good.

Can't you come over and spend a few days while I am here? I expect Ma will be up here all of the week. All are well here and at Alice's, but there has been a good deal of sickness in town. Maj. Smith's wife lost one of their twins a few days ago. I think it died from flux. Kate Cooper Smith's baby has been very low, but is improving. Several have had typhoid fever and one or two have died from it.

I hope you and the children are well, and that I can see you soon. Love to all

Your Sister
M. W. Hughes

Mary Matthews to Mary W. Butler in Malvern

Tulip, Ark.
Oct. 6, 1885

My Dear Mamma:

I was much disappointed yesterday not to hear something from you. Sent up early for the mail, fully expecting a letter. Thought I would hear from you Saturday. Is Sister still at Malvern or have they gone to Little Rock? A letter came for you from Ira yesterday, and I received one from Emma. Her chills were broken, but still not feeling well. Bro. Billy expected to go to St Louis this week, and she would have to wait until his return before coming over. I felt so rejoiced and thankful to hear of your safe return. Now I'm getting impatient to see you.

Miss Pattie staid with me last night. Neither of us felt well enough to go to church. She is suffering with rheumatism and I have a bad cold. Miss P says she can hardly wait to see you. I look for Mr. M to-day. He is so anxious to see you that he concluded to come home this week. He will have a long ride. Our meeting has resulted in much good, four conversions all joined the church last Sunday. Herbert hasn't come to his breakfast yet. He is staying late. I haven't heard whether the meeting closed last night or not. I suppose the meeting at Malvern is still going on. Would like to hear from it. It is clouding up this morning and turning much cooler. Let us know when you wish to come home, and we will send up the wagon. Sorry we have no buggy to send—hope you keep well. Much love to all and a large share for your dear self.

> Lovingly your daughter
> Mary

Get some of them to write if you can't. I send you Ira's letter. Mrs. Cooper looked for you yesterday. Said she felt like you were coming. Herbert has come. Said there were six conversions last night and all joined the church, Hunter Green, Eddie Daniel, young Welsh, Bettie Welsh, Dora Laurence and Nellie Taylor. The meeting closed, appointed prayer meeting every Wednesday night. What a glorious thing if all these will be faithful working members.

D. L. (Lacy) Paisley to William Paisley in Dobyville

Bennettsville, S.C.
Nov. 22, 1885

Dear Cousin and Family:

Three months have gone by since I come to this place to begin old work in a new place. The time has seemed very short indeed. I guess it ought to, to a man having a sweet new wife. I often think of the day we were made one with much pleasure, and the brightest ray that shines is one cast from an unknown, yet known face over in the amen corner. I never shall forget how I eyed you that day in Greensboro, and I will always wish that I had grabbed hold of you. These things are pleasant to think of. How I wish there were no such thing as distance. Man with his steam and electricity has not yet been able to set it at naught. He never can be God in his kindness to man, who has promised to us a place where there will be no such word known to the happy inhabitants as separation. Oh! most kind and just God, Grant that we may all at last meet in that blest abode.

We are all well now. Porter has been sick a week or more, and has had the Dr. to see him every day—but I am glad to say that he is out again. Our schools are good. I have twenty-seven, which gives me my hands full. Lou is going to take two or three of the least in toe. This no. gives me a salary of over $70 per mo. I could save more if we could keep house. I have concluded to wait until next June. Then we will rent the buildings for a no. of years if that seems best. I then expect to buy a small house for my own and get to myself. Lou is as happy now as she can well be, but I know she wants to get to keeping house.

I wish I could have your boys in my school. That is, if they would work. And you did not buck when per chance I went for one a little. How I know you will hoot at this. I have had to collar one great big chap.

We have a knobby choir at our church—will soon have a grand pipe organ. We have a fine cornette player.

Give my love to all of yours and my regards to your pastor, Mr. W. Lou would be so glad to hear from some of your girls. Sends much love. This is my second letter to you, old fellow, since I come down here. You will get a third tho' if you do not get time to write. All well at home by last advice. Porter & Sallie would send love if they knew that I were writing. Your affec. cousin

Lacy

Was glad to see Dr. Woodrow come out so well "Right is might" Truth tho' crushed to earth will rise again.

Minerva Paisley to William and Emma Paisley in Dobyville

Mcleansville, N.C.
Dec. 22, 1885

My Dearest Nephew & Niece

I am afraid you have thought me tardy about writing, but I hope you will excuse me, for I assure you, it is not because I have not thought of you, or because you have any less hold of my warmest thought and affections. I often think of you all, and there is *no family* outside of my own children that I would rather correspond with. I would like so much to see you *all*, but if this is denied us, *do* let us write to each other as long as we live.

We are near the close of another year, and Oh! how much we have to be thankful for. When I am thinking about this, I think of the almost unexpressible pleasure your visit gave us all. You never will know the extent of that pleasure. I feel like it will do me good as long as I live, and I know the children feel the same way. You will believe me when I tell you Jno and Bessie have named their boy William. He is a bright little fellow, made his appearance the 28 of Nov. Percy is fond of his brother, says they will have a big time rabbit hunting. Bessie and babe are doing well—for which we ought to be so thankful.

Walter Linsay's wife gave birth to an infant which died one week afterward. She has never been well since. We had letters from Porter and Lacy last week. They are well and have a fine school. Annie is well, is coming home to take her Christmas. Jim and Jno are going to have a grand time hunting—you must remember than Jno is in a big way about his boy.

We were at Alamance Sunday, heard Mr. Miller preach a good sermon. It was the funeral occasion of the old gentleman that was sick between our house and Mr. Joe Gilmers. You remember, you and Jno. passed his house on the way. Poor man, he suffered a great deal, but he is doubtless at rest. He was a good man and a sincere lover of old Alamance. I reckon you will have a jolly time with all of your little fellows Christmas, if they make as much fuss over it as Percy. He has been writing notes to Old Santa, and counting the days till C. for a week or two.

Porter and Lacy are not coming home this C., so I reckon we will have a quiet time, as Jim and Annie are not very fussy. I reckon baby will be apt to make some music for us. Bessie and Jno. are down stairs now. I am glad of it. It is more convenient for them and more company for me. I have taken Percy for a bedfellow, and we get on finely. We had a visit from my brother's daughter, who lives in Virginia this fall. I had not seen her since she was two years old. That was a great pleasure to me. She is a nice intelligent young lady. She is the daughter of Rev. W. P. Wharton.

Will, there is one thing that I wish I had given you when you were here, that is the old family Bible. I did not think of it, but I would just as leave you would have it as any one, and you have just as much right to it as any of my children. I want it kept in the family. Give my love to Maryannie, and tell her to write to me. Our very best love and wishes to every one of you. Please write soon. God bless you from

> your loving
> Aunt Minerva

P.S. We have had a beautiful fall, and Jno. has got on finely with his work. Got a very good price for his Tobacco. With all the good wishes I can give, I am still your loving

> Aunt

Lacy Paisley to William Paisley in Dobyville

Bennettsville, S.C.
Jan. 8, 1886

Mr. Wm Paisley

Mr. Dear cousin:

You know I told you that if you did not write me soon, I would inflict you with another document, so here goes. We are all well except Porter. He fell off of his bicycle and got one of his feet hurt right bad. He has to ride to school. Our schools are doing well. We did not have a long vacation for Christmas. None of us left here. We had a very pleasant time here, so many of us in the same house, we have lots of fun all of the time. Col Dudley has a large family, and then all of we teachers boarding here makes some fifteen.

Lou has turned teacher, and helps me with my little fellows. I have one boy nearly grown that does not know anything at all. Poor boy, he does not know what two and two makes. So you see we have some very ignorant people in this state too. When I see the amount of ignorance in the world, I can but think my calling is second to none. My boys seem to like me very much.

We all had to stand an examination in the branches taught in free schools, yesterday. We get help from the county; that is, we are payed $30 per mo., which we deduct from the bills of the patrons. This helps them, and I do not see that it hurts us any. The examinations were not easy, and to do your work in an honest way was no fun. Now each one has to sign a pledge at the end of the examination, that we have not recd. any help. How some of the teachers could do that is more than we can see. I tell you one crowd took the cake. I just believe if Porter and I had said so, I think we could have made some of those teachers put California on the Atlantic coast.

There were in all twenty examined. I am anxious to know how many got first grade certificates. I don't see how some of them will get any at all. I worked on my papers from ten o'clock till after four, and wrote as hard as I could all of the time, and you know I, like yourself, do not write very slow.

We heard from home last night. They are all well. Jno. has another boy by name William. Jno. and Jim had a grand hunt Christmas. I wish I could have been with them. I can't get over my longing after that old home. (Blotter slipped here!) There are charms there for me that no place can ever have.

Jim's Bro Edd. is to come by to see us, on his way from a visit to his uncle in Wadesboro. I will feel like I had been at home after seeing he and Miss Lillie.

Lou just seems to be as well satisfied here as if she had been here all of her life. She is so kind and good that she is a general favorite in the house. I am so glad that she is contented and happy. I do hope that our schools will hold up well. I want to do well here and have a good and lasting school. I like the people very much. They are kind, too much so for the good of their children— let them have there own way too much. That is natural I know. Will, I wish we could all live in one place. I would like to teach those boys of yours, and I imagine you would not send many such notes to school as this: Please excuse Johnnie for being late it was not his fault. I require an excuse of this kind, and I get lots of them too. When I know it is the parents' fault for excusing, but what am I to do? We cannot have things just as we would like. I wish you could drop in and see us. I think we have well managed schools.

I guess you heard of Walter Lindsey's loosing his little one. Connie has been very sick for a long time, but is better now. She stayed at her Pa's for three or four months. The school that they had so much trouble to get up has busted all to flinders, and Frontes and his crowd have gone home, blessing out the Guilford people, & they in turn bless him out. He was not the man & that is a hard place, on acct of a very ignorant set near McLeansville. Mr. Alexander is very much put out about it.

We have a small church here, but fine music I tell you. Pipe organ. Large one too, cornett, and good voices. I wish you could hear Porter sing tenor.

We had a very nice little play to wind up our school with. Will send program. I was the Frost King, and my costume was very frosty. Porter was Santa. That is, some Porter & some pillows. The thing was good, everyone said.

Well, I guess you all have snow. We had a little this morning the first of the season. Now old chap, I am going to look for a letter from you in earnest this time. Lou said tell you she was as much devoted to her new cousin as ever, and wanted to hear from him soon.

Give our love to each one of your family, and thank your wife again for allowing you to come to see us this last summer. With best wishes and a happy and prosperous new year, with much love to all, your affec. cousin

Lacy.

Mattie Hughes to Emma Paisley in Dobyville

Little Rock, Ark.
Jan. 12, 1886

Dear Sister Emma:

Your letter written on the first, was received last week, and I was very glad to hear from you. I had been thinking of you, and wondering how you all were getting on. I was surprised that you hadn't heard from Tulip, though it seems to me that I hear from there very seldom. Ma scarcely ever writes, and sister Mary is slow about answering letters, but of late she hasn't had any help.

I expect she has suffered during this extremely cold weather—you know how she can't endure cold. I hope bro. Matthews has been at home. If so, he will do all he can to help her. How have you and the children stood the cold? As I am boarding and don't have to expose myself, I hardly feel it. Reavis says, he feels the cold here, more than he did in Boston. Last Friday was one of the most disagreeable days, I believe, I ever saw—a cold north wind blowing all day. I felt sorry for any one who had to be out. I know many a poor person suffered, for the want of fire and warm clothing.

George has kept very well, and has been free from cold. Reavis goes out a good deal—somewhere every night, and for a while he had a bad cough, but he is very well now. We enjoyed Walter's visit, Christmas—he spent three or four days with us, and we were very glad to have two of the boys with us. We hear from West quite often. He is in New York Hospital, and seems to be well pleased. He says, he is kept quite busy and time passes very rapidly.

I didn't see Ira, although I was at Malvern while he was at Tulip. I kept house for Mollie, while she was at Conference. Mamma was very glad to have Ira with her while sister Mary and bro. M. were at Conference. She would have been lonely without him. I received a letter from him since he returned to Abilene. He is much more cheerful than he was.

Alice wrote me that Olin was going to commence drumming some time this month, and that Ma had promised to come and stay some with her, but I don't suppose she came up before this bad weather.

I haven't heard from California very lately—all well when we heard. Bro Charlie has rented a place near bro George, and Kate is better pleased than she was living in Downey. They have two or three cows and plenty of room for raising chickens. Mrs. Colburn thinks she will go out to see them during the summer.

I hope I can make you a visit during the Summer—tell Mattie and Lula, if I come, I'll bring Annie with me. Annie has been going to school and was delighted. I hope Alice will not let her go while it is so cold. Have you a school near for your children? Is Billy any better contented? and how has he been getting on with his business?

We have a new preacher at our church, Dr. G. W. Miller, from Mo., and every body seems to be pleased with him. I like him very much—he is very bold in denouncing the sins of the day. He doesn't want any theater going, dancing, or card playing members.

Much love to Billy and the children, and write whenever you can.

> Your Devoted Sister
> M. W. Hughes

Maj. Coulter [Mollie Butler's father] had a slight attack of paralysis, but is about well.

Ira Butler to Emma and Billy Paisley in Dobyville

> Abilene
> Jan. 17, 1886

Dear Sister Emma:

Ike and Eugean Cheatham spent last Sunday with us. The latter said you were all well, and have not left Dobyville. Think Eugean told me he took dinner with you before leaving for Texas. Was very glad to hear you were all well. We were so glad to see them both. Eugean is in Jones County, joining Taylor (our county) on the north. Think Ike is on a section of land by his brother Eugean. Tried to find a position here as clerk but could not. Was sorry he could not, for he seemed like a good boy and would I guess make a good clerk. Ike is clerking for a firm in Belton. I am reducing my stock, with an eye to selling out. The grocery business is very much overdone here, so much so that there is no money to be made in it at present. Sister Emma: I commenced this letter to you, but since so much is of a business nature will direct it to Bro. Billy.

Bro. Billy: I am thinking of going in the hardware business. Don't you think that business would be more profitable than handling groceries? Isn't there a better profit in hardware than in groceries, & can't you buy hardware on much better terms than you can groceries?

Our county is settling up with farmers rapidly, and from the experience of three years: this county is well adapted to farming purposes. The furniture business also has been very remunerative to those who have followed it here. Thought I would follow one or the other. Which in your opinion would be more profitable in this western country? How is Ben Logan getting on at Prescott? Believe he is in an exclusive hardware business. My idea is to go to a smaller place than Abilene to open up. Which in your opinion is more prefable to doing, a small business on the railroad or in some small inland town? I propound these questions because I know you are capable of giving good advice. My capital will be quite small, after I sell what goods I have on hand and pay what I am owing. Don't expect to sell my house & lot. We have been counting pretty heavy on getting another railroad at Abilene, but it is right uncertain now.

Gus is getting along finely now in his law. He is now all alone in his profession, and is much better pleased and will get on better I believe.

How are you getting on in your business? Haven't heard from you in a long time in that particular. Hope you are doing well. How are money matters in your part of Arkansas? They have been exceedingly tight here. Where ever I move have decided to sell exclusively for cash. Am sick of the credit system. How does your pulse beat on that subject: Don't you think it the best policy? Guess you think I ask a great many questions, but I do so not through mere idle curiosity.

Gus came in my room and I told him I was writing to you and requested me to remember him very kindly to you and Sister Emma. Mrs. Smith is still with us, and will remain I guess until spring. She is a great deal of company and assistance to Sis M.

[final page missing]

William Paisley to Emma Paisley in Dobyville

[Billy is now keeping a store at Gurdon]

Gurdon, Ark.
Jan. 22, 1886

My very dear one:

I am sorry to tell you that I am again sick & in bed. My bowels seemed to get wrong the night I was at home, but I was so much in hopes that it would amount to nothing that I said but little about it. After leaving you Saturday morning, I stopped at Mr. Billy Jones on or near the road by Clarks Mill, out of the rain. While there I got very sleepy. Mr. Jones had me to lie down & I slept for an hour & a half or near that time. Mrs. Jones prepared a good dinner & when I got up I ate heartily, but soon found that I would not digest it properly. I reached Gurdon between three & four o'clock, feeling weak & tired, & that night my bowels got very wrong again. I sent for Dr. Moore and told him if he thought I was going to have a spell & it would do, that I wanted to go home at once. He game me some medicine which acted very promptly & relieved me greatly. The bloody actions ceased, & the medicine appeared to be acting on the liver very well. Yesterday I remained quiet and in bed most of the day, but felt tolerably well. Slept well last night, but am not feeling quite so well this morning & consequently am a little low-spirited. Mr. Boyce & his family are here, spent last night at Billy's, & as I suppose they will go out in the morning, I write this to send by them. If you get this in time, you might let Henry come down on Dock this evening, & if I am well enough I will get a buggy & come out home. If not I will try & get a buggy here & send out for you to come in & stay with me.

Tell Jno & Willie to be sure & look after the oats—even undo the binds & sun them if necessary, in order to keep them from moulding, & just as soon as they are dry enough to put in a house, to haul them up & house them, even if they have to keep some plows idle to do it. *It is very important that the oats should be saved.* They must go to the field with the horse just as soon as the ground will do at all, & then with the plows. The fence row in the Big New ground next to the lane can be hoed any time. Will stop now & add more after a while.

It is now 5 minutes to 8 A.M. Mr. Boyce has been in & says he will want to start out soon. I am not suffering any pain but have a languid sick feeling. Think I have suffered a little more from impatience this spell than I did before, & the fact of my having to be away from home has worried me some. You must not be at all uneasy about me, though it may take me some little time to get well, as the causes that are operating have existed a long time. When I am alone & in bed, my thoughts, my dear one, turn to you & the dear children with the tenderest love, & I then realize more fully than ever how dear & precious you all are to me. I think & hope that when I get over this spell, my health will be better than for a long time. On the other hand, should it be the will of God that my sickness should be unto death, I feel that I can safely leave you & our children in the hand of Him whom we love & who has always taken care of us. Now my dear one do not imagine from that that I am low spirited or desponding, for that is not the case.

Mr. Boyce is about ready & I must close.

> As ever your devoted husband
> Wm Paisley

L. D. Lipscomb to William Paisley in Dobyville

> Waxahachie, Ellis Co., Texas
> Jan. 23, 1886

Dere William:

I was delited too recve a letter from you again, and here that you and family ware all well. I have bin suffering with a very bad cold and cof ever sence that very bad cold spel of wether that come about the 8 day of Januay, my birth day. I was 66 my 3 score and ten will soone wind up, if I live to se it. I pray God too make and keep me reddy.

Claud has not bin very well this winter. He is having chills and fever, and it semes hard to brake them up and keep them broke. Lorenzo D. and family are well. Dr. Bentley and family are all well. The doctor is dooing better I think tan I ever nue him. I hope he may continue.

I saw Henry Bronen some days ago and he spoke very kindly of you. I se Tom Phillips some times. He is selling goods at Mountain Peek now. I rote to Mr. White that I would be at Dobevill in Januey, but I cant say now when I will come. I dont like to be on the rode in bad wether. This is a pretty country in pretty wether, but rather ruf now. Quite cold here to day but not so cold as the other spel. Fine crops here last year.

Well William I dont no what else to rite. I recon by the time gets thare you will be back from St. Louis. I am glad you made the trip to North Caroliner and enjoied it so much.

I think of Dobeville and the graveyard often. Let us live nearer ower god more prarful and watchful.

Rite often, William. give my love to Emma and the children. give my love to Mr. White and family.

Your Devoted Farther
L. D. Lipscomb

William Paisley to Emma Paisley in Dobyville

Gurdon, Ark
3/6/1886

My dear one:

I am very busy but will say a word. I was a little unwell yesterday, but took some pills last night, & feel better to day. Am very busy, and fear that the work & worry I have had may make me sick, but hope not. Went to prayer meeting last Thursday night, but found few there. Am still pleased with every thing, except being away from you all.

Your devoted husband
W. P.

March 7, 1886

My dearest one:

Your note came yesterday & I was glad to get it but sorry to hear that you were not feeling well. I am feeling all right again & hope that I will not get sick but will be sure to let you know if I do. Went to ch yesterday & heard two excellent sermons from Rev. Mr. Hill, a Baptist Brother who preaches here once a month. Am bothered considerably about freights. The R R hands are on a strike & but few trains running. Love to all.

Yrs. devotedly
W. P.

March 9, 1886

My dear one,

As Walter is here & will go out to day, I write to say that if you have more chickens than you need, now is a good time to sell them here. Grown chickens are worth 25¢ a piece & sell very readily at that price. I think you might pick out 25 or 30 that you could spare very well, & then have plenty left, but you be the judge of that. If you think of sending them, let some of them make a frame that will fit the wagon bed—like the body out of the 3 in slats i.e. the sides ends & top. the bottom can be made solid out of box tops or something like the red fruit dryers, & put the chickens in that, & when they get here the whole thing can be lifted off, & I will have a place to keep the chickens until they are sold. 25 or 30 would be as many as I would want at a time. You need say nothing of the price, for while I can sell them at 25¢ I ought to buy them for 20¢.

I am feeling very well, but am muchly bothered by not getting my plows & other goods. The

R R hands are on a strike, and nearly all the trains have stopped except passenger trains. I am thinking something of hiring Inman for a few months to make a corn crop. Would you object?

Hoping to see you Saturday, I am yours hurriedly with much love

Wm Paisley

Should Willie bring the chickens ask him to bring as much of the scale lumber as he can haul.

.W. P.

Tell him to bring all the faucets out of the molasses boles, except the one you need at home. I also want the cotton scales as soon as I can get them here.

W. P.

Mary Matthews to Emma Paisley in Dobyville

Tulip, Ark.
Mar. 10, 1886

Dear Sister Emma:

Your letter was received some time ago—very glad to hear from you. Ma went up with Herbert to Malvern Monday, so I will be very lonely again. I don't know how long she will remain. Mr. M is at home now, but will have to leave Friday. He is in the garden getting ready to finish planting Irish potatoes. Our early vegetables are coming up very nicely, the strawberries are just beginning to put out. Everything very backward this spring. I do hope we will have plenty of fruit.

Just before Ma left she received a letter from Sister containing the sad news of the sudden death of Mrs. Cates. Her son found her dead in bed just after breakfast. He was in her room twice during the night to put wood in the stove, and thought she was sleeping well. She had been suffering with severe pain near the heart which the doctor had relieved, but it is supposed it reached her heart and killed her immediately. We have heard of so many sudden deaths lately, it is a warning to us to be always ready "for in such an hour as ye think not the son of man cometh". Hasn't Bettie Strong been sorely afflicted? Just after the burning of her house comes the unexpected news of the sudden death of her oldest daughter who was buried here beside her father. Bob Smith was the only relative that came with the corpse.

Aunt Lucy was here a few days ago and requested me to be sure to ask you if Sarah was still living in Clark, and ask her if she has heard any thing more from Billy, whether he is dead or not. Tell her to write to her mother when you write. Don't forget to let her know, as she seems so anxious about it.

It turned very cold last night. There was some ice this morning, but the sun has been shining very brightly today. I hope it will continue clear and turn warmer, so that vegetables will grow rapidly. The turkeys destroyed all our turnip salad and we miss it so much. I think it so healthy to eat in the spring.

A letter came to Ma yesterday from Johnny. Think I will send it to her in the morning—all were well. Johnny has determined to do better about writing, especially to Ma, and wonders now why he has been so neglectful.

I have only 3 hens sitting. The turkeys will soon be laying. Ma was anxious to be at home to look after them, but Alice seemed so anxious for her to come up and stay some with her while Olin is away. How are you getting on gardening &c? Tell bro. Billy he must bring you over to see us. Wish you could be with me now while ma is gone. I would enjoy having you with me *so* much. Miss Pattie is so good and kind. She will stay with me at night some times, but Mrs. Cooper talks of going to see her son Jim, and then Miss Pattie can't leave. I ought to have one of your girls.

Love to Bro. Billy and the children. Write soon to your loving sister

Mary

William Paisley to Emma Paisley in Dobyville

Gurdon, Ark.
Mch. 12, 1886

My dearest one:

I read your note by Willie again last night, and knowing that you were going about, made me so uneasy about you that I became excited & could not sleep until after 2 o'clock this morning. My dear one, you must be very cautious. Even if household matters should seem to require your attention, Emma could stay home from school or every thing could take care of itself rather than for you to run any risk. I do hope that you are still improving, but if you are not, send for Dr. Cargile, go to bed & remain there until you get entirely well.

I was strongly tempted last night to decide to start home this morning, but Billy will not be of much service until he gets fixed, and he seems to me to be almost as helpless as a child.

Lizzie went up to Sis's last evening & stayed there last night. They will move in this morning. I shall expect to take supper with you tomorrow night, unless I hear from you to come sooner & should you feel that I should come at any time, do not fail to send for me, no matter what the trip may be.

No freight trains yet & no telling how long the strike may last. As ever your devoted husband

Wm. Paisley

Do not exert or expose yourself fixing for Sunday.

William Paisley to Emma Paisley in Dobyville

Gurdon, Ark.
Mch. 15, 1886

My dearest one

Thinking about the dreariness of being separated from my dear & interesting wife & little ones gave me the blues badly this morning, & I felt that I could hardly indure it, but as soon as I got into the house, I had to get to work selling goods for cash, & now the cash sales for the day foot up over $50.00, which is mighty good considering the stock we have over.

But it will not do to speak of this to any one, & would really rather that none of the children know it, because I am determined to keep our own secrets. The day's work has encouraged me considerably, & I hope all will work out right yet.

I saw Stan Harley this morning. He may be over to eat with you while assessing. I am boarding with Lizzie, & find it very convenient.

Yours in haste,
Wm Paisley

[Marked *Private* in red ink]

Emma Paisley to William Paisley in Gurdon

Dobyville, Ark.
April 14, 1886

My dear one,

As John has written to you, I will add a few lines to send in his. I took all the things out of the desk thinking, as it rained very hard, probably Willie could go to Gurdon to morrow. John thinks if it does not rain any more they can plow by tomorrow evening.

Manerva was over and washed today. Said she wanted you to send her a barrel of flour like the one Bill got—a keg of molasses and *five yds* of pant goods, for her children. I told her she better not get so much at once, for she might get sick and could not do the work. She said, well, she wanted a barrel of your best flour—that she did not want any dark stuff. She has done 7 washings since she got anything except 25 cents worth of tobacco, which leaves us owing her $5.00 (five dollars). I don't know what the flour will come to, but by the time she gets it, she may do enough washing to pay for it. She did not say anything about wanting money to me.

If you think she ought not to have flour till she pays for it, it will be all right with me. I don't believe in paying before the work is done, though if Manerva keeps well she will pay for all she gets. Sophie has been saying to Manerva that she wanted money to pay her preacher next Sunday, and she was going to have it.

I have finished my callico dress and expect to wear it to Sunday school next Sabbath. Much obliged for the domestic and triming. All have gone to bed except myself, so I will bid you good night.

Write and come when you can. Love to friends. Ever your loving and devoted

Emma E. Paisley

William Paisley to Emma Paisley in Dobyville

Gurdon, Ark.
Apl. 15, 1886

My dear one,

Sammie Orr is here & I will send a line. Henry told you about Robt's having Roseola. He was quite sick Saturday night & Sunday, but has been at work all week. They were crowded Monday before I got here, & we have had a good trade all week.

The new City Council was sworn in Monday night, of which I am a member. Have been sleeping like a log for past few nights, & am feeling much better than when I was out at home. Think I must have had a touch of the Roseola my self.

You must arrange to come over as soon as you can, and bring the smaller children. Let me know how Emma is getting along. I forgot to inquire very particularly. I want to report to Dr. Cargile. All are well here, haven't time to write more. I will have to go to Arkadelphia Saturday to attend meeting of the County Central Committee.

Much love to all, as ever your devoted husband

Wm. Paisley

William Paisley to Emma Paisley in Dobyville

Gurdon, Ark.
Apl. 22, 1886

My very dear one:

Your letter of yesterday just received and I am pained to hear of your and the children's sickness. Your expression of disappointment causes me to censure myself severely for not writing you, but you can be assured, my darling, that my not doing so was not all due to indifference or anything of the kind, & while the rush of business some times prevents my writing you, when I have a chance of sending by hand there is nothing in the way of business or social duties that I put ahead in point of importance to writing to you my dear one.

Sunday morning I went to Sunday School (Mr. Baker was sick & did not preach) &, as Miss Louise Hall was at Sis', went there for dinner—in the evening went to see Mr. Baker & then back home. Went to bed early, was very busy Monday. Monday night had to attend the meeting of the council. All last week we were very busy. Yesterday & to day being the only quiet days we have had since the goods came. I acknowledge the justness of your censure for not writing, but you must not imagine for a moment that it is owing to any feeling of indifference, for you are uppermost in my thoughts, & it seems to me that since I was at home last, I have been more home sick than ever. Had I known of your sickness I would have been with you before this, would start now but it is so late & will be so dark I will put it off, hoping to be with you to morrow.

Miss Lizzie had a chill Monday. I have been feeling very well—have quit drinking coffee except for breakfast & have no trouble sleeping.

Have had a good deal of new trade since I saw you, & am much encouraged with my business prospects. Hoping to see you soon, & hoping that you will not have any more chills, & that the children will soon be well, & that you will forgive me for my seeming negligence.

I am as ever your devoted husband with much love

Wm Paisley

M. Grier to Emma Paisley in Dobyville

Yorkville, S.C.
April 26, 1886

My ever dear friend

I was agreeably surprised to receive your kind letter yesterday sent me by Maggie Miller from Charlotte, & to shew you my appreciation of it I answer by to days mail. Tho I assure you I did not forget my obligation to such a friend as yourself, but was waiting a little while longer so as to tell you my various plans of visiting, for tho I've been in Carolina more than 4 months, I've not yet gotten around to see all my relatives. After seeing my Charlotte friends, the day William left me, my son Dr. Jim took me to his home 12 miles in the country, had not seen his wife & children in 10 years. There I staid the cold month of Feb.

I then went to Concord Town, visiting 4 families of Nephews & nieces besides cousins, was there two weeks. Then to Charlotte & then to this place, where for the first time I've seen any one of my sainted Elva's family. I met with a warm welcome, but oh, how I miss her dear presence. The first time in 24 years that I've been here & she was absent. I've visited her grave, & find a beautiful monument to her memory there, and a number of her & my friends have called to see me & so many expressions of praise I hear from them regarding her life among them here.

I have still to go to Mr. Jones and to Chester & Back Hill visiting granddaughters who reside there, before my return to Charlotte. & in July some time I hope to see Mr. Tidball & Mary, beside other relatives in Statesville. My reunion with dear friends has been a great pleasure. All give me warm welcomes, & I often think, if such joys are realized in this fleeting life, what must it be in that world where there is no ending to all Eternity. I often think of my pleasant intercourse with my Arkansas friends, among whom you & Capt. P are prominent ones, & wonder if it will ever be my pleasure to be with you all again. I surely enjoyed my 8 years sojourn among you greatly.

Tell the Capt. I think with him that Old North Carolina, with the numerous R Road & No Fence Laws and increased number of churches, is surely in a general progressive State. The hard times is the general cry.

I was a little surprised to hear of the Capt. moving his store to Gurdon. I have wondered if he intends moving his family there too. The copartnership surprised me more of the firm of Boswell, Stitt & Davies. I presume they will prosper with no competition, & one store is surely enough for the little village of "Dobyville".

I was truly sorry to hear of Dr. Cargle's affliction in the case of his wife. Such tumors as you wrote of bodes no good, and I predict there is little to hope for. My friends write me, as well as yourself of the continued favor Mr. Williams is held among the people of "Carolina Church," &

I've little doubt he will grow in their esteem. I was so pleased with his instructive preaching as well as its deep spiritual teaching, & I do hope the Church there may long be blessed with his ministry. Where does he board now since the Davies has moved?

The Churches here and in the Co of York & in and around Charlotte are being greatly revived, & I believe a time of refreshing from the presence of the Lord and the glory of His power is awaiting them in common. No great excitement, but a deep feeling & reverence in attending the ministrations of the Word. I attended a communion at Charlotte 1st Sabbath of this month & it was a very solemn one. I attended then on 3rd Sabbath at Bethel Church in this county, where some 400 communicants participated. Mr. Welch the minister, said he had never in his ministry witnessed so many communicants & so large a congregation so reverant, & yesterday we had communion here, a protracted meeting of 4 days & very solemn. 1 old gentleman, Mr. Theodore Moore, made a profession aged 75 years. If you see Mr Adams tell him of it. I think he must know him. He is the elder brother of Rufus Moore & Adolphus. Tell him too that I have seen & been with his friends since I came to the Co., & all are well. Miss Lilla Crenshaw is in Nashville, Tennessee, teaching music.

The farming is backward, cold wet weather, & now dry are retarding labor. Gardens too are backward. Spinage, lettuce, & radishes, shelots are all I have eaten of early gardening, not a pea blooming or potatoe formed. Say to Altona I will write her before I leave Yorkville, & after seeing Mrs. Jones about the last of next week, I will write to Lizzie Grier.

Say to the Capt. I hope to be able to send him a remittance after 1st July. Am sorry to have been unable to do so before. Don't let your little ones forget me. I think the older ones won't. Tell Lula when she learns to write, she must write "Grandma" a little letter & send it in yours. I had a letter from Mary Tidball last week. She was getting on nicely with her housekeeping & little school about 200 yard distant. Mr. T had gone to Presbytery & his health greatly improved. Give my congratulations to Mr. Bayre & Fannie on the birth of their daughter. Hope mother & Babe are doing well, & always remember me to your good mother, & tell her I believe we will meet again in the Better World if never here. With many kind regards for you & yours, I must close, hoping to hear from you again when, amid your cares, you can find it convenient to write. Remember me to your children and to Capt & accept a large share for yourself from your affectionate friend,

M Grier

Address to Box 12 Charlotte N.C. until I inform you otherwise. M.G.

Mattie Hughes to Emma Paisley in Dobyville

Malvern, Ark.
May 7, 1886

Dear Sister Emma:

I came here about ten days ago, to keep house for Mollie, while she is gone with brother Henry to General Conference. I received a postal yesterday from bro. Henry written from Louisville, and he said they were having a splendid time. They spent nearly two days in Nashville—stopped with Cousin James Manire, who had asked for them. Saw all of our relatives there and were delighted with them. I am so glad that Mollie went, and hope she will have a pleasant time.

George [Hughes] came out yesterday, and will spend a few days here. He thinks of going to California the last of the month, and Alice Steel is going with him, to spend the Summer. Reavis is here too—he came out the day before his pa. He had been having fever for several days, and thought a stay of a few days here might be beneficial. He is looking quite thin, and is feeling badly.

Walter returned, from a two weeks stay in Abilene, last night. He is well pleased with the town, and has decided to locate there, and form a partnership with Gus Tillett. I hate to think of his going so far, but believe he will do better there than here—so much more outcome in that country. He says Ira is looking thin, and hasn't been making more than expenses. Gus is looking well, and very happy with his wife and baby. Maj. Coulter is doing very well, and expects to go to Texas in two weeks, to spend the summer.

George [Henry's son] is with bro. Johnnie, learning to be a farmer, and very much pleased. May [Henry's daughter] will return home with her pa and ma, the 12th of June. They are coming by, and will be at her commencement. I had an interesting letter from her the other day—she is quite anxious to get home. Coulter is staying in the store and has splendid health.

I saw Alice yesterday. She is very well. William and Annie are at Tulip, but will come up the first opportunity. Ma expected to come back and stay while I was here, but I think it doubtful about her coming. She is so well pleased at the old home, and it is so difficult to find a good way to come. I expect to spend part of the summer at Tulip, and will visit West in August or Sept, when he can have a vacation of three weeks. His health is good, and he is well pleased at the hospital.

Alice received your letter, and we sent it to Ma. I know you find it disagreeable living like you are, and after getting so well fixed, to leave your home. But I suppose Billy will do better at Gurdon.

They were all well in California when we last heard from them.

Much love to the children, and write when you can.

> Your Loving Sister
> Mattie W. Hughes

Alice Moores to Emma Paisley in Dobyville

> Malvern, Ark.
> May 7, 1886

Dear Sister Emma:

Your letter was received several days ago, and I was glad to hear from you, for it had been some time since I received a letter, and think I had written last.

Edwin is writing to Henry, so I thought I would put my letter in his. William and Annie have been at Tulip now for some time, am looking for them up every day.

Olin is about through drumming now until the fall trade sets in; he had thought of going to Cal. a week ago, but just at the time he had expected to get off, the rates, which had been so low, were reestablished, so he concluded not to go at present. Although I had been away from him a good while, I would have been so glad if he could have made the trip to see his mother and father. Tickets were sold as low as ten dollars, from here to Cal. If he could have gotten off from his work, then was the time for him to have gone.

Mattie is running all about now and can talk a little; she is always into some mischief, and one of the most restless children I ever saw. We tried several times to get her picture, but she wouldn't sit still long enough to have it taken. I took her to Little Rock especially to get one, but could not.

We have had two messes of strawberries, but not of our raising, however. Mr. Draper has some very fine ones for sale.

We have a "Ladies Aid Society" organized here, which is for the benefit of the poor, and to assist in furnishing the parsonage. We have an entertainment tonight, which will be at bro Henry's, and we will also have cake and lemonade to sell. This is furnished by the members. I succeeded very well with a silver cake.

It is indeed a great pleasure to have Ma with me, and I wish it was so that she could live with us. Walter went out to Abilene last week, Sister is looking for him back today. I think it is very probable that he will return there to live.

Am glad to hear that Bro B. is getting on so well at Gurdon; it is indeed bad to be separated so much, I know how to sympathize with you. Wish you could come over to see us; you may look for me some of these days.

Love to all

Your Afft. sister
Alice

William Paisley to Emma Paisley in Dobyville

Gurdon, Ark.
May 18, 1886

My very dear one,

Mr. Ellis whom I was surprised to see this morning, is now about ready to start back, and I only have a moment to write.

I am very much afraid the hands do not realize the importance of rushing work on the farm, and that the outcome will show a fearful falling off.

I have been unwell ever since I was at home. My tongue is badly coated and I have but little appetite. Am taking medicine but it seems to do but little good. Have not stopped work, but feel but little like it. Hope though I will get better soon. Do not be uneasy for if I get sick will let you know.

Today has been rather an idle day so far as trade was concerned, but have had a good trade every other day since I was at home. Last Saturday was the best day since I was at home.

Mr. Baker went off to Magnolia to attend Harry May's meeting, and expecting to get him to come here to assist him, but Baker got sick and is still away, and Harry May could not come. Rev. John R. Saunders is here, and will preach until Thursday. I do not know whether it will close then or not. I went out to prayer meeting this morning at 10 o'clock. A genuine revival is much needed here, and there are many here that ought to be brought into the church. But the means used are so questionable that I fear the results.

Must close.

Your devoted husband
W.P.

Henry Butler to William Paisley in Gurdon

Malvern, Ark.
June 23, 1886

Dear Billy:

I had a pleasant trip to Ky—enjoyed the commencement exercises. My daughters acquitted themselves with credit, & it was gratifying to see in what esteem they were held by the teachers as well as the citizens of Millersburg. May graduated with second honors & would have been first in the class of eight, but for the fact she did not study Latin. She did study German and excelled in that, but the curriculum of the college required Latin in order to attain first honors.

Dr. Pope has a fine school in a town of enlightened religious people—healthy beautiful country—the blue grass and clover looks charming at this season. Mrs. Duffie met Miss Sidney here. I had charge of 21 girls on my return—a splendid lot of girls they are. Most all from Ark. Five went on to Texas, among them Miss Wells a daughter of Rev. Marshall Wells, whom you remember.

May has an invitation to visit Cal. & leaves this evening with Sister. Mrs. Dr. Bond & Mrs. Dotter of L.R., also Reavis Hughes will be of the party.

I am fearful sister is going to stay, as Mr. H has invested largely in real estate & making money. He has rented a cottage at "Long Beach" (not far from Los Angeles & Downey) for the months of July, Aug. & Sept.

We hate to give May up so soon after returning, but this is such a fine opportunity for a splendid trip, & then she needs rest &c after close application to studies. May is a little thin. Mattie [his daughter] is in fine health. I took Nannie with me to Ky, and she made the most of the trip, noticed everything.

[No closing]

Mattie Hughes to Emma Paisley in Dobyville

Tulip, Ark.
June 30, 1886

Dear Sister Emma:

You will notice from the heading of my letter, that I am once more at the dear old home. I never had been away so long, and you don't know how it affected me coming back after so long an absence. When I passed the church, I thought of the dear ones who were buried near, and by the time I entered the grove, I was so full I could with difficulty keep back the tears. And when I entered the dining room where I met sister Mary and Ma, I couldn't restrain my feelings, and had to take a good cry.

I came down in a loaded wagon with George Matthews, and brought Annie with me—we were very tired, and for a day or two I felt sore from the long rough ride, but now I am feeling all right, and expect to enjoy my stay here.

I think I'll be here about a month, and if I can I want to make you a visit, before going to see West, though I may have to go to New York first. Mr. John Hughes thinks of going there after goods, and I'll have to go when it suits him. If I don't get to see you before going, I will after I return, I hope.

Sister Mary was feeling badly when I came (last Saturday) but she is well now, though she is quite thin. She has a little negro girl to help about the work, but she knows very little, and sister M. has to be with her all the time. Ma is looking well, and seems cheerful—she seems better contented here than anywhere, though she would like so much to have one of the boys with her. We are having so many nice vegetables, and I enjoy eating them—nobody enjoys them more than Ma and Annie. Brother Matthews is at home now, but he will leave the last of the week to be gone sometime. He is out now, busy at work, trying to get rid of some of the grass and weeds.

I had a pleasant stay at Malvern, though after Maj. Coulter and Walter left it was quite lonely, and about the same time, too, George left, though he came back and spent a week with me, before he went to California. I hear from him quite often and he seems to be having a pleasant time. Alice Steele and George (brother John's son), have gained so much in weight, and both are delighted with California. I suppose they will be gone until the last of Sept. Did you know that Jimmie's wife had twins? born on the 16th-a girl and boy, the boy weighed 6½ and the girl 4½, and from last accounts they were doing well.

July 1st. Yesterday I received a long and interesting letter from Walter—he is well pleased with Abilene, though he says times are dull on account of the severe drouth. He and Gus have made something over expenses, and his health has been very good.

Brother Henry wasn't well when I left Malvern, had a bilious attack. Herbert [Matthews] came from there yesterday, said he had been up attending to business, but had to go to bed again. Mollie came home sick with asthma, but was nearly well when I left.

Reavis is coming here next week, and May expects to come with him—she is looking thin and pale. I hope a visit here will be beneficial to both. Reavis hasn't looked well for a long time. West says, his health is very good and he thinks he can take a vacation in August—about two weeks, and that is the time I want to be with him.

Hattie Boyd and Dudley Green were married about two weeks ago; very much against the wishes of her family. I think he has eight children. Olin returned from Cal last Saturday night and brought some nice honey—a few lemons—some wine, about 8 gallons, a few apricots and oranges. Alice wrote Ma. He was gone a little over three weeks, and had a pleasant visit. Much love to all—and write soon.

Your Sister,
M. W. H.

Mary Wyche Butler to daughter Emma Paisley in Dobyville

Tulip, Ark.
June 30, 1886

My Dear Daughter,

Your sister is writing to you. I would like to add a few lines though I have but a short while to write. She wants to send it off this morning. I didn't know she was writing to you. I feel so much for you over there alone, so far away from the rest of us.

Can't you make a visit this summer, or must we go to see you? Martha says she would like right well to go, but it seems so hard to get over there. I would like so much to be with you some. It is to bad to be so far away, can't hear any thing from home. John writes that he is expecting me to visit him this summer. I don't see how I can get over there. We are delighted to have your sister with us. She gets news every day from some of the family. Geo writes most every day. She had a good long letter from Walter. I expect she has written all the newes. The latest is Jimmie's twins. Everyone is excited about that. I don't know whether they send you one or not.

I had a fine drove of turkeys. Well, we had 24 but I am losing them. I have only 14 now. I am afraid they will have the colera, so much rain is not good for them.

I hope you have plenty of watter now. I was glad on your account. We are all well, have plenty of vegetables, fine garden, had some good plums all gone. I can't write any more.

Good bye my Dear one, much love to Billy and all the children. Herbert is waiting. The Lord bless you all

Your Mother

William Paisley to Emma Paisley in Dobyville

St. Louis, Mo.
July 3, 1886

My very dear one

I arrived here this evening about 6 o'clock, and am stopping at the above Hotel. Stood the trip very well and with the exception of feeling a little tired, am suffering no inconvenience whatever. This being Saturday evening and celebrated as the 4th of July, nearly all the business houses closed at 1 o'clock, so I have not met any of the merchants as yet. The city is in a constant noise from the fireing of fire crackers & other fire works. By Monday I shall hope to be feeling better, as I shall expect to rest to morrow, & think, I hope, that I will get through my work all right.

I can but feel some uneasiness about Willie & Jimmie, & hope you will write me by Monday's mail so that I may know how they are. I did not think to ask you to do so in my letter yesterday. I had the letter I wrote yesterday mailed at Smithton last night, so that you would be sure to get it today.

473

The train was crowded today with persons going from one point to another to attend public picnics &c. Haven't time to write more now, but may write again tomorrow. With much love for all, as ever your devoted husband

Wm Paisley

Emma Paisley (15) to her Mother Emma Paisley in Dobyville

Gurdon, Ark.
July 5, 1886

My dear Mamma

I have just written to Papa and thought I would write to you. I suppose Mattie and Lula told you how I got here. I came as far as the picnic in Mr. Hall's wagon, and the rest in Mr. Pugh's wagon. The reason I did not come all the way in his wagon is because there was not enough room and he told me if I got any other way as far as the picnic, I could go in his wagon the rest of the way.

I went first to Papa's store, and found he had gone to St. Louis the night before. Mr. Davies asked me to go home with him, and as I did not know the way to Aunt Mollie's from his store, I went, but I did not know the way from his house to here, and did not come here until that evening after supper, and Cousin Robert came with me then. I heard Mr. Hit preach, but not until last night, as the train was behind time.

How have the sick ones got? I hope there are well. I suppose Mattie and Lula told you I forgot to tell them goodby until after I got in the wagon. Write and tell me how the sick ones are. I will add a few lines to brother Henry. Write soon to your little daughter

Emma

P.S. Sophie asked me to bring her a pair of white stockings. Must I?

E.P.

Brother Henry:

As I did not tell you goodby I will write you a short note I ought told you goodby at the picnic, but forgot it until after I left, so I will tell you goodby now. *Good by.* You might write a little note when Mamma writes and put it in her envelope. Tell her to be sure to write.

Lovingly your sister
Emma

Minerva Paisley to William Paisley in Gurdon

Mcleansville, N.C.
Aug. 3, 1886

My Dear Will,

My heart is so full this morning that I don't know that I can write any thing to interest you. You must know that it is a hard trial for me to part with my dear boy and Lou. They are both dear to me, and nothing but the hope that it will be better for them can reconcile me to the separation. There is no one in the round world that I would rather they would be near than you, except our own immediate family. I hope you can be a mutual help to each other, not only in this world, but what is far more important, do all in your power to prepare for a happier world beyond this vale of tears, where we hope to meet all of our dear kindred who have gone before, and who will be there to welcome us, as your dear uncle told me not long before he died. Oh! happy day when that time shall come to free us from all the cares and sorrows to which we are all subject. I hope you will love Lacy and his wife more and more the better you get acquainted. You will pardon me when I say that I think Lacy has a noble Christian character, and I think he has a sweet amiable wife, who will do all in her power to help him to make a living. God grant that they may be useful and happy.

Porter seems to be full of the prospect of his work. Think he reproaches himself for ever faltering at first. Says though he hopes God in infinite mercy has been training him for his work. He will spend a week with us before he goes on to seminary, which meets the 10 of Sep. He is now at Cleveland Springs recruiting his health. I hope his life may be long spared, and he may have health to make a useful man. I know that he will throw his whole heart and soul in his work, for that has always been his character, and I believe is one cause of his delicate health.

Jno and family are well, and my health is as good as I could expect. Jno has a very good prospect for a crop. Annie and her little family are well. She has one of the sweetest little babes. She is looking well. Your little namesake is growing fast, is trying to step around a chair. Percy feels his importance.

I will close with good wishes for you and wife and dear little ones. Tell them I love them all. Goodbye, may God bless you, is the prayer of your loving

Aunt Minerva

William Paisley to Emma Paisley in Dobyville

[Gurdon]
Aug. 10/86

My dear one,

Lacy & Lou [his cousins] came yesterday evening & are stopping at Mr. Hall's. Let Jno or Willie borrow Mr. Fletcher Logan's horse, & bring the wagon down after Lacy, Lou & myself to morrow, unless they can learn of a wagon coming from the neighbors that will bring us back.

Some of the millet will have to be hauled to morrow. Should my wagon come, tell Jno or Willie to get Mr. White's wagon & team if they can, or if they cannot, hire Mr. Gardner to haul up the millet that is ready. You can get Sophie to help you make preparation for your company.

Mr. Cheatham & Mr. Ewing Williams have gone out. Wish I could be with you for the meeting.

Yours
W.P.

Jimmie Butler to Emma Paisley in Dobyville

Downey, Cal.
Aug. 13, 1886

My Dear Sister:

Your kind and interesting letter was received some time ago, but I have not had time to write in reply. I had not written a letter in a long time until today. I got off from the store today, and employed a man to stay in my place just so that I could write some letters. I had gotten so far behind with my correspondents that it looked like an utter impossibility to catch up and attend to the store. I am still clerking for Jenison and Greening. I did think of trying to buy a stock for groceries in a town about 40 miles above here, but Jenison and Greening raised my salary $10 pr. month and agreed to secure me 12% on what money I have. My salary together with the interest will amount to about $1150.00 a year. I concluded to stay for a time until I could have more capital.

You were about the first to *congratulate* or *condole* with us over our twins. Ma must have been so completely shocked by the news of the arrival of twins that she has not recovered sufficiently to write to me. Several have sent word that they did not know whether to congratulate or condole, and consequently could not write. We think we have inherited quite a fortune. I don't remember to have heard of such an event in the history of any of our families. Tell brother Billy that we accept the belt, and will wear it with all the grace and dignity that we can command.

We have not found names pretty enough for the twins yet, and consequently they go nameless. They are very healthy babies, and have more than doubled their first weight. Both of them have not been the trouble that our little Walter was. He was not well at all for about a year after his birth, but is now in splendid health, and is but little trouble. He is beginning to talk a little now.

How is your little boy James Ira? and all the other children? I would like so much to see you all. Have you moved to Gurdon yet? I am glad to hear that brother Billy is doing so well. I expect Gurdon is a very good point for business. The only fear that I would have would be sickness. You wrote that brother Billy was sick in your last letter. I suppose he has gotten stout & healthy long before this.

Will you sell your farm at Dobyville or let the boys take care of it? John and Willie are large enough now to do considerable work. Who has brother Billy helping him in the store? Does he do a cash or credit business?

Ira wants me to go back to Malvern and join him in business. I think Malvern is rather overdone now, and besides, the customers around there are very close and hard to deal with, and hardly enough money to justify a cash business. The people here are much more liberal in trading than they were around Malvern. There is at most all times of the year some crop being harvested, and that keeps money in circulation. There are quite a number of advantages in this state over Arkansas. It may not be any better for making money, but it is more pleasant to live here.

Brother Charlie has never bought him a place yet. He has been renting a place near here, and running a peddling wagon. I don't think he has been making much over a good living. It would be better if he would get him a farm where his boys could help him. His wife and Mrs. Colburn and John Colburn's wife and mother have been down on the coast bathing for about a week.

Brother George & family are all well, also bro. Moores & family. I must now close. Let me hear from you soon. Maria joins me in love to all.

Your affectionate bro.

J. O. Butler

Mattie Hughes to Emma Paisley in Dobyville

Malvern, Ark.
Aug. 26, 1886

Dear Sister Emma,

I write this morning only to let you know how very sick Alice is. She has been confined to the bed for more than a week with something on the order of flux, and her condition makes her case very critical. Dr. Reamey has visited her quite often—he has been twice today, and says, he will be back again. Her pulse was 120 this morning, she is resting quietly now, and it has been more than two hours since she has had an action from the bowels, and if we can keep them checked there is some hope of her recovery. I sat up with her last night (until Olin came on the train at 3 o'clock this morning), and I can't tell you how many discharges she had, although she was taking opium and using injections with a good deal of morphine. Olin was in St. Louis and we dispatched for him to come.

Coulter has gone for Ma and I suppose, she will be here late this evening. Ma hadn't been very well and I hated to have to send for her, but I knew she would want to be with Alice. We are trying to keep her very quiet—don't allow any visitors, only some one to sit by and fan her. Olin is with her now. I hope you all keep well.

I have been very well, and stand the loss of sleep and fatigue of nursing better than one would think.

I heard from George [Hughes, her husband] this morning, he was in Honolulu and in fine health. My boys were well when I heard from them. I have been disappointed in getting to see West.

I would write more but have so much to do, and I must take some rest. William has had fever for a week, and Mattie (the baby) is sick too. Much love to all.

Your Sister

M. W. Hughes

Dr. R says Alice is doing better. She is as thin as any one you ever saw. Ma will feel shocked when she sees her.

477

Henry Butler to William Paisley in Gurdon

Sept. 4, 86

Alice died last night at 9 o'clock, being unconscious the whole day. She died easy *without a struggle*. We take the precious body to Tulip to-day. Her example will yet do much good for this community.

Your Bro. Henry

Mattie Hughes to Emma Paisley in Dobyville

Malvern, Ark.
Sept. 7, 1886

Dear Sister Emma:

You have heard of the death of our dear sister, which occurred so soon after you left. I regret that you and sister Mary didn't stay. Ma takes her death very hard, she says it is the greatest trial of her life.

Alice suffered so much Thursday night from severe pains in her lower bowels—they would come and go. Ma and myself worked with her and did what we could to relieve her, by putting hot poultices and cloths out of hot water—it looked like it would nearly kill Ma to see her suffer so much. She was restless all night, and her mind wandering—she didn't seem to be rational Friday morning, and lay in a stupor most of the day. I don't think she had any pain, but I don't believe she was conscious that she was dying. From 12 o'clock, I think she was dying, and breathed her last at nine. She died so quietly, without a struggle or a groan.

We would have liked for her to have been conscious and talked some—she was stupefied with morphine. Olin took her death very hard, but he will get over it, and I don't believe Ma ever will. She seems so weak and looks so stooped ever since. She hasn't had a good night's rest since, but slept better last night. and today after dinner she took a good nap.

Olin and brother Henry went to Tulip with the body and it was buried about 6 o'clock Saturday evening (sister Annie's birthday) and they were each 31 years old when they died. Ma thought of going down, but there wasn't a seat for her in the buggy, and she was very glad afterwards that she didn't go. It was so warm and dusty, for her to go down and come back the next day, I believe it would have made her sick. We had funeral services here in the parlor, and brother Stone's remarks were beautiful. There were a good many present, and all seemed most affected.

Brother Henry said there were a good many out at the burial, and bro. Caldwell made such a good talk. We had some beautiful flowers sent in. Nannie Strong made a lovely cross of white and green—Mollie brought two magnolias, and Alice Robertson a pretty crown or wreath of white flowers.

Mattie is a good deal better, but not able to walk yet. She is lying in her crib now begging for something to eat. She and William too have such an appetite. Ma has gone with William to brother Henry's. It is the first time she has been away, and I was glad for her to go—except Mattie, I am the only person on the place.

Olin left for St. Louis yesterday, and said it would take him two or three weeks to finish up his business there. Ma and myself are staying here with the children. Poor little Mattie, I feel so much for her—so young and left without a mother. I don't know what Olin intends doing—Ma is too old to have the care of the children. When Mattie was so sick, I felt if her mother was taken, it would be so much better for her to go too. But we don't know what is best, and can't see now, why these afflictions are sent. I know Alice is at rest, and all is well with her. Soon after they left for Tulip, Mattie called for her "Mamma" the only time she had asked for her. Ma wanted to show her to her, while she was in the parlor, but she wouldn't look at her face, and cried to be taken out. Ma received a letter from Mrs. Feild this morning full of sympathy—said she would have been so glad to have helped nurse her, if she had known that she was sick.

I received a telegram from George on the 4th informing me of his safe return to San Francisco. I hope you found all well. Love to Billy and the children.

> Your Sister
> M. W. Hughes

William Paisley to Emma Paisley in Dobyville

> [Gurdon]
> Sept. 8, 86

My dear one

I opened Mrs. Hughes letter, which came this morning—I had not been able to realize Alice's death until after reading it. I retired to my room & found relief in tears.

Have learned nothing definite yet as to Whitman's place, but will know soon.

> Yours affectionately
> Wm Paisley

Mary Matthews to Emma Paisley in Dobyville

> Tulip, Ark.
> Sept. 24, 86

Dear Sister Emma:

I have been wanting to write you for a long time. The short while I met you at Malvern seems almost like a dream. I did want to be with you longer so much, and regretted that both of us didn't remain the short while longer that our dear sister lived. I had no idea the end was so near when I left, and even hoped she would get well: but an all wise, and mysterious Providence saw best to take her to himself; we must bow in submission to his will. Her work was ended and she was fully ready. O that we may be as well prepared when our time comes—only three sisters now left—and

I feel that the ties of love for each other grow stronger as the dear ones are taken from us; earth has fewer attractions and Heaven more.

It makes me sad to think of the changes that are taking place. I don't know what arrangement is to be made about the dear little children, nor how long Ma will remain at Malvern. I am very lonely here without her, and it may be that I'll have to give up house keeping after this year. It will be sad indeed to have the pleasant old homestead deserted.

Annie went to Mal. last Monday. I miss her very much, but she was anxious to go back, to be with little Mattie and the boys. Ma says she is so much company for Mattie that she is glad she came back.

If I could get a good white girl or woman to live with me I could get along very well. The girl Alice had came home last week, and is sick with typhoid fever, so Dr. Cooper says. They have a white woman without children, a widow, and she is doing very well.

I received a short note from sister which I'll send you; they sent me your letter to sister with it. One came from Johnny to me which I sent to her this morning, he says Kellie's health has not been so good this summer, thinks she has been doing too much work. Johnny says he wants to take Alice's baby to live with them, and expected to write to bro. Olin for her. Says he would like to have two or three children. I would like so much to see Johnny and his wife.

Cousin Maggie Dean and her children staid with me Monday night, on their way home from Hot Springs. I was so glad to see them, for I was feeling so lonely, Mr. Matthews not being at home. He left again this morning.

I expected to go visiting this evening, but it has commenced raining. Sent word to one of the girls to come and stay with me tonight. I still have Bettie to help night and morning. She goes to school. I wouldn't keep her if I could do any better, but we are compelled to have some one to do the milking. We are milking 5 cows, & I ought to make more butter than I do. Don't think she takes time to milk well. Mr. M. will try to get a white girl while on this trip.

You will soon leave your old home. I hope you will all have good health in Gurdon—wish you lived near me, then I could have some of your children with me all the time. Sister looks for bro. G. the last of this month, then she will have to go to L.R. Bro. G wrote her to get a home there if she wished to keep house this winter and longer. Said he wouldn't be hard to please. If my health was good and I had some one to do the work, I would be glad to take care of little Mattie. Love to all the children. Write.

Lovingly
sister Mary

John A. Paisley to his father William Paisley in Gurdon

Dobyville, Ark.
Sept 30, 86

Dear Pa

I will write you a few lines to let you know how we are getting along. We will get through pulling corn to day, but not through hauling. Mr. Crews is very anxious for John Crews' corn to be pulled and cotton picked. We have gathered all of the corn in the little new ground, and we will put the cows and hogs in right away.

Your Son
J. A. Paisley

P.S. I think there will be about 15 loads of corn on that side next to the road.

J. A. P.

Emma Paisley to William Paisley in Gurdon

Dobyville, Ark.
Sept. 30, 1886

My *very* dear one,

I am sorry you are so distressed about my condition, for I think I am getting on as well as could be expected. Dr. Cargile called yesterday and gave me a vial of drops to take three times a day. I neglected saying anything to him about my bowels, which still act too freely—he did not sit down and seemed in a great hurry. Mrs. Ben McGill came over yesterday evening, and spent a few hours very pleasantly (to me). I will give this to Willie, thinking he may see some one going to Gurdon. I received a letter from sister Mary which I will send to you.

Sorry you could not get off to St. Louis, as it will put off our moving till the roads get bad I am afraid. Don't think I am impatient, but I can assure you I am very tired of living like we have for the past seven months.

I have not heard any news, so good bye. I wrote to you by last mail a short letter. Ever your loving wife

E. E. Paisley

Dobyville, Ark.
Oct. 2, 1886

My dearest one

As Willie is going off with some corn, and as I am needing some things I will write a few lines. I saw the doctor yesterday, and he told me to take some laudanum, which I did. I feel right well this morning with the exception of a slight headache. I will have to have some more flour, sugar, and molasses. Mr. Craig says he wants $1.00 (One dollar) worth of coffee and 1 lb of tobacco, which you can do as you please about letting him have.

Got through gathering corn Thursday evening. Ed did not help after Tuesday, but is picking cotton. I think the children have been very busy this week. Billie Peters helped a day and a half. Willie carried cotton seed yesterday evening after getting through hauling corn. John and the children will finish picking peas today, I reckon.

481

Come home to night if you are not too busy, for I would like to see you before you get off to St. Louis. I am ever yours lovingly

Emma

I send you Mrs. Grier's letter which you will please send back or take care of.

George Hughes to William Paisley in Gurdon

Malvern, Ark.
Oct. 3, 1886

Dear Billy:

The postal sent you told the sad news that George Butler was dying [Henry & Mollie's younger son]. No danger was feared until Friday just before noon, when he had a spasmodic attack, losing consciousness which never returned. Other convulsions followed at intervals though not violent. at 11.40 last night, thirty-six hours after the first convulsion, he passed away as easily as an infant falling asleep.

The many friends which you know the family have here are offering all the consolation and sympathy possible.

He will be buried late this evening in the Malvern cemetery. Say to Emma that my wife will write her in a few days.

Your Bro.
Geo. W. Hughes

[Sent on to Emma Paisley in Dobyville with this note from Wm Paisley]

My dearest one

I am all in a flurry trying to take the 10.18 train to night. It is now after nine—I send you the enclosed letter giving account of Geo's death.

Take good care of yourself. Will try to write you from St. Louis.

Your devoted husband with love & goodbye to all

W. Paisley

Oct. 4, 86

William Paisley to Emma Paisley in Dobyville

St. Louis, M.
Oct. 8, 1886

My very dear one:

I reached here Tuesday evening about sundown, got supper, and that night witnessed the Veiled Prophet procession. The weather is fine, and it is thought that there are more visitors in the city

482

than ever before on a similar occasion. I am rooming again with Maj. Wilkins and have plenty of room there, but at the eating houses I find such crowds that some times I have to wait some time before I can get my meals.

Yesterday was a general Holiday, in order to give the business men & clerks an opportunity to get out to the Fair. I worked in the morning, but spent the afternoon at the Fair grounds, and enjoyed the sights very much. Found Ben Logan, Jimmie Pattillo, Billie Cooper & several other acquaintances out here. The three mentioned left for home last night. I have bot shoes & boots & part of my dry [goods] but can hardly expect to get thru this week. Do what you can towards getting ready to move, as I shall want to get you over in Gurdon as soon as possible after I get back, tho I may have to open the goods first, as some will want them by the time I get back.

I am very well. Haven't time to write more. With much love to all. Yours devotedly

Wm Paisley

Should Willie catch up with his hauling, tell him to haul 40 Bas Cot send to Mr. Andrews at Keons Mill.

W. P.

Mary Matthews to Emma Paisley at Dobyville

Tulip, Ark.
Oct. 27, 1886

Dear Sister Emma:

Your letter was received yesterday—very glad to hear from you. I was just thinking of writing you again, as I knew you had your hands full, but didn't know whether you had moved or not; it does seem real strange that you have been married 20 years—hadn't thought of its being that long; the years pass rapidly away, and ere we are aware of it, find ourselves growing old. You will very soon have several grown children.

I received a letter from Sister day before yesterday, she was at Malvern again, but expected to leave today. Ma has never been down yet; but expect to send the wagon up for her the last of this or the first of next week. It seemed that she couldn't leave the children.

She will bring Annie & Mattie with her, and they will probably be here until next fall: Bro. Olin is selling out every thing and making his arrangements to go to Cal. as soon as possible—will take the two boys. Ma wrote for Sister to come, she didn't want to come down without seeing her again. Sister is anxious to have Annie, and I expect she and I together will keep her. I don't know whether Olin will consent to give up Mattie, but she is too young to go well without a mother. I suppose he thinks in a year he could come back for her. Sister wrote me to know if I would be willing to keep the children, if Olin would pay the hire for a cook. I wrote her I would. I am willing to do what I can for the little motherless children. If I can have health and keep some help, think we can get on very well.

George [Matthews, her step-son] expects to go to Va. soon to live with his uncle, who has written for him and will pay his expenses there. Mr. Matthews will have to get a good farm hand to look after things, get wood &c. I wish we knew of some good white man that would take an interest in things so as to relieve Mr. M. while he attends to his ministerial work.

Our sweet potatoes turned out very well—have a few Irish potatoes yet. Digging our goober peas today, will have about 2½ bushels—half a barrel of pop corn after being shucked; so you see we will have something to eat this winter. You know Ma is as fond of such things as any child. Also saved a few hickory nuts—they are scarce this year. We had some nice turnip greens for dinner today. I enjoyed them so much: ours were sowed very late.

Herbert [Matthews] went to Malvern yesterday, and will return tonight, so I'll hear from them up there.

I have been afraid Ma would get sick; there is still a great deal of sickness, "slow fever," as they call it. George [Butler] was not considered dangerous 'till the day before he died, when he was taken with convulsions. Sister Mollie especially took his death very hard, and talks about him a great deal; not being at home when he was first taken sick, grieves her. Maj. Coulter has returned from Texas, and sister writes that sister Mollie seems more cheerful. He will be a great deal of company for them. I have not seen any of them since George's death. May and Mattie being away at school makes the family seem small.

I suppose bro Billy is getting on well in business—love to him, also the children. Mr. Matthews is now at home, and sends love to you all. I am very lonely when he is away. Ira staid with us nearly two weeks. I was very glad to see him.

Herbert and Judge Green are getting on very well in business.

Write whenever you can to your loving sister

Mary J. Matthews.

Kate Ryland is to be married tomorrow night to Mr. Lee, brother to Mr. Anson Lee, Banks Lee's father. He is a widower with one daughter. Kate has just been here with her two little girls, and invited me to see her married. She will not have any supper. Will leave for her new home next day in the neighborhood of Rock Springs. She is greatly delighted at the prospect of marrying again. I hope she will be happy.

28th. Herbert came late, and brought Annie with him—will send the wagon for Ma tomorrow, and will soon have plenty of company. Sister wrote a few lines—she will keep Annie when she goes to housekeeping—she will stay with me this winter.

Minerva Paisley to Lacy and Lou Paisley in Gurdon

Mcleansville, N.C.
Nov. 8, 1886

My Dear Children,

It is raining this morning, and Jno is in the house helping Bessie with the little ones, and I thought I would slip off and talk awhile with you. I am glad to say that we are all well, Bessie and I went to see Eugenie yesterday. Had a pleasant visit. They are all well and fixed up so nicely. I tell you, Walter has a smart woman for his wife. She has made quite a change in the looks of things around there.

Well, Lacy your furniture came all right. We went upstairs this morning thinking, that we would unpack it. But do hate to do it, it is packed so nicely. Do you reckon there is any hope that you will ever get it? If we thought there was, we would never unpack it. It is packed so securely. Tell us what you think about it. Forbes said he could not do anything with it. He has gone in copartnership with a man who belongs to a firm who makes furniture for sale. Said if he was situated like he was when you bought it, he would love to accommodate you. We are perfectly willing to put it up in our company room and take as good care of it as we can, but do feel so sorry for you that you cannot have it. We know of no chance to sell it at present. We thought it might be if Jno Mc and Alamy Forbes hitched up that Capt. might buy it for her, but we do not know. We will do the best we can for you. Those folks did not pay the freight for you as you expected. Jno paid it, it was $21.38. Jno says for you not to bother about that, as he does not need the money. Maybe he will take some of your pieces.

Bessie wants your tin set awful bad. Did you know it was coming? I think it is one of the prettiest I ever saw, so neat and plain. But I hope, if Providence smiles on your efforts, that you will be able some day to get fixed up and forget all the trouble you have had thus far. But Oh! how I wish I was near enough to *help you a little*. If you think you will never want or be able to get your feather bed, I think I can sell that and send you the money.

I think you will have a comfortable house if you build on the plan you sent us. Don't have too many windows. They are nothing but a botheration. I hope your other things have reached you before this. I think they have had time to have gone around the world by this time.

Annie and Jim are right well now. Jim is sick about not getting down here to hunt, but is so busy he don't do it. I heard from Porter last week. He was well, and said he hoped his life which he was living would restore him to perfect health. May God grant it may be so, and that he may yet be permitted to carry out his long cherished desire to preach the gospel. All join in love to you both. Write soon. We are so glad to hear from you at any time. Tell cousin Will I hope there will come a big snow this winter, and then it may be he will have time to write. Love to cousin Mary. Tell her to write to me. Good bye from your

Devoted Mother

Lacy, our rooms below have 9 ft pitch the dining room is 10 I would suggest to you if you are going to have one story to have yours 10. Jim's and Ed's I think is 10.

Mrs. Mary W. Butler to Emma Paisley in Gurdon

Nov. 2, 1886

My Dear Daughter

I have been wishing to write for a long time, but it seems to me I could not write. I had my heart and hands so full, it seemed all most impossible. I thought of you a great deal and felt so hurt that you left when you did. I want so much for you to be with me in that sad hour. Oh it was a tryin time indeed. Aunt Mare said she knew she was worse that morn when she came. Said she didn't notice her like she had. I didn't know she was worse until the eve, then I wished so much you had not left. I blamed myself for leting you leave. I felt I needed all the help & sympathy I could have.

I was glad you sent Mrs. Greyers letter. It was good letter, glad to hear from her. I sufered Sundy night it was the most misarible night I ever felt. I felt like ther was no chance for Alice to get well. I would go to the door every few minutes, and ask Henry how she was. He would say she was doing well. I told him I felt so burdened and heavy ladend, I couldn't sleep. He said I had been dreaming. I knew I haden't been sleep.

I know she was ready, but it was so hard to go & leave the little babe behind. I almost wished for her to go too, but we can't tell what is best. I wish I had talked more to her than I did. I wish you had talked with her. She would liked it if she was able, but it is all over now. Let us live so as to be as well prepared as she was, so that we may meet her in Heaven. She had done what she could. She is such a loss to the church. I know it better for her but we do miss her so much.

I came down from Ma[lvern] on the 30, your Birthday. The text for that day is: I will strengthen thee, yea, I will help thee. Isa 41 10 vers. I read it on the way. This is your Bro Geo's Birth day 2nd Nov.

I brought the children with me. Your sister expects to take Ana. I have the little Baby sleeping with me. I don't know what they will do with her I feel like I would like to keep her, but Olin talks of taking her to Cal. She has improved very much running all about. I do hate to see the little thing leave. I think she looks like her mother. The Boys are delighted here. Edwin has a gun, shot 2 birds, he is so proud he shout.

I never heard of your sickness until today. Why didnt you let me kno of it? I was suprised to read it in your letter. I left a box of things for you at Henry's. You can get them from ther easer than from here. I asked Mollie to keep them for you. We having most beautiful weather. Your sister has a basket of things for Ana. She is so anxious to keep house and take Anna with her, I recon.

I have writen enough to night, it is so dark I can hardly see. The lamp gives a poor light, I recon. I can finish in the morn. good night.

It is after nine o c. I went to the church yard Sunday eve. How strange, my two younger daughters lying together.

I've a good long letter from cou. Magi Dean. Said they had the greatest revival in Hamburg she ever saw. Henry May's wife was caring it on. Said she never saw anything like it before.

When can you come to see me? I wanted you to have some of your sister things. I hope you can get them. We are all well. Little Matty sleped so well last night. She's dear, she looks so sweet. I wish we could call her Alice. Good by.

All send love to you & Billy.

Your Mother

Love to all the children. Little Mattie is pulling at me now. Tell Henry to write to Edwin & William.

Mattie Hughes to Emma Paisley in Gurdon

Little Rock, Ark's.
Nov. 24, 1886

Dear Sister Emma:

It has been a long time since we wrote to each other, though I have heard from you occasionally through others. While I was at Malvern a few days ago, Nannie received a letter from Mary—a nice letter it was too—I was surprised that she could write so well.

West is here on a visit—he came two weeks ago, and will return to New York the last of this week. We went to Malvern last Saturday, and after spending Sunday there, returned here Monday. I thought of you, and would like to have made you a visit. I was anxious too, for West to visit Tulip, especially for him to see his Grandma, but he hardly thought he had the time, and then we were having such rainy disagreeable weather. West was feeling very well the first week, but for the last three or four days, he has had a bad cold and sore throat. I regret his taking cold so much, for I hoped he would improve during his vacation, for he is quite thin. He and Reavis have been to several entertainments, and are out tonight calling on some young ladies.

Mollie continues very sad, and wants to talk about George all the time—brother Henry feels anxious about her. It seemed strange not to see Alice and the children. I think Olin was at Tulip while I was at Malvern. I don't know when he expects to leave for Cal. Ma wants to keep Mattie, for awhile anyway—says she is becoming so fond of her. But Ma is too old to have the care of her, and the longer she keeps her, the harder it will be for her to give her up.

I expect to keep Annie, and if we were keeping house I would have her with me now. George says he expects me to have a home some time, but I don't know when or where. We are boarding now on Scott and 8th, next door to Mrs. Feild, and I see Mrs. F. and Florrie quite often.

I am convenient to the different churches—just three blocks from Methodist, Presbyterian and Episcopal. Sam Small was here most of last week, and I heard him preach some good sermons— he had a full house every night. I like our preacher, Dr. Miller, so much—he had been carrying on a protracted meeting for two weeks or more, before Sam Small came, though there were very few conversions. But I think the church has been much revived. Judge English's only son, who has been very dissipated, made a profession, and joined the church. It distresses me that my husband and sons care so little for religious matters. George seldom goes to church. He is wholly taken up with the things of this life. My dear sister, you must pray for us—it is hard for me to be religious, living as I am. The family we are boarding with, are Episcopalians, and you know they dance, play cards, and do about what the world does—one can't see any difference.

John Colburn and wife are in California, boarding at bro. Charlie's, and expect to spend the winter there—they left here about two weeks ago.

Sister Mary expects to attend Conference at Hot Springs—she wrote me that she was busy getting ready. How are you pleased with Gurdon? and how are the children doing at school?

We heard from Walter a few days ago—he is in good health. Much love to all. Write soon.

> Your Sister
> Mattie W. Hughes

Mary Matthews to Emma Paisley in Gurdon

> Tulip, Ark.
> Dec. 27, 1886

Dear sister Emma:

Your letter received some time ago, which I've been wanting to answer ever since my return from Conference on Tuesday 14th. The next day we killed 7 hogs, so I was kept busy all that week about the lard, sausage &c. We had a delightful time at Con. Staid at the St. James hotel, occupied a room in the cottage part of the building across the street, which was nicely furnished, and so much more private.

Mrs. Cook from Little Rock occupied a room adjoining, which made it pleasant for me to have some one to go with me to get hot water, walk down town, or go to Conference room when we pleased &c. We had a very harmonious session, and was delighted with our new bishop Galloway. The appointments as a general thing gave satisfaction. Mr. M. returned to New Edinburgh, which was not unexpected.

Ma received a letter from Sister yesterday, written 25th. She had a nice turkey and other good things, but no one but themselves to enjoy it. Bro. Caldwell, his wife and little Jamie, ate dinner with us, besides the family. Mr. Matthews was not here. He had an appointment to preach at New Edinburgh—returned yesterday.

Annie and Mattie enjoyed the good things found in their stockings, as well as our hired girl. You have quite a number to fill if all hang up stockings—hope all had a pleasant Christmas. Sister wants Annie to come up, and I think probably I'll go up with her next week, if the weather is good. I suppose you have heard she was keeping house—rented Dr. Thompson's place ready furnished for six months. They have a very good servant, and like housekeeping.

Olin and the boys reached Cal. safely, had a pleasant time—didn't have to pay anything for William. Ira seems to be doing very well now. He sent Ma a sack of pecans and box of candy, which came just in time for Christmas. Brother Henry also sent her a box of candies, oranges, and apples with an affectionate little note, which almost made her cry to think what kind thoughtful children she had.

I don't think Olin and Jimmie ought to keep writing for Mamma to come out there. Olin thinks she will go when he comes for Mattie, as she will hate to give her up. She is a very sweet child and a great pet with all of us. Ma enjoys good health, cheerful and well satisfied here at the old home, and I think ought to remain. Ma sends love, and wants to know if you have ever gotten your box from Malvern.

Sister Mollie is still sad at times, and dwells on her sorrow too much. Maj Coulter was looking very well. Bro Henry was looking well and cheerful, but didn't attend Conference. Was our cousin Johnson there? Nannie went over and staid a while after with Mrs. Henderson who used to live at Malvern. Coulter went over on Sunday. Did you get the Advocate containing Alice's obituary?

Mr. M. and Ma unite with me in love and greetings for a happy new year to all!

Affectionately your sister
M. J. Matthews

Little Mattie is sassy and fat as a little pig. You would not know her now.
George Matthews [Mary's older step-son] is well pleased in Virginia.

Mattie Hughes to brother-in-law William Paisley

Little Rock, Ark.
Jan. 20, 1887

Dear Brother Billy:

What can I say to comfort you in this the greatest sorrow of your life? Would that it were in my power to do or say something to lessen your grief. You are a Christian, and know where to go for comfort. I believe you will bear this severe affliction with Christian fortitude, and thank our heavenly Father for having given you such a good wife. What consolation to know that her death was so peaceful and triumphant. Oh that I could have been with her, and received from her a parting message. Even in death I would have been so glad to have seen her sweet face. Rest assured you have my prayers and sympathy. The dear children, how much I feel for them.

I didn't get your postal until 10 o'clock Monday morning—too late for me to attend the burial, and then I didn't know where she would be buried. This morning I received a letter from sister Mary, giving me some of the particulars of her death, but I want to hear more, and when you can, do write me. I feel more determined to get to Heaven than ever—I want to see the dear loved ones again, and live with them forever. If my husband and children were trying to be Christians, how happy it would make me. Pray for them, and me.

May God comfort and sustain you, and the precious children is the prayer of

Your Devoted Sister
M. W. Hughes

[Emma Butler Paisley died of pneumonia, January 16, 1887]

APPENDIX

Butler Family

Alexander Butler married Mary Wyche Reavis

1. Sarah Frances   b. 1833, died in childhood

2. Martha Wyche   b. 1835
   m   children: Walter, West, George Reavis
 George Hughes

3. Henry Alexander b. 1836
   m   children: Coulter, May, Mattie, Nannie, George
 Mary E. Coulter

4. Mary Jane   b. 1838
   m
 George Matthews

5. Lewis Peter   b. 1839
   m   children: Jessie, Willard
 Jennie Bowman

6. George Emery   b. 1840
   m   children: Moores, Alice, Lou, George, Anna, Julia
 *Julia Moores

7. Charles Albert   b. 1843
   m   children: 5 sons and 4 daughters
 Kate Colburn

8. Emma Eliza   b. 1844
   m   children: 4 sons and 5 daughters
 William McLean Paisley

9. John Reavis   b. 1846
   m
 Malinda Clardy

10. Anna Louise   b. 1849
   m   children: Edwin, William, Annie
 *Olin Moores

11. Ira Wyche   b. 1852
   m
 Fannie John Smith

12. Alice Palmer   b. 1855
   m   children: Olin Alex, Alice
 *Olin Moores

13. James Oliver   b. 1857
     m   children: Walter Hughes, and twins
 *Mariah Moores

*These members of the Moores family are siblings.

Paisley Family

William McLean Paisley married 1866 Emma Eliza Butler
       1842–1891   1844–1887

1. John Alexander Paisley
   b. Oct. 11, 1867

2. William Butler Paisley (Willie)
   b. March 15, 1869

3. Emma Paisley
   b. Nov. 30, 1870

4. Henry Lewis Paisley
   b. July 11, 1873

5. Mary Eliza Paisley
   b. Aug. 24, 1875

6. Martha Wyche Paisley (Mattie)
   b. Oct. 17, 1877

7. Lula Grier Paisley
   b. Nov. 1879

8. Annie Orr Paisley
   b. Nov. 10, 1882 d. 1883

9. James Ira Paisley (Jimmy)
   b. Aug. 23, 1884

William McLean Paisley's father (a Presbyterian minister) died of typhoid fever in Billy's childhood. His mother married a second time to L. D. Lipscomb, a tailor. William had one sister, Mary Anne, and several stepbrothers and stepsisters, among them Willis, Claude, Emma, Eliza, and Ella. He called his stepfather "Father."